Contents

Indice

	Page		Pagina
Preface	6	Prefazione	7
Introduction	11	Introduzione	191
Guide to Pronunciation	12	Guida della pronuncia	192

ITALIAN-ENGLISH DICTIONARY	15	DIZIONARIO ITALIANO-INGLESE	15

Menu Reader	151	Lessico gastronomico	323
Mini-Grammar	167	Mini-grammatica	335
Italian Abbreviations	179	Abbreviazioni inglesi	343
Numerals	181	Numeri	346
Time	182	L'ora	347
Some Basic Phrases	183	Alcune espressioni utili	183
Measures and Temperature	342	Misure e temperatura	342

ENGLISH-ITALIAN DICTIONARY	195	DIZIONARIO INGLESE-ITALIANO	195

Preface

In selecting the 12.500 word-concepts in each language for this dictionary, the editors have had the traveller's needs foremost in mind. This book will prove invaluable to all the millions of travellers, tourists and business people who appreciate the reassurance a small and practical dictionary can provide. It offers them—as it does beginners and students—all the basic vocabulary they are going to encounter and to have to use, giving the key words and expressions to allow them to cope in everyday situations.

Like our successful phrase books and travel guides, these dictionaries—created with the help of a computer data bank—are designed to slip into pocket or purse, and thus have a role as handy companions at all times.

Besides just about everything you normally find in dictionaries, there are these Berlitz bonuses:

- imitated pronunciation next to each foreign-word entry, making it easy to read and enunciate words whose spelling may look forbidding

- a unique, practical glossary to simplify reading a foreign restaurant menu and to take the mystery out of complicated dishes and indecipherable names on bills of fare

- useful information on how to tell the time and how to count, on conjugating irregular verbs, commonly seen abbreviations and converting to the metric system, in addition to basic phrases.

While no dictionary of this size can pretend to completeness, we expect the user of this book will feel well armed to affront foreign travel with confidence. We should, however, be very pleased to receive comments, criticism and suggestions that you think may be of help in preparing future editions.

Berlitz®

Italian-English Dictionary

Dizionario Inglese-Italiano

Berlitz Publishing Company, Inc.

Princeton   Mexico City   Dublin   Eschborn   Singapore

Library of Congress
Catalog Card Number: 78-78081

ISBN 2-8315-6569-3

Revised 1994
Sixth Printing - August 1997
Printed in the Netherlands

Berlitz Dictionaries

Dansk	Engelsk, Fransk, Italiensk, Spansk, Tysk
Deutsch	Dänisch, Englisch, Finnisch, Französisch, Italienisch, Niederländisch, Norwegisch, Portugiesisch, Schwedish, Spanisch
English	Danish, Dutch, Finnish, French, German, Italian, Norwegian, Portuguese, Spanish, Swedish, Turkish
Español	Alemán, Danés, Finlandés, Francés, Holandés, Inglés, Noruego, Sueco
Français	Allemand, Anglais, Danois, Espagnol, Finnois, Italien, Néerlandais, Norvégien, Portugais, Suédois
Italiano	Danese, Finlandese, Francese, Inglese, Norvegese, Olandese, Svedese, Tedesco
Nederlands	Duits, Engels, Frans, Italiaans, Portugees, Spaans
Norsk	Engelsk, Fransk, Italiensk, Spansk, Tysk
Português	Alemão, Francês, Holandês, Inglês, Sueco
Suomi	Englanti, Espanja, Italia, Ranska, Ruotsi, Saksa
Svenska	Engelska, Finska, Franska, Italienska, Portugisiska, Spanska, Tyska

Prefazione

Selezionando le 12.500 parole-concetti in ogni lingua di questo dizionario, i nostri redattori hanno tenuto conto innanzitutto delle necessità di
chi viaggia. Questo libro si rivelerà prezioso per i milioni di turisti, viag-
giatori, uomini d'affari che apprezzano il contributo che può dare un
dizionario pratico e di formato ridotto. Di grande utilità sarà anche per
i principianti e gli studenti, perchè contiene tutti i vocaboli di base che
sentiranno e dovranno usare, oltre a parole-chiave ed espressioni che
permettono di affrontare situazioni correnti.

Come i nostri manuali di conversazione e le nostre guide turistiche,
già molto apprezzate, questi dizionari – realizzati grazie a una banca
dei dati su ordinatore – hanno la dimensione giusta per scivolare in una
tasca o in una borsetta, diventando così i compagni indispensabili di
ogni momento.

Oltre a tutto quanto si trova normalmente in un dizionario, i nostri
volumetti contengono:

- una trascrizione fonetica accanto a ogni lemma, al fine di facilitarne
  la lettura; ciò si rivela particolarmente utile per quelle parole che
  sembrano impronunciabili
- un pratico lessico gastronomico, inteso a semplificare la lettura del
  menù in un ristorante straniero e a svelare i misteri di pietanze com-
  plicate e di nomi indecifrabili sui conti
- preziose informazioni sul modo di esprimere il tempo, di contare,
  sui verbi irregolari, sulle abbreviazioni e le conversioni nel sistema
  metrico, oltre alle espressioni più correnti.

Nessun dizionario di questo formato può pretendere di essere completo,
ma il suo scopo è di permettere a chi lo usa di affrontare con fiducia
un viaggio all'estero. Naturalmente saremo lieti di ricevere commenti,
critiche e suggerimenti che potrebbero essere di aiuto nella preparazione di future edizioni.

italian-english

italiano-inglese

Introduction

The dictionary has been designed to take account of your practical needs. Unnecessary linguistic information has been avoided. The entries are listed in alphabetical order, regardless of whether the entry word is printed in a single word or in two or more separate words. As the only exception to this rule, a few idiomatic expressions are listed alphabetically as main entries, by order of the most significant word in the expression. When an entry is followed by sub-entries such as expressions and locutions, these, too, have been listed in alphabetical order.

Each main-entry word is followed by a phonetic transcription (see Guide to pronunciation). Following the transcription is the part of speech of the entry word, whenever applicable. When an entry word may be used as more than one part of speech, the translations are grouped together after the respective part of speech.

Irregular plurals of nouns are shown in brackets after the part of speech.

Whenever an entry word is repeated in irregular plurals or in sub-entries, a tilde (~) is used to represent the full entry word.

An asterisk (*) in front of a verb indicates that the verb is irregular. For details, refer to the lists or irregular verbs.

Abbreviations

adj	adjective	*num*	numeral
adv	adverb	*p*	past tense
Am	American	*pl*	plural
art	article	*plAm*	plural (American)
conj	conjunction	*pp*	past participle
f	feminine	*pr*	present tense
fpl	feminine plural	*pref*	prefix
m	masculine	*prep*	preposition
mpl	masculine plural	*pron*	pronoun
n	noun	*v*	verb
nAm	noun (American)	*vAm*	verb (American)

Guide to Pronunciation

Each main entry in this part of the dictionary is followed by a phonetic transcription which shows you how to pronounce the words. This transcription should be read as if it were English. It is based on Standard British pronunciation, though we have tried to take account of General American pronunciation also. Below, only those letters and symbols are explained which we consider likely to be ambiguous or not immediately understood.

The syllables are separated by hyphens, and stressed syllables are printed in *italics*.

Of course, the sounds of any two languages are never exactly the same, but if you follow carefully our indications, you should be able to pronounce the foreign words in such a way that you'll be understood. To make your task easier, our transcriptions occasionally simplify slightly the sound system of the language while still reflecting the essential sound differences.

Consonants

g	always hard, as in go
l^y	like **lli** in million
ñ	as in Spanish se**ñ**or, or like **ni** in o**ni**on
r	slightly rolled in the front of the mouth
s	always hard, as in so
y	always as in **y**et, not as in eas**y**

Vowels and Diphthongs

aa	long **a**, as in car
ah	a short version of **aa**; between **a** in cat and **u** in cut
ai	like **air**, without any **r**-sound
eh	like **e** in get
igh	as in sigh
o	always as in hot (British pronunciation)
ou	as in loud

1) A bar over a vowel symbol (e.g. $\overline{oo}$) shows that this sound is long.

2) Raised letters (e.g. **ah^{ay}**, **eh^{oo}**) should be pronounced only fleetingly.

3) Italian vowels (i.e. not diphthongs) are pure. Therefore, you should try to read a transcription like **oa** without moving tongue or lips while pronouncing the sound.

4) A few Italian words borrowed from French contain nasal vowels, which we transcribe with a vowel symbol plus **ng** (e.g. **ong**). This **ng** should *not* be pronounced, and serves solely to indicate nasal quality of the preceding vowel. A nasal vowel is pronounced simultaneously through the mouth and the nose.

A

a (ah) *prep* at; to; on

abbagliante (ahb-bah-*lʸahn*-tay) *adj* glaring

abbagliare (ahb-bah-*lʸaa*-ray) *v* blind

abbaiare (ahb-bah-*yaa*-ray) *v* bark

abbandonare (ahb-bahn-doa-*naa*-ray) *v* abandon

abbassare (ahb-bahss-*saa*-ray) *v* lower

abbastanza (ahb-bah-*stahn*-tsah) *adv* enough; fairly, rather, pretty, quite

abbattere (ahb-*baht*-tay-ray) *v* knock down, fell; dishearten

abbattuto (ahb-bah-*tōō*-toa) *adj* low, down

abbigliamento sportivo (ahb-bee-lʸah-mayn-toa spoar-*tee*-voa) sportswear

abbigliare (ahb-bee-*lʸaa*-ray) *v* dress

abbonamento (ahb-boa-nah-*mayn*-toa) *m* subscription; season-ticket

abbonato (ahb-boa-*naa*-toa) *m* subscriber

abbondante (ahb-boan-*dahn*-tay) *adj* plentiful, abundant

abbondanza (ahb-boan-*dahn*-tsah) *f* plenty, abundance

abbottonare (ahb-boat-toa-*naa*-ray) *v* button

abbozzare (ahb-boat-*tsaa*-ray) *v* sketch

abbracciare (ahb-braht-*chaa*-ray) *v* embrace, hug

abbraccio (ahb-*braht*-choa) *m* embrace, hug

abbreviazione (ahb-bray-vyah-*tsyōā*-nay) *f* abbreviation

abbronzato (ahb-broan-*dzaa*-toa) *adj* tanned

abbronzatura (ahb-broan-dzah-*tōō*-rah) *f* sunburn

aberrazione (ah-bayr-rah-*tsyōā*-nay) *f* aberration

abete (ah-*bāy*-tay) *m* fir-tree

abile (*aa*-bee-lay) *adj* able; skilled, skilful

abilità (ah-bee-lee-*tah*) *f* capacity, ability; art, skill

abilitare (ah-bee-lee-*taa*-ray) *v* enable

abisso (ah-*beess*-soa) *m* abyss

abitabile (ah-bee-*taa*-bee-lay) *adj* inhabitable, habitable

abitante (ah-bee-*tahn*-tay) *m* inhabitant

abitare (ah-bee-*taa*-ray) *v* live; inhabit; reside

abitazione (ah-bee-tah-*tsyōā*-nay) *f* house; home

abito (*aa*-bee-toa) *m* frock; suit; **abiti** clothes *pl*; **~ da sera** evening dress; **~ femminile** robe, dress

abituale (ah-bee-*twaa*-lay) *adj* common, customary

abitualmente (ah-bee-twahl-*mayn*-tay) *adv* usually

abituare (ah-bee-*twaa*-ray) *v* accustom

abitudine (ah-bee-*tōō*-dee-nay) *f* habit; custom; routine

abolire (ah-boa-*lee*-ray) *v* abolish

aborto (ah-*bor*-toa) *m* miscarriage; abortion

abramide (ah-brah-*mee*-day) *m* bream

abuso (ah-*bōō*-zoa) *m* misuse, abuse

accademia (ahk-kah-*dai*-myah) *f* academy; ~ **di belle arti** art school

*__accadere__ (ahk-kah-*dāy*-ray) *v* occur, happen

accamparsi (ahk-kahm-*pahr*-see) *v* camp

accanto (ahk-*kahn*-toa) *adv* next-door; ~ **a** beside

accappatoio (ahk-kahp-pah-*tōā*-yoa) *m* bathrobe

accelerare (aht-chay-lay-*raa*-ray) *v* accelerate

accelerato (aht-chay-lay-*raa*-toa) *m* stopping train

acceleratore (aht-chay-lay-rah-*tōā*-ray) *m* accelerator

*__accendere__ (aht-*chehn*-day-ray) *v* *light; turn on, switch on

accendino (aht-chayn-*dee*-noa) *m* cigarette-lighter, lighter

accennare (aht-chayn-*naa*-ray) *v* beckon; ~ **a** allude to

accensione (aht-chayn-*syōā*-nay) *f* ignition; contact; **bobina di** ~ ignition coil

accento (aht-*chehn*-toa) *m* accent; stress

accerchiare (aht-chayr-*kyaa*-ray) *v* circle, encircle

accertare (aht-chayr-*taa*-ray) *v* ascertain

accessibile (aht-chayss-*see*-bee-lay) *adj* accessible

accesso (aht-*chehss*-soa) *m* access; approach, entrance

accessori (aht-chayss-*sōā*-ree) *mpl* accessories *pl*

accessorio (aht-chayss-*sōā*-ryoa) *adj* additional

accettare (aht-chayt-*taa*-ray) *v* accept

acchiappare (ahk-kyahp-*paa*-ray) *v* *catch

acciaio (aht-*chaa*-yoa) *m* steel; ~ **inossidabile** stainless steel

accidentato (aht-chee-dayn-*taa*-toa) *adj* bumpy

acciuga (aht-*chōō*-gah) *f* anchovy

acclamare (ahk-klah-*maa*-ray) *v* cheer

*__accludere__ (ahk-*klōō*-day-ray) *v* enclose

accoglienza (ahk-koa-*lʸehn*-tsah) *f* reception, welcome

*__accogliere__ (ahk-*kaw*-lʸay-ray) *v* welcome; accept

accomodamento (ahk-koa-moa-dah-*mayn*-toa) *m* arrangement, settlement

accompagnare (ahk-koam-pah-*ña*-ray) *v* accompany; *take

acconciatura (ahk-koan-chah-*tōō*-rah) *f* hair-do

acconsentire (ahk-koan-sayn-*tee*-ray) *v* consent

accontentato (ahk-koan-tayn-*taa*-toa) *adj* satisfied

acconto (ahk-*koan*-toa) *m* down payment

accordare (ahk-koar-*daa*-ray) *v* grant, extend; **accordarsi** *v* agree

accordo (ahk-*kor*-doa) *m* agreement, settlement; approval; deal; **d'accordo!** okay!

*__accorgersi di__ (ahk-*kor*-jayr-see) notice

*__accorrere__ (ahk-*koar*-ray-ray) *v* rush

accreditare (ahk-kray-dee-*taa*-ray) *v* credit

*__accrescersi__ (ahk-kraysh-*shayr*-see) *v* increase

accudire a (ahk-koo-*dee*-ray) attend to

accumulatore (ahk-koo-moo-lah-*tōa*-ray) *m* battery

accurato (ahk-koo-*raa*-toa) *adj* careful, accurate; thorough

accusa (ahk-*kōō*-zah) *f* charge

accusare (ahk-koo-*zaa*-ray) *v* accuse; charge

accusato (ahk-koo-*zaa*-toa) *m* accused

acero (*ah*-chay-roa) *m* maple

aceto (ah-*chāy*-toa) *m* vinegar

acido (*ah*-chee-doa) *m* acid

acne (*ahk*-nay) *f* acne

acqua (*ahk*-kwah) *f* water; ~ **corrente** running water; ~ **dentifricia** mouthwash; ~ **di mare** sea-water; ~ **di seltz** soda-water; ~ **dolce** fresh water; ~ **ghiacciata** iced water; ~ **minerale** mineral water; ~ **ossigenata** *m* peroxide; ~ **potabile** drinking-water

acquaforte (ahk-kwah-*for*-tay) *f* etching

acquazzone (ahk-kwaht-*tsōa*-nay) *m* shower, downpour

acquerello (ahk-kway-*rehl*-loa) *m* water-colour

acquisizione (ahk-kwee-zee-*tsyōa*-nay) *f* acquisition

acquistare (ahk-kwee-*staa*-ray) *v* *buy

acquisto (ahk-*kwee*-stoa) *m* purchase

acuto (ah-*kōō*-toa) *adj* acute

adattare (ah-daht-*taa*-ray) *v* adapt; adjust, suit

adattatore (ah-daht-tah-*tōa*-ray) *m* adaptor

adatto (ah-*daht*-toa) *adj* proper, suitable, fit; appropriate

addestramento (ahd-day-strah-*mayn*-toa) *m* training

addestrare (ahd-day-*straa*-ray) *v* train, drill

addio (ahd-*dee*-oa) *m* parting

***addirsi** (ahd-*deer*-see) *v* *become, suit; qualify

additare (ahd-dee-*taa*-ray) *v* point

addizionare (ahd-dee-tsyoa-*naa*-ray) *v* add, count

addizione (ahd-dee-*tsyōa*-nay) *f* addition

addolcitore (ahd-doal-chee-*tōa*-ray) *m* water-softener

addomesticare (ahd-doa-may-stee-*kaa*-ray) *v* tame; **addomesticato** tame

addormentato (ahd-doar-mayn-*taa*-toa) *adj* asleep

adeguato (ah-day-*gwaa*-toa) *adj* adequate; suitable

adempiere (ah-*dehm*-pyay-ray) *v* accomplish

adempimento (ah-daym-pee-*mayn*-toa) *m* achievement

adesso (ah-*dehss*-soa) *adv* now

adiacente (ah-dyah-*chehn*-tay) *adj* neighbouring

adolescente (ah-doa-laysh-*shehn*-tay) *m* teenager

adoperare (ah-doa-pay-*raa*-ray) *v* use

adorabile (ah-doa-*raa*-bee-lay) *adj* adorable

adottare (ah-doat-*taa*-ray) *v* adopt; borrow

adulto (ah-*dool*-toa) *adj* grown-up, adult; *m* grown-up, adult

aerare (ah^{ay}-*raa*-ray) *v* ventilate

aerazione (ah^{ay}-rah-*tsyōa*-nay) *f* ventilation

aereo (ah-*ai*-ray-oa) *m* plane, aircraft; ~ **a reazione** turbojet

aerodromo (ah^{ay}-*ro*-dro-moa) *m* airfield

aeroplano (ah^{ay}-roa-*plaa*-noa) *m* aeroplane; airplane *nAm*

aeroporto (ah^{ay}-roa-*por*-toa) *m* airport

affabile (ahf-*faa*-bee-lay) *adj* friendly

affacciarsi (ahf-faht-*chahr*-see) *v* appear

affamato (ahf-fah-*maa*-toa) *adj* hungry

affare (ahf-*faa*-ray) *m* matter, affair,

business; bargain; deal; **affari** business; ***fare affari con** *deal with; **per affari** on business

affascinante (ahf-fahsh-shee-*nahn*-tay) *adj* glamorous, enchanting, charming

affascinare (ahf-fahsh-shee-*naa*-ray) *v* fascinate

affastellare (ahf-fah-stayl-*laa*-ray) *v* bundle

affaticato (ahf-fah-tee-*kaa*-toa) *adj* weary, tired

affatto (ahf-*faht*-toa) *adv* at all

affermare (ahf-fayr-*maa*-ray) *v* state

affermativo (ahf-fayr-mah-*tee*-voa) *adj* affirmative

afferrare (ahf-fayr-*raa*-ray) *v* grasp, *catch, seize; *take

affettato (ahf-fayt-*taa*-toa) *adj* affected

affetto (ahf-*feht*-toa) *m* affection

affettuoso (ahf-fayt-*twōa*-soa) *adj* affectionate

affezionato a (ahf-fay-tsyoa-*naa*-toa ah) attached to

affezione (ahf-fay-*tsyoa*-nay) *f* affection, ailment

affidare (ahf-fee-*daa*-ray) *v* commit

affilare (ahf-fee-*laa*-ray) *v* sharpen

affilato (ahf-fee-*laa*-toa) *adj* sharp

affinché (ahf-feeng-*kay*) *conj* so that

affisso (ahf-*feess*-soa) *m* placard

affittacamere (ahf-feet-tah-*kaa*-may-ray) *m* landlord; *f* landlady

affittare (ahf-feet-*taa*-ray) *v* *let; rent

affitto (ahf-*feet*-toa) *m* rent; ***dare in ~** lease; ***prendere in ~** lease

*affliggersi (ahf-fleed-*jayr*-see) *v* grieve

afflitto (ahf-*fleet*-toa) *adj* sad

afflizione (ahf-flee-*tsyoa*-nay) *f* affliction; grief

affogare (ahf-foa-*gaa*-ray) *v* drown; **affogarsi** *v* *be drowned

affollato (ahf-foal-*laa*-toa) *adj* crowded

affondare (ahf-foan-*daa*-ray) *v* *sink

affrancare (ahf-frahng-*kaa*-ray) *v* stamp

affrancatura (ahf-frahng-kah-*tōō*-rah) *f* postage

affrettarsi (ahf-frayt-*tahr*-see) *v* rush, hasten, hurry

affrontare (ahf-froan-*taa*-ray) *v* tackle, face

Africa (*aa*-free-kah) *f* Africa; **Africa del Sud** South Africa

africano (ah-free-*kaa*-noa) *adj* African; *m* African

agenda (ah-*jehn*-dah) *f* diary; agenda

agente (ah-*jehn*-tay) *m* policeman; agent; **~ di viaggio** travel agent; **~ immobiliare** house agent

agenzia (ah-jayn-*tsee*-ah) *f* agency; **~ viaggi** travel agency

agevolazione (ah-jay-voa-lah-*tsyoa*-nay) *f* facility

aggeggio (ahd-*jayd*-joa) *m* gadget

aggettivo (ahd-jayt-*tee*-voa) *m* adjective

aggiudicare (ahd-joo-dee-*kaa*-ray) *v* award

*aggiungere (ahd-*joon*-jay-ray) *v* add

aggiunta (ahd-*joon*-tah) *f* addition; **in ~ a** beyond

aggiustamento (ahd-joo-stah-*mayn*-toa) *m* settlement

aggredire (ahg-gray-*dee*-ray) *v* assault

aggressivo (ahg-grayss-*see*-voa) *adj* aggressive

agiato (ah-*jaa*-toa) *adj* well-to-do

agile (*ah*-jee-lay) *adj* supple

agio (*aa*-joa) *m* comfort, ease

agire (ah-*jee*-ray) *v* act; operate

agitare (ah-jee-*taa*-ray) *v* *shake

agitazione (ah-jee-tah-*tsyoa*-nay) *f* excitement, unrest

aglio (*aa*-lᶦyoa) *m* garlic

agnello (ah-*ñehl*-loa) *m* lamb

ago (*aa*-goa) *m* needle

agosto (ah-*goa*-stoa) August

agricolo (ah-*gree*-koa-loa) *adj* agrarian

agricoltura (ah-gree-koal-*too*-rah) *f* agriculture

agro (*aa*-groa) *adj* sour

aguzzo (ah-*goot*-tsoa) *adj* keen

aiola (igh-*aw*-lah) *f* flowerbed

airone (igh-*rōa*-nay) *m* heron

aiutante (ah-yoo-*tahn*-tay) *m* helper

aiutare (ah-yoo-*taa*-ray) *v* aid, help

aiuto (ah-*yōō*-toa) *m* assistance, help; relief

ala (*aa*-lah) *f* wing

alba (*ahl*-bah) *f* dawn

albergatore (ahl-bayr-gah-*tōa*-ray) *m* inn-keeper

albergo (ahl-*behr*-goa) *m* hotel

albero (*ahl*-bay-roa) *m* tree; mast; ~ **a camme** camshaft; ~ **a gomiti** crankshaft

albicocca (ahl-bee-*kok*-kah) *f* apricot

album (*ahl*-boom) *m* album; ~ **da disegno** sketch-book; ~ **per ritagli** scrap-book

alce (*ahl*-chay) *m* moose

alcool (*ahl*-koa-oal) *m* alcohol; ~ **metilico** methylated spirits

alcoolico (ahl-*kaw*-lee-koa) *adj* alcoholic

alcuno (ahl-*kōō*-noa) *adj* any; **alcuni** *adj* some; *pron* some

alfabeto (ahl-fah-*bai*-toa) *m* alphabet

algebra (*ahl*-jay-brah) *f* algebra

Algeria (ahl-jay-*ree*-ah) *f* Algeria

algerino (ahl-jay-*ree*-noa) *adj* Algerian; *m* Algerian

aliante (ah-*lyahn*-tay) *m* glider

alimentari (ah-lee-mayn-*taa*-ree) *mpl* groceries *pl*, foodstuffs *pl*

alimento (ah-lee-*mayn*-toa) *m* food; **alimenti** alimony

allacciare (ahl-laht-*chaa*-ray) *v* fasten

allargare (ahl-lahr-*gaa*-ray) *v* widen; extend; expand

allarmante (ahl-lahr-*mahn*-tay) *adj* scary

allarmare (ahl-lahr-*maa*-ray) *v* alarm

allarme (ahl-*lahr*-may) *m* alarm; ~ **d'incendio** fire-alarm

allattare (ahl-laht-*taa*-ray) *v* nurse

alleanza (ahl-lay-*ahn*-tsah) *f* alliance

alleato (ahl-lay-*aa*-toa) *m* associate; **Alleati** Allies *pl*

allegare (ahl-lay-*gaa*-ray) *v* enclose

allegato (ahl-lay-*gaa*-toa) *m* annex, enclosure

allegria (ahl-lay-*gree*-ah) *f* gaiety

allegro (ahl-*lāy*-groa) *adj* merry, joyful, gay, cheerful; jolly

allenatore (ahl-lay-nah-*tōa*-ray) *m* coach

allergia (ahl-layr-*jee*-ah) *f* allergy

allevare (ahl-lay-*vaa*-ray) *v* raise; rear; *breed

allibrare (ahl-lee-*braa*-ray) *v* book

allibratore (ahl-lee-brah-*tōa*-ray) *m* bookmaker

allievo (ahl-*lyai*-voa) *m* scholar

allodola (ahl-*law*-doa-lah) *f* lark

alloggiare (ahl-load-*jaa*-ray) *v* accommodate, lodge

alloggio (ahl-*lod*-joa) *m* accommodation, lodgings *pl*; apartment *nAm*; ~ **e colazione** bed and breakfast

allontanare (ahl-loan-tah-*naa*-ray) *v* remove; **allontanarsi** depart; deviate

allora (ahl-*lōa*-rah) *adv* then; **da** ~ since

allungare (ahl-loong-*gaa*-ray) *v* lengthen; dilute

almanacco (ahl-mah-*nahk*-koa) *m* almanac

almeno (ahl-*māy*-noa) *adv* at least

alpinismo (ahl-pee-*nee*-zmoa) *m* mountaineering

alquanto (ahl-*kwahn*-toa) *adv* fairly, rather, pretty, quite; somewhat

alt! (ahlt) stop!

altalena (ahl-tah-*lāy*-nah) f swing; see-saw

altare (ahl-*taa*-ray) m altar

alternativa (ahl-tayr-nah-*tee*-vah) f alternative

alternato (ahl-tayr-*naa*-toa) adj alternate

altezza (ahl-*tayt*-tsah) f height

altezzoso (ahl-tayt-*tsōa*-soa) adj haughty

altitudine (ahl-tee-*tōo*-dee-nay) f altitude

alto (*ahl*-toa) adj high; tall; loud; **verso l'alto** up

altoparlante (ahl-toa-pahr-*lahn*-tay) m loud-speaker

altopiano (ahl-toa-*pyaa*-noa) m (pl altipiani) plateau, uplands pl

altrettanto (ahl-trayt-*tahn*-toa) adv as much

altrimenti (ahl-tree-*mayn*-tee) adv otherwise, else; conj otherwise

altro (*ahl*-troa) adj other; different; **l'un l'altro** each other; **l'uno o l'altro** either; **tra l'altro** among other things; **un ~** another

d'altronde (dahl-*troan*-day) besides

altrove (ahl-*trōa*-vay) adv elsewhere

altura (ahl-*tōo*-rah) f rise

alveare (ahl-vay-*aa*-ray) m beehive

alzare (ahl-*tsaa*-ray) v lift; **alzarsi** *get up, *rise

amabile (ah-*maa*-bee-lay) adj gentle

amaca (ah-*maa*-kah) f hammock

amante (ah-*mahn*-tay) m lover; f mistress

amare (ah-*maa*-ray) v love; *be fond of

amaro (ah-*maa*-roa) adj bitter

amato (ah-*maa*-toa) adj beloved

ambasciata (ahm-bahsh-*shaa*-tah) f embassy

ambasciatore (ahm-bahsh-shah-*tōa*-ray) m ambassador

ambiente (ahm-*byayn*-tay) m milieu, environment

ambiguo (ahm-*bee*-gwoa) adj ambiguous

ambizioso (ahm-bee-*tsyōa*-soa) adj ambitious

ambra (*ahm*-brah) f amber

ambulante (ahm-boo-*lahn*-tay) adj itinerant

ambulanza (ahm-boo-*lahn*-tsah) f ambulance

America (ah-*mai*-ree-kah) f America; **~ Latina** Latin America

americano (ah-may-ree-*kaa*-noa) adj American; m American

ametista (ah-may-*tee*-stah) f amethyst

amianto (ah-*myahn*-toa) m asbestos

amica (ah-*mee*-kah) f friend

amichevole (ah-mee-*kāy*-voa-lay) adj friendly

amicizia (ah-mee-*chee*-tsyah) f friendship

amico (ah-*mee*-koa) m friend

amido (*aa*-mee-doa) m starch

ammaccare (ahm-mahk-*kaa*-ray) v bruise

ammaccatura (ahm-mahk-kah-*tōo*-rah) f dent

ammaestrare (ahm-mah^{ay}-*straa*-ray) v train

ammainare (ahm-migh-*naa*-ray) v *strike

ammalato (ahm-mah-*laa*-toa) adj ill, sick

ammazzare (ahm-maht-*tsaa*-ray) v kill

*ammettere (ahm-*mayt*-tay-ray) v admit; acknowledge

amministrare (ahm-mee-nee-*straa*-ray) v direct

amministrativo (ahm-mee-nee-strah-*tee*-voa) adj administrative

amministrazione (ahm-mee-nee-strah-*tsyōa*-nay) f administration; direction

ammiraglio (ahm-mee-*rah*-l^Yoa) *m* admiral

ammirare (ahm-mee-*raa*-ray) *v* admire

ammirazione (ahm-mee-rah-*tsyōā*-nay) *f* admiration

ammissione (ahm-meess-*syōā*-nay) *f* admittance, admission

ammobiliare (ahm-moa-bee-l^Y*aa*-ray) *v* furnish; **non ammobiliato** unfurnished

ammollare (ahm-moal-*laa*-ray) *v* soak

ammoniaca (ahm-moa-*nee*-ah-kah) *f* ammonia

ammonire (ahm-moa-*nee*-ray) *v* caution

ammontare (ahm-moan-*taa*-ray) *m* amount

ammontare a (ahm-moan-*taa*-ray) amount to

ammorbidire (ahm-moar-bee-*dee*-ray) *v* soften

ammortizzatore (ahm-moar-teed-dzah-*tōā*-ray) *m* shock absorber

ammucchiare (ahm-mook-*kyaa*-ray) *v* pile

ammuffito (ahm-moof-*fee*-toa) *adj* mouldy

ammutinamento (ahm-moo-tee-nah-*mayn*-toa) *m* mutiny

amnistia (ahm-nee-*stee*-ah) *f* amnesty

amo (*aa*-moa) *m* fishing hook; **pescare con l'amo** fish

amore (ah-*mōā*-ray) *m* love; darling, sweetheart

amoretto (ah-moa-*rayt*-toa) *m* affair

ampio (*ahm*-pyoa) *adj* extensive, broad

ampliamento (ahm-plyah-*mayn*-toa) *m* extension

ampliare (ahm-*plyaa*-ray) *v* enlarge

amuleto (ah-moo-*lāy*-toa) *m* charm

analfabeta (ah-nahl-fah-*bai*-tah) *m* illiterate

analisi (ah-*naa*-lee-zee) *f* analysis

analista (ah-nah-*lee*-stah) *m* analyst

analizzare (ah-nah-leed-*dzaa*-ray) *v* analyse; *break down

analogo (ah-*naa*-loa-goa) *adj* similar

ananas (*ah*-nah-nahss) *m* pineapple

anarchia (ah-nahr-*kee*-ah) *f* anarchy

anatomia (ah-nah-toa-*mee*-ah) *f* anatomy

anche (*ahng*-kay) *adv* too, also; even

ancora[1] (ahng-*kōā*-rah) *adv* yet, still; again; some more; ~ **una volta** once more

ancora[2] (*ahng*-koa-rah) *f* anchor

*andare (ahn-*daa*-ray) *v* *go; ~ **a prendere** *get, fetch; ~ **carponi** crawl; ~ **in macchina** *ride; *andarsene *go away, depart

andata (ahn-*daa*-tah) *f* going

andatura (ahn-dah-*tōō*-rah) *f* walk; pace, gait

andirivieni (ahn-dee-ree-*vyai*-nee) *m* bustle

anello (ah-*nehl*-loa) *m* ring; ~ **di fidanzamento** engagement ring; ~ **per stantuffo** piston ring

anemia (ah-nay-*mee*-ah) *f* anaemia

anestesia (ah-nay-stay-*see*-ah) *f* anaesthesia

anestetico (ah-nay-*stai*-tee-koa) *m* anaesthetic

angelo (*ahn*-jay-loa) *m* angel

angolo (*ahng*-goa-loa) *m* corner; angle

angora (*ahng*-go-rah) *f* mohair

anguilla (ahng-*gweel*-lah) *f* eel

anguria (ahng-*gōō*-ryah) *f* watermelon

angusto (ahng-*goo*-stoa) *adj* narrow

anima (*aa*-nee-mah) *f* soul; essence

animale (ah-nee-*maa*-lay) *m* animal; beast; ~ **da preda** beast of prey; ~ **domestico** pet

animato (ah-nee-*maa*-toa) *adj* busy

animo (*aa*-nee-moa) *m* heart; intention; courage

anitra (*aa*-nee-trah) *f* duck

***annettere** (ahn-*neht*-tay-ray) *v* annex; attach

anniversario (ahn-nee-vayr-*saa*-ryoa) *m* anniversary; jubilee

anno (*ahn*-noa) *m* year; **all'anno** per annum; ~ **bisestile** leap-year; ~ **nuovo** New Year

annodare (ahn-noa-*daa*-ray) *v* knot, tie

annoiare (ahn-noa-*yaa*-ray) *v* annoy; bore

annotare (ahn-noa-*taa*-ray) *v* *write down, note

annuale (ahn-*nwaa*-lay) *adj* yearly, annual

annuario (ahn-*nwaa*-ryoa) *m* annual

annuire (ahn-*nwee*-ray) *v* nod

annullamento (ahn-nool-lah-*mayn*-toa) *m* cancellation

annullare (ahn-nool-*laa*-ray) *v* cancel

annunziare (ahn-noon-*tsyaa*-ray) *v* announce

annunzio (ahn-*noon*-tsyoa) *m* announcement; ~ **pubblicitario** commercial

anonimo (ah-*naw*-nee-moa) *adj* anonymous

anormale (ah-noar-*maa*-lay) *adj* abnormal

ansia (*ahn*-syah) *f* worry

ansietà (ahn-syay-*tah*) *f* anxiety, concern

ansimare (ahn-see-*maa*-ray) *v* pant

ansioso (ahn-*syōā*-soa) *adj* anxious, eager

d'anteguerra (dahn-tay-*gwehr*-rah) pre-war

antenato (ahn-tay-*naa*-toa) *m* ancestor

antenna (ahn-*tayn*-nah) *f* aerial

anteriore (ahn-tay-*ryōā*-ray) *adj* prior, previous

anteriormente (ahn-tay-ryoar-*mayn*-tay) *adv* formerly

antibiotico (ahn-tee-*byaw*-tee-koa) *m* antibiotic

anticaglia (ahn-tee-*kaa*-l^yah) *f* antique

antichità (ahn-tee-kee-*tah*) *fpl* antiquities *pl*; **Antichità** *f* antiquity

anticipare (ahn-tee-chee-*paa*-ray) *v* anticipate

anticipatamente (ahn-tee-chee-pah-tah-*mayn*-tay) *adv* in advance

anticipo (ahn-*tee*-chee-poa) *m* advance; **in** ~ in advance

antico (ahn-*tee*-koa) *adj* ancient; antique; former

anticoncezionale (ahn-tee-koan-chay-tsyoa-*naa*-lay) *m* contraceptive

anticongelante (ahn-tee-koan-jay-*lahn*-tay) *m* antifreeze

antipasto (ahn-tee-*pah*-stoa) *m* hors-d'œuvre

antipatia (ahn-tee-pah-*tee*-ah) *f* antipathy, dislike

antipatico (ahn-tee-*paa*-tee-koa) *adj* unpleasant, nasty

antiquario (ahn-tee-*kwaa*-ryoa) *m* antique dealer

antiquato (ahn-tee-*kwaa*-toa) *adj* ancient, old-fashioned; quaint

antisettico (ahn-tee-*seht*-tee-koa) *m* antiseptic

antologia (ahn-toa-loa-*jee*-ah) *f* anthology

anzi (*ahn*-tsee) *adv* rather, on the contrary

anziano (ahn-*tsyaa*-noa) *adj* aged, elderly

ape (*aa*-pay) *f* bee

aperitivo (ah-pay-ree-*tee*-voa) *m* aperitif, drink

aperto (ah-*pehr*-toa) *adj* open; **all'aperto** outdoors

apertura (ah-payr-*tōō*-rah) *f* opening

apice (*aa*-pee-chay) *m* zenith

appagamento (ahp-pah-gah-*mayn*-toa) *m* satisfaction

apparato (ahp-pah-*raa*-toa) *m* appliance; pomp

apparecchio (ahp-pah-*rayk*-kyoa) *m* appliance, apparatus, machine

apparente (ahp-pah-*rehn*-tay) *adj* apparent

apparentemente (ahp-pah-rayn-tay-*mayn*-tay) *adv* apparently

apparenza (ahp-pah-*rehn*-tsah) *f* appearance; semblance

*****apparire** (ahp-pah-*ree*-ray) *v* appear

apparizione (ahp-pah-ree-*tsyōa*-nay) *f* apparition

appartamento (ahp-pahr-tah-*mayn*-toa) *m* flat; suite; apartment *nAm*; **blocco di appartamenti** apartment house *Am*

*****appartenere** (ahp-pahr-tay-*nāy*-ray) *v* belong

appassionato (ahp-pahss-syoa-*naa*-toa) *adj* passionate; keen

appello (ahp-*pehl*-loa) *m* appeal; call

appena (ahp-*pai*-nah) *adv* hardly, barely; just; **non ~** as soon as

*****appendere** (ahp-*pehn*-day-ray) *v* *hang

appendice (ahp-payn-*dee*-chay) *f* appendix

appendicite (ahp-payn-dee-*chee*-tay) *f* appendicitis

appetito (ahp-pay-*tee*-toa) *m* appetite

appetitoso (ahp-pay-tee-*tōa*-soa) *adj* appetizing

appezzamento (ahp-payt-tsah-*mayn*-toa) *m* plot

appiccicare (ahp-peet-chee-*kaa*-ray) *v* *stick

appiccicaticcio (ahp-peet-chee-kah-*teet*-choa) *adj* sticky

applaudire (ahp-plou-*dee*-ray) *v* clap

applauso (ahp-*plou*-zoa) *m* applause

applicare (ahp-plee-*kaa*-ray) *v* apply; **applicarsi** apply

applicazione (ahp-plee-kah-*tsyōa*-nay) *f* application

appoggiare (ahp-poad-*jaa*-ray) *v* support; **appoggiarsi** *lean

apposta (ahp-*po*-stah) *adv* on purpose

*****apprendere** (ahp-*prehn*-day-ray) *v* learn; *hear

apprezzamento (ahp-prayt-tsah-*mayn*-toa) *m* appreciation

apprezzare (ahp-prayt-*tsaa*-ray) *v* appreciate

approfittare (ahp-proa-feet-*taa*-ray) *v* profit, benefit

appropriato (ahp-proa-*pryaa*-toa) *adj* appropriate, proper

approssimativo (ahp-proass-see-mah-*tee*-voa) *adj* approximate

approvare (ahp-proa-*vaa*-ray) *v* approve; approve of

approvazione (ahp-proa-vah-*tsyōa*-nay) *f* approval

appuntamento (ahp-poon-tah-*mayn*-toa) *m* appointment, date

appuntare (ahp-poon-*taa*-ray) *v* pin

appuntato (ahp-poon-*taa*-toa) *adj* pointed

appunto (ahp-*poon*-toa) *m* note; **blocco per appunti** pad, writing-pad

apribottiglie (ah-pree-boat-*tee*-l^yay) *m* bottle opener

aprile (ah-*pree*-lay) April

*****aprire** (ah-*pree*-ray) *v* open; unlock; turn on

apriscatole (ah-pree-*skaa*-toa-lay) *m* tin-opener, can opener

aquila (*ah*-kwee-lah) *f* eagle

Arabia Saudita (ah-*raa*-byah sou-*dee*-tah) Saudi Arabia

arabo (*ah*-rah-boa) *adj* Arab; *m* Arab

arachide (ah-*raa*-kee-day) *f* peanut

aragosta (ah-rah-*goa*-stah) *f* lobster

aragostina (ah-rah-goa-*stee*-nah) *f* prawn

arancia (ah-*rahn*-chah) *f* orange

arancione (ah-rahn-*chōa*-nay) *adj* orange

arare (ah-*raa*-ray) *v* plough

aratro (ah-*raa*-troa) *m* plough

arazzo (ah-*raht*-tsoa) *m* tapestry

arbitrario (ahr-bee-*traa*-ryoa) *adj* arbitrary

arbitro (*ahr*-bee-troa) *m* umpire

arbusto (ahr-*boo*-stoa) *m* shrub

arcata (ahr-*kaa*-tah) *f* arch; arcade

arcato (ahr-*kaa*-toa) *adj* arched

archeologia (ahr-kay-oa-loa-*jee*-ah) *f* archaeology

archeologo (ahr-kay-*o*-loa-goa) *m* archaeologist

architetto (ahr-kee-*tayt*-toa) *m* architect

architettura (ahr-kee-tayt-*toō*-rah) *f* architecture

archivio (ahr-*kee*-vyoa) *m* archives *pl*

arcivescovo (ahr-chee-*vay*-skoa-voa) *m* archbishop

arco (*ahr*-koa) *m* bow; arch

arcobaleno (ahr-koa-bah-*lāy*-noa) *m* rainbow

***ardere** (*ahr*-day-ray) *v* *burn; glow

ardesia (ahr-*dāy*-syah) *f* slate

ardore (ahr-*dōā*-ray) *m* glow

area (*aa*-ray-ah) *f* area

arena (ah-*rāy*-nah) *f* bullring

argenteria (ahr-jayn-tay-*ree*-ah) *f* silverware

argentiere (ahr-jayn-*tyai*-ray) *m* silversmith

Argentina (ahr-jayn-*tee*-nah) *f* Argentina

argentino (ahr-jayn-*tee*-noa) *adj* Argentinian; *m* Argentinian

argento (ahr-*jehn*-toa) *m* silver; **d'argento** silver

argilla (ahr-*jeel*-lah) *f* clay

argine (*ahr*-jee-nay) *m* dike, dam; river bank, embankment

argomentare (ahr-goa-mayn-*taa*-ray) *v* argue

argomento (ahr-goa-*mayn*-toa) *m* argument; theme

aria (*aa*-ryah) *f* air, sky; tune; **ad ~ condizionata** air-conditioned; **a tenuta d'aria** airtight; *aver l'aria look; **condizionamento dell'aria** air-conditioning

arido (*aa*-ree-doa) *adj* arid

arieggiare (ah-ryayd-*jaa*-ray) *v* air

aringa (ah-*reeng*-gah) *f* herring

arioso (ah-*ryōā*-soa) *adj* airy

aritmetica (ah-reet-*mai*-tee-kah) *f* arithmetic

arma (*ahr*-mah) *f* (*pl* armi) arm, weapon

armadio (ahr-*maa*-dyoa) *m* cupboard; closet *nAm*

armare (ahr-*maa*-ray) *v* arm

armatore (ahr-mah-*tōā*-ray) *m* shipowner

armonia (ahr-moa-*nee*-ah) *f* harmony

arnese (ahr-*nāy*-say) *m* tool, utensil; **cassetta degli arnesi** tool kit

aroma (ah-*raw*-mah) *m* aroma

arpa (*ahr*-pah) *f* harp

arrabbiato (ahr-rahb-*byaa*-toa) *adj* angry, cross

arrampicare (ahr-rahm-pee-*kaa*-ray) *v* climb

arrangiarsi con (ahr-rahn-*jahr*-see) *make do with

arredare (ahr-ray-*daa*-ray) *v* furnish

***arrendersi** (ahr-*rehn*-dayr-see) *v* surrender

arrestare (ahr-ray-*staa*-ray) *v* arrest

arresto (ahr-*reh*-stoa) *m* arrest

arretrato (ahr-ray-*traa*-toa) *adj* overdue

arricciacapelli (ahr-reet-chah-kah-*payl*-lee) *m* curling-tongs *pl*

arricciare (ahr-reet-*chaa*-ray) *v* curl

arrischiare (ahr-ree-*skyaa*-ray) *v* venture

arrivare (ahr-ree-*vaa*-ray) *v* arrive

arrivederci! (ahr-ree-vay-*dayr*-chee)

good-bye!

arrivo (ahr-*ree*-voa) *m* arrival; **in ~ due**

arrogante (ahr-roa-*gahn*-tay) *adj* snooty

arrossire (ahr-roass-*see*-ray) *v* blush

arrostire (ahr-roa-*stee*-ray) *v* roast

arrotondato (ahr-roa-toan-*daa*-toa) *adj* rounded

arrugginito (ahr-rood-jee-*nee*-toa) *adj* rusty

arte (*ahr*-tay) *f* art; **arti e mestieri** arts and crafts; **belle arti** fine arts; **opera d'arte** work of art

arteria (ahr-*tai*-ryah) *f* artery; thoroughfare

articolazione (ahr-tee-koa-lah-*tsyoā*-nay) *f* joint

articolo (ahr-*tee*-koa-loa) *m* article; item; **articoli da toeletta** toiletry

artificiale (ahr-tee-fee-*chaa*-lay) *adj* artificial

artificio (ahr-tee-fee-*choa*) *m* artifice

artigianato (ahr-tee-jah-*naa*-toa) *m* handicraft

artiglio (ahr-*tee*-lYoa) *m* claw

artista (ahr-*tee*-stah) *m* artist

artistico (ahr-*tee*-stee-koa) *adj* artistic

***ascendere** (ahsh-*shayn*-day-ray) *v* ascend

ascensione (ahsh-shayn-*syoā*-nay) *f* ascent

ascensore (ahsh-shayn-*soā*-ray) *m* lift; elevator *nAm*

ascesa (ahsh-*shāy*-sah) *f* rise; climb; ascent

ascesso (ahsh-*shehss*-soa) *m* abscess

ascia (*ahsh*-shah) *f* axe

asciugacapelli (ahsh-shoo-gah-kah-*payl*-lee) *m* hair-dryer

asciugamano (ahsh-shoo-gah-*maa*-noa) *m* towel, bath towel

asciugare (ahsh-shoo-*gaa*-ray) *v* dry; wipe

asciutto (ahsh-*shoot*-toa) *adj* dry

ascoltare (ah-skoal-*taa*-ray) *v* listen

ascoltatore (ah-skoal-tah-*toā*-ray) *m* listener

asfalto (ah-*sfahl*-toa) *m* asphalt

Asia (*aa*-zyah) *f* Asia

asiatico (ah-*zyaa*-tee-koa) *adj* Asian; *m* Asian

asilo (ah-*zee*-loa) *m* asylum; **~ infantile** kindergarten

asino (*aa*-see-noa) *m* ass, donkey

asma (*ah*-zmah) *f* asthma

asola (*aa*-zoa-lah) *f* buttonhole

asparago (ah-*spaa*-rah-goa) *m* asparagus

aspettare (ah-spayt-*taa*-ray) *v* wait, await; expect

aspettativa (ah-spayt-tah-*tee*-vah) *f* expectation

aspetto (ahss-*speht*-toa) *m* look; appearance; aspect; **di bell'aspetto** good-looking

aspirapolvere (ah-spee-rah-*poal*-vay-ray) *m* vacuum cleaner; **pulire con l'aspirapolvere** hoover; vacuum *vAm*

aspirare (ah-spee-*raa*-ray) *v* inhale; aspire; **~ a** aim at

aspirazione (ah-spee-rah-*tsyoā*-nay) *f* suction; aspiration

aspirina (ah-spee-*ree*-nah) *f* aspirin

aspro (*ah*-sproa) *adj* harsh

assaggiare (ahss-sahd-*jaa*-ray) *v* taste

assai (ahss-*sigh*) *adv* very, quite

***assalire** (ahss-sah-*lee*-ray) *v* attack

assassinare (ahss-sahss-see-*naa*-ray) *v* murder

assassinio (ahss-sahss-*see*-ñoa) *m* assassination, murder

assassino (ahss-sahss-*see*-noa) *m* murderer

asse (*ahss*-say) *m* axle; *f* plank, board

assedio (ahss-*sāy*-dyoa) *m* siege

assegnare (ahss-say-*ñaa*-ray) *v* allot;

~ **a** assign to

assegno (ahss-*say*-ñoa) *m* allowance; cheque; check *nAm*; ~ **turistico** traveller's cheque; **libretto di assegni** cheque-book; check-book *nAm*

assemblea (ahss-saym-*blai*-ah) *f* assembly, meeting

assennato (ahss-sayn-*naa*-toa) *adj* sober

assente (ahss-*sehn*-tay) *adj* absent

assenza (ahss-*sehn*-tsah) *f* absence

asserire (ahss-say-*ree*-ray) *v* claim

assetato (ahss-say-*taa*-toa) *adj* thirsty

assicurare (ahss-see-koo-*raa*-ray) *v* assure; insure; **assicurarsi** secure

assicurazione (ahss-see-koo-rah-*tsyoā*-nay) *f* insurance; ~ **sulla vita** life insurance; ~ **viaggi** travel insurance

assieme (ahss-*syai*-may) *m* set

assistente (ahss-see-*stehn*-tay) *m* assistant

assistenza (ahss-see-*stehn*-tsah) *f* assistance

*assistere** (ahss-*see*-stay-ray) *v* assist, aid; ~ **a** attend, assist at

associare (ahss-soa-*chaa*-ray) *v* associate; **associarsi** *v* join

associato (ahss-soa-*chaa*-toa) *adj* affiliated

associazione (ahss-soa-chah-*tsyoā*-nay) *f* association; society, club

assolutamente (ahss-soa-loo-tah-*mayn*-tay) *adv* absolutely

assoluto (ahss-soa-*loō*-toa) *adj* sheer; total

assoluzione (ahss-soa-loo-*tsyoā*-nay) *f* acquittal

assomigliare a (ahss-soa-mee-*lɪ^yaa*-ray) resemble

assonnato (ahss-soan-*naa*-toa) *adj* sleepy

assortimento (ahss-soar-tee-*mayn*-toa) *m* assortment

assortire (ahss-soar-*tee*-ray) *v* assort; sort

assortito (ahss-soar-*tee*-toa) *adj* varied

*assumere** (ahss-*soō*-may-ray) *v* assume; engage

assurdo (ahss-*soor*-doa) *adj* absurd

asta (*ah*-stah) *f* auction

astemio (ah-*stai*-myoa) *m* teetotaller

*astenersi da** (ah-stay-*nayr*-see) abstain from

astore (ah-*stoā*-ray) *m* hawk

astratto (ah-*straht*-toa) *adj* abstract

astronomia (ah-stroa-noa-*mee*-ah) *f* astronomy

astuccio (ah-*stoot*-choa) *m* case; ~ **di toeletta** toilet case; ~ **per tabacco** tobacco pouch

astuto (ah-*stoō*-toa) *adj* sly

astuzia (ah-*stoō*-tsyah) *f* ruse

ateo (*aa*-tay-oa) *m* atheist

Atlantico (aht-*lahn*-tee-koa) *m* Atlantic

atleta (aht-*lai*-tah) *m* athlete

atletica (aht-*lai*-tee-kah) *f* athletics *pl*

atmosfera (aht-moa-*sfai*-rah) *f* atmosphere

atomico (ah-*taw*-mee-koa) *adj* atomic

atomizzatore (ah-toa-meed-dzah-*toā*-ray) *m* atomizer

atomo (*aa*-toa-moa) *m* atom

atrio (*aa*-tryoa) *m* lobby

atroce (ah-*troā*-chay) *adj* horrible

attaccapanni (aht-tahk-kah-*pahn*-nee) *m* hat rack; coat-hanger, hanger

attaccare (aht-tahk-*kaa*-ray) *v* attach; assault

attacco (aht-*tahk*-koa) *m* attack; fit; ~ **cardiaco** heart attack

atteggiamento (aht-tayd-jah-*mayn*-toa) *m* position

attempato (aht-taym-*paa*-toa) *adj* aged

*attendere** (aht-*tehn*-day-ray) *v* await, wait; ~ **a** attend to

attento (aht-*tehn*-toa) *adj* attentive;

careful; *stare ~ look out

attenzione (aht-tayn-*tsyoā*-nay) f attention; consideration, notice; *fare ~ mind, *pay attention, look out, beware; **prestare ~ a** attend to

atterrare (aht-tayr-*raa*-ray) v knock down; land

attesa (aht-*tāy*-sah) f waiting

attestato (aht-tay-*staa*-toa) m certificate

attillato (aht-teel-*laa*-toa) adj tight

attimo (*aht*-tee-moa) m moment

attinenza (aht-tee-*nehn*-tsah) f relation

attitudine (aht-tee-*tōō*-dee-nay) f faculty, talent; attitude

attività (aht-tee-vee-*tah*) f activity; work

attivo (aht-*tee*-voa) adj active

atto (*aht*-toa) m deed, act; certificate

attore (aht-*tōā*-ray) m actor

attorno (aht-*toar*-noa) adv about; ~ a round

attraccare (aht-trahk-*kaa*-ray) v dock

attraente (aht-trah-*ehn*-tay) adj attractive

*attrarre (aht-*trahr*-ray) v attract

attrattiva (aht-trah-*tee*-vah) f attraction

attraversare (aht-trah-vayr-*saa*-ray) v cross; pass through

attraverso (aht-trah-*vehr*-soa) prep across; through

attrazione (aht-trah-*tsyoā*-nay) f attraction

attrezzatura (aht-trayt-tsah-*tōō*-rah) f gear

attrezzo (aht-*trayt*-tsoa) m tool; **attrezzi da pesca** fishing tackle, fishing gear

attribuire a (aht-tree-*bwee*-ray) assign to

attrice (aht-*tree*-chay) f actress

attrito (aht-*tree*-toa) m friction

attuale (aht-*twaa*-lay) adj present;

topical

attualmente (aht-twahl-*mayn*-tay) adv at present

attuare (aht-*twaa*-ray) v realize

audace (ou-*daa*-chay) adj brave

audacia (ou-*daa*-chah) f courage; nerve

auditorio (ou-dee-*tōā*-ryoa) m auditorium

augurare (ou-goo-*raa*-ray) v wish

aula (*ou*-lah) f classroom

aumentare (ou-mayn-*taa*-ray) v increase; raise

aumento (ou-*mayn*-toa) m rise, increase; raise nAm

aureo (*ou*-ray-oa) adj golden

aurora (ou-*raw*-rah) f daybreak, dawn; sunrise

Australia (ou-*straa*-lYah) f Australia

australiano (ou-strah-lYaa-noa) adj Australian; m Australian

Austria (*ou*-stryah) f Austria

austriaco (ou-*stree*-ah-koa) adj Austrian; m Austrian

autentico (ou-*tehn*-tee-koa) adj original, authentic; true

autista (ou-*tee*-stah) m driver, chauffeur

autobus (*ou*-toa-booss) m (pl ~) bus; coach

autocarro (ou-toa-*kahr*-roa) m lorry; truck nAm

autogoverno (ou-toa-goa-*vehr*-noa) m self-government

automatico (ou-toa-*maa*-tee-koa) adj automatic

automazione (ou-toa-mah-*tsyoā*-nay) f automation

automobile (ou-toa-*maw*-bee-lay) f automobile, motor-car; ~ **club** automobile club

automobilismo (ou-toa-moa-bee-*lee*-zmoa) m motoring

automobilista (ou-toa-moa-bee-*lee*-

stah) *m* motorist

autonoleggio (ou-toa-noa-*layd*-joa) *m* car hire; car rental *Am*

autonomo (ou-*taw*-noa-moa) *adj* autonomous, independent

autore (ou-*tōa*-ray) *m* author

autorità (ou-toa-ree-*tah*) *f* authority

autoritario (ou-toa-ree-*taa*-ryoa) *adj* authoritarian

autorizzare (ou-toa-reed-*dzaa*-ray) *v* license

autorizzazione (ou-toa-reed-dzah-*tsyōā*-nay) *f* authorization, permission

autostello (ou-toa-*stehl*-loa) *m* motel

autostoppista (ou-toa-stoap-*pee*-stah) *m* hitchhiker; *fare l'autostop* hitchhike

autostrada (ou-toa-*straa*-dah) *f* motorway; highway *nAm*

autunno (ou-*toon*-noa) *m* autumn; fall *nAm*

avanti (ah-*vahn*-tee) *adv* onwards, forward; ahead; ~ **dritto** straight on

avant'ieri (ah-vahn-*tyai*-ree) *adv* the day before yesterday

avanzamento (ah-vahn-tsah-*mayn*-toa) *m* advance

avanzare (ah-vahn-*tsaa*-ray) *v* advance; *get on

avanzo (ah-*vahn*-tsoa) *m* remainder

avaria (ah-vah-*ree*-ah) *f* breakdown

avaro (ah-*vaa*-roa) *adj* avaricious

avena (ah-*vāy*-nah) *f* oats *pl*

***avere** (ah-*vāy*-ray) *v* *have

avido (*aa*-vee-doa) *adj* greedy

aviogetto (ah-vyoa-*jeht*-toa) *m* jet

avorio (ah-*vaw*-ryoa) *m* ivory

avvelenare (ahv-vay-lay-*naa*-ray) *v* poison

avvenente (ahv-vay-*nehn*-tay) *adj* handsome

avvenimento (ahv-vay-nee-*mayn*-toa) *m* event

avvenire (ahv-vay-*nee*-ray) *m* future

***avvenire** (ahv-vay-*nee*-ray) *v* happen

avventato (ahv-vayn-*taa*-toa) *adj* rash

avventore (ahv-vayn-*tōā*-ray) *m* customer

avventura (ahv-vayn-*tōō*-rah) *f* adventure

avverbio (ahv-*vehr*-byoa) *m* adverb

avversario (ahv-vayr-*saa*-ryoa) *m* opponent

avversione (ahv-vayr-*syōā*-nay) *f* aversion, dislike

avversità (ahv-vayr-see-*tah*) *f* misfortune

avverso (ahv-*vehr*-soa) *adj* averse

avvertimento (ahv-vayr-teé-*mayn*-toa) *m* warning

avvertire (ahv-vayr-*tee*-ray) *v* warn; notice

avviatore (ahv-vyah-*taw*-ray) *m* starter motor

avvicinare (ahv-vee-chee-*naa*-ray) *v* approach

avvisare (ahv-vee-*zaa*-ray) *v* warn; notify

avviso (ahv-*vee*-zoa) *m* notice, announcement; advertisement

avvitare (ahv-vee-*taa*-ray) *v* screw

avvocato (ahv-voa-*kaa*-toa) *m* lawyer; barrister, solicitor, attorney

***avvolgere** (ahv-*vol*-jay-ray) *v* *wind; wrap

avvolgibile (ahv-voal-*jee*-bee-lay) *m* blind

avvoltoio (ahv-voal-*tōā*-yoa) *m* vulture

azienda (ah-*dzyehn*-dah) *f* concern, business

azione (ah-*tsyōā*-nay) *f* deed, action; share

azoto (ah-*dzaw*-toa) *m* nitrogen

azzardo (ahd-*dzahr*-doa) *m* chance

azzurro (ahd-*dzoor*-roa) *adj* sky-blue

B

babbo (*bahb*-boa) *m* dad

babordo (bah-*boar*-doa) *m* port

baby-pullman (*bay*-bee-pool-mahn) *m* carry-cot

bacca (*bahk*-kah) *f* berry

baccano (bahk-*kaa*-noa) *m* noise

bacheca (bah-*kai*-kah) *f* show-case

baciare (bah-*chaa*-ray) *v* kiss

bacino (bah-*chee*-noa) *m* basin; dock; pelvis

bacio (*baa*-choa) *m* kiss

badare a (bah-*daa*-ray) tend, look after; mind

badia (bah-*dee*-ah) *f* abbey

baffi (*bahf*-fee) *mpl* moustache

bagagliaio (bah-gah-*lΥaa*-yoa) *m* luggage van; boot; trunk *nAm*

bagaglio (bah-*gaa*-lΥoa) *m* luggage, baggage; ~ **a mano** hand luggage; hand baggage *Am*

bagliore (bah-*lΥōā*-ray) *m* glare

bagnarsi (bah-*ñahr*-see) *v* bathe

bagnato (bah-*ñaa*-toa) *adj* wet; moist

bagno (*baa*-ñoa) *m* bath; ~ **turco** Turkish bath; **costume da** ~ bathing-suit; **cuffia da** ~ bathing-cap; *fare il* ~ bathe

baia (*baa*-yah) *f* bay

balbettare (bahl-bayt-*taa*-ray) *v* falter

balconata (bahl-koa-*naa*-tah) *f* circle

balcone (bahl-*kōā*-nay) *m* balcony

balena (bah-*lāy*-nah) *f* whale

baleno (bah-*lāy*-noa) *m* flash

ballare (bahl-*laa*-ray) *v* dance

balletto (bahl-*layt*-toa) *m* ballet

ballo (*bahl*-loa) *m* dance; ball

balsamo (*bahl*-sah-moa) *m* conditioner

balzare (bahl-*dzaa*-ray) *v* *leap

bambina (bahm-*bee*-nah) *f* little girl

bambinaia (bahm-bee-*naa*-yah) *f* nurse; babysitter

bambino (bahm-*bee*-noa) *m* child; kid

bambola (*bahm*-boa-lah) *f* doll

bambù (bahm-*boo*) *m* bamboo

banana (bah-*naa*-nah) *f* banana

banca (*bahng*-kah) *f* bank

bancarella (bahng-kah-*rehl*-lah) *f* stall

banchetto (bahng-*kayt*-toa) *m* banquet

banchina (bahng-*kee*-nah) *f* platform

banco (*bahng*-koa) *m* bench; counter; stand; reef; ~ **di scuola** desk

banconota (bahng-koa-*naw*-tah) *f* banknote

banda (*bahn*-dah) *f* gang; band

bandiera (bahn-*dyai*-rah) *f* flag

bandito (bahn-*dee*-toa) *m* bandit

bar (bahr) *m* bar; saloon, café, pub

baracca (bah-*rahk*-kah) *f* shed; booth

baratro (*baa*-rah-troa) *m* chasm

barattare (bah-raht-*taa*-ray) *v* swap

barattolo (bah-*raht*-toa-loa) *m* tin, canister

barba (*bahr*-bah) *f* beard

barbabietola (bahr-bah-*byai*-toa-lah) *f* beetroot, beet

barbiere (bahr-*byai*-ray) *m* barber

barbone (bahr-*bōā*-nay) *m* tramp

barca (*bahr*-kah) *f* boat; ~ **a remi** rowing-boat; ~ **a vela** sailing-boat

barchetta (bahr-*kayt*-tah) *f* dinghy

barcollante (bahr-koal-*lahn*-tay) *adj* unsteady

bar-emporio (bahr-aym-*paw*-ryoa) *m* drugstore *nAm*

barile (bah-*ree*-lay) *m* cask, barrel

bariletto (bah-ree-*layt*-toa) *m* keg

barista (bah-*ree*-stah) *m* bartender, barman; *f* barmaid

baritono (bah-*ree*-toa-noa) *m* baritone

barocco (bah-*rok*-koa) *adj* baroque

barometro (bah-*raw*-may-troa) *m* barometer

barra (*bahr*-rah) *f* rod

barriera (bahr-*ryai*-rah) *f* barrier; ~ **di**

sicurezza crash barrier
basamento (bah-zah-*mayn*-toa) m crankcase
basare (bah-*zaa*-ray) v base
base (*baa*-zay) f base; basis
basette (bah-*zayt*-tay) fpl sideburns pl, whiskers pl
basilica (bah-*zee*-lee-kah) f basilica
basso (*bahss*-soa) adj low; short; m bass
bassopiano (bahss-soa-*pyaa*-noa) m lowlands pl
bastante (bah-*stahn*-tay) adj sufficient
bastardo (bah-*stahr*-doa) m bastard
bastare (bah-*staa*-ray) v suffice, *do
bastone (bah-*stoa*-nay) m stick; cane; ~ **da passeggio** walking-stick; **bastoni da sci** ski sticks; ski poles Am
battaglia (baht-*taa*-lᵛah) f battle
battello (baht-*tehl*-loa) m boat
battere (*baht*-tay-ray) v *beat; ~ **le mani** clap
batteria (baht-tay-*ree*-ah) f battery
batterio (baht-*tai*-ryoa) m bacterium
battesimo (baht-*tāy*-zee-moa) m christening, baptism
battezzare (baht-tayd-*dzaa*-ray) v christen, baptize
baule (bah-*ōō*-lay) m chest; trunk
becco (*bayk*-koa) m beak; nozzle; goat
beffare (bayf-*faa*-ray) v fool
beige (baizh) adj beige
belga (*behl*-gah) adj (pl belgi) Belgian; m Belgian
Belgio (*behl*-joa) m Belgium
bellezza (bayl-*layt*-tsah) f beauty
bellino (bayl-*lee*-noa) adj nice
bello (*behl*-loa) adj beautiful; fair, lovely, fine, pretty
benché (behng-*kay*) conj although, though
benda (*bayn*-dah) f band
bendare (bayn-*daa*-ray) v dress

bene (*bai*-nay) adv well; **va bene!** all right!
***benedire** (bay-nay-*dee*-ray) v bless
benedizione (bay-nay-dee-*tsyōā*-nay) f blessing
beneficiario (bay-nay-fee-*chaa*-ryoa) m payee
beneficio (bay-nay-*fee*-choa) m benefit
benessere (bay-*nehss*-say-ray) m welfare
benevolenza (bay-nay-voa-*lehn*-tsah) f goodwill
benevolo (bay-*nai*-voa-loa) adj kind
benvenuto (behn-vay-*nōō*-toa) adj welcome
benzina (bayn-*dzee*-nah) f fuel, petrol; gasoline nAm; gas nAm; ~ **senza piombo** unleaded petrol
***bere** (*bāy*-ray) v *drink
berretto (bayr-*rayt*-toa) m cap; beret
bersaglio (bayr-*saa*-lᵛoa) m mark; target
bestemmia (bay-*staym*-myah) f curse
bestemmiare (bay-staym-*myaa*-ray) v curse, *swear
bestia (*beh*-styah) f beast
bestiame (bay-*styaa*-may) m cattle pl
bevanda (bay-*vahn*-dah) f beverage; **bevande alcooliche** spirits, liquor
biancheria (byahng-kay-*ree*-ah) f linen; lingerie; ~ **da letto** bedding; ~ **personale** underwear
bianco (*byahng*-koa) adj white
biasimare (byah-zee-*maa*-ray) v blame
biasimo (*byaa*-zee-moa) m blame
bibbia (*beeb*-byah) f bible
bibita (*bee*-bee-tah) f drink; ~ **analcoolica** soft drink
biblioteca (bee-blyoa-*tai*-kah) f library
bicchiere (beek-*kyai*-ray) m glass; tumbler
bicicletta (bee-chee-*klayt*-tah) f cycle, bicycle
biforcarsi (bee-foar-*kahr*-see) v fork

biglietteria (bee-lʸayt-tay-*ree*-ah) *f*
box-office; ~ **automatica** ticket
machine

biglietto (bee-lʸayt-toa) *m* note; ticket; ~ **da visita** visiting-card; ~ **gratuito** free ticket

bigodino (bee-goa-*dee*-noa) *m* curler

bilancia (bee-*lahn*-chah) *f* weighing-machine, scales *pl*

bilancio (bee-*lahn*-choa) *m* budget;
balance

bile (*bee*-lay) *f* gall, bile

biliardo (bee-lʸahr-doa) *m* billiards *pl*

bilingue (bee-*leeng*-gway) *adj* bilingual

bimbetto (beem-*bayt*-toa) *m* tot

bimbo (*beem*-boa) *m* toddler

binario (bee-*naa*-ryoa) *m* track

binocolo (bee-*naw*-koa-loa) *m* binoculars *pl*; field glasses

biologia (byoa-loa-*jee*-ah) *f* biology

bionda (*byoan*-dah) *f* blonde

biondo (*byoan*-doa) *adj* fair

birbante (beer-*bahn*-tay) *m* rascal

birichinata (bee-ree-kee-*naa*-tah) *f*
mischief

birra (*beer*-rah) *f* beer, ale

birreria (beer-ray-*ree*-ah) *f* brewery

bisaccia (bee-*zaht*-chah) *f* haversack

biscottino (bee-skoat-*tee*-noa) *m* biscuit; cracker *nAm*

biscotto (bee-*skot*-toa) *m* cookie *nAm*

bisognare (bee-zoa-*ñaa*-ray) *v* need

bisogno (bee-*zōā*-ño) *m* want; need;
misery; ***aver ~ di** need

bistecca (bee-*stayk*-kah) *f* steak

bivio (*bee*-vyoa) *m* road fork, fork

bizzarro (beed-*dzahr*-roa) *adj* odd,
strange, queer, quaint

bloccare (bloak-*kaa*-ray) *v* block

blu (bloo) *adj* blue

blusa (*blōō*-zah) *f* blouse

boa (*baw*-ah) *f* buoy

bocca (*boak*-kah) *f* mouth

boccale (boak-*kaa*-lay) *m* mug

boccaporto (boak-kah-*por*-toa) *m* porthole

bocchino (boak-*kee*-noa) *m* cigarette-holder

bocciare (boat-*chaa*-ray) *v* fail

bocciolo (boat-*chaw*-loa) *m* bud

boccone (boak-*kōā*-nay) *m* bite

boia (*boi*-ah) *m* (pl ~) executioner

Bolivia (boa-*lee*-vyah) *f* Bolivia

boliviano (boa-lee-*vyaa*-noa) *adj* Bolivian; *m* Bolivian

bolla (*boal*-lah) *f* bubble; blister

bollettino meteorologico (boal-layt-*tee*-noa may-tay-oa-roa-*law*-jee-koa)
weather forecast

bollire (boal-*lee*-ray) *v* boil

bollitore (boal-lee-*tōā*-ray) *m* kettle

bomba (*boam*-bah) *f* bomb

bombardare (boam-bahr-*daa*-ray) *v*
bomb

bordello (boar-*dehl*-loa) *m* brothel

bordo (*boar*-doa) *m* edge; border,
verge; **a ~** aboard

borghese (boar-*gāy*-say) *adj* middle-class, bourgeois; *m* civilian

borsa[1] (*boar*-sah) *f* bag; ~ **da ghiaccio** ice-bag; ~ **dell'acqua calda**
hot-water bottle; ~ **per la spesa**
shopping bag

borsa[2] (*boar*-sah) *f* grant; ~ **di studio**
scholarship

borsa[3] (*boar*-sah) *f* exchange; stock
market, stock exchange

borsellino (boar-sayl-*lee*-noa) *m* purse

borsetta (boar-*sayt*-tah) *f* handbag,
bag

boschetto (boa-*skayt*-toa) *m* grove

bosco (*bo*-skoa) *m* wood

boscoso (boa-*skōā*-soa) *adj* wooded

botanica (boa-*taa*-nee-kah) *f* botany

botola (*bo*-toa-lah) *f* hatch

botte (*boat*-tay) *f* cask, barrel

bottega (boat-*tāy*-gah) *f* store

botteghino (boat-tay-*gee*-noa) *m* box-office

bottiglia (boat-*tee*-lʸah) *f* bottle

bottone (boat-*tōā*-nay) *m* button

boutique (boo-*teek*) *m* boutique

a braccetto (ah braht-*chayt*-toa) arm-in-arm

braccialetto (braht-chah-*layt*-toa) *m* bracelet, bangle

braccio[1] (*braht*-choa) *m* (pl le braccia) arm

braccio[2] (*braht*-choa) *m* (pl bracci) arm; tributary

brachetta (brah-*kayt*-tah) *f* fly

braciola (brah-*chaw*-lah) *f* chop

bramare (brah-*maa*-ray) *v* long for

bramosia (brah-moa-*zee*-ah) *f* longing

branchia (*brahng*-kyah) *f* gill

branda (*brahn*-dah) *f* camp-bed

brano (*braa*-noa) *m* excerpt, passage

branzino (brahn-*dzee*-noa) *m* bass

Brasile (brah-*zee*-lay) *m* Brazil

brasiliano (brah-zee-lʸaa-noa) *adj* Brazilian; *m* Brazilian

bravo (*braa*-voa) *adj* clever; honest

breccia (*brayt*-chah) *f* gap; breach

bretelle (bray-*tehl*-lay) *fpl* braces *pl*; suspenders *plAm*

breve (*brāy*-vay) *adj* brief; concise; **tra ~** shortly

brevetto (bray-*vayt*-toa) *m* patent

brezza (*brayd*-dzah) *f* breeze

briciola (*bree*-choa-lah) *f* crumb

brillante (breel-*lahn*-tay) *adj* brilliant, bright

brillantina (breel-lahn-*tee*-nah) *f* hair cream

brillare (breel-*laa*-ray) *v* *shine

brindisi (*breen*-dee-zee) *m* toast

britannico (bree-*tahn*-nee-koa) *adj* British

britanno (bree-*tahn*-noa) *m* Briton

brivido (*bree*-vee-doa) *m* chill, shudder, shiver

brocca (*brok*-kah) *f* pitcher, jug

bronchite (broang-*kee*-tay) *f* bronchitis

brontolare (broan-toa-*laa*-ray) *v* growl; grumble

bronzeo (*broan*-dzay-oa) *adj* bronze

bronzo (*broan*-dzoa) *m* bronze

bruciare (broo-*chaa*-ray) *v* *burn

bruciatura (broo-chah-*tōō*-rah) *f* burn

brughiera (broo-*gyāy*-rah) *f* moor

bruna (*brōō*-nah) *f* brunette

bruno (*brōō*-noa) *adj* brown

brutale (broo-*taa*-lay) *adj* brutal

brutto (*broot*-toa) *adj* ugly; bad

buca (*bōō*-kah) *f* pit, hole; **~ delle lettere** pillar-box

bucato (boo-*kaa*-toa) *adj* punctured; *m* washing, laundry

bucatura (boo-kah-*tōō*-rah) *f* flat tyre, puncture

buccia (*boot*-chah) *f* skin, peel

buco (*bōō*-koa) *m* hole; **~ della serratura** keyhole

budella (boo-*dehl*-lah) *fpl* bowels *pl*

bue (*bōō*-ay) *m* ox

buffé (boof-*feh*) *m* buffet

buffo (*boof*-foa) *adj* funny

buffonata (boof-foa-*naa*-tah) *f* farce

buio (*bōō*-yoa) *adj* obscure, dark; *m* dark

bulbo (*bool*-boa) *m* bulb; light bulb

Bulgaria (bool-gah-*ree*-ah) *f* Bulgaria

bulgaro (*bool*-gah-roa) *adj* Bulgarian; *m* Bulgarian

bullone (bool-*lōā*-nay) *m* bolt

buongustaio (bwon-goo-*staa*-yoa) *m* gourmet

buono (*bwaw*-noa) *adj* good; kind; nice; *m* voucher

burocrazia (boo-roa-krah-*tsee*-ah) *f* bureaucracy

burrasca (boor-*rah*-skah) *f* gale

burro (*boor*-roa) *m* butter

bussare (booss-*saa*-ray) *v* knock, tap

bussola (*booss*-soa-lah) f compass

busta (*boo*-stah) f envelope; sleeve

busto (*boo*-stoa) m bust; corset, girdle

buttare (boot-*taa*-ray) v *throw; **da ~** disposable

C

cabaret (kah-bah-*ray*) m cabaret

cabina (kah-*bee*-nah) f booth, cabin; **~ di coperta** deck cabin; **~ telefonica** telephone booth

caccia (*kaht*-chah) f chase, hunt

cacciare (kaht-*chaa*-ray) v hunt; chase; **~ di frodo** poach

cacciatore (kaht-chah-*tōā*-ray) m hunter

cacciavite (kaht-chah-*vee*-tay) m screw-driver

cachemire (kahsh-*meer*) m cashmere

cadavere (kah-*daa*-vay-ray) m corpse

***cadere** (kah-*dāy*-ray) v *fall; *far ~** drop

caduta (kah-*dōō*-tah) f fall

caffè (kahf-*feh*) m coffee; public house

caffeina (kahf-fay-*ee*-nah) f caffeine

calare (kah-*laa*-ray) v lower

calce (*kahl*-chay) f lime

calcestruzzo (kahl-chay-*stroot*-tsoa) m concrete

calcio (*kahl*-choa) m kick; soccer; calcium; **~ d'inizio** kick-off; **~ di rigore** penalty kick; *prendere a calci** kick

calcolare (kahl-koa-*laa*-ray) v calculate

calcolatrice (kahl-koa-laa-*tree*-chay) f calculator

calcolo (*kahl*-koa-loa) m calculation; **calcolo biliare** gallstone; *fare i calcoli** reckon

caldo (*kahl*-doa) adj warm, hot; m heat

calendario (kah-layn-*daa*-ryoa) m calendar

callista (kahl-*lee*-stah) m chiropodist

callo (*kahl*-loa) m callus; corn

calma (*kahl*-mah) f calm

calmare (kahl-*maa*-ray) v calm down; **calmarsi** calm down

calmo (*kahl*-moa) adj calm; serene, quiet

calore (kah-*lōā*-ray) m warmth, heat

caloria (kah-loa-*ree*-ah) f calorie

calunnia (kah-*loon*-ñah) f slander

calvinismo (kahl-vee-*nee*-zmoa) m Calvinism

calvo (*kahl*-voa) adj bald

calza (*kahl*-tsah) f sock; stocking; **calze elastiche** support hose

calzamaglia (kahl-tsah-*maa*-lᵛah) f panty-hose, tights pl

calzatura (kahl-tsah-*tōō*-rah) f footwear

calzolaio (kahl-tsoa-*laa*-yoa) m shoemaker

calzoleria (kahl-tsoa-lay-*ree*-ah) f shoeshop

calzoncini (kahl-tsoan-*chee*-nee) mpl shorts pl; trunks pl

calzoni (kahl-*tsōā*-nee) mpl slacks pl; pants plAm; **~ da sci** ski pants

cambiamento (kahm-byah-*mayn*-toa) m alteration, change

cambiare (kahm-*byaa*-ray) v change; alter, vary; exchange, switch; **~ marcia** change gear; **cambiarsi** change

cambio (*kahm*-byoa) m change; exchange; **~ di velocità** gear-box; **corso del ~** exchange rate; *dare il ~** relieve

camera (*kaa*-may-rah) f room, chamber; **~ blindata** vault; **~ da letto** bedroom; **~ d'aria** inner tube; **~**

degli ospiti guest-room; **~ dei bambini** nursery

cameriera (kah-may-*ryai*-rah) *f* maid; chambermaid; waitress

cameriere (kah-may-*ryai*-ray) *m* valet; waiter

camerino (kah-may-*ree*-noa) *m* dressing-room

camicia (kah-*mee*-chah) *f* shirt; **~ da notte** nightdress

camino (kah-*mee*-noa) *m* chimney

camionetta (kah-myoa-*nayt*-tah) *f* pick-up van

cammello (kahm-*mehl*-loa) *m* camel

cammeo (kahm-*mai*-oa) *m* cameo

camminare (kahm-mee-*naa*-ray) *v* *go, walk; step; hike

campagna (kahm-*paa*-ñah) *f* countryside, country; campaign

campana (kahm-*paa*-nah) *f* bell

campanello (kahm-pah-*nehl*-loa) *m* bell, doorbell

campanile (kahm-pah-*nee*-lay) *m* steeple

campeggiatore (kahm-payd-jah-*tōā*-ray) *m* camper

campeggio (kahm-*payd*-joa) *m* camping; camping site

campione (kahm-*pyōā*-nay) *m* champion; sample

campo (*kahm*-poa) *m* field; camp; **~ di gioco** recreation ground; **~ di golf** golf-course; **~ di grano** cornfield; **~ di tennis** tennis-court

camposanto (kahm-poa-*sahn*-toa) *m* churchyard

Canadà (kah-nah-*dah*) *m* Canada

canadese (kah-nah-*dāy*-zay) *adj* Canadian; *m* Canadian

canale (kah-*naa*-lay) *m* canal; channel

canapa (*kah*-nah-pah) *f* hemp

canarino (kah-nah-*ree*-noa) *m* canary

cancello (kahn-*chehl*-loa) *m* gate

cancro (*kahng*-kroa) *m* cancer

candela (kahn-*dāy*-lah) *f* candle; **~ d'accensione** sparking-plug

candelabro (kahn-day-*laa*-broa) *m* candelabrum

candidato (kahn-dee-*daa*-toa) *m* candidate

cane (*kaa*-nay) *m* dog; **~ guida** guide-dog

canguro (kahng-*gōō*-roa) *m* kangaroo

canile (kah-*nee*-lay) *m* kennel

canna (*kahn*-nah) *f* cane; **~ da pesca** fishing rod

cannella (kahn-*nehl*-lah) *f* cinnamon

cannone (kahn-*nōā*-nay) *m* gun

canoa (kah-*nōā*-ah) *f* canoe

cantante (kahn-*tahn*-tay) *m* singer, vocalist

cantare (kahn-*taa*-ray) *v* *sing

canticchiare (kahn-teek-*kyaa*-ray) *v* hum

cantina (kahn-*tee*-nah) *f* cellar; wine-cellar

cantiniere (kahn-tee-*nyai*-ray) *m* wine-waiter

canto (*kahn*-toa) *m* song *c*

canzonare (kahn-tsoa-*naa*-ray) *v* mock

canzone (kahn-*tsōā*-nay) *f* song; **~ popolare** folk song

caos (*kaa*-oass) *m* chaos

caotico (kah-*aw*-tee-koa) *adj* chaotic

capace (kah-*paa*-chay) *adj* able; capable

capacità (kah-pah-chee-*tah*) *f* capacity; faculty

capanna (kah-*pahn*-nah) *f* hut; cabin

caparbio (kah-*pahr*-byoa) *adj* obstinate

capello (kah-*payl*-loa) *m* hair; **fissatore per capelli** setting lotion

capigliatura (kah-pee-lᵞah-*tōō*-rah) *f* hair-do

capire (kah-*pee*-ray) *v* *understand, *see, *take

capitale (kah-pee-*taa*-lay) *m* capital

capitalismo (kah-pee-tah-*lee*-zmoa) *m*

capitalism

capitano (kah-pee-*taa*-noa) *m* captain

capitare (kah-pee-*taa*-ray) *v* occur

capitolazione (kah-pee-toa-lah-*tsyoā*-nay) *f* capitulation

capitolo (kah-*pee*-toa-loa) *m* chapter

capo (*kaa*-poa) *m* head; manager, boss, chieftain, chief; cape; ~ **di stato** head of state

capocameriere (kah-poa-kah-may-*ryai*-ray) *m* head-waiter

capocuoco (kah-poa-*kwaw*-koa) *m* chef

capogiro (kah-poa-*jee*-roa) *m* dizziness

capolavoro (kah-poa-lah-*vōā*-roa) *m* masterpiece

capomastro (kah-poa-*mah*-stroa) *m* foreman

capostazione (kah-poa-stah-*tsyoā*-nay) *m* station-master

capoverso (kah-poa-*vehr*-soa) *m* paragraph

*•***capovolgere** (kah-poa-*vol*-jay-ray) *v* turn over

cappella (kahp-*pehl*-lah) *f* chapel

cappellano (kahp-payl-*laa*-noa) *m* chaplain

cappello (kahp-*pehl*-loa) *m* hat

cappotto (kahp-*pot*-toa) *m* coat; ~ **di pelliccia** fur coat

cappuccio (kahp-*poot*-choa) *m* hood

capra (*kaa*-prah) *f* goat

capretto (kah-*prayt*-toa) *m* kid

capriccio (kah-*preet*-choa) *m* fancy, fad, whim

capsula (*kah*-psoo-lah) *f* capsule

caraffa (kah-*rahf*-fah) *f* carafe

caramella (kah-rah-*mehl*-lah) *f* toffee; sweet; candy *nAm*

carato (kah-*raa*-toa) *m* carat

carattere (kah-*raht*-tay-ray) *m* character

caratteristica (kah-raht-tay-*ree*-steekah) *f* feature, characteristic, quality

caratteristico (kah-raht-tay-*ree*-steekoa) *adj* typical, characteristic

caratterizzare (kah-raht-tay-reed-*dzaa*-ray) *v* mark, characterize

carbone (kahr-*bōā*-nay) *m* coal; ~ **di legno** charcoal

carburatore (kahr-boo-rah-*tōā*-ray) *m* carburettor

carcere (*kahr*-chay-ray) *m* gaol

carceriere (kahr-chay-*ryai*-ray) *m* jailer

carciofo (kahr-*chaw*-foa) *m* artichoke

cardinale (kahr-dee-*naa*-lay) *m* cardinal; *adj* cardinal

cardine (*kahr*-dee-nay) *m* hinge

cardo (*kahr*-doa) *m* thistle

carenza (kah-*rehn*-tsah) *f* shortage

caricare (kah-ree-*kaa*-ray) *v* load, charge; *wind

carico (*kaa*-ree-koa) *m* cargo, load, freight, charge

carillon (kah-ree-*yoyah*) *m* chimes *pl*

carino (kah-*ree*-noa) *adj* nice; pretty

carità (kah-ree-*tah*) *f* charity

carnagione (kahr-nah-*jōā*-nay) *f* complexion

carne (*kahr*-nay) *f* flesh; meat

carnevale (kahr-nay-*vaa*-lay) *m* carnival

caro (*kaa*-roa) *adj* dear; expensive; *m* darling

carota (kah-*raw*-tah) *f* carrot

carovana (kah-roa-*vah*-nah) *f* caravan

carpa (*kahr*-pah) *f* carp

carriera (kahr-*ryai*-rah) *f* career

carriola (kahr-*ryaw*-lah) *f* wheelbarrow

carro (*kahr*-roa) *m* cart

carrozza (kahr-*rot*-tsah) *f* coach, carriage

carrozzeria (kahr-roat-tsay-*ree*-ah) *f* coachwork; motor body *Am*

carrozzina (kahr-roat-*tsee*-nah) *f* pram; baby carriage *Am*

carrozzone (kahr-roat-*tsōā*-nay) *m* caravan

carrucola (kahr-*roo*-koa-lah) *f* pulley

carta (*kahr*-tah) *f* paper; map; menu; ~ **assorbente** blotting paper; ~ **carbone** carbon paper; ~ **da gioco** playing-card; ~ **da imballaggio-** wrapping paper; ~ **da lettere** writing-paper; notepaper; ~ **da macchina** typing paper; ~ **da parati** wallpaper; ~ **di credito** credit card; charge plate *Am*; ~ **d'identità** identity card; ~ **igienica** toilet-paper; ~ **nautica** chart; ~ **stradale** road map; ~ **verde** green card; ~ **vetrata** sandpaper; **di** ~ paper

cartella (kahr-*tehl*-lah) *f* briefcase; satchel

cartello indicatore (kahr-*tehl*-loa een-dee-kah-*tōā*-ray) milepost, signpost

cartellone (kahr-tayl-*lōā*-nay) *m* poster

cartilagine (kahr-tee-*laa*-jee-nay) *f* cartilage

cartoleria (kahr-toa-lay-*ree*-ah) *f* stationer's; stationery

cartolina (kahr-toa-*lee*-nah) *f* card, postcard; ~ **illustrata** picture postcard

cartoncino (kahr-toan-*chee*-noa) *m* card

cartone (kahr-*tōā*-nay) *m* cardboard; ~ **animato** cartoon; **di** ~ cardboard

cartuccia (kahr-*toot*-chah) *f* cartridge

casa (*kaa*-sah) *f* house; home; **a** ~ home; ~ **di campagna** country house; ~ **di riposo** rest-home; ~ **galleggiante** houseboat; ~ **padronale** manor-house; **in** ~ at home

casalinga (kah-sah-*leeng*-gah) *f* housewife

casalingo (kah-sah-*leeng*-goa) *adj* home-made

cascata (kah-*skaa*-tah) *f* waterfall

cascina (kah-*shee*-nah) *f* farmhouse

casco (*kah*-skoa) *m* helmet

caseggiato (kah-sayd-*jaa*-toa) *m* block

of flats

caserma (kah-*zehr*-mah) *f* barracks *pl*

casinò (kah-see-*noa*) *m* casino

caso *m* luck, chance; case, instance, event; ~ **di emergenza** emergency; **in** ~ **di** in case of; **in ogni** ~ anyway; **per** ~ by chance

cassa (*kahss*-sah) *f* pay-desk; ~ **di risparmio** savings bank; ~ **mobile** container

cassaforte (kahss-sah-*for*-tay) *f* safe

casseruola (kahss-say-*rwaw*-lah) *f* saucepan

cassetta postale (kahss-*sayt*-tah poa-*staa*-lay) letter-box; mailbox *nAm*

cassetto (kahss-*sayt*-toa) *m* drawer

cassettone (kahss-sayt-*tōā*-nay) *m* chest of drawers

cassiera (kahss-*syai*-rah) *f* cashier

cassiere (kahss-*syai*-ray) *m* cashier

castagna (kah-*staa*-ñah) *f* chestnut

castano (kah-*staa*-noa) *adj* auburn

castello (kah-*stehl*-loa) *m* castle

casto (*kah*-stoa) *adj* chaste, pure

castoro (kah-*staw*-roa) *m* beaver

catacomba (kah-tah-*koam*-bah) *f* catacomb

catalogo (kah-*taa*-loa-goa) *m* catalogue

catarro (kah-*tahr*-roa) *m* catarrh

catastrofe (kah-*tah*-stroa-fay) *f* catastrophe, disaster

categoria (kah-tay-goa-*ree*-ah) *f* category

categorico (kah-tay-*gaw*-ree-koa) *adj* explicit

catena (kah-*tāy*-nah) *f* chain; ~ **di montagne** mountain range

catino (kah-*tee*-noa) *m* basin

catrame (kah-*traa*-may) *m* tar

cattedra (*kaht*-tay-drah) *f* pulpit

cattedrale (kaht-tay-*draa*-lay) *f* cathedral

cattivo (kaht-*tee*-voa) *adj* bad; ill,

evil; naughty

cattolico (kaht-*taw*-lee-koa) *adj* Roman Catholic, catholic

cattura (kaht-*tōō*-rah) *f* capture

catturare (kaht-too-*raa*-ray) *v* capture

cauicciù (kou-*choo*) *m* rubber

causa (*kou*-zah) *f* cause; reason; case; lawsuit; **a ~ di** owing to; because of, for, on account of

causare (kou-*zaa*-ray) *v* cause

cautela (kou-*tai*-lah) *f* caution

cauto (*kou*-toa) *adj* cautious

cauzione (kou-*tsyōa*-nay) *f* guarantee, security; bail

cava (*kaa*-vah) *f* quarry

cavalcare (kah-vahl-*kaa*-ray) *v* *ride

cavaliere (kah-vah-*lYai*-ray) *m* knight

cavalla (kah-*vahl*-lah) *f* mare

cavallerizzo (kah-vahl-lay-*reet*-tzoa) *m* rider, horseman

cavalletta (kah-vahl-*layt*-tah) *f* grasshopper

cavallino (kah-vahl-*lee*-noa) *m* pony

cavallo (kah-*vahl*-loa) *m* horse; **~ da corsa** race-horse; **~ vapore** horse-power

cavatappi (kah-vah-*tahp*-pee) *m* corkscrew

caverna (kah-*vehr*-nah) *f* cavern, cave

caviale (kah-*vyaa*-lay) *m* caviar

caviglia (kah-*vee*-lYah) *f* ankle

cavità (kah-vee-*tah*) *f* cavity

cavo (*kaa*-voa) *m* cable

cavolfiore (kah-voal-*fyōa*-ray) *m* cauliflower

cavolini (kah-voa-*lee*-nee) *mpl* sprouts *pl*

cavolo (*kaa*-voa-loa) *m* cabbage

ceco (*chai*-koa) *adj* Czech; *m* Czech; **Repubblica ceca** (ray-*poob*-blee-kah *chai*-kah) *f* Czech Republic

cedere (*chai*-day-ray) *v* *give in, indulge

cedola (*chai*-doa-lah) *f* coupon

cedro (*chāy*-droa) *m* lime

ceffone (chayf-*fōa*-nay) *m* smack

celare (chay-*laa*-ray) *v* *hide

celebrare (chay-lay-*braa*-ray) *v* celebrate

celebrazione (chay-lay-brah-*tsyōa*-nay) *f* celebration

celebre (*chai*-lay-bray) *adj* famous

celebrità (chay-lay-bree-*tah*) *f* celebrity

celibato (chay-lee-*baa*-toa) *m* celibacy

celibe (*chai*-lee-bay) *adj* single; *m* bachelor

cella (*chehl*-lah) *f* cell

cellofan (*chehl*-loa-fahn) *m* cellophane

cemento (chay-*mayn*-toa) *m* cement

cena (*chāy*-nah) *f* dinner, supper

cenere (*chāy*-nay-ray) *f* ash

cenno (*chayn*-noa) *m* sign

censura (chayn-*sōō*-rah) *f* censorship

centigrado (chayn-*tee*-grah-doa) *adj* centigrade

centimetro (chayn-*tee*-may-troa) *m* centimetre; tape-measure

cento (*chehn*-toa) *num* hundred

centrale (chayn-*traa*-lay) *adj* central; **~ elettrica** power-station

centralinista (chayn-trah-lee-*nee*-stah) *f* operator

centralino (chayn-trah-*lee*-noa) *m* telephone exchange

centralizzare (chayn-trah-leed-*dzaa*-ray) *v* centralize

centro (*chehn*-troa) *m* centre; **~ commerciale** shopping centre; **~ della città** town centre; **~ di ricreazione** recreation centre; **~ sanitario** health centre

ceppo (*chayp*-poa) *m* block; log

cera (*chāy*-rah) *f* wax

ceramica (chay-*raa*-mee-kah) *f* faience, ceramics *pl*, pottery

cerbiatto (chayr-*byaht*-toa) *m* fawn

cercare (chayr-*kaa*-ray) *v* look for; *seek, search, hunt for; look up

cerchio (*chayr*-kyoa) *m* circle, ring

cerchione (chayr-*kyoā*-nay) *m* rim

cerimonia (chay-ree-*maw*-ñah) *f* ceremony

cerotto (chay-*rot*-toa) *m* plaster, adhesive tape

certamente (chayr-tah-*mayn*-tay) *adv* surely

certezza (chayr-*tayt*-tsah) *f* certainty

certificato (chayr-tee-fee-*kaa*-toa) *m* certificate; ~ **di sanità** health certificate

certo (*chehr*-toa) *adj* certain

cervello (chayr-*vehl*-loa) *m* brain

cervo (*chehr*-voa) *m* deer

cespuglio (chay-*spōō*-l^{y}oa) *m* scrub, bush

cessare (chayss-*saa*-ray) *v* end; stop, discontinue,.quit

cestino (chay-*stee*-noa) *m* wastepaper-basket

ceto (*chai*-toa) *m* rank; ~ **medio** middle class

cetriolo (chay-*tryaw*-loa) *m* cucumber

chalet (shah-*lay*) *m* chalet

champagne (shah~~ng~~-*pahñ*) *m* champagne

che (kay) *pron* that, who, which; how; *conj* that; as, than

chi (kee) *pron* who; **a** ~ whom

chiacchierare (kyahk-kyay-*raa*-ray) *v* chat

chiacchierata (kyahk-kyay-*raa*-tah) *f* chat

chiacchierone (kyahk-kyay-*rōā*-nay) *m* chatterbox

chiamare (kyah-*maa*-ray) *v* call; **chiamarsi** *be called

chiamata (kyah-*maa*-tah) *f* telephone call; ~ **locale** local call

chiarificare (kyah-ree-fee-*kaa*-ray) *v* clarify

chiarire (kyah-*ree*-ray) *v* clarify, explain

chiaro (*kyaa*-roa) *adj* clear; pale, light; plain, distinct; ~ **di luna** moonlight

chiasso (*kyahss*-soa) *m* noise, racket

chiave (*kyaa*-vay) *f* key; wrench; ~ **di casa** latchkey

chiavistello (kyah-vee-*stehl*-loa) *m* bolt

chiazza (*keeaht*-tsah) *f* spot

chiazzato (kyaht-*tsaa*-toa) *adj* spotted

*****chiedere** (*kyai*-day-ray) *v* ask; beg; *****chiedersi** wonder

chierico (*kyai*-ree-koa) *m* clergyman

chiesa (*kyai*-zah) *f* church, chapel

chiglia (*kee*-l^{y}ah) *f* keel

chilo (*kee*-loa) *m* kilogram

chilometraggio (kee-loa-may-*trahd*-joa) *m* distance in kilometres

chilometro (kee-*law*-may-troa) *m* kilometre

chimica (*kee*-mee-kah) *f* chemistry

chimico (*kee*-mee-koa) *adj* chemical

chinarsi (kee-*nahr*-see) *v* *bend down

chinino (kee-*nee*-noa) *m* quinine

chiocciola di mare (*kyot*-choa-lah dee *maa*-ray) winkle

chiodo (*kyaw*-doa) *m* nail

chiosco (*kyo*-skoa) *m* kiosk

chirurgo (kee-*roor*-goa) *m* surgeon

chitarra (kee-*tahr*-rah) *f* guitar

*****chiudere** (*kyōō*-day-ray) *v* close; fasten, *shut; turn off; ~ **a chiave** lock; lock up

chiunque (*kyoong*-kway) *pron* anybody, whoever; anyone

chiusa (*kyōō*-sah) *f* sluice, lock

chiuso (*kyōō*-soa) *adj* closed, shut

chiusura lampo (kyoo-*sōō*-rah *lahm*-poa) zip; zipper

ci (chee) *pron* ourselves, us

ciabatta (chah-*baht*-tah) *f* slipper

cialda (*chahl*-dah) *f* waffle

ciancia (*chahn*-chah) *f* chat

ciao! (*chaa*-oa) hello!

ciarlare (chahr-*laa*-ray) *v* chat

ciarlata (chahr-*laa*-tah) *f* chat

ciarlatano (chahr-lah-*taa*-noa) *m* quack

ciascuno (chah-*skoo*-noa) *adj* every, each

cibo (*chee*-boa) *m* fare, food; ~ **surgelato** frozen food

cicatrice (chee-kah-*tree*-chay) *f* scar

ciclista (chee-*klee*-stah) *m* cyclist

ciclo (*chee*-kloa) *m* cycle; bicycle

cicogna (chee-*kōā*-ñah) *f* stork

cieco (*chai*-koa) *adj* blind

cielo (*chai*-loa) *m* sky; heaven

cifra (*chee*-frah) *f* number, figure

ciglio (*chee*-lᵞoa) *m* (pl le ciglia) eyelash

cigno (*chee*-ñoa) *m* swan

cigolare (chee-goa-*laa*-ray) *v* creak

Cile (*chee*-lay) *m* Chile

cileno (chee-*lāy*-noa) *adj* Chilean; *m* Chilean

ciliegia (chee-lᵞ*āy*-jah) *f* cherry

cilindro (chee-*leen*-droa) *m* cylinder

cima (*chee*-mah) *f* top; peak; **in ~ a** on top of

cimice (*chee*-mee-chay) *f* bug

cimitero (chee-mee-*tai*-roa) *m* graveyard, cemetery

Cina (*chee*-nah) *f* China

cinegiornale (chee-nay-joar-*naa*-lay) *m* newsreel

cinema (*chee*-nay-mah) *m* pictures; movie theater *Am*, movies *Am*

cinematografo (chee-nay-mah-*taw*-grah-foa) *m* cinema

cinepresa (chee-nay-*prāy*-sah) *f* camera

cinese (chee-*nāy*-say) *adj* Chinese; *m* Chinese

*cingere (*cheen*-jay-ray) *v* encircle

cinghia (*cheeng*-gyah) *f* strap; belt; ~ **del ventilatore** fan belt

cinquanta (cheeng-*kwahn*-tah) *num* fifty

cinque (*cheeng*-kway) *num* five

ciò (cho) *pron* that, this

cioccolata (choak-koa-*laa*-tah) *f* chocolate

cioccolatino (choak-koa-lah-*tee*-noa) *m* chocolate

cioccolato (choak-koa-*laa*-toa) *m* chocolate

cioè (choa-*ai*) *adv* namely

ciottolo (*chot*-toa-loa) *m* pebble

cipolla (chee-*poal*-lah) *f* onion

cipollina (chee-poal-*lee*-nah) *f* chives *pl*

cipria (*chee*-pryah) *f* face-powder; **piumino da ~** powder-puff

circa (*cheer*-kah) *adv* approximately, about; *prep* about

circo (*cheer*-koa) *m* circus

circolazione (cheer-koa-lah-*tsyōā*-nay) *f* circulation; ~ **del sangue** circulation

circolo (*cheer*-koa-loa) *m* circle; club; ~ **nautico** yacht-club

circondare (cheer-koan-*daa*-ray) *v* circle, encircle, surround

circonvallazione (cheer-koan-vahl-lah-*tsyōā*-nay) *f* by-pass

circostante (cheer-koa-*stahn*-tay) *adj* surrounding

circostanza (cheer-koa-*stahn*-tsah) *f* circumstance, condition

cistifellea (chee-stee-*fehl*-lay-ah) *f* gall bladder

cistite (chee-*stee*-tay) *f* cystitis

citare (chee-*taa*-ray) *v* quote

citazione (chee-tah-*tsyōā*-nay) *f* mention, quotation; summons

città (cheet-*tah*) *f* city, town

cittadinanza (cheet-tah-dee-*nahn*-tsah) *f* townspeople *pl*; citizenship

cittadino (cheet-tah-*dee*-noa) *m* citizen

civico (*chee*-vee-koa) *adj* civic

civile (chee-*vee*-lay) *adj* civilian, civil

civilizzato (chee-vee-leed-*dzaa*-toa) *adj* civilized

civiltà (chee-veel-*tah*) f civilization

clacson (*klahk*-soan) m hooter; horn

classe (*klahss*-say) f class; grade; form; ~ **turistica** tourist class

classico (*klahss*-see-koa) adj classical

classificare (klahss-see-fee-*kaa*-ray) v classify, grade; sort

clausola (*klou*-zoa-lah) f clause

clava (*klaa*-vah) f club

clavicembalo (klah-vee-*chaym*-bah-loa) m harpsichord

clavicola (klah-*vee*-koa-lah) f collarbone

clemenza (klay-*mehn*-tsah) f mercy

cliente (*klyehn*-tay) m client, customer

clima (*klee*-mah) m climate

clinica (*klee*-nee-kah) f clinic

cloro (*klaw*-roa) m chlorine

coagulare (koa-ah-goo-*laa*-ray) v coagulate

cocaina (koa-kah-*ee*-nah) f cocaine

cocciuto (koat-*chōō*-toa) adj stubborn

cocco (*kok*-koa) m pet

coccodrillo (koak-koa-*dreel*-loa) m crocodile

coda (*kōā*-dah) f tail; queue; *****fare la ~** queue; stand in line Am

codardo (koa-*dahr*-doa) m coward

codice (*kaw*-dee-chay) m code; ~ **postale** zip code Am

coerenza (koa-ay-*rehn*-tsah) f coherence

cofano (*kaw*-fah-noa) m bonnet; hood nAm

*****cogliere** (*kaw*-lyay-ray) v pick; *****catch

cognac (koa-*ñahk*) m cognac

cognata (koa-*ñaa*-tah) f sister-in-law

cognato (koa-*ñaa*-toa) m brother-in-law

cognome (koa-*ñōā*-may) m family name, surname; ~ **da nubile** maiden name

coincidenza (koa-een-chee-*dehn*-tsah) f connection

*****coincidere** (koa-een-*chee*-day-ray) v coincide

*****coinvolgere** (koa-een-*vol*-jay-ray) v involve

colapasta (koa-lah-*pah*-stah) m strainer

colazione (koa-lah-*tsyōā*-nay) f luncheon, lunch; **prima ~** breakfast; **seconda ~** lunch

colla (*koal*-lah) f gum, glue

collaborazione (koal-lah-boa-rah-*tsyōā*-nay) f collaboration

collana (koal-*laa*-nah) f beads pl, necklace

collare (koal-*laa*-ray) m collar

collega (koal-*lai*-gah) m colleague

collegare (koal-lay-*gaa*-ray) v connect, link

collera (*kol*-lay-rah) f anger, passion

collettivo (koal-layt-*tee*-voa) adj collective

colletto (koal-*layt*-toa) m collar; **bottoncino per ~** collar stud

collettore (koal-layt-*tōā*-ray) m collector

collezione (koal-lay-*tsyōā*-nay) f collection; ~ **d'arte** art collection

collezionista (koal-lay-tsyoa-*nee*-stah) m collector

collina (koal-*lee*-nah) f hill

collinoso (koal-lee-*nōā*-soa) adj hilly

collisione (koal-lee-*zyōā*-nay) f collision

collo (*kol*-loa) m throat, neck

collocare (koal-loa-*kaa*-ray) v *lay, *put

colmo (*koal*-moa) adj full up; m height

Colombia (koa-*loam*-byah) f Colombia

colombiano (koa-loam-*byaa*-noa) adj Colombian; m Colombian

colonia (koa-*law*-ñah) f colony; ~ **di vacanze** holiday camp

colonna (koa-*lon*-nah) f pillar, column
colonnello (koa-loan-*nehl*-loa) m colonel
colore (koa-*lōa*-ray) m paint; colour; **di ~** coloured
colorito (koa-loa-*ree*-toa) adj colourful
colpa (*koal*-pah) f guilt, fault, blame
colpetto (koal-*payt*-toa) m tap
colpevole (koal-*pāy*-voa-lay) adj guilty; **dichiarare ~** convict
colpire (koal-*pee*-ray) v *hit; *strike; touch
colpo (*koal*-poa) m knock, blow; stroke; **~ di sole** sunstroke
coltello (koal-*tehl*-loa) m knife
coltivare (koal-tee-*vaa*-ray) v cultivate; *grow, raise
colto (*koal*-toa) adj cultured
coltura (koal-*tōō*-rah) f culture
coma (*kaw*-mah) m coma
comandante (koa-mahn-*dahn*-tay) m commander; captain
comandare (koa-mahn-*daa*-ray) v command, order
comando (koa-*mahn*-doa) m order; leadership
combattere (koam-*baht*-tay-ray) v combat, *fight, battle
combattimento (koam-baht-tee-*mayn*-toa) m combat, battle; fight, struggle
combinare (koam-bee-*naa*-ray) v combine
combinazione (koam-bee-nah-*tsyōā*-nay) f combination
combustibile (koam-boo-*stee*-bee-lay) m fuel
come (*kōā*-may) adv such as, like; how; conj as; **~ pure** as well; as well as; **~ se** as if
comico (*kaw*-mee-koa) adj comic, humorous; m comedian, entertainer
cominciare (koa-meen-*chaa*-ray) v *begin, start

comitato (koa-mee-*taa*-toa) m committee, commission
commedia (koam-*mai*-dyah) f comedy; **~ musicale** musical comedy, musical
commediante (koam-may-*dyahn*-tay) m comedian
commemorazione (koam-may-moa-rah-*tsyōā*-nay) f commemoration
commentare (koam-mayn-*taa*-ray) v comment
commento (koam-*mayn*-toa) m comment; note
commerciale (koam-mayr-*chaa*-lay) adj commercial
commerciante (koam-mayr-*chahn*-tay) m tradesman, merchant, dealer
commerciare (koam-mayr-*chaa*-ray) v trade
commercio (koam-*mehr*-choa) m trade, commerce, business; **~ al minuto** retail trade
commessa (koam-*mayss*-sah) f salesgirl
commesso (koam-*mayss*-soa) m salesman, shop assistant; **~ d'ufficio** clerk
commestibile (koam-may-*stee*-bee-lay) adj edible
*commettere** (koam-*mayt*-tay-ray) v commit
commissione (koam-meess-*syōā*-nay) f message, errand; committee
commozione (koam-moa-*tsyōā*-nay) f emotion; **~ cerebrale** concussion
*commuovere** (koam-*mwaw*-vay-ray) v move
comò (koa-*mo*) m (pl ~) bureau nAm
comodità (koa-moa-dee-*tah*) f comfort
comodo (*kaw*-moa-doa) adj convenient; comfortable, easy; m leisure
compact disc (*kom*-pahkt-disk) m compact disc; compact disc player
compagnia (koam-pah-*ñee*-ah) f com-

pany; society

compagno (koam-*paa*-ñoa) *m* companion; partner; comrade; ~ **di classe** class-mate

*comparire** (koam-pah-*ree*-ray) *v* appear

compassione (koam-pahss-*syōā*-nay) *f* sympathy; **provare** ~ **per** pity

compatire (koam-pah-*tee*-ray) *v* pity

compatriota (koam-pah-*tryaw*-tah) *m* countryman

compatto (koam-*paht*-toa) *adj* compact

compensare (koam-payn-*saa*-ray) *v* compensate, *make good

compensazione (koam-payn-sah-*tsyōā*-nay) *f* compensation

compera (*koam*-pay-rah) *f* purchase

competente (koam-pay-*tehn*-tay) *adj* expert; qualified

competere (koam-*pai*-tay-ray) *v* compete

competizione (koam-pay-tee-*tsyōā*-nay) *f* contest

compiacente (koam-pyah-*chehn*-tay) *adj* willing

compiere (*koam*-pyay-ray) *v* accomplish; commit; perform

compilare (koam-pee-*laa*-ray) *v* compile; *make up; fill out *Am*

compitare (koam-pee-*taa*-ray) *v* *spell

compito (*koam*-pee-toa) *m* duty, task

compleanno (koam-play-*ahn*-noa) *m* birthday

complesso (koam-*plehss*-soa) *adj* complex; *m* complex

completamente (koam-play-tah-*mayn*-tay) *adv* wholly, completely, quite

completare (koam-play-*taa*-ray) *v* complete, finish; fill in; fill out *Am*

completo (koam-*plai*-toa) *adj* total, complete, whole, utter

complicato (koam-plee-*kaa*-toa) *adj* complicated

complice (*kom*-plee-chay) *m* accessary

complimentare (koam-plee-mayn-*taa*-ray) *v* compliment

complimento (koam-plee-*mayn*-toa) *m* compliment

complotto (koam-*plot*-toa) *m* plot

componimento (koam-poa-nee-*mayn*-toa) *m* essay

*comporre** (koam-*poar*-ray) *v* compose

comportamento (koam-poar-tah-*mayn*-toa) *m* behaviour

comportare (koam-poar-*taa*-ray) *v* imply; **comportarsi** behave, act; **comportarsi male** misbehave

compositore (koam-poa-zee-*tōā*-ray) *m* composer

composizione (koam-poa-zee-*tsyōā*-nay) *f* composition

comprare (koam-*praa*-ray) *v* *buy, purchase

compratore (koam-prah-*tōā*-ray) *m* buyer, purchaser

*comprendere** (koam-*prehn*-day-ray) *v* contain, include, comprise; conceive, *understand

comprensione (koam-prayn-*syōā*-nay) *f* understanding

comprensivo (koam-prayn-*see*-voa) *adj* comprehensive; sympathetic

compreso (koam-*prāy*-soa) *adj* inclusive

compromesso (koam-proa-*mayss*-soa) *m* compromise

computare (koam-poo-*taa*-ray) *v* calculate

computer (koam-*poo*-tayr) *m* computer

comune (koa-*mōō*-nay) *adj* common

comunicare (koa-moo-nee-*kaa*-ray) *v* communicate, inform

comunicato (koa-moo-nee-*kaa*-toa) *m* communiqué

comunicazione (koa-moo-nee-kah-*tsyōā*-nay) *f* communication, information

comunione (koa-moo-*nyōa*-nay) *f* congregation

comunismo (koa-moo-*nee*-zmoa) *m* communism

comunista (koa-moo-*nee*-stah) *m* communist

comunità (koa-moo-nee-*tah*) *f* community

comunque (koa-*moong*-kway) *adv* at any rate, any way; though, still

con (koan) *prep* with; by

*****concedere** (koan-*chai*-day-ray) *v* grant

concentrare (koan-chayn-*traa*-ray) *v* concentrate

concentrazione (koan-chayn-trah-*tsyōa*-nay) *f* concentration

concepimento (koan-chay-pee-*mayn*-toa) *m* conception

concepire (koan-chay-*pee*-ray) *v* conceive

concernere (koan-*chehr*-nay-ray) *v* concern

concerto (koan-*chehr*-toa) *m* concert

concessione (koan-chayss-*syōa*-nay) *f* concession

concetto (koan-*cheht*-toa) *m* idea

concezione (koan-chay-*tsyōa*-nay) *f* conception

conchiglia (koang-*kee*-lᶦªah) *f* sea-shell, shell

concime (koan-*chee*-may) *m* manure

conciso (koan-*chee*-zoa) *adj* concise

*****concludere** (koang-*klōō*-day-ray) *v* conclude

conclusione (koang-kloo-*zyōa*-nay) *f* conclusion, issue

concordanza (koang-koar-*dahn*-tsah) *f* agreement

concorrente (koang-koar-*rehn*-tay) *m* rival, competitor

concorrenza (koang-koar-*rehn*-tsah) *f* rivalry, competition

concorso (koang-*koar*-soa) *m* concurrence

concreto (koang-*krai*-toa) *adj* concrete

concupiscenza (koang-koo-peesh-*shehn*-tsah) *f* lust

condanna (koan-*dahn*-nah) *f* conviction

condannare (koan-dahn-*naa*-ray) *v* sentence

condannato (koan-dahn-*naa*-toa) *m* convict

condire (koan-*dee*-ray) *v* flavour

condito (koan-*dee*-toa) *adj* spiced

*****condividere** (koan-dee-*vee*-day-ray) *v* share

condizionale (koan-dee-tsyoa-*naa*-lay) *adj* conditional

condizione (koan-dee-*tsyōa*-nay) *f* term, condition

condotta (koan-*doat*-tah) *f* conduct

*****condurre** (koan-*door*-ray) *v* conduct, carry; *drive

conduttore (koan-doot-*tōa*-ray) *m* conductor

confederazione (koan-fay-day-rah-*tsyōa*-nay) *f* union, federation

conferenza (koan-fay-*rehn*-tsah) *f* lecture; conference; ~ **stampa** press conference

conferma (koan-*fayr*-mah) *f* confirmation

confermare (koan-fayr-*maa*-ray) *v* confirm, acknowledge

confessare (koan-fayss-*saa*-ray) *v* confess

confessione (koan-fayss-*syōa*-nay) *f* confession

confezionare (koan-fay-tsyoa-*naa*-ray) *v* manufacture

confezionato (koan-fay-tsyoa-*naa*-toa) *adj* ready-made

confidente (koan-fee-*dehn*-tay) *adj* confident

confidenziale (koan-fee-dayn-*tsyaa*-lay)

adj confidential; familiar

confine (koan-*fee*-nay) *m* border

confiscare (koan-fee-*skaa*-ray) *v* confiscate

conflitto (koan-*fleet*-toa) *m* conflict

*confondere (koan-*foan*-day-ray) *v* *mistake, confuse

in conformità con (een koan-foar-mee-*tah* koan) in accordance with

confortevole (koan-foar-*tāy*-voa-lay) *adj* cosy, comfortable

conforto (koan-*for*-toa) *m* comfort

confronto (koan-*froan*-toa) *m* comparison; confrontation

confusione (koan-foo-*zyōā*-nay) *f* confusion, disorder

confuso (koan-*fōō*-zoa) *adj* confused

congedare (koan-jay-*daa*-ray) *v* dismiss

congedo (koan-*jai*-doa) *m* leave

congelarsi (koan-jay-*lahr*-see) *v* *freeze

congelato (koan-jay-*laa*-toa) *adj* frozen

congelatore (koan-jay-lah-*tōā*-ray) *m* deep-freeze

congettura (koan-jayt-*tōō*-rah) *f* guess

congetturare (koan-jayt-too-*raa*-ray) *v* guess

congiunto (koan-*joon*-toa) *adj* joint; related

congiura (koan-*jōō*-rah) *f* plot

congratularsi (koang-grah-too-*lahr*-see) *v* congratulate

congratulazione (koang-grah-too-lah-*tsyōā*-nay) *f* congratulation

congregazione (koang-gray-gah-*tsyōā*-nay) *f* congregation

congresso (koang-*grehss*-soa) *m* congress

coniglio (koa-*nee*-lʸoa) *m* rabbit

coniugi (*kaw*-ñoo-jee) *mpl* married couple

connessione (koan-nayss-*syōā*-nay) *f* connection

*connettere (koan-*neht*-tay-ray) *v* connect; plug in

connotati (koan-noa-*taa*-tee) *mpl* description

conoscenza (koa-noash-*shehn*-tsah) *f* knowledge; acquaintance

*conoscere (koa-*noash*-shay-ray) *v* *know

conquista (koang-*kwee*-stah) *f* conquest

conquistare (koang-kwee-*staa*-ray) *v* conquer

conquistatore (koang-kwee-stah-*tōā*-ray) *m* conqueror

consapevole (koan-sah-*pāy*-voa-lay) *adj* aware

conscio (*kon*-shoa) *adj* conscious

consegna (koan-*sāy*-ñah) *f* delivery

consegnare (koan-say-*ñaa*-ray) *v* deliver; commit

conseguentemente (koan-say-gwayn-tay-*mayn*-tay) *adv* consequently

conseguenza (koan-say-*gwehn*-tsah) *f* result, consequence; issue; **in ~ di** because of, for

conseguibile (koan-say-*gwee*-bee-lay) *adj* attainable

conseguire (koan-say-*gwee*-ray) *v* obtain

consenso (koan-*sehn*-soa) *m* consent

consentire (koan-sayn-*tee*-ray) *v* agree, consent

conservare (koan-sayr-*vaa*-ray) *v* preserve; *hold

conservatore (koan-sayr-vah-*tōā*-ray) *adj* conservative

conservatorio (koan-sayr-vah-*taw*-ryoa) *m* music academy

conserve (koan-*sehr*-vay) *fpl* tinned food; ***mettere in conserva** preserve

considerare (koan-see-day-*raa*-ray) *v* consider, regard; count, reckon

considerato (koan-see-day-*raa*-toa)

prep considering

considerazione (koan-see-day-rah-tsyōā-nay) *f* consideration

considerevole (koan-see-day-*rāy*-voalay) *adj* considerable

consigliare (koan-see-*lᵞaa*-lay) *v* recommend, advise

consigliere (koan-see-*lᵞai*-ray) *m* counsellor; councillor

consiglio (koan-*see*-lᵞoa) *m* board; advice; counsel, council

consistere in (koan-*see*-stay-ray) consist of

consolare (koan-soa-*laa*-ray) *v* comfort

consolato (koan-soa-*laa*-toa) *m* consulate

consolazione (koan-soa-lah-*tsyōā*-nay) *f* comfort

console (*kon*-soa-lay) *m* consul

consorte (koan-*sor*-tay) *f* wife

constante (koan-*stahn*-tay) *adj* constant

constatare (koan-stah-*taa*-ray) *v* ascertain

consueto (koan-*swai*-toa) *adj* habitual

consulta (koan-*sool*-tah) *f* consultation

consultare (koan-sool-*taa*-ray) *v* consult

consultazione (koan-sool-tah-*tsyōā*-nay) *f* consultation

consultorio (koan-sool-*taw*-ryoa) *m* surgery

consumare (koan-soo-*maa*-ray) *v* use up

consumato (koan-soo-*maa*-toa) *adj* worn

consumatore (koan-soo-mah-*tōā*-ray) *m* consumer

contadino (koan-tah-*dee*-noa) *m* peasant

contagioso (koan-tah-*jōā*-soa) *adj* contagious, infectious

contaminazione (koan-tah-mee-nah-tsyōā-nay) *f* pollution

contanti (koan-*tahn*-tee) *mpl* cash

contare (koan-*taa*-ray) *v* count; ~ **su** rely on

contattare (koan-taht-*taa*-ray) *v* contact

contatto (koan-*taht*-toa) *m* touch, contact

conte (*koan*-tay) *m* count, earl

contea (koan-*tai*-ah) *f* county

contemporaneo (koan-taym-poa-*raa*-nay-oa) *adj* contemporary; *m* contemporary

*contenere** (koan-tay-*nāy*-ray) *v* contain; comprise; restrain

contento (koan-*tehn*-toa) *adj* content; glad, happy

contenuto (koan-tay-*nōō*-toa) *m* contents *pl*

contessa (koan-*tayss*-sah) *f* countess

contiguo (koan-*tee*-gwoa) *adj* neighbouring

continentale (koan-tee-nayn-*taa*-lay) *adj* continental

continente (koan-tee-*nehn*-tay) *m* continent

continuamente (koan-tee-nwah-*mayn*-tay) *adv* all the time, continually

continuare (koan-tee-*nwaa*-ray) *v* continue, carry on; *go on, *go ahead, *keep on, *keep

continuazione (koan-tee-nwah-*tsyōā*-nay) *f* sequel

continuo (koan-*tee*-nwoa) *adj* continuous, continual

conto (*koan*-toa) *m* account; bill; check *nAm*; ~ **bancario** bank account; **per** ~ **di** on behalf of; *** rendere** ~ **di** account for

contorno (koan-*toar*-noa) *m* outline, contour

contrabbandare (koan-trahb-bahn-*daa*-ray) *v* smuggle

*contraddire** (koan-trahd-*dee*-ray) *v*

contradict

contraddittorio (koan-trahd-deet-*taw*-ryoa) *adj* contradictory

contraffatto (koan-trahf-*faht*-toa) *adj* false

contralto (koan-*trahl*-toa) *m* alto

contrario (koan-*traa*-ryoa) *adj* contrary, opposite; *m* reverse, contrary; **al ~** on the contrary

*****contrarre** (koan-*trahr*-ray) *v* contract

contrasto (koan-*trah*-stoa) *m* contrast

contratto (koan-*traht*-toa) *m* agreement, contract; **~ di affitto** lease

contravvenzione (koan-trahv-vayn-*tsyōa*-nay) *f* ticket

contribuire (koan-tree-*bwee*-ray) *v* contribute

contributo (koan-tree-*bōō*-toa) *m* contribution

contribuzione (koan-tree-boo-*tsyōa*-nay) *f* contribution

contro (*koan*-troa) *prep* against; versus

controllare (koan-troal-*laa*-ray) *v* control

controllo (koan-*trol*-loa) *m* control, inspection; **~ passaporti** passport control

controllore (koan-troal-*lōa*-ray) *m* ticket collector

controversia (koan-troa-*vehr*-syah) *f* dispute

controverso (koan-troa-*vehr*-soa) *adj* controversial

contusione (koan-too-*zyōa*-nay) *f* bruise

conveniente (koan-vay-*ñehn*-tay) *adj* convenient, proper

*****convenire** (koan-vay-*nee*-ray) *v* suit, fit

convento (koan-*vehn*-toa) *m* convent; nunnery

conversazione (koan-vayr-sah-*tsyōa*-nay) *f* conversation, discussion, talk

convertire (koan-vayr-*tee*-ray) *v* convert; cash

*****convincere** (koan-*veen*-chay-ray) *v* convince, persuade

convinzione (koan-veen-*tsyōa*-nay) *f* conviction, persuasion

convitto (koan-*veet*-toa) *m* boarding-school

convulsione (koan-vool-*syōa*-nay) *f* convulsion

cooperante (koa-oa-pay-*rahn*-tay) *adj* co-operative

cooperativa (koa-oa-pay-rah-*tee*-vah) *f* co-operative

cooperativo (koa-oa-pay-rah-*tee*-voa) *adj* co-operative

cooperatore (koa-oa-pay-rah-*tōa*-ray) *adj* co-operative

cooperazione (koa-oa-pay-rah-*tsyōa*-nay) *f* co-operation

coordinare (koa-oar-dee-*naa*-ray) *v* co-ordinate

coordinazione (koa-oar-dee-nah-*tsyōa*-nay) *f* co-ordination

coperchio (koa-*pehr*-kyoa) *m* top, cover, lid

coperta (koa-*pehr*-tah) *f* blanket; quilt; deck

copertina (koa-payr-*tee*-nah) *f* cover, jacket

coperto (koa-*pehr*-toa) *adj* overcast

copertone (koa-payr-*tōa*-nay) *m* tyre

copia (*kaw*-pyah) *f* copy; **~ fotostatica** photostat

copiare (koa-*pyaa*-ray) *v* copy

coppa (*kop*-pah) *f* cup

coppia (*kop*-pyah) *f* couple

copriletto (koa-pree-*leht*-toa) *m* counterpane

*****coprire** (koa-*pree*-ray) *v* cover

coraggio (koa-*rahd*-joa) *m* guts, courage

coraggioso (koa-rahd-*jōa*-soa) *adj* courageous; plucky, brave, bold

corallo (koa-*rahl*-loa) *m* coral

corazza (koa-*raht*-tsah) *f* armour

corda (*kor*-dah) *f* cord, rope; string

cordiale (koar-*dyaa*-lay) *adj* cordial; hearty, sympathetic

cordicella (koar-dee-*chehl*-lah) *f* line

cordoglio (koar-*daw*-l^yoa) *m* grief

cordone elettrico (koar-*dōa*-nay ay-*leht*-tree-koa) electric cord

cornacchia (koar-*nahk*-kyah) *f* crow

cornice (koar-*nee*-chay) *f* frame

corno¹ (*kor*-noa) *m* (pl le corna) horn

corno² (*kor*-noa) *m* (pl i corni) horn

coro (*kaw*-roa) *m* choir

corona (koa-*rōa*-nah) *f* crown

coronare (koa-roa-*naa*-ray) *v* crown

corpo (*kor*-poa) *m* body

corpulento (koar-poo-*lehn*-toa) *adj* corpulent, stout

corredo (koar-*rai*-doa) *m* kit

***correggere** (koar-*rehd*-jay-ray) *v* correct

corrente (koar-*rehn*-tay) *adj* current; *f* current, stream; **con la** ~ downstream; **contro** ~ upstream; ~ **alternata** alternating current; ~ **continua** direct current; ~ **d'aria** draught; ***mettere al** ~ inform

***correre** (*koar*-ray-ray) *v* *run; *speed; *~ **troppo** *speed

correttezza (koar-rayt-*tayt*-tsah) *f* correctness

corretto (koar-*reht*-toa) *adj* correct, right

correzione (koar-ray-*tsyōa*-nay) *f* correction

corrida (koar-*ree*-dah) *f* bullfight

corridoio (koar-ree-*dōa*-yoa) *m* corridor

corriera *f* coach

corrispondente (koar-ree-spoan-*dehn*-tay) *m* correspondent; reporter

corrispondenza (koar-ree-spoan-*dehn*-tsah) *f* correspondence

***corrispondere** (koar-ree-*spoan*-day-ray) *v* correspond, agree

***corrompere** (koar-*roam*-pay-ray) *v* corrupt, bribe

corrotto (koar-*roat*-toa) *adj* corrupt; vicious

corruzione (koar-roo-*tsyōa*-nay) *f* corruption, bribery

corsa (*koar*-sah) *f* ride; race; ~ **di cavalli** horserace

corsia (koar-*see*-ah) *f* lane

corso (*koar*-soa) *m* course; promenade; ~ **accelerato** intensive course; ~ **del cambio** exchange rate, rate of exchange

corte (*koar*-tay) *f* court

corteccia (koar-*tayt*-chah) *f* bark

corteo (koar-*tai*-oa) *m* procession

cortese (koar-*tāy*-zay) *adj* civil, courteous, polite

cortile (koar-*tee*-lay) *m* yard; ~ **di ricreazione** playground

corto (*koar*-toa) *adj* short; ~ **circuito** short circuit

corvo (*kor*-voa) *m* raven

cosa (*kaw*-sah) *f* thing; **che** ~ what; **qualunque** ~ anything

coscia (*kosh*-shah) *f* thigh

coscienza (koash-*shehn*-tsah) *f* consciousness; conscience

coscritto (koa-*skreet*-toa) *m* conscript

così (koa-*see*) *adv* so, thus, such; as; ~ **che** so that; **e** ~ **via** and so on

cosiddetto (koa-seed-*dayt*-toa) *adj* so-called

cosmetici (koa-*zmai*-tee-chee) *mpl* cosmetics *pl*

cospirare (koa-spee-*raa*-ray) *v* conspire

costa (*ko*-stah) *f* coast

costante (koa-*stahn*-tay) *adj* even

costare (koa-*staa*-ray) *v* *cost

costatare (koa-stah-*taa*-ray) *v* diagnose

costernato (koa-stayr-*naa*-toa) *adj* upset

costituire (koa-stee-*twee*-ray) *v* constitute

costituzione (koa-stee-too-*tsyōa*-nay) *f* constitution

costo (*ko*-stoa) *m* cost; charge

costola (*ko*-stoa-lah) *f* rib

costoletta (koa-stoa-*layt*-tah) *f* cutlet

costoso (koa-*stōa*-soa) *adj* expensive

*costringere (koa-*streen*-jay-ray) *v* compel, force

costruire (koa-*strwee*-ray) *v* construct, *build

costruzione (koa-stroo-*tsyōa*-nay) *f* construction

costume (koa-*stōo*-may) *m* custom; ~ **da bagno** bathing-suit, swim-suit; ~ **nazionale** national dress; **costumi** *mpl* morals

cotoletta (koa-toa-*layt*-tah) *f* chop

cotone (koa-*tōa*-nay) *m* cotton; **di ~** cotton

cozza (*koat*-tsah) *f* mussel

cozzare (koat-*tsaa*-ray) *v* collide, bump

crampo (*krahm*-poa) *m* cramp

cranio (*kraa*-ño-a) *m* skull

cratere (krah-*tai*-ray) *m* crater

cravatta (krah-*vaht*-tah) *f* tie, necktie; ~ **a farfalla** bow tie

cravattino (krah-vaht-*tee*-noa) *m* bow tie

creare (kray-*aa*-ray) *v* create

creatura (kray-ah-*tōo*-rah) *f* creature

credenza (kray-*dehn*-tsah) *f* closet

credere (*krāy*-day-ray) *v* believe; guess, reckon

credibile (kray-*dee*-bee-lay) *adj* credible

credito (*krāy*-dee-toa) *m* credit

creditore (kray-dee-*tōa*-ray) *m* creditor

credulo (*krai*-doo-loa) *adj* credulous

crema (*krai*-mah) *f* cream; ~ **da barba** shaving-cream; ~ **di bellezza** face-cream; ~ **idratante** moisturizing cream; ~ **per la notte** night-cream; ~ **per la pelle** skin cream; ~ **per le mani** hand cream

cremare (kray-*maa*-ray) *v* cremate

cremazione (kray-mah-*tsyōa*-nay) *f* cremation

cremisino (kray-mee-*zee*-noa) *adj* crimson

cremoso (kray-*mōa*-soa) *adj* creamy

crepa (*krai*-pah) *f* cleft

crepuscolo (kray-*poo*-skoa-loa) *m* twilight, dusk

*crescere (*kraysh*-shay-ray) *v* *grow

crescione (kraysh-*shōa*-nay) *m* watercress

crescita (*kraysh*-shee-tah) *f* growth

cresta (*kray*-stah) *f* ridge

creta (*krāy*-tah) *f* chalk

cricco (*kreek*-koa) *m* jack

criminale (kree-mee-*naa*-lay) *adj* criminal; *m* criminal

criminalità (kree-mee-nah-lee-*tah*) *f* criminality

crimine (*kree*-mee-nay) *m* crime

crisi (*kree*-zee) *f* crisis

cristallino (kree-stahl-*lee*-noa) *adj* crystal

cristallo (kree-*stahl*-loa) *m* crystal

cristiano (kree-*styaa*-noa) *adj* Christian; *m* Christian

Cristo (*kree*-stoa) *m* Christ

critica (*kree*-tee-kah) *f* criticism

criticare (kree-tee-*kaa*-ray) *v* criticize

critico (*kree*-tee-koa) *adj* critical; *m* critic

croccante (kroak-*kahn*-tay) *adj* crisp

croce (*krōa*-chay) *f* cross

crocevia (kroa-chay-*vee*-ah) *m* junction, crossing

crociata (kroa-*chaa*-tah) *f* crusade

crocicchio (kroa-*cheek*-kyoa) *m* crossroads

crociera (kroa-*chai*-rah) *f* cruise

*crocifiggere (kroa-chee-*feed*-jay-ray) *v* crucify

crocifissione (kroa-chee-feess-*syōā*-nay) f crucifixion

crocifisso (kroa-chee-*feess*-soa) m crucifix

crollare (kroal-*laa*-ray) v collapse

cromo (*kraw*-moa) m chromium

cronico (*kraw*-nee-koa) adj chronic

cronologico (kroa-noa-*law*-jee-koa) adj chronological

crosta (*kro*-stah) f crust

crostaceo (kroa-*staa*-chay-oa) m shellfish

crostino (kroa-*stee*-noa) m toast

crudele (kroo-*dai*-lay) adj cruel, harsh

crudo (*krōō*-doa) adj raw

cruscotto (kroo-*skot*-toa) m dashboard

Cuba (*kōō*-bah) f Cuba

cubano (koo-*baa*-noa) adj Cuban; m Cuban

cubo (*kōō*-boa) m cube

cuccetta (koot-*chayt*-tah) f berth, bunk

cucchiaiata (kook-kyah-*yaa*-tah) f spoonful

cucchiaino (kook-kyah-*ee*-noa) m teaspoon; teaspoonful

cucchiaio (kook-*kyaa*-yoa) m spoon, tablespoon; ~ **da minestra** soupspoon

cucina (koo-*chee*-nah) f kitchen; stove; ~ **a gas** gas cooker

cucinare (koo-chee-*naa*-ray) v cook; ~ **alla griglia** grill

cucire (koo-*chee*-ray) v sew

cucitura (koo-chee-*tōō*-rah) f seam; **senza** ~ seamless

cuculo (*kōō*-koo-loa) m cuckoo

cugina (koo-*jee*-nah) f cousin

cugino (koo-*jee*-noa) m cousin

cui (*koo*-ee) pron whose; of which; whom; to which

culla (*kool*-lah) f cradle

culmine (*kool*-mee-nay) m height

culto (*kool*-toa) m worship

cultura (kool-*tōō*-rah) f culture

cumulo (*koo*-moo-loa) m heap

cuneo (*kōō*-nay-oa) m wedge

cunetta (koo-*nayt*-tah) f gutter

cuoco (*kwaw*-koa) m cook

cuore (*kwaw*-ray) m heart

cupidigia (koo-pee-*dee*-jah) f greed

cupo (*kōō*-poa) adj gloomy

cupola (*kōō*-poa-lah) f dome

cura (*kōō*-rah) f care; cure; *aver ~ di *take care of; ~ **di bellezza** beauty treatment

curapipe (koo-rah-*pee*-pay) m pipe cleaner

curare (koo-*raa*-ray) v nurse; cure; ~ **le unghie** manicure

curato (koo-*raa*-toa) adj neat

curiosità (koo-ryoa-see-*tah*) f curiosity; sight, curio

curioso (koo-*ryōa*-soa) adj curious

curva (*koor*-vah) f bend; curve

curvare (koor-*vaa*-ray) v *bend

curvatura (koor-vah-*tōō*-rah) f bend

curvo (*koor*-voa) adj curved

cuscinetto (koosh-shee-*nayt*-toa) m pad

cuscino (koosh-*shee*-noa) m cushion; ~ **elettrico** heating pad

custode (koo-*staw*-day) m warden; custodian; caretaker

custodia (koo-*staw*-dyah) f custody

custodire (koo-stoa-*dee*-ray) v guard

D

da (dah) prep out of, from; at, to; as from; since; by

dabbasso (dahb-*bahss*-soa) adv downstairs; down

dacché (dahk-*kay*) adv since

dado (*daa*-doa) m nut

daltonico (dahl-*taw*-nee-koa) adj colour-blind

danese (dah-*nāy*-say) *adj* Danish; *m* Dane

Danimarca (dah-nee-*mahr*-kah) *f* Denmark

danneggiare (dahn-nayd-*jaa*-ray) *v* damage

danno (*dahn*-noa) *m* damage; mischief, harm

dannoso (dahn-*nōā*-soa) *adj* harmful

dappertutto (dahp-payr-*toot*-toa) *adv* throughout

*****dare** (*daa*-ray) *v* *give

data (*daa*-tah) *f* date

dato (*daa*-toa) *m* data *pl*

dattero (*daht*-tay-roa) *m* date

dattilografa (daht-tee-*law*-grah-fah) *f* typist

dattilografare (daht-tee-loa-grah-*faa*-ray) *v* type

dattiloscritto (daht-tee-loa-*skreet*-toa) *adj* typewritten

davanti (dah-*vahn*-tee) *prep* before

davanzale (dah-vahn-*tsaa*-lay) *m* window-sill

davvero (dahv-*vāy*-roa) *adv* really

dazio (*daa*-tsyoa) *m* Customs duty, duty

dea (*dai*-ah) *f* goddess

debito (*dai*-bee-toa) *m* debt; debit

debole (*dāy*-boa-lay) *adj* weak; faint; dim

debolezza (day-boa-*layt*-tsah) *f* weakness

decaffeinizzato (day-kahf-fay-neet-*tsaa*-toa) *adj* decaffeinated

deceduto (day-chay-*dōō*-toa) *adj* dead

decente (day-*chehn*-tay) *adj* decent, proper

decenza (day-*chehn*-tsah) *f* decency

*****decidere** (day-*chee*-day-ray) *v* decide

decimo (*dai*-chee-moa) *num* tenth

decisione (day-chee-*zyōā*-nay) *f* decision

deciso (day-*chee*-zoa) *adj* resolute

decollare (day-koal-*laa*-ray) *v* *take off

decollo (day-*kol*-loa) *m* take-off

decrepito (day-*krai*-pee-toa) *adj* dilapidated

*****decrescere** (day-*kraysh*-shay-ray) *v* decrease

dedicare (day-dee-*kaa*-ray) *v* dedicate; devote

*****dedurre** (day-*door*-ray) *v* infer, deduce

deferenza (day-fay-*rehn*-tsah) *f* respect

deficienza (day-fee-*chehn*-tsah) *f* deficiency, shortcoming

deficit (*dai*-fee-cheet) *m* deficit

definire (day-fee-*nee*-ray) *v* define

definitivo (day-fee-nee-*tee*-voa) *adj* definitive

definizione (day-fee-nee-*tsyōā*-nay) *f* definition

deformato (day-foar-*maa*-toa) *adj* deformed

deforme (day-*foar*-may) *adj* deformed

degno di (*day*-ño dee) worthy of

delegato (day-lay-*gaa*-toa) *m* delegate

delegazione (day-lay-gah-*tsyōā*-nay) *f* delegation

deliberare (day-lee-bay-*raa*-ray) *v* deliberate

deliberazione (day-lee-bay-rah-*tsyōā*-nay) *f* deliberation

delicato (day-lee-*kaa*-toa) *adj* delicate; tender; gentle

delinquente (day-leeng-*kwehn*-tay) *m* criminal

delizia (day-*lee*-tsyah) *f* delight, joy

deliziare (day-lee-*tsyaa*-ray) *v* delight

delizioso (day-lee-*tsyōā*-soa) *adj* delicious, lovely, wonderful

delucidare (day-loo-chee-*daa*-ray) *v* elucidate

*****deludere** (day-*lōō*-day-ray) *v* disappoint, *let down; *be disappointing

delusione (day-loo-*zyōā*-nay) *f* disappointment

democratico (day-moa-*kraa*-tee-koa)
adj democratic

democrazia (day-moa-krah-*tsee*-ah) *f*
democracy

demolire (day-moa-*lee*-ray) *v* demolish

demolizione (day-moa-lee-*tsyōa*-nay) *f*
demolition

denaro (day-*naa*-roa) *m* money

denominazione (day-noa-mee-nah-
tsyōa-nay) *f* denomination

denso (*dehn*-soa) *adj* dense, thick

dente (*dehn*-tay) *m* tooth

dentiera (dayn-*tyai*-rah) *f* denture,
false teeth

dentifricio (dayn-tee-*free*-choa) *m*
toothpaste

dentista (dayn-*tee*-stah) *m* dentist

dentro (*dayn*-troa) *adv* in, inside;
prep inside, within

denutrizione (day-noo-tree-*tsyōa*-nay) *f*
malnutrition

deodorante (day-oa-doa-*rahn*-tay) *m*
deodorant

deperibile (day-pay-*ree*-bee-lay) *adj*
perishable

depositare (day-poa-zee-*taa*-ray) *v* deposit, bank

deposito (day-*paw*-zee-toa) *m* deposit;
depot, warehouse; ~ **bagagli** left
luggage office; baggage deposit office *Am*

depressione (day-prayss-*syōa*-nay) *f*
depression

depresso (day-*prehss*-soa) *adj* de-
pressed, blue

deprimente (day-pree-*mayn*-tay) *adj*
depressing

***deprimere** (day-*pree*-may-ray) *v* de-
press

deputato (day-poo-*taa*-toa) *m* deputy;
Member of Parliament

derisione (day-ree-*zyōa*-nay) *f* mockery

derivare (day-ree-*vaa*-ray) *v* divert; ~

da derive from

***descrivere** (day-*skree*-vay-ray) *v* de-
scribe

descrizione (day-skree-*tsyōa*-nay) *f* description

deserto (day-*zehr*-toa) *adj* desert; *m*
desert

desiderabile (day-see-day-*raa*-bee-lay)
adj desirable

desiderare (day-see-day-*raa*-ray) *v*
want, desire, wish

desiderio (day-see-*dai*-ryoa) *m* desire,
wish

desideroso (day-see-day-*rōa*-soa) *adj*
eager

designare (day-see-*ñaa*-ray) *v* designate; appoint

desistere (day-*see*-stay-ray) *v* *give up

destarsi (day-*stahr*-see) *v* wake up

destinare (day-stee-*naa*-ray) *v* destine

destinatario (day-stee-nah-*taa*-ryoa) *m*
addressee

destinazione (day-stee-nah-*tsyōa*-nay)
f destination

destino (day-*stee*-noa) *m* fate, destiny,
fortune

destro (*deh*-stroa) *adj* right; right-
hand; skilful

detenuto (day-tay-*nōō*-toa) *m* prisoner

detenzione (day-tayn-*tsyōa*-nay) *f* custody

detergente (day-tayr-*jehn*-tay) *m* detergent

determinare (day-tayr-mee-*naa*-ray) *v*
define, determine; **determinato**
definite

determinazione (day-tayr-mee-nah-
tsyōa-nay) *f* determination

detersivo (day-tayr-*see*-voa) *m* washing-powder

detestare (day-tay-*staa*-ray) *v* hate,
dislike

dettagliante (dayt-tah-*lʸahn*-tay) *m* retailer

dettagliato (dayt-tah-*lYaa*-toa) *adj* detailed

dettaglio (dayt-*taa*-lYoa) *m* detail

dettare (dayt-*taa*-ray) *v* dictate

dettato (dayt-*taa*-toa) *m* dictation

deviare (day-*vyaa*-ray) *v* deviate

deviazione (day-vyah-*tsyoā*-nay) *f* detour, diversion

di (dee) *prep* of

diabete (dyah-*bai*-tay) *m* diabetes

diabetico (dyah-*bai*-tee-koa) *m* diabetic

diagnosi (*dyaa*-ñoa-zee) *f* diagnosis

diagnosticare (dyah-ñoa-stee-*kaa*-ray) *v* diagnose

diagonale (dyah-goa-*naa*-lay) *adj* diagonal; *f* diagonal

diagramma (dyah-*grahm*-mah) *m* chart; diagram

dialetto (dyah-*leht*-toa) *m* dialect

diamante (dyah-*mahn*-tay) *m* diamond

diapositiva (dyah-poa-zee-*tee*-vah) *f* slide

diario (*dyaa*-ryoa) *m* diary

diarrea (dyahr-*rai*-ah) *f* diarrhoea

diavolo (*dyaa*-voa-loa) *m* devil

dibattere (dee-*baht*-tay-ray) *v* discuss

dibattito (dee-*baht*-tee-toa) *m* debate, discussion

dicembre (dee-*chehm*-bray) December

diceria (dee-chay-*ree*-ah) *f* rumour

dichiarare (dee-kyah-*raa*-ray) *v* declare

dichiarazione (dee-kyah-rah-*tsyoā*-nay) *f* declaration, statement

diciannove (dee-chahn-*naw*-vay) *num* nineteen

diciannovesimo (dee-chahn-noa-*vai*-zee-moa) *num* nineteenth

diciassette (dee-chahss-*seht*-tay) *num* seventeen

diciassettesimo (dee-chahss-sayt-*tai*-zee-moa) *num* seventeenth

diciottesimo (dee-choat-*tai*-zee-moa) *num* eighteenth

diciotto (dee-*chot*-toa) *num* eighteen

didietro (dee-*dyai*-troa) *m* bottom

dieci (*dyai*-chee) *num* ten

dieta (*dyai*-tah) *f* diet

dietro (*dyai*-troa) *prep* behind

***difendere** (dee-*fehn*-day-ray) *v* defend

difensore (dee-fayn-*soā*-ray) *m* champion

difesa (dee-*faȳ*-sah) *f* defence; plea

difetto (dee-*feht*-toa) *m* fault

difettoso (dee-fayt-*toā*-soa) *adj* defective, faulty

differente (deef-fay-*rehn*-tay) *adj* different

differenza (deef-fay-*rehn*-tsah) *f* difference; contrast, distinction

differire (deef-fay-*ree*-ray) *v* differ, vary; delay

difficile (deef-*fee*-chee-lay) *adj* difficult, hard

difficoltà (deef-fee-koal-*tah*) *f* difficulty

diffidare di (deef-fee-*daa*-ray) mistrust

***diffondere** (deef-*foan*-day-ray) *v* *shed

diffusione (deef-foo-*zyoā*-nay) *f* diffusion

difterite (deef-tay-*ree*-tay) *f* diphtheria

diga (*dee*-gah) *f* dike, dam

digeribile (dee-jay-*ree*-bee-lay) *adj* digestible

digerire (dee-jay-*ree*-ray) *v* digest

digestione (dee-jay-*styoā*-nay) *f* digestion

digitale (dee-*jee*-taa-lay) *adj* digital

dignità (dee-ñee-*tah*) *f* dignity; rank

dignitoso (dee-ñee-*toā*-soa) *adj* dignified

dilettevole (dee-layt-*tāȳ*-voa-lay) *adj* delightful

diletto (dee-*leht*-toa) *adj* dear; *m* delight, pleasure

diligente (dee-lee-*jehn*-tay) *adj* diligent

diligenza (dee-lee-*jehn*-tsah) f diligence

diluire (dee-*lwee*-ray) v dilute

diluito (dee-*lwee*-toa) adj weak

dimagrire (dee-mah-*gree*-ray) v slim

dimensione (dee-mayn-*syoā*-nay) f extent, size

dimenticare (dee-mayn-tee-*kaa*-ray) v *forget

*dimettersi** (dee-*mayt*-tayr-see) v resign

dimezzare (dee-mayd-*dzaa*-ray) v halve

diminuire (dee-mee-*nwee*-ray) v reduce; decrease, lessen

diminuzione (dee-mee-noo-*tsyoā*-nay) f decrease

dimissioni (dee-meess-*syoā*-nee) fpl resignation

dimostrare (dee-moa-*straa*-ray) v demonstrate, prove, *show

dimostrazione (dee-moa-strah-*tsyoā*-nay) f demonstration; *fare una ~ demonstrate

dinamo (*dee*-nah-moa) f dynamo

dinanzi a (dee-*nahn*-tsee ah) before

dintorni (deen-*toar*-nee) mpl environment, surroundings pl

dio (*dee*-oa) m (pl dei) god

dipendente (dee-payn-*dehn*-tay) adj dependant

dipendenza (dee-payn-*dehn*-tsah) f annex

*dipendere da** (dee-*pehn*-day-ray) depend on

diploma (dee-*plaw*-mah) m certificate; diploma

diplomarsi (dee-ploa-*mahr*-see) v graduate

diplomatico (dee-ploa-*maa*-tee-koa) m diplomat

*dire** (*dee*-ray) v *say, *tell; *voler ~ *mean

direttamente (dee-rayt-tah-*mayn*-tay)

*adv straight away

direttiva (dee-rayt-*tee*-vah) f directive

diretto (dee-*reht*-toa) adj direct; ~ a bound for

direttore (dee-rayt-*tōā*-ray) m director, manager; executive; ~ di scuola head teacher, headmaster; ~ d'orchestra conductor

direzione (dee-ray-*tsyoā*-nay) f way, direction; management; indicatore di ~ trafficator; directional signal Am

dirigente (dee-ree-*jehn*-tay) m leader

*dirigere** (dee-*ree*-jay-ray) v direct, head, *lead; conduct; manage

diritto (dee-*reet*-toa) adj erect, upright; m right; ~ amministrativo administrative law; ~ civile civil law; ~ commerciale commercial law; ~ elettorale franchise; ~ penale criminal law; sempre ~ straight ahead

dirottare (dee-roat-*taa*-ray) v hijack

dirottatore (dee-roat-tah-*tōā*-ray) m hijacker

disabitato (dee-zah-bee-*taa*-toa) adj uninhabited

disadatto (dee-zah-*daht*-toa) adj unfit

disapprovare (dee-zahp-proa-*vaa*-ray) v disapprove

disastro (dee-*zah*-stroa) m disaster, calamity

disastroso (dee-zah-*strōā*-soa) adj disastrous

discendente (deesh-shayn-*dehn*-tay) m descendant

discendenza (deesh-shayn-*dehn*-tsah) f origin

discernimento (deesh-shayr-nee-*mayn*-toa) m sense

discesa (deesh-*shāy*-sah) f descent; in ~ downwards

disciplina (deesh-shee-*plee*-nah) f discipline

disco (dee-skoa) m disc; record

discorso (dee-skoar-soa) m speech; conversation

discussione (dee-skooss-syōā-nay) f argument, discussion

*****discutere** (dee-skōō-tay-ray) v argue, discuss; dispute

disdegno (deez-dāy-ñoa) m contempt

*****disdire** (deez-dee-ray) v cancel; check out

disegnare (dee-say-ñaa-ray) v sketch, *draw

disegno (dee-sāy-ñoa) m sketch, drawing; pattern; design; **puntina da disegno** drawing-pin; thumbtack nAm

disertare (dee-zayr-taa-ray) v desert

*****disfare** (dee-sfaa-ray) v *undo; unpack, unwrap

disgelarsi (deez-jay-lahr-see) v thaw

disgelo (deez-jai-loa) m thaw

*****disgiungere** (deez-joon-jay-ray) v disconnect

disgrazia (deez-graa-tsyah) f accident; disgrace

disgraziatamente (deez-grah-tsyah-tah-mayn-tay) adv unfortunately

disgustoso (deez-goo-stōā-soa) adj revolting, disgusting

disimparare (dee-zeem-pah-raa-ray) v unlearn

disinfettante (dee-zeen-fayt-tahn-tay) m disinfectant

disinfettare (dee-zeen-fayt-taa-ray) v disinfect

disinserire (dee-zeen-say-ree-ray) v disconnect

disinteressato (dee-zeen-tay-rayss-saa-toa) adj unselfish

disinvoltura (dee-zeen-voal-tōō-rah) f ease

disoccupato (dee-zoak-koo-paa-toa) adj unemployed

disoccupazione (dee-zoak-koo-pah-tsyōā-nay) f unemployment

disonesto (dee-zoa-neh-stoa) adj crooked, unfair, dishonest

disonore (dee-zoa-nōā-ray) m disgrace, shame

disordinato (dee-zoar-dee-naa-toa) adj sloppy, untidy

disordine (dee-zoar-dee-nay) m mess, disorder

disossare (dee-zoass-saa-ray) v bone

dispari (dee-spah-ree) adj odd

dispensa (dee-spehn-sah) f larder

dispensare (dee-spayn-saa-ray) v exempt

disperare (dee-spay-raa-ray) v despair

disperato (dee-spay-raa-toa) adj desperate; hopeless

disperazione (dee-spay-rah-tsyōā-nay) f despair

dispiacere (dee-spyah-chāy-ray) m sorrow

*****dispiacere** (dee-spyah-chāy-ray) v displease

disponibile (dee-spoa-nee-bee-lay) adj available; spare

*****disporre di** (dee-spoar-ray) dispose of

dispositivo (dee-spoa-zee-tee-voa) m apparatus

disposizione (dee-spoa-zee-tsyōā-nay) f disposal

disprezzare (dee-sprayt-tsaa-ray) v despise, scorn

disprezzo (dee-spreht-tsoa) m contempt, scorn

disputa (dee-spoo-tah) f argument, dispute

disputare (dee-spoo-taa-ray) v argue; dispute

dissenteria (deess-sayn-tay-ree-ah) f dysentery

dissentire (deess-sayn-tee-ray) v disagree

dissimile (deess-see-mee-lay) adj unlike

*dissuadere (deess-swah-*dáy*-ray) v dissuade from

distante (dee-*stahn*-tay) adj far-away, remote

distanza (dee-*stahn*-tsah) f distance; space, way

*distinguere (dee-*steeng*-gway-ray) v distinguish

distinto (dee-*steen*-toa) adj distinct; separate; distinguished

distinzione (dee-steen-*tsyóa*-nay) f difference, distinction

*distogliere (dee-*staw*-lYay-ray) v avert

distorsione (dee-stoar-*syóa*-nay) f sprain

distretto (dee-*strayt*-toa) m district

distribuire (dee-stree-*bwee*-ray) v *deal, distribute; issue

distributore (dee-stree-boo-*tóa*-ray) m distributor; ~ automatico slot-machine; ~ di benzina petrol station, filling station, service station

distribuzione (dee-stree-boo-*tsyóa*-nay) f distribution; disposition

*distruggere (dee-*strood*-jay-ray) v destroy, wreck

distruzione (dee-stroo-*tsyóa*-nay) f destruction

disturbare (dee-stoor-*baa*-ray) v trouble, disturb; disturbarsi bother

disturbo (dee-*stoor*-boa) m disturbance

ditale (dee-*taa*-lay) m thimble

dito (*dee*-toa) m (pl le dita) finger; ~ del piede toe

ditta (*deet*-tah) f company, firm; business

dittafono (deet-*taa*-foa-noa) m dictaphone

dittatore (deet-tah-*tóa*-ray) m dictator

divano (dee-*vaa*-noa) m couch

*divenire (dee-vay-*nee*-ray) v *become

diventare (dee-vayn-*taa*-ray) v *grow,

*go, *get

diversione (dee-vayr-*syóa*-nay) f diversion

diverso (dee-*vehr*-soa) adj different; diversi several

divertente (dee-vayr-*tehn*-tay) adj funny, entertaining, enjoyable, amusing

divertimento (dee-vayr-tee-*mayn*-toa) m pleasure, fun, entertainment, amusement

divertire (dee-vayr-*tee*-ray) v entertain, amuse

*dividere (dee-*vee*-day-ray) v divide

divieto (dee-*vyai*-toa) m prohibition; ~ di sorpasso no overtaking; no passing Am; ~ di sosta no parking

divino (dee-*vee*-noa) adj divine

divisa estera (dee-*vee*-zah eh-stay-rah) foreign currency

divisione (dee-vee-*zyóa*-nay) f division; agency

divisorio (dee-vee-*zaw*-ryoa) m partition

divorziare (dee-voar-*tsyaa*-ray) v divorce

divorzio (dee-*vor*-tsyoa) m divorce

dizionario (dee-tsyoa-*naa*-ryoa) m dictionary

doccia (*doat*-chah) f shower

docente (doa-*chehn*-tay) m teacher

documento (doa-koo-*mayn*-toa) m document

dodicesimo (doa-dee-*chai*-zee-moa) num twelfth

dodici (*dóa*-dee-chee) num twelve

dogana (doa-*gaa*-nah) f Customs pl

doganiere (doa-gah-*ñai*-ray) m Customs officer

doglie (*daw*-lYay) fpl labour

dolce (*doal*-chay) adj sweet; gentle, tender; m cake; dessert, sweet

dolciumi (doal-*chóo*-mee) mpl sweets; candy nAm

*dolere (doa-*láy*-ray) v ache, *hurt

dolore (doa-*lōā*-ray) *m* pain, ache; grief, sorrow

doloroso (doa-loa-*rōā*-soa) *adj* sorrowful, painful

domanda (doa-*mahn*-dah) *f* inquiry, query; request; demand

domandare (doa-mahn-*daa*-ray) *v* ask; query

domani (doa-*maa*-nee) *adv* tomorrow

domenica (doa-*māy*-nee-kah) *f* Sunday

domestica (doa-*meh*-stee-kah) *f* housemaid

domestico (doa-*meh*-stee-koa) *adj* domestic; *m* domestic; **faccende domestiche** housekeeping

domicilio (doa-mee-*chee*-lyoa) *m* domicile

dominante (doa-mee-*nahn*-tay) *adj* leading

dominare (doa-mee-*naa*-ray) *v* master; rule

dominazione (doa-mee-nah-*tsyōā*-nay) *f* domination

dominio (doa-*mee*-ñoa) *m* rule, dominion

donare (doa-*naa*-ray) *v* donate

donatore (doa-nah-*tōā*-ray) *m* donor

donazione (doa-nah-*tsyōā*-nay) *f* donation

dondolare (doan-doa-*laa*-ray) *v* rock, *swing

donna (*don*-nah) *f* woman

dono (*dōā*-noa) *m* gift, present

dopo (*daw*-poa) *prep* after; ~ **che** after

doppio (*doap*-pyoa) *adj* double

dorato (doa-*raa*-toa) *adj* gilt

dormire (doar-*mee*-ray) *v* *sleep

dormitorio (doar-mee-*taw*-ryoa) *m* dormitory

dorso (*dawr*-soa) *m* back

dose (*daw*-zay) *f* dose

dotato (doa-*taa*-toa) *adj* talented

dottore (doat-*tōā*-ray) *m* doctor

dove (*dōā*-vay) *adv* where; *conj* where

dovere (doa-*vāy*-ray) *m* duty

***dovere** (doa-*vāy*-ray) *v* need to, *have to, *be obliged to, *be bound to, *must, *ought to, *should, *shall; owe

dovunque (doa-*voong*-kway) *adv* anywhere; *conj* wherever

dovuto (doa-*vōō*-toa) *adj* due

dozzina (doad-*dzee*-nah) *f* dozen

drago (*draa*-goa) *m* dragon

dramma (*drahm*-mah) *m* drama

drammatico (drahm-*maa*-tee-koa) *adj* dramatic

drammaturgo (drahm-mah-*toor*-goa) *m* playwright, dramatist

drapperia (drahp-pay-*ree*-ah) *f* drapery

drenare (dray-*naa*-ray) *v* drain

dritto (*dreet*-toa) *adj* straight; *adv* straight

drogheria (droa-gay-*ree*-ah) *f* grocer's

droghiere (droa-*gyai*-ray) *m* grocer

dubbio (*doob*-byoa) *m* doubt; ***mettere in** ~ query

dubbioso (doob-*byōā*-soa) *adj* doubtful

dubitare (doo-bee-*taa*-ray) *v* doubt

duca (*dōō*-kah) *m* (pl duchi) duke

duchessa (doo-*kayss*-sah) *f* duchess

due (*dōō*-ay) *num* two; **tutti e** ~ either

duna (*dōō*-nah) *f* dune

dunque (*doong*-kway) *conj* so; then

duomo (*dwaw*-moa) *m* cathedral

durante (doo-*rahn*-tay) *prep* for, during

durare (doo-*raa*-ray) *v* last

durata (doo-*raa*-tah) *f* duration

duraturo (doo-rah-*tōō*-roa) *adj* permanent, lasting

durevole (doo-*rāy*-voa-lay) *adj* lasting

duro (*dōō*-roa) *adj* tough, hard

E

e (ay) *conj* and

ebano (*ai*-bah-noa) *m* ebony

ebbene! (ayb-*bai*-nay) well!

ebraico (ay-*braa*-ee-koa) *adj* Jewish; *m* Hebrew

ebreo (ay-*brai*-oa) *m* Jew

eccedenza (ayt-chay-*dehn*-tsah) *f* surplus

eccedere (ayt-*chai*-day-ray) *v* exceed

eccellente (ayt-chayl-*lehn*-tay) *adj* excellent

****eccellere** (ayt-*chehl*-lay-ray) *v* excel

eccentrico (ayt-*chehn*-tree-koa) *adj* eccentric

eccessivo (ayt-chayss-*see*-voa) *adj* excessive

eccesso (ayt-*chehss*-soa) *m* excess; ~ **di velocità** speeding

eccetera (ayt-*chai*-tay-rah) etcetera

eccetto (ayt-*cheht*-toa) *prep* except

eccezionale (ayt-chayss-syoa-*naa*-lay) *adj* exceptional

eccezione (ayt-chayss-*syōā*-nay) *f* exception

eccitante (ayt-chee-*tahn*-tay) *adj* exciting

eccitare (ayt-chee-*taa*-ray) *v* excite

eccitazione (ayt-chee-tah-*tsyōā*-nay) *f* excitement

ecco (*ehk*-koa) here you are; *adv* here is

eclissi (ay-*kleess*-see) *f* eclipse

eco (*ai*-koa) *m/f* echo

economia (ay-koa-noa-*mee*-ah) *f* economy

economico (ay-koa-*naw*-mee-koa) *adj* economic; inexpensive, cheap, economical

economista (ay-koa-noa-*mee*-stah) *m* economist

economizzare (ay-koa-noa-meed-*dzaa*-ray) *v* economize

Ecuador (*ay*-kwah-doar) *m* Ecuador

ecuadoriano (ay-kwah-doa-*ryaa*-noa) *m* Ecuadorian

eczema (ayk-*jai*-mah) *m* eczema

edera (*ai*-day-rah) *f* ivy

edicola (ay-*dee*-koa-lah) *f* newsstand, bookstand

edificare (ay-dee-fee-*kaa*-ray) *v* construct

edificio (ay-dee-*fee*-choa) *m* construction, building

editore (ay-dee-*tōā*-ray) *m* publisher

edizione (ay-dee-*tsyōā*-nay) *f* issue, edition; ~ **del mattino** morning edition

educare (ay-doo-*kaa*-ray) *v* educate; *bring up

educazione (ay-doo-kah-*tsyōā*-nay) *f* education

effervescenza (ayf-fayr-vaysh-*shehn*-tsah) *f* fizz

effettivamente (ayf-fayt-tee-vah-*mayn*-tay) *adv* as a matter of fact; indeed

effetto (ayf-*feht*-toa) *m* effect; **effetti personali** belongings *pl*

effettuare (ayf-fayt-*twaa*-ray) *v* implement, effect; achieve

efficace (ayf-fee-*kaa*-chay) *adj* effective

efficiente (ayf-fee-*chehn*-tay) *adj* efficient

Egitto (ay-*jeet*-toa) *m* Egypt

egiziano (ay-jee-*tsyaa*-noa) *adj* Egyptian; *m* Egyptian

egli (*āy*-lʸee) *pron* he; ~ **stesso** himself

egocentrico (ay-goa-*chehn*-tree-koa) *adj* self-centred

egoismo (ay-goa-*ee*-zmoa) *m* selfishness

egoista (ay-goa-*ee*-stah) *adj* selfish

egoistico (ay-goa-*ee*-stee-koa) *adj* egoistic

elaborare (ay-lah-boa-*raa*-ray) v elaborate

elasticità (ay-lah-stee-chee-*tah*) f elasticity

elastico (ay-*lah*-stee-koa) adj elastic; m rubber band, elastic

elefante (ay-lay-*fahn*-tay) m elephant

elegante (ay-lay-*gahn*-tay) adj smart, elegant

eleganza (ay-lay-*gahn*-tsah) f elegance

***eleggere** (ay-*lehd*-jay-ray) v elect

elementare (ay-lay-mayn-*taa*-ray) adj primary

elemento (ay-lay-*mayn*-toa) m element

elencare (ay-layng-*kaa*-ray) v list

elenco (ay-*lehng*-koa) m list; ~ **telefonico** telephone directory; telephone book Am

elettricista (ay-layt-tree-*chee*-stah) m electrician

elettricità (ay-layt-tree-chee-*tah*) f electricity

elettrico (ay-*leht*-tree-koa) adj electric

elettronico (ay-layt-*traw*-nee-koa) adj electronic

elevare (ay-lay-*vaa*-ray) v raise; elevate; **elevato** high; lofty

elevazione (ay-lay-vah-*tsyōā*-nay) f mound

elezione (ay-lay-*tsyōā*-nay) f election

elica (*ai*-lee-kah) f propeller

eliminare (ay-lee-mee-*naa*-ray) v eliminate

ella (*ayl*-lah) pron she

elogio (ay-*law*-joa) m praise

emancipazione (ay-mahn-chee-pah-*tsyōā*-nay) f emancipation

emblema (aym-*blai*-mah) m emblem

emergenza (ay-mayr-*jehn*-tsah) f emergency

***emergere** (ay-*mehr*-jay-ray) v appear, emerge; *stand out

***emettere** (ay-*mayt*-tay-ray) v utter

emicrania (ay-mee-*kraa*-ñah) f migraine

emigrante (ay-mee-*grahn*-tay) m emigrant

emigrare (ay-mee-*graa*-ray) v emigrate

emigrazione (ay-mee-grah-*tsyōā*-nay) f emigration

eminente (ay-mee-*nehn*-tay) adj outstanding

emissione (ay-meess-*syōā*-nay) f issue; broadcast

emorragia (ay-moar-rah-*jee*-ah) f haemorrhage

emorroidi (ay-moar-*raw*-ee-dee) fpl haemorrhoids pl, piles pl

emozione (ay-moa-*tsyōā*-nay) f emotion

enciclopedia (ayn-chee-kloa-pay-*dee*-ah) f encyclopaedia

energia (ay-nayr-*jee*-ah) f energy; power; ~ **nucleare** nuclear energy

energico (ay-*nehr*-jee-koa) adj energetic

enigma (ay-*neeg*-mah) m enigma, mystery; puzzle

enorme (ay-*nor*-may) adj tremendous, immense, enormous, huge

ente (*ehn*-tay) m being; society

entrambi (ayn-*trahm*-bee) adj both

entrare (ayn-*traa*-ray) v *go in, enter

entrata (ayn-*traa*-tah) f way in, entry, entrance; **entrate** revenue

entro (*ayn*-troa) prep in

entusiasmo (ayn-too-*zyah*-zmoa) m enthusiasm

entusiastico (ayn-too-*zyah*-stee-koa) adj enthusiastic

epico (*ai*-pee-koa) adj epic

epidemia (ay-pee-day-*mee*-ah) f epidemic

epilessia (ay-pee-layss-*seeah*) f epilepsy

epilogo (ay-*pee*-loa-goa) m epilogue

episodio (ay-pee-*zaw*-dyoa) m episode

epoca (ai-poa-kah) f period

eppure (ayp-pōō-ray) conj yet, however

equatore (ay-kwah-tōa-ray) m equator

equilibrio (ay-kwee-lee-bryoa) m balance

equipaggiamento (ay-kwee-pahd-jah-mayn-toa) m outfit, equipment

equipaggiare (ay-kwee-pahd-jaa-ray) v equip

equipaggio (ay-kwee-pahd-joa) m crew

equitazione (ay-kwee-tah-tsyōa-nay) f riding

equivalente (ay-kwee-vah-lehn-tay) adj equivalent

equivoco (ay-kwee-voa-koa) adj ambiguous

equo (ai-kwoa) adj right

erba (ehr-bah) f grass; herb

erbaccia (ayr-baht-chah) f weed

eredità (ay-ray-dee-tah) f inheritance

ereditare (ay-ray-dee-taa-ray) v inherit

ereditario (ay-ray-dee-taa-ryoa) adj hereditary

erica (ai-ree-kah) f heather

***erigere** (ay-ree-jay-ray) v erect

ernia (ehr-ñah) f hernia, slipped disc

eroe (ay-raw-ay) m hero

errare (ayr-raa-ray) v wander, err

erroneo (ayr-raw-nay-oa) adj mistaken, wrong

errore (ayr-rōa-ray) m mistake, error

erudito (ay-roo-dee-toa) m scholar

eruzione (ay-roo-tsyōa-nay) f rash

esagerare (ay-zah-jay-raa-ray) v exaggerate

esalare (ay-zah-laa-ray) v exhale

esame (ay-zaa-may) m examination; test

esaminare (ay-zah-mee-naa-ray) v examine

esantema (ay-zahn-tai-mah) m rash

esattamente (ay-zaht-tah-mayn-tay) adv just

esatto (ay-zaht-toa) adj exact, precise; correct, just

esaurire (ay-zou-ree-ray) v exhaust; **esaurito** sold out; **esausto** overtired, overstrung

esca (ay-skah) f bait

esclamare (ay-sklah-maa-ray) v exclaim

esclamazione (ay-sklah-mah-tsyōa-nay) f exclamation

***escludere** (ay-sklōō-day-ray) v exclude

esclusivamente (ay-skloo-zee-vah-mayn-tay) adv solely, exclusively

esclusivo (ay-skloo-zee-voa) adj exclusive

escogitare (ay-skoa-jee-taa-ray) v devise

escoriazione (ay-skoa-ryah-tsyōa-nay) f graze

escrescenza (ay-skraysh-shehn-tsah) f growth

escursione (ay-skoor-syōa-nay) f excursion

esecutivo (ay-zay-koo-tee-voa) adj executive

esecuzione (ay-zay-koo-tsyōa-nay) f execution

eseguire (ay-zay-gwee-ray) v execute, perform, carry out

esempio (ay-zaym-pyoa) m instance, example; **per ~** for instance, for example

esemplare (ay-zaym-plaa-ray) m specimen

esentare (ay-zayn-taa-ray) v exempt

esente (ay-zehn-tay) adj exempt; **~ da tassa** tax-free

esenzione (ay-zayn-tsyōa-nay) f exemption

esercitare (ay-zayr-chee-taa-ray) v exercise; **esercitarsi** practise

esercito (ay-zehr-chee-toa) m army

esercizio (ay-zayr-chee-tsyoa) m exercise

esibire (ay-zee-*bee*-ray) *v* exhibit; *show

esigente (ay-zee-*jehn*-tay) *adj* particular

esigenza (ay-zee-*jehn*-tsah) *f* demand; requirement

*esigere** (ay-zee-jay-ray) *v* demand; require

esiguo (ay-zee-gwoa) *adj* minor

esilio (ay-zee-lᵛoa) *m* exile

esistenza (ay-zee-*stehn*-tsah) *f* existence

*esistere** (ay-zee-stay-ray) *v* exist

esitare (ay-zee-*taa*-ray) *v* hesitate

esito (*ai*-zee-toa) *m* result; issue

esonerare da (ay-zoa-nay-*raa*-ray) discharge of

esotico (ay-*zaw*-tee-koa) *adj* exotic

*espandere** (ay-*spahn*-day-ray) *v* expand

*espellere** (ay-*spehl*-lay-ray) *v* expel

esperienza (ay-spay-*ryehn*-tsah) *f* experience

esperimento (ay-spay-ree-*mayn*-toa) *m* experiment

esperto (ay-*spehr*-toa) *adj* experienced; skilful, skilled; *m* expert

espirare (ay-spee-*raa*-ray) *v* expire

esplicazione (ay-splee-kah-*tsyōā*-nay) *f* explanation

esplicito (ay-*splee*-chee-toa) *adj* explicit; express, definite

*esplodere** (ay-*splaw*-day-ray) *v* explode

esplorare (ay-sploa-*raa*-ray) *v* explore

esplosione (ay-sploa-*zyōā*-nay) *f* explosion, blast

esplosivo (ay-sploa-zee-voa) *adj* explosive; *m* explosive

*esporre** (ay-*spoar*-ray) *v* exhibit, display

esportare (ay-spoar-*taa*-ray) *v* export

esportazione (ay-spoar-tah-*tsyōā*-nay) *f*

exports *pl*, exportation, export

esposimetro (ay-spoa-*zee*-may-troa) *m* exposure meter

esposizione (ay-spoa-zee-*tsyōā*-nay) *f* exposition, exhibition, display, show; exposure

espressione (ay-sprayss-*syōā*-nay) *f* expression

espresso (ay-*sprehss*-soa) *adj* express; **per ~** special delivery

*esprimere** (ay-*spree*-may-ray) *v* express

essa (*ayss*-sah) *pron* she; **~ stessa** herself

essenza (ayss-*sehn*-tsah) *f* essence

essenziale (ayss-sayn-*tsyaa*-lay) *adj* essential

essenzialmente (ayss-sayn-tsyahl-*mayn*-tay) *adv* essentially

essere (*ehss*-say-ray) *m* creature; being; **~ umano** human being

*essere** (*ehss*-say-ray) *v* *be

essi (*ayss*-see) *pron* they; **~ stessi** themselves

essiccatoio (ayss-see-tᵛah-*tōā*-yoa) *m* dryer

est (ehst) *m* east

estasi (*eh*-stah-zee) *f* ecstasy

estate (ay-*staa*-tay) *f* summer; **piena ~** midsummer

*estendere** (ay-*stehn*-day-ray) *v* extend; expand

esteriore (ay-stay-*ryōā*-ray) *adj* external; *m* outside

esterno (ay-*stehr*-noa) *adj* outward, exterior; *m* outside, exterior

all'estero (ahl-*leh*-stay-roa) abroad

esteso (ay-*stāy*-soa) *adj* broad

*estinguere** (ay-*steeng*-gway-ray) *v* extinguish

estintore (ay-steen-*tōā*-ray) *m* fire-extinguisher

*estorcere** (ay-*stor*-chay-ray) *v* extort

estorsione (ay-stoar-*syōā*-nay) *f* extortion

estradare (ay-strah-*daa*-ray) *v* extradite

estraneo (ay-*straa*-nay-oa) *adj* foreign; *m* stranger

*estrarre (ay-*strahr*-ray) *v* extract

estremità (ay-stray-mee-*tah*) *f* end

estremo (ay-*strāy*-moa) *adj* extreme; very, utmost; *m* extreme

estuario (ay-stwaa-ryoa) *m* estuary

esuberante (ay-zoo-bay-*rahn*-tay) *adj* exuberant

esule (*ai*-zoo-lay) *m* exile

età (ay-*tah*) *f* age

etere (*ai*-tay-ray) *m* ether

eternità (ay-tayr-nee-*tah*) *f* eternity

eterno (ay-*tehr*-noa) *adj* eternal

eterosessuale (ay-tay-roa-sayss-*swaa*-lay) *adj* heterosexual

etichetta (ay-tee-*kayt*-tah) *f* label, tag

etichettare (ay-tee-kayt-*taa*-ray) *v* label

Etiopia (ay-*tyaw*-pyah) *f* Ethiopia

etiopico (ay-*tyaw*-pee-koa) *adj* Ethiopian; *m* Ethiopian

Europa (ay^{oo}-*raw*-pah) *f* Europe

europeo (ay^{oo}-roa-*pai*-oa) *adj* European; *m* European

evacuare (ay-vah-*kwaa*-ray) *v* evacuate

evaporare (ay-vah-poa-*raa*-ray) *v* evaporate

evasione (ay-vah-*zyōa*-nay) *f* escape

evento (ay-*vehn*-toa) *m* occurrence, event, happening

eventuale (ay-vayn-*twaa*-lay) *adj* eventual, possible

evidente (ay-vee-*dehn*-tay) *adj* evident

evidentemente (ay-vee-dehn-tay-*mayn*-tay) *adv* apparently

evitare (ay-vee-*taa*-ray) *v* avoid

evoluzione (ay-voa-loo-*tsyōa*-nay) *f* evolution

F

fa (fah) *adv* ago

fabbrica (*fahb*-bree-kah) *f* factory, mill, works *pl*

fabbricante (fahb-bree-*kahn*-tay) *m* manufacturer

fabbricare (fahb-bree-*kaa*-ray) *v* construct; manufacture

fabbricazione (fahb-bree-kah-*tsyōa*-nay) *f* construction

fabbro (*fahb*-broa) *m* smith, blacksmith

faccenda (faht-*chehn*-dah) *f* matter, concern; **faccende di casa** housekeeping

facchino (fahk-*kee*-noa) *m* porter

faccia (*faht*-chah) *f* face; **in ~ a** *prep* facing

facciata (faht-*chaa*-tah) *f* façade; front

facile (*faa*-chee-lay) *adj* easy

facilità (fah-chee-lee-*tah*) *f* ease

facilone (fah-chee-*lōa*-nay) *adj* easygoing

facoltà (fah-koal-*tah*) *f* faculty

facoltativo (fah-koal-tah-*tee*-voa) *adj* optional

faggio (*fahd*-joa) *m* beech

fagiano (fah-*jaa*-noa) *m* pheasant

fagiolo (fah-*jaw*-loa) *m* bean

fagotto (fah-*got*-toa) *m* bundle

falcone (fahl-*kōa*-nay) *m* hawk

falegname (fah-lay-*ñaa*-may) *m* carpenter

fallace (fahl-*laa*-chay) *adj* false

fallimento (fahl-lee-*mayn*-toa) *m* failure

fallire (fahl-*lee*-ray) *v* fail

fallito (fahl-*lee*-toa) *adj* bankrupt

fallo (*fahl*-loa) *m* mistake

falsificare (fahl-see-fee-*kaa*-ray) *v* counterfeit, forge

falsificazione (fahl-see-fee-kah-tsyōa-nay) f fake

falso (fahl-soa) adj untrue; false

fama (faa-mah) f fame; reputation; **di ~ mondiale** world-famous

fame (faa-may) f hunger

famigerato (fah-mee-jay-raa-toa) adj notorious

famiglia (fah-mee-lɩ̯ah) f family

familiare (fah-mee-lɩ̯aa-ray) adj familiar

famoso (fah-mōa-soa) adj famous

fanale (fah-naa-lay) m headlamp; ~ **antinebbia** foglamp; **fanalino posteriore** rear-light

fanatico (fah-naa-tee-koa) adj fanatical

fanciulla (fahn-chool-lah) f young girl

fanciullo (fahn-chool-loa) m boy

fanfara (fahn-faa-rah) f brass band

fango (fahng-goa) m mud

fangoso (fahng-gōa-soa) adj muddy

fantasia (fahn-tah-zee-ah) f fantasy

fantasma (fahn-tah-zmah) m spirit, phantom

fantastico (fahn-tah-stee-koa) adj fantastic

fante (fahn-tay) m knave

fanteria (fahn-tay-ree-ah) f infantry

fantino (fahn-tee-noa) m jockey

***fare** (faa-ray) v *do; *make; *have

farfalla (fahr-fahl-lah) f butterfly

farina (fah-ree-nah) f flour

farmacia (fahr-mah-chee-ah) f pharmacy, chemist's; drugstore nAm

farmacista (fahr-mah-chee-stah) m chemist

farmaco (fahr-mah-koa) m drug

farmacologia (fahr-mah-koa-loa-jee-ah) f pharmacology

faro (faa-roa) m lighthouse; headlight

farsa (fahr-sah) f farce

fasciatura (fahsh-shah-tōō-rah) f bandage

fascino (fahsh-shee-noa) m glamour, charm

fascismo (fahsh-shee-zmoa) m fascism

fascista (fahsh-shee-stah) m fascist

fascistico (fahsh-shee-stee-koa) adj fascist

fase (faa-zay) f phase; stage

fastidioso (fah-stee-dyōa-soa) adj inconvenient, difficult

fata (faa-tah) f fairy

fatale (fah-taa-lay) adj fatal

faticare (fah-tee-kaa-ray) v labour

faticoso (fah-tee-kōa-soa) adj tiring

fato (faa-toa) m fate

fatto (faht-toa) m fact

fattore (faht-tōa-ray) m factor; farmer

fattoressa (faht-toa-rayss-sah) f farmer's wife

fattoria (faht-toa-ree-ah) f farm

fattorino d'albergo (faht-toa-ree-noa dahl-behr-goa) bellboy

fattura (faht-tōō-rah) f bill, invoice

fatturare (faht-too-raa-ray) v bill

fauci (fou-chee) fpl mouth

favola (faa-voa-lah) f fable

favore (fah-vōa-ray) m favour; **a ~ di** on behalf of; **per ~** please

favorevole (fah-voa-rāy-voa-lay) adj favourable

favorire (fah-voa-ree-ray) v favour

favorito (fah-voa-ree-toa) adj pet; m favourite

fax (fahkss) m fax, telefax

fazzoletto (faht-tsoa-layt-toa) m handkerchief; ~ **di carta** paper tissue

febbraio (fayb-braa-yoa) February

febbre (fehb-bray) f fever; ~ **del fieno** hay fever

febbricitante (fayb-bree-chee-tahn-tay) adj feverish

fecondo (fay-koan-doa) adj fertile

fede (fāy-day) f belief, faith; wedding-ring

fedele (fay-dāy-lay) adj true, faithful

federa (*fai*-day-rah) *f* pillow-case

federale (fay-day-*raa*-lay) *adj* federal

federazione (fay-day-rah-*tsyoā*-nay) *f* federation

fegato (*fāy*-gah-toa) *m* liver

felice (fay-*lee*-chay) *adj* happy

felicissimo (faylee-*cheess*-see-moa) *adj* delighted

felicità (fay-lee-chee-*tah*) *f* happiness

felicitarsi con (fay-lee-chee-*tahr*-see) compliment, congratulate

felicitazione (fay-lee-chee-tah-*tsyoā*-nay) *f* congratulation

feltro (*fayl*-troa) *m* felt

femmina (*faym*-mee-nah) *f* female; girl

femminile (faym-mee-*nee*-lay) *adj* female; feminine

*fendere (*fayn*-day-ray) *v* *split

fenicottero (fay-nee-*kot*-tay-roa) *m* flamingo

fenomeno (fay-*naw*-may-noa) *m* phenomenon

ferie (*fai*-ryay) *fpl* holiday; **in ~** on holiday

ferire (fay-*ree*-ray) *v* injure, wound, *hurt

ferita (fay-*ree*-tah) *f* injury, wound

ferito (fay-*ree*-toa) *adj* injured

fermaglio (fayr-*maa*-lᵞoa) *m* fastener; **~ per capelli** bobby pin *Am*

fermarsi (fayr-*mahr*-see) *v* halt, pull up

fermata (fayr-*maa*-tah) *f* stop

fermentare (fayr-mayn-*taa*-ray) *v* ferment

fermo (*fayr*-moa) *adj* steadfast; **~ posta** poste restante

feroce (fay-*rōā*-chay) *adj* wild, fierce

ferramenta (fayr-rah-*mayn*-tah) *fpl* hardware

ferriera (fayr-*ryai*-rah) *f* ironworks

ferro (*fehr*-roa) *m* iron; **di ~** iron; **~ da stiro** iron; **~ di cavallo** horse-shoe; **rottame di ~** scrap-iron

ferrovia (fayr-roa-*vee*-ah) *f* railway; railroad *nAm*

fertile (*fehr*-tee-lay) *adj* fertile

fessura (fayss-*sōō*-rah) *f* crack, chink; slot

festa (*feh*-stah) *f* holiday; feast; party

festival (*fay*-stee-vahl) *m* festival

festivo (fay-*stee*-voa) *adj* festive

fetta (*fayt*-tah) *f* slice

feudale (fayºº-*daa*-lay) *adj* feudal

fiaba (*fyaa*-bah) *f* fairytale

fiacco (*fyahk*-koa) *adj* feeble, faint

fiamma (*fyahm*-mah) *f* flame

fiammifero (fyahm-*mee*-fay-roa) *m* match

fianco (*fyahng*-koa) *m* hip

fiato (*fyaa*-toa) *m* breath

fibbia (*feeb*-byah) *f* buckle

fibra (*fee*-brah) *f* fibre

fico (*fee*-koa) *m* fig

fidanzamento (fee-dahn-tsah-*mayn*-toa) *m* engagement

fidanzata (fee-dahn-*tsaa*-tah) *f* fiancée

fidanzato (fee-dahn-*tsaa*-toa) *adj* engaged; *m* fiancé

fidarsi (fee-*dahr*-see) *v* trust

fidato (fee-*daa*-toa) *adj* trustworthy, reliable; **non ~** unreliable

fiducia (fee-*dōō*-chah) *f* faith, trust, confidence

fieno (*fyai*-noa) *m* hay

fiera (*fyai*-rah) *f* fair

fierezza (fyay-*rayt*-tsah) *f* pride

fiero (*fyai*-roa) *adj* proud

figlia (*fee*-lᵞah) *f* daughter

figliastro (fee-*lᵞah*-stroa) *m* stepchild

figliata (fee-*lᵞaa*-tah) *f* litter

figlio (*fee*-lᵞoa) *m* son

figliolo (fee-*lᵞaw*-loa) *m* son; boy

figura (fee-*gōō*-rah) *f* figure; picture

figurarsi (fee-goo-*rahr*-see) *v* imagine; fancy

fila (*fee*-lah) *f* row, rank, file, line

filare (fee-*laa*-ray) v *spin

filippino (fee-leep-*pee*-noa) adj Philippine; m Filipino

film (feelm) m (pl ~) film, movie

filmare (feel-*maa*-ray) v film

filo (*fee*-loa) m thread, wire, yarn

filobus (fee-loa-*booss*) m trolley-bus

filosofia (fee-loa-zoa-*fee*-ah) f philosophy

filosofo (fee-*law*-zoa-foa) m philosopher

filtrare (feel-*traa*-ray) v strain

filtro (*feel*-troa) m filter; percolator; ~ **dell'aria** air-filter; ~ **dell'olio** oil filter

finale (fee-*naa*-lay) adj eventual, final

finalmente (fee-nahl-*mayn*-tay) adv at last

finanze (fee-*nahn*-tsay) fpl finances pl

finanziare (fee-nahn-*tsyaa*-ray) v finance

finanziario (fee-nahn-*tsyaa*-ryoa) adj financial

finanziatore (fee-nahn-tsyah-*tōa*-ray) m investor

finché (feeng-*kay*) conj until, till; ~ **non** till

fine (*fee*-nay) f ending, end; m purpose; **fine-settimana** weekend

finestra (fee-*nay*-strah) f window

***fingere** (*feen*-jay-ray) v pretend

finire (fee-*nee*-ray) v end, finish; expire; **finito** finished; over

finlandese (feen-lahn-*dāy*-say) adj Finnish; m Finn

Finlandia (feen-*lahn*-dyah) f Finland

fino (*fee*-noa) adj fine; sheer

fino a (*fee*-noa ah) prep until, to, till

finora (fee-*nōā*-rah) adv so far

finzione (feen-*tsyōa*-nay) f fiction

fioraio (fyoa-*raa*-yoa) m florist

fiore (*fyōa*-ray) m flower

fiorente (fyoa-*rehn*-tay) adj prosperous

firma (*feer*-mah) f signature

firmare (feer-*maa*-ray) v sign

fischiare (fee-*skyaa*-ray) v whistle

fischio (*fee*-skyoa) m whistle

fisica (*fee*-zee-kah) f physics

fisico (*fee*-zee-koa) adj physical; m physicist

fisiologia (fee-zyoa-loa-*jee*-ah) f physiology

fissare (feess-*saa*-ray) v gaze, stare; settle

fisso (*feess*-soa) adj permanent, fixed

fitta (*feet*-tah) f stitch

fiume (*fyōō*-may) m river

flacone (flah-*koa*-nay) m flask

flagello (flah-*jehl*-loa) m plague

flanella (flah-*nehl*-lah) f flannel

flauto (*flou*-toa) m flute

flessibile (flayss-*see*-bee-lay) adj supple, flexible, elastic

floscio (*flosh*-shoa) adj limp

flotta (*flot*-tah) f fleet

fluente (*flwehn*-tay) adj fluent

fluido (*flōō*-ee-doa) adj fluid; m fluid

flusso (*flooss*-soa) m flood

foca (*faw*-kah) f seal

foce (*faw*-chay) f mouth

focolare (foa-koa-*laa*-ray) m fireplace, hearth

fodera (*faw*-day-rah) f lining

foglia (*faw*-lˠah) f leaf

foglio (*faw*-lˠoa) m sheet; ~ **di registrazione** registration form

fogna (*fōa*-ñah) f sewer

folklore (foal-*klaw*-ray) m folklore

folla (*fol*-lah) f crowd

folle (*fol*-lay) adj crazy, mad

folletto (foal-*layt*-toa) m elf

fondamentale (foan-dah-mayn-*taa*-lay) adj fundamental, essential, basic

fondamento (foan-dah-*mayn*-toa) m base; basis

fondare (foan-*daa*-ray) v found; **fondato** well-founded

fondazione (foan-dah-*tsyoā*-nay) *f* foundation

*****fondere** (*foan*-day-ray) *v* melt

fondo (*foan*-doa) *m* ground, bottom; **fondi** fund; ~ **tinta** foundation cream

fonetico (foa-*nai*-tee-koa) *adj* phonetic

fontana (foan-*taa*-nah) *f* fountain

fonte (*foan*-tay) *f* spring; source

foratura (foa-rah-*tōo*-rah) *f* puncture, blow-out

forbici (*for*-bee-chee) *fpl* scissors *pl*; **forbicine per le unghie** nail-scissors *pl*

forca (*foar*-kah) *f* gallows *pl*

forchetta (foar-*kayt*-tah) *f* fork

forcina (foar-*chee*-nah) *f* hairpin, hair-grip

foresta (foa-*reh*-stah) *f* forest

forestiero (foa-ray-*styai*-roa) *m* foreigner

forfora (*foar*-foa-rah) *f* dandruff

forma (*foar*-mah) *f* form, shape; figure; condition

formaggio (foar-*mahd*-joa) *m* cheese

formale (foar-*maa*-lay) *adj* formal

formalità (foar-mah-lee-*tah*) *f* formality

formare (foar-*maa*-ray) *v* form, shape

formato (foar-*maa*-toa) *m* size

formazione (foar-mah-*tsyoā*-nay) *f* formation

formica (foar-*mee*-kah) *f* ant

formidabile (foar-mee-*daa*-bee-lay) *adj* terrific

formula (*for*-moo-lah) *f* formula

formulario (foar-moo-*laa*-ryoa) *m* form

fornace (foar-*naa*-chay) *f* furnace

fornello (foar-*nehl*-loa) *m* cooker; ~ **a gas** gas cooker; ~ **a spirito** spirit stove

fornire (foar-*nee*-ray) *v* furnish, provide, supply

fornitura (foar-nee-*tōo*-rah) *f* supply

forno (*foar*-noa) *m* oven; ~ **a microonde** microwave oven

forse (*foar*-say) *adv* maybe, perhaps

forte (*for*-tay) *adj* strong, powerful; loud; *m* fort

fortezza (foar-*tayt*-tsah) *f* fortress

fortuito (foar-*tōo*-ee-toa) *adj* casual, accidental

fortuna (foar-*tōo*-nah) *f* lot; luck

fortunato (foar-too-*naa*-toa) *adj* lucky, fortunate

foruncolo (foa-*roong*-koa-loa) *m* boil

forza (*for*-tsah) *f* energy, strength, force; ~ **di volontà** will-power; ~ **motrice** driving force; **forze militari** military force

forzare (foar-*tsaa*-ray) *v* force; strain

foschia (foa-*skee*-ah) *f* mist, haze

fosco (*foa*-skoa) *adj* hazy

fossato (foass-*saa*-toa) *m* ditch; moat

fosso (*foass*-soa) *m* ditch

foto (*faw*-toa) *f* photo; ~ **per passaporto** passport photograph

fotocopia (foa-toa-*kaw*-pyah) *f* photocopy

fotografare (foa-toa-grah-*faa*-ray) *v* photograph

fotografia (foa-toa-grah-*fee*-ah) *f* photography; photograph

fotografo (foa-*taw*-grah-foa) *m* photographer

fra (frah) *prep* among; amid

fragile (*fraa*-jee-lay) *adj* fragile

fragola (*fraa*-goa-lah) *f* strawberry

*****fraintendere** (frah-een-*tehn*-day-ray) *v* *misunderstand

francese (frahn-*chāy*-zay) *adj* French; *m* Frenchman

Francia (*frahn*-chah) *f* France

franco (*frahng*-koa) *adj* open; ~ **di dazio** duty-free; ~ **di porto** postage paid

francobollo (frahng-koa-*boal*-loa) *m* postage stamp

frangia (*frahn*-jah) *f* fringe

frappé (frahp-*pay*) *m* milk-shake

frase (*fraa*-zay) *f* sentence; phrase

fratello (frah-*tehl*-loa) *m* brother

fraternità (frah-tayr-nee-*tah*) *f* fraternity

frattanto (fraht-*tahn*-toa) *adv* meanwhile

nel frattempo (nayl fraht-*tehm*-poa) in the meantime

frattura (fraht-*tōō*-rah) *f* fracture; break

fratturare (fraht-too-*raa*-ray) *v* fracture

frazione (frah-*tsyōā*-nay) *f* fraction; hamlet

freccia (*frayt*-chah) *f* arrow; indicator

freddino (frayd-*dee*-noa) *adj* chilly

freddo (*frayd*-doa) *adj* cold; *m* cold

freno (*frāy*-noa) *m* brake; ~ **a mano** hand-brake; ~ **a pedale** foot-brake

frequentare (fray-kwayn-*taa*-ray) *v* mix with, associate with

frequente (fray-*kwehn*-tay) *adj* frequent

frequenza (fray-*kwehn*-tsah) *f* frequency; attendance

fresco (*fray*-skoa) *adj* fresh; cool

fretta (*frayt*-tah) *f* speed, haste, hurry; **in** ~ in a hurry

frettoloso (frayt-toa-*lōā*-soa) *adj* hasty

friggere (*freed*-jay-ray) *v* fry

frigorifero (free-goa-*ree*-fay-roa) *m* refrigerator, fridge

fringuello (freeng-*gwehl*-loa) *m* finch

frittata (freet-*taa*-tah) *f* omelette

frizione (free-*tsyōā*-nay) *f* clutch

frode (*fraw*-day) *f* fraud

fronte (*froan*-tay) *f* forehead; **di** ~ **a** in front of; opposite; **far** ~ **a** face

frontiera (froan-*tyai*-rah) *f* frontier; boundary

frontone (froan-*tōā*-nay) *m* gable

frullatore (frool-lah-*tōā*-ray) *m* mixer

frumento (froo-*mayn*-toa) *m* corn, grain; wheat

frusta (*froo*-stah) *f* whip

frutta (*froot*-tah) *f* fruit

frutteto (froot-*tāy*-toa) *m* orchard

fruttivendolo (froot-tee-*vayn*-doa-loa) *m* greengrocer; vegetable merchant

frutto (*froot*-toa) *m* fruit

fruttuoso (froot-*twōā*-soa) *adj* profitable

fucile (foo-*chee*-lay) *m* gun, rifle

fuga (*fōō*-gah) *f* flight; leak

fuggire (food-*jee*-ray) *v* escape

fuggitivo (food-jee-*tee*-voa) *m* runaway

fulvo (*fool*-voa) *adj* fawn

fumare (foo-*maa*-ray) *v* smoke

fumatore (foo-mah-*tōā*-ray) *m* smoker; **compartimento per fumatori** smoking-compartment

fumo (*fōō*-moa) *m* smoke

funerale (foo-nay-*raa*-lay) *m* funeral

fungo (*foong*-goa) *m* toadstool, mushroom

funzionamento (foon-tsyoa-nah-*mayn*-toa) *m* working, operation

funzionare (foon-tsyoa-*naa*-ray) *v* work, operate

funzionario (foon-tsyoa-*naa*-ryoa) *m* civil servant

funzione (foon-*tsyōā*-nay) *f* function; office

fuoco (*fwaw*-koa) *m* fire; focus

fuori (*fwaw*-ree) *adv* out; outside; **al di** ~ outwards; ~ **di** outside, out of

furbo (*foor*-boa) *adj* cunning

furfante (foor-*fahn*-tay) *m* villain

furgone (foor-*gōā*-nay) *m* delivery van, van

furibondo (foo-ree-*boan*-doa) *adj* furious

furioso (foo-*ryōā*-soa) *adj* furious

furore (foo-*rōā*-ray) *m* rage

furto (*foor*-toa) *m* robbery, theft

fusibile (foo-*zee*-bee-lay) *m* fuse

fusione (foo-*zyōa*-nay) *f* merger

futile (*fōō*-tee-lay) *adj* insignificant, petty

futuro (foo-*tōō*-roa) *m* future; *adj* future

G

gabbia (*gahb*-byah) *f* cage; ~ **da imballaggio** crate

gabbiano (gahb-*byaa*-noa) *m* gull; seagull

gabinetto (gah-bee-*nayt*-toa) *m* toilet, bathroom, lavatory; cabinet; ~ **per signore** ladies' room, powder-room; ~ **per signori** men's room

gaiezza (gah-*yayt*-tsah) *f* gaiety

gaio (*gaa*-yoa) *adj* cheerful

galleggiante (gahl-layd-*jahn*-tay) *m* float

galleggiare (gahl-layd-*jaa*-ray) *v* float

galleria (gahl-lay-*ree*-ah) *f* tunnel; gallery; ~ **d'arte** art gallery

gallina (gahl-*lee*-nah) *f* hen

gallo (*gahl*-loa) *m* cock

galoppo (gah-*lop*-poa) *m* gallop

gamba (*gahm*-bah) *f* leg

gamberetto (gahm-bay-*rayt*-toa) *m* shrimp

gambero (*gahm*-bay-roa) *m* prawn

gambo (*gahm*-boa) *m* stem

gancio (*gahn*-choa) *m* peg

gara (*gaa*-rah) *f* competition; race

garante (gah-*rahn*-tay) *m* guarantor

garantire (gah-rahn-*tee*-ray) *v* guarantee

garanzia (gah-rahn-*tsee*-ah) *f* guarantee

gargarizzare (gahr-gah-reed-*dzaa*-ray) *v* gargle

garza (*gahr*-dzah) *f* gauze

gas (gahz) *m* gas; ~ **di scarico** exhaust gases

gastrico (*gah*-stree-koa) *adj* gastric

gatto (*gaht*-toa) *m* cat

gazza (*gahd*-dzah) *f* magpie

gelare (jay-*laa*-ray) *v* *freeze

gelatina (jay-lah-*tee*-nah) *f* jelly

gelato (jay-*laa*-toa) *m* ice-cream

gelo (*jai*-loa) *m* frost

gelone (jay-*lōā*-nay) *m* chilblain

gelosia (jay-loa-*see*-ah) *f* jealousy

geloso (jay-*lōā*-soa) *adj* envious, jealous

gemelli (jay-*mehl*-lee) *mpl* twins *pl*; cuff-links *pl*

gemere (*jai*-may-ray) *v* groan, moan

gemma (*jehm*-mah) *f* gem

generale (jay-nay-*raa*-lay) *adj* general; universal, broad, public; *m* general; **in** ~ in general

generalmente (jay-nay-rahl-*mayn*-tay) *adv* as a rule

generare (jay-nay-*raa*-ray) *v* generate

generatore (jay-nay-rah-*tōā*-ray) *m* generator

generazione (jay-nay-rah-*tsyōā*-nay) *f* generation

genere (*jai*-nay-ray) *m* sort, kind; gender

genero (*jai*-nay-roa) *m* son-in-law

generosità (jay-nay-roa-see-*tah*) *f* generosity

generoso (jay-nay-*rōā*-soa) *adj* generous, liberal

gengiva (jayn-*jee*-vah) *f* gum

genio (*jai*-ñoa) *m* genius

genitale (jay-nee-*taa*-lay) *adj* genital

genitori (jay-nee-*tōā*-ree) *mpl* parents *pl*

gennaio (jayn-*naa*-yoa) January

gente (*jehn*-tay) *f* people *pl*

gentile (jayn-*tee*-lay) *adj* good-natured; kind

genuino (jay-*nwee*-noa) *adj* genuine

geografia (jay-oa-grah-*fee*-ah) *f* geography

geologia (jay-oa-loa-*jee*-ah) f geology

geometria (jay-oa-may-*tree*-ah) f geometry

gerarchia (jay-rahr-*kee*-ah) f hierarchy

Germania (jayr-*maa*-nyah) f Germany

germe (*jehr*-may) m germ

gesso (*jehss*-soa) m plaster

gesticolare (jay-stee-koa-*laa*-ray) v gesticulate

gestione (jay-*styōa*-nay) f management

gesto (*jeh*-stoa) m sign

gettare (jayt-*taa*-ray) v toss, *throw, *cast

getto (*jeht*-toa) m spout, jet

gettone (jayt-*tōa*-nay) m token, chip

ghiacciaio (gyaht-*chaa*-yoa) m glacier

ghiaccio (*gyaht*-choa) m ice

ghiaia (*gyaa*-yah) f gravel

ghianda (*gyahn*-dah) f acorn

ghiandola (*gyahn*-doa-lah) f gland

ghignare (gee-*ñaa*-ray) v grin

ghiottoneria (gyoat-toa-nay-*ree*-ah) f delicacy

ghiribizzo (gee-ree-*beed*-dzoa) m whim

ghisa (*gee*-zah) f cast iron

già (jah) adv already; formerly

giacca (*jahk*-kah) f jacket; ~ **e calzoni** pant-suit; ~ **sportiva** blazer

giacché (jahk-*kay*) conj since

giacchetta (jahk-*kayt*-tah) f jacket; ~ **sportiva** sports-jacket

giaccone (jahk-*kōa*-nay) m cardigan

giacimento (jah-chee-*mayn*-toa) m deposit

giada (*jaa*-dah) f jade

giallo (*jahl*-loa) adj yellow

Giappone (jahp-*pōa*-nay) m Japan

giapponese (jahp-poa-*nāy*-say) adj Japanese; m Japanese

giara (*jaa*-rah) f jar

giardiniere (jahr-dee-*ñai*-ray) m gardener

giardino (jahr-*dee*-noa) m garden; ~ **d'infanzia** kindergarten; ~ **pubblico** public garden; ~ **zoologico** zoological gardens, zoo

gigante (jee-*gahn*-tay) m giant

gigantesco (jee-gahn-*tay*-skoa) adj gigantic

giglio (*jee*-lYoa) m lily

ginecologo (jee-nay-*kaw*-loa-goa) m gynaecologist

ginnasta (jeen-*nah*-stah) m gymnast

ginnastica (jeen-*nah*-stee-kah) f gymnastics pl

ginocchio (jee-*nok*-kyoa) m (pl le ginocchia) knee

giocare (joa-*kaa*-ray) v play

giocatore (joa-kah-*tōa*-ray) m player

giocattolo (joa-*kaht*-toa-loa) m toy

gioco (*jaw*-koa) m play; **carta da ~** playing-card; ~ **della dama** draughts; checkers plAm; ~ **delle bocce** bowling

giogo (*jōa*-goa) m yoke

gioia (*jaw*-yah) f gladness, joy; **gioie** jewellery

gioielliere (joa-yayl-lYai-ray) m jeweller

gioiello (joa-*yehl*-loa) m gem, jewel; **gioielli** jewellery

gioioso (joa-*yōa*-soa) adj joyful

Giordania (joar-*daa*-ñah) f Jordan

giordano (joar-*daa*-noa) adj Jordanian; m Jordanian

giornalaio (joar-nah-*laa*-yoa) m newsagent

giornale (joar-*naa*-lay) m paper, newspaper; journal; ~ **del mattino** morning paper

giornaliero (joar-nah-*lYai*-roa) adj daily

giornalismo (joar-nah-*lee*-zmoa) m journalism

giornalista (joar-nah-*lee*-stah) m journalist

giornata (joar-*naa*-tah) f day

giorno (*joar*-noa) m day; **al ~ per**

day; **di** ~ by day; ~ **feriale** week-day; ~ **lavorativo** working day; ~ **quindicina di giorni** fortnight; **un** ~ some time; **un** ~ **o l'altro** some day

giostra (*jo*-strah) *f* merry-go-round

giovane (*jōā*-vah-nay) *adj* young; *m* lad; ~ **esploratore** boy scout; ~ **esploratrice** girl guide

giovanile (joa-vah-*nee*-lay) *adj* juvenile

giovanotto (joa-vah-*not*-toa) *m* youth

giovare (joa-*vaa*-ray) *v* *be of use

giovedì (joa-vay-*dee*) *m* Thursday

gioventù (joa-vayn-*too*) *f* youth

giovinezza (joa-vee-*nayt*-tsah) *f* youth

giradischi (jee-rah-*dee*-skee) *m* record-player

girare (jee-*raa*-ray) *v* turn; endorse; *far* ~ *spin; ~ **intorno a** by-pass

giro (*jee*-roa) *m* turn; day trip; detour; ~ **d'affari** turnover

gita (*jee*-tah) *f* trip, excursion; ~ **turistica** tour

giù (joo) *adv* beneath, below, down; over; ~ **da** off; **in** ~ downwards, down

giudicare (joo-dee-*kaa*-ray) *v* judge

giudice (*jōō*-dee-chay) *m* judge

giudizio (joo-*dee*-tsyoa) *m* judgment

giugno (*jōō*-ño-a) June

giunco (*joong*-koa) *m* reed; rush

giungere (*joon*-jay-ray) *v* arrive

giungla (*joong*-glah) *f* jungle

giuoco (*jwaw*-koa) *m* game

giuramento (joo-rah-*mayn*-toa) *m* oath, vow

giurare (joo-*raa*-ray) *v* vow, *swear

giuria (joo-*ree*-ah) *f* jury

giuridico (joo-*ree*-dee-koa) *adj* legal

giurista (joo-*ree*-stah) *m* lawyer

giustamente (joo-stah-*mayn*-tay) *adv* rightly

giustificare (joo-stee-fee-*kaa*-ray) *v* justify

giustizia (joo-*stee*-tsyah) *f* justice

giusto (*joo*-stoa) *adj* righteous, right, fair, just; proper

glaciale (glah-*chaa*-lay) *adj* freezing

gli (l*ʸ*ee) *pron* him

globale (gloa-*baa*-lay) *adj* overall

globo (*glaw*-boa) *m* globe

gloria (*glaw*-ryah) *f* glory

glossario (gloass-*saa*-ryoa) *m* vocabulary

goccia (*goat*-chah) *f* drop

godere (goa-*dāy*-ray) *v* enjoy

godimento (goa-dee-*mayn*-toa) *m* enjoyment

goffo (*gof*-foa) *adj* clumsy, awkward

gola (*gōā*-lah) *f* throat; gorge, glen

golf (goalf) *m* jumper; golf; **campo di** ~ golf-links

golfo (*goal*-foa) *m* gulf

goloso (goa-*lōā*-soa) *adj* greedy

gomito (*gaw*-mee-toa) *m* elbow

gomma (*goam*-mah) *f* gum; ~ **da masticare** chewing-gum; ~ **per cancellare** rubber, eraser

gommapiuma (goam-mah-*pyōā*-mah) *f* foam-rubber

gondola (*goan*-doa-lah) *f* gondola

gonfiabile (goan-*fyaa*-bee-lay) *adj* inflatable

gonfiare (goan-*fyaa*-ray) *v* inflate; *swell

gonfiore (goan-*fyōā*-ray) *m* swelling

gonna (*goan*-nah) *f* skirt

gotta (*goat*-tah) *f* gout

governante (goa-vayr-*nahn*-tay) *f* governess; housekeeper

governare (goa-vayr-*naa*-ray) *v* govern, rule; navigate

governatore (goa-vayr-nah-*tōā*-ray) *m* governor

governo (goa-*vehr*-noa) *m* government, rule

gradevole (grah-*dāy*-voa-lay) *adj*

pleasing, pleasant, enjoyable, agreeable

gradire (grah-*dee*-ray) v fancy, like

grado (*graa*-doa) m degree; ***essere in ~ di** *be able to

graduale (grah-*dwaa*-lay) adj gradual

graffetta (grahf-*fayt*-tah) f staple

graffiare (grahf-*fyaa*-ray) v scratch

graffio (*grahf*-fyoa) m scratch

grafico (*graa*-fee-koa) adj graphic; m graph, diagram

grammatica (grahm-*maa*-tee-kah) f grammar

grammaticale (grahm-mah-tee-*kaa*-lay) adj grammatical

grammo (*grahm*-moa) m gram

grammofono (grahm-*maw*-foa-noa) m gramophone

granaio (grah-*naa*-yoa) m barn

Gran Bretagna (grahn bray-*taa*-ñah) Great Britain, Britain

granchio (*grahng*-kyoa) m crab

grande (*grahn*-day) adj big; great, large, major

grandezza (grahn-*dayt*-tsah) f size

grandine (*grahn*-dee-nay) f hail

grandioso (grahn-*dyōa*-soa) adj magnificent, superb

granello (grah-*nehl*-loa) m corn, grain

graniglia (grah-*nee*-lᴵah) f grit

granito (grah-*nee*-toa) m granite

grano (*graa*-noa) m corn, grain

granturco (grahn-*toor*-koa) m maize; **pannocchia di ~** corn on the cob

grasso (*grahss*-soa) adj fat; corpulent; greasy; m grease, fat

grassottello (grahss-soat-*tehl*-loa) adj plump

grata (*graa*-tah) f grate

gratis (*graa*-teess) adj gratis

gratitudine (grah-tee-*tōō*-dee-nay) f gratitude

grato (*graa*-toa) adj grateful

grattacielo (graht-tah-*chai*-loa) m skyscraper

grattugia (graht-*tōō*-jah) f grater

gratuito (grah-*tōō*-ee-toa) adj free of charge, free

grave (*graa*-vay) adj grave

gravità (grah-vee-*tah*) f gravity

grazia (*graa*-tsyah) f grace; pardon

grazie (*graa*-tsyay) thank you

grazioso (grah-*tsyōa*-soa) adj graceful

Grecia (*grai*-chah) f Greece

greco (*grai*-koa) adj (pl greci) Greek; m Greek

gregge (*grayd*-jay) m herd, flock

grembiule (graym-*byōa*-lay) m apron

gremito (gray-*mee*-toa) adj chock-full

gridare (gree-*daa*-ray) v cry; shout

grido (*gree*-doa) m cry, scream, shout

grigio (*gree*-joa) adj grey

griglia (*gree*-lᴵah) f grill

grilletto (greel-*layt*-toa) m trigger

grillo (*greel*-loa) m cricket

grinza (*green*-tsah) f crease

grossa (*gross*-sah) f gross

grossista (groass-*see*-stah) m wholesale dealer

grosso (*gross*-soa) adj big, stout

grossolano (groass-soa-*laa*-noa) adj coarse; rude

grotta (*grot*-tah) f grotto

gru (groo) f crane

grullo (*grool*-loa) adj silly

grumo (*grōō*-moa) m lump

grumoso (groo-*mōa*-soa) adj lumpy

gruppo (*groop*-poa) m group, party, set; bunch

guadagnare (gwah-dah-*ñaa*-ray) v *make, earn; gain

guadagno (gwah-*daa*-ñoa) m profit

guadare (gwah-*daa*-ray) v wade

guado (*gwaa*-doa) m ford

guaio (*gwaa*-yoa) m trouble

guancia (*gwahn*-chah) f cheek

guanciale (gwahn-*chaa*-lay) m pillow

guanto (*gwahn*-toa) m glove

guardare (gwahr-*daa*-ray) v look;
watch, look at, view; **guardarsi** beware

guardaroba (gwahr-dah-*raw*-bah) m
wardrobe; checkroom nAm

guardia (*gwahr*-dyah) f attendant; ~
del corpo bodyguard; ~ **forestale**
forester

guardiano (gwahr-*dyaa*-noa) m guard,
warden

guarigione (gwah-ree-*joa*-nay) f recovery, cure

guarire (gwah-*ree*-ray) v heal; recover

guastare (gwah-*staa*-ray) v *spoil;
guastarsi *break down

guasto (*gwah*-stoa) adj broken; m
breakdown

guerra (*gwehr*-rah) f war; ~ **mondiale** world war

gufo (*goo*-foa) m owl

guglia (*goo*-lᵞah) f spire

guida (*gwee*-dah) f lead; guide;
guidebook; **patente di** ~ driving licence

guidare (gwee-*daa*-ray) v guide, conduct; *drive

guinzaglio (gween-*tsaa*-lᵞoa) m leash,
lead

guscio (*goosh*-shoa) m shell; ~ **di noce** nutshell

gustare (goo-*staa*-ray) v enjoy

gusto (*goo*-stoa) m taste; flavour;
zest

gustoso (goo-*stoa*-soa) adj enjoyable,
tasty

I

icona (ee-*koa*-nah) f icon

idea (ee-*dai*-ah) f idea; ~ **luminosa**
brain-wave

ideale (ee-day-*aa*-lay) adj ideal; m
ideal

identico (ee-*dehn*-tee-koa) adj identical

identificare (ee-dayn-tee-fee-*kaa*-ray) v
identify

identificazione (ee-dayn-tee-fee-kah-
tsyoa-nay) f identification

identità (ee-dayn-tee-*tah*) f identity

idillio (ee-*deel*-lᵞoa) m romance

idioma (ee-*dyaw*-mah) m idiom

idiomatico (ee-dyoa-*maa*-tee-koa) adj
idiomatic

idiota (ee-*dyaw*-tah) adj idiotic; m
fool, idiot

idolo (*ee*-doa-loa) m idol

idoneo (ee-*daw*-nay-oa) adj adequate

idraulico (ee-*drou*-lee-koa) m plumber

idrogeno (ee-*draw*-jay-noa) m hydrogen

ieri (*yai*-ree) adv yesterday

igiene (ee-*jai*-nay) f hygiene

igienico (ee-*jai*-nee-koa) adj hygienic

ignorante (ee-ñoa-*rahn*-tay) adj ignorant

ignorare (ee-ñoa-*raa*-ray) v ignore

ignoto (ee-*ñaw*-toa) adj unknown

il (eel) art (f la;pl i, gli, le) the art

illecito (eel-*lay*-chee-toa) adj unauthorized

illegale (eel-lay-*gaa*-lay) adj unlawful,
illegal

illeggibile (eel-layd-*jee*-bee-lay) adj illegible

illimitato (eel-lee-mee-*taa*-toa) adj unlimited

illuminare (eel-loo-mee-*naa*-ray) v illuminate

illuminazione (eel-loo-mee-nah-*tsyōā*-nay) *f* lighting, illumination

illusione (eel-loo-*zyō*-nay) *f* illusion

illustrare (eel-loo-*straa*-ray) *v* illustrate

illustrazione (eel-loo-strah-*tsyōā*-nay) *f* illustration; picture

illustre (eel-*loo*-stray) *adj* noted

imballaggio (eem-bahl-*lahd*-joa) *m* packing

imballare (eem-bahl-*laa*-ray) *v* pack up, pack

imbarazzante (eem-bah-raht-*tsahn*-tay) *adj* awkward, embarrassing; puzzling

imbarazzare (eem-bah-raht-*tsaa*-ray) *v* embarrass

imbarcare (eem-bahr-*kaa*-ray) *v* embark

imbarco (eem-*bahr*-koa) *m* embarkation

imbiancare (eem-byahng-*kaa*-ray) *v* bleach

imboscata (eem-boa-*skaa*-tah) *f* ambush

imbrogliare (eem-broa-*lʸaa*-ray) *v* cheat

imbroglio (eem-*braw*-lʸoa) *m* muddle

imbronciato (eem-broan-*chaa*-toa) *adj* cross

imbuto (eem-*bōō*-toa) *m* funnel

imitare (ee-mee-*taa*-ray) *v* copy, imitate

imitazione (ee-mee-tah-*tsyōā*-nay) *f* imitation

immacolato (eem-mah-koa-*laa*-toa) *adj* stainless, spotless

immagazzinare (eem-mah-gahd-dzee-*naa*-ray) *v* store

immaginare (eem-mah-jee-*naa*-ray) *v* fancy, imagine

immaginario (eem-mah-jee-*naa*-ryoa) *adj* imaginary

immaginazione (eem-mah-jee-nah-

tsyōā-nay) *f* fancy, imagination

immagine (eem-*maa*-jee-nay) *f* image; ~ **riflessa** reflection

immangiabile (eem-mahn-*jaa*-bee-lay) *adj* inedible

immediatamente (eem-may-dyah-tah-*mayn*-tay) *adv* instantly, immediately

immediato (eem-may-*dyaa*-toa) *adj* immediate

immenso (eem-*mehn*-soa) *adj* vast, immense, huge

immigrante (eem-mee-*grahn*-tay) *m* immigrant

immigrare (eem-mee-*graa*-ray) *v* immigrate

immigrazione (eem-mee-grah-*tsyōā*-nay) *f* immigration

imminente (eem-mee-*nehn*-tay) *adj* oncoming

immobile (eem-*maw*-bee-lay) *m* house

immodesto (eem-moa-*deh*-stoa) *adj* immodest

immondizia (eem-moan-*dee*-tsyah) *f* rubbish, refuse, garbage

immunità (eem-moo-nee-*tah*) *f* immunity

immunizzare (eem-moo-need-*dzaa*-ray) *v* immunize

impalcatura (eem-pahl-kah-*tōō*-rah) *f* scaffolding

imparare (eem-pah-*raa*-ray) *v* *learn; ~ **a memoria** memorize

imparziale (eem-pahr-*tsyaa*-lay) *adj* impartial

impasticciare (eem-pah-steet-*chaa*-ray) *v* muddle

impasto (eem-*pah*-stoa) *m* batter

impaurito (eem-pou-*ree*-toa) *adj* afraid

impaziente (eem-pah-*tsyehn*-tay) *adj* eager, impatient

impeccabile (eem-payk-*kaa*-bee-lay) *adj* faultless

impedimento (eem-pay-dee-*mayn*-toa)

m impediment

impedire (eem-pay-*dee*-ray) *v* prevent; impede

impegnare (eem-pay-*ñaa*-ray) *v* pawn; **impegnarsi** engage

impegno (eem-*pāy*-ñoa) *m* engagement

imperatore (eem-pay-rah-*tōa*-ray) *m* emperor

imperatrice (eem-pay-rah-*tree*-chay) *f* empress

imperfetto (eem-payr-*feht*-toa) *adj* imperfect

imperfezione (eem-payr-fay-*tsyōa*-nay) *f* fault

imperiale (eem-pay-*ryaa*-lay) *adj* imperial

impermeabile (eem-payr-may-*aa*-bee-lay) *adj* waterproof, rainproof; *m* mackintosh, raincoat

impero (eem-*pai*-roa) *m* empire

impersonale (eem-payr-soa-*naa*-lay) *adj* impersonal

impertinente (eem-payr-tee-*nehn*-tay) *adj* insolent, impertinent

impertinenza (eem-payr-tee-*nehn*-tsah) *f* impertinence

impetuoso (eem-pay-*twōa*-soa) *adj* violent

impianto (eem-*pyahn*-toa) *m* plant

impiegare (eem-pyay-*gaa*-ray) *v* employ; *spend

impiegato (eem-pyay-*gaa*-toa) *m* clerk, employee

impiego (eem-*pyai*-goa) *m* job, post; employment; **domanda d'impiego** application

implicare (eem-plee-*kaa*-ray) *v* imply

imponente (eem-poa-*nehn*-tay) *adj* imposing, grand

impopolare (eem-poa-poa-*laa*-ray) *adj* unpopular

*imporre (eem-*poar*-ray) *v* impose; order; *imporsi assert oneself

importante (eem-poar-*tahn*-tay) *adj* important, capital; big

importanza (eem-poar-*tahn*-tsah) *f* importance; *avere ~ matter

importare (eem-poar-*taa*-ray) *v* import

importatore (eem-poar-tah-*tōa*-ray) *m* importer

importazione (eem-poar-tah-*tsyōa*-nay) *f* import

importunare (eem-poar-too-*naa*-ray) *v* disturb, bother

impossibile (eem-poass-*see*-bee-lay) *adj* impossible

imposta[1] (eem-*po*-stah) *f* shutter

imposta[2] (eem-*poa*-stah) *f* taxation; ~ **sul reddito** income-tax

impostare (eem-poa-*staa*-ray) *v* mail, post

impostazione (eem-poa-stah-*tsyōa*-nay) *f* approach

impotente (eem-poa-*tehn*-tay) *adj* powerless; impotent

impotenza (eem-poa-*tehn*-tsah) *f* impotence

impraticabile (eem-prah-tee-*kaa*-bee-lay) *adj* impassable

imprenditore (eem-prayn-dee-*tōa*-ray) *m* contractor

impresa (eem-*prāy*-sah) *f* enterprise, concern, undertaking

impressionante (eem-prayss-syoa-*nahn*-tay) *adj* impressive; striking

impressionare (eem-prayss-syoa-*naa*-ray) *v* impress

impressione (eem-prayss-*syōa*-nay) *f* impression

imprigionamento (eem-pree-joa-nah-*mayn*-toa) *m* imprisonment

imprigionare (eem-pree-joa-*naa*-ray) *v* imprison

improbabile (eem-proa-*baa*-bee-lay) *adj* improbable, unlikely

improprio (eem-*praw*-pryoa) *adj* improper

improvvisamente (eem-proav-vee-zah-*mayn*-tay) *adv* suddenly

improvvisare (eem-proav-vee-*zaa*-ray) *v* improvise

improvviso (eem-proav-*vee*-zoa) *adj* sudden

impudente (eem-poo-*dehn*-tay) *adj* impudent

impugnare (eem-poo-*ñaa*-ray) *v* grip

impugnatura (eem-poo-ñah-*tōō*-rah) *f* handle

impulsivo (eem-pool-*see*-voa) *adj* impulsive

impulso (eem-*pool*-soa) *m* impulse; urge

in (een) *prep* in, into; at

inabilitato (ee-nah-bee-lee-*taa*-toa) *adj* disabled

inabitabile (ee-nah-bee-*taa*-bee-lay) *adj* uninhabitable

inaccessibile (ee-naht-chayss-*see*-bee-lay) *adj* inaccessible

inaccettabile (ee-naht-chayt-*taa*-bee-lay) *adj* unacceptable

inadatto (ee-nah-*daht*-toa) *adj* unsuitable

inadeguato (ee-nah-day-*gwaa*-toa) *adj* inadequate

inamidare (ee-nah-mee-*daa*-ray) *v* starch

inaspettato (ee-nah-spayt-*taa*-toa) *adj* unexpected

inatteso (ee-naht-*tāy*-soa) *adj* unexpected

inaugurare (ee-nou-goo-*raa*-ray) *v* open, inaugurate

incantare (eeng-kahn-*taa*-ray) *v* bewitch

incantevole (eeng-kahn-*tāy*-voa-lay) *adj* enchanting

incanto (eeng-*kahn*-toa) *m* spell, charm

incapace (eeng-kah-*paa*-chay) *adj* incapable, unable

incaricare (eeng-kah-ree-*kaa*-ray) *v* charge; **incaricarsi di** *take charge of; **incaricato di** in charge of

incarico (eeng-*kaa*-ree-koa) *m* assignment

incassare (eeng-kahss-*saa*-ray) *v* cash

incauto (eeng-*kou*-toa) *adj* unwise

incendio (een-*chehn*-dyoa) *m* fire

incenso (een-*chehn*-soa) *m* incense

incerto (een-*chehr*-toa) *adj* uncertain, doubtful

inchiesta (eeng-*kyeh*-stah) *f* enquiry, inquiry

inchinare (eeng-kee-*naa*-ray) *v* bow

inchiostro (eeng-*kyo*-stroa) *m* ink

inciampare (een-chahm-*paa*-ray) *v* stumble

incidentale (een-chee-dayn-*taa*-lay) *adj* incidental, casual

incidente (een-chee-*dehn*-tay) *m* accident; incident; ~ **aereo** plane crash

*incidere** (een-*chee*-day-ray) *v* engrave

incinta (een-*cheen*-tah) *adj* pregnant

incisione (een-chee-*zyoa*-nay) *f* cut; engraving

incisore (een-chee-*zōā*-ray) *m* engraver

incitare (een-chee-*taa*-ray) *v* incite

inclinare (eeng-klee-*naa*-ray) *v* slant; **inclinato** slanting, sloping

inclinazione (eeng-klee-nah-*tsyōā*-nay) *f* gradient; inclination, tendency

*includere** (eeng-*klōō*-day-ray) *v* count, include

incollare (eeng-koal-*laa*-ray) *v* paste, *stick

incolto (eeng-*koal*-toa) *adj* desert, waste, uncultivated; uneducated

incolume (eeng-*kaw*-loo-may) *adj* unhurt

incombustibile (eeng-koam-boo-*stee*-bee-lay) *adj* fireproof

incompetente (eeng-koam-pay-*tehn*-tay) *adj* incompetent; unqualified

incompleto (eeng-koam-*plai*-toa) *adj*

incomplete

inconcepibile (eeng-koan-chay-*pee*-bee-lay) *adj* inconceivable

incondizionato (eeng-koan-dee-tsyoa-*naa*-toa) *adj* unconditional

inconscio (eeng-*kon*-shoa) *adj* unconscious

inconsueto (eeng-koan-*swai*-toa) *adj* unusual

incontrare (eeng-koan-*traa*-ray) *v* *meet, run into, *come across, encounter

incontro (eeng-*koan*-troa) *m* meeting, encounter

inconveniente (eeng-koan-vay-*ñehn*-tay) *adj* inconvenient; *m* inconvenience

incoraggiare (eeng-koa-rahd-*jaa*-ray) *v* encourage

incoronare (eeng-koa-roa-*naa*-ray) *v* crown

incosciente (eeng-koash-*shehn*-tay) *adj* unaware

incredibile (eeng-kray-*dee*-bee-lay) *adj* incredible

incremento (eeng-kray-*mayn*-toa) *m* increase

increscioso (eeng-kraysh-*shōa*-soa) *adj* unpleasant

increspare (eeng-kray-*spaa*-ray) *v* crease

incrinarsi (eeng-kree-*nahr*-see) *v* crack

incrocio (eeng-*krōa*-choa) *m* junction

incurabile (eengkoo-*raa*-bee-lay) *adj* incurable

indaffarato (een-dahf-fah-*raa*-toa) *adj* busy

indagare (een-dah-*gaa*-ray) *v* enquire; inquire

indagine (een-*daa*-jee-nay) *f* inquiry; examination

indecente (een-day-*chehn*-tay) *adj* indecent

indefinito (een-day-fee-*nee*-toa) *adj* indefinite

indemoniato (een-day-moa-*ñaa*-toa) *adj* possessed

indennità (een-dayn-nee-*tah*) *f* indemnity, compensation

indesiderabile (een-day-see-day-*raa*-bee-lay) *adj* undesirable

India (*een*-dyah) *f* India

indiano (een-*dyaa*-noa) *adj* Indian; *m* Indian

indicare (een-dee-*kaa*-ray) *v* point out; indicate, declare

indicazione (een-dee-kah-*tsyōa*-nay) *f* indication; direction

indice (*een*-dee-chay) *m* index finger; index; table of contents

indietro (een-*dyai*-troa) *adv* behind; back; **all'indietro** backwards

indifeso (een-dee-*fāy*-soa) *adj* unprotected

indifferente (een-deef-fay-*rehn*-tay) *adj* indifferent

indigeno (een-*dee*-jay-noa) *m* native

indigestione (een-dee-jay-*styōa*-nay) *f* indigestion

indignazione (een-dee-ñah-*tsyōa*-nay) *f* indignation

indipendente (een-dee-payn-*dehn*-tay) *adj* independent, self-employed

indipendenza (een-dee-payn-*dehn*-tsah) *f* independence

indiretto (een-dee-*reht*-toa) *adj* indirect

indirizzare (een-dee-reet-*tsaa*-ray) *v* address

indirizzo (een-dee-*reet*-tsoa) *m* address

indispensabile (een-dee-spayn-*saa*-bee-lay) *adj* essential

indisposto (een-dee-*spoa*-stoa) *adj* unwell

individuale (een-dee-vee-*dwaa*-lay) *adj* individual

individuo (een-dee-*vee*-dwoa) *m* individual

indiziato (een-dee-*tsyaa*-toa) *m* suspect

indizio (een-*dee*-tsyoa) *m* indication

indole (*een*-doa-lay) *f* nature

indolenzito (een-doa-layn-*jee*-toa) *adj* sore

indolore (een-doa-*lōa*-ray) *adj* painless

Indonesia (een-doa-*nai*-zyah) *f* Indonesia

indonesiano (een-doa-nay-*zyaa*-noa) *adj* Indonesian; *m* Indonesian

indossare (een-doass-*saa*-ray) *v* *put on; *wear

indossatrice (een-doass-sah-*tree*-chay) *f* model, mannequin

indovinare (een-doa-vee-*naa*-ray) *v* guess

indovinello (een-doa-vee-*nehl*-loa) *m* riddle

indubbiamente (een-doob-byah-*mayn*-tay) *adv* undoubtedly

indugio (een-*dōō*-joa) *m* delay

***indurre a** (een-*door*-ray) cause to

industria (een-*doo*-stryah) *f* industry; ~ **mineraria** mining

industriale (een-doo-*stryaa*-lay) *adj* industrial

inefficace (een-ayf-fee-*kaa*-chay) *adj* inefficient

ineguale (ee-nay-*gwaa*-lay) *adj* uneven, unequal

inesatto (ee-nay-*zaht*-toa) *adj* incorrect, inaccurate

inesperto (ee-nay-*spehr*-toa) *adj* inexperienced

inesplicabile (ee-nay-splee-*kaa*-bee-lay) *adj* unaccountable

inestimabile (ee-nay-stee-*maa*-bee-lay) *adj* priceless

inevitabile (ee-nay-vee-*taa*-bee-lay) *adj* inevitable, unavoidable

infastidire (een-fah-stee-*dee*-ray) *v* annoy; bother

infatti (een-*faht*-tee) *conj* as a matter of fact, in fact

infedele (een-fay-*dai*-lay) *adj* unfaithful

infelice (een-fay-*lee*-chay) *adj* unhappy

inferiore (een-fay-*ryōa*-ray) *adj* inferior, bottom

infermeria (een-fayr-may-*ree*-ah) *f* infirmary

infermiera (een-fayr-*myai*-rah) *f* nurse

inferno (een-*fehr*-noa) *m* hell

inferriata (een-fayr-*ryaa*-tah) *f* railing

infettare (een-fayt-*taa*-ray) *v* infect

infezione (een-fay-*tsyōa*-nay) *f* infection

infiammabile (een-fyahm-*maa*-bee-lay) *adj* inflammable

infiammarsi (een-fyahm-*mahr*-see) *v* *become septic

infiammazione (een-fyahm-mah-*tsyōa*-nay) *f* inflammation

infierire (een-fyay-*ree*-ray) *v* rage

infilare (een-fee-*laa*-ray) *v* thread

infine (een-*fee*-nay) *adv* at last

infinito (een-fee-*nee*-toa) *adj* infinite, endless; *m* infinitive

inflazione (een-flah-*tsyōa*-nay) *f* inflation

influente (een-*flwehn*-tay) *adj* influential

influenza (een-*flwehn*-tsah) *f* influence; influenza, flu

influenzare (een-floo-ayn-*tsaa*-ray) *v* affect

influire (een-*flwee*-ray) *v* influence

informale (een-foar-*maa*-lay) *adj* informal, casual

informare (een-foar-*maa*-ray) *v* inform; **informarsi** enquire, inquire

informazione (een-foar-mah-*tsyōa*-nay) *f* information, enquiry

infornare (een-foar-*naa*-ray) *v* bake

infrangibile (een-frahn-*jee*-bee-lay) *adj* unbreakable

infrarosso (een-frah-*roass*-soa) *adj* infra-red

infreddolito (een-frayd-doa-*lee*-toa) *adj* shivery

infrequente (een-fray-*kwehn*-tay) *adj* infrequent

infruttuoso (een-froot-*twōā*-soa) *adj* unsuccessful

ingannare (eeng-gahn-*naa*-ray) *v* deceive, cheat

inganno (eeng-*gahn*-noa) *m* deceit; illusion

ingegnere (een-jay-*ñai*-ray) *m* engineer

ingente (een-*jehn*-tay) *adj* enormous

ingenuo (een-*jai*-nwoa) *adj* simple, naïve

Inghilterra (eeng-geel-*tehr*-rah) *f* England

inghiottire (eeng-gyoat-*tee*-ray) *v* swallow

inginocchiarsi (een-jee-noak-*kyahr*-see) *v* *kneel

ingiuriare (een-joo-*ryaa*-ray) *v* call names

ingiustizia (een-joo-*stee*-tsyah) *f* injustice

ingiusto (een-*joo*-stoa) *adj* unjust, unfair

inglese (eeng-*glāy*-say) *adj* English; British; *m* Englishman; Briton

ingoiare (een-goa-*yaa*-ray) *v* swallow

ingorgo (eeng-*goar*-goa) *m* traffic jam; bottleneck

ingrandimento (eeng-grahn-dee-*mayn*-toa) *m* enlargement

ingrandire (eeng-grahn-*dee*-ray) *v* enlarge

ingrato (eeng-*graa*-toa) *adj* ungrateful

ingrediente (eeng-gray-*dyehn*-tay) *m* ingredient

ingresso (eeng-*grehss*-soa) *m* entry; entrance; appearance, admission; entrance-fee

ingrosso (eeng-*gross*-soa) *m* wholesale

inguine (*eeng*-gwee-nay) *m* groin

iniettare (ee-*ñayt*-*taa*-ray) *v* inject

iniezione (ee-ñay-*tsyōā*-nay) *f* injection, shot

ininterrotto (ee-neen-tayr-*roat*-toa) *adj* continuous

iniziale (ee-nee-*tsyaa*-lay) *adj* initial; *f* initial; *apporre le iniziali initial

iniziare (ee-nee-*tsyaa*-ray) *v* *begin, commence

iniziativa (ee-nee-tsyah-*tee*-vah) *f* initiative

inizio (ee-*nee*-tsyoa) *m* beginning, start

innalzare (een-nahl-*tsaa*-ray) *v* erect

innamorato (een-nah-moa-*raa*-toa) *adj* in love

innanzi (een-*nahn*-tsee) *adv* forwards; before; ~ **a** before

innato (een-*naa*-toa) *adj* natural

inno (*een*-noa) *m* hymn; ~ **nazionale** national anthem

innocente (een-noa-*chehn*-tay) *adj* innocent

innocenza (een-noa-*chehn*-tsah) *f* innocence

innocuo (een-*naw*-kwoa) *adj* harmless

inoculare (ee-noa-koo-*laa*-ray) *v* inoculate

inoculazione (ee-noa-koo-lah-*tsyōā*-nay) *f* inoculation

inoltrare (ee-noal-*traa*-ray) *v* forward

inoltre (ee-*noal*-tray) *adv* moreover, besides, furthermore; likewise

inondazione (ee-noan-dah-*tsyōā*-nay) *f* flood

inopportuno (ee-noap-poar-*tōō*-noa) *adj* misplaced

inquieto (eeng-kwee-*ai*-toa) *adj* restless, uneasy

inquietudine (eeng-kwee-ay-*tōō*-dee-nay) *f* unrest

inquilino (eeng-kwee-*lee*-noa) *m* tenant; lodger

inquinamento (eeng-kwee-nah-*mayn*-toa) *m* pollution

inquisitivo (eeng-kwee-zee-*tee*-voa) *adj* inquisitive

insalata (een-sah-*laa*-tah) *f* salad

insano (een-*saa*-noa) *adj* insane

insegnamento (een-say-ñah-*mayn*-toa) *m* tuition; teachings *pl*

insegnante (een-say-*ñahn*-tay) *m* teacher; master, schoolteacher, schoolmaster

insegnare (een-say-*ña*-ray) *v* *teach

inseguire (een-say-*gwee*-ray) *v* chase

insenatura (een-say-nah-*tōō*-rah) *f* creek, inlet

insensato (een-sayn-*saa*-toa) *adj* senseless; meaningless

insensibile (een-sayn-*see*-bee-lay) *adj* insensitive

inserire (een-say-*ree*-ray) *v* insert

insetticida (een-sayt-tee-*chee*-dah) *m* insecticide

insettifugo (een-sayt-tee-*fōō*-goa) *m* insect repellent

insetto (een-*seht*-toa) *m* insect; bug *nAm*

insieme (een-*syai*-may) *adv* together; jointly

insignificante (een-see-ñee-fee-*kahn*-tay) *adj* unimportant, insignificant; petty; inconspicuous

insipido (een-*see*-pee-doa) *adj* tasteless

insistere (een-*see*-stay-ray) *v* insist

insoddisfacente (een-soad-dee-sfah-*chehn*-tay) *adj* unsatisfactory

insolente (een-soa-*lehn*-tay) *adj* insolent, impertinent

insolenza (een-soa-*lehn*-tsah) *f* insolence

insolito (een-*saw*-lee-toa) *adj* uncommon, unusual

insomma (een-*soam*-mah) *adv* in short

insonne (een-*son*-nay) *adj* sleepless

insonnia (een-*son*-ñah) *f* insomnia

insonorizzato (een-soa-noa-reed-*jaa*-toa) *adj* soundproof

insopportabile (een-soap-poar-*taa*-bee-lay) *adj* unbearable

instabile (een-*staa*-bee-lay) *adj* unstable

installare (een-stahl-*laa*-ray) *v* install

installazione (een-stahl-lah-*tsyōā*-nay) *f* installation

insuccesso (een-soot-*chehss*-soa) *m* failure

insufficiente (een-soof-fee-*chehn*-tay) *adj* insufficient

insultante (een-sool-*tahn*-tay) *adj* offensive

insultare (een-sool-*taa*-ray) *v* insult

insulto (een-*sool*-toa) *m* insult

insuperato (een-soo-pay-*raa*-toa) *adj* unsurpassed

insurrezione (een-soor-ray-*tsyōā*-nay) *f* rising

intagliare (een-tah-*lʸaa*-ray) *v* carve

intanto (een-*tahn*-toa) *adv* in the meantime

intatto (een-*taht*-toa) *adj* unbroken, whole, intact

intelletto (een-tayl-*leht*-toa) *m* intellect

intellettuale (een-tayl-layt-*twaa*-lay) *adj* intellectual

intelligente (een-tayl-lee-*jehn*-tay) *adj* intelligent; clever, smart, bright

intelligenza (een-tayl-lee-*jehn*-tsah) *f* intelligence; brain

*intendere (een-*tehn*-day-ray) *v* *mean; intend

intenditore (een-tayn-dee-*tōā*-ray) *m* connoisseur

intensità (een-tayn-see-*tah*) *f* intensity

intenso (een-*tehn*-soa) *adj* intense, violent

intento (een-*tehn*-toa) *m* aim

intenzionale (een-tayn-tsyoa-*naa*-lay)

adj intentional

intenzione (een-tayn-*tsyōā*-nay) *f* intention, purpose

interamente (een-tay-rah-*mayn*-tay) *adv* completely, entirely, altogether, quite

interessamento (een-tay-rayss-sah-*mayn*-toa) *m* interest

interessante (een-tay-rayss-*sahn*-tay) *adj* interesting

interessare (een-tay-rayss-*saa*-ray) *v* interest; **interessato** concerned

interesse (een-tay-*rehss*-say) *m* interest

interferenza (een-tayr-fay-*rehn*-tsah) *f* interference

interferire (een-tayr-fay-*ree*-ray) *v* interfere

interim (*een*-tay-reem) *m* interim

interiora (een-tay-*ryōā*-rah) *fpl* insides

interiore (een-tay-*ryōā*-ray) *m* interior

intermediario (een-tayr-may-*dyaa*-ryoa) *m* intermediary; ***fare da ~** mediate

intermezzo (een-tayr-*mehd*-dzoa) *m* interlude

internazionale (een-tayr-nah-tsyoa-*naa*-lay) *adj* international

interno (een-*tehr*-noa) *adj* inner, internal, inside; resident; domestic; *m* inside; **all'interno** within; **verso l'interno** inwards

intero (een-*tāy*-roa) *adj* entire, whole

interpretare (een-tayr-pray-*taa*-ray) *v* interpret

interprete (een-*tehr*-pray-tay) *m* interpreter

interrogare (een-tayr-roa-*gaa*-ray) *v* interrogate

interrogativo (een-tayr-roa-gah-*tee*-voa) *adj* interrogative

interrogatorio (een-tayr-roa-gah-*taw*-ryoa) *m* interrogation

interrogazione (een-tayr-roa-gah-*tsyōā*-

nay) *f* examination

***interrompere** (een-tayr-*roam*-pay-ray) *v* interrupt; ***interrompersi** pause

interruttore (een-tayr-root-*tōā*-ray) *m* switch

interruzione (een-tayr-roo-*tsyōā*-nay) *f* interruption

intersezione (een-tay-say-*tsyōā*-nay) *f* intersection

interurbana (een-tay-roor-*baa*-nah) *f* trunk-call

intervallo (een-tayr-*vahl*-loa) *m* interval; intermission, break; half-time

***intervenire** (een-tayr-vay-*nee*-ray) *v* intervene

intervista (een-tayr-*vee*-stah) *f* interview

intestino (een-tay-*stee*-noa) *m* gut, intestine; bowels *pl*

intimità (een-tee-mee-*tah*) *f* privacy

intimo (*een*-tee-moa) *adj* intimate; cosy

intirizzito (een-tee-reed-*dzee*-toa) *adj* numb

intollerabile (een-toal-lay-*raa*-bee-lay) *adj* intolerable

intonarsi con (een-toa-*nahr*-see) match

intorno (een-*toar*-noa) *adv* around; **~ a** around, round, about

intorpidito (een-toar-pee-*dee*-toa) *adj* numb

intossicazione alimentare (een-toass-see-kah-*tsyōā*-nay ah-lee-mayn-*taa*-ray) food poisoning

***intraprendere** (een-trah-*prehn*-day-ray) *v* *undertake

***intrattenere** (een-traht-tay-*nāy*-ray) *v* entertain

***intravvedere** (een-trahv-vay-*dāy*-ray) *v* glimpse

intricato (een-tree-*kaa*-toa) *adj* complex

intrigo (een-*tree*-goa) *m* intrigue

***introdurre** (een-troa-*door*-ray) *v* introduce

introduzione (een-troa-doo-*tsyoā*-nay) f introduction

intromettersi in (een-troa-*mayt*-tayr-see) interfere with

intuire (een-*twee*-ray) v *understand

inumidire (ee-noo-mee-*dee*-ray) v moisten, damp

inutile (ee-*noō*-tee-lay) adj useless; vain

inutilmente (ee-noo-teel-*mayn*-tay) adv in vain

*****invadere** (een-*vaa*-day-ray) v invade

invalido (een-*vaa*-lee-doa) adj disabled, invalid; m invalid

invano (een-*vaa*-noa) adv in vain

invasione (een-vah-*zyoā*-nay) f invasion

invece di (een-*vāy*-chay dee) instead of

inveire (een-vay-*ee*-ray) v scold

inventare (een-vayn-*taa*-ray) v invent

inventario (een-vayn-*taa*-ryoa) m inventory

inventivo (een-vayn-*tee*-voa) adj inventive

inventore (een-vayn-*tōā*-ray) m inventor

invenzione (een-vayn-*tsyoā*-nay) f invention

inverno (een-*vehr*-noa) m winter

inverso (een-*vehr*-soa) adj reverse

invertire (een-vayr-*tee*-ray) v invert

investigare (een-vay-stee-*gaa*-ray) v investigate

investigatore (een-vay-stee-gah-*tōā*-ray) m detective

investigazione (een-vay-stee-gah-*tsyoā*-nay) f enquiry, investigation

investimento (een-vay-stee-*mayn*-toa) m investment

investire (een-vay-*stee*-ray) v invest

inviare (een-*vyaa*-ray) v dispatch

inviato (een-*vyaa*-toa) m envoy

invidia (een-*vee*-dyah) f envy

invidiare (een-vee-*dyaa*-ray) v grudge, envy

invidioso (een-vee-*dyoā*-soa) adj envious

invio (een-*vee*-oa) m expedition

invisibile (een-vee-*zee*-bee-lay) adj invisible

invitare (een-vee-*taa*-ray) v ask, invite

invito (een-*vee*-toa) m invitation

invocare (een-voa-*kaa*-ray) v invoke

involontario (een-voa-loan-*taa*-ryoa) adj unintentional

inzuppare (een-tsoop-*paa*-ray) v soak

io (*ee*-oa) pron I; ~ **stesso** myself

iodio (*yaw*-dyoa) m iodine

ipocrisia (ee-poa-kree-*see*-ah) f hypocrisy

ipocrita (ee-*paw*-kree-tah) m hypocrite; adj hypocritical

ipoteca (ee-poa-*tai*-kah) f mortgage

ipotesi (ee-*paw*-tay-zee) f supposition

ippodromo (eep-*paw*-droa-moa) m race-course

ippoglosso (eep-poa-*gloss*-soa) m halibut

ira (*ee*-rah) f anger

iracheno (ee-rah-*kāy*-noa) adj Iraqi; m Iraqi

Iran (*ee*-rahn) m Iran

iraniano (ee-rah-*nyaa*-noa) adj Iranian; m Iranian

Iraq (*ee*-rahk) m Iraq

irascibile (ee-rahsh-*shee*-bee-lay) adj irascible, hot-tempered, quick-tempered

irato (ee-*raa*-toa) adj angry

Irlanda (eer-*lahn*-dah) f Ireland

irlandese (eer-lahn-*dāy*-say) adj Irish; m Irishman

ironia (ee-roa-*nee*-ah) f irony

ironico (ee-*raw*-nee-koa) adj ironical

irragionevole (eer-rah-joa-*nāy*-voa-lay) adj unreasonable

irreale (eer-ray-*aa*-lay) adj unreal

irregolare (eer-ray-goa-*laa*-ray) *adj* irregular; uneven

irreparabile (eer-ray-pah-*raa*-bee-lay) *adj* irreparable

irrequieto (eer-ray-kwee-*ai*-toa) *adj* restless

irrestringibile (eer-ray-streen-*jee*-bee-lay) *adj* shrinkproof

irrevocabile (eer-ray-voa-*kaa*-bee-lay) *adj* irrevocable

irrilevante (eer-ree-lay-*vahn*-tay) *adj* insignificant

irrisorio (eer-ree-*zaw*-ryoa) *adj* ludicrous

irritabile (eer-ree-*taa*-bee-lay) *adj* irritable

irritare (eer-ree-*taa*-ray) *v* irritate

irruzione (eer-roo-*tsyōa*-nay) *f* invasion, raid

*__iscrivere__ (ee-*skree*-vay-ray) *v* enter; **per iscritto** in writing, written

iscrizione (ee-skree-*tsyōa*-nay) *f* inscription

Islanda (ee-*zlahn*-dah) *f* Iceland

islandese (ee-zlahn-*dāy*-say) *adj* Icelandic; *m* Icelander

isola (*ee*-zoa-lah) *f* island

isolamento (ee-zoa-lah-*mayn*-toa) *m* isolation; insulation

isolare (ee-zoa-*laa*-ray) *v* isolate; insulate

isolato (ee-zoa-*laa*-toa) *adj* isolated; *m* house block *Am*

isolatore (ee-zoa-lah-*tōa*-ray) *m* insulator

Isole Filippine (*ee*-zoa-lay fee-leep-*pee*-nay) Philippines *pl*

ispessire (ee-spayss-*see*-ray) *v* thicken

ispettore (ee-spayt-*tōa*-ray) *m* inspector; supervisor

ispezionare (ee-spay-tsyoa-*naa*-ray) *v* inspect

ispezione (ee-spay-*tsyōa*-nay) *f* inspection

ispirare (ee-spee-*raa*-ray) *v* inspire

Israele (ee-zrah-*ai*-lay) *m* Israel

israeliano (ee-zrah-ay-*lYaa*-noa) *adj* Israeli; *m* Israeli

issare (eess-*saa*-ray) *v* hoist

istantanea (ee-stahn-*taa*-nay-ah) *f* snapshot

istante (ee-*stahn*-tay) *m* instant, second; while; **all'istante** instantly

istanza (ee-*stahn*-tsah) *f* petition, application

isterico (ee-*stai*-ree-koa) *adj* hysterical

istigare (ee-stee-*gah*-ray) *v* investigate; stir up

istinto (ee-*steen*-toa) *m* instinct

istituire (ee-stee-*twee*-ray) *v* institute; found

istituto (ee-stee-*tōō*-toa) *m* institute; institution

istituzione (ee-stee-too-*tsyōa*-nay) *f* institution, institute

istmo (*eest*-moa) *m* isthmus

istruire (ee-*strwee*-ray) *v* instruct; educate

istruttivo (ee-stroot-*tee*-voa) *adj* instructive

istruttore (ee-stroot-*tōa*-ray) *m* instructor

istruzione (ee-stroo-*tsyōa*-nay) *f* instruction; background; **istruzioni per l'uso** directions for use

Italia (ee-*taa*-lYah) *f* Italy

italiano (ee-tah-*lYaa*-noa) *adj* Italian; *m* Italian

itinerario (ee-tee-nay-*raa*-ryoa) *m* itinerary

itterizia (eet-tay-*ree*-tsyah) *f* jaundice

K

kaki (*kaa*-kee) *m* khaki

Kenia (*kai*-nyah) *m* Kenya

L

la (lah) *pron* her

là (lah) *adv* there; **al di ~** beyond; **al di ~ di** past; **di ~** there

labbro (*lahb*-broa) *m* (pl le labbra) lip; **pomata per le labbra** lipsalve

labirinto (lah-bee-*reen*-toa) *m* labyrinth, maze

laboratorio (lah-boa-rah-*taw*-ryoa) *m* laboratory; **~ linguistico** language laboratory

laborioso (lah-boa-*ryōa*-soa) *adj* industrious

lacca (*lahk*-kah) *f* lacquer; varnish; **~ per capelli** hair-spray

laccio (*laht*-choa) *m* lace

lacrima (*laa*-kree-mah) *f* tear

ladro (*laa*-droa) *m* robber, thief

laggiù (lahd-*joo*) *adv* over there

lagnanza (lah-*ñahn*-tsah) *f* complaint

lagnarsi (lah-*ñahr*-see) *v* complain

lago (*laa*-goa) *m* lake

laguna (lah-*gōō*-nah) *f* lagoon

lama (*laa*-mah) *f* blade; **~ di rasoio** razor-blade

lamentevole (lah-mayn-*tāy*-voa-lay) *adj* lamentable

lamiera (lah-*myai*-rah) *f* plate

lamina (*laa*-mee-nah) *f* sheet

lampada (*lahm*-pah-dah) *f* lamp; **~ da tavolo** reading-lamp; **~ flash** flash-bulb; **~ portatile** flash-light

lampadina (lahm-pah-*dee*-nah) *f* light bulb; **~ tascabile** torch

lampante (lahm-*pahn*-tay) *adj* self-evident

lampione (lahm-*pyōa*-nay) *m* lamp-post

lampo (*lahm*-poa) *m* lightning

lampone (lahm-*pōa*-nay) *m* raspberry

lana (*laa*-nah) *f* wool; **di ~** woollen; **~ da rammendo** darning wool; **~ pettinata** worsted

lancia (*lahn*-chah) *f* spear

lanciare (lahn-*chaa*-ray) *v* *throw, *cast; launch

lancio (*lahn*-choa) *m* cast

landa (*lahn*-dah) *f* moor, heath

lanterna (lahn-*tehr*-nah) *f* lantern; **~ vento** hurricane lamp

lanugine (lah-*nōō*-jee-nay) *f* down

lapide (*laa*-pee-day) *f* gravestone

lardo (*lahr*-doa) *m* bacon

larghezza (lahr-*gayt*-tsah) *f* width, breadth

largo (*lahr*-goa) *adj* wide, broad; ***farsi ~** push

laringite (lah-reen-*jee*-tay) *f* laryngitis

lasca (*lah*-skah) *f* roach

lasciare (lahsh-*shaa*-ray) *v* desert, *leave; *leave behind; allow to, *let

lassativo (lahss-sah-*tee*-voa) *m* laxative

lassù (lahss-*soo*) *adv* up there

lastricare (lah-stree-*kaa*-ray) *v* pave

lateralmente (lah-tay-rahl-*mayn*-tay) *adv* sideways

laterizio (lah-tay-*ree*-tsyoa) *m* brick

latino americano (lah-*tee*-noa ah-may-ree-*kaa*-noa) Latin-American

latitudine (lah-tee-*tōō*-dee-nāy) *f* latitude

lato (*laa*-toa) *m* way, side

latrare (lah-*traa*-ray) *v* bay

latta (*laht*-tah) *f* tin, can

lattaio (laht-*taa*-yoa) *m* milkman

latte (*laht*-tay) *m* milk

latteo (*laht*-tay-oa) *adj* milky

latteria (laht-tay-*ree*-ah) *f* dairy

lattuga (laht-*tōō*-gah) *f* lettuce

lavabile (lah-*vaa*-bee-lay) *adj* washable

lavaggio (lah-*vahd*-joa) *m* washing; **inalterabile al ~** fast-dyed

lavagna (lah-*vaa*-ñah) *f* blackboard

lavanderia (lah-vahn-day-*ree*-ah) f laundry; ~ **automatica** launderette
lavandino (lah-vahn-*dee*-noa) m wash-stand; wash-basin
lavare (lah-*vaa*-ray) v wash; ~ **i piatti** wash up
lavatrice (lah-vah-*tree*-chay) f washing-machine
lavello (lah-*vehl*-loa) m sink
lavorare (lah-voa-*raa*-ray) v work; ~ **all'uncinetto** crochet; ~ **a maglia** *knit; ~ **sodo** labour; ~ **troppo** overwork
lavoratore (lah-voa-rah-*tōa*-ray) m worker
lavoro (lah-*vōa*-roa) m work; labour; job; **datore di** ~ employer; **lavori domestici** housework; ~ **fatto a mano** handwork; ~ **manuale** handicraft
Le (lay) *pron* you
le (lay) *pron* her
leale (lay-*aa*-lay) *adj* true, loyal
lebbra (*layb*-brah) f leprosy
leccare (layk-*kaa*-ray) v lick
leccornia (layk-*koar*-ñah) f delicatessen
lega (*lāy*-gah) f union, league
legale (lay-*gaa*-lay) *adj* lawful, legal; **procuratore** ~ solicitor
legalizzazione (lay-gah-leed-dzah-*tsyōa*-nay) f legalization
legame (lay-*gaa*-may) m link
legare (lay-*gaa*-ray) v *bind, tie; ~ **insieme** bundle
legato (lay-*gaa*-toa) m legacy
legatura (lay-gah-*tōō*-rah) f binding
legazione (lay-gah-*tsyōa*-nay) f legation
legge (*lehd*-jay) f law
leggenda (layd-*jehn*-dah) f legend; caption
***leggere** (*lehd*-jay-ray) v *read
leggero (layd-*jai*-roa) *adj* light; slight; gentle
leggibile (layd-*jee*-bee-lay) *adj* legible
leggio (layd-*jee*-oa) m desk
legittimo (lay-*jeet*-tee-moa) *adj* legitimate, legal
legname (lay-*ñaa*-may) m timber
legno (*lāy*-ñoa) m wood; **di** ~ wooden
Lei (*lai*-ee) *pron* you; ~ **stesso** yourself
lente (*lehn*-tay) f lens; ~ **d'ingrandimento** magnifying glass; **lenti a contatto** contact lenses
lento (*lehn*-toa) *adj* slack, slow
lenza (*lehn*-tsah) f fishing line
lenzuolo (layn-*tswaw*-loa) m sheet
leone (lay-*ōa*-nay) m lion
lepre (*lai*-pray) f hare
lesione (lay-*zyōa*-nay) f injury
letale (lay-*taa*-lay) *adj* mortal
letamaio (lay-tah-*maa*-yoa) m dunghill
letame (lay-*taa*-may) m dung
lettera (*leht*-tay-rah) f letter; **carta da lettere** notepaper; ~ **di credito** letter of credit; ~ **di raccomandazione** letter of recommendation
letterario (layt-tay-*raa*-ryoa) *adj* literary
letteratura (layt-tay-rah-*tōō*-rah) f literature
letto (*leht*-toa) m bed; **letti gemelli** twin beds; **lettino da campeggio** camp-bed; **cot** *nAm*
lettura (layt-*tōō*-rah) f reading
leva (*lāy*-vah) f lever; ~ **del cambio** gear lever
levare (lay-*vaa*-ray) v *take away
levata (lay-*vaa*-tah) f collection
levatrice (lay-vah-*tree*-chay) f midwife
levigato (lay-vee-*gaa*-toa) *adj* smooth
levriere (lay-*vryai*-ray) m greyhound
lezione (lay-*tsyōa*-nay) f lesson, lecture
li (lee) *pron* (f le) them
lì (lee) *adv* there

libanese (lee-bah-*náy*-say) *adj* Lebanese; *m* Lebanese

Libano (*lee*-bah-noa) *m* Lebanon

libbra (*leeb*-brah) *f* pound

liberale (lee-bay-*raa*-lay) *adj* liberal

liberare (lee-bay-*raa*-ray) *v* deliver

liberazione (lee-bay-rah-*tsyóā*-nay) *f* liberation; delivery

Liberia (lee-*bai*-ryah) *f* Liberia

liberiano (lee-bay-*ryaa*-noa) *adj* Liberian; *m* Liberian

libero (*lee*-bay-roa) *adj* free

libertà (lee-bayr-*tah*) *f* freedom, liberty

libraio (lee-*braa*-yoa) *m* bookseller

libreria (lee-bray-*ree*-ah) *f* bookstore

libro (*lee*-broa) *m* book; ~ **dei reclami** complaints book; ~ **di cucina** cookery-book; cookbook *nAm*; ~ **in brossura** paperback

licenza (lee-*chehn*-tsah) *f* permission, licence

licenziare (lee-chayn-*tsyaa*-ray) *v* fire

lieto (*lYai*-toa) *adj* pleased, glad

lieve (*lYai*-vay) *adj* light

lievito (*lYai*-vee-toa) *m* yeast

lilla (*leel*-lah) *adj* mauve

lima (*lee*-mah) *f* file; **limetta per le unghie** nail-file

limitare (lee-mee-*taa*-ray) *v* limit

limite (*lee*-mee-tay) *m* boundary, bound; limit; ~ **di velocità** speed limit

limonata (lee-moa-*naa*-tah) *f* lemonade

limone (lee-*móā*-nay) *m* lemon

limpido (*leem*-pee-doa) *adj* limpid

lindo (*leen*-doa) *adj* neat

linea (*lee*-nayah) *f* line; ~ **aerea** airline; ~ **di navigazione** shipping line; ~ **principale** main line

lineetta (lee-nay-*ayt*-tah) *f* dash; hyphen

lingua (*leeng*-gwah) *f* tongue; language; ~ **materna** mother tongue, native language

linguaggio (leeng-*gwahd*-joa) *m* speech

lino (*lee*-noa) *m* linen

liquido (*lee*-kwee-doa) *adj* liquid

liquirizia (lee-kwee-*ree*-tsyah) *f* liquorice

liquore (lee-*kwaw*-ray) *m* liqueur; **spaccio di liquori** off-licence

lisca (*lee*-skah) *f* fishbone

liscio (*leesh*-shoa) *adj* smooth

liso (*lee*-zoa) *adj* threadbare

lista (*lee*-stah) *f* strip; list; ~ **dei vini** wine-list; ~ **di attesa** waiting-list; **listino prezzi** price list

lite (*lee*-tay) *f* row, dispute, quarrel

litigare (lee-tee-*gaa*-ray) *v* quarrel

litigio (lee-*tee*-joa) *m* quarrel

litorale (lee-toa-*raa*-lay) *m* sea-coast

litro (*lee*-troa) *m* litre

livella (lee-*vehl*-lah) *f* level

livellare (lee-vayl-*laa*-ray) *v* level

livello (lee-*vehl*-loa) *m* level; ~ **di vita** standard of living

livido (*lee*-vee-doa) *m* bruise

lo (loa) *pron* him

locale (loa-*kaa*-lay) *adj* local

località (loa-kah-lee-*tah*) *f* spot, locality

localizzare (loa-kah-leed-*dzaa*-ray) *v* locate

locanda (loa-*kahn*-dah) *f* inn, roadhouse; roadside restaurant

locazione (loa-kah-*tsyóā*-nay) *f* lease; *dare in ~ lease

locomotiva (loa-koa-moa-*tee*-vah) *f* locomotive

locomotrice (loa-koa-moa-*tree*-chay) *f* engine

lodare (loa-*daa*-ray) *v* praise

lode (*law*-day) *f* glory

loggione (load-*jóā*-nay) *m* gallery

logica (*law*-jee-kah) *f* logic

logico (*law*-jee-koa) *adj* logical

logorare (loa-goa-*raa*-ray) *v* wear out

lombaggine (loam-*bahd*-jee-nay) *f* lumbago

longitudine (loan-jee-*tōō*-dee-nay) *f* longitude

lontano (loan-*taa*-noa) *adj* far-off, far, distant

loquace (loa-*kwaa*-chay) *adj* talkative

lordo (*loar*-doa) *adj* gross

loro (*lōā*-roa) *adj* their; *pron* them

lotta (*lot*-tah) *f* combat, fight, battle; contest, struggle, strife

lottare (loat-*taa*-ray) *v* *fight, struggle

lotteria (loat-tay-*ree*-ah) *f* lottery

lozione (loa-*tsyōā*-nay) *f* lotion; ~ **dopo barba** aftershave lotion

lubrificante (loo-bree-fee-*kahn*-tay) *m* lubrication oil

lubrificare (loo-bree-fee-*kaa*-ray) *v* grease, lubricate

lubrificazione (loo-bree-fee-kah-*tsyōā*-nay) *f* lubrication

lucchetto (look-*kayt*-toa) *m* padlock

luccio (*loot*-choa) *m* pike

luce (*lōō*-chay) *f* light; ~ **del giorno** daylight; ~ **del sole** sunshine, sunlight; ~ **di posizione** parking light; ~ **laterale** sidelight; ~ **posteriore** tail-light; **luci di arresto** brake lights

lucentezza (loo-chayn-*tayt*-tsah) *f* gloss

lucidare (loo-chee-*daa*-ray) *v* polish

lucido (*lōō*-chee-doa) *adj* bright; glossy

luglio (*lōō*-lʸoa) July

lui (looæħ) *pron* him; he

lumaca (loo-*maa*-kah) *f* snail

lume (*lōō*-may) *m* light; lamp

luminoso (loo-mee-*nōā*-soa) *adj* luminous

luna (*lōō*-nah) *f* moon; ~ **di miele** honeymoon

lunedì (loo-nay-*dee*) *m* Monday

lunghezza (loong-*gayt*-tsah) *f* length; ~ **d'onda** wave-length

lungo (*loong*-goa) *adj* long; tall; *prep* along, past; **di gran lunga** by far; **per il** ~ lengthways

lungofiume (loong-goa-*fyōō*-may) *m* riverside

luogo (*lwaw*-goa) *m* spot; *aver ~ *take place; **in nessun** ~ nowhere; ~ **di nascita** place of birth; ~ **di riunione** meeting-place; ~ **di villeggiatura** holiday resort

lupo (*lōō*-poa) *m* wolf

luppolo (*loop*-poa-loa) *m* hop

lusso (*looss*-soa) *m* luxury

lussuoso (looss-*swōā*-soa) *adj* luxurious

lutto (*loot*-toa) *m* mourning

M

ma (mah) *conj* but; yet

macchia (*mahk*-kyah) *f* stain, spot, blot

macchiare (mahk-*kyaa*-ray) *v* stain

macchina (*mahk*-kee-nah) *f* engine, machine; car; ~ **da cucire** sewing-machine; ~ **da scrivere** typewriter; ~ **fotografica** camera; ~ **sportiva** sports-car

macchinario (mahk-kee-*naa*-ryoa) *m* machinery

macchiolina (mahk-kyoa-*lee*-nah) *f* speck

macellaio (mah-chayl-*laa*-yoa) *m* butcher

macinare (mah-chee-*naa*-ray) *v* *grind

macinino (mah-chee-*nee*-noa) *m* mill

madre (*maa*-dray) *f* mother

madreperla (mah-dray-*pehr*-lah) *f* mother-of-pearl

maestro (mah-*eh*-stroa) *m* master;

schoolmaster, teacher
magari (mah-*gaa*-ree) *adv* even; *conj* even if
magazzinaggio (mah-gahd-dzee-*nahd*-joa) *m* storage
magazzino (mah-gahd-*dzee*-noa) *m* depository, warehouse, store-house; **grande** ~ department store; ***tenere in** ~ stock
maggio (*mahd*-joa) May
maggioranza (mahd-joa-*rahn*-tsah) *f* majority
maggiore (mahd-*jōā*-ray) *adj* major, main, superior; elder; eldest; *m* major
maggiorenne (mahd-joa-*rehn*-nay) *adj* of age
magia (mah-*jee*-ah) *f* magic
magico (*maa*-jee-koa) *adj* magic
magistrato (mah-jee-*straa*-toa) *m* magistrate
maglia (*maa*-l*ah) *f* link; mesh; vest
maglieria (mah-l*ay-*ree*-ah) *f* hosiery
maglietta (mah-l*ayt-tah) *f* undershirt
maglio (*maa*-l*oa) *m* mallet
maglione (mah-l*ōā-nay) *m* jersey, pullover, sweater
magnete (mah-*ñai*-tay) *m* magneto
magnetico (mah-*ñai*-tee-koa) *adj* magnetic
magnetofono (mah-ñay-*taw*-foa-noa) *m* recorder, tape-recorder
magnifico (mah-*ñee*-fee-koa) *adj* gorgeous, splendid, magnificent, swell
magro (*maa*-groa) *adj* thin, lean
mai (migh) *adv* ever; **non...** ~ never
maiale (mah-*yaa*-lay) *m* pig
maiuscola (mah-*yoo*-skoa-lah) *f* capital letter
malacca (mah-*lahk*-kah) *f* rattan
malagevole (mah-lah-*jāy*-voa-lay) *adj* rough
malaria (mah-*laa*-ryah) *f* malaria
malato (mah-*laa*-toa) *adj* ill

malattia (mah-laht-*tee*-ah) *f* disease, ailment, illness; ~ **venerea** venereal disease
male (*maa*-lay) *m* mischief, evil, harm; sickness; **mal d'aria** air-sickness; **mal di denti** toothache; **mal di gola** sore throat; **mal di mare** seasickness; **mal di pancia** stomach-ache; **mal di schiena** backache; **mal di stomaco** stomach-ache; **mal di testa** headache; **mal d'orecchi** earache
*maledire (mah-lay-*dee*-ray) *v* curse
malese (mah-*lāy*-say) *adj* Malaysian; *m* Malay
Malesia (mah-*lai*-zyah) *f* Malaysia
malessere (mah-*lehss*-say-ray) *m* hangover
malevolo (mah-*lāy*-voa-loa) *adj* spiteful, malicious
malfermo (mahl-*fayr*-moa) *adj* unsteady
malfido (mahl-*fee*-doa) *adj* untrustworthy
malgrado (mahl-*graa*-doa) *prep* in spite of, despite
maligno (mah-*lee*-ña) *adj* malignant
malinconia (mah-leeng-koa-*nee*-ah) *f* melancholy
malinconico (mah-leeng-*kaw*-nee-koa) *adj* sad
malinteso (mah-leen-*tāy*-soa) *m* misunderstanding
malizia (mah-*lee*-tsyah) *f* mischief
malizioso (mah-lee-*tsyōā*-soa) *adj* mischievous
malsano (mahl-*saa*-noa) *adj* unsound, unhealthy
malsicuro (mahl-see-*kōō*-roa) *adj* unsafe
malvagio (mahl-*vaa*-joa) *adj* evil, ill
mamma (*mahm*-mah) *f* mum
mammifero (mahm-*mee*-fay-roa) *m* mammal

mammut (mahm-*moot*) *m* mammoth

mancante (mahng-*kahn*-tay) *adj* missing

mancanza (mahng-*kahn*-tsah) *f* want, lack, shortage; fault

mancare (mahng-*kaa*-ray) *v* lack; fail

mancia (*mahn*-chah) *f* gratuity, tip

manciata (mahn-*chaa*-tah) *f* handful

mancino (mahn-*chee*-noa) *adj* left-handed

mandare (mahn-*daa*-ray) *v* *send

mandarino (mahn-dah-*ree*-noa) *m* mandarin, tangerine

mandato (mahn-*daa*-toa) *m* mandate

mandorla (*mahn*-doar-lah) *f* almond

maneggevole (mah-nayd-*jāy*-voa-lay) *adj* handy

maneggiabile (mah-nayd-*jaa*-bee-lay) *adj* manageable

maneggiare (mah-nayd-*jaa*-ray) *v* handle

manette (mah-*nayt*-tay) *fpl* handcuffs *pl*

mangiare (mahn-*jaa*-ray) *v* *eat; *m* food

mangiatoia (mahn-jah-*tōā*-yah) *f* manger

mania (mah-*nee*-ah) *f* craze

manica (*maa*-nee-kah) *f* sleeve; **La Manica** English Channel

manico (*maa*-nee-koa) *m* handle

manicure (mah-nee-*kōō*-ray) *f* manicure

maniera (mah-*ñāy*-rah) *f* way, manner; **maniere** manners *pl*

manifestare (mah-nee-fay-*staa*-ray) *v* express

manifestazione (mah-nee-fay-stah-*tsyōā*-nay) *f* expression

mano (*maa*-noa) *f* hand; **fatto a ~** hand-made

manopola (mah-*naw*-poa-lah) *f* knob

manoscritto (mah-noa-*skreet*-toa) *m* manuscript

mansueto (mahn-*swai*-toa) *adj* tame

mantella (mahn-*tehl*-lah) *f* cape

mantello (mahn-*tehl*-loa) *m* cloak

*mantenere (mahn-tay-*nāy*-ray) *v* maintain; *keep

mantenimento (mahn-tay-nee-*mayn*-toa) *m* upkeep

manuale (mah-*nwaa*-lay) *adj* manual; *m* handbook, textbook; **~ di conversazione** phrase-book

manutenzione (mah-noo-tayn-*tsyōā*-nay) *f* maintenance

manzo (*mahn*-dzoa) *m* beef

mappa (*mahp*-pah) *f* map

marca (*mahr*-kah) *f* brand

marcare (mahr-*kaa*-ray) *v* mark; score

marchio (*mahr*-kyoa) *m* brand; **~ di fabbrica** trademark

marcia (*mahr*-chah) *f* march; ***far ~ indietro** reverse; **~ indietro** reverse

marciapiede (mahr-chah-*pyai*-day) *m* pavement; sidewalk *nAm*

marciare (mahr-*chaa*-ray) *v* march

marcio (*mahr*-choa) *adj* rotten

mare (*maa*-ray) *m* sea; **riva del ~** seaside

marea (mah-*rai*-ah) *f* tide; **alta ~** high tide; **bassa ~** low tide

margarina (mahr-gah-*ree*-nah) *f* margarine

margine (*mahr*-jee-nay) *m* edge; margin; **~ della strada** wayside, roadside

marina (mah-*ree*-nah) *f* navy; seascape

marinaio (mah-ree-*naa*-yoa) *m* sailor, seaman

marito (mah-*ree*-toa) *m* husband

marittimo (mah-*reet*-tee-moa) *adj* maritime

marmellata (mahr-mayl-*laa*-tah) *f* marmalade, jam

marmo (*mahr*-moa) *m* marble

marocchino (mah-roak-*kee*-noa) *adj*

Moroccan; *m* Moroccan

Marocco (mah-*rok*-koa) *m* Morocco

martedì (mahr-tay-*dee*) *m* Tuesday

martello (mahr-*tehl*-loa) *m* hammer

martire (*mahr*-tee-ray) *m* martyr

marzo (*mahr*-tsoa) March

mascalzone (mah-skahl-*tsoā*-nay) *m* bastard

mascella (mahsh-*shehl*-lah) *f* jaw

maschera (*mah*-skay-rah) *f* mask; usherette; ~ **di bellezza** face-pack

maschile (mah-*skee*-lay) *adj* masculine

maschio (*mah*-skyoa) male

massa (*mahss*-sah) *f* lot, bulk; mass, crowd

massaggiare (mahss-sahd-*jaa*-ray) *v* massage

massaggiatore (mahss-sahd-jah-*tōā*-ray) *m* masseur

massaggio (mahss-*sahd*-joa) *m* massage; ~ **facciale** face massage

massiccio (mahss-*seet*-choa) *adj* solid, massive

massimo (*mahss*-see-moa) *adj* greatest; **al** ~ at most

masso (*mahss*-soa) *m* boulder

masticare (mah-stee-*kaa*-ray) *v* chew

matematica (mah-tay-*maa*-tee-kah) *f* mathematics

matematico (mah-tay-*maa*-tee-koa) *adj* mathematical

materasso (mah-tay-*rahss*-soa) *m* mattress

materia (mah-*tai*-ryah) *f* matter; ~ **prima** raw material

materiale (mah-tay-*ryaa*-lay) *adj* material, substantial; *m* material

matita (mah-*tee*-tah) *f* pencil; ~ **per gli occhi** eye-pencil

matrice (mah-*tree*-chay) *f* stub

matrigna (mah-*tree*-ñah) *f* stepmother

matrimoniale (mah-tree-moa-*ñaa*-lay) *adj* matrimonial

matrimonio (mah-tree-*maw*-ñoa) *m* marriage; matrimony; wedding

mattina (maht-*tee*-nah) *f* morning

mattino (maht-*tee*-noa) *m* morning

matto (*maht*-toa) *adj* mad

mattone (maht-*tōā*-nay) *m* brick

mattonella (maht-toa-*nehl*-lah) *f* tile

mattutino (maht-too-*tee*-noa) *adj* early

maturità (mah-too-ree-*tah*) *f* maturity

maturo (mah-*tōō*-roa) *adj* ripe, mature

mausoleo (mou-zoa-*lai*-oa) *m* mausoleum

mazza (*maht*-tsah) *f* club; ~ **da golf** golf-club

mazzo (*maht*-tsoa) *m* bunch, bouquet

me (may) *pron* me

meccanico (mayk-*kaa*-nee-koa) *adj* mechanical; *m* mechanic

meccanismo (mayk-kah-*nee*-zmoa) *m* mechanism, machinery

medaglia (may-*daa*-lᵛah) *f* medal

medesimo (may-*dāy*-zee-moa) *adj* same

media (*mai*-dyah) *f* average, mean; **in** ~ on the average

mediante (may-*dyahn*-tay) *prep* by means of

mediatore (may-dyah-*tōā*-ray) *m* mediator; broker

medicamento (may-dee-kah-*mayn*-toa) *m* medicine

medicina (may-dee-*chee*-nah) *f* medicine

medico (*mai*-dee-koa) *adj* medical; *m* physician, doctor; ~ **generico** general practitioner

medicone (may-dee-*kōā*-nay) *m* quack

medievale (may-dyay-*vaa*-lay) *adj* mediaeval

medio (*mai*-dyoa) *adj* medium; average

mediocre (may-*dyaw*-kray) *adj* moderate, medium

medioevo (may-dyoa-*ai*-voa) *m* Middle Ages

meditare (may-dee-*taa*-ray) *v* meditate

Mediterraneo (may-dee-tayr-*raa*-nay-oa) *m* Mediterranean

medusa (may-*dōō*-zah) *f* jelly-fish

meglio (*mai*-lYoa) *adv* better; best

mela (*māy*-lah) *f* apple

melanzana (may-lahn-*tsaa*-nah) *f* eggplant

melma (*mayl*-mah) *f* muck

melodia (may-loa-*dee*-ah) *f* tune, melody

melodioso (may-loa-*dyōā*-soa) *adj* tuneful

melodramma (may-loa-*drahm*-mah) *m* melodrama

melone (may-*lōā*-nay) *m* melon

membrana (maym-*braa*-nah) *f* diaphragm

membro[1] (*mehm*-broa) *m* (pl le membra) limb

membro[2] (*mehm*-broa) *m* (pl i membri) member; **qualità di ~** membership

memorabile (may-moa-*raa*-bee-lay) *adj* memorable

memoria (may-*maw*-ryah) *f* memory; **a ~** by heart

ménage (may-*naazh*) *m* household

mendicante (mayn-dee-*kahn*-tay) *m* beggar

mendicare (mayn-dee-*kaa*-ray) *v* beg

meno (*māy*-noa) *adv* less; minus; **a ~ che** unless; ***fare a ~ di** spare

mensa (*mayn*-sah) *f* canteen

mensile (mayn-*see*-lay) *adj* monthly

menta (*mayn*-tah) *f* mint; **~ peperina** peppermint

mentale (mayn-*taa*-lay) *adj* mental

mente (*mayn*-tay) *f* mind

mentire (mayn-*tee*-ray) *v* lie

mento (*mayn*-toa) *m* chin

mentre (*mayn*-tray) *conj* whilst, while

menu (may-*noo*) *m* menu

menzionare (mayn-tsyoa-*naa*-ray) *v* mention

menzione (mayn-*tsyōā*-nay) *f* mention

menzogna (mayn-*tsōā*-ñah) *f* lie

meraviglia (may-rah-*vee*-lYah) *f* surprise; marvel

meravigliarsi (may-rah-vee-*lYahr*-see) *v* marvel

meraviglioso (may-rah-vee-*lYōā*-soa) *adj* marvellous, fine, wonderful

mercante (mayr-*kahn*-tay) *m* trader, merchant; **~ di vini** wine-merchant

mercanteggiare (mayr-kahn-tayd-*jaa*-ray) *v* bargain

mercanzia (mayr-kahn-*tsee*-ah) *f* merchandise

mercato (mayr-*kaa*-toa) *m* market; **a buon ~** cheap; **~ nero** black market

merce (*mehr*-chay) *f* merchandise; **merci** goods *pl*, wares *pl*

merceria (mayr-chay-*ree*-ah) *f* haberdashery

mercoledì (mayr-koa-lay-*dee*) *m* Wednesday

mercurio (mayr-*kōō*-ryoa) *m* mercury

merenda (may-*rehn*-dah) *f* tea

meridionale (may-ree-dyoa-*naa*-lay) *adj* southern, southerly

meritare (may-ree-*taa*-ray) *v* deserve, merit

merito (*mai*-ree-toa) *m* merit

merlano (mayr-*laa*-noa) *m* whiting

merletto (mayr-*layt*-toa) *m* lace

merlo (*mehr*-loa) *m* blackbird

merluzzo (mayr-*loot*-tsoa) *m* cod; haddock

meschino (may-*skee*-noa) *adj* mean; narrow-minded

mescolare (may-skoa-*laa*-ray) *v* mix; stir; shuffle

mese (*māy*-say) *m* month

messa (*mayss*-sah) *f* Mass

messaggero (mayss-sahd-*jai*-roa) *m*

messenger

messaggio (mayss-*sahd*-joa) *m* message

messicano (mayss-see-*kaa*-noa) *adj* Mexican; *m* Mexican

Messico (*mehss*-see-koa) *m* Mexico

mestiere (may-*styai*-ray) *m* trade; business

mesto (*meh*-stoa) *adj* sad

mestruazione (may-strwah-*tsyoā*-nay) *f* menstruation

metà (may-*tah*) *f* half; **a ~** half

metallico (may-*tahl*-lee-koa) *adj* metal

metallo (may-*tahl*-loa) *m* metal

meticoloso (may-tee-koa-*loā*-soa) *adj* precise

metodico (may-*taw*-dee-koa) *adj* methodical

metodo (*mai*-toa-doa) *m* method

metrico (*mai*-tree-koa) *adj* metric

metro (*mai*-troa) *m* metre; meter; **~ a nastro** tape-measure

metropolitana (may-troa-poa-lee-*taa*-nah) *f* underground; subway *nAm*

*mettere (*mayt*-tay-ray) *v* *set, *put; *lay; **~ in imbarazzo** embarrass

mezzanino (mayd-dzah-*nee*-noa) *m* mezzanine

mezzanotte (mayd-dzah-*not*-tay) *f* midnight

mezzo (*mehd*-dzoa) *adj* half; middle; *m* midst, middle; means; **in ~ a** amid; among

mezzogiorno (mayd-dzoa-*joar*-noa) *m* midday, noon

mi (mee) *pron* me; myself

miccia (*meet*-chah) *f* fuse

micia (*mee*-chah) *f* pussy-cat

microfono (mee-*kraw*-foa-noa) *m* microphone

micromotore (mee-kroa-moa-*toā*-ray) *m* moped

microsolco (mee-kroa-*soal*-koa) *m* long-playing record

midollo (mee-*doal*-loa) *m* marrow

miele (*myai*-lay) *m* honey

miglio (*mee*-lᵞoa) *m* (pl le miglia) mile; **distanza in miglia** mileage

miglioramento (mee-lᵞoa-rah-*mayn*-toa) *m* improvement

migliorare (mee-lᵞoa-*raa*-ray) *v* improve

migliore (mee-lᵞoā-ray) *adj* better; superior

mignolo (*mee*-ñoa-loa) *m* little finger

milionario (mee-lᵞoa-naa-ryoa) *m* millionaire

milione (mee-lᵞoā-nay) *m* million

militare (mee-lee-*taa*-ray) *adj* military; *m* soldier

mille (*meel*-lay) *num* thousand

minaccia (mee-*naht*-chah) *f* threat

minacciare (mee-naht-*chaa*-ray) *v* threaten

minaccioso (mee-naht-*choā*-soa) *adj* threatening

minatore (mee-nah-*toā*-ray) *m* miner

minerale (mee-nay-*raa*-lay) *m* mineral; ore

minestra (mee-*neh*-strah) *f* soup

miniatura (mee-ñah-*too*-rah) *f* miniature

miniera (mee-*ñai*-rah) *f* mine, pit; **~ d'oro** goldmine

minimo (*mee*-nee-moa) *adj* least; *m* minimum

ministero (mee-nee-*stai*-roa) *m* ministry

ministro (mee-*nee*-stroa) *m* minister; **primo ~** Prime Minister, premier

minoranza (mee-noa-*rahn*-tsah) *f* minority

minore (mee-*noā*-ray) *adj* minor; junior

minorenne (mee-noa-*rehn*-nay) *adj* under age; *m* minor

minuscolo (mee-*noo*-skoa-loa) *adj* tiny

minuto (mee-*noō*-toa) *adj* minute; *m*

minute

minuzioso (mee-noo-*tsyōa*-soa) *adj* thorough

mio (*mee*-oa) *adj* (f mia; pl miei, mie) my

miope (*mee*-oa-pay) *adj* short-sighted

miracolo (mee-*raa*-koa-loa) *m* miracle, wonder

miracoloso (mee-rah-koa-*lōa*-soa) *adj* miraculous

mirare a (mee-*raa*-ray) aim at

mirino (mee-*ree*-noa) *m* view-finder

miscuglio (mee-*skōo*-lᵞoa) *m* mixture

miserabile (mee-zay-*raa*-bee-lay) *adj* miserable

miseria (mee-*zai*-ryah) *f* misery

misericordia (mee-zay-ree-*kor*-dyah) *f* mercy

misericordioso (mee-zay-ree-koar-*dyōa*-soa) *adj* merciful

misero (*mee*-zay-roa) *adj* miserable; poor

missione (meess-*syōa*-nay) *f* mission

misterioso (mee-stay-*ryōa*-soa) *adj* mysterious

mistero (mee-*stai*-roa) *m* mystery

misto (*mee*-stoa) *adj* mixed, miscellaneous

misura (mee-*zōo*-rah) *f* measure; size; **fatto su ~** made to order, tailor-made

misurare (mee-zoo-*raa*-ray) measure

misuratore (mee-zoo-rah-*tōa*-ray) *m* gauge

mite (*mee*-tay) *adj* mild

mitigare (mee-tee-*gaa*-ray) relieve

mito (*mee*-toa) *m* myth

mobile (*maw*-bee-lay) *adj* mobile; movable

mobilia (moa-*bee*-lᵞah) *f* furniture

moda (*maw*-dah) *f* fashion; **alla ~** fashionable; **fuori ~** out of date

modellare (moa-dayl-*laa*-ray) model

modello (moa-*dehl*-loa) *m* model

moderato (moa-day-*raa*-toa) *adj* moderate

moderno (moa-*dehr*-noa) *adj* modern

modestia (moa-*deh*-styah) *f* modesty

modesto (moa-*deh*-stoa) *adj* modest

modifica (moa-*dee*-fee-kah) *f* alteration

modificare (moa-dee-fee-*kaa*-ray) modify, change, alter

modista (moa-*dee*-stah) *f* milliner

modo (*maw*-doa) *m* way, fashion, manner; **ad ogni ~** at any rate; **in nessun ~** by no means; **in ogni ~** anyhow; **nello stesso ~** likewise

moglie (*mōa*-lᵞay) *f* wife

molare (moa-*laa*-ray) *m* molar

molesto (moa-*leh*-stoa) *adj* troublesome

molla (*mol*-lah) *f* spring

molleggio (moal-*layd*-joa) *m* suspension

molo (*maw*-loa) *m* pier, jetty; wharf, quay

moltiplicare (moal-tee-plee-*kaa*-ray) multiply

moltiplicazione (moal-tee-plee-kah-*tsyōa*-nay) *f* multiplication

molto (*moal*-toa) *adj* much; *adv* very, quite; far, much; **molti** *adj* many

momentaneo (moa-mayn-*taa*-nay-oa) *adj* momentary

momento (moa-*mayn*-toa) *m* moment; **a momenti** presently

monaca (*maw*-nah-kah) *f* nun

monaco (*maw*-nah-koa) *m* monk

monarca (moa-*nahr*-kah) *m* monarch, ruler

monarchia (moa-nahr-*kee*-ah) *f* monarchy

monastero (moa-nah-*stai*-roa) *m* cloister, monastery

mondiale (moan-*dyaa*-lay) *adj* world-wide

mondo (*moan*-doa) *m* world

monello (moa-*nehl*-loa) *m* rascal

moneta (moa-*nāy*-tah) *f* coin; ~ **spicciola** petty cash

monetario (moa-nay-*taa*-ryoa) *adj* monetary

monologo (moa-*naw*-loa-goa) *m* monologue

monopattino (moa-noa-*paht*-tee-noa) *m* scooter

monopolio (moa-noa-*paw*-lyoa) *m* monopoly

monotono (moa-*naw*-toa-noa) *adj* monotonous, dull

montagna (moan-*taa*-ñah) *f* mountain

montagnoso (moan-tah-*ñōā*-soa) *adj* mountainous

montare (moan-*taa*-ray) *v* mount; *get on; assemble

montatura (moan-tah-*tōō*-rah) *f* frame

monte (*moan*-tay) *m* mount

montone (moan-*tōā*-nay) *m* mutton

monumento (moa-noo-*mayn*-toa) *m* monument; ~ **commemorativo** memorial

mora (*maw*-rah) *f* mulberry; blackberry

morale (moa-*raa*-lay) *adj* moral; *f* moral; *m* spirits

moralità (moa-rah-lee-*tah*) *f* morality

morbido (*mor*-bee-doa) *adj* soft, smooth

morbillo (moar-*beel*-loa) *m* measles

***mordere** (*mor*-day-ray) *v* *bite

morfina (moar-*fee*-nah) *f* morphine, morphia

***morire** (moa-*ree*-ray) *v* die

mormorare (moar-moa-*raa*-ray) *v* whisper

morsa (*mor*-sah) *f* clamp

morsetto (moar-*sayt*-toa) *m* clamp

morso (*mor*-soa) *m* bite

mortale (moar-*taa*-lay) *adj* fatal; mortal

morte (*mor*-tay) *f* death

morto (*mor*-toa) *adj* dead

mosaico (moa-*zaa*-ee-koa) *m* mosaic

mosca (*moa*-skah) *f* fly

moschea (moa-*skai*-ah) *f* mosque

mossa (*moss*-sah) *f* move

mostra (*moa*-strah) *f* display; exhibition; ***mettere in** ~ display; ~ **d'arte** art exhibition

mostrare (moa-*straa*-ray) *v* display, *show; **mostrarsi** prove

motivo (moa-*tee*-voa) *m* cause, occasion; **a** ~ **di** owing to

moto (*maw*-toa) *m* motion

motocicletta (moa-toa-chee-*klayt*-tah) *f* motor-cycle

motonave (moa-toa-*naa*-vay) *f* launch

motore (moa-*tōā*-ray) *m* motor, engine

motorino (moa-toa-*ree*-noa) *m* motorbike *nAm*

motoscafo (moa-toa-*skaa*-foa) *m* motor-boat

motto (*mot*-toa) *m* motto, slogan

movente (moa-*vehn*-tay) *m* motive

movimento (moa-vee-*mayn*-toa) *m* movement

mozione (moa-*tsyōā*-nay) *f* motion

mucchio (*mook*-kyoa) *m* pile, heap

muffa (*moof*-fah) *f* mildew

muffole (*moof*-foa-lay) *fpl* mittens *pl*

mugghiare (moog-*gyaa*-ray) *v* roar

mugnaio (moo-*ñaa*-yoa) *m* miller

mulino a vento (moo-*lee*-noa ah *vayn*-toa) windmill

mulo (*mōō*-loa) *m* mule

multa (*mool*-tah) *f* fine

municipale (moo-nee-chee-*paa*-lay) *adj* municipal

municipalità (moo-nee-chee-pah-lee-*tah*) *f* municipality

municipio (moo-nee-*chee*-pyoa) *m* town hall

munifico (moo-*nee*-fee-koa) *adj* generous

***muovere** (*mwaw*-vay-ray) *v* move,

stir

murare (moo-*raa*-ray) v *lay bricks

muratore (moo-rah-*tōā*-ray) m brick-layer

muro (*mōō*-roa) m wall

muschio (*moo*-skyoa) m moss

muscolo (*moo*-skoa-loa) m muscle

muscoloso (moo-skoa-*lōā*-soa) adj muscular

museo (moo-*zai*-oa) m museum; ~ **delle cere** waxworks pl

musica (*mōō*-zee-kah) f music

musicale (moo-zee-*kaa*-lay) adj musical

musicista (moo-zee-*chee*-stah) m musician

muso (*mōō*-zoa) m snout

mussolina (mooss-soa-*lee*-nah) f muslin

mutamento (moo-tah-*mayn*-toa) m variation

mutande (moo-*tahn*-day) fpl drawers; panties pl, pants pl; shorts plAm

mutandine (moo-tahn-*dee*-nay) fpl panties pl, briefs pl; knickers pl; underpants plAm; ~ **da bagno** bathing-trunks, swimming-trunks

mutare (moo-*taa*-ray) v change

muto (*mōō*-toa) adj mute, dumb; speechless

mutuo (*mōō*-twoa) adj mutual

N

nafta (*nahf*-tah) f fuel oil

nailon (*nigh*-loan) m nylon

nano (*naa*-noa) m dwarf

narciso (nahr-*chee*-zoa) m daffodil

narcosi (nahr-*kaw*-zee) f narcosis

narcotico (nahr-*kaw*-tee-koa) m narcotic, drug

narice (nah-*ree*-chay) f nostril

nascere (*nahsh*-shay-ray) v *be born

nascita (*nahsh*-shee-tah) f birth

nascondere (nah-*skoan*-day-ray) v *hide; conceal

naso (*naa*-soa) m nose

nastro (*nah*-stroa) m ribbon; tape; ~ **adesivo** adhesive tape

Natale (nah-*taa*-lay) Xmas, Christmas

natica (*naa*-tee-kah) f buttock

nativo (nah-*tee*-voa) adj native

nato (*naa*-toa) adj born

natura (nah-*tōō*-rah) f nature

naturale (nah-too-*raa*-lay) adj natural

naturalmente (nah-too-rahl-*mayn*-tay) adv of course, naturally

nausea (*nou*-zay-ah) f nausea, sickness

nauseante (nou-zay-*ahn*-tay) adj disgusting

nauseato (nou-zay-*aa*-toa) adj sick

navale (nah-*vaa*-lay) adj naval; **cantiere** ~ shipyard

nave (*naa*-vay) f ship; vessel; ~ **da guerra** man-of-war; ~ **di linea** liner

navigabile (nah-vee-*gaa*-bee-lay) adj navigable

navigare (nah-vee-*gaa*-ray) v sail, navigate

navigazione (nah-vee-gah-*tsyōā*-nay) f navigation

nazionale (nah-tsyoa-*naa*-lay) adj national

nazionalità (nah-tsyoā-nah-lee-*tah*) f nationality

nazionalizzare (nah-tsyoa-nah-leed-*dzaa*-ray) v nationalize

nazione (nah-*tsyōā*-nay) f nation

ne (nay) pron of it; about him

né... né (nay) neither ... nor

neanche (nay-*ahng*-kay) adv not even; conj nor

nebbia (*nayb*-byah) f mist, fog

nebbioso (nayb-*byōā*-soa) adj misty, hazy, foggy

necessario (nay-chayss-*saa*-ryoa) *adj* necessary

necessità (nay-chayss-see-*tah*) *f* necessity; need

necroscopia (nay-kroa-skoa-*pee*-ah) *f* autopsy

negare (nay-*gaa*-ray) *v* deny

negativa (nay-gah-*tee*-vah) *f* negative

negativo (nay-gah-*tee*-voa) *adj* negative

negligente (nay-glee-*jehn*-tay) *adj* neglectful

negligenza (nay-glee-*jehn*-tsah) *f* neglect

negoziante (nay-goa-*tsyahn*-tay) *m* dealer; shopkeeper; ~ **di stoffe** draper

negoziare (nay-goa-*tsyaa*-ray) *v* negotiate

negozio (nay-*gaw*-tsyoa) *m* shop; ~ **di ferramenta** hardware store; ~ **di fiori** flower-shop; ~ **di giocattoli** toyshop

negro (*nãy*-groa) *m* Negro

nemico (nay-*mee*-koa) *m* enemy

nemmeno (naym-*mãy*-noa) *adv* not even; *conj* nor

neon (*nai*-oan) *m* neon

neonato (nay-oa-*naa*-toa) *m* infant

neppure (nayp-*pōō*-ray) *adv* not even; *conj* nor

nero (*nãy*-roa) *adj* black

nervo (*nehr*-voa) *m* nerve

nervoso (nayr-*võã*-soa) *adj* nervous

nessuno (nayss-*sōō*-noa) *adj* no; *pron* none, nobody, no one

nettare (nayt-*taa*-ray) *v* clean

netto (*nayt*-toa) *adj* net

neutrale (nay°°-*traa*-lay) *adj* neutral

neutro (*neh*°°-troa) *adj* neuter

neve (*nãy*-vay) *f* snow; ~ **fangosa** slush

nevicare (nay-vee-*kaa*-ray) *v* snow

nevoso (nay-*võã*-soa) *adj* snowy

nevralgia (nay-vrahl-*jee*-ah) *f* neuralgia

nevrosi (nay-*vraw*-zee) *f* neurosis

nichelio (nee-kai-lᵞoa) *m* nickel

nicotina (nee-koa-*tee*-nah) *f* nicotine

nido (*nee*-doa) *m* nest; nursery

niente (*ñehn*-tay) *pron* nothing; nil

Nigeria (nee-*jai*-ryah) *f* Nigeria

nigeriano (nee-jay-*ryaa*-noa) *adj* Nigerian; *m* Nigerian

nipote (nee-*põã*-tay) *m* grandson; nephew; *f* granddaughter; niece

nipotina (nee-poa-*tee*-nah) *f* granddaughter

nipotino (nee-poa-*tee*-noa) *m* grandson

no (no) no

nobile (*naw*-bee-lay) *adj* noble

nobiltà (noa-beel-*tah*) *f* nobility

nocca (*nok*-kah) *f* knuckle

nocciola (noat-*chaw*-lah) *f* hazelnut

nocciolo (*not*-choa-loa) *m* stone; essence, heart

noce (*nõã*-chay) *f* nut; walnut; ~ **di cocco** coconut; ~ **moscata** nutmeg

nocivo (noa-*chee*-voa) *adj* harmful, hurtful

nodo (*naw*-doa) *m* knot; lump; ~ **scorsoio** loop

noi (noi) *pron* we; ~ **stessi** ourselves

noia (*naw*-yah) *f* annoyance; bother

noioso (noa-*yõã*-soa) *adj* annoying, dull, boring

noleggiare (noa-layd-*jaa*-ray) *v* hire

a nolo (ah *naw*-loa) for hire

nome (*nõã*-may) *m* name; first name; denomination; noun; **a ~ di** in the name of, on behalf of; ~ **di battesimo** Christian name

nomignolo (noa-*mee*-ñoa-loa) *m* nickname

nomina (*naw*-mee-nah) *f* appointment, nomination

nominale (noa-mee-*naa*-lay) *adj* nominal

nominare (noa-mee-*naa*-ray) v mention, name; appoint, nominate

non (noan) not; ~... **mai** never; ~... **più** no longer

nonché (noang-*kay*) conj as well as

noncurante (noang-koo-*rahn*-tay) adj careless

nonna (*non*-nah) f grandmother

nonno (*non*-noa) m grandfather, granddad; **nonni** grandparents pl

nono (*naw*-noa) num ninth

nonostante (noa-noa-*stahn*-tay) prep in spite of

nord (nord) m north; **polo Nord** North Pole

nord-est (nor-*dehst*) m north-east

nordico (*nor*-dee-koa) adj northern

nord-ovest (nor-*daw*-vayst) m north-west

norma (*nor*-mah) f standard; **di** ~ as a rule

normale (noar-*maa*-lay) adj normal; standard, regular

norvegese (noar-vay-*jāȳ*-say) adj Norwegian; m Norwegian

Norvegia (noar-*vāȳ*-jah) f Norway

nostalgia (noa-stahl-*jee*-ah) f homesickness

nostro (*no*-stroa) adj our

nota (*naw*-tah) f memo

notaio (noa-*taa*-yoa) m notary

notare (noa-*taa*-ray) v note; notice

notevole (noa-*tāȳ*-voa-lay) adj considerable, remarkable, noticeable, striking

notificare (noa-tee-fee-*kaa*-ray) v notify

notizia (noa-*tee*-tsyah) f notice; **notizie** tidings pl, news

notiziario (noa-tee-*tsyaa*-ryoa) m news

noto (*naw*-toa) adj well-known

notte (*not*-tay) f night; **di** ~ by night; overnight

notturno (noat-*toor*-noa) adj nightly; **locale** ~ nightclub

novanta (noa-*vahn*-tah) num ninety

nove (*naw*-vay) num nine

novembre (noa-*vehm*-bray) November

novità (noa-vee-*tah*) f news

nozione (noa-*tsyōā*-nay) f notion; idea

nubifragio (noo-bee-*fraa*-joa) m cloudburst

nuca (*nōō*-kah) f nape of the neck

nucleare (noo-klay-*aa*-ray) adj nuclear

nucleo (*nōō*-klay-oa) m core, nucleus

nudo (*nōō*-doa) adj nude, bare, naked; m nude

nulla (*nool*-lah) m nothing

nullo (*nool*-loa) adj invalid, void

numerale (noo-may-*raa*-lay) m numeral

numero (*nōō*-may-roa) m number; digit; quantity; act; ~ **di targa** registration number; licence number Am

numeroso (noo-may-*rōā*-soa) adj numerous

*__nuocere__ (*nwaw*-chay-ray) v harm

nuotare (nwoa-*taa*-ray) v *swim

nuotatore (nwoa-tah-*tōā*-ray) m swimmer

nuoto (*nwaw*-toa) m swimming; ~ **a farfalla** butterfly stroke; ~ **a rana** breaststroke

nuovamente (nwaw-vah-*mayn*-tay) adv again

Nuova Zelanda (*nwaw*-vah tsay-*lahn*-dah) New Zealand

nuovo (*nwaw*-voa) adj new; **di** ~ again; ~ **fiammante** brand-new

nutriente (noo-*tryehn*-tay) adj nutritious, nourishing

nutrire (noo-*tree*-ray) v *feed

nuvola (*nōō*-voa-lah) f cloud

nuvoloso (noo-voa-*lōā*-soa) adj cloudy

O

o (oa) *conj* or; ~... **o** either ... or

oasi (*aw*-ah-zee) *f* oasis

obbligare (oab-blee-*gaa*-ray) *v* oblige

obbligatorio (oab-blee-gah-*taw*-ryoa) *adj* compulsory, obligatory

obbligazione (oab-blee-gah-*tsyoa*-nay) *f* bond

obbligo (*ob*-blee-goa) *m* obligation

obeso (oa-*bai*-zoa) *adj* corpulent, stout

obiettare (oa-byayt-*taa*-ray) *v* object

obiettivo (oa-byayt-*tee*-voa) *m* objective, object

obiezione (oa-byay-*tsyoa*-nay) *f* objection; *fare ~ **a mind**

obliquo (oa-*blee*-kwoa) *adj* slanting

oblungo (oa-*bloong*-goa) *adj* oblong

oca (*aw*-kah) *f* goose

occasionalmente (oak-kah-zyoa-nahl-*mayn*-tay) *adv* occasionally

occasione (oak-kah-*zyoa*-nay) *f* chance, occasion, opportunity; **d'occasione** second-hand

occhiali (oak-*kyaa*-lee) *mpl* spectacles, glasses; ~ **da sole** sun-glasses *pl*; ~ **di protezione** goggles *pl*

occhiata (oak-*kyaa*-tah) *f* glimpse, glance, look; *dare un'occhiata glance

occhio (*ok*-kyoa) *m* eye; ~ **di pernice** corn; *tenere d'occhio watch

occidentale (oat-chee-dayn-*taa*-lay) *adj* western; westerly

occidente (oat-chee-*dehn*-tay) *m* west

*occorrere (oak-*koar*-ray-ray) *v* need

occupante (oak-koo-*pahn*-tay) *m* occupant

occupare (oak-koo-*paa*-ray) *v* occupy, *take up; **occuparsi di** attend to, look after, see to, *take care of; **oc-**

cupato *adj* busy, engaged; occupied

occupazione (oak-koo-pah-*tsyoa*-nay) *f* occupation; employment

oceano (oa-*chai*-ah-noa) *m* ocean; **Oceano Pacifico** Pacific Ocean

oculista (oa-koo-*lee*-stah) *m* oculist

odiare (oa-*dyaa*-ray) *v* hate

odio (*aw*-dyoa) *m* hatred, hate

odorare (oa-doa-*raa*-ray) *v* *smell

odore (oa-*doa*-ray) *m* odour, smell

*offendere (oaf-*fehn*-day-ray) *v* injure, offend, wound, *hurt

offensiva (oaf-fayn-*see*-vah) *f* offensive

offensivo (oaf-fayn-*see*-voa) *adj* offensive

offerta (oaf-*fehr*-tah) *f* offer; supply

offesa (oaf-*fay*-sah) *f* offence

officina (oaf-fee-*chee*-nah) *f* workshop; ~ **del gas** gasworks

*offrire (oaf-*free*-ray) *v* offer

offuscato (oaf-foo-*skaa*-toa) *adj* dim

oggettivo (oad-jayt-*tee*-voa) *adj* objective

oggetto (oad-*jeht*-toa) *m* object; **oggetti smarriti** lost and found

oggi (*od*-jee) *adv* today

oggigiorno (oad-jee-*joar*-noa) *adv* nowadays

ogni (*oā*-ñee) *adj* every, each

ogniqualvolta (oa-ñee-kwahl-*vol*-tah) *conj* whenever

ognuno (oa-*ñōō*-noa) *pron* everyone, everybody

Olanda (oa-*lahn*-dah) *f* Holland

olandese (oa-lahn-*dāy*-say) *adj* Dutch; *m* Dutchman

oleoso (oa-lay-*oa*-soa) *adj* oily

olio (*aw*-lᶦyoa) *m* oil; ~ **abbronzante** suntan oil; ~ **da tavola** salad-oil; ~ **d'oliva** olive oil; ~ **per capelli** hairoil

oliva (oa-*lee*-vah) *f* olive

olmo (*oal*-moa) *m* elm

oltraggio (oal-*trahd*-joa) *m* outrage

oltre (*oal*-tray) *prep* beyond; over; ~ **a** besides

oltremarino (oal-tray-mah-*ree*-noa) *adj* overseas

oltrepassare (oal-tray-pahss-*saa*-ray) *v* *overtake; pass *vAm*

omaggio (oa-*mahd*-joa) *m* tribute, homage

ombelico (oam-bay-*lee*-koa) *m* navel

ombra (*oam*-brah) *f* shadow, shade

ombreggiato (oam-brayd-*jaa*-toa) *adj* shady

ombrellino (oam-brayl-*lee*-noa) *m* sunshade

ombrello (oam-*brehl*-loa) *m* umbrella

ombretto (oam-*brayt*-toa) *m* eye-shadow

*omettere (oa-*mayt*-tay-ray) *v* omit, *leave out; skip

omosessuale (oa-moa-sayss-*swaa*-lay) *adj* homosexual

onda (*oan*-dah) *f* wave

ondulare (oan-doo-*laa*-ray) *v* curl

ondulato (oan-doo-*laa*-toa) *adj* wavy, undulating

onestà (oa-nay-*stah*) *f* honesty

onesto (oa-*neh*-stoa) *adj* honest; fair, straight; honourable

onice (*aw*-nee-chay) *f* onyx

onnipotente (oan-nee-poa-*tehn*-tay) *adj* omnipotent

onorare (oa-noa-*raa*-ray) *v* honour

onorario (oa-noa-*raa*-ryoa) *m* fee

onore (oa-*nōā*-ray) *m* glory, honour

onorevole (oa-noa-*rāy*-voa-lay) *adj* honourable

opaco (oa-*paa*-koa) *adj* dim, mat

opale (oa-*paa*-lay) *m* opal

opera (*aw*-pay-rah) *f* opera

operaio (oa-pay-*raa*-yoa) *m* labourer, workman

operare (oa-pay-*rah*-ray) *v* operate

operazione (oa-pay-rah-*tsyōā*-nay) *f* surgery, operation

operetta (oa-pay-*rayt*-tah) *f* operetta

opinione (oa-pee-*ñōā*-nay) *f* view, opinion

*opporsi (oap-*poar*-see) *v* oppose; ~ **a** object to

opportunità (oap-poar-too-nee-*tah*) *f* chance, opportunity

opportuno (oap-poar-*tōō*-noa) *adj* opportune

opposizione (oap-poa-zee-*tsyōā*-nay) *f* opposition

opposto (oap-*poa*-stoa) *adj* opposite

*opprimere (oap-*pree*-may-ray) *v* oppress

oppure (oap-*pōō*-ray) *conj* or

opuscolo (oa-*poo*-skoa-loa) *m* brochure

ora (*ōā*-rah) *f* hour; *adv* now; **d'ora innanzi** henceforth; ~ **di arrivo** time of arrival; ~ **di partenza** time of departure; ~ **di punta** rush-hour, peak hour; **ore di visita** visiting hours; **ore d'ufficio** office hours, business hours; **quarto d'ora** quarter of an hour

orale (oa-*raa*-lay) *adj* oral

oramai (oa-rah-*mahæh*) *adv* by now; by then

orario (oa-*raa*-ryoa) *m* timetable, schedule; ~ **di apertura** business hours; ~ **di ricevimento** consultation hours; ~ **estivo** summer time

orchestra (oar-*keh*-strah) *f* orchestra

ordinare (oar-dee-*naa*-ray) *v* arrange; order

ordinario (oar-dee-*naa*-ryoa) *adj* ordinary; plain, common, simple

ordinato (oar-dee-*naa*-toa) *adj* tidy

ordinazione (oar-dee-nah-*tsyōā*-nay) *f* order; **modulo di** ~ order-form

ordine (*oar*-dee-nay) *m* order; method; command; **in** ~ in order; ***mettere in** ~ arrange

orecchino (oa-rayk-*kee*-noa) *m* earring

orecchio (oa-*rayk*-kyoa) *f* ear

orecchioni (oa-rayk-*kyoa*-nee) *mpl* mumps

orefice (oa-*ray*-fee-chay) *m* goldsmith

orfano (*or*-fah-noa) *m* orphan

organico (oar-*gaa*-nee-koa) *adj* organic

organismo (oar-gah-*nee*-zmoa) *m* organism

organizzare (oar-gah-need-*dzaa*-ray) *v* organize; arrange

organizzazione (oar-gah-need-dzah-*tsyoa*-nay) *f* organization

organo (*or*-gah-noa) *m* organ; **organetto di Barberia** street-organ

orgoglio (oar-*gaw*-lYoa) *m* pride

orgoglioso (oar-goa-*lYoa*-soa) *adj* proud

orientale (oa-ryayn-*taa*-lay) *adj* eastern; easterly; oriental

orientarsi (oa-ryayn-*tahr*-see) *v* orientate

oriente (oa-*ryehn*-tay) *m* east; Orient

originale (oa-ree-jee-*naa*-lay) *adj* original

originariamente (oa-ree-jee-nah-ryah-*mayn*-tay) *adv* originally

origine (oa-*ree*-jee-nay) *f* origin

origliare (oa-ree-*lYaa*-ray) *v* eavesdrop

orizzontale (oa-reed-dzoan-*taa*-lay) *adj* horizontal

orizzonte (oa-reed-*dzoan*-tay) *m* horizon

orlo (*oar*-loa) *m* rim, brim; hem; ~ **del marciapiede** curb

orlon (*or*-loan) *m* orlon

ornamentale (oar-nah-mayn-*taa*-lay) *adj* ornamental

ornamento (oar-nah-*mayn*-toa) *m* decoration, ornament

oro (*aw*-roa) *m* gold; ~ **laminato** gold leaf

orologiaio (oa-roa-loa-*jaa*-yoa) *m* watch-maker

orologio (oa-roa-*law*-joa) *m* watch; clock; **cinturino da** ~ watch-strap; ~ **da polso** wrist-watch; ~ **da tasca** pocket-watch

orrendo (oar-*rehn*-doa) *adj* hideous

orribile (oar-*ree*-bee-lay) *adj* horrible

orrore (oar-*roa*-ray) *m* horror

orso (*oar*-soa) *m* bear

orticoltura (oar-tee-koal-*too*-rah) *f* horticulture

orto (*or*-toa) *m* kitchen garden

ortodosso (oar-toa-*doss*-soa) *adj* orthodox

ortografia (oar-toa-grah-*fee*-ah) *f* spelling

orzo (*or*-dzoa) *m* barley

osare (oa-*zaa*-ray) *v* dare

osceno (oash-*shai*-noa) *adj* obscene

oscurità (oa-skoo-ree-*tah*) *f* gloom, dark

oscuro (oa-*skoo*-roa) *adj* dim, dark; obscure

ospedale (oa-spay-*daa*-lay) *m* hospital

ospitale (oa-spee-*taa*-lay) *adj* hospitable

ospitalità (oa-spee-tah-lee-*tah*) *f* hospitality

ospitare (oa-spee-*taa*-ray) *v* entertain

ospite (*o*-spee-tay) *f* hostess, host; *m* guest; **camera degli ospiti** spare room

ospizio (oa-*spee*-tsyoa) *m* asylum, home

osservare (oass-sayr-*vaa*-ray) *v* observe; watch, regard; remark, note

osservatorio (oass-sayr-vah-*toa*-ryoa) *m* observatory

osservazione (oass-sayr-vah-*tsyoa*-nay) *f* observation; remark

ossessione (oass-sayss-*syoa*-nay) *f* obsession

ossia (oass-*see*-ah) *conj* that is; or rather

ossigeno (oass-*see*-jay-noa) *m* oxygen

osso (*oss*-soa) *m* (pl le ossa) bone

ostacolare (oa-stah-koa-*laa*-ray) *v* hinder, embarrass

ostacolo (oa-*staa*-koa-loa) *m* obstacle

ostaggio (oa-*stahd*-joa) *m* hostage

ostello (oa-*stehl*-loa) *m* hostel; ~ **della gioventù** youth hostel

ostia (*o*-styah) *f* wafer

ostile (oa-*stee*-lay) *adj* hostile

ostinato (oa-stee-*naa*-toa) *adj* obstinate, dogged

ostrica (*o*-stree-kah) *f* oyster

ostruire (o-*strwee*-ray) *v* block

ottanta (oat-*tahn*-tah) *num* eighty

ottavo (oat-*taa*-voa) *num* eighth

* **ottenere** (oat-tay-*nāy*-ray) *v* *get, obtain; acquire

ottenibile (oat-tay-*nee*-bee-lay) *adj* available, obtainable

ottico (*ot*-tee-koa) *m* optician

ottimismo (oat-tee-*mee*-zmoa) *m* optimism

ottimista (oat-tee-*mee*-stah) *m* optimist

ottimistico (oat-tee-*mee*-stee-koa) *adj* optimistic

ottimo (*ot*-tee-moa) *adj* excellent, first-rate, fine; best

otto (*ot*-toa) *num* eight

ottobre (oat-*tōā*-bray) October

ottoname (oat-toa-*naa*-may) *m* brassware

ottone (oat-*tōā*-nay) *m* brass

otturazione (oat-too-rah-*tsyōā*-nay) *f* filling

ottuso (oat-*tōō*-zoa) *adj* blunt; slow, dumb

ovale (oa-*vaa*-lay) *adj* oval

ovatta (oa-*vaht*-tah) *f* cotton-wool

ovest (*aw*-vayst) *m* west

ovunque (oa-*voong*-kway) *adv* anywhere, everywhere

ovvio (*ov*-vyoa) *adj* obvious, apparent

ozioso (oa-*tsyōā*-soa) *adj* idle

P

pacchetto (pahk-*kayt*-toa) *m* parcel, packet

pacco (*pahk*-koa) *m* parcel, package

pace (*paa*-chay) *f* peace

pachistano (pah-kee-*staa*-noa) *adj* Pakistani; *m* Pakistani

pacifico (pah-*chee*-fee-koa) *adj* peaceful

pacifismo (pah-chee-*fee*-zmoa) *m* pacifism

pacifista (pah-chee-*fee*-stah) *m* pacifist; *adj* pacifist

padella (pah-*dehl*-lah) *f* frying-pan

padiglione (pah-dee-*lʸōā*-nay) *m* pavilion

padre (*paa*-dray) *m* father; dad

padrino (pah-*dree*-noa) *m* godfather

padrona (pah-*drōā*-nah) *f* mistress

padrone (pah-*drōā*nay) *m* master, boss; ~ **di casa** landlord

paesaggio (pahᵃʸ-*zahd*-joa) *m* landscape, scenery

paese (pah-*āy*-zay) *m* country, land; ~ **natio** native country

Paesi Bassi (pah-*āy*-zee *bahss*-see) the Netherlands

paga (*paa*-gah) *f* pay

pagamento (pah-gah-*mayn*-toa) *m* payment

pagano (pah-*gaa*-noa) *adj* pagan, heathen; *m* pagan, heathen

pagare (pah-*gaa*-ray) *v* *pay; *far ~ charge; ~ **a rate** *pay on account; **pagato in anticipo** prepaid

paggio (*pahd*-joa) *m* page-boy

pagina (*paa*-jee-nah) *f* page

paglia (*paa*-lʸah) *f* straw

pagliaccio (pah-*lʸaht*-choa) *m* clown

pagnotta (pah-*ñot*-tah) *f* loaf

paio (*paa*-yoa) *m* (pl le paia) pair

Pakistan (pah-kee-*stahn*) *m* Pakistan

pala (*paa*-lah) *f* shovel

palazzo (pah-*laht*-tsoa) *m* palace; mansion

palco (*pahl*-koa) *m* antlers *pl*

palestra (pah-*leh*-strah) *f* gymnasium

palla (*pahl*-lah) *f* ball

pallido (*pahl*-lee-doa) *adj* pale; dim, mat, dull

pallina (pahl-*lee*-nah) *f* marble

pallino (pahl-*lee*-noa) *m* hobby-horse

palloncino (pahl-loan-*chee*-noa) *m* balloon

pallone (pahl-*lōā*-nay) *m* football

pallottola (pahl-*lot*-toa-lah) *f* bullet

palma (*pahl*-mah) *f* palm

palo (*paa*-loa) *m* pole, post

palpabile (pahl-*paa*-bee-lay) *adj* palpable

palpare (pahl-*paa*-ray) *v* *feel

palpebra (*pahl*-pay-brah) *f* eyelid

palpitazione (pahl-pee-tah-*tsyōā*-nay) *f* palpitation

palude (pah-*lōō*-day) *f* marsh, swamp, bog

paludoso (pah-loo-*dōā*-soa) *adj* marshy

pancia (*pahn*-chah) *f* belly

panciotto (pahn-*chot*-toa) *m* waistcoat; vest *nAm*

pane (*paa*-nay) *m* bread; ~ **integrale** wholemeal bread

panetteria (pah-nayt-tay-*ree*-ah) *f* bakery

panettiere (pah-nayt-*tyai*-ray) *m* baker

panfilo (*pahn*-fee-loa) *m* yacht

panico (*paa*-nee-koa) *m* panic

paniere (pah-*ñai*-ray) *m* hamper, basket

panino (pah-*nee*-noa) *m* roll, bun

panna (*pahn*-nah) *f* cream

pannello (pahn-*nehl*-loa) *m* panel; **rivestimento a pannelli** panelling

panno (*pahn*-noa) *m* cloth

pannolino (pahn-noa-*lee*-noa) *m* nappy; diaper *nAm*; ~ **igienico** sanitary towel

pantaloni (pahn-tah-*lōā*-nee) *mpl* trousers *pl*

pantofola (pahn-*taw*-foa-lah) *f* slipper

Papa (*paa*-pah) *m* pope

papà (pah-*pah*) *m* daddy

papavero (pah-*paa*-vay-roa) *m* poppy

pappagallo (pahp-pah-*gahl*-loa) *m* parrot

parabrezza (pah-rah-*brayd*-dzah) *m* windscreen; windshield *nAm*

parafango (pah-rah-*fahng*-goa) *m* mud-guard

paragonare (pah-rah-goa-*naa*-ray) *v* compare

paragone (pah-rah-*gōā*-nay) *m* comparison

paragrafo (pah-*raa*-grah-foa) *m* paragraph

paralitico (pah-rah-*lee*-tee-koa) *adj* lame

paralizzare (pah-rah-leed-*dzaa*-ray) *v* paralise

parallela (pah-rahl-*lai*-lah) *f* parallel

parallelo (pah-rahl-*lai*-loa) *adj* parallel

paralume (pah-rah-*lōō*-may) *m* lampshade

parata (pah-*raa*-tah) *f* parade

paraurti (pah-rah-*oor*-tee) *m* fender, bumper

parcheggio (pahr-*kehd*-joa) *m* parking; car park; parking lot *Am*

parchimetro (pahr-*kee*-may-troa) *m* parking meter

parco (*pahr*-koa) *m* park; ~ **nazionale** national park

parecchi (pah-*rayk*-kee) *adj* several, various

pareggiare (pah-rayd-*jaa*-ray) *v* level; equalize

parente (pah-*rehn*-tay) *m* relative,

relation

parere (pah-*rāy*-ray) *m* view, opinion

*** parere** (pah-*rāy*-ray) *v* seem

parete (pah-*rāy*-tay) *f* wall

pari (*paa*-ree) *adj* even

parlamentare (pahr-lah-mayn-*taa*-ray) *adj* parliamentary

parlamento (pahr-lah-*mayn*-toa) *m* parliament

parlare (pahr-*laa*-ray) *v* *speak, talk

parola (pah-*raw*-lah) *f* word; speech; ~ **d'ordine** password

parrocchetto (pahr-roak-*kayt*-toa) *m* parakeet

parrocchia (pah-*rok*-kyah) *f* parish

parrucca (pah-*rook*-kah) *f* wig

parrucchiere (pah-rook-*kyai*-ray) *m* hairdresser

parsimonioso (pahr-see-moa-*nyōā*-soa) *adj* thrifty, economical

parte (*pahr*-tay) *f* part; share; side; **a ~** apart, separately; **dall'altra ~** across; **dall'altra ~ di** across; **da ~** aside; **in ~** partly; **una ~** some

partecipante (pahr-tay-chee-*pahn*-tay) *m* participant

partecipare (pahr-tay-chee-*paa*-ray) *v* participate

partenza (pahr-*tehn*-tsah) *f* departure

particolare (pahr-tee-koa-*laa*-ray) *adj* particular, special, peculiar; *m* detail; **in ~** in particular

particolareggiato (pahr-tee-koa-lah-rayd-*jaa*-toa) *adj* detailed

particolarmente (pahr-tee-koa-lahr-*mayn*-tay) *adv* specially

partire (pahr-*tee*-ray) *v* depart, *leave; *set out; pull out; **a ~ da** as from

partita (pahr-*tee*-tah) *f* batch; match; ~ **di calcio** football match; ~ **di pugilato** boxing match

partito (pahr-*tee*-toa) *m* party

parto (*pahr*-toa) *m* delivery, childbirth

parziale (pahr-*tsyaa*-lay) *adj* partial

pascolare (pah-skoa-*laa*-ray) *v* graze

pascolo (*pah*-skoa-loa) *m* pasture

Pasqua (*pah*-skwah) Easter

passaggio (pahss-*sahd*-joa) *m* passage; aisle; ~ **a livello** level crossing; ~ **pedonale** crossing, pedestrian crossing; crosswalk *nAm*

passante (pahss-*sahn*-tay) *m* passer-by

passaporto (pahss-sah-*por*-toa) *m* passport

passare (pahss-*saa*-ray) *v* pass; ~ **accanto** pass by

passarella (pahss-sah-*rehl*-lah) *f* gangway

passatempo (pahss-sah-*tehm*-poa) *m* entertainment, amusement; hobby

passato (pahss-*saa*-toa) *adj* past; *m* past

passeggero (pahss-sayd-*jāy*-roa) *m* passenger

passeggiare (pahss-sayd-*jaa*-ray) *v* walk, stroll

passeggiata (pahss-sayd-*jaa*-tah) *f* walk, stroll

passera di mare (*pahss*-say-rah dee *maa*-ray) plaice

passero (*pahss*-say-roa) *m* sparrow

passione (pahss-*syōā*-nay) *f* passion

passivo (pahss-*see*-voa) *adj* passive

passo (*pahss*-soa) *m* pace, step; gait; mountain pass; extract; *stare al ~ con *keep up with

pasta (*pah*-stah) *f* dough; paste

pasticca (pah-*steek*-kah) *f* tablet

pasticceria (pah-steet-chay-*ree*-ah) *f* pastry, cake; pastry shop, sweetshop; candy store *Am*

pasticciare (pah-steet-*chaa*-ray) *v* mess up

pasticciere (pah-steet-*chai*-ray) *m* confectioner

pasticcio (pah-*steet*-choa) *m* muddle

pasto (*pah*-stoa) *m* meal

pastore (pah-*stōā*-ray) *m* shepherd;

clergyman, parson, minister, rector

patata (pah-*taa*-tah) *f* potato; **patatine fritte** chips

patria (*paa*-tryah) *f* fatherland, native country

patrigno (pah-*tree*-ñoa) *m* stepfather

patriota (pah-*tryaw*-tah) *m* patriot

patrocinatore (pah-troa-chee-nah-*tōa*-ray) *m* advocate

pattinaggio (paht-tee-*nahd*-joa) *m* skating; ~ **a rotelle** roller-skating

pattinare (paht-tee-*naa*-ray) *v* skate

pattino (*paht*-tee-noa) *m* skate

patto (*paht*-toa) *m* agreement; term

pattuglia (paht-*tōō*-lʸah) *f* patrol

pattugliare (paht-too-*lʸaa*-ray) *v* patrol

pattumiera (paht-too-*myai*-rah) *f* rubbish-bin, dustbin; trash can *Am*

paura (pah-*ōō*-rah) *f* fear, fright; *aver ~ *be afraid

pausa (*pou*-zah) *f* pause

pavimentare (pah-vee-mayn-*taa*-ray) *v* pave

pavimento (pah-vee-*mayn*-toa) *m* floor; pavement

pavoncella (pah-voan-*chehl*-lah) *f* pewit

pavone (pah-*vōa*-nay) *m* peacock

paziente (pah-*tsyehn*-tay) *adj* patient; *m* patient

pazienza (pah-*tsyehn*-tsah) *f* patience

pazzia (paht-*tsee*-ah) *f* madness, lunacy

pazzo (*paht*-tsoa) *adj* crazy, mad, lunatic; *m* lunatic

peccato (payk-*kaa*-toa) *m* sin; **peccato!** what a pity!

pecora (*pai*-koa-rah) *f* sheep

pedaggio (pay-*dahd*-joa) *m* toll

pedale (pay-*daa*-lay) *m* pedal

pedata (pay-*daa*-tah) *f* kick

pedicure (pay-dee-*kōō*-ray) *m* pedicure

pedina (pay-*dee*-nah) *f* pawn

pedone (pay-*dōa*-nay) *m* pedestrian

peggio (*pehd*-joa) *adv* worse; worst

peggiore (payd-*jōa*-ray) *adj* worse

pelle (*pehl*-lay) *f* skin; hide; leather; **di ~** leather; ~ **di cinghiale** pigskin; ~ **di vacca** cow-hide; ~ **di vitello** calf skin; ~ **d'oca** goose-flesh; ~ **scamosciata** suede

pellegrinaggio (payl-lay-gree-*nahd*-joa) *m* pilgrimage

pellegrino (payl-lay-*gree*-noa) *m* pilgrim

pellicano (payl-lee-*kaa*-noa) *m* pelican

pelliccia (payl-*leet*-chah) *f* fur

pellicciaio (payl-lee-*chaa*-yoa) *m* furrier

pellicola (payl-*lee*-koa-lah) *f* film; ~ **a colori** colour film

peloso (pay-*lōa*-soa) *adj* hairy

peltro (*payl*-troa) *m* pewter

pena (*pāy*-nah) *f* trouble, pains, difficulty; penalty; ~ **di morte** death penalty; *valer la ~ *be worthwhile

penalità (pay-nah-lee-*tah*) *f* penalty

pendente (payn-*dehn*-tay) *adj* slanting; *m* pendant

pendere (*pehn*-day-ray) *v* *hang; slope

pendio (payn-*dee*-oa) *m* incline, hillside, slope

pendolare (payn-doa-*laa*-ray) *m* commuter

penetrare (pay-nay-*traa*-ray) *v* penetrate

penetrazione (pay-nay-trah-*tsyōa*-nay) *f* insight

penicillina (pay-nee-cheel-*lee*-nah) *f* penicillin

penisola (pay-*nee*-zoa-lah) *f* peninsula

penna (*payn*-nah) *f* feather; pen; ~ **a sfera** Biro, ballpoint-pen; ~ **stilografica** fountain-pen

pennello (payn-*nehl*-loa) *m* brush; paint-brush; ~ **da barba** shaving-brush

penoso (pay-*nōā*-soa) *adj* painful

pensare (payn-*saa*-ray) *v* *think; ~ **a** *think of

pensatore (payn-sah-*tōā*-ray) *m* thinker

pensiero (payn-*syai*-roa) *m* thought, idea

pensieroso (payn-syay-*rōā*-soa) *adj* thoughtful

pensionante (payn-syoa-*nahn*-tay) *m* boarder

pensionato (payn-syoa-*naa*-toa) *adj* retired

pensione (payn-*syōā*-nay) *f* board; guest-house, pension, boarding-house; ~ **completa** bed and board, full board, board and lodging

Pentecoste (payn-tay-*ko*-stay) *f* Whitsun

pentimento (payn-tee-*mayn*-toa) *m* repentance

pentola (*pehn*-toa-lah) *f* pot; ~ **a pressione** pressure-cooker

penuria (pay-*nōō*-ryah) *f* scarcity

pepe (*pāy*-pay) *m* pepper

per (payr) *prep* for; to; with; times

pera (*pāy*-rah) *f* pear

percento (payr-*chehn*-toa) *m* percent

percentuale (payr-chayn-*twaa*-lay) *f* percentage

percepire (payr-chay-*pee*-ray) *v* perceive, sense

percettibile (payr-chayt-*tee*-bee-lay) *adj* perceptible, noticeable

percezione (payr-chay-*tsyōā*-nay) *f* perception

perché (payr-*kay*) *adv* what for, why; *conj* because

perciò (payr-*cho*) *conj* therefore

***percorrere** (payr-*koar*-ray-ray) *v* cover; *go through

***percuotere** (payr-*kwaw*-tay-ray) *v* thump

perdente (payr-*dehn*-tay) *adj* leaky

***perdere** (*pehr*-day-ray) *v* *lose

perdita (*pehr*-dee-tah) *f* loss

perdonare (payr-doa-*naa*-ray) *v* *forgive

perdono (payr-*dōā*-noa) *m* pardon; grace

perfetto (payr-*feht*-toa) *adj* perfect; faultless

perfezione (payr-fay-*tsyōā*-nay) *f* perfection

perfido (*pehr*-fee-doa) *adj* foul

perforare (payr-foa-*raa*-ray) *v* pierce

pericolo (pay-*ree*-koa-loa) *m* danger; risk, peril; distress

pericoloso (pay-ree-koa-*lōā*-soa) *adj* perilous, dangerous

periodico (pay-*ryaw*-dee-koa) *adj* periodical; *m* periodical

periodo (pay-*ree*-oa-doa) *m* period, term

perire (pay-*ree*-ray) *v* perish

perito (pay-*ree*-toa) *m* expert

perla (*pehr*-lah) *f* pearl

perlina (payr-*lee*-nah) *f* bead

perlustrare (payr-loo-*straa*-ray) *v* search

permanente (payr-mah-*nehn*-tay) *adj* permanent; *f* permanent wave

permesso (payr-*mayss*-soa) *m* authorization, permission; permit; ***avere il ~ di** *be allowed to; ~ **di lavoro** work permit; labor permit *Am*; ~ **di pesca** fishing licence; ~ **di soggiorno** residence permit

***permettere** (payr-*mayt*-tay-ray) *v* allow, permit; ***permettersi** afford

pernice (payr-*nee*-chay) *f* partridge

però (pay-*roa*) *conj* but; only, yet

perorare (pay-roa-*raa*-ray) *v* plead

perpendicolare (payr-payn-dee-koa-*laa*-ray) *adj* perpendicular

perquisire (payr-kwee-*zee*-ray) *v* search

perseguire (payr-say-*gwee*-ray) *v* pursue

perseverare (payr-say-vay-*raa*-ray) v
*keep up

Persia (*pehr*-syah) f Persia

persiana (payr-*syaa*-nah) f shutter,
blind

persiano (payr-*syaa*-noa) adj Persian;
m Persian

persistere (payr-*see*-stay-ray) v insist

persona (payr-*soā*-nah) f person; **per
~ per** person

personaggio (payr-soa-*nahd*-joa) m
personality; character

personale (payr-soa-*naa*-lay) adj personal, private; m staff, personnel

personalità (payr-soa-nah-lee-*tah*) f
personality

perspicace (payr-spee-*kaa*-chay) adj
clever

***persuadere** (payr-swah-*dāy*-ray) v
persuade

pesante (pay-*sahn*-tay) adj heavy

pesare (pay-*saa*-ray) v weigh

pesca[1] (*peh*-skah) f peach

pesca[2] (*pay*-skah) f fishing industry

pescare (pay-*skaa*-ray) v fish; **~ con
l'amo** angle

pescatore (pay-skah-*tōā*-ray) m fisherman

pesce (*paysh*-shay) m fish; **~ persico**
perch

pescecane (paysh-shay-*kaa*-nay) m
shark

pescheria (pay-skay-*ree*-ah) f fish shop

pesciolino (paysh-shoa-*lee*-noa) m
whitebait

peso (*pāy*-soa) m weight; load, burden

pessimismo (payss-see-*mee*-zmoa) m
pessimism

pessimista (payss-see-*mee*-stah) m
pessimist

pessimistico (payss-see-*mee*-stee-koa)
adj pessimistic

pessimo (*pehss*-see-moa) adj worst

pestare (pay-*staa*-ray) v stamp

petalo (*pai*-tah-loa) m petal

petizione (pay-tee-*tsyōā*-nay) f petition

petroliera (pay-troa-*lʸai*-rah) f tanker

petrolio (pay-*traw*-lʸoa) m petroleum;
oil; paraffin, kerosene

pettegolare (payt-tay-goa-*laa*-ray) v
gossip

pettegolezzo (payt-tay-goa-*layt*-tsoa) m
gossip

pettinare (payt-tee-*naa*-ray) v comb

pettine (*peht*-tee-nay) m comb; **~ tascabile** pocket-comb

pettirosso (payt-tee-*roass*-soa) m robin

petto (*peht*-toa) m chest, bosom

pezzetto (payt-*tsayt*-toa) m bit; morsel, scrap

pezzo (*peht*-tsoa) m piece; part,
lump; fragment; **in due pezzi** two-
piece; **~ di ricambio** spare part

piacere (pyah-*chāy*-ray) m pleasure;
con ~ gladly

***piacere** (pyah-*chāy*-ray) v please

piacevole (pyah-*chāy*-voa-lay) adj
pleasant, enjoyable, nice

piacevolissimo (pyah-chay-voa-*leess*-
see-moa) adj delightful

piaga (*pyaa*-gah) f sore

pianeta (pyah-*nāy*-tah) m planet

***piangere** (*pyahn*-jay-ray) v *weep,
cry

pianista (pyah-*nee*-stah) m pianist

piano (*pyaa*-noa) adj plane, smooth,
even, flat, level; m floor, storey;
project; **primo ~** foreground

pianoforte (pyah-noa-*for*-tay) m piano; **~ a coda** grand piano

pianta (*pyahn*-tah) f plant; map, plan

piantagione (pyahn-tah-*jōā*-nay) f
plantation

piantare (pyahn-*taa*-ray) v plant

pianterreno (pyahn-tayr-*rāy*-noa) m
ground floor

pianura (pyah-*nōō*-rah) *f* plain

piattino (pyaht-*tee*-noa) *m* saucer

piatto (*pyaht*-toa) *adj* even, flat, level; *m* plate, dish

piazza (*pyaht*-tsah) *f* square; ~ **del mercato** market-place

piccante (peek-*kahn*-tay) *adj* savoury; spicy

picchiare (peek-*kyaa*-ray) *v* *strike, *beat; smack

piccino (peet-*chee*-noa) *m* baby

piccione (peet-*chōa*-nay) *m* pigeon

piccolo (*peek*-koa-loa) *adj* small, little; minor, petty

piccone (peek-*kōā*-nay) *m* pick-axe

*fare un picnic picnic

pidocchio (pee-*dok*-kyoa) *m* louse

piede (*pyai*-day) *m* foot; leg; **a piedi** walking, on foot; **in piedi** upright; ~ **di porco** crowbar

piega (*pyai*-gah) *f* fold; crease

piegare (pyay-*gaa*-ray) *v* fold

pieghevole (pyay-*gāy*-voa-lay) *adj* flexible, supple

pieno (*pyai*-noa) *adj* full; ***fare il** ~ fill up; ~ **zeppo** chock-full

pietà (pyay-*tah*) *f* pity

pietanza (pyay-*tahn*-tsah) *f* dish

pietra (*pyai*-trah) *f* stone; **di** ~ stone; ~ **miliare** milestone; landmark; ~ **pomice** pumice stone; ~ **preziosa** stone; ~ **sepolcrale** tombstone

pietrina (pyay-*tree*-nah) *f* flint

pigiama (pee-*jaa*-mah) *m* pyjamas *pl*

pigliare (pee-*lʸaa*-ray) *v* *take

pigro (*pee*-groa) *adj* lazy; idle

pila (*pee*-lah) *f* stack

pilastro (pee-*lah*-stroa) *m* column, pillar

pillola (*peel*-loa-lah) *f* pill

pilota (pee-*law*-tah) *m* pilot

pinguedine (peeng-*gwai*-dee-nay) *f* fatness

pinguino (peeng-*gwee*-noa) *m* penguin

pinze (*peen*-tsay) *fpl* pliers *pl*, tongs *pl*

pinzette (peen-*tsayt*-tay) *fpl* tweezers *pl*

pio (*pee*-oa) *adj* pious

pioggerella (pyoad-jay-*rehl*-lah) *f* drizzle

pioggia (*pyod*-jah) *f* rain

piombo (*pyoam*-boa) *m* lead

pioniere (pyoa-*ñai*-ray) *m* pioneer

*piovere (*pyaw*-vay-ray) *v* rain

piovoso (pyoa-*vōā*-soa) *adj* rainy

pipa (*pee*-pah) *f* pipe

pirata (pee-*raa*-tah) *m* pirate

piroscafo (pee-*raw*-skah-foa) *m* steamer

piscina (peesh-*shee*-nah) *f* swimming pool

pisello (pee-*sehl*-loa) *m* pea

pisolino (pee-zoa-*lee*-noa) *m* nap

pista (*pee*-stah) *f* track; ring; ~ **da corsa** race-course, race-track; ~ **di bocce** bowling alley; ~ **di decollo** runway; ~ **di pattinaggio** skating-rink

pistola (pee-*staw*-lah) *f* pistol

pittore (peet-*tōā*-ray) *m* painter

pittoresco (peet-toa-*ray*-skoa) *adj* picturesque, scenic

pittura (peet-*tōō*-rah) *f* painting, picture; ~ **ad olio** oil-painting

pitturare (peet-too-*raa*-ray) *v* paint

più (pyoo) *adv* more; *prep* plus; **il** ~ most; **per lo** ~ mostly; ~ ... **più** the ... the; ~ **in là di** beyond; ~ **lontano** further; **sempre** ~ more and more; **tutt'al** ~ at most

piuttosto (pee°°t-*to*-stoa) *adv* sooner, rather; fairly, pretty, quite

pizzicare (peet-tsee-*kaa*-ray) *v* pinch

planetario (plah-nay-*taa*-ryoa) *m* planetarium

plasmare (plah-*zmaa*-ray) *v* model

plastica (*plah*-stee-kah) *f* plastic

plastico (*plah*-stee-koa) *adj* plastic

platino (*plaa*-tee-noa) *m* platinum

plurale (ploo-*raa*-lay) *m* plural

pneumatico (pnay°°-*maa*-tee-koa) *adj* pneumatic; *m* tire; ~ **di ricambio** spare tyre

poco (*paw*-koa) *adj* little; *m* bit; **pochi** *adj* few; **press'a** ~ about; **tra** ~ soon

poderoso (poa-day-*rōā*-soa) *adj* mighty, powerful

poema (poa-*ai*-mah) *m* poem; ~ **epico** epic

poesia (poa-ay-*zee*-ah) *f* poetry

poeta (poa-*ai*-tah) *m* poet

poi (poi) *adv* then; afterwards

poiché (poay-*kay*) *conj* as, since, because; for

polacco (poa-*lahk*-koa) *adj* Polish; *m* Pole

polio (*paw*-l^yoa) *f* polio

polipo (*paw*-lee-poa) *m* octopus

politica (poa-*lee*-tee-kah) *f* politics; policy

politico (poa-*lee*-tee-koa) *adj* political

polizia (poa-lee-*tsee*-ah) *f* police *pl*

poliziotto (poa-lee-*tsyot*-toa) *m* policeman

polizza (poa-*leet*-tsah) *f* policy; ~ **di assicurazione** insurance policy

pollame (poal-*laa*-may) *m* fowl; poultry

pollice (*pol*-lee-chay) *m* thumb

pollivendolo (poal-lee-*vayn*-doa-loa) *m* poulterer

pollo (*poal*-loa) *m* chicken

polmone (poal-*mōā*-nay) *m* lung

polmonite (poal-moa-*nee*-tay) *f* pneumonia

Polonia (poa-*law*-ñah) *f* Poland

polpaccio (poal-*paht*-choa) *m* calf

polposo (poal-*pōā*-soa) *adj* mellow

polsino (poal-*see*-noa) *m* cuff

polso (*poal*-soa) *m* pulse; wrist

poltrona (poal-*trōā*-nah) *f* armchair, easy chair; ~ **d'orchestra** orchestra seat *Am*; ~ stall

polvere (*poal*-vay-ray) *f* dust; powder; ~ **da sparo** gunpowder; ~ **dentifricia** toothpowder

polveroso (poal-vay-*rōā*-soa) *adj* dusty

pomeriggio (poa-may-*reed*-joa) *m* afternoon; **oggi nel** ~ this afternoon

pomodoro (poa-moa-*daw*-roa) *m* tomato

pompa (*poam*-pah) *f* pump; ~ **ad acqua** water pump; ~ **di benzina** petrol pump; gas pump *Am*

pompare (poam-*paa*-ray) *v* pump

pompelmo (poam-*pehl*-moa) *m* grapefruit

pompieri (poam-*pyai*-ree) *mpl* firebrigade

ponderare (poan-day-*raa*-ray) *v* deliberate

ponte (*poan*-tay) *m* bridge; ~ **di coperta** main deck; ~ **levatoio** drawbridge; ~ **sospeso** suspension bridge

pontefice (poan-*tāy*-fee-chay) *m* pontiff

popelina (poa-pay-*lee*-nah) *f* poplin

popolano (poa-poa-*laa*-noa) *adj* vulgar

popolare (poa-poa-*laa*-ray) *adj* popular; **danza** ~ folk-dance

popolazione (poa-poa-lah-*tsyōā*-nay) *f* population

popolo (*paw*-poa-loa) *m* people; nation, folk

popoloso (poa-poa-*lōā*-soa) *adj* populous

porcellana (poar-chayl-*laa*-nah) *f* porcelain, china

porcellino (poar-chayl-*lee*-noa) *m* piglet; ~ **d'India** guinea-pig

porco (*por*-koa) *m* (pl porci) pig

porcospino (poar-koa-*spee*-noa) *m* porcupine

*porgere (*por*-jay-ray) v hand, *give

porporino (poar-poa-*ree*-noa) adj purple

*porre (*poar*-ray) v place; *put

porta (*por*-tah) f door; ~ **girevole** revolving door; ~ **scorrevole** sliding door

portabagagli (poar-tah-bah-*gaa*-lʸee) m luggage rack

portacarte (poar-tah-*kahr*-tay) m attaché case

portacenere (poar-tah-*chāy*-nay-ray) m ashtray

portacipria (poar-tah-*chee*-pryah) m powder compact

portafoglio (poar-tah-*fōā*-lʸoa) m pocket-book, wallet

portafortuna (poar-tah-foar-*tōō*-nah) m lucky charm

portalampada (poar-tah-*lahm*-pah-dah) m socket

portare (poar-*taa*-ray) v *bring; fetch; carry, *bear; **portar via** *take away

portasigarette (poar-tah-see-gah-*rayt*-tay) m cigarette-case

portata (poar-*taa*-tah) f course; reach, range

portatile (poar-*taa*-tee-lay) adj portable

portatore (poar-tah-*tōā*-ray) m bearer

portauovo (poar-tah-*waw*-voa) m egg-cup

portico (*por*-tee-koa) m arcade

portiere (poar-*tyai*-ray) m porter; goalkeeper

portinaio (poar-tee-*naa*-yoa) m concierge, janitor; doorman, door-keeper

porto (*por*-toa) m harbour, port; ~ **di mare** seaport

Portogallo (poar-toa-*gahl*-loa) m Portugal

portoghese (poar-toa-*gāy*-say) adj Portuguese; m Portuguese

portuale (poar-*twaa*-lay) m docker

porzione (poar-*tsyōā*-nay) f portion, helping

posare (poa-*saa*-ray) v *lay, *put; place

posate (poa-*saa*-tay) fpl cutlery

positiva (poa-zee-*tee*-vah) f positive, print

positivo (poa-zee-*tee*-voa) adj positive

posizione (poa-zee-*tsyōā*-nay) f position; site, location

*possedere (poass-say-*dāy*-ray) v possess, own

possedimenti (poass-say-dee-*mayn*-tee) mpl possessions

possesso (poass-*sehss*-soa) m possession

possibile (poass-*see*-bee-lay) adj possible

possibilità (poass-see-bee-lee-*tah*) f possibility

posta (*po*-stah) f post, mail; bet; ~ **aerea** airmail

posteggiare (poa-stayd-*jaa*-ray) v park

posteggio di autopubbliche (poa-*stayd*-joa dee ou-toa-*poob*-blee-kay) taxi rank; taxi stand Am

posteriore (poa-stay-*ryōā*-ray) adj rear; later

postino (poa-*stee*-noa) m postman

posto (*poa*-stoa) m place; seat; station; **in qualche** ~ somewhere; ***mettere a** ~ *put away; ~ **di polizia** police-station; ~ **di pronto soccorso** first-aid post; ~ **libero** vacancy

potabile (poa-*taa*-bee-lay) adj for drinking

potente (poa-*tehn*-tay) adj powerful

potenza (poa-*tehn*-tsah) f might; power; capacity

potere (poa-*tāy*-ray) m authority, power; faculty

*potere (poa-*tāy*-ray) v *can, *be able to; *might, *may

povero (*paw*-vay-roa) *adj* poor

povertà (poa-vayr-*tah*) *f* poverty

pozzanghera (poat-*tsahng*-gay-rah) *f* puddle

pozzo (*poat*-tsoa) *m* well; ~ **di petrolio** oil-well

pranzare (prahn-*dzaa*-ray) *v* *eat; dine

pranzo (*prahn*-dzoa) *m* dinner; lunch; ~ **a prezzo fisso** set menu

pratica (*praa*-tee-kah) *f* practice

praticamente (prah-tee-kah-*mayn*-tay) *adv* practically

praticare (prah-tee-*kaa*-ray) *v* practise

pratico (*praa*-tee-koa) *adj* practical

prato (*praa*-toa) *m* meadow; lawn

precario (pray-*kaa*-ryoa) *adj* critical, precarious

precauzione (pray-kou-*tsyōa*-nay) *f* precaution

precedente (pray-chay-*dehn*-tay) *adj* previous, former, preceding

precedentemente (pray-chay-dayn-tay-*mayn*-tay) *adv* before

precedenza (pray-chay-*dehn*-tsah) *f* right of way; priority

precedere (pray-*chai*-day-ray) *v* precede

precettore (pray-chayt-*tōa*-ray) *m* tutor

precipitare (pray-chee-pee-*taa*-ray) *v* crash; **precipitarsi** dash

precipitazione (pray-chee-pee-tah-*tsyōa*-nay) *f* shower; precipitation

precipizio (pray-chee-*pee*-tsyoa) *m* precipice

precisamente (pray-chee-zah-*mayn*-tay) *adv* exactly

precisare (pray-chee-*zaa*-ray) *v* specify

precisione (pray-chee-*zyōa*-nay) *f* precision

preciso (pray-*chee*-zoa) *adj* very, precise

predecessore (pray-day-chayss-*sōa*-ray) *m* predecessor

predicare (pray-dee-*kaa*-ray) *v* preach

*predire (pray-*dee*-ray) *v* predict

preferenza (pray-fay-*rehn*-tsah) *f* preference

preferibile (pray-fay-*ree*-bee-lay) *adj* preferable

preferire (pray-fay-*ree*-ray) *v* prefer; **preferito** favourite

prefisso (pray-*feess*-soa) *m* prefix; area code

pregare (pray-*gaa*-ray) *v* ask; pray

preghiera (pray-*gyai*-rah) *f* prayer

pregiudizio (pray-joo-*dee*-tsyoa) *m* prejudice

preliminare (pray-lee-mee-*naa*-ray) *adj* preliminary

prematuro (pray-mah-*tōō*-roa) *adj* premature

premeditato (pray-may-dee-*taa*-toa) *adj* deliberate

premere (*prai*-may-ray) *v* press

premio (*prai*-myoa) *m* award, prize; premium; ~ **di consolazione** consolation prize

premura (pray-*mōō*-rah) *f* haste

premuroso (pray-moo-*rōa*-soa) *adj* thoughtful

*prendere (*prehn*-day-ray) *v* *take; *catch; capture

prenotare (pray-noa-*taa*-ray) *v* reserve, book

prenotazione (pray-noa-tah-*tsyōa*-nay) *f* reservation, booking

preoccuparsi (pray-oak-koo-*pahr*-see) *v* worry; ~ **di** care about

preoccupato (pray-oak-koo-*paa*-toa) *adj* concerned, anxious, worried

preoccupazione (pray-oak-koo-pah-*tsyōa*-nay) *f* worry; trouble, care

preparare (pray-pah-*raa*-ray) *v* prepare; cook

preparazione (pray-pah-rah-*tsyōa*-nay) *f* preparation

preposizione (pray-poa-zee-*tsyōa*-nay) *f* preposition

presa (*prāy*-sah) *f* grip; capture

presbiterio (pray-zbee-*tai*-ryoa) *m* parsonage, rectory, vicarage

a prescindere da (ah pray-*sheen*-day-ray dah) apart from

*__prescrivere__ (pray-*skree*-vay-ray) *v* prescribe

presentare (pray-zayn-*taa*-ray) *v* offer, present; introduce; **presentarsi** report; appear

presentazione (pray-zayn-tah-*tsyoā*-nay) *f* introduction

presente (pray-*zehn*-tay) *adj* present; *m* present

presenza (pray-*zehn*-tsah) *f* presence

preservativo (pray-*sayr*-vah-tee-voa) *m* condom

preservazione (pray-zayr-vah-*tsyoā*-nay) *f* preservation

preside (*prai*-see-day) *m* headmaster, principal

presidente (pray-see-*dehn*-tay) *m* chairman, president

pressante (prayss-*sahn*-tay) *adj* pressing

pressione (prayss-*syoā*-nay) *f* pressure; ~ **atmosferica** atmospheric pressure; ~ **dell'olio** oil pressure; ~ **gomme** tyre pressure; ~ **sanguigna** blood pressure

presso (*prehss*-soa) *prep* with

prestare (pray-*staa*-ray) *v* *lend

prestazione (pray-stah-*tsyoā*-nay) *f* feat

prestigiatore (pray-stee-jah-*toā*-ray) *m* magician

prestigio (pray-*stee*-joa) *m* prestige

prestito (*preh*-stee-toa) *m* loan; *__prendere in__ ~ borrow

presto (*preh*-stoa) *adv* soon, shortly

*__presumere__ (pray-*zōō*-may-ray) *v* assume

presuntuoso (pray-zoon-*twoā*-soa) *adj* conceited, presumptuous

prete (*prai*-tay) *m* priest

*__pretendere__ (pray-*tehn*-day-ray) *v* pretend

pretesa (pray-*tāy*-sah) *f* pretence; claim

pretesto (pray-*teh*-stoa) *m* pretext

*__prevedere__ (pray-vay-*dāy*-ray) *v* forecast; anticipate

*__prevenire__ (pray-vay-*nee*-ray) *v* anticipate, prevent

preventivo (pray-vayn-*tee*-voa) *adj* preventive; *m* budget

previo (*prai*-vyoa) *adj* previous

previsione (pray-vee-*zyoā*-nay) *f* forecast

prezioso (pray-*tsyoā*-soa) *adj* valuable, precious

prezzare (prayt-*tsaa*-ray) *v* price

prezzemolo (prayt-*tsāy*-moa-loa) *m* parsley

prezzo (*preht*-tsoa) *m* price-list; cost, rate; **calo di** ~ slump; ~ **d'acquisto** purchase price; ~ **del biglietto** fare; ~ **del coperto** cover charge

prigione (pree-*joā*-nay) *m* jail, prison

prigioniero (pree-joa-*ñai*-roa) *m* prisoner; *__far__ ~ capture

prima (*pree*-mah) *adv* at first; before; ~ **che** before; ~ **di** before

primario (pree-*maa*-ryoa) *adj* primary

primato (pree-*maa*-toa) *m* record

primavera (pree-mah-*vāy*-rah) *f* springtime, spring

primitivo (pree-mee-*tee*-voa) *adj* primitive

primo (*pree*-moa) *num* first, foremost, primary, chief

principale (preent-shee-*paa*-lay) *adj* leading, main, cardinal, principal, primary, chief

principalmente (preen-chee-pahl-*maynt*-tay) *adv* mainly

principe (*preen*-chee-pay) *m* prince

principessa (preen-chee-*payss*-sah) *f*

princess

principiante (preen-chee-*pyahn*-tay) *m* beginner, learner

principio (preen-*chee*-pyoa) *m* beginning; principle; **al** ~ at first

priorità (pryoa-ree-*tah*) *f* priority

privare di (pree-*vaa*-ray) deprive of

privato (pree-*vaa*-toa) *adj* private

privazioni (pree-vah-*tsyoa*-nee) *fpl* exposure

privilegiare (pree-vee-lay-*jaa*-ray) *v* favour

privilegio (pree-vee-*lai*-joa) *m* privilege

probabile (proa-*baa*-bee-lay) *adj* probable, likely

probabilmente (proa-bah-beel-*mayn*-tay) *adv* probably

problema (proa-*blai*-mah) *m* problem, question

procedere (proa-*chai*-day-ray) *v* proceed

procedimento (proa-chay-dee-*mayn*-toa) *m* procedure; process

processione (proa-chayss-*syoa*-nay) *f* procession

processo (proa-*chehss*-soa) *m* trial, lawsuit; process

proclamare (proa-klah-*maa*-ray) *v* proclaim

procurare (proa-koo-*raa*-ray) *v* furnish

prodigo (*praw*-dee-goa) *adj* lavish; liberal

prodotto (proa-*doat*-toa) *m* product; produce

***produrre** (proa-*door*-ray) *v* produce

produttore (proa-doot-*toā*-ray) *m* producer

produzione (proa-doo-*tsyoā*-nay) *f* production, output; ~ **in serie** mass production

profano (proa-*faa*-noa) *m* layman

professare (proa-fayss-*saa*-ray) *v* confess

professionale (proa-fayss-syoa-*naa*-lay)

adj professional

professione (proa-fayss-*syoā*-nay) *f* profession

professore (proa-fayss-*soā*-ray) *m* master; professor

professoressa (proa-fayss-soa-*rayss*-sah) *f* teacher

profeta (proa-*fai*-tah) *m* prophet

profitto (proa-*feet*-toa) *m* benefit, gain; profit

profondità (proa-foan-dee-*tah*) *f* depth

profondo (proa-*foan*-doa) *adj* deep; profound

profumo (proa-*fōō*-moa) *m* scent; perfume

progettare (proa-jayt-*taa*-ray) *v* plan; design

progetto (proa-*jeht*-toa) *m* plan, scheme; project

programma (proa-*grahm*-mah) *m* programme

progredire (proa-gray-*dee*-ray) *v* *get on

progressista (proa-grayss-*see*-stah) *adj* progressive

progressivo (proa-grayss-*see*-voa) *adj* progressive

progresso (proa-*grehss*-soa) *m* progress

proibire (proa-ee-*bee*-ray) *v* *forbid, prohibit; **proibito passare** no entry

proibitivo (proa-ee-bee-*tee*-voa) *adj* prohibitive

proiettore (proa-yayt-*tōā*-ray) *m* spotlight

prolunga (proa-*loong*-gah) *f* extension cord

prolungamento (proa-loong-gah-*mayn*-toa) *m* extension

promessa (proa-*mayss*-sah) *f* promise; vow

***promettere** (proa-*mayt*-tay-ray) *v* promise

promontorio (proa-moan-*taw*-ryoa) *m*

headland

promozione (proa-moa-*tsyōā*-nay) *f* promotion

***promuovere** (proa-*mwaw*-vay-ray) *v* promote

pronome (proa-*nōā*-may) *m* pronoun

pronto (*proan*-toa) *adj* ready; prompt

pronuncia (proa-*noon*-chah) *f* pronunciation

pronunciare (proa-noon-*chaa*-ray) *v* pronounce

propaganda (proa-pah-*gahn*-dah) *f* propaganda

propenso (proa-*pehn*-soa) *adj* inclined

***proporre** (proa-*poar*-ray) *v* propose

proporzionale (proa-poar-tsyoa-*naa*-lay) *adj* proportional

proporzione (proa-poar-*tsyōā*-nay) *f* proportion

proposito (proa-*paw*-zee-toa) *m* purpose; **a ~** by the way

proposta (proa-*poa*-stah) *f* proposition, proposal

proprietà (proa-pryay-*tah*) *f* property; estate

proprietario (proa-pryay-*taa*-ryoa) *m* proprietor, owner; landlord

proprio (*pro*-pryoa) *adj* own

propulsare (proa-pool-*saa*-ray) *v* propel

prosaico (proa-*zigh*-koa) *adj* matter-of-fact

prosciugare (proash-shoo-*gaa*-ray) *v* drain

prosciutto (proash-*shoot*-toa) *m* ham

proseguire (proa-say-*gwee*-ray) *v* continue, carry on

prosperità (proa-spay-ree-*tah*) *f* prosperity

prospettiva (proa-spayt-*tee*-vah) *f* perspective; prospect, outlook

prospetto (proa-*speht*-toa) *m* prospectus

prossimamente (proass-see-mah-*mayn*-tay) *adv* shortly

prossimità (proass-see-mee-*tah*) *f* vicinity

prossimo (*pross*-see-moa) *adj* next

prostituta (proa-stee-*tōō*-tah) *f* prostitute

protagonista (proa-tah-goa-*nee*-stah) *m* protagonist

***proteggere** (proa-*tehd*-jay-ray) *v* protect

proteina (proa-tay-*ee*-nah) *f* protein

protesta (proa-*teh*-stah) *f* protest

protestante (proa-tay-*stahn*-tay) *adj* Protestant

protestare (proa-tay-*staa*-ray) *v* protest

protezione (proa-tay-*tsyōā*-nay) *f* protection

protuberanza (proa-too-bay-*rahn*-tsah) *f* lump

prova (*praw*-vah) *f* trial, experiment, test; evidence, token, proof; rehearsal; ***fare le prove** rehearse; **in ~** on approval

provare (proa-*vaa*-ray) *v* attempt, test; prove; experience; try on

provenienza (proa-vay-*ñehn*-tsah) *f* origin

***provenire da** (proa-vay-*nee*-ray) *come from; originate from

proverbio (proa-*vehr*-byoa) *m* proverb

provincia (proa-*veen*-chah) *f* province

provinciale (proa-veen-*chaa*-lay) *adj* provincial

provocare (proa-voa-*kaa*-ray) *v* cause

***provvedere** (proav-vay-*dāy*-ray) *v* provide; **~ di** furnish with

provvedimento (proav-vay-dee-*mayn*-toa) *m* measure

provvisioni (proav-vee-*zyōā*-nee) *fpl* provisions *pl*

provvisorio (proav-vee-*zaw*-ryoa) *adj* provisional, temporary

provvista (proav-*vee*-stah) *f* supply

prudente (proo-*dehn*-tay) *adj* wary

prudere (*proō*-day-ray) v itch

prurito (proo-*ree*-toa) m itch

psichiatra (psee-*kyaa*-trah) m psychiatrist

psichico (*psee*-kee-koa) adj psychic

psicoanalista (psee-koa-ah-nah-*lee*-stah) m psychoanalyst

psicologia (psee-koa-loa-*jee*-ah) f psychology

psicologico (psee-koa-*law*-jee-koa) adj psychological

psicologo (psee-*kaw*-loa-goa) m psychologist

pubblicare (poob-blee-*kaa*-ray) v publish

pubblicazione (poob-blee-kah-*tsyōa*-nay) f publication

pubblicità (poob-blee-chee-*tah*) f advertising, publicity

pubblico (*poob*-blee-koa) adj public; m public

pudore (poo-*dōa*-ray) m shame

pugno (*pōō*-ñoa) m fist; punch; **sferrare pugni** punch

pulcino (pool-*chee*-noa) m chicken

pulire (poo-*lee*-ray) v clean; ~ **a secco** dry-clean

pulito (poo-*lee*-toa) adj clean

pulitura (poo-lee-*tōō*-rah) f cleaning

pulizia (poo-lee-*tsee*-ah) f cleaning

pulpito (*pool*-pee-toa) m pulpit

pulsante (pool-*sahn*-tay) m push-button

*pungere (*poon*-jay-ray) v *sting, prick

punire (poo-*nee*-ray) v punish

punizione (poo-nee-*tsyōa*-nay) f punishment

punta (*poon*-tah) f point, tip

puntare su (poon-*taa*-ray) aim at

punteggio (poon-*tehd*-joa) m score

punto (*poon*-toa) m point; period, full stop; item, issue; stitch; ~ **decisivo** turning-point; ~ **di congelamento**

freezing-point; ~ **di partenza** starting-point; ~ **di riferimento** landmark; ~ **di vista** point of view, outlook; ~ **e virgola** semi-colon; ~ **interrogativo** question mark

puntuale (poon-*twaa*-lay) adj punctual

puntura (poon-*tōō*-rah) f bite, sting

purché (poor-*kay*) conj provided that

pure (*pōō*-ray) adv as well, also

puro (*pōō*-roa) adj clean, pure; neat, sheer

purosangue (poo-roa-*sahng*-gway) adj thoroughbred

pus (pooss) m pus

pustoletta (poo-stoa-*layt*-tah) f pimple

puttana (poot-*taa*-nah) f whore

puzzare (poot-*tsa*-ray) v *smell, *stink

puzzle (pahzl) jigsaw puzzle

puzzolente (poot-tsoa-*lehn*-tay) adj smelly

Q

qua (kwah) adv here

quadrato (kwah-*draa*-toa) adj square; m square

quadrettato (kwah-drayt-*taa*-toa) adj chequered

quadretto (kwah-*drayt*-toa) m check

quadro (*kwaa*-droa) m picture; cadre; ~ **di distribuzione** switchboard

quaglia (*kwaa*-lʸah) f quail

qualche (*kwahl*-kay) adj some

qualcosa (kwahl-*kaw*-sah) pron something

qualcuno (kwahl-*kōō*-noa) pron someone, somebody

quale (*kwaa*-lay) pron which

qualifica (kwah-*lee*-fee-kah) f qualification

qualificato (kwah-lee-fee-*kaa*-toa) adj

qualified; **non ~** unskilled

qualità (kwah-lee-tah) f quality; **di prima ~** first-rate, first-class

qualora (kwah-lōā-rah) conj when, in case

qualsiasi (kwahl-see-ah-see) adj whatever; whichever

quando (kwahn-doa) adv when; conj when

quantità (kwahn-tee-tah) f amount, quantity; number; lot

quanto (kwahn-toa) adj how much, how many

quantunque (kwahn-toong-kway) conj though

quaranta (kwah-rahn-tah) num forty

quarantena (kwah-rahn-tai-nah) f quarantine

quartiere (kwahr-tyai-ray) m district, quarter; **~ generale** headquarters pl; **~ povero** slum

quarto (kwahr-toa) num fourth; m quarter

quasi (kwaa-zee) adv almost, nearly

quattordicesimo (kwaht-toar-dee-chai-zee-moa) num fourteenth

quattordici (kwaht-tor-dee-chee) num fourteen

quattro (kwaht-troa) num four

quello[1] (kwayl-loa) pron that; **quelli** those; **~ che** what

quello[2] (kwayl-loa) adj that; **quei** adj those

quercia (kwehr-chah) f oak

questione (kway-styōā-nay) f matter, issue, question

questo (kway-stoa) adj this; **questi** these

qui (kwee) adv here

quiete (kwee-ai-tay) f stillness, quiet

quieto (kwee-ai-toa) adj quiet

quindi (kween-dee) conj therefore

quindicesimo (kween-dee-chai-zee-moa) num fifteenth

quindici (kween-dee-chee) num fifteen

quinto (kween-toa) num fifth

quota (kwaw-tah) f quota

quotidiano (kwoa-tee-dyaa-noa) adj daily; everyday; m daily

R

rabarbaro (rah-bahr-bah-roa) m rhubarb

rabbia (rahb-byah) f anger, rage; rabies

rabbioso (rahb-byōā-soa) adj mad

rabbrividire (rahb-bree-vee-dee-ray) v shiver

raccapricciante (rahk-kahp-preet-chahn-tay) adj creepy

raccapriccio (rahk-kahp-preet-choa) m horror

racchetta (rahk-kayt-tah) f racquet

*****raccogliere** (rahk-kaw-lYay-ray) v pick up; gather; collect; *****raccogliersi** gather

raccolta (rahk-kol-tah) f crop; **~ di documenti** file

raccolto (rahk-kol-toa) m harvest

raccomandare (rahk-koa-mahn-daa-ray) v recommend; register

raccomandata (rahk-koa-mahn-daa-tah) f registered letter

raccomandazione (rahk-koa-mahn-dah-tsyōā-nay) f recommendation

raccontare (rahk-koan-taa-ray) v relate; *****tell

racconto (rahk-koan-toa) m story, tale; **~ a fumetti** comics pl

raccorciare (rahk-koar-chaa-ray) v shorten; trim

*****radere** (raa-day-ray) v shave

radiatore (rah-dyah-tōā-ray) m radiator

radicale (rah-dee-kaa-lay) adj radical

radice (rah-*dee*-chay) f root

radio (*raa*-dyoa) f wireless, radio

radiografare (rah-dyoa-grah-*faa*-ray) v X-ray

radiografia (rah-dyoa-grah-*fee*-ah) f X-ray

raduno (rah-*dōō*-noa) m rally

radura (rah-*dōō*-rah) f clearing

rafano (*raa*-fah-noa) m horseradish

raffermo (rahf-*fayr*-moa) adj stale

raffica (*rahf*-fee-kah) f gust, blow

raffigurare (rahf-fee-goo-*raa*-ray) v represent

raffineria (rahf-fee-nay-*ree*-ah) f refinery; ~ **di petrolio** oil-refinery

raffreddore (rahf-frayd-*dōā*-ray) m cold; *prendere un ~ catch a cold

ragazza (rah-*gaht*-tsah) f girl

ragazzino (rah-gaht-*tsee*-noa) m boy

ragazzo (rah-*gaht*-tsoa) m lad, boy

raggio (*rahd*-joa) m beam, ray; radius; spoke

*raggiungere** (rahd-*joon*-jay-ray) v attain, achieve, reach

raggiungibile (rahd-joon-*jee*-bee-lay) adj attainable

ragguaglio (rahg-*gwaa*-lʸoa) m information

ragionamento (rah-joa-nah-*mayn*-toa) m reasoning

ragionare (rah-joa-*naa*-ray) v reason

ragione (rah-*jōā*-nay) f reason, wits pl, sense; cause; *avere ~* be right

ragionevole (rah-joa-*nāy*-voa-lay) adj reasonable; sensible

ragnatela (rah-ñah-*tāy*-lah) f cobweb, spider's web

ragno (*raa*-ñoa) m spider

raion (*raa*-yoan) m rayon

rallegrare (rahl-lay-*graa*-ray) v cheer up

rallentare (rahl-layn-*taa*-ray) v slow down

rame (*raa*-may) m copper

rammendare (rahm-mayn-*daa*-ray) v mend, darn

rammentare (rahm-mayn-*taa*-ray) v remind of; **rammentarsi** remember

ramo (*raa*-moa) m branch, bough

ramoscello (rah-moash-*shehl*-loa) m twig

rampa (*rahm*-pah) f ramp

rana (*raa*-nah) f frog

rancido (*rahn*-chee-doa) adj rancid

randello (rahn-*dehl*-loa) m cudgel

rapida (*raa*-pee-dah) f rapids pl

rapidità (rah-pee-dee-*tah*) f speed

rapido (*raa*-pee-doa) adj fast; swift, rapid

rapina (rah-*pee*-nah) f robbery, hold-up

rappezzare (rahp-payt-*tsaa*-ray) v patch

rapporto (rahp-*por*-toa) m report; affair, intercourse

rappresentante (rahp-pray-zayn-*tahn*-tay) m agent

rappresentanza (rahp-pray-zayn-*tahn*-tsah) f representation

rappresentare (rahp-pray-zayn-*taa*-ray) v represent

rappresentativo (rahp-pray-zayn-tah-*tee*-voa) adj representative

rappresentazione (rahp-pray-zayn-tah-*tsyōā*-nay) f performance, show; ~ **di marionette** puppet-show; ~ **teatrale** play

raramente (rah-rah-*mayn*-tay) adv seldom, rarely

raro (*raa*-roa) adj uncommon, rare

raschiare (rah-*skyaa*-ray) v scrape

raso (*raa*-soa) m satin

rasoio (rah-*sōā*-yoa) m safety-razor, razor; ~ **elettrico** electric razor; shaver

raspare (rah-*spaa*-ray) v grate

rassegna (rahss-*sāy*-ñah) f survey

rassomiglianza (rahss-soa-mee-lʸahntsah) f similarity

rastrello (rah-*strehl*-loa) m (pl ~n) rake

rata (*raa*-tah) f instalment

ratto (*raht*-toa) m rat

rauco (*rou*-koa) adj hoarse

ravanello (rah-vah-*nehl*-loa) m radish

razione (rah-tsyō*a*-nay) f ration

razza (*raht*-tsah) f breed, race

razziale (raht-*tsyaa*-lay) adj racial

razzo (*raht*-tsoa) m rocket

re (ray) m (pl ~) king

reale (ray-*aa*-lay) adj true, factual, actual, substantial, real; royal

realizzabile (ray-ah-leed-*dzaa*-bee-lay) adj feasible, realizable

realizzare (ray-ah-leed-*dzaa*-ray) v realize

realtà (ray-ahl-*tah*) f reality; **in** ~ actually, in effect; really

reato (ray-*aa*-toa) m offence

reazione (ray-ah-tsyō*a*-nay) f reaction

recapitare (ray-kah-pee-*taa*-ray) v deliver

recare (ray-*kaa*-ray) v *bring; cause; **recarsi** *go

recensione (ray-chayn-*syō*ā-nay) f review

recente (ray-*chehn*-tay) adj recent; **di** ~ recently

recentemente (ray-chayn-tay-*mayn*-tay) adv lately, recently

recessione (ray-chayss-*syōā*-nay) f recession

recinto (ray-*cheen*-toa) m fence

recipiente (ray-chee-*pyehn*-tay) m container, vessel

reciproco (ray-*chee*-proa-koa) adj mutual

recital (ray-see-*tahl*) m recital

recitare (ray-chee-*taa*-ray) v act

reclamare (ray-klah-*maa*-ray) v claim

recluta (*ray*-kloo-tah) f recruit

redattore (ray-daht-*tōā*-ray) m editor

reddito (*rehd*-dee-toa) m revenue, income; **redditi** earnings pl

*****redigere** (ray-*dee*-jay-ray) v *draw up

*****redimere** (ray-*dee*-may-ray) v redeem

refe (*rāy*-fay) m thread

referenza (ray-fay-*rehn*-tsah) f reference

regalo (ray-*gaa*-loa) m gift, present

regata (ray-*gaa*-tah) f regatta

*****reggersi** (*rehd*-jayr-see) v *hold on

reggicalze (rayd-jee-*kahl*-tsay) m suspender belt; garter belt *Am*

reggipetto (rayd-jee-*peht*-toa) m brassiere, bra

reggiseno (rayd-jee-*sāy*-noa) m brassiere, bra

regia (ray-*jee*-ah) f direction

regime (ray-*jee*-may) m rule, régime

regina (ray-*jee*-nah) f queen

regionale (ray-joa-*naa*-lay) adj regional

regione (ray-*jōā*-nay) f region; country, district

regista (ray-*jee*-stah) m director

registrare (ray-jee-*straa*-ray) v record, book; **registrarsi** register, check in

registrazione (ray-jee-strah-*tsyōā*-nay) f registration; record, entry; recording

regnare (ray-*ñaa*-ray) v reign

regno (*rāy*-ñoa) m kingdom; reign

regola (*rai*-goa-lah) f rule

regolamentazione (ray-goa-lah-*mayn*-tah-*tsyōā*-nay) f regulation

regolamento (ray-goa-lah-*mayn*-toa) m regulation

regolare (ray-goa-*laa*-ray) adj regular; v regulate; adjust; **regolato** regular

relativo (ray-lah-*tee*-voa) adj relative; comparative

relazione (ray-lah-*tsyōā*-nay) f relation; reference, connection; report; **in** ~ **a** regarding

religione (ray-lee-*jōā*-nay) f religion

religioso (ray-lee-jōā-soa) *adj* religious

reliquia (ray-*lee*-kwee-ah) *f* relic

relitto (ray-*leet*-toa) *m* wreck

remare (ray-*maa*-ray) *v* row

remo (*rai*-moa) *m* oar; paddle

remoto (ray-*maw*-toa) *adj* remote, out of the way

****rendere** (*rehn*-day-ray) *v* reimburse; **pay; ~ **conto di** account for; ~ **omaggio** honour

rene (*rai*-nay) *m* kidney

renna (*rehn*-nah) *f* reindeer

reparto (ray-*pahr*-toa) *m* section, division

repellente (ray-payl-*lehn*-tay) *adj* repellent

repertorio (ray-payr-*taw*-ryoa) *m* repertory

****reprimere** (ray-*pree*-may-ray) *v* suppress

repubblica (ray-*poob*-blee-kah) *f* republic

repubblicano (ray-poob-blee-*kaa*-noa) *adj* republican

reputare (ray-poo-*taa*-ray) *v* consider

reputazione (ray-poo-tah-*tsyōā*-nay) *f* fame, reputation

resa (*rāy*-sah) *f* surrender

residente (ray-see-*dehn*-tay) *adj* resident; *m* resident

residenza (ray-see-*dehn*-tsah) *f* residence

residuo (ray-*see*-dwoa) *m* remnant, remainder

resina (*rai*-zee-nah) *f* resin

resistenza (ray-see-*stehn*-tsah) *f* resistance; strength

resistere (ray-*see*-stay-ray) *v* resist

resoconto (ray-soa-*koan*-toa) *m* account

****respingere** (ray-*speen*-jay-ray) *v* turn down, reject

respirare (ray-spee-*raa*-ray) *v* breathe

respiratore (ray-spee-rah-*tōā*-ray) *m* snorkel

respirazione (ray-spee-rah-*tsyōā*-nay) *f* respiration, breathing

respiro (ray-*spee*-roa) *m* breath

responsabile (ray-spoan-*saa*-bee-lay) *adj* responsible; liable

responsabilità (ray-spoan-sah-bee-lee-*tah*) *f* responsibility; liability

restare (ray-*staa*-ray) *v* remain

restauro (ray-*stou*-roa) *m* repair

restio (ray-*stee*-oa) *adj* unwilling

resto (*reh*-stoa) *m* rest; remnant, remainder

****restringersi** (ray-*streen*-jayr-see) *v *shrink; tighten

restrizione (ray-stree-*tsyōā*-nay) *f* restriction, qualification

rete (*rāy*-tay) *f* net; network; goal; ~ **da pesca** fishing net; ~ **stradale** road system

reticella (ray-tee-*chehl*-lah) *f* hair-net

retina (*rai*-tee-nah) *f* retina

rettangolare (rayt-tahng-goa-*laa*-ray) *adj* rectangular

rettangolo (rayt-*tahng*-goa-loa) *m* rectangle, oblong

rettifica (rayt-*tee*-fee-kah) *f* correction

rettile (*reht*-tee-lay) *m* reptile

retto (*reht*-toa) *adj* right; *m* rectum

reumatismo (ray∞-mah-*tee*-zmoa) *m* rheumatism

revisionare (ray-vee-zyoa-*naa*-ray) *v* revise, overhaul

revisione (ray-vee-*zyōā*-nay) *f* revision

revocare (ray-voa-*kaa*-ray) *v* recall

rialzo (*ryahl*-tsoa) *m* rise

riassunto (ryahss-*soon*-toa) *m* résumé

ribassare (ree-bahss-*saa*-ray) *v* lower

ribasso (ree-*bahss*-soa) *m* reduction

ribellione (ree-bayl-*lʸōā*-nay) *f* revolt, rebellion

ribes (*ree*-bayss) *m* currant; ~ **nero** black-currant

ributtante (ree-boot-*tahn*-tay) *adj*

creepy, repulsive

ricamare (ree-kah-*maa*-ray) v embroider

ricambio (ree-*kahm*-byoa) m refill

ricamo (ree-*kaa*-moa) m embroidery

ricchezza (reek-*kayt*-tsah) f riches pl, wealth, fortune

riccio (*reet*-choa) m hedgehog; ~ **di mare** sea-urchin

ricciolo (*reet*-choa-loa) m curl; wave

ricciuto (reet-*chōō*-toa) adj curly

ricco (*reek*-koa) adj rich, wealthy

ricerca (ree-*chehr*-kah) f research; search

ricetta (ree-*cheht*-tah) f prescription; recipe

ricevere (ree-*chāy*-vay-ray) v receive

ricevimento (ree-chay-vee-*mayn*-toa) m reception, receipt; **capo ufficio** ~ receptionist

ricevitore (ree-chay-vee-*tōā*-ray) m receiver

ricevuta (ree-chay-*vōō*-tah) f receipt; voucher

richiamare (ree-kyah-*maa*-ray) v recall

richiamo (ree-*kiæħa*-moa) m recall m; allurement; cross-reference

* **richiedere** (ree-*kyai*-day-ray) v request; demand

richiesta (ree-*kyeh*-stah) f request; application

richiesto (ree-*keeeh*-stoa) adj requisite

riciclabile (ree-chee-*klah*-bee-lay) adj recyclable

riciclare (ree-chee-*klah*-ray) v recycle

ricominciare (ree-koa-meen-*chaa*-ray) v recommence

ricompensa (ree-koam-*pehn*-sah) f reward, prize

ricompensare (ree-koam-payn-*saa*-ray) v reward

riconciliazione (ree-koan-chee-lyah-*tsyōā*-nay) f reconciliation

riconoscente (ree-koa-noash-*shehn*-tay) adj grateful, thankful

* **riconoscere** (ree-koa-*noash*-shay-ray) v recognize; acknowledge; admit, confess

riconoscimento (ree-koa-noash-shee-*mayn*-toa) m recognition

ricordare (ree-koar-*daa*-ray) v remember; *think of; *far ~ remind; **ricordarsi** recollect, remember, recall

ricordo (ree-*kor*-doa) m memory, remembrance; souvenir

* **ricorrere** (ree-*koar*-ray-ray) v recur; appeal; ~ **a** apply to

ricostruire (ree-koa-*strwee*-ray) v *rebuild; reconstruct

ricreazione (ree-kray-ah-*tsyōā*-nay) f recreation

ricuperare (ree-koo-pay-*raa*-ray) v recover

ricusare (ree-koo-*zaa*-ray) v deny

ridacchiare (ree-dahk-*kyaa*-ray) v giggle, chuckle

* **ridere** (*ree*-day-ray) v laugh

ridicolizzare (ree-dee-koa-leed-*dzaa*-ray) v ridicule

ridicolo (ree-*dee*-koa-loa) adj ridiculous, ludicrous

ridondante (ree-doan-*dahn*-tay) adj redundant

ridotto (ree-*doat*-toa) m lobby, foyer

* **ridurre** (ree-*door*-ray) v reduce, *cut

riduzione (ree-doo-*tsyōā*-nay) f discount, reduction, rebate

rieducazione (ryay-doo-kah-*tsyōā*-nay) f rehabilitation

riempire (ryaym-*pee*-ray) v fill

rientrare (ræħyn-*traa*-ray) v return; ~ **in** *be part of

riferimento (ree-fay-ree-*mayn*-toa) m reference

riferire (ree-fay-*ree*-ray) v report

rifiutare (ree-fyoo-*taa*-ray) v deny, refuse; reject

rifiuto (ree-*fyōō*-toa) m refusal; **rifiuti** litter

riflessione (ree-flayss-syōā-nay) f deliberation

riflesso (ree-flehss-soa) m reflection

***riflettere¹** (ree-fleht-tay-ray) v (pp riflesso) reflect

***riflettere²** (ree-fleht-tay-ray) v (pp riflettuto) *think

riflettore (ree-flayt-tōā-ray) m searchlight; reflector

riforma (ree-foar-mah) f reformation

rifornimento (ree-foar-nee-mayn-toa) m supply

rifugiarsi (ree-foo-jahr-see) v *seek refuge

rifugio (ree-fōō-joa) m cover, shelter

riga (ree-gah) f line; ruler

rigettare (ree-jayt-taa-ray) v reject; vomit

rigido (ree-jee-doa) adj stiff; bleak; strict

rigirarsi (ree-jee-rahr-see) v turn round

rigoroso (ree-goa-rōā-soa) adj severe

riguardare (ree-gwahr-daa-ray) v concern, affect; **per quanto riguarda** as regards; **riguardante** concerning

riguardo (ree-gwahr-doa) m regard, consideration; ~ **a** regarding; concerning, with reference to

riguardoso (ree-gwahr-dōā-soa) adj considerate

rilassamento (ree-lahss-sah-mayn-toa) m relaxation

rilassarsi (ree-lahss-sahr-see) v relax

rilevante (ree-lay-vahn-tay) adj important

rilevare (ree-lay-vaa-ray) v notice; collect, pick up; *take over

rilievo (ree-lʸai-voa) m relief; importance

rima (ree-mah) f rhyme

rimandare (ree-mahn-daa-ray) v postpone; ~ **a** refer to

rimanente (ree-mah-nehn-tay) adj remaining

rimanenza (ree-mah-nehn-tsah) f remnant

***rimanere** (ree-mah-nāy-ray) v stay, remain

rimborsare (reem-boar-saa-ray) v reimburse, refund, *repay

rimborso (reem-boar-soa) m refund, repayment

rimedio (ree-māy-dyoa) m remedy

rimessa (ree-mayss-sah) f remittance; garage; ***mettere in** ~ garage

***rimettere** (ree-mayt-tay-ray) v remit

rimorchiare (ree-moar-kyaa-ray) v tug

rimorchiatore (ree-moar-kyah-tōā-ray) m tug

rimorchio (ree-mor-kyoa) m trailer

***rimpiangere** (reem-pyahn-jay-ray) v regret; miss

rimpianto (reem-pyahn-toa) m regret

rimproverare (reem-proa-vay-raa-ray) v reproach, reprimand; blame

rimprovero (reem-praw-vay-roa) m reproach

rimunerare (ree-moo-nay-raa-ray) v remunerate

rimunerativo (ree-moo-nay-rah-tee-voa) adj paying

rimunerazione (ree-moo-nay-rah-tsyōā-nay) f remuneration

rincasare (reeng-kah-saa-ray) v *go home

***rinchiudere** (reeng-kyōō-day-ray) v *shut in

rinfrescare (reen-fray-skaa-ray) v refresh

rinfresco (reen-fray-skoa) m refreshment

ringhiera (reeng-gyai-rah) f banisters pl, rail

ringraziare (reeng-grah-tsyaa-ray) v thank

rinnovare (reen-noa-vaa-ray) v renew

rinoceronte (ree-noa-chay-roan-tay) m rhinoceros

rinomanza (ree-noa-*mahn*-tsah) f fame

rinorragia (ree-noar-rah-*jee*-ah) f nosebleed

rintracciare (reen-traht-*chaa*-ray) v trace

rinviare (reen-*vyaa*-ray) v *send back; adjourn, *put off

rinvio (reen-*vee*-oa) m delay

riordinare (ryoar-dee-*naa*-ray) v tidy up

riparare (ree-pah-*raa*-ray) v shelter; mend, repair, fix

riparazione (ree-pah-rah-tsyō*a*-nay) f reparation

riparo (ree-*paa*-roa) m shelter; screen

ripartire (ree-pahr-*tee*-ray) v divide

riparto (ree-*pahr*-toa) m department

ripensare (ree-payn-*saa*-ray) v *think over

ripetere (ree-*pai*-tay-ray) v repeat

ripetizione (ree-pay-tee-tsyō*a*-nay) f repetition

ripetutamente (ree-pay-too-tah-*mayn*-tay) adv again and again

ripido (*ree*-pee-doa) adj steep

ripieno (ree-*pyai*-noa) adj stuffed; m filling; stuffing

riportare (ree-poar-*taa*-ray) v *bring back

riposante (ree-poa-*sahn*-tay) adj restful

riposarsi (ree-poa-*sahr*-see) v rest

riposo (ree-*paw*-soa) m rest

*riprendere (ree-*prehn*-day-ray) v resume

ripresa (ree-*prāy*-sah) f round

ripristino (ree-pree-*stee*-noa) m revival

*riprodurre (ree-proa-*door*-ray) v reproduce

riproduzione (ree-proa-doo-tsyō*a*-nay) f reproduction

riprovare (ree-proa-*vaa*-ray) v scold

ripugnante (ree-poo-*ñahn*-tay) adj repellent

ripugnanza (ree-poo-*ñahn*-tsah) f dislike

risarcimento (ree-sahr-chee-*mayn*-toa) m indemnity

risata (ree-*saa*-tah) f laughter

riscaldamento (ree-skahl-dah-*mayn*-toa) m heating

riscaldatore (ree-skahl-dah-tō*a*-ray) m heater

riscatto (ree-*skaht*-toa) m ransom

rischiare (ree-*skyaa*-ray) v risk

rischio (*ree*-skyoa) m risk; chance, hazard

rischioso (ree-*skyoa*-soa) adj risky

*riscuotere (ree-*skwaw*-tay-ray) v cash, raise

risentirsi per (ree-sayn-*teer*-see) resent

riserva (ree-*sehr*-vah) f reserve; store; qualification; di ~ spare; ~ di selvaggina game reserve

riservare (ree-sayr-*vaa*-ray) v reserve, engage

riservato (ree-sayr-*vaa*-toa) adj reserved; modest

riso¹ (*ree*-soa) m laugh

riso² (*ree*-soa) m rice

risoluto (ree-soa-*lōō*-toa) adj determined, resolute

*risolvere (ree-*sol*-vay-ray) v solve

risparmi (ree-*spahr*-mee) mpl savings pl

risparmiare (ree-spahr-*myaa*-ray) v save

rispedire (ree-spay-*dee*-ray) v *send back

rispettabile (ree-spayt-*taa*-bee-lay) adj respectable

rispettare (ree-spayt-*taa*-ray) v respect

rispettivo (ree-spayt-*tee*-voa) adj respective

rispetto (ree-*speht*-toa) m esteem, respect

rispettoso (ree-spayt-tō*a*-soa) adj respectful

risplendere (ree-*splehn*-day-ray) v *shine

*__rispondere__ (ree-*spoan*-day-ray) v answer; reply

risposta (ree-*spoa*-stah) f answer, reply; **in ~** in reply; **senza ~** unanswered

ristorante (ree-stoa-*rahn*-tay) m restaurant

risultare (ree-sool-*taa*-ray) v result; appear

risultato (ree-sool-*taa*-toa) m result; issue, effect, outcome

risvolta (ree-*svol*-tah) f lapel

ritardare (ree-tahr-*daa*-ray) v delay

ritardo (ree-*tahr*-doa) m delay; **in ~** late, overdue

*__ritenere__ (ree-tay-*nāy*-ray) v consider

ritirare (ree-tee-*raa*-ray) v *withdraw; *draw

ritmo (*reet*-moa) m rhythm

ritornare (ree-toar-*naa*-ray) v turn back, return

ritorno (ree-*toar*-noa) m return; way back; **andata e ~** round trip *Am*

ritratto (ree-*traht*-toa) m portrait

ritrovare (ree-troa-*vaa*-ray) v recover, *find back

ritto (*reet*-toa) adj erect

riunione (ryoo-*nyōā*-nay) f assembly, meeting

riunire (ryoo-*nee*-ray) v reunite; assemble; join

*__riuscire__ (ryoosh-*shee*-ray) v manage, succeed; *make; **riuscito** successful

riva (*ree*-vah) f bank, shore; **~ del mare** seashore

rivale (ree-*vaa*-lay) m rival

rivaleggiare (ree-vah-layd-*jaa*-ray) v rival

rivalità (ree-vah-lee-*tah*) f rivalry

*__rivedere__ (ree-vay-*dāy*-ray) v check

rivelare (ree-vay-*laa*-ray) v reveal

rivelazione (ree-vay-lah-*tsyōā*-nay) f revelation

rivendicare (ree-vayn-dee-*kaa*-ray) v claim

rivendicazione (ree-vayn-dee-kah-*tsyōā*-nay) f claim

rivenditore (ree-vayn-dee-*tōā*-ray) m retailer

rivista (ree-*vee*-stah) f magazine, review; revue; **~ mensile** monthly magazine

*__rivolgersi a__ (ree-*vol*-jayr-see) address

rivolgimento (ree-voal-jee-*mayn*-toa) m reverse

rivolta (ree-*vol*-tah) f revolt, rebellion

rivoltante (ree-voal-*tahn*-tay) adj revolting

rivoltarsi (ree-voal-*tahr*-see) v revolt

rivoltella (ree-voal-*tehl*-lah) f gun, revolver

rivoluzionario (ree-voa-loo-tsyoa-*naa*-ryoa) adj revolutionary

rivoluzione (ree-voa-loo-*tsyōā*-nay) f revolution

roba (*raw*-bah) f stuff

robaccia (roa-*baht*-chah) f trash

robusto (roa-*boo*-stoa) adj robust, solid, strong

roccaforte (roak-kah-*for*-tay) f stronghold

rocchetto (roak-*kayt*-toa) m spool

roccia (*rot*-chah) f rock

roccioso (roat-*chōā*-soa) adj rocky

roco (*raw*-koa) adj hoarse

Romania (roa-mah-*nee*-ah) f Rumania

romantico (roa-*mahn*-tee-koa) adj romantic

romanziere (roa-mahn-*dzyai*-ray) m novelist

romanzo (roa-*mahn*-dzoa) m novel; **~ a puntate** serial; **~ poliziesco** detective story

rombo¹ (*roam*-boa) m roar

rombo² (*roam*-boa) m brill

romeno (roa-*mai*-noa) adj Rumanian;

m Rumanian

*rompere (*roam*-pay-ray) *v* *break

rompicapo (roam-pee-*kaa*-poa) *m* puzzle

rondine (*roan*-dee-nay) *f* swallow

rosa (*raw*-zah) *f* rose; *adj* rose, pink

rosario (roa-*zaa*-ryoa) *m* rosary, beads *pl*

rosolaccio (roa-zoa-*laht*-choa) *m* poppy

rospo (*ro*-spoa) *m* toad

rossetto (roass-*sayt*-toa) *f* lipstick; rouge

rosso (*roass*-soa) *adj* red

rosticceria (roa-steet-chay-*ree*-ah) *f* grill-room

rotabile (roa-*taa*-bee-lay) *f* carriage-way; roadway *nAm*

rotolare (roa-toa-*laa*-ray) *v* roll

rotolo (*raw*-toa-loa) *m* roll

rotonda (roa-*toan*-dah) *f* roundabout

rotondo (roa-*toan*-doa) *adj* round

rotta (*roat*-tah) *f* route; course

rotto (*roat*-toa) *adj* broken

rottura (roat-*tōō*-rah) *f* break

rotula (*raw*-too-lah) *f* kneecap

roulette (roo-*leht*) *f* roulette

roulotte (roo-*lot*-tay) *f* trailer *nAm*

rovesciare (roa-vaysh-*shaa*-ray) *v* *spill, knock over; *overthrow; turn inside out; **rovesciarsi** over-turn

rovescio (roa-*vehsh*-shoa) *m* reverse; **alla rovescia** the other way round; inside out

rovina (roa-*vee*-nah) *f* destruction, ruination, ruin; **rovine** ruins

rovinare (roa-vee-*naa*-ray) *v* ruin

rozzo (*road*-dzoa) *adj* gross

rubare (roo-*baa*-ray) *v* *steal; rob

rubinetto (roo-bee-*nayt*-toa) *m* tap; faucet *nAm*

rubino (roo-*bee*-noa) *m* ruby

rubrica (roo-*bree*-kah) *f* column

ruga (*rōō*-gah) *f* wrinkle

ruggine (*rood*-jee-nay) *f* rust

ruggire (rood-*jee*-ray) *v* roar

ruggito (rood-*jee*-toa) *m* roar

rugiada (roo-*jaa*-dah) *f* dew

rumore (roo-*mōa*-ray) *m* noise

rumoroso (roo-moa-*rōa*-soa) *adj* noisy

ruota (*rwaw*-tah) *f* wheel; ~ **di ricam-bio** spare wheel

rurale (roo-*raa*-lay) *adj* rural

ruscello (roosh-*shehl*-loa) *m* brook, stream

russare (rooss-*saa*-ray) *v* snore

Russia (*rooss*-syah) *f* Russia

russo (*rooss*-soa) *adj* Russian; *m* Russian

rustico (*roo*-stee-koa) *adj* rustic

ruvido (*rōō*-vee-doa) *adj* uneven

S

sabato (*saa*-bah-toa) *m* Saturday

sabbia (*sahb*-byah) *f* sand

sabbioso (sahb-*byōa*-soa) *adj* sandy

saccarina (sahk-kah-*ree*-nah) *f* saccharin

sacchetto (sahk-*kayt*-toa) *m* paper bag; pouch

sacco (*sahk*-koa) *m* bag, sack; ~ **a pe-lo** sleeping-bag

sacerdote (sah-chayr-*daw*-tay) *m* priest

sacrificare (sah-kree-fee-*kaa*-ray) *v* sac-rifice

sacrificio (sah-kree-*fee*-choa) *m* sacri-fice

sacrilegio (sah-kree-*lai*-joa) *m* sacri-lege

sacro (*saa*-kroa) *adj* sacred

saggezza (sahd-*jayt*-tsah) *f* wisdom

saggiare (sahd-*jaa*-ray) *v* test

saggio (*sahd*-joa) *adj* wise; *m* essay

sagrestano (sah-gray-*staa*-noa) *m* sexton

sala (saa-lah) f hall; ~ **da ballo** ballroom; ~ **da banchetto** banqueting-hall; ~ **da concerti** concert hall; ~ **da pranzo** dining-room; ~ **d'aspetto** waiting-room; ~ **da tè** tea-shop; ~ **di esposizione** showroom; ~ **di lettura** reading-room; ~ **per fumatori** smoking-room

salariato (sah-lah-ryaa-toa) m employee

salario (sah-laa-ryoa) m salary, pay

salassare (sah-lahss-saa-ray) v *bleed

salato (sah-laa-toa) adj salty

saldare (sahl-daa-ray) v weld, solder; *pay off

saldatore (sahl-dah-toa-ray) m soldering-iron

saldatura (sahl-dah-too-rah) f joint

saldo (sahl-doa) adj firm; m balance; **saldi** sales

sale (saa-lay) m salt; **sali da bagno** bath salts

saliera (sah-lyai-rah) f salt-cellar

***salire** (sah-lee-ray) v ascend; *rise, increase

saliva (sah-lee-vah) f spit

salmone (sahl-moa-nay) m salmon

salone (sah-loa-nay) m salon; lounge; ~ **di bellezza** beauty salon, beauty parlour

salotto (sah-lot-toa) m drawing-room, living-room; **salottino di prova** fitting room

salsa (sahl-sah) f sauce

salsiccia (sahl-seet-chah) f sausage

saltare (sahl-taa-ray) v jump

saltellare (sahl-tayl-laa-ray) v skip, hop

saltello (sahl-tehl-loa) m hop

salto (sahl-toa) m leap, jump

salubre (sah-loo-bray) adj wholesome

salutare (sah-loo-taa-ray) v greet; salute

salute (sah-loo-tay) f health

saluto (sah-loo-toa) m greeting

salvare (sahl-vaa-ray) v save, rescue

salvataggio (sahl-vah-tahd-joa) m rescue; **cintura di** ~ lifebelt

salvatore (sahl-vah-toa-ray) m saviour

salvo (sahl-voa) prep except

sanatorio (sah-nah-taw-ryoa) m sanatorium

sandalo (sahn-dah-loa) m sandal

sangue (sahng-gway) m blood

sanguinare (sahng-gwee-naa-ray) v *bleed

sanitario (sah-nee-taa-ryoa) adj sanitary

sano (saa-noa) adj healthy; well

santo (sahn-toa) adj holy; m saint

santuario (sahn-twaa-ryoa) m shrine

***sapere** (sah-pay-ray) v.taste; *know; *be able to

sapone (sah-poa-nay) m soap; ~ **da barba** shaving-soap; ~ **in polvere** soap powder

sapore (sah-poa-ray) m taste

saporito (sah-poa-ree-toa) adj savoury, tasty

sardina (sahr-dee-nah) f sardine

sarta (sahr-tah) f dressmaker

sarto (sahr-toa) m tailor

sasso (sahss-soa) m stone

satellite (sah-tehl-lee-tay) m satellite

saudita (sou-dee-tah) adj Saudi Arabian

sauna (sou-nah) f sauna

sbadigliare (zbah-dee-lyaa-ray) v yawn

sbagliarsi (zbah-lyahr-see) v *be mistaken

sbagliato (zbah-lyaa-toa) adj false, wrong; misplaced

sbaglio (zbaa-lyoa) m mistake, error

sbalordire (zbah-loar-dee-ray) v astonish

sbarcare (zbahr-kaa-ray) v land, disembark

sbarra (zbahr-rah) f bar; rail

sbattere (zbaht-tay-ray) v slam; whip

sbiadire (zbyah-dee-ray) v fade

sbottonare (zboat-toa-naa-ray) v unbutton

sbucciare (zboot-chaa-ray) v peel

scaccato (skahk-kaa-toa) adj chequered

scacchi (skahk-kee) mpl chess

scacchiera (skahk-kyai-rah) f draughtboard; checkerboard nAm

scacciare (skaht-chaa-ray) v chase

scacco! (skahk-koa) check!

scadente (skah-dehn-tay) adj poor

scadenza (skah-dehn-tsah) f expiry

*__scadere__ (skah-dāy-ray) v expire

scaffale (skahf-faa-lay) m shelf

scala (skaa-lah) f stairs pl, staircase; ladder; scale; ~ di sicurezza fire-escape; ~ mobile escalator; ~ musicale scale

scaldare (skahl-daa-ray) v warm, heat; scaldacqua ad immersione immersion heater

scalfire (skahl-fee-ray) v scratch

scalfittura (skahl-feet-tōō-rah) f scratch

scalino (skah-lee-noa) m step

scalo (skaa-loa) m dock

scalpello (skahl-pehl-loa) m chisel

scalpore (skahl-pōā-ray) m fuss

scambiare (skahm-byaa-ray) v exchange

scambio (skahm-byoa) m exchange; points pl

scandalo (skahn-dah-loa) m scandal; offence

Scandinavia (skahn-dee-naa-vyah) f Scandinavia

scandinavo (skahn-dee-naa-voa) adj Scandinavian; m Scandinavian

scappamento (skahp-pah-mayn-toa) m exhaust

scappare (skahp-paa-ray) v escape; slip

scarabeo (skah-rah-bai-oa) m beetle

scaricare (skah-ree-kaa-ray) v discharge, unload

scarlatto (skahr-laht-toa) adj scarlet

scarpa (skahr-pah) f shoe; lucido per scarpe shoe polish; scarpe da ginnastica gym shoes, plimsolls pl; sneakers plAm; scarpe da tennis tennis shoes; stringa per scarpe shoe-lace

scarrozzata (skahr-roat-tsaa-tah) f drive

scarsamente (skahr-sah-mayn-tay) adv scarcely

scarsezza (skahr-sayt-tsah) f want

scarso (skahr-soa) adj scarce; slight, small

scartare (skahr-taa-ray) v discard

scassinare (skahss-see-naa-ray) v burgle

scassinatore (skahss-see-nah-tōā-ray) m burglar

scatola (skaa-toa-lah) f box; ~ di colori paint-box; ~ di fiammiferi match-box

scatolone (skah-toa-lōā-nay) m carton

scavare (skah-vaa-ray) v *dig

scavo (skaa-voa) m excavation

*__scegliere__ (shai-lʸay-ray) v *choose; pick, select; elect

scellerato (shayl-lay-raa-toa) adj wicked

scelta (shayl-tah) f choice; pick, selection

scelto (shayl-toa) adj select

scena (shai-nah) f scene; stage

scenario (shay-naa-ryoa) m setting

*__scendere__ (shayn-day-ray) v descend; *get off

scheggia (skayd-jah) f splinter, chip

scheggiare (skayd-jaa-ray) v chip

scheletro (skai-lay-troa) m skeleton

schema (skai-mah) m scheme; diagram

schermo (*skayr*-moa) *m* screen

scherno (*skayr*-noa) *m* scorn

scherzare (skayr-*tsaa*-ray) *v* joke

scherzo (*skayr*-tsoa) *m* joke; fun

schiaccianoci (skyaht-chah-*nōā*-chee) *m* nutcrackers *pl*

schiacciare (skyaht-*chaa*-ray) *v* mash; press; overwhelm

schiaffeggiare (skyahf-fayd-*jaa*-ray) *v* slap

schiaffo (*skyahf*-foa) *m* slap

schiarimento (skyah-ree-*mayn*-toa) *m* explanation

schiavo (*skyaa*-voa) *m* slave

schioccare (skyoak-*kaa*-ray) *v* crack

schiocco (skyok-koa) *m* crack

schiuma (*skyōō*-mah) *f* lather, foam, froth

schivo (*skee*-voa) *adj* shy

schizzare (skeet-*tsaa*-ray) *v* splash

schizzo (*skeet*-tsoa) *m* sketch

sci (shee) *m* ski; skiing; **scarponi da ~** ski boots; **~ d'acqua** water ski

sciacquare (shahk-*kwaa*-ray) *v* rinse

sciacquata (shahk-*kwaa*-tah) *f* rinse

sciagura (shah-*gōō*-rah) *f* disaster

scialle (*shahl*-lay) *m* scarf, shawl

sciare (*shyaa*-ray) *v* ski

sciarpa (*shahr*-pah) *f* scarf

sciatore (shyah-*tōā*-ray) *m* skier

sciatto (*shaht*-toa) *adj* slovenly

scientifico (shayn-*tee*-fee-koa) *adj* scientific

scienza (*shehn*-tsah) *f* science

scienziato (shayn-*tsyaa*-toa) *m* scientist

scimmia (*sheem*-myah) *f* monkey

scintilla (sheen-*teel*-lah) *f* spark

scintillante (sheen-teel-*lahn*-tay) *adj* sparkling

scintillare (sheen-teel-*laa*-ray) *v* *shine

sciocchezza (shoak-*kayt*-tsah) *f* rubbish, nonsense

sciocco (*shok*-koa) *adj* crazy, foolish,
silly; *m* fool

* **sciogliere** (shaw-*lʸay*-ray) *v* dissolve

scioperare (shoa-pay-*raa*-ray) *v* *strike

sciopero (*shaw*-pay-roa) *m* strike

sciroppo (shee-*rop*-poa) *m* syrup

scivolare (shee-voa-*laa*-ray) *v* glide, slip; skid

scivolata (shee-voa-*laa*-tah) *f* slide

scivolo (*shee*-voa-loa) *m* slide

scodella (skoa-*dehl*-lah) *f* soup-plate

scogliera (skoa-*lʸay*-rah) *f* cliff

scoglio (*skaw*-lʸoa) *m* cliff

scoiattolo (skoa-*yaht*-toa-loa) *m* squirrel

scolara (skoa-*laa*-rah) *f* schoolgirl

scolaro (skoa-*laa*-roa) *m* schoolboy; pupil

scolo (*skōā*-loa) *m* drain

scolorirsi (skoa-loa-*reer*-see) *v* fade, discolour

scommessa (skoam-*mayss*-sah) *f* bet

* **scommettere** (skoam-*mayt*-tay-ray) *v* *bet

scomodità (skoa-moa-dee-*tah*) *f* inconvenience

scomodo (*skaw*-moa-doa) *adj* uncomfortable

* **scomparire** (skoam-pah-*ree*-ray) *v* disappear

scompartimento (skoam-pahr-tee-*mayn*-toa) *m* compartment; **~ per fumatori** smoker

scomparto (skoam-*pahr*-toa) *m* section

* **sconfiggere** (skoan-*feed*-jay-ray) *v* defeat

sconfinato (skoan-fee-*naa*-toa) *adj* unlimited

sconfitta (skoan-*feet*-tah) *f* defeat

sconosciuto (skoa-noash-*shōō*-toa) *adj* unfamiliar

sconsiderato (skoan-see-day-*raa*-toa) *adj* rash

scontentare (skoan-tayn-*taa*-ray) *v* displease

scontento (skoan-*tehn*-toa) *adj* dissatisfied, discontented

sconto (*skoan*-toa) *m* discount, rebate; **tasso di ~** bank-rate

scontrarsi (skoan-*trahr*-see) *v* crash

scontro (*skoan*-troa) *m* collision, crash

scopa (*skoā*-pah) *f* broom

scopare (skoa-*paa*-ray) *v* *sweep

scoperta (skoa-*pehr*-tah) *f* discovery

scopo (*skaw*-poa) *m* design; **allo ~ di** to, in order to

scoppiare (skoap-*pyaa*-ray) *v* *burst

scoppio (*skop*-pyoa) *m* outbreak

***scoprire** (skoa-*pree*-ray) *v* uncover; detect, discover

***scorgere** (*skor*-jay-ray) *v* perceive

***scorrere** (*skoar*-ray-ray) *v* flow, stream

scorretto (skoar-*reht*-toa) *adj* incorrect

scorso (*skoar*-soa) *adj* past, last

scorta (*skor*-tah) *f* escort; stock

scortare (skoar-*taa*-ray) *v* escort

scortese (skoar-*tāy*-zay) *adj* unkind, impolite

scossa (*skoss*-sah) *f* shock

Scozia (*skaw*-tsyah) *f* Scotland

scozzese (skoat-*tsāy*-say) *adj* Scottish, Scotch; *m* Scot

scriminatura (skree-mee-nah-*tōō*-rah) *f* parting

scritto (*skreet*-toa) *m* writing

scrittoio (skreet-*tōā*-yoa) *m* bureau

scrittore (skreet-*tōā*-ray) *m* writer

scrittura (skreet-*tōō*-rah) *f* handwriting

scrivania (skree-vah-*nee*-ah) *f* desk

scrivano (skree-*vaa*-noa) *m* clerk

***scrivere** (*skree*-vay-ray) *v* *write

scrupoloso (skroo-poa-*lōā*-soa) *adj* careful

sculacciata (skoo-laht-*chaa*-tah) *f* spanking

scultore (skool-*tōā*-ray) *m* sculptor

scultura (skool-*tōō*-rah) *f* sculpture; ~

in legno wood-carving, carving

scuola (*skwaw*-lah) *f* school; **marinare la ~** play truant; **~ di equitazione** riding-school; **~ media** secondary school

***scuotere** (*skwaw*-tay-ray) *v* shock

scuro (*skōō*-roa) *adj* obscure

scusa (*skōō*-zah) *f* apology, excuse

scusare (skoo-*zaa*-ray) *v* excuse; **scusa!** sorry!; **scusarsi** apologize

sdolcinatura (zdoal-chee-nah-*tōō*-rah) *f* tear-jerker

sdraiarsi (zdrah-*yahr*-see) *v* *lie down

sdrucciolevole (zdroot-choa-*lāy*-voa-lay) *adj* slippery

se (say) *conj* if; whether; **se ... o** whether ... or

sé (say) *pron* oneself

sebbene (sayb-*bai*-nay) *conj* though, although

seccatore (sayk-kah-*tōā*-ray) *m* bore

seccatura (sayk-kah-*tōō*-rah) *f* nuisance

secchio (*sayk*-kyoa) *m* pail, bucket

secolo (*sai*-koa-loa) *m* century

secondario (say-koan-*daa*-ryoa) *adj* secondary, subordinate

secondo[1] (say-*koan*-doa) *num* second

secondo[2] (say-*koan*-doa) *prep* according to

secondo[3] (say-*koan*-doa) *m* second

sedano (*sai*-dah-noa) *m* celery

sedativo (say-dah-*tee*-voa) *m* sedative

sede (*sai*-day) *f* seat

sedere (say-*dāy*-ray) *m* bottom

***sedere** (say-*dāy*-ray) *v* *sit; *sedersi* *sit down

sedia (*sai*-dyah) *f* chair, seat; **~ a rotelle** wheelchair; **~ a sdraio** deck chair

sedicesimo (say-dee-*chai*-zee-moa) *num* sixteenth

sedici (*sāy*-dee-chee) *num* sixteen

sedimento (say-dee-*mayn*-toa) *m* de-

posit
*sedurre (say-*door*-ray) v seduce
seduta (say-*doo*-tah) f session
sega (*say*-gah) f saw
segatura (say-gah-*too*-rah) f sawdust
seggio (*sehd*-joa) m chair
segheria (say-gay-*ree*-ah) f saw-mill
segmento (sayg-*mayn*-toa) m stretch
segnalare (say-ñah-*laa*-ray) v signal; indicate
segnale (say-*ñaa*-lay) m signal; ~ di soccorso distress signal
segnare (say-*ñaa*-ray) v tick off, mark
segno (*say*-ñoa) m sign; mark; token, signal
segretaria (say-gray-*taa*-ryah) f secretary
segretario (say-gray-*taa*-ryoa) m clerk, secretary
segreto (say-*gray*-toa) adj secret; m secret
seguente (say-*gwehn*-tay) adj following
seguire (say-*gwee*-ray) v follow; in seguito then, afterwards
seguitare (say-gooæ̃h-*taa*-ray) v continue
sei (say) num six
selezionare (say-lay-tsyoa-*naa*-ray) v select; selezionato select
selezione (say-lay-*tsyoa*-nay) f selection; choice
sella (*sehl*-lah) f saddle
selvaggina (sayl-vahd-*jee*-nah) f game
selvaggio (sayl-*vahd*-joa) adj fierce, savage
selvatico (sayl-*vaa*-tee-koa) adj wild
semaforo (say-*maa*-foa-roa) m traffic light
sembrare (saym-*braa*-ray) v appear, seem, look
seme (*say*-may) m pip
semenza (say-*mehn*-tsah) f seed
semi- (say-mee) semi-

semicerchio (say-mee-*chehr*-kyoa) m semicircle
seminare (say-mee-*naa*-ray) v *sow
seminterrato (say-meen-tayr-*raa*-toa) m basement
semplice (*saym*-plee-chay) adj simple; plain
sempre (*sehm*-pray) adv always, ever; ~ diritto straight ahead
senape (*sai*-nah-pay) f mustard
senato (say-*naa*-toa) m senate
senatore (say-nah-*toā*-ray) m senator
senile (say-*nee*-lay) adj senile
seno (*say*-noa) m breast, bosom
sensato (sayn-*saa*-toa) adj down-to-earth
sensazionale (sayn-sah-tsyoa-*naa*-lay) adj sensational
sensazione (sayn-sah-*tsyoā*-nay) f feeling; sensation
sensibile (sayn-*see*-bee-lay) adj sensitive
sensibilità (sayn-see-bee-lee-*tah*) f sensibility
senso (*sehn*-soa) m sense; reason; ~ unico one-way traffic
sentenza (sayn-*tehn*-tsah) f sentence, verdict
sentiero (sayn-*tyai*-roa) m trail, path, lane, footpath
sentimentale (sayn-tee-mayn-*taa*-lay) adj sentimental
sentimento (sayn-tee-*mayn*-toa) m feeling
sentire (sayn-*tee*-ray) v *feel; listen
senza (*sehn*-tsah) prep without; senz'altro without fail
separare (say-pah-*raa*-ray) v part, separate, divide; separato separate
separatamente (say-pah-rah-tah-*mayn*-tay) adv apart
sepoltura (say-poal-*too*-rah) f burial
seppellimento (sayp-payl-lee-*mayn*-toa) m burial

seppellire (sayp-payl-*lee*-ray) v bury

sequenza (say-*kwehn*-tsah) f shot

sequestrare (say-kway-*straa*-ray) v confiscate, impound

sera (*sāy*-rah) f evening, night

serbatoio (sayr-bah-*tōa*-yoa) m reservoir, tank; ~ **di benzina** petrol tank

sereno (say-*rāy*-noa) adj serene

serie (*sai*-ryay) f (pl~) series, sequence

serietà (say-ryay-*tah*) f seriousness; gravity

serio (*sai*-ryoa) adj serious

sermone (sayr-*mōa*-nay) m sermon

serpeggiante (sayr-payd-*jahn*-tay) adj winding

serpente (sayr-*pehn*-tay) m snake

serra (*sehr*-rah) f greenhouse

serrare (sayr-*raa*-ray) v tighten

serratura (sayr-rah-*tōo*-rah) f lock

servire (sayr-*vee*-ray) v attend on, serve, wait on

servitore (sayr-vee-*tōa*-ray) m servant

servizievole (sayr-vee-*tsyāy*-voa-lay) adj obliging, helpful

servizio (sayr-*vee*-tsyoa) m service; service charge; ~ **da tavola** dinner-service; ~ **da tè** tea-set; ~ **in camera** room service; ~ **postale** postal service

servo (*sehr*-voa) m boy

sessanta (sayss-*sahn*-tah) num sixty

sessione (sayss-*syōa*-nay) f session

sesso (*sehss*-soa) m sex

sessuale (sayss-*swaa*-lay) adj sexual

sessualità (sayss-swah-lee-*tah*) f sexuality

sesto (*seh*-stoa) num sixth

seta (*sāy*-tah) f silk; **di** ~ silken

setacciare (say-taht-*chaa*-ray) v sieve

setaccio (say-*taht*-choa) m sieve

sete (*sāy*-tay) f thirst

settanta (sayt-*tahn*-tah) num seventy

sette (*seht*-tay) num seven

settembre (sayt-*tehm*-bray) September

settentrionale (sayt-tayn-tryoa-*naa*-lay) adj northerly, north

settentrione (sayt-tayn-*tryōa*-nay) m north

setticemia (sayt-tee-chay-*mee*-ah) f blood-poisoning

settico (*seht*-tee-koa) adj septic

settimana (sayt-tee-*maa*-nah) f week

settimanale (sayt-tee-mah-*naa*-lay) adj weekly

settimo (*seht*-tee-moa) num seventh

settore (sayt-*tōa*-ray) m field

severo (say-*vai*-roa) adj harsh, strict, severe

sezione (say-*tsyōa*-nay) f department; section

sfacciato (sfaht-*chaa*-toa) adj bold

sfavorevole (sfah-voa-*rāy*-voa-lay) adj unfavourable

sfera (*sfai*-rah) f sphere

sfida (*sfee*-dah) f challenge

sfidare (sfee-*daa*-ray) v challenge, dare

sfilacciarsi (sfee-laht-*chahr*-see) v fray

sfiorare (sfyoa-*raa*-ray) v skim over; touch on

sfondo (*sfoan*-doa) m background

sfortuna (sfoar-*tōo*-nah) f bad luck, misfortune

sfortunato (sfoar-too-*naa*-toa) adj unfortunate, unlucky

sforzarsi (sfoar-*tsahr*-see) v try

sforzo (*sfor*-tsoa) m effort; strain

sfrontato (sfroan-*taa*-toa) adj bold

sfruttare (sfroot-*taa*-ray) v exploit

sfuggire (sfood-*jee*-ray) v escape

sfumatura (sfoo-mah-*tōo*-rah) f nuance

sgangerato (zgahng-gay-*raa*-toa) adj ramshackle

sgarbato (zgahr-*baa*-toa) adj unkind

sgocciolamento (zgoat-choa-lah-*mayn*-toa) m leak

sgombrare (zgoam-*braa*-ray) v vacate

sgombro (*zgoam*-broa) *m* mackerel

sgomentare (zgoa-mayn-*taa*-ray) *v* terrify

sgradevole (zgrah-*dāy*-voa-lay) *adj* disagreeable, unpleasant, nasty

sguardo (*zgwahr*-doa) *m* look

si (see) *pron* himself; herself; themselves

sì (see) yes

sia ... sia (*see*-ah) both ... and

Siam (syahm) *m* Siam

siamese (syah-*māy*-zay) *adj* Siamese; *m* Siamese

siccità (seet-chee-*tah*) *f* drought

siccome (seek-*kōā*-may) *conj* as

sicurezza (see-koo-*rayt*-tsah) *f* safety, security; **cintura di ~** safety-belt, seat-belt

sicuro (see-*kōō*-roa) *adj* safe, secure; sure

siepe (*syai*-pay) *f* hedge

siero (*syai*-roa) *m* serum

sifone (see-*fōā*-nay) *m* siphon, syphon

sigaretta (see-gah-*rayt*-tah) *f* cigarette

sigaro (*see*-gah-roa) *m* cigar

sigillo (see-*jeel*-loa) *m* seal

significare (see-*ñee*-fee-*kaa*-ray) *v* *mean

significativo (see-*ñee*-fee-kah-*tee*-voa) *adj* significant

significato (see-*ñee*-fee-*kaa*-toa) *m* meaning, sense

signora (see-*ñōā*-rah) *f* lady; mistress; madam

signore (see-*ñōā*-ray) *m* gentleman; mister; sir

signorina (see-*ñoa*-ree-nah) *f* miss

silenziatore (see-layn-tsyah-*tōā*-ray) *m* silencer; muffler *nAm*

silenzio (see-*lehn*-tsyoa) *m* silence

silenzioso (see-layn-*tsyoā*-soa) *adj* silent

sillaba (*seel*-lah-bah) *f* syllable

simbolo (*seem*-boa-loa) *m* symbol

simile (*see*-mee-lay) *adj* alike, like; such; similar

simpatia (seem-pah-*tee*-ah) *f* sympathy

simpatico (seem-*paa*-tee-koa) *adj* pleasant, nice

simulare (see-moo-*laa*-ray) *v* simulate

simultaneo (see-mool-*taa*-nay-oa) *adj* simultaneous

sinagoga (see-nah-*gaw*-gah) *f* synagogue

sincero (seen-*chai*-roa) *adj* honest, sincere

sindacato (seen-dah-*kaa*-toa) *m* trade-union

sindaco (*seen*-dah-koa) *m* mayor

sinfonia (seen-foa-*nee*-ah) *f* symphony

singhiozzo (seeng-*geeot*-tsoa) *m* hiccup

singolare (seeng-goa-*laa*-ray) *adj* queer; *m* singular

singolarità (seeng-goa-lah-ree-*tah*) *f* peculiarity

singolo (*seeng*-goa-loa) *adj* individual, single; *m* individual

sinistro (see-*nee*-stroa) *adj* left-hand, left; ominous, sinister; **a sinistra** left-hand

sino a (*see*-noa ah) as far as, till

sinonimo (see-*naw*-nee-moa) *m* synonym

sintetico (seen-*tai*-tee-koa) *adj* synthetic

sintomo (*seen*-toa-moa) *m* symptom

sintonizzare (seen-toa-need-*dzaa*-ray) *v* tune in

sipario (see-*paa*-ryoa) *m* curtain

sirena (see-*rai*-nah) *f* siren; mermaid

Siria (*see*-ryah) *f* Syria

siriano (see-*ryaa*-noa) *adj* Syrian; *m* Syrian

siringa (see-*reeng*-gah) *f* syringe

sistema (see-*stai*-mah) *m* system; **~ decimale** decimal system; **~ di raf-**

freddamento cooling system; ~ **lubrificante** lubrication system

sistemare (see-stay-*maa*-ray) v settle; **sistemarsi** settle down

sistematico (see-stay-*maa*-tee-koa) adj systematic

sistemazione (see-stay-mah-*tsyoā*-nay) f accommodation

sito (*see*-toa) m site

situato (see-*twaa*-toa) adj situated

situazione (see-twah-*tsyoā*-nay) f situation; position

slacciare (zlaht-*chaa*-ray) v unfasten, untie

slegare (zlay-*gaa*-ray) v loosen; **slegato** loose

slip (zleep) mpl briefs pl

slitta (*zleet*-tah) f sleigh, sledge

slittare (zleet-*taa*-ray) v *slide

slogato (zloa-*gaa*-toa) adj dislocated

smacchiatore (zmahk-kyah-*tōā*-ray) m stain remover, cleaning fluid

smaltare (zmahl-*taa*-ray) v glaze; **smaltato** enamelled

smalto (*zmahl*-toa) m enamel; ~ **per unghie** nail-polish

smarrire (zmahr-*ree*-ray) v *lose; *mislay; **smarrito** lost

smemorato (zmay-moa-*raa*-toa) adj forgetful

smeraldo (zmay-*rahl*-doa) m emerald

***smettere** (*zmayt*-tay-ray) v cease, stop, quit

smisurato (zmee-zoo-*raa*-toa) adj immense

smoking (*zmo*-keeng) m dinner-jacket; tuxedo nAm

smorfia (*zmoar*-fyah) f grin

smorto (*zmor*-toa) adj dull

smussato (zmooss-*saa*-toa) adj dull

snello (*znehl*-loa) adj slim, slender

sobborgo (soab-*boar*-goa) m suburb; outskirts pl

sobrio (*saw*-bryoa) adj sober

soccombere (soak-*koam*-bay-ray) v succumb

soccorso (soak-*koar*-soa) m assistance, aid; **equipaggiamento di pronto ~** first-aid kit; **pronto ~** first-aid

sociale (soa-*chaa*-lay) adj social

socialismo (soa-chah-*lee*-zmoa) m socialism

socialista (soa-chah-*lee*-stah) adj socialist; m socialist

società (soa-chyay-*tah*) f community; society; company

socio (*saw*-choa) m associate; partner

***soddisfare** (soad-dee-*sfaa*-ray) v satisfy

soddisfazione (soad-dee-sfah-*tsyoā*-nay) f satisfaction

sofà (soa-*fah*) m sofa

sofferenza (soaf-fay-*rehn*-tsah) f suffering

soffiare (soaf-*fyaa*-ray) v *blow

soffione (soaf-*fyōā*-nay) m dandelion

soffitta (soaf-*feet*-tah) f attic

soffitto (soaf-*feet*-toa) m ceiling

soffocare (soaf-foa-*kaa*-ray) v choke

***soffrire** (soaf-*free*-ray) v suffer

soggetto (soad-*jeht*-toa) m topic, subject; **soggetto a** subject to, liable to

soggiornare (soad-joar-*naa*-ray) v stay

soggiorno (soad-*joar*-noa) m stay; sitting-room, living-room

soglia (*saw*-lYah) f threshold

sogliola (*saw*-lYoa-lah) f sole

sognare (soa-*ñaa*-ray) v *dream

sogno (*sōā*-ñoa) m dream

solamente (soa-lah-*mayn*-tay) adv only

solco (*soal*-koa) m groove

soldato (soal-*daa*-toa) m soldier

sole (*sōā*-lay) m sun

soleggiato (soa-layd-*jaa*-toa) adj sunny

solenne (soa-*lehn*-nay) adj solemn

solido (*saw*-lee-doa) adj sound, solid, firm; m solid

solitario (soa-lee-*taa*-ryoa) *adj* lonely

solito (*saw*-lee-toa) *adj* customary, usual, ordinary

solitudine (soa-lee-*tōō*-dee-nay) *f* loneliness

sollecito (soal-*lāy*-chee-toa) *adj* prompt

solleticare (soal-lay-tee-*kaa*-ray) *v* tickle

sollevare (soal-lay-*vaa*-ray) *v* lift, raise; *bring up

sollievo (soal-*lʸai*-voa) *m* relief

solo (*sōā*-loa) *adj* only; *adv* only, alone

soltanto (soal-*tahn*-toa) *adv* only, merely

solubile (soa-*lōō*-bee-lay) *adj* soluble

soluzione (soa-loo-*tsyōā*-nay) *f* solution

somiglianza (soa-mee-*lʸahn*-tsah) *f* resemblance

somma (*soam*-mah) *f* amount, sum; ~ **globale** lump sum

sommario (soam-*maa*-ryoa) *m* summary

somministrare (soam-mee-nee-*straa*-ray) *v* administer

sommo (*soam*-moa) *adj* top

sommossa (soam-*moss*-sah) *f* riot

sonare (soa-*naa*-ray) *v* play

sonnifero (soan-*nee*-fay-roa) *m* sleeping-pill

sonno (*soan*-noa) *m* sleep

sonoro (soa-*naw*-roa) *adj* noisy

sopportare (soap-poar-*taa*-ray) *v* *bear, sustain, endure; *go through

sopra (*sōā*-prah) *prep* over; *adv* above; **al di** ~ over; **di** ~ upstairs

soprabito (soa-*praa*-bee-toa) *m* coat; topcoat, overcoat

sopracciglio (soa-praht-*chee*-lʸoa) *m* eyebrow

***sopraffare** (soa-prahf-*faa*-ray) *v* overwhelm

soprappeso (soa-prahp-*pāy*-soa) *m* overweight

soprattutto (soa-praht-*toot*-toa) *adv* most of all, especially

sopravvivenza (soa-prahv-vee-*vehn*-tsah) *f* survival

***sopravvivere** (soa-prahv-*vee*-vay-ray) *v* survive

soprintendenza (soa-preen-tayn-*dehn*-tsah) *f* supervision

***soprintendere** (soa-preen-*tehn*-day-ray) *v* supervise

sordido (*sor*-dee-doa) *adj* filthy

sordo (*soar*-doa) *adj* deaf

sorella (soa-*rehl*-lah) *f* sister

sorgente (soar-*jehn*-tay) *f* source, spring, fountain

***sorgere** (*sor*-jay-ray) *v* *rise; *arise

sorpassare (soar-pahss-*saa*-ray) *v* pass

sorprendente (soar-prayn-*dehn*-tay) *adj* astonishing

***sorprendere** (soar-*prehn*-day-ray) *v* surprise

sorpresa (soar-*prāy*-sah) *f* astonishment, surprise

***sorridere** (soar-*ree*-day-ray) *v* smile

sorriso (soar-*ree*-soa) *m* smile

sorsetto (soar-*sayt*-toa) *m* sip

sorte (*sor*-tay) *f* destiny, lot

sorteggio (soar-*tayd*-joa) *m* draw

sorveglianza (soar-vay-*lʸahn*-tsah) *f* supervision

sorvegliare (soar-vay-*lʸaa*-ray) *v* patrol

***sospendere** (soa-*spehn*-day-ray) *v* discontinue, suspend

sospensione (soa-spayn-*syōā*-nay) *f* suspension

sospettare (soa-spayt-*taa*-ray) *v* suspect

sospetto (soa-*speht*-toa) *adj* suspicious; *m* suspicion

sospettoso (soa-spayt-*tōā*-soa) *adj* suspicious

sostanza (soa-*stahn*-tsah) *f* substance

sostanziale (soa-stahn-*tsyaa*-lay) *adj* substantial

sostare (soa-*staa*-ray) *v* stop

sostegno (soa-*stāy*-ñoa) *m* support

*****sostenere** (soa-stay-*nāy*-ray) *v* *hold up, support

sostituire (soa-stee-*twee*-ray) *v* replace, substitute

sostituto (soa-stee-*tōō*-toa) *m* deputy, substitute

sottaceti (soat-tah-*chāy*-tee) *mpl* pickles *pl*

sottacqua (soat-*tahk*-kwah) *adj* underwater

sotterraneo (soa-tayr-*raa*-nay-oa) *adj* underground

sottile (soat-*tee*-lay) *adj* thin, sheer; subtle

sotto (*soat*-toa) *prep* beneath, below, under; *adv* underneath

sottolineare (soat-toa-lee-nay-*aa*-ray) *v* underline; stress, emphasize

*****sottomettere** (soat-toa-*mayt*-tay-ray) *v* subject; *sottomettersi submit

*****sottoporre** (soat-toa-*poar*-ray) *v* subject; submit

sottoscritto (soat-toa-*skreet*-toa) *m* undersigned

*****sottoscrivere** (soat-toa-*skree*-vay-ray) *v* sign

sottosopra (soat-toa-*sōā*-prah) upside-down

sottotitolo (soat-toa-*tee*-toa-loa) *m* subtitle

sottovalutare (soat-toa-vah-loo-*taa*-ray) *v* underestimate

*****sottrarre** (soat-*trahr*-ray) *v* subtract; deduct

sovrano (soa-*vraa*-noa) *m* sovereign; ruler

sovvenzione (soav-vayn-*tsyōā*-nay) *f* subsidy

sozzo (*soad*-dzoa) *adj* dirty

spaccare (spahk-*kaa*-ray) *v* crack; chop; **spaccarsi** *burst

spada (*spaa*-dah) *f* sword

Spagna (*spaa*-ñah) *f* Spain

spagnolo (spah-*ñōā*-loa) *adj* Spanish; *m* Spaniard

spago (*spaa*-goa) *m* twine, cord, string

spalancare (spah-lahng-*kaa*-ray) *v* open wide

spalla (*spahl*-lah) *f* shoulder

*****spandere** (*spahn*-day-ray) *v* *spill

sparare (spah-*raa*-ray) *v* fire, *shoot

*****spargere** *v* *strew; *shed, spill; *spread

sparire (spah-*ree*-ray) *v* disappear, vanish

sparo (*spaa*-roa) *m* shot

sparpagliare (spahr-pah-*lʸaa*-ray) *v* scatter

spaventare (spah-vayn-*taa*-ray) *v* scare, frighten; **spaventarsi** *be frightened

spaventevole (spah-vayn-*tāy*-voa-lay) *adj* horrible, terrifying

spavento (spah-*vehn*-toa) *m* scare, fright

spaventoso (spah-vayn-*tōā*-soa) *adj* dreadful, terrible

spaziare (spah-*tsyaa*-ray) *v* space

spazio (*spaa*-tsyoa) *m* room, space

spazioso (spah-*tsyōā*-soa) *adj* roomy, spacious, large

spazzare (spaht-*tsaa*-ray) *v* wipe

spazzatura (spaht-tsah-*tōō*-rah) *f* junk, garbage

spazzola (*spaht*-tsoa-lah) *f* brush; ~ per capelli hairbrush; ~ per vestiti clothes-brush; **spazzolino da denti** toothbrush; **spazzolino per le unghie** nailbrush

spazzolare (spaht-tsoa-*laa*-ray) *v* brush

specchio (*spehk*-kyoa) *m* mirror, looking-glass

speciale (spay-*chaa*-lay) *adj* particular, special, peculiar

specialista (spay-chah-*lee*-stah) *m* specialist

specialità (spay-chah-lee-*tah*) *f* speciality

specializzarsi (spay-chah-leed-*dzahr*-see) *v* specialize

specialmente (spay-chahl-*mayn*-tay) *adv* especially

specie (*spai*-chay) *f* (pl ~) species, breed; sort

specifico (spay-*chee*-fee-koa) *adj* specific

speculare (spay-koo-*laa*-ray) *v* speculate

spedire (spay-*dee*-ray) *v* despatch, dispatch, *send off, *send; ship·

spedizione (spay-dee-*tsyōā*-nay) *f* consignment; expedition

***spegnere** (*spai*-ñay-ray) *v* extinguish; *put out, switch off

spelonca (spay-*loang*-kah) *f* cave

***spendere** (*spehn*-day-ray) *v* *spend

spendereccio (spayn-day-*rayt*-choa) *adj* wasteful

spensierato (spayn-syay-*raa*-toa) *adj* carefree

speranza (spay-*rahn*-tsah) *f* hope

speranzoso (spay-rahn-*tsōā*-soa) *adj* hopeful

sperare (spay-*raa*-ray) *v* hope

spergiuro (spayr-*jōō*-roa) *m* perjury

sperimentare (spay-ree-mayn-*taa*-ray) *v* experiment; experience

spesa (*spāy*-sah) *f* expense, expenditure; *fare la ~ shop; spese expenses *pl*, expenditure; **spese di viaggio** fare; travelling expenses

spesso (*spayss*-soa) *adj* thick; *adv* often

spessore (spayss-*sōā*-ray) *m* thickness

spettacolo (spayt-*taa*-koa-loa) *m* spectacle, show; sight; ~ **di varietà** floor show, variety show

spettatore (spayt-tah-*tōā*-ray) *m* spectator

spettro (*speht*-troa) *m* spook, ghost

spezie (*spai*-tsyay) *fpl* spices

spezzare (spayt-*tsaa*-ray) *v* *break; interrupt

spia (*spee*-ah) *f* spy

spiacente (spyah-*chehn*-tay) *adj* sorry

spiacevole (spyah-*chāy*-voa-lay) *adj* unpleasant

spiaggia (*spyahd*-jah) *f* beach; ~ **per nudisti** nudist beach

spianata (spyah-*naa*-tah) *f* esplanade

spianato (spyah-*naa*-toa) *adj* level

spiare (*spyaa*-ray) *v* peep

spicciarsi (speet-*chahr*-see) *v* hurry

spiccioli (*speet*-choa-lee) *mpl* change

spiedo (*spyai*-doa) *m* spit

spiegabile (spyay-*gaa*-bee-lay) *adj* accountable

spiegare (spyay-*gaa*-ray) *v* unfold; explain

spiegazione (spyay-gah-*tsyōā*-nay) *f* explanation

spietato (spyay-*taa*-toa) *adj* heartless

spilla (*speel*-lah) *f* brooch

spillo (*speel*-loa) *m* pin; ~ **di sicurezza** safety-pin

spina (*spee*-nah) *f* thorn; plug; ~ **di pesce** fishbone; ~ **dorsale** spine, backbone

spinaci (spee-*naa*-chee) *mpl* spinach

***spingere** (*speen*-jay-ray) *v* push

spinta (*speen*-tah) *f* push

spirare (spee-*raa*-ray) *v* expire

spirito (*spee*-ree-toa) *m* spirit; soul; humour; ghost

spiritoso (spee-ree-*tōā*-soa) *adj* witty, humorous

spirituale (spee-ree-*twaa*-lay) *adj* spiritual

splendido (*splehn*-dee-doa) *adj* splendid; glorious, magnificent, lovely

splendore (splayn-*dōā*-ray) *m* glare; splendour

spogliarsi (spoa-*lᵞahr*-see) v undress

spogliatoio (spoa-lᵞah-*tōa*-yoa) m cloakroom

spoglio (*spaw*-lᵞoa) adj bare, naked

sponda (*spoan*-dah) f shore

sporco (*spor*-koa) adj dirty, foul

sporgere (*spor*-jay-ray) v *put out; protrude

sport (sport) m sport; ~ **invernali** winter sports; ~ **velico** yachting

sportivo (spoar-*tee*-voa) m sportsman

sportello automatico (spor-*tehl*-loa ou-toa-*maa*-tee-koa) m cash dispenser, automatic teller

sposa (*spaw*-zah) f bride

sposalizio (spoa-zah-*lee*-tsyoa) m wedding

sposare (spoa-*zaa*-ray) v marry

sposo (*spaw*-zoa) m bridegroom

spostamento (spoa-stah-*mayn*-toa) m removal

spostare (spoa-*staa*-ray) v move, remove

sprecare (spray-*kaa*-ray) v waste

spreco (*sprai*-koa) m waste

spruzzatore (sproot-tsah-*tōa*-ray) m atomizer

spugna (*spōō*-ñah) f sponge

spumante (spoo-*mahn*-tay) adj sparkling

spumare (spoo-*maa*-ray) v foam

spuntato (spoon-*taa*-toa) adj blunt

spuntino (spoon-*tee*-noa) m snack

sputare (spoo-*taa*-ray) v *spit

sputo (*spōō*-toa) m spit

squadra (*skwaa*-drah) f team; shift, gang; soccer team

squama (*skwaa*-mah) f scale

squattrinato (skwaht-tree-*naa*-toa) adj broke

squisito (skwee-*zee*-toa) adj exquisite, delicious

stabile (*staa*-bee-lay) adj steady, stable, permanent; m premises pl

stabilire (stah-bee-*lee*-ray) v establish; determine

staccare (stahk-*kaa*-ray) v detach

stadio (*staa*-dyoa) m stadium; stage

staffa (*stahf*-fah) f stirrup

stagione (stah-*jōa*-nay) f season; **alta ~** peak season, high season; **bassa ~** low season; **fuori ~** off season

stagno (*staa*-ñoa) m tin; pond

stagnola (stah-*ñaw*-lah) f tinfoil

stalla (*stahl*-lah) f stable

stamani (stah-*maa*-nee) adv this morning

stampa (*stahm*-pah) f press; picture, print, engraving; **stampe** printed matter

stampare (stahm-*paa*-ray) v print

stampella (stahm-*pehl*-lah) f crutch

stancare (stahng-*kaa*-ray) v tire

stanco (*stahng*-koa) adj weary, tired

stanotte (stah-*not*-tay) adv tonight

stantio (stahn-*tee*-oa) adj stuffy

stantuffo (stahn-*toof*-foa) m piston; **asta dello ~** piston-rod

stanza (*stahn*-tsah) f room; ~ **da bagno** bathroom

stappare (stahp-*paa*-ray) v uncork

stare (*staa*-ray) v stay; **lasciar ~** *keep off; ***star disteso** *lie; ~ **attento a** *pay attention to; ~ **in guardia** watch out; ~ **in piedi** *stand

starnutire (stahr-noo-*tee*-ray) v sneeze

stasera (stah-*sai*-rah) adv tonight

statale (stah-*taa*-lay) adj national

statistica (stah-*tee*-stee-kah) f statistics pl

Stati Uniti (*staa*-tee oo-*nee*-tee) United States, the States

stato (*staa*-toa) m state; condition; ~ **di emergenza** emergency

statua (*staa*-twah) f statue

stazionario (stah-tsyoa-*naa*-ryoa) adj stationary

stazione (stah-*tsyōā*-nay) *f* station; depot *nAm*; ~ **balneare** seaside resort; ~ **centrale** central station; ~ **di servizio** gas station *Am*; ~ **termale** spa

stecca (*stayk*-kah) *f* rod; splint; carton

steccato (stayk-*kaa*-toa) *m* fence

stella (*stayl*-lah) *f* star

stendardo (stayn-*dahr*-doa) *m* banner

***stendere** (*stehn*-day-ray) *v* *spread

stenografia (stay-noa-grah-*fee*-ah) *f* shorthand

stenografo (stay-*naw*-grah-foa) *m* stenographer

sterile (*stai*-ree-lay) *adj* sterile

sterilizzare (stay-ree-leed-*dzaa*-ray) *v* sterilize

stesso (*stayss*-soa) *adj* same

stile (*stee*-lay) *m* style

stima (*stee*-mah) *f* esteem, respect; ***fare la** ~ estimate

stimare (stee-*maa*-ray) *v* esteem

stimolante (stee-moa-*lahn*-tay) *m* stimulant

stimolare (stee-moa-*laa*-ray) *v* stimulate, urge

stimolo (*stee*-moa-loa) *m* impulse

stipendio (stee-*pehn*-dyoa) *m* salary, wages *pl*

stipulare (stee-poo-*laa*-ray) *v* stipulate

stipulazione (stee-poo-lah-*tsyōā*-nay) *f* stipulation

stirare (stee-*raa*-ray) *v* iron, press; **non si stira** wash and wear, drip-dry; **senza stiratura** drip-dry; **stiratura permanente** permanent press

stitichezza (stee-tee-*kayt*-tsah) *f* constipation

stitico (*stee*-tee-koa) *adj* constipated

stiva (*stee*-vah) *f* hold

stivale (stee-*vaa*-lay) *m* boot

stizza (*steet*-tsah) *f* temper

stoffa (*stof*-fah) *f* cloth, fabric, material

stola (*staw*-lah) *f* stole

stolto (*stoal*-toa) *adj* foolish

stomachevole (stoa-mah-*kāӯ*-voa-lay) *adj* revolting

stomaco (*staw*-mah-koa) *m* stomach; **bruciore di** ~ heartburn

***storcere** (*stor*-chay-ray) *v* wrench; sprain

stordito (stoar-*dee*-toa) *adj* giddy, dizzy

storia (*staw*-ryah) *f* history; tale; ~ **d'amore** love-story; ~ **dell'arte** art history

storico (*staw*-ree-koa) *adj* historical, historic; *m* historian

stornello (stoar-*nehl*-loa) *m* starling

storta (*stor*-tah) *f* wrench

storto (*stor*-toa) *adj* crooked

stoviglie (stoa-*vee*-lʸay) *fpl* pottery; **canovaccio per** ~ tea-cloth

strabico (*straa*-bee-koa) *adj* cross-eyed

straccio (*straht*-choa) *m* rag

strada (*straa*-dah) *f* road, street; drive; **a mezza** ~ halfway; ~ **a pedaggio** turnpike *nAm*; ~ **ferrata** railroad *nAm*; ~ **in riparazione** road up; ~ **maestra** thoroughfare

strangolare (strahng-goa-*laa*-ray) *v* strangle

straniero (strah-*ñai*-roa) *adj* alien, foreign; *m* alien, stranger, foreigner

strano (*straa*-noa) *adj* strange; odd, curious, peculiar, queer, singular, funny

straordinario (strah-oar-dee-*naa*-ryoa) *adj* extraordinary, exceptional

strappare (strahp-*paa*-ray) *v* rip, *tear

strappo (*strahp*-poa) *m* tear

strato (*straa*-toa) *m* layer

strattone (straht-*tōā*-nay) *m* tug

stravagante (strah-vah-*gahn*-tay) *adj* extravagant

strega (*strāy*-gah) *f* witch

stregare (stray-*gaa*-ray) *v* bewitch

stretta (*strayt*-tah) *f* clutch, grip, grasp; ~ **di mano** handshake

strettamente (strayt-tah-*mayn*-tay) *adv* tight

stretto (*strayt*-toa) *adj* narrow; tight

stria (*stree*-ah) *f* stripe

striato (*stryaa*-toa) *adj* striped

strillare (streel-*laa*-ray) *v* scream, yell, shriek

strillo (*streel*-loa) *m* scream, yell, shriek

*stringere (*streen*-jay-ray) *v* tighten

striscia (*streesh*-shah) *f* strip

strisciare (streesh-*shaa*-ray) *v* *creep

strofa (*straw*-fah) *f* stanza

strofinare (stroa-fee-*naa*-ray) *v* rub, scrub; wipe

strozzare (stroat-*tsaa*-ray) *v* choke

strumento (stroo-*mayn*-toa) *m* implement; instrument; ~ **musicale** musical instrument

struttura (stroot-*tōō*-rah) *f* fabric, structure, texture

struzzo (*stroot*-tsoa) *m* ostrich

stucco (*stook*-koa) *m* plaster

studente (stoo-*dehn*-tay) *m* student

studentessa (stoo-dayn-*tayss*-sah) *f* student

studiare (stoo-*dyaa*-ray) *v* study

studio (*stōō*-dyoa) *m* study

stufa (*stōō*-fah) *f* stove; ~ **a gas** gas stove

stufo di (*stōō*-foa dee) fed up with, tired of

stuoia (*stwaw*-yah) *f* mat

*stupefare (stoo-pay-*faa*-ray) *v* amaze

stupendo (stoo-*pehn*-doa) *adj* wonderful

stupidaggini (stoo-pee-*dahd*-jee-nee) *fpl* rubbish; ***dire** ~ talk rubbish

stupido (*stōō*-pee-doa) *adj* stupid; foolish, dumb

stupire (stoo-*pee*-ray) *v* amaze, surprise

stupore (stoo-*pōā*-ray) *m* amazement, wonder

stuzzicadenti (stoot-tsee-kah-*dehn*-tee) *m* toothpick

stuzzicare (stoot-tsee-*kaa*-ray) *v* kid, tease

stuzzichino (stoot-tsee-*kee*-noa) *m* appetizer

su (soo) *prep* on, upon, in; above; about; *adv* up; upstairs; **in** ~ upwards, up; overhead

subacqueo (soo-*bahk*-kway-oa) *adj* underwater

subalterno (soo-bahl-*tehr*-noa) *adj* subordinate

subire (soo-*bee*-ray) *v* suffer

subito (*sōō*-bee-toa) *adv* at once, instantly, straight away, presently, immediately

subordinato (soo-boar-dee-*naa*-toa) *adj* minor

suburbano (soo-boor-*baa*-noa) *adj* suburban

*succedere (soot-*chai*-day-ray) *v* succeed; happen, occur

successione (soot-chayss-*syōā*-nay) *f* sequence

successivo (soot-chayss-*see*-voa) *adj* following, subsequent

successo (soot-*chehss*-soa) *m* success; hit

succhiare (sook-*kyaa*-ray) *v* suck

succo (*sook*-koa) *m* juice; ~ **di frutta** squash

succoso (sook-*kōā*-soa) *adj* juicy

succursale (sook-koor-*saa*-lay) *f* branch

sud (sood) *m* south; **polo Sud** South Pole

sudare (soo-*daa*-ray) *v* perspire, sweat

suddito (*sood*-dee-toa) *m* subject

sud-est (soo-*dehst*) *m* south-east

sudicio (*sŏo*-dee-choa) *adj* dirty; filthy, unclean, soiled

sudiciume (soo-dee-*chŏo*-may) *m* dirt

sudore (soo-*dōa*-ray) *m* perspiration, sweat

sud-ovest (sood-*aw*-vayst) *m* southwest

sufficiente *adj* enough, sufficient

suffragio (soof-*fraa*-joa) *m* suffrage

suggerimento (sood-jay-ree-*mayn*-toa) *m* suggestion

suggerire (sood-jay-*ree*-ray) *v* suggest

sughero (*sŏo*-gay-roa) *m* cork

sugo (*sŏo*-goa) *m* gravy

suicidio (wake-*chee*-dyoa) *m* suicide

sunto (*soon*-toa) *m* summary

suo (*sŏo*-oa) *adj* (f sua;pl suoi,sue) his; her; **Suo** *adj* your

suocera (*swaw*-chay-rah) *f* mother-in-law

suocero (*swaw*-chay-roa) *m* father-in-law; **suoceri** parents-in-law *pl*

suola (*swaw*-lah) *f* sole

suolo (*swaw*-loa) *m* soil, earth

suonare (swoa-*naa*-ray) *v* sound; *ring; ~ il clacson hoot; toot vAm, honk vAm

suono (*swaw*-noa) *m* sound

superare (soo-pay-*raa*-ray) *v* exceed, *outdo

superbo (soo-*pehr*-boa) *adj* superb

superficiale (soo-payr-fee-*chaa*-lay) *adj* superficial

superficie (soo-payr-*fee*-chay) *f* surface

superfluo (soo-*pehr*-flwoa) *adj* unnecessary, superfluous

superiore (soo-pay-*ryōa*-ray) *adj* upper, superior

superlativo (soo-payr-lah-*tee*-voa) *adj* superlative; *m* superlative

supermercato (soo-payr-mayr-*kaa*-toa) *m* supermarket

superstizione (soo-payr-stee-*tsyōa*-nay) *f* superstition

supplementare (soop-play-mayn-*taa*-ray) *adj* extra, additional

supplemento (soop-play-*mayn*-toa) *m* supplement; surcharge

supplicare (soop-plee-*kaa*-ray) *v* beg

*supporre (soop-*poar*-ray) *v* suppose; suspect; **supposto che** supposing that

supposta (soop-*poa*-stah) *f* suppository

suscitare (soosh-shee-*taa*-ray) *v* stir up

susina (soo-*see*-nah) *f* plum

sussidio (sooss-*see*-dyoa) *m* grant

sussistenza (sooss-see-*stehn*-tsah) *f* livelihood

sussurro (sooss-*soor*-roa) *m* whisper

suturare (soo-too-*raa*-ray) *v* sew up

svago (*zvaa*-goa) *m* recreation

svalutare (zvah-loo-*taa*-ray) *v* devalue

svalutazione (zvah-loo-tah-*tsyōa*-nay) *f* devaluation

svantaggio (zvahn-*tahd*-joa) *m* disadvantage

svedese (zvay-*dāy*-zay) *adj* Swedish; *m* Swede

sveglia (*zvāy*-lʸah) *f* alarm-clock

svegliare (zvay-*lʸaa*-ray) *v* *awake, *wake; **svegliarsi** wake up

sveglio (*zvāy*-lʸoa) *adj* awake; clever, smart, bright

svelare (zvay-*laa*-ray) *v* reveal

svelto (*zvehl*-toa) *adj* quick

svendita (*zvayn*-dee-tah) *f* clearance sale

*svenire (zvay-*nee*-ray) *v* faint

sventolare (zvayn-toa-*laa*-ray) *v* wave

Svezia (*zvai*-tsyah) *f* Sweden

sviluppare (zvee-loop-*paa*-ray) *v* develop

sviluppo (zvee-*loop*-poa) *m* development

svista (*zvee*-stah) *f* slip, oversight

svitare (zvee-*taa*-ray) *v* unscrew

Svizzera (*zveet*-tsay-rah) *f* Switzerland

svizzero (*zveet*-tsay-roa) *adj* Swiss; *m* Swiss

*svolgere (*zvol*-jay-ray) *v* *unwind; treat; carry out

svolta (*zvol*-tah) *f* turning, curve

swahili (zvah-*ee*-lee) *m* Swahili

T

tabaccaio (tah-bahk-*kaa*-yoa) *m* tobacconist

tabaccheria (tah-bahk-kay-*ree*-ah) *f* tobacconist's, cigar shop

tabacco (tah-*bahk*-koa) *m* tobacco; ~ **da pipa** pipe tobacco

tabella (tah-*behl*-lah) *f* chart, table; ~ **di conversione** conversion chart

tabù (tah-*boo*) *m* taboo

taccagno (tahk-*kaa*-ñoa) *adj* stingy

tacchino (tahk-*kee*-noa) *m* turkey

tacco (*tahk*-koa) *m* heel

taccuino (tahk-*kwee*-noa) *m* notebook

*tacere (tah-*chāy*-ray) *v* *keep quiet, *be silent; *far ~ silence

tachimetro (tah-*kee*-may-troa) *m* speedometer

tagliacarte (tah-l^yah-*kahr*-tay) *m* paper-knife

tagliando (tah-*l^yahn*-doa) *m* coupon

tagliare (tah-*l^yaa*-ray) *v* *cut; *cut off, carve, chop

taglio (*taa*-l^yoa) *m* cut; ~ **di capelli** haircut

tailandese (tigh-lahn-*dāy*-say) *adj* Thai; *m* Thai

Tailandia (tigh-*lahn*-dyah) *f* Thailand

talco (*tahl*-koa) *m* talc powder; ~ **per piedi** foot powder

tale (*taa*-lay) *adj* such

talento (tah-*lehn*-toa) *m* gift, talent; **di** ~ gifted

talloncino (tahl-loan-*cheenoa*) *m* counterfoil

tallone (tahl-*lōā*-nay) *m* heel

talmente (tahl-*mayn*-tay) *adv* so

taluni (tah-*lōō*-nee) *pron* some

talvolta (tahl-*vol*-tah) *adv* sometimes

tamburo (tahm-*bōō*-roa) *m* drum; ~ **del freno** brake drum

tampone (tahm-*pōā*-nay) *m* tampon

tana (*taa*-nah) *f* den

tangibile (tahn-*jee*-bee-lay) *adj* tangible

tanto (*tahn*-toa) *adv* as much; **di** ~ in **tanto** now and then; **ogni** ~ occasionally

tappa (*tahp*-pah) *f* stage

tappeto (tahp-*pāy*-toa) *m* carpet; rug

tappezzare (tahp-payt-*tsaa*-ray) *v* upholster

tappezzeria (tahp-payt-tsay-*ree*-ah) *f* tapestry

tappo (*tahp*-poa) *m* cork, stopper

tardi (*tahr*-dee) *adv* late

tardivo (tahr-*dee*-voa) *adj* late

tardo (*tahr*-doa) *adj* late; slow

targa automobilistica (*tahr*-gah ou-toa-moa-bee-*lee*-stee-kah) registration plate; licence plate *Am*

tariffa (tah-*reef*-fah) *f* tariff, rate; ~ **del parcheggio** parking fee; ~ **doganale** Customs duty; ~ **notturna** night rate

tarma (*tahr*-mah) *f* moth

tartaruga (tahr-tah-*rōō*-gah) *f* turtle

tasca (*tah*-skah) *f* pocket

tassa (*tahss*-sah) *f* tax; ~ **sugli affari** turnover tax, sales tax; ~ **di scambio** sales tax

tassabile (tahs-*saa*-bee-lay) *adj* dutiable

tassametro (tahss-*saa*-may-troa) *m* taxi-meter

tassare (tahss-*saa*-ray) *v* tax

tassì (tahss-*see*) *m* cab, taxi

tassista (tahss-*see*-stah) *m* cab-driver,

taxi-driver

tattica (*taht*-tee-kah) *f* tactics *pl*

tatto (*taht*-toa) *m* touch

taverna (tah-*vehr*-nah) *f* public house, pub; tavern

tavola (*taa*-voa-lah) *f* table; ~ **calda** snack-bar, cafeteria

tavoletta (tah-voa-*layt*-tah) *f* board

tazza (*taht*-tsah) *f* cup; mug; **tazzina da tè** teacup

te (tay) *pron* you

tè (teh) *m* tea

teatro (tay-*aa*-troa) *m* theatre; drama; ~ **dell'opera** opera house; ~ **di varietà** music-hall, variety theatre

tecnica (*tehk*-nee-kah) *f* technique

tecnico (*tehk*-nee-koa) *adj* technical; *m* technician

tecnologia (tayk-noa-loa-*jee*-ah) *f* technology

tedesco (tay-*day*-skoa) *adj* German; *m* German

tegame (tay-*gaa*-may) *m* pan

tegola (*tāy*-goa-lah) *f* tile

teiera (tay-*yai*-rah) *f* teapot

telaio (tay-*laa*-yoa) *m* chassis

telecamera (tay-lay-*kaa*-may-rah) *f* video camera

telefonare (tay-lay-foa-*naa*-ray) *v* ring up, phone, call; call up *Am*

telefonata (tay-lay-foa-*naa*-tah) *f* call

telefonista (tay-lay-foa-*nee*-stah) *f* telephonist, telephone operator

telefono (tay-*lai*-foa-noa) *m* phone, telephone; ~ **interno** extension

telegrafare (tay-lay-grah-*faa*-ray) *v* cable, telegraph

telegramma (tay-lay-*grahm*-mah) *m* cable, telegram

telemetro (tay-*lai*-may-troa) *m* range-finder

teleobbiettivo (tay-lay-oab-byayt-*tee*-voa) *m* telephoto lens

televisione (tay-lay-vee-*zyōā*-nay) *f*

television; ~ **cavo** cable television; ~ **satellite** satellite television

televisore (tay-lay-vee-*zōā*-ray) *m* television set

telex (tay-*lehks*) *m* telex

tema (*tai*-mah) *m* theme

temere (tay-*māy*-ray) *v* fear, dread

temperamatite (taym-pay-rah-mah-*tee*-tay) *m* pencil-sharpener

temperatura (taym-pay-rah-*tōō*-rah) *f* temperature; ~ **ambientale** room temperature

temperino (taym-pay-*ree*-noa) *m* pocket-knife, penknife

tempesta (taym-*peh*-stah) *f* storm, tempest

tempestoso (taym-pay-*stōā*-soa) *adj* stormy

tempia (*tehm*-pyah) *f* temple

tempio (*tehm*-pyoa) *m* temple

tempo (*tehm*-poa) *m* time; weather; **in** ~ in time; ~ **libero** spare time

temporale (taym-poa-*raa*-lay) *m* thunderstorm

temporalesco (taym-poa-rah-*lay*-skoa) *adj* thundery

temporaneo (taym-poa-*raa*-nay-oa) *adj* temporary

tenace (tay-*naa*-chay) *adj* tough

tenaglie (tay-*naa*-lʸay) *fpl* pincers *pl*

tenda (*tehn*-dah) *f* curtain; tent; ~ **di riparo** awning

tendenza (tayn-*dehn*-tsah) *f* tendency

*****tendere** (*tehn*-day-ray) *v* stretch; *be inclined to; *~ **a** tend to

tendine (tayn-*dee*-nay) *m* sinew, tendon

*****tenere** (tay-*nāy*-ray) *v* *keep; *hold

tenero (*tai*-nay-roa) *adj* tender

tennis (*tehn*-neess) *m* tennis; **campo di** ~ tennis-court; ~ **da tavolo** ping-pong

tensione (tayn-*syōā*-nay) *f* tension;

stress, pressure

tentare (tayn-*taa*-ray) *v* try, attempt; tempt

tentativo (tayn-tah-*tee*-voa) *m* try, attempt, effort

tentazione (tayn-tah-*tsyōā*-nay) *f* temptation

teologia (tay-oa-loa-*jee*-ah) *f* theology

teoria (tay-oa-*reeah*) *f* theory

teorico (tay-*aw*-ree-koa) *adj* theoretical

terapia (tay-rah-*pee*-ah) *f* therapy

tergicristallo (tayr-jee-kree-*stahl*-loa) *m* windscreen wiper; windshield wiper *Am*

terital (tay-ree-*tahl*) *m* terylene

terminare (tayr-mee-*naa*-ray) *v* finish; stop

termine (*tehr*-mee-nay) *m* term; finish, end; terminal

termometro (tayr-*maw*-may-troa) *m* thermometer

termos (*tehr*-moass) *m* vacuum flask, thermos flask

termostato (tayr-*mo*-stah-toa) *m* thermostat

terra (*tehr*-rah) *f* earth; land; ground, soil; **a** ~ ashore; down

terracotta (tayr-rah-*kot*-tah) *f* faience

terraferma (tayr-rah-*fayr*-mah) *f* mainland

terraglie (tayr-*raa*-lᵛay) *fpl* crockery, ceramics *pl*, earthenware

terrazza (tayr-*raht*-tsah) *f* terrace

terremoto (tayr-ray-*maw*-toa) *m* earthquake

terreno (tayr-*rāy*-noa) *m* soil; grounds, terrain

terribile (tayr-*ree*-bee-lay) *adj* terrible; awful, dreadful, frightful

territorio (tayr-ree-*taw*-ryoa) *m* territory

terrore (tayr-*rōā*-ray) *m* terror

terrorismo (tayr-roa-*ree*-zmoa) *m* terrorism

terrorista (tayr-roa-*ree*-stah) *m* terrorist

terzo (*tehr*-tsoa) *num* third

tesi (*tai*-zee) *f* thesis

teso (*tāy*-soa) *adj* tense

tesoriere (tay-zoa-*ryai*-ray) *m* treasurer

tesoro (tay-*zaw*-roa) *m* treasure; **Tesoro** *m* treasury

tessere (*tehss*-say-ray) *v* *weave

tessitore (tayss-see-*tōā*-ray) *m* weaver

tessuto (tayss-*sōō*-toa) *m* tissue; textile

testa (*teh*-stah) *f* head; **in** ~ **a** ahead of; ~ **cilindro** cylinder head

testamento (tay-stah-*mayn*-toa) *m* will

testardo (tay-*stahr*-doa) *adj* pigheaded, head-strong

testimone (tay-stee-*maw*-nay) *m* witness; ~ **oculare** eye-witness

testimoniare (tay-stee-moa-*ñaa*-ray) *v* testify

testo (*teh*-stoa) *m* text

tetro (*tai*-troa) *adj* sombre

tetto (*tayt*-toa) *m* roof; ~ **di paglia** thatched roof

ti (tee) *pron* you; yourself

tiepido (*tyai*-pee-doa) *adj* lukewarm, tepid

tifoidea (tee-foa-ee-*dai*-ah) *f* typhoid

tifoso (tee-*fōā*-soa) *m* fan; supporter

tiglio (*tee*-lᵛoa) *m* limetree, lime

tigre (*tee*-gray) *f* tiger

timbro (*teem*-broa) *m* stamp; tone

timidezza (tee-mee-*dayt*-tsah) *f* timidity, shyness

timido (*tee*-mee-doa) *adj* timid, shy

timo (*tee*-moa) *m* thyme

timone (tee-*mōā*-nay) *m* rudder, helm

timoniere (tee-moa-*ñai*-ray) *m* steersman, helmsman

timore (tee-*mōā*-ray) *m* fear, dread

timpano (*teem*-pah-noa) *m* ear-drum

*tingere (*teen*-jay-ray) *v* dye

tinta (*teen*-tah) *f* shade; **a ~ solida** fast-dyed

tintoria (teen-toa-*ree*-ah) *f* dry-cleaner's

tintura (teen-*tōō*-rah) *f* colourant, dye

tipico (*tee*-pee-koa) *adj* typical, characteristic

tipo (*tee*-poa) *m* type; guy, fellow

tiranno (tee-*rahn*-noa) *m* tyrant

tirare (tee-*raa*-ray) *v* *draw, pull; *blow; **~ di scherma** fence

tiratura (tee-rah-*tōō*-rah) *f* issue

tiro (*tee*-roa) *m* throw; trick

titolo (*tee*-toa-loa) *m* title; headline, heading; degree; **titoli** stocks and shares

tizio (*tee*-tsyoa) *m* chap

toccare (toak-*kaa*-ray) *v* touch; *hit

tocco (*toak*-koa) *m* touch

***togliere** (*taw*-l[y]ay-ray) *v* *take out, *take away

toletta (toa-*leht*-tah) *f* dressing-table; washroom *nAm*

tollerabile (toal-lay-*raa*-bee-lay) *adj* tolerable

tollerare (toal-lay-*raa*-ray) *v* *bear

tomba (*toam*-bah) *f* grave, tomb

tonico (*taw*-nee-koa) *m* tonic; **~ per capelli** hair tonic

tonnellata (toan-nayl-*laa*-tah) *f* ton

tonno (*toan*-noa) *m* tuna

tono (*taw*-noa) *m* tone; note

tonsille (toan-*seel*-lay) *fpl* tonsils *pl*

tonsillite (toan-seel-*lee*-tay) *f* tonsilitis

topo (*taw*-poa) *m* mouse

torace (toa-*raa*-chay) *m* chest

***torcere** (*tor*-chay-ray) *v* twist

torcia (*tor*-chah) *f* torch

tordo (*tor*-doa) *m* thrush

tormenta (toar-*mayn*-tah) *f* blizzard, snowstorm

tormentare (toar-mayn-*taa*-ray) *v* torment

tormento (toar-*mayn*-toa) *m* torment

tornante (toar-*nahn*-tay) *m* turn

tornare (toar-*naa*-ray) *v* *go back, *get back

torneo (toar-*nai*-oa) *m* tournament

toro (*taw*-roa) *m* bull

torre (*toar*-ray) *f* tower

torrone (toar-*rōā*-nay) *m* nougat

torsione (toar-*syōā*-nay) *f* twist

torsolo (*toar*-soa-loa) *m* core

torta (*toar*-tah) *f* cake

torto (*tor*-toa) *m* wrong; ***avere ~** *be wrong; ***fare un ~** wrong

tortuoso (toar-*twōā*-soa) *adj* crooked

tortura (toar-*tōō*-rah) *f* torture

torturare (toar-too-*raa*-ray) *v* torture

tosse (*toass*-say) *f* cough

tossico (*toss*-see-koa) *adj* toxic

tossire (toass-*see*-ray) *v* cough

totale (toa-*taa*-lay) *adj* total; utter; *m* whole; total

totalitario (toa-tah-lee-*taa*-ryoa) *adj* totalitarian

totalizzatore (toa-tah-leed-dzah-*tōā*-ray) *m* totalizator

totalmente (toa-tahl-*mayn*-tay) *adv* completely

toupet (too-*pay*) *m* hair piece

tovaglia (toa-*vaa*-l[y]ah) *f* table-cloth

tovagliolo (toa-vah-*l[y]aw*-loa) *m* napkin, serviette; **~ di carta** paper napkin

tra (trah) *prep* between; among, amid

traccia (*traht*-chah) *f* trail, trace

tradimento (trah-dee-*mayn*-toa) *m* treason

tradire (trah-*dee*-ray) *v* betray; *give away

traditore (trah-dee-*tōā*-ray) *m* traitor

tradizionale (trah-dee-tsyoa-*naa*-lay) *adj* traditional

tradizione (trah-dee-*tsyōā*-nay) *f* tradition

***tradurre** (trah-*door*-ray) *v* translate

traduttore (trah-doot-*tōā*-ray) *m* translator

traduzione (trah-doo-*tsyōā*-nay) *f* translation, version

traffico (*trahf*-fee-koa) *m* traffic

tragedia (trah-*jai*-dyah) *f* tragedy; drama

traghetto (trah-*gayt*-toa) *m* ferry-boat

tragico (*traa*-jee-koa) *adj* tragic

traguardo (trah-*gwahr*-doa) *m* finish; goal

trainare (trigh-*naa*-ray) *v* tow, haul

tralasciare (trah-lahsh-*shaa*-ray) *v* fail

tram (trahm) *m* tram; streetcar *nAm*

trama (*traa*-mah) *f* plot

trambusto (trahm-*boo*-stoa) *m* fuss

tramezzino (trah-mayd-*dzee*-noa) *m* sandwich

tramonto (trah-*moan*-toa) *m* sunset

tranne (*trahn*-nay) *prep* but

tranquillante (trahng-kweel-*lahn*-tay) *m* tranquilizer

tranquillità (trahng-kweel-lee-*tah*) *f* quiet

tranquillizzare (trahng-kweel-leed-*dzaa*-ray) *v* reassure

tranquillo (trahng-*kweel*-loa) *adj* calm; still, tranquil, quiet

transatlantico (trahn-saht-*lahn*-tee-koa) *adj* transatlantic

transazione (trahn-sah-*tsyōā*-nay) *f* transaction

transizione (trahn-see-*tsyōā*-nay) *f* transition

trapanare (trah-pah-*naa*-ray) *v* drill, bore

trapano (*traa*-pah-noa) *m* drill

trapassare (trah-pahss-*saa*-ray) *v* depart

trappola (*trahp*-poa-lah) *f* trap

***trarre** (*trahr*-ray) *v* *draw

trascinare (trahsh-shee-*naa*-ray) *v* drag

***trascorrere** (trah-*skoar*-ray-ray) *v* pass

trascurare (trah-skoo-*raa*-ray) *v* neglect; overlook; **trascurato** careless

trasferire (trah-sfay-*ree*-ray) *v* transfer

trasformare (trah-sfoar-*maa*-ray) *v* transform

trasformatore (trah-sfoar-mah-*tōā*-ray) *m* transformer

trasgredire (trahz-gray-*dee*-ray) *v* trespass, offend

trasgressore (trah-zgrayss-*sōā*-ray) *m* trespasser

traslocare (trah-zloa-*kaa*-ray) *v* move

trasloco (trah-*zlaw*-koa) *m* move

***trasmettere** (trah-*zmayt*-tay-ray) *v* transmit, *broadcast

trasmettitore (trah-zmayt-tee-*tōā*-ray) *m* transmitter

trasmissione (trah-zmeess-*syōā*-nay) *f* transmission

trasparente (trah-spah-*rehn*-tay) *adj* transparent, sheer

traspirare (trah-spee-*raa*-ray) *v* perspire

traspirazione (trah-spee-rah-*tsyōā*-nay) *f* perspiration

trasportare (trah-spoar-*taa*-ray) *v* transport

trasporto (trah-*spor*-toa) *m* transportation, transport

tratta (*traht*-tah) *f* draft

trattamento (traht-tah-*mayn*-toa) *m* treatment

trattare (traht-*taa*-ray) *v* handle, treat; ~ **con** *deal with

trattativa (traht-tah-*tee*-vah) *f* negotiation

trattato (traht-*taa*-toa) *m* essay; treaty

***trattenere** (traht-tay-*nāy*-ray) *v* restrain; ***trattenersi** stay

tratto (*traht*-toa) *m* line; feature, trait; ~ **del carattere** characteristic

trattore (traht-*tōā*-ray) *m* tractor

trave (*traa*-vay) *f* beam

traversa (trah-*vehr*-sah) *f* side-street

traversata (trah-vayr-*saa*-tah) *f* passage, crossing

travestimento (trah-vay-stee-*mayn*-toa) *m* disguise

travestirsi (trah-vay-*steer*-see) *v* disguise

tre (tray) *num* three; ~ **quarti** three-quarter

tredicesimo (tray-dee-*chai*-zee-moa) *num* thirteenth

tredici (*trāy*-dee-chee) *num* thirteen

tremare (tray-*maa*-ray) *v* tremble, shiver

tremendo (tray-*mehn*-doa) *adj* terrible

trementina (tray-mayn-*tee*-nah) *f* turpentine

treno (*trai*-noa) *m* train; ~ **direttissimo** express train; ~ **diretto** through train; ~ **locale** local train; ~ **merci** goods train; freight-train *nAm*; ~ **notturno** night train; ~ **passeggeri** passenger train

trenta (*trayn*-tah) *num* thirty

trentesimo (trayn-*tai*-zee-moa) *num* thirtieth

triangolare (tryahng-goa-*laa*-ray) *adj* triangular

triangolo (*tryahng*-goa-loa) *m* triangle

tribordo (tree-*boar*-doa) *m* starboard

tribù (tree-*boo*) *f* tribe

tribuna (tree-*bōō*-nah) *f* stand

tribunale (tree-boo-*naa*-lay) *m* law court

trifoglio (tree-*faw*-lᵞoa) *m* clover; shamrock

triglia (*tree*-lᵞah) *f* mullet

trimestrale (tree-may-*straa*-lay) *adj* quarterly

trimestre (tree-*meh*-stray) *m* quarter

trinciato (treen-*chaa*-toa) *m* cigarette tobacco

trionfante (tryoan-*fahn*-tay) *adj* triumphant

trionfare (tryoan-*faa*-ray) *v* triumph

trionfo (*tryoan*-foa) *m* triumph

triste (*tree*-stay) *adj* sad

tristezza (tree-*stayt*-tsah) *f* sadness, sorrow

tritare (tree-*taa*-ray) *v* *grind, mince

triviale (tree-*vyaa*-lay) *adj* vulgar

tromba (*troam*-bah) *f* trumpet

troncare (troang-*kaa*-ray) *v* *cut off

tronco (*troang*-koa) *m* trunk

trono (*traw*-noa) *m* throne

tropicale (troa-pee-*kaa*-lay) *adj* tropical

tropici (*traw*-pee-chee) *mpl* tropics *pl*

troppo (*trop*-poa) *adv* too

trota (*traw*-tah) *f* trout

trovare (troa-*vaa*-ray) *v* *find, *come across

trovata (troa-*vaa*-tah) *f* idea

trucco (*trook*-koa) *m* make-up; trick

truffa (*troof*-fah) *f* swindle

truffare (troof-*faa*-ray) *v* swindle

truffatore (troof-fah-*tōā*-ray) *m* swindler

truppe (*troop*-pay) *fpl* troops *pl*

tu (too) *pron* you; ~ **stesso** yourself

tubatura (too-bah-*tōō*-rah) *f* pipe

tubercolosi (too-bayr-koa-*law*-zee) *f* tuberculosis

tubetto (too-*bayt*-toa) *m* tube

tubo (*tōō*-boa) *m* tube

tuffare (toof-*faa*-ray) *v* dive

tulipano (too-lee-*paa*-noa) *m* tulip

tumore (too-*mōā*-ray) *m* tumour

tumulto (too-*mool*-toa) *m* disturbance

tunica (*tōō*-nee-kah) *f* tunic

Tunisia (too-nee-*zee*-ah) *f* Tunisia

tunisino (too-nee-*zee*-noa) *adj* Tunisian; *m* Tunisian

tuo (*tōō*-oa) *adj* (f tua;pl tuoi,tue) your

tuonare (twoa-*naa*-ray) *v* thunder

tuono (*twaw*-noa) *m* thunder

tuorlo (*twor*-loa) *m* egg-yolk

turbare (toor-*baa*-ray) *v* upset

turbina (toor-*bee*-nah) *f* turbine

turbolento (toor-boa-*lehn*-toa) *adj* rowdy

Turchia (toor-*kee*-ah) *f* Turkey

turco (*toor*-koa) *adj* Turkish; *m* Turk

turismo (too-ree-zmoa) *m* tourism

turista (too-*ree*-stah) *m* tourist

turno (*toor*-noa) *m* turn

tuta (*tōō*-tah) *f* overalls *pl*

tutela (too-*tai*-lah) *f* custody

tutore (too-*tōā*-ray) *m* guardian, tutor

tuttavia (toot-tah-*vee*-ah) *adv* however, nevertheless

tutto (*toot*-toa) *adj* all; entire; *pron* everything; **in ~** altogether; **~ compreso** all in

tuttora (toot-*tōā*-rah) *adv* still

tweed (tweed) *m* tweed

U

ubbidiente (oob-bee-*dyehn*-tay) *adj* obedient

ubbidienza (oob-bee-*dyehn*-tsah) *f* obedience

ubbidire (oob-bee-*dee*-ray) *v* obey

ubicazione (oo-bee-kah-*tsyōā*-nay) *f* situation

ubriaco (oo-*bryaa*-koa) *adj* intoxicated, drunk

uccello (oot-*chehl*-loa) *m* bird; **~ marino** sea-bird

*****uccidere** (oot-*chee*-day-ray) *v* kill

udibile (oo-*dee*-bee-lay) *adj* audible

udienza (oo-*dyehn*-tsah) *f* audience

*****udire** (oo-*dee*-ray) *v* *hear

udito (oo-*dee*-toa) *m* hearing

uditore (oo-dee-*tōā*-ray) *m* auditor

ufficiale (oof-fee-*chaa*-lay) *adj* official; *m* officer

ufficio (oof-*fee*-choa) *m* office; **~ cambio** money exchange, exchange office; **~ di collocamento** employ-

ment exchange; **~ informazioni** inquiry office, information bureau; **~ oggetti smarriti** lost property office; **~ postale** post-office; **~ ricevimento** reception office; **~ turistico** tourist office

ufficioso (oof-fee-*chōā*-soa) *adj* unofficial

uguaglianza (oo-gwah-*lᵛahn*-tsah) *f* equality

uguagliare (oo-gwah-*lᵛaa*-ray) *v* equal

uguale (oo-*gwaa*-lay) *adj* even, equal; alike

ulcera (*ool*-chay-rah) *f* ulcer, sore; **~ gastrica** gastric ulcer

ulteriore (ool-tay-*ryōā*-ray) *adj* further

ultimamente (ool-tee-mah-*mayn*-tay) *adv* lately

ultimo (*ool*-tee-moa) *adj* last, ultimate

ultravioletto (ool-trah-vyoa-*layt*-toa) *adj* ultraviolet

umanità (oo-mah-nee-*tah*) *f* humanity, mankind

umano (oo-*maa*-noa) *adj* human

umidità (oo-mee-dee-*tah*) *f* moisture, humidity, damp

umido (*ōō*-mee-doa) *adj* wet, moist, humid, damp

umile (*ōō*-mee-lay) *adj* humble

umore (oo-*mōā*-ray) *m* spirit, mood; **di buon ~** good-tempered, good-humoured

un (oon) *art* (uno; f una) a *art*

unanime (oo-*naa*-nee-may) *adj* unanimous; like-minded

uncino (oon-*chee*-noa) *m* hook

undicesimo (oon-dee-*chai*-zee-moa) *num* eleventh

undici (*oon*-dee-chee) *num* eleven

ungherese (oong-gay-*rāȳ*-zay) *adj* Hungarian; *m* Hungarian

Ungheria (oong-gay-*ree*-ah) *f* Hungary

unghia (*oong*-gyah) *f* nail

unguento (oong-*gwehn*-toa) *m* salve,

ointment

unicamente (oo-nee-kah-*mayn*-tay) *adv* exclusively

unico (*ōō*-nee-koa) *adj* sole; unique

uniforme (oo-nee-*foar*-may) *adj* uniform; *f* uniform

unilaterale (oo-nee-lah-tay-*raa*-lay) *adj* one-sided

unione (oo-*ñōā*-nay) *f* union

unire (oo-*nee*-ray) *v* join; unite; combine; **unirsi a** join

unità (oo-nee-*tah*) *f* unity; unit; **~ monetaria** monetary unit

unito (oo-*nee*-toa) *adj* joint

universale (oo-nee-vayr-*saa*-lay) *adj* universal, global; all-round

università (oo-nee-vayr-see-*tah*) *f* university

universo (oo-nee-*vehr*-soa) *m* universe

uno (*ōō*-noa) *num* one; *pron* one

unto (*oon*-toa) *adj* greasy

untuoso (oon-*twōā*-soa) *adj* fatty

uomo (*waw*-moa) *m* (pl uomini) man; **~ d'affari** businessman; **~ di stato** statesman; **~ politico** politician

uovo (*waw*-voa) *m* (pl le uova) egg; **uova di pesce** roe

uragano (oo-rah-*gaa*-noa) *m* hurricane

urbano (oor-*baa*-noa) *adj* urban

urgente (oor-*jehn*-tay) *adj* urgent, pressing

urgenza (oor-*jehn*-tsah) *f* urgency

urina (oo-*ree*-nah) *f* urine

urlare (oor-*laa*-ray) *v* scream, shout

urlio (oor-*lee*-oa) *m* shouting

urlo (*oor*-loa) *m* cry

urtante (oor-*tahn*-tay) *adj* shocking, irritating, annoying

urtare (oor-*taa*-ray) *v* bump

urto (*oor*-toa) *m* bump; push

uruguaiano (oo-roo-gwah-*yaa*-noa) *adj* Uruguayan; *m* Uruguayan

Uruguay (oo-roo-*gwaa*-ee) *m* Uruguay

usabile (oo-*zaa*-bee-lay) *adj* usable

usanza (oo-*zahn*-tsah) *f* usage

usare (oo-*zaa*-ray) *v* use; **usato** worn-out

usciere (oosh-*shai*-ray) *m* usher; bailiff

uscio (*oosh*-shoa) *m* door

*uscire (oosh-*shee*-ray) *v* *go out

uscita (oosh-*shee*-tah) *f* way out, exit; issue; **~ di sicurezza** emergency exit

usignolo (oo-zee-*ñōā*-loa) *m* nightingale

uso (*ōō*-zoa) *m* use; **fuori ~** out of order

usuale (oo-*zwaa*-lay) *adj* customary

utensile (oo-tayn-*see*-lay) *m* utensil, implement

utente (oo-*tehn*-tay) *m* user

utero (*ōō*-tay-roa) *m* womb

utile (*ōō*-tee-lay) *adj* useful

utilità (oo-tee-lee-*tah*) *f* utility, use

utilizzare (oo-tee-leed-*dzaa*-ray) *v* utilize, employ; exploit

uva (*ōō*-vah) *f* grapes *pl*; **~ di Corinto** currant; **~ spina** gooseberry

uvetta (oo-*vayt*-tah) *f* raisin

V

vacante (vah-*kahn*-tay) *adj* unoccupied, vacant

vacanza (vah-*kahn*-tsah) *f* vacation

vacca (*vahk*-kah) *f* cow

vaccinare (vaht-chee-*naa*-ray) *v* vaccinate

vaccinazione (vaht-chee-nah-*tsyōā*-nay) *f* vaccination

vacillante (vah-cheel-*lahn*-tay) *adj* shaky; unsteady

vacillare (vah-cheel-*laa*-ray) *v* falter

vagabondaggio (vah-gah-boan-*dahd*-joa) *m* vagrancy

vagabondare (vah-gah-boan-*daa*-ray) *v* roam, tramp

vagabondo (vah-gah-*boan*-doa) *m* tramp

vagare (vah-*gaa*-ray) *v* wander

vaglia (*vaa*-lᵞah) *m* money order; ~ **postale** postal order; mail order *Am*

vagliare (vah-*lᵞaa*-ray) *v* sift

vago (*vaa*-goa) *adj* faint, vague

vagone (vah-*gōa*-nay) *m* coach, carriage; waggon; passenger car *Am*; ~ **letto** sleeping-car; ~ **ristorante** dining-car

vaiolo (vah-*yaw*-loa) *m* smallpox

valanga (vah-*lahng*-gah) *f* avalanche

*valere (vah-*lāy*-ray) *v* *be worth

valido (*vaa*-lee-doa) *adj* valid

valigia (vah-*lee*-jah) *f* bag, case, suitcase

valle (*vahl*-lay) *f* valley

valletto (vahl-*layt*-toa) *m* valet

valore (vah-*lōa*-ray) *m* value, worth; **senza~** worthless; **valori** valuables *pl*

valoroso (vah-loa-*rōa*-soa) *adj* courageous

valuta (vah-*lōō*-tah) *f* currency

valutare (vah-loo-*taa*-ray) *v* evaluate, estimate, appreciate, value

valutazione (vah-loo-tah-*tsyōa*-nay) *f* estimate

valvola (*vahl*-voa-lah) *f* valve; ~ **dell'aria** choke

valzer (*vahl*-tsayr) *m* waltz

vanga (*vahng*-gah) *f* spade

vangelo (vahn-*jai*-loa) *m* gospel

vaniglia (vah-*nee*-lᵞah) *f* vanilla

vanità (vah-nee-*tah*) *f* vanity

vano (*vaa*-noa) *adj* vain, idle; *m* room

vantaggio (vahn-*tahd*-joa) *m* benefit, advantage; profit; lead

vantaggioso (vahn-tahd-*jōa*-soa) *adj* advantageous

vantarsi (vahn-*tahr*-see) *v* boast

vapore (vah-*pōa*-ray) *m* steam, vapour

vaporizzatore (vah-poa-reed-dzah-*tōa*-ray) *m* atomizer

vari (*vaa*-ree) *adj* various

variabile (vah-*ryaa*-bee-lay) *adj* variable

variare (vah-*ryaa*-ray) *v* vary

variazione (vah-ryah-*tsyōa*-nay) *f* variation

varicella (vah-ree-*chehl*-lah) *f* chickenpox

varietà (vah-ryay-*tah*) *f* variety

varo (*vaa*-roa) *m* launching

vascello (vahsh-*shehl*-loa) *m* vessel

vasellame (vah-zayl-*laa*-may) *m* crockery

vasellina (vah-zayl-*lee*-nah) *f* vaseline

vaso (*vaa*-zoa) *m* vase; bowl; ~ **sanguigno** blood-vessel

vassoio (vahss-*sōa*-yoa) *m* tray

vasto (*vah*-stoa) *adj* vast; extensive, wide

vecchiaia (vayk-*kyaa*-yah) *f* old age

vecchio (*vehk*-keeoa) *adj* old; ancient

*vedere (vay-*dāy*-ray) *v* *see; notice; ***far ~** *show

vedova (*vāy*-doa-vah) *f* widow

vedovo (*vāy*-doa-voa) *m* widower

veduta (vay-*dōō*-tah) *f* sight

veemente (vay-ay-*mayn*-tay) *adj* fierce, intense

vegetariano (vay-jay-tah-*ryaa*-noa) *m* vegetarian

vegetazione (vay-jay-tah-*tsyōa*-nay) *f* vegetation

veicolo (vay-*ee*-koa-loa) *m* vehicle

vela (*vāy*-lah) *f* sail; ~ **di trinchetto** foresail

veleno (vay-*lāy*-noa) *m* poison

velenoso (vay-lay-*nōa*-soa) *adj* poisonous

velivolo (vay-*lee*-voa-loa) *m* aircraft

velluto (vayl-*lōō*-toa) *m* velvet; ~ **a**

coste corduroy; **~ di cotone** velveteen

velo (*vāy*-loa) *m* veil

veloce (vay-*lōā*-chay) *adj* fast, rapid

velocità (vay-loa-chee-*tah*) *f* speed; pace, rate; gear; **limite di ~** speed limit; **~ di crociera** cruising speed

vena (*vāy*-nah) *f* vein; **~ varicosa** varicose vein

vendemmia (vayn-*daym*-myah) *f* vintage

vendere (*vayn*-day-ray) *v* *sell; **~ al minuto** retail

vendetta (vayn-*dayt*-tah) *f* revenge

vendibile (vayn-*dee*-bee-lay) *adj* saleable

vendita (*vayn*-dee-tah) *f* sale; **in ~** for sale; **~ al minuto** retail trade

venerabile (vay-nay-*raa*-bee-lay) *adj* venerable

venerare (vay-nay-*raa*-ray) *v* worship

venerdì (vay-nayr-*dee*) *m* Friday

venezolano (vay-nay-tsoa-*laa*-noa) *adj* Venezuelan; *m* Venezuelan

Venezuela (vay-nay-*tswai*-lah) *m* Venezuela

*venire** (vay-*nee*-ray) *v* *come; *far ~** *send for

ventaglio (vayn-*taa*-lʸoa) *m* fan

ventesimo (vayn-*tai*-zee-moa) *num* twentieth

venti (*vayn*-tee) *num* twenty

ventilare (vayn-tee-*laa*-ray) *v* ventilate

ventilatore (vayn-tee-lah-*tōā*-ray) *m* fan, ventilator

ventilazione (vayn-tee-lah-*tsyōā*-nay) *f* ventilation

vento (*vehn*-toa) *m* wind

ventoso (vayn-*tōā*-soa) *adj* gusty, windy

veramente (vay-rah-*mayn*-tay) *adv* really

veranda (vay-*rahn*-dah) *f* veranda

verbale (vayr-*baa*-lay) *adj* verbal; *m* minutes

verbo (*vehr*-boa) *m* verb

verde (*vayr*-day) *adj* green

verdetto (vayr-*dayt*-toa) *m* verdict

verdura (vayr-*dōō*-rah) *f* greens *pl*, vegetable

vergine (*vehr*-jee-nay) *f* virgin

vergogna (vayr-*gōā*-ñah) *f* shame; *aver ~** *be ashamed; **vergogna!** shame!

vergognoso (vayr-goa-*ñōā*-soa) *adj* ashamed

verificare (vay-ree-fee-*kaa*-ray) *v* check, verify

verità (vay-ree-*tah*) *f* truth

veritiero (vay-ree-*tyai*-roa) *adj* truthful

verme (*vehr*-may) *m* worm

vernice (vayr-*nee*-chay) *f* varnish

verniciare (vayr-nee-*chaa*-ray) *v* varnish, paint

vero (*vāy*-roa) *adj* true; very

versamento (vayr-sah-*mayn*-toa) *m* deposit

versare (vayr-*saa*-ray) *v* pour; *shed

versione (vayr-*syōā*-nay) *f* version

verso[1] (*vehr*-soa) *prep* to; at, towards

verso[2] (*vehr*-soa) *m* verse

verticale (vayr-tee-*kaa*-lay) *adj* vertical

vertigine (vayr-*tee*-jee-nay) *f* vertigo; giddiness

vescica (vaysh-*shee*-kah) *f* bladder

vescovo (*vāy*-skoa-voa) *m* bishop

vespa (*vay*-spah) *f* wasp

vestaglia (vay-*staa*-lʸah) *f* negligee; dressing-gown

veste (*veh*-stay) *f* frock; robe

vestibolo (vayss-*tee*-boa-loa) *m* hall

vestire (vay-*stee*-ray) *v* dress; *wear

vestiti (vayss-*tee*-tee) *mpl* clothes *pl*; **vestito da donna** gown, dress; **vestito da uomo** *m* suit

veterinario (vay-tay-ree-*naa*-ryoa) *m* veterinary surgeon

vetrina (vay-*tree*-nah) *f* shop-window

vetro (*vāy*-troa) *m* glass; pane; **di ~** glass; **~ colorato** stained glass

vetta (*vayt*-tah) *f* peak, summit

vi (vee) *pron* you; yourselves

via¹ (*vee*-ah) *f* way; **~ d'acqua** waterway; **~ principale** main street; **~ selciata** causeway

via² (*vee*-ah) *adv* away, gone, off; *prep* via

viadotto (vyah-*doat*-toa) *m* viaduct

viaggiare (veeahd-*jaa*-ray) *v* travel

viaggiatore (vyahd-jah-*tōā*-ray) *m* traveller

viaggio (*vyahd*-joa) *m* journey; trip, voyage; **~ d'affari** business trip; **~ di ritorno** return journey

viale (*vyaa*-lay) *m* avenue

vibrare (vee-*braa*-ray) *v* tremble, vibrate

vibrazione (vee-brah-*tsyōā*-nay) *f* vibration

vicenda (vee-*chehn*-dah) *f* vicissitude; event

vicepresidente (vee-chay-pray-see-*dehn*-tay) *m* vice-president

vicinanza (vee-chee-*nahn*-tsah) *f* vicinity

vicinato (vee-chee-*naa*-toa) *m* neighbourhood

vicino (vee-*chee*-noa) *adj* close, nearby, near; *m* neighbour; **~ a** near; beside, next to, by

vicolo (*vee*-koa-loa) *m* lane, alley; **~ cieco** cul-de-sac

video (*vee*-day-oa) *m* screen

videocassetta (vee-day-oa-kahss-*sayt*-tah) *f* video cassette

videoregistratore (vee-day-oa-ray-jee-straa-toa-ray) *m* video recorder

vietato (vyay-*taa*-toa) *adj* prohibited; **~ ai pedoni** no pedestrians; **~ fumare** no smoking; **~ l'ingresso** no admittance

vigna (*vee*-ña) *f* vineyard

vigore (vee-*gōā*-ray) *m* stamina

vile (*vee*-lay) *adj* cowardly

villa (*veel*-lah) *f* villa

villaggio (veel-*lahd*-joa) *m* village

villino (veel-*lee*-noa) *m* cottage

*vincere (*veen*-chay-ray) *v* conquer, *overcome; *win

vincita (veen-*chee*-tah) *f* winnings *pl*

vincitore (veen-chee-*tōā*-ray) *m* winner

vino (*vee*-noa) *m* wine

violazione (vyoa-lah-*tsyōā*-nay) *f* violation

violentare (vyoa-layn-*taa*-ray) *v* rape

violento (vyoa-*lehn*-toa) *adj* violent, severe

violenza (vyoa-*lehn*-tsah) *f* violence

violetta (vyoa-*layt*-tah) *f* violet

violetto (vyoa-*layt*-toa) *adj* violet

violino (vyoa-*lee*-noa) *m* violin

virgola (*veer*-goa-lah) *f* comma

virgolette (veer-goa-*layt*-tay) *fpl* quotation marks

virtù (veer-*too*) *f* virtue

virtuoso (veer-*twōā*-soa) *adj* good

viscido (*veesh*-shee-doa) *adj* slippery

visibile (vee-*zee*-bee-lay) *adj* visible

visibilità (vee-zee-bee-lee-*tah*) *f* visibility

visione (vee-*zyōā*-nay) *f* vision

visita (*vee*-zee-tah) *f* visit, call; **~ medica** check-up

visitare (vee-zee-*taa*-ray) *v* call on; visit

visitatore (vee-zee-tah-*tōā*-ray) *m* visitor

viso (*vee*-zoa) *m* face

visone (vee-*zōā*-nay) *m* mink

vista (*vee*-stah) *f* sight; view

vistare (vee-*staa*-ray) *v* endorse

visto (*vee*-stoa) *m* visa

vistoso (vee-*stōā*-soa) *adj* striking

vita (*vee*-tah) *f* life; waist

vitale (vee-*taa*-lay) *adj* vital

vitamina (vee-tah-*mee*-nah) *f* vitamin

vite (*vee*-tay) f screw; vine

vitello (vee-*tehl*-loa) m calf; veal

vittima (*veet*-tee-mah) f victim; casualty

vitto (*veet*-toa) m fare, food; **~ e alloggio** room and board, bed and board, board and lodging

vittoria (veet-*taw*-ryah) f victory

vivace (vee-*vaa*-chay) adj active, brisk, lively; gay

vivaio (vee-*vaa*-yoa) m nursery

vivente (vee-*vehn*-tay) adj alive

***vivere** (*vee*-vay-ray) v live

vivido (*vee*-vee-doa) adj vivid

vivo (vee-voa) adj alive, live

viziare (vee-*tsyaa*-ray) v *spoil

vizio (*vee*-tsiœh) m vice

vocabolario (voa-kah-boa-*laa*-ryoa) m vocabulary

vocale (voa-*kaa*-lay) adj vocal; f vowel

voce (*vōa*-chay) f voice; **ad alta ~** aloud

voglia (*vaw*-lyah) f fancy; ***aver ~ di** fancy, *feel like

voi (*vōa*-ee) pron you; **~ stessi** yourselves

volante (voa-*lahn*-tay) m steering-wheel

volare (voa-*laa*-ray) v *fly

volentieri (voa-layn-*tyai*-ree) adv gladly, willingly

***volere** (voa-*lāy*-ray) v *will, want; ***voler bene** care for, like

volgare (voal-*gaa*-ray) adj coarse, vulgar

***volgere** (*vol*-jay-ray) v turn

volo (*vōa*-loa) m flight; **~ charter** charter flight; **~ di ritorno** return flight; **~ notturno** night flight

volontà (voa-loan-*tah*) f will

volontario (voa-loan-*taa*-ryoa) adj voluntary; m volunteer

volpe (*voal*-pay) f fox

volt (voalt) m volt

volta (*vol*-tah) f time; vault; **ancora una ~** once more; **due volte** twice; **qualche ~** sometimes; **una ~** once

voltaggio (voal-*tahd*-joa) m voltage

voltare (voal-*taa*-ray) v turn; turn round

volume (voa-*lōō*-may) m volume

voluminoso (voa-loo-mee-*nōa*-soa) adj big, bulky

vomitare (voa-mee-*taa*-ray) v vomit

vostro (*vo*-stroa) adj your

votare (voa-*taa*-ray) v vote

votazione (voa-tah-*tsyōa*-nay) f vote

voto (*vōa*-toa) m vote; mark

vulcano (vool-*kaa*-noa) m volcano

vulnerabile (vool-nay-*raa*-bee-lay) adj vulnerable

vuotare (vwo-*taa*-ray) v empty

vuoto (*vwaw*-toa) adj empty; hollow; m vacuum

Z

zaffiro (dzahf-*fee*-roa) m sapphire

zaino (*dzigh*-noa) m rucksack, knapsack

zampa (*tsahm*-pah) f paw

zampillo (tsahm-*peel*-loa) m squirt

zanzara (dzahn-*dzaa*-rah) f mosquito

zanzariera (dzahn-dzah-*ryai*-rah) f mosquito-net

zappa (*tsahp*-pah) f spade

zattera (*tsaht*-tay-rah) f raft

zebra (*dzai*-brah) f zebra

zelante (dzay-*lahn*-tay) adj diligent, zealous

zelo (*dzai*-loa) m diligence, zeal

zenit (*dzai*-neet) m zenith

zenzero (*dzehn*-dzay-roa) m ginger

zero (*dzai*-roa) m nought, zero

zia (*tsee*-ah) f aunt

zigomo (*dzee*-goa-moa) *m* cheek-bone

zigzagare (dzeeg-dzah-*gaa*-ray) *v* *wind

zinco (*dzeeng*-koa) *m* zinc

zingaro (*tseeng*-gah-roa) *m* gipsy

zio (*tsee*-oa) *m* uncle

zitella (tsee-*tehl*-lah) *f* spinster

zitto (*tseet*-toa) *adj* silent

zoccolo (*tsok*-koa-loa) *m* wooden shoe; hoof

zodiaco (dzoa-*dee*-ah-koa) *m* zodiac

zona (*dzōa*-nah) *f* zone; area; ~ **di**

parcheggio parking zone; ~ **industriale** industrial area

zoologia (dzoa-oa-loa-*jee*-ah) *f* zoology

zoom (zōōm) *m* zoom lens

zoppicante (tsoap-pee-*kahn*-tay) *adj* lame

zoppicare (tsoap-pee-*kaa*-ray) *v* limp

zoppo (*tsop*-poa) *adj* crippled, lame

zuccherare (tsook-kay-*raa*-ray) *v* sweeten

zucchero (*tsook*-kay-roa) *m* sugar; **zolletta di** ~ lump of sugar

Menu Reader

Food

abbacchio grilled lam

~ **alla cacciatora** pieces of lamb, often braised with garlic, rosemary, white wine, anchovy paste and hot peppers

(all') abruzzese Abruzzi style; with red peppers and sometimes ham

acciughe anchovies

~ **al limone** fresh anchovies served with a sauce of lemon, oil, breadcrumbs and oregano

(all')aceto (in) vinegar

acetosella sorrel

acquacotta soup of bread and vegetables, sometimes with eggs and cheese

affettati sliced cold meat, ham and salami (US cold cuts)

affumicato smoked

agliata garlic sauce; garlic mashed with breadcrumbs

aglio garlic

agnello lamb

agnolotti kind of ravioli with savoury filling of vegetables, chopped meats, sometimes with garlic and herbs

(all')agro dressing of lemon juice and oil

agrodolce sweet-sour dressing of caramelized sugar, vinegar and flour to which capers, raisins or lemon may be added

al, all', alla in the style of: with

ala wing

albicocca apricot

alice anchovy

allodola lark

alloro bay leaf

ananas pineapple

anguilla eel

~ **alla veneziana** braised with tunny (tuna) and lemon sauce

anguria watermelon

anice aniseed

animelle (di vitello) (veal) sweetbreads

anitra duck

~ **selvatica** wild duck

annegati slices of meat in white wine or Marsala wine

antipasto hors-d'oeuvre

~ **di mare** seafood

~ **a scelta** to one's own choosing

arachide peanuts

aragosta spiny lobster

arancia orange

aringa herring

arista loin of pork

arrosto roast(ed)

arsella kind of mussel

asiago cheese made of skimmed milk, semi hard to hard, sweet when young

asparago asparagus

assortito assorted

astice lobster

attorta flaky pastry filled with fruit and almonds

avellana hazelnut

babbaluci snails in olive-oil sauce with tomatoes and onions

baccalà stockfish, dried cod

~ **alla fiorentina** floured and fried in oil

~ **alla vicentina** poached in milk with onion, garlic, parsley, anchovies and cinnamon

(con) bagna cauda simmering sauce of butter, olive oil, garlic and chopped anchovies, into which raw vegetables and bread are dipped

barbabietola beetroot

basilico basil

beccaccia woodcock

Bel Paese smooth cheese with delicate taste

ben cotto well-done

(alla) besciamella (with) white sauce

bigoli in salsa noodles with an anchovy or sardine sauce

biscotto rusk, biscuit (US zwieback, cookie)

bistecca steak, usually beef, but may be another kind of meat

~ **di manzo** beef steak

~ **(alla) pizzaiola** with tomatoes, basil and sometimes garlic

~ **di vitello** veal scallop

bocconcini diced meat with herbs

bollito 1) boiled 2) meat or fish stew

(alla) bolognese in a sauce of tomatoes and meat or ham and cheese

(alla) brace on charcoal

braciola di maiale pork chop

bracioletta small slice of meat

~ **a scottadito** charcoal-grilled lamb chops

braciolone alla napoletana breaded rumpsteak with garlic, parsley, ham and currants; rolled, sautéed and stewed

branzino bass

brasato braised

broccoletti strascinati brocoli sautéed with pork fat and garlic

brodetto fish soup with onions and tomato pulp

brodo bouillon, broth, soup

~ **vegetale** vegetable broth

bruschetta a thick slice of countrystyle bread, grilled, rubbed with garlic and sprinkled with olive oil

budino blancmange, custard

bue beef

burrida fish casserole strongly flavoured with spices and herbs

burro butter

~ **maggiordomo** with lemon juice and parsley

busecca thick tripe and vegetable soup

cacciagione game

(alla) cacciatora often with mushrooms, herbs, shallots, wine, tomatoes, strips of ham and tongue

cacciucco spicy fish soup, usually with onions, green pepper, garlic and red wine topped with garlic flavoured croutons

caciocavallo firm, slightly sweet cheese from cow's or sheep's milk

calamaretto young squid

calamaro squid

caldo hot

calzone pizza dough envelope with ham, cheese, herbs and baked

(alla) campagnola with vegetables, especially onions and tomatoes

canederli dumplings made from ham, sausage and breadcrumbs

cannella cinnamon

cannelloni tubular dough stuffed with meat, cheese or vegetables, covered with a white sauce and baked

~ **alla Barbaroux** with chopped ham, veal, cheese and covered with white sauce

~ **alla laziale** with meat and onion filling and baked in tomato sauce

~ **alla napoletana** with cheese and ham filling in tomato and herb sauce

cannolo rolled pastry filled with sweet, white cheese, sometimes nougat and crystallized fruit

capitone large eel

capocollo smoked salt pork

caponata aubergine, green pepper, tomato, vegetable marrow, garlic, oil and herbs; usually served cold

cappelletti small ravioli filled with meat, herbs, cheese and eggs

cappero caper·

cappon magro pyramid of cooked vegetables and fish salad

cappone capon

capretto kid

~ **ripieno al forno** stuffed with herbs and roasted

caprino a soft goat's cheese

~ **romano** hard goat's milk cheese

capriolo roebuck

caramellato caramelized

(alla) carbonara *pasta* with smoked ham, cheese, eggs and olive oil

carbonata 1) grilled pork chop 2) beef stew in red wine

carciofo artichoke

~ **alla romana** stuffed, sautéed in oil, garlic and white wine

carciofino small artichoke

cardo cardoon

carne meat

~ **a carrargiu** spit-roasted

carota carrot

carpa, carpione carp

(della) casa chef's speciality

(alla) casalinga home-made

cassata ice-cream with a crystallized fruit filling

~ **(alla) siciliana** sponge cake garnished with sweet cream cheese, chocolate and crystallized fruit

(in) casseruola (in a) casserole

castagnaccio chestnut cake with pine kernels, raisins, nuts, cooked in oil

castagne chestnuts

caviale caviar

cavolfiore cauliflower

cavolino di Bruxelles brussels sprout

cavolo cabbage

cazzoeula a casserole of pork, celery, onions, cabbage and spices

cece chick-pea

cena dinner, supper

cerfoglio chervil

cervella brains ·

cervo stag
cetriolino gherkin (US pickle)
cetriolo cucumber
chiodo di garofano cloves
ciambella ringshaped bun
cicoria endive (US chicory)
ciliegia cherry
cima cold, stuffed veal
~ **alla genovese** stuffed with eggs, sausage and mushrooms
cinghiale (wild) boar
cioccolata chocolate
cipolla onion
cipollina pearl onion
ciuppin thick fish soup
cocomero watermelon
coda di bue oxtail
colazione lunch
composta stewed fruit
coniglio rabbit
~ **all'agro** stewed in red wine, with the addition of lemon juice
contorno garnish
copata small wafer of honey and nuts
coppa kind of raw ham, usually smoked
corda lamb tripes roasted or braised in tomato sauce with peas
cornetti 1) string beans 2) crescent rolls
cosce di rana frogs' legs
coscia leg, thigh
cosciotto leg
costata beef steak or chop, entre-côte
~ **alla fiorentina** grilled over an olive-wood fire, served with lemon juice and parsley
~ **alla pizzaiola** braised in sauce with tomatoes, marjoram, parsley and *mozzarella* cheese
~ **al prosciutto** with ham,

cheese and truffles; breaded and fried
costoletta cutlet, chop (veal or pork)
~ **alla bolognese** breaded veal cutlet topped with a slice of ham, cheese and tomato sauce
~ **alla milanese** veal cutlet, breaded, then fried
~ **alla parmigiana** breaded and baked with parmesan cheese
~ **alla valdostana** with ham and *fontina* cheese
~ **alla viennese**. breaded veal scallop, wiener schnitzel
cotechino spiced pork sausage, served hot in slices
cotto cooked
~ **a puntino** medium (done)
cozza mussel
cozze alla marinara mussels cooked in white wine with parsley and garlic
crauti sauerkraut
crema cream, custard
cremino 1) soft cheese 2) type of ice-cream bar
crescione watercress
crespolino spinach-filled pancake baked in cheese sauce
crocchetta potato or rice croquette
crostaceo shellfish
crostata pie, flan
crostini small pieces of toast, croutons
~ **in brodo** broth with croutons
~ **alla provatura** diced bread and *provatura* cheese toasted on a spit
crostino alla napoletana small toast with anchovies and melted cheese
crudo raw
culatello type of raw ham, cured

in white wine

cuore heart

  ~ di sedano celery heart

cuscusu di Trapani fish soup with semolina flakes

dattero date

datteri di mare mussels, small clams

dentice dentex (Mediterranean fish, similar to sea bream)

(alla) diavola usually grilled with a lavish amount of pepper, chili pepper or pimento

diverso varied

dolce sweet, dessert

dolci pastries, cakes

(alla) Doria with cucumbers

dragoncello tarragon

fagiano pheasant

fagiolino French bean (US green bean)

fagiolo haricot bean

faraona guinea hen

farcito stuffed

farsumagru rolled beef or veal stuffed with bacon, ham, eggs, cheese, parsley and onions; braised with tomatoes

fatto in casa home-made

fava broad bean

favata casserole of beans, bacon, sausage and seasoning

fegatelli di maiale alla Fiorentina pork liver grilled on a skewer with bay leaves and diced, fried croutons

fegato liver

  ~ alla veneziana slices of calf's liver fried with onions

(ai) ferri on the grill, grilled

fesa round cut taken from leg of veal

  ~ in gelatina roast veal in aspic jelly

fettina small slice

fettuccine flat narrow noodles

  ~ verdi green noodles

fico fig

filetto fillet

finocchio fennel

  ~ in salsa bianca in white sauce

(alla) fiorentina with herbs, oil and often spinach

focaccia 1) flat bread, sprinkled with olive oil, sometimes with fried chopped onions or cheese 2) sweet ring-shaped cake

  ~ di vitello veal patty

fondo di carciofo artichoke heart (US bottom)

fonduta melted cheese with egg-yolk, milk and truffles

fontina a soft, creamy cheese from Piedmont, chiefly used in cooking

formaggio cheese

(al) forno baked

forte hot, spicy

fra diavolo with a spicy tomato sauce

fragola strawberry

  ~ di bosco wild

frattaglie giblets

fregula soup with semolina and saffron dumplings

fresco cool, fresh, uncooked

frittata omelet

  ~ semplice plain

frittatina di patate potato omelet

frittella fritter, pancake, often filled with ham and cheese or with an apple

fritto deep-fried

  ~ alla milanese breaded

  ~ misto deep-fried bits of seafood, vegetables or meat

  ~ alla napoletana fried fish, vegetables and cheese

~ alla romana sweetbread, artichokes and cauliflower

~ di verdura fried vegetables

frutta fruit

~ candita crystallized (US candied)

~ cotta stewed

frutti di mare shellfish

fungo mushroom

galantina tartufata truffles in aspic jelly

gallina hen

gallinaccio 1) chanterelle mushroom 2) woodcock

gallinella water-hen

gallo cedrone grouse

gamberetto shrimp

gambero crayfish, crawfish

garofolato beef stew with cloves

(in) gelatina (in) aspic jelly

gelato ice-cream; iced dessert

(alla) genovese with basil and other herbs, pine kernels, garlic and oil

ghiacciato iced, chilled

ginepro juniper (berry)

girello round steak from the leg

gnocchi dumplings

gorgonzola most famous of the Italian blue-veined cheese, rich with a tangy flavour

grana hard cheese; also known as *parmigiano(-reggiano)*

granchio crab

grasso rich with fat or oil

(alla) graticola grilled

gratinata sprinkled with breadcrumbs and grated cheese and oven-browned

grattugiato grated

(alla) griglia from the grill

grissino breadstick

gruviera mild cheese with holes, Italian version of Swiss *gruyère*

guazzetto meat stew with garlic, rosemary, tomatoes and pimentos

incasciata layers of dough, meat sauce, hard-boiled eggs and grated cheese

indivia chicory (US endive)

insalata salad

~ all'americana mayonnaise and shrimps

~ russa diced boiled vegetables in mayonnaise

~ verde green

~ di verdura cotta boiled vegetables

involtino stuffed meat or ham roll

lampone raspberry

lampreda lamprey

lardo bacon

lasagne thin layers of generally green noodle dough alternating with tomato, sausage meat, ham, white sauce and grated cheese; baked in the oven

latte alla portoghese baked custard with liquid caramel

lattuga lettuce

lauro bay leaf

(alla) laziale with onions

legume vegetable

lenticchia lentil

lepre hare

~ al lardo con funghi with bacon and mushrooms

~ in salmì jugged

leprotto leveret

lesso 1) boiled 2) meat or fish stew

limone lemon

lingua tongue

linguine flat noodles

lista dei vini wine list

lodigiano kind of parmesan cheese

lombata loin

luganega pork sausage

lumaca snail
lupo di mare sea perch
maccheroni macaroni
macedonia di frutta fruit salad
maggiorana marjoram
magro 1) lean 2) dish without meat
maiale pork
  ~ al latte cooked in milk
  ~ ubriaco cooked in red wine
maionese mayonnaise
mandarino mandarin
mandorla almond
manzo beef
  ~ arrosto ripieno stuffed roast
  ~ lesso boiled
  ~ salato corned beef
(alla) marinara sauce of tomatoes, olives, garlic, clams and mussels
marinato marinated
maritozzo soft roll
marmellata jam
  ~ d'arance marmalade
marrone chestnut
mascarpone soft, butter-coloured cheese, often served as a sweet dish
medaglione round fillet of beef or veal
mela apple
  ~ cotogna quince
melanzana aubergine (US eggplant)
melanzane alla parmigiana aubergines baked with tomatoes, parmesan cheese and spices
melanzane ripiene stuffed with various ingredients and gratinéed
melone melon
  ~ con prosciutto with cured ham
menta mint
meringa meringue

merlano whiting
merluzzo cod
messicani veal scallops rolled around a meat, cheese or herb stuffing
midollo marrow (bone)
miele honey
(alla) milanese 1) Milanese style of cooking 2) breaded (of meat)
millefoglie custard slice (US napoleon)
minestra soup
  ~ in brodo bouillon with noodles or rice and chicken liver
  ~ di funghi cream of mushroom
minestrone thick vegetable soup
  ~ alla genovese with spinach, basil, macaroni
  ~ verde with French beans and herbs
mirtillo bilberry (US blueberry)
misto mixed
mitilo mussel
(alla) montanara with different root vegetables
montone mutton
mora blackberry, mulberry
mortadella bologna (sausage)
mostarda mustard
  ~ di frutta spiced crystallized fruits (US candied fruits) in a sweet-sour syrup
mozzarella soft, unripened cheese with a bland, slightly sweet flavour, made from buffalo's milk in southern Italy, elsewhere with cow's milk
(alla) napoletana with cheese, tomatoes, herbs and sometimes anchovies
nasello whiting
naturale plain, without sauce or

filling

navone yellow turnip

nocciola hazelnut

noce nut

~ **di cocco** coconut

~ **moscata** nutmeg

nostrano local, home-grown

oca goose

olio oil

~ **d'arachide** peanut oil

~ **di semi** seed oil

olive agrodolci olives in vinegar and sugar

olive ripiene stuffed olives (e.g. with meat, cheese, pimento)

ombrina umbrine (fish)

orata John Dory (fish)

origano oregano

osso bone

~ **buco** veal shanks cooked in various ways depending on the region

ostrica oyster

ovalina small *mozzarella* cheese from buffalo's milk

ovolo egg mushroom

(alla) paesana with bacon, potatoes, carrots, vegetable marrow and other root vegetables

pagliarino medium-soft cheese from Piedmont

palomba wood-pigeon, ring-dove

pan di Genova almond cake

pan di Spagna sponge cake

pan tostato toasted Italian bread

pancetta bacon

pandolce heavy cake with dried fruit and pine kernels

pane bread

~ **casareccio** home-made

~ **scuro** dark

~ **di segale** rye

panettone tall light cake with a few raisins and crystallized fruit

panforte di Siena flat round slab made mostly of spiced crystallized fruit

pangrattato breadcrumbs

panicielli d'uva passula grapes wrapped in citron leaves and baked

panino roll

~ **imbottito** sandwich

panna cream

~ **montata** whipped

panzarotti fried or baked large dough envelopes often with a filling of pork, eggs, cheese, anchovies and tomatoes

pappardelle long, broad noodles

~ **con la lepre** garnished with spiced hare

parmigiano(-reggiano) parmesan, a hard cheese generally grated for use in hot dishes

passatelli pasta made from a mixture of egg, parmesan cheese, breadcrumbs, often with a pinch of nutmeg

passato purée, creamed

~ **di verdura** mashed vegetable soup, generally with croutons

pasta the traditional Italian first course; essentially a dough consisting of flour, water, oil (or butter) and eggs; produced in a variety of shapes and sizes (e.g. spaghetti, macaroni, broad noodles, ravioli, shell- and star-shaped *pasta*); may be eaten on its own, in a bouillon, seasoned with butter or olive oil, stuffed or accompanied by a savoury sauce, sprinkled with grated cheese

~ **asciutta** any pasta not eaten in a bouillon; served with any of various dressings

pasticcino tart, cake, small pastry

pasticcio 1) pie 2) type of *pasta* like *lasagne*

pastina small *pasta* in various shapes used principally as a bouillon or soup ingredient

pasto meal

patate potatoes

~ **fritte** deep fried

~ **lesse** boiled

~ **novelle** new

~ **in padella** fried in a pan

~ **rosolate** roasted

~ **saltate** sliced and sautéed

patatine small, new potatoes

pecorino a hard cheese made from sheep's milk

pepato peppered

pepe pepper

peperonata stew of peppers, tomatoes and sometimes onions

peperone green or red sweet pepper

~ **arrostito** roasted sweet pepper

~ **ripieno** stuffed, usually with rice and chopped meat

pera pear

pernice partridge

pesca peach

~ **melba** peach-halves poached in syrup over vanilla ice-cream, topped with raspberry sauce and whipped cream

pescatrice angler fish, frog fish

pesce fish

~ **spada** swordfish

pesto sauce of basil leaves, garlic, cheese and sometimes with pine kernels and majoram; used in *minestrone* or with *pasta*

petto breast

(a) piacere to your own choosing

piatto dish

~ **del giorno** the day's speciality

~ **principale** main course

primo ~ first course

piccante highly seasoned

piccata thin veal scallop

~ **al marsala** braised in Marsala sauce

piccione pigeon (US squab)

piede trotter (US foot)

(alla) piemontese Piedmontese style; with truffles and rice

pignoli pine kernels

pinoccate pine kernel and almond cake

pisello pea

pistacchi pistachio nuts

piviere plover (bird)

pizza flat, open(-faced) pie, tart, flan; bread dough bottom with any of a wide variety of toppings

pizzetta small *pizza*

polenta pudding of maizemeal (US cornmeal)

~ **pasticciata** *polenta*, sliced and served with meat sauce, mushrooms, white sauce, butter and cheese

~ **e uccelli** small birds spit-roasted and served with *polenta*

pollame fowl

pollo chicken

~ **alla diavola** highly spiced and grilled

~ **novello** spring chicken

polpetta di carne meatball

polpettone meat loaf of seasoned beef or veal

polpo octopus

~ **in purgatorio** sautéed in oil with tomatoes, parsley, garlic and peppers

(salsa di) pommarola tomato sauce

for *pasta*

pomodoro tomato

pompelmo grapefruit

popone melon

porchetta roast suck(l)ing pig

porcini boletus mushrooms

porro leek

pranzo lunch or dinner

prezzemolo parsley

prezzo price

  ~ fisso fixed price

prima colazione breakfast

primizie spring fruit or vegetables

profiterole filled cream puff

  ~ alla cioccolata with chocolate frosting

prosciutto ham

  ~ affumicato cured, smoked

  ~ di cinghiale smoked wild boar

  ~ di Parma cured ham from Parma

provatura soft, mild and slightly sweet cheese made from buffalo's milk

provolone white, medium-hard cheese

prugna plum

  ~ secca prune

punte di asparagi asparagus tips

purè di patate mashed potatoes

quaglia quail

rabarbaro rhubarb

rafano horse-radish

ragù meat sauce for *pasta*

ragusano hard and slightly sweet cheese

rapa turnip

ravanello radish

raviggiolo cheese made from sheep's or goat's milk

razza ray

ribes currants

  ~ neri blackcurrants

~ rossi redcurrants

riccio di mare sea urchin

ricotta soft cow's or sheep's milk cheese

rigaglie giblets

rigatoni 1) type of *pasta* similar to *cannelloni* 2) type of macaroni

ripieno stuffing, stuffed

risi e bisi rice and peas cooked in chicken bouillon

riso rice

  ~ in bianco white rice with butter

risotto dish made of boiled rice served as a first course, with various ingredients according to the region

(brodo) ristretto consommé

robiola soft, rich and sweet sheep's milk cheese

robiolina goat's or sheep's milk cheese

rognoni kidneys

(alla) romana with vegetables, particularly onions, mint and sometimes anchovies

rombo turbot, brill

rosbif roast beef

rosmarino rosemary

rotolo rolled, stuffed meat

salame salami

salato salted

sale salt

salmone salmon

salsa sauce

salsiccia any spiced pork sausage to be served cooked

saltimbocca veal slices with ham, sage, herbs and wine

  ~ alla romana veal cutlet flavoured with ham and sage, sautéed in butter and white wine

(al) sangue underdone (US rare)

sarda pilchard, sardine

sardina small sardine

sardo sheep's milk cheese, hard, pungent and aromatic

sartù oven-baked rice with tomatoes, meat balls, chicken giblets, mushrooms and peas

scalogno shallot

scaloppa, scaloppina veal scallop
~ **alla fiorentina** with spinach and white sauce

scamorza aged *mozzarella*, firmer and saltier

scampi Dublin Bay prawns

scapece fried fish preserved in white vinegar with saffron

(allo) sciroppo in syrup

scorfano rascasse, a Mediterranean fish, used for fish soup

scorzonera salsify

sedano celery

selvaggina game

senape mustard

seppia cuttlefish, squid

servizio (non) compreso service (not) included

sfogliatelle puff pastry with custard or fruit-preserve filling

sgombro mackerel

silvano chocolate meringue or tart

soffritto sautéed

sogliola sole
~ **arrosto** baked in olive oil, herbs and white wine
~ **dorata** breaded and fried
~ **ai ferri** grilled
~ **alla mugnaia** sautéed in butter with lemon juice and parsley

soppressata 1) sausage 2) preserved pig's head with pistachio nuts

sottaceti pickled vegetables

sottaceto pickled

spaghetti spaghetti

~ **aglio e olio** with olive oil and fried garlic

~ **all'amatriciana** with tomato sauce, garlic and parmesan cheese

~ **alla carbonara** with oil, cheese, bacon and eggs

~ **pomodoro e basilico** fresh tomatoes and basil leaves

~ **alle vongole** with clam or mussel sauce, tomatoes, garlic and pimento

spalla shoulder

specialità speciality

spezzatino meat or fowl stew

spiedino pieces of meat grilled or roasted on a skewer
~ **di mare** pieces of fish and seafood skewered and roasted

(allo) spiedo (on a) spit

spigola sea bass

spinaci spinach

spugnola morel mushroom

spumone foamy ice-cream dessert with crystallized fruit, whipped cream and nuts

(di) stagione (in) season

stellette star-shaped *pasta*

stinco knuckle (of veal), shin (of beef)

stoccafisso stockfish, dried cod

storione sturgeon

stracchino creamy, soft to medium-soft cheese

stracciatella consommé with semolina or breadcrumbs, eggs and grated cheese

stracotto meat stew, slowly cooked for several hours

strascinati shell-shaped fresh *pasta* with different sauces

stufato 1) stew(ed) 2) beef stew

succu tunnu soup with semolina and saffron dumplings

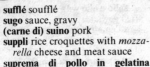

sufflé soufflé

sugo sauce, gravy

(carne di) suino pork

suppli rice croquettes with *mozzarella* cheese and meat sauce

suprema di pollo in gelatina chicken breast in aspic jelly

susina plum

tacchino turkey

tagliatelle flat noodles

tagliolini thin flat noodles

taleggio medium-hard cheese with a mild flavour

tartaruga turtle

tartina open(-faced) sandwich

tartufo truffle

tartufi di mare cockles or small clams

(al) tegame sautéed

(alla) teglia fried in a pan

testa di vitello calf's head

timo thyme

tinca tench (fish)

tonnato in tunny (tuna) sauce

tonno tunny (US tuna)

topinambur Jerusalem artichoke

tordo thrush

torrone nougat

torta pie, tart, flan

tortelli small fritters

tortellini ringlets of dough filled with seasoned minced meat

tortiglione almond cake

tortino savoury tart filled with cheese and vegetables

~ **di carciofi** fried artichokes mixed with beaten eggs

(alla) toscana with tomatoes, celery and herbs

tostato toasted

totano young squid

tramezzino small sandwich

trenette noodles

triglia red mullet

trippe alla fiorentina slowly braised tripe and minced beef with tomato sauce, marjoram, parmesan cheese

trippe alla milanese tripe stewed with onions, leek, carrots, tomatoes, beans, sage and nutmeg

trippe alla romana cooked in sweet-and-sour sauce with cheese

tritato minced

trota trout

~ **alle mandorle** stuffed, seasoned, baked in cream and topped with almonds

~ **di ruscello** river trout

tutto compreso everything included

uccelletti, uccelli small birds, usually spit-roasted

~ **in umido** stewed

uovo egg

~ **affogato nel vino** poached in wine

~ **al burro** fried in butter

~ **in camicia** poached

~ **alla coque** boiled

~ **alla fiorentina** fried, served on a bed of spinach

~ **(al) forno** baked

~ **fritto** fried

~ **molle** soft-boiled

~ **ripieno** stuffed

~ **sodo** hard-boiled

~ **strapazzato** scrambled

uva grape

vaniglia vanilla

vario assorted

(alla) veneziana with onions or shallots, white wine and mint

verdura green vegetables

vermicelli thin noodles

verza green cabbage

vitello veal

~ **all'uccelletto** diced veal, sage, simmered in wine

vongola small clam

zaba(gl)ione dessert of egg-yolks, sugar and Marsala wine; served warm

zampone pig's trotter filled with seasoned pork, boiled and served in slices

zèppola fritter, doughnut

zimino fish stew

zucca pumpkin, gourd

zucchero sugar

zucchino small vegetable marrow (US zucchini)

zuppa soup

~ **fredda** cold

~ **di frutti di mare** seafood

~ **inglese** sponge cake steeped in rum with candied fruit and custard or whipped cream

~ **alla pavese** consommé with poached egg, croutons and grated cheese

~ **di vongole** clam soup with white wine

Drinks

abboccato medium dry (wine)

acqua water

~ **fredda** ice-cold

~ **gasata** soda water

acquavite brandy, spirits

Aleatico a dessert wine made from muscat grapes

amabile slightly sweet (wine)

Americano a popular aperitif made with *Campari*, vermouth, angostura and lemon peel

aperitivo aperitif

aranciata orangeade

asciutto dry (wine)

Asti Spumante the renowned sparkling white wine from Piedmont

Aurum an orange liqueur

Barbaresco a red wine from Piedmont resembling *Barolo*, but lighter and slightly drier

Barbera a dark red, full-bodied wine from Piedmont and Lombardy with a rich bouquet

Bardolino a very pale red wine, from the Lago di Garda near Verona

Barolo a high quality red wine from Piedmont, can be compared to wines from the Rhone Valley

bibita beverage, drink

birra beer

~ **di barile** draught (US draft)

~ **chiara** lager, light

~ **scura** dark

~ **alla spina** draught (US draft)

caffè coffee

~ **corretto** espresso laced with a shot of liquor or brandy

~ **freddo** iced

~ **macchiato** with a few drops of warm milk

~ **nero** black

~ **ristretto** small and concentrated

caffellatte coffee with milk

Campania the region around Naples is noted for its fine red and white wines like *Capri*, *Falerno* and *Lacrima Christi*

Campari a reddish bitter aperitif with a quinine taste

cappuccino black coffee and whipped milk, sometimes with grated chocolate

caraffa carafe

Castelli Romani a common dry white wine from south-east of Rome

Centerbe a strong, green herb liqueur

Cerasella a cherry liqueur

Certosino a yellow or green herb liqueur

Chianti the renowned red and white table wines of Tuscany, traditionally bottled in a *fiasco*; there are many different qualities depending on the vineyards

Chiaretto one of Italy's most famous rosé wines; best when drunk very young; produced south of Lago di Garda

Cortese a dry white wine from Piedmont with limited production

dolce sweet (wine)

Emilia-Romagna the region around Bologna produces chiefly red wine like *Lambrusco*, which is sparkling and has a certain tang, and *Sangiovese*, a still type

Est! Est! Est! a semi-sweet white wine from the region north of Rome

Etna wines from the west slopes of Mount Etna (Sicily)

Falerno red and white dry wines produced in Campania

Fernet-Branca a bitter digestive

fiasco a straw-covered flask

frappè milk shake

Frascati a *Castelli Romani* white wine which can be dry or slightly sweet

Freisa red wines from Piedmont; one type is dry and fruity, the other is lighter and can be slightly sweet or semi-sparkling; one of Italy's best red wines produced south-west of Lago Maggiore

frizzante semi-sparkling (wine)

Gattinara a red, high-quality full-bodied wine from Piedmont, south-east of Lago Maggiore

granatina, granita fruit syrup or coffee served over crushed ice

grappa spirit distilled from grape mash

Grignolino good quality red wine with a special character and scent; often with a high alcoholic content

Lacrima Christi the most well-known wine from the Vesuvian slopes (Campania); the white wine is the best, but there are also red and rosé versions

Lago di Caldaro light red wine produced in the Italian Tyrol

Lagrein Rosato a good rosé from the region around Bolzano in the Italian Tyrol

Lambrusco a sparkling and tingling red wine from Emilia-Romagna

latte milk

~ **al cacao** chocolate drink

Lazio Latium; the region princi-

limonata lemonade

Lombardia Lombardy; the region around Milan produces various red wines like the *Bonarda*, *Inferno*, *Spanna* and *Valtellina*, the rosé *Chiaretto* and the white *Lugana*

Lugana a good dry white wine from the region of Lago di Garda

Marsala the renowned red dessert wine from Sicily

Martini a brand-name of white and red vermouth

Millefiori a liqueur distilled from herbs and alpine flowers

Moscatello, Moscato muscatel; name for different dessert and table wines produced from the muscat grapes; there are some red, but most are white

Orvieto light, white wine from Umbria; three versions exist: dry, slightly sweet and sweet

Piemonte Piedmont; the north-western region of Italy reputedly produces the highest quality wine in the country and is best known for its sparkling wine *Asti Spumante*; among its red wines are *Barbaresco*, *Barbera*, *Barolo*, *Dolcetto*, *Freisa*, *Gattinara*, *Grignolino*, *Nebbiolo*; *Cortese* is a light white wine

porto port (wine)

Puglia Apulia; at the south-eastern tip of Italy, this region produces the greatest quantity of the nation's wine, mainly table wine and some dessert wine

pally to the south of Rome produces chiefly white wine like *Castelli Romani*, *Est! Est! Est!* and *Frascati*

Punt e Mès a brand-name vermouth

Sangiovese a red table wine from Emilia-Romagna

Santa Giustina a good red table wine from the Italian Tyrol

Santa Maddalena a good quality red wine from the Italian Tyrol, light in colour and rather fruity

sciroppo fruit syrup diluted with water

secco dry (wine)

Sicilia Sicily; this island is noted for its dessert wine, particularly the celebrated *Marsala*; among many table wines the red, white and rosé *Etna* wines are the best known

sidro cider

Silvestro a herb and mint liqueur

Soave very good dry white wine, which is best when drunk young (from the east ov Verona)

spremuta fresh fruit drink

spumante sparkling

Stock a wine-distilled brandy

Strega a strong herb liqueur

succo juice

tè tea

~ **al latte** with milk

~ **al limone** with lemon

Terlano Tyrolean white wine, renowned, well balanced, greenish yellow in colour and with a delicate taste

Toscana Tuscany; the region around Florence is particularly noted for its red and white *Chianti*, a good table wine, and the dessert wines *Aleatico* and *Vin Santo*

Traminer a Tyrolean white wine from the region which gave the grape and the name to the renowned Alsatian *Traminer* and *Gewürztraminer* white wines

Trentino-Alto Adige the alpine region produces red wines like *Lago di Caldaro, Santa Giustina, Santa Maddalena; Terlano* and *Traminer* are notable white wines; *Lagrein Rosato* is a rosé to remember while *Vin Santo* is a good dessert wine

Valpolicella a light red wine with a rich cherry colour and a trace of bitterness; it is best when drunk young

Valtellina region near the Swiss border which produces good, dark red wine

Vecchia Romagna a wine-distilled brandy

Veneto the north-eastern region of Italy produces high quality wines; among its red wines are *Amarone, Bardolino, Merlot, Pinot Nero, Valpolicella;* among the whites, *Pinot Grigio, Soave. Recioto* is a sparkling red wine

Vin Santo (Vinsanto) a fine dessert wine produced chiefly in Tuscany but also in Trentino, the Italian Tyrol

vino wine

~ **aperto** open

~ **bianco** white

~ **del paese** local

~ **rosatello, rosato** rosé

~ **rosso** red

Mini-Grammar

Articles

There are two genders in Italian—masculine (masc.) and feminine (fem.).

1. Definite article (the):

	singular	plural
masc.	**l'** before a vowel	**gli**
	lo before **z** or **s + consonant**	**gli**
	il before all other consonants	**i**
	l'amico (the friend)	**gli amici** (the friends)
	lo studente (the student)	**gli studenti** (the students)
	il treno (the train)	**i treni** (the trains)
fem.	**l'** before a vowel	**le**
	la before a consonant	**le**
	l'arancia (the orange)	**le arance** (the oranges)
	la casa (the house)	**le case** (the houses)

2. Indefinite article (a/an):

masc.   **un** (**uno** before **z** or **s + consonant***)
    un piatto (a plate)
    uno specchio (a mirror)

fem.   **una** (**un'** before a vowel)
    una strada (a street)
    un'amica (a girl friend)

3. Partitive (some/any)

In affirmative sentences and some interrogatives, **some** and **any** are expressed by **di + definite article**, which has the following contracted forms:

masc.	**dell'** before a vowel	**degli**
	dello before **z** or **s + consonant**	**degli**
	del before other consonants	**dei**
fem.	**dell'** before a vowel	**delle**
	della before a consonant	**delle**

Desidero del vino.	I want some wine.
Vorrei delle sigarette.	I'd like some cigarettes.
Ha degli amici a Roma?	Have you any friends in Rome?

Nouns

Nouns ending in **o** are generally masculine. To form the plural, change **o** to **i**.

il tavolo (the table)   **i tavoli** (the tables)

Nouns ending in **a** are usually feminine. To form the plural, change **a** to **e**.

la casa (the house)   **le case** (the houses)

Nouns ending in **e**—no rule as to gender. Learn each noun individually. Plurals are formed by changing the **e** to **i**.

il piede (the foot)   **i piedi** (the feet)   **la notte** (the night)   **le notti** (the nights)

---

*When **s** is followed by a vowel, the masculine articles are **il/i** (definite) and **un** (indefinite).

Adjectives

They agree with the noun they modify in number and gender. There are two basic types—ending in **o** and ending in **e**.

	singular	plural		singular	plural
masc.	**leggero** light (in weight)	**leggeri**	fem.	**leggera**	**leggere**
	grande big	**grandi**		**grande**	**grandi**

They usually follow the noun but certain common adjectives precede the noun.

un caro amico (a dear friend)   **una strada lunga** (a long street)

Demonstratives

this	**questo/questa** (contracted to **quest'** before a vowel)
these	**questi/queste** (no contraction)
that	**quell', quello, quel** (masc.)/**quell', quella*** (fem.)
those	**quegli, quei** (masc.)/**quelle** (fem.)

Possessive adjectives and pronouns

These agree in number and gender *with the nouns they modify* (or replace).

	masculine		feminine	
	singular	plural	singular	plural
my, mine	**il mio**	**i miei**	**la mia**	**le mie**
your, yours	**il tuo**	**i tuoi**	**la tua**	**le tue**
his, her, hers, its	**il suo**	**i suoi**	**la sua**	**le sue**
our, ours	**il nostro**	**i nostri**	**la nostra**	**le nostre**
your, yours	**il vostro**	**i vostri**	**la vostra**	**le vostre**
their, theirs	**il loro**	**i loro**	**la loro**	**le loro**
**your, yours (sing.)	**il suo**	**i suoi**	**la sua**	**le sue**
**your, yours (plur.)	**il loro**	**i loro**	**la loro**	**le loro**

Thus, depending on the context, **il suo cane** can mean *his, her* or *your dog*.

* These forms follow the same system as **dell'/dello/della**, etc. (see p. 167).
**This is the formal form—used in addressing people you do not know well.

Personal pronouns

	Subject	Direct Object	Indirect Object	After a Preposition
I	**io**	**mi**	**mi**	**me**
you	**tu**	**ti**	**ti**	**te**
he, it (masc.)	**lui/egli**	**lo**	**gli**	**lui**
she, it (fem.)	**lei/ella**	**la**	**le**	**lei**
we	**noi**	**ci**	**ci**	**noi**
you	**voi**	**vi**	**vi**	**voi**
they (masc.)	**loro/essi**	**li**	**loro**	**loro**
they (fem.)	**loro/esse**	**le**	**loro**	**loro**

Note: There are two forms for "you" in Italian: **tu** (singular) is used when talking to relatives, close friends and children (and between young people); the plural of **tu** is **voi**. **Lei** (singular) and **Loro** (plural) are used in all other cases (with the 3rd person singular/plural of the verb).

Italian verbs

Below is a list of Italian verbs in three regular conjugations, grouped by families according to their infinitive endings, *-are*, *-ere* and *-ire*. Within the *-ire* group is one category that lengthens its stem by the addition of *-isc-* in the singular and the third person plural of the present tense (e.g. *fiorire* – *fiorisco*). Verbs which do not follow the conjugations below are considered irregular (see irregular verb list). Note that there are some verbs which follow the regular conjugation of the category they belong to, but present some minor changes in spelling. Examples: *mangiare, mangerò; cominciare, comincerò; navigare, navigherò*. The personal pronoun is not generally expressed since the verb endings clearly indicate the person.

		1st conj.	2nd conj.	3rd conj.
Infinitive		**am are** *(love)*	**tem ere** *(fear)*	**vest ire** *(dress)*
Present	(io)	am **o**	tem **o**	vest **o**
	(tu)	am **i**	tem **i**	vest **i**
	(egli)	am **a**	tem **e**	vest **e**
	(noi)	am **iamo**	tem **iamo**	vest **iamo**
	(voi)	am **ate**	tem **ete**	vest **ite**
	(essi)	am **ano**	tem **ono**	vest **ono**
Imperfect	(io)	am **avo**	tem **evo**	vest **ivo**
	(tu)	am **avi**	tem **evi**	vest **ivi**
	(egli)	am **ava**	tem **eva**	vest **iva**
	(noi)	am **avamo**	tem **evamo**	vest **ivamo**
	(voi)	am **avate**	tem **evate**	vest **ivate**
	(essi)	am **avano**	tem **evano**	vest **ivano**
Past Definit	(io)	am **ai**	tem **ei**	vest **ii**
	(tu)	am **asti**	tem **esti**	vest **isti**
	(egli)	am **ò**	tem **è**	vest **ì**
	(noi)	am **ammo**	tem **emmo**	vest **immo**
	(voi)	am **aste**	tem **este**	vest **iste**
	(essi)	am **arono**	tem **erono**	vest **irono**
Future	(io)	am **erò**	tem **erò**	vest **irò**
	(tu)	am **erai**	tem **erai**	vest **irai**
	(egli)	am **erà**	tem **erà**	vest **irà**
	(noi)	am **eremo**	tem **eremo**	vest **iremo**
	(voi)	am **erete**	tem **erete**	vest **irete**
	(essi)	am **eranno**	tem **eranno**	vest **iranno**
Conditional	(io)	am **erei**	tem **erei**	vest **irei**
	(tu)	am **eresti**	tem **eresti**	vest **iresti**
	(egli)	am **erebbe**	tem **erebbe**	vest **irebbe**
	(noi)	am **eremmo**	tem **eremmo**	vest **iremmo**
	(voi)	am **ereste**	tem **ereste**	vest **ireste**
	(essi)	am **erebbero**	tem **erebbero**	vest **irebbero**

Pres. subj.	(io) am **i**	tem **a**	vest **a**
	(tu) am **i**	tem **a**	vest **a**
	(egli) am **i**	tem **a**	vest **a**
	(noi) am **iamo**	tem **iamo**	vest **iamo**
	(voi) am **iate**	tem **iate**	vest **iate**
	(essi) am **ino**	tem **ano**	vest **ano**
Pres. part./gerund	am **ando**	tem **endo**	vest **endo**
Past. part.	am **ato**	tem **uto**	vest **ito**

Auxiliary verbs

avere
(to have)

essere
(to be)

	Present	Imperfect	Present	Imperfect
(io)	ho	avevo	sono	ero
(tu)	hai	avevi	sei	eri
(egli)	ha	aveva	è	era
(noi)	abbiamo	avevamo	siamo	eravamo
(voi)	avete	avevate	siete	eravate
(essi)	hanno	avevano	sono	erano

	Future	Conditional	Future	Conditional
(io)	avrò	avrei	sarò	sarei
(tu)	avrai	avresti	sarai	saresti
(egli)	avrà	avrebbe	sarà	sarebbe
(noi)	avremo	avremmo	saremo	saremmo
(voi)	avrete	avreste	sarete	sareste
(essi)	avranno	avrebbero	saranno	sarebbero

	Pres. subj.	Pres. perf.	Pres. subj.	Pres. perf.
(io)	abbia	ho avuto	sia	sono stato
(tu)	abbia	hai avuto	sia	sei stato
(egli)	abbia	ha avuto	sia	è stato
(noi)	abbiamo	abbiamo avuto	siamo	siamo stati
(voi)	abbiate	avete avuto	siate	siete stati
(essi)	abbiano	hanno avuto	siano	sono stati

	Past definit		Past definit	
(io)	ebbi		fui	
(tu)	avesti		fosti	
(egli)	ebbe		fu	
(noi)	avemmo		fummo	
(voi)	aveste		foste	
(essi)	ebbero		furono	

Irregular verbs

Below is a list of the verbs and tenses commonly used in spoken Italian. In the listing, a) stands for the present tense, b) for the past definit, c) for the future, d) for the conditional and e) for the past participle. Certain verbs are considered irregular although often only their past participles have an irregular form while, for the rest, they are conjugated like regular verbs. A few verbs are conjugated irregularly in the present tense. Such cases are shown below in all persons, the first person singular only is given for all other tenses. Unless otherwise indicated, the verbs with prefixes like *ac-, am-, ap-, as-, at-, av-, co-, com-, con-, cor-, de-, di-, dis-, e-, es-, im-, in-, inter-, intra-, ot-, per-, pro-, re-, ri-, sopra-, sup-, tra(t)-,* etc. are conjugated like the stem verb.

accendere
light
a) accendo; b) accesi; c) accenderò; d) accenderei; e) acceso

accludere
enclose
a) accludo; b) acclusi; c) accluderò; d) accluderei; e) accluso

accorgersi
perceive
a) mi accorgo, ti accorgi, si accorge, ci accorgiamo, vi accorgete, si accorgono; b) mi accorsi; c) mi accorgerò; d) mi accorgerei; e) accorto

addurre
bring, result in
a) adduco; b) addussi; c) addurrò; d) addurrei; e) addotto

affliggere
afflict, upset
a) affliggo; b) afflissi; c) affliggerò; d) affliggerei; e) afflitto

alludere
allude
a) alludo; b) allusi; c) alluderò; d) alluderei; e) alluso

andare
go
a) vado, vai, va, andiamo, andate, vanno; b) andai; c) andrò; d) andrei; e) andato

annettere
annex
a) annetto; b) annettei; c) annetterò; d) annetterei; e) annesso

apparire
appear
a) appaio, apparisci, appare, appariamo, apparite, appaiono; b) apparsi; c) apparirò; d) apparirei; e) apparso

appendere
hang
a) appendo; b) appesi; c) appenderò; d) appenderei; e) appeso

aprire
open
a) apro; b) aprii; c) aprirò; d) aprirei; e) aperto

ardere
burn
a) ardo; b) arsi; c) arderò; d) arderei; e) arso

assistere
assist
a) assisto; b) assistei; c) assisterò; d) assisterei; e) assistito

assolvere
absolve
a) assolvo; b) assolsi; c) assolverò; d) assolverei; e) assolto

assumere
employ; assume
a) assumo; b) assunsi; c) assumerò; d) assumerei; e) assunto

avere
have
a) ho, hai, ha, abbiamo, avete, hanno; b) ebbi; c) avrò; d) avrei; e) avuto

bere *drink*	a) bevo, bevi, beve, beviamo, bevete, bevono; b) bevvi; c) berrò; d) berrei; e) bevuto
cadere *fall*	a) cado; b) caddi; c) cadrò; d) cadrei; e) caduto
capire *understand*	a) capisco, capisci, capisce, capiamo, capite, capiscono; b) capii; c) capirò; d) capirei; e) capito
chiedere *ask*	a) chiedo; b) chiesi; c) chiederò; d) chiederei; e) chiesto
chiudere *close*	a) chiudo; b) chiusi; c) chiuderò; d) chiuderei; e) chiuso
cingere *gird*	a) cingo; b) cinsi; c) cingerò; d) cingerei; e) cinto
cogliere *pick*	a) colgo, cogli, coglie, cogliamo, cogliete, colgono; b) colsi; c) coglierò; d) coglierei; e) colto
compiere *complete, do*	a) compio, compi, compie, compiamo, compiete, compiono; b) compiei; c) compierò; d) compierei; e) compiuto
comprimere *squeeze; press*	a) comprimo; b) compressi; c) comprimerò; d) comprimerei; e) compresso
concludere *conclude*	→chiudere
condurre *escort, drive*	a) conduco; b) condussi; c) condurrò; d) condurrei; e) condotto
connetere *connect, join*	a) connetto; b) connessi; c) connetterò; d) connetterei; e) connesso
conoscere *know, be aware of*	a) conosco; b) conobbi; c) conoscerò; d) conoscerei; e) conosciuto
coprire *cover*	a) copro; b) coprii; c) coprirò; d) coprirei; e) coperto
correre *run*	a) corro; b) corsi; c) correrò; d) correrei; e) corso
costruire *construct*	→ capire
crescere *grow*	a) cresco; b) crebbi; c) crescerò; d) crescerei; e) cresciuto
cucire *sew*	a) cucio, cuci, cuce, cuciamo, cucite, cuciono; b) cucii; c) cucirò; d) cucirei; e) cucito
cuocere *cook*	a) cuocio, cuoci, cuoce, cuociamo, cuocete, cuociono; b) cossi; c) cuocerò; d) cuocerei; e) cotto
dare *give*	a) do, dai, dà, diamo, date, danno; b) diedi; c) darò; d) darei; e) dato

decidere
decide
a) decido; b) decisi; c) deciderò; d) deciderei; e) deciso

dedurre
deduct
→ condurre

deludere
disappoint
→ alludere

deprimere
depress
→ comprimere

difendere
defend
a) difendo; b) difesi; c) difenderò; d) difenderei; e) difeso

dipendere
depend
→ appendere

dipingere
paint
a) dipingo; b) dipinsi; c) dipingerò; d) dipingerei; e) dipinto

dire
say, tell
a) dico, dici, dice, diciamo, dite, dicono; b) dissi; c) dirò; d) direi; e) detto

dirigere
manage; conduct
a) dirigo; b) diressi; c) dirigerò; d) dirigerei; e) diretto

discutere
discuss
a) discuto; b) discussi; c) discuterò; d) discuterei; e) discusso

dissuadere
dissuade
a) dissuado; b) dissuasi; c) dissuaderò; d) dissuaderei; e) dissuaso

distinguere
distinguish
a) distinguo; b) distinsi; c) distinguerò; d) distinguerei; e) distinto

dividere
divide
a) divido; b) divisi; c) dividerò; d) divederei; e) diviso

dolere
hurt; ache
a) dolgo, duoli, duole, dogliamo, dolete, dolgono; b) dolsi; c) dorrò; d) dorrei; e) doluto

dovere
have to, ought to
a) devo, devi, deve, dobbiamo, dovete, debbono (devono); b) dovetti; c) dovrò; d) dovrei; e) dovuto

eccellere
excel, outshine
a) eccello; b) eccelsi; c) eccellerò; d) eccellerei; e) eccelso

emergere
rise; distinguish oneself
a) emergo; b) emersi; c) emergerò; d) emergerei; e) emerso

erigere
erect, build
a) erigo; b) eressi; c) erigerò; d) erigerei; e) eretto

escludere
exclude
→ alludere

esigere
demand, require
a) esigo; b) esigei; c) esigerò; d) esigerei; e) esatto

esistere
exist, live
a) esisto; b) esistei; c) esisterò; d) esisterei; e) esistito

espellere — *expel*
a) espello; b) espulsi; c) espellerò; d) espellerei; d) espulso

esplodere — *explode*
a) esplodo: b) esplosi; c) esploderò; d) esploderei; e) esploso

esprimere — *express*
→comprimere

essere — *be*
a) sono, sei, è, siamo, siete, sono; b) fui; c) sarò; d) sarei; e) stato

estinguere — *extinguish*
→ distinguere

fare — *do, make*
a) faccio, fai, fa, facciamo, fate, fanno; b) feci; c) farò; d) farei; e) fatto

fendere — *split*
a) fendo; b) fendei; c) fenderò; d) fenderei; e) fesso

ferire — *wound, hurt*
→capire

figgere — *fasten*
a) figgo; b) fissi; c) figgerò; d) figgerei; e) fitto

fingere — *pretend*
a) fingo; b) finsi; c) fingerò; d) fingerei; e) finto

flettere — *bend*
a) fletto; b) flettei; c) fletterò; d) fletterei; e) flesso

fondere — *melt*
a) fondo; b) fusi; c) fonderò; d) fonderei; e) fuso

frangere — *break*
a) frango; b) fransi; c) frangerò; d) frangerei; e) franto

friggere — *fry*
→ affliggere

giacere — *lie, rest*
a) giaccio, giaci, giace, giaciamo, giacete, giacciono; b) giacqui; c) giacerò; d) giacerei; e) giaciuto

giungere — *arrive*
a) giungo; b) giunsi; c) giungerò; d) giungerei; e) giunto

immergere — *dip, immerse*
a) immergo; b) immersi; c) immergerò; d) immergerei; e) immerso

incidere — *engrave; record; have influence*
a) incido; b) incisi; c) inciderò; d) inciderei; e) inciso

includere — *include*
→ alludere

indurre — *induce*
→ condurre

introdurre — *insert, introduce*
→condurre

invadere — *invade*
a) invado; b) invasi; c) invaderò; d) invaderei; e) invaso

leggere *read*	a) leggo; b) lessi; c) leggerò; d) leggerei; e) letto
mettere *put*	a) metto; b) misi; c) metterò; d) metterei; e) messo
mordere *bite*	a) mordo; b) morsi; c) morderò; d) morderei; e) morso
morire *die*	a) muoio, muori, muore, moriamo, morite, muoiono; b) morii; c) morirò; d) morirei; e) morto
muovere *move*	→mordere; e) mosso
nascere *be born*	→conoscere; e) nato
nascondere *hide*	→mordere; e) nascosto
nuocere *harm, damage*	a) nuoccio, nuoci, nuoce, nociamo, nocete, nuociono; b) nocqui; c) nocerò; d) nocerei; e) nuociuto
nutrire *nourrish*	→capire
offendere *offend*	a) offendo; b) offesi; c) offenderò; d) offenderei; e) offeso
offrire *offer*	a) offro; b) offrii; c) offrirò; d) offrirei; e) offerto
opprimere *oppress*	→comprimere
parere *seem*	a) paio, pari, pare, paiamo, parete, paiono; b) parvi; c) parrò; d) parrei; e) parso
percuotere *hit, strike*	a) percuoto; b) percossi; c) percuoterò; d) percuoterei; e) percosso
perdere *lose*	a) perdo; b) persi; c) perderò; d) perderei; e) perso
persuadere *persuade*	→dissuadere
piacere *like; please*	a) piaccio, piaci, piace, piacciamo, piacete, piacciono; b) piacqui; c) piacerò; d) piacerei; e) piaciuto
piangere *cry*	a) piango; b) piansi; c) piangerò; d) piangerei; e) pianto
piovere *rain*	a) piove; b) piovve; c) pioverà; d) pioverebbe; e) piovuto
porgere *hand over, offer*	→leggere; e) porto
porre *place, put*	a) pongo, poni, pone, poniamo, ponete, pongono; b) posi; c) porrò; d) porrei; e) posto
potere *be able to*	a) posso, puoi, può, possiamo, potete, possono; b) potei; c) potrò; d) potrei; e) potuto

prendere
take
a) prendo; b) presi; c) prenderò; d) prenderei; e) preso

presumere
presume
→ assumere

produrre
produce
→ condurre

proteggere
protect
a) proteggo; b) protessi; c) proteggerò; d) proteggerei; e) protetto

pungere
sting
a) pungo; b) punsi; c) pungerò; d) pungerei; e) punto

radere
shave, raze
a) rado; b) rasi; c) raderò; d) raderei; e) raso

redigere
edit, write
a) redigo; b) redassi; c) redigerò; d) redigerei; e) redatto

redimere
redeem
a) redimo; b) redensi; c) redimerò; d) redimerei; e) redento

reggere
uphold, support
→ leggere

rendere
render, give up
→ prendere

reprimere
repress
→ comprimere

retrocedere
retreat
a) retrocedo; b) retrocedei; c) retrocederò; d) retrocederei; e) retroceduto

ridere
laugh
→ prendere

ridurre
reduce
→ condurre

rimanere
remain
a) rimango, rimani, rimane, rimaniamo, rimanete, rimangono; b) rimasi; c) rimarrò; d) rimarrei; e) rimasto

riprodurre
reproduce
→ condurre

risolvere
resolve
→ assolvere

rispondere
answer
a) rispondo; b) risposi; c) risponderò; d) risponderei; e) risposto

rompere
break
a) rompo; b) ruppi; c) romperò; d) romperei; e) rotto

salire
go up, climb
a) salgo, sali, sale, saliamo, salite, salgono; b) salii; c) salirò; d) salirei; e) salito

sapere
know
a) so, sai, sa, sappiamo, sapete, sanno; b) seppi; c) saprò; d) saprei; e) saputo

scegliere
choose
a) scelgo, scegli, sceglie, scegliamo, scegliete, scelgono; b) scelsi; c) sceglierò; d) sceglierei; e) scelto

scendere *get down*	a) scendo; b) scesi; c) scenderò; d) scenderei; e) sceso
sciogliere *solve*	→ cogliere
scomparire *disappear*	→ apparire
scoprire *dis-, uncover*	→ coprire
scorgere *notice, see*	a) scorgo; b) scorsi; c) scorgerò; d) scorgerei; e) scorto
scrivere *write*	→ leggere
scuotere *shake*	→ percuotere
sedere *sit*	a) siedo, siedi, siede, sediamo, sedete, siedono; b) sedei; c) sederò; d) sederei; e) seduto
sedurre *seduce*	→ condurre
smettere *put a stop to*	→ mettere
soffrire *suffer*	→ offrire
solere *be used to*	a) soglio, suoli, suole, sogliamo, solete, sogliono; b) solei; c) –; d) –; e) solito
sommergere *flood, sink*	→ immergere
sopprimere *suppress, abolish*	→ comprimere
sorgere *rise, ascend; be due to*	→ leggere; e) sorto
sospendere *suspend*	→ appendere
spandere *spread*	a) spando; b) spansi; c) spanderò; d) spanderei; e) spanto
spargere *scatter, strew*	a) spargo; b) sparsi; c) spargerò; d) spargerei; e) sparso
spegnere *extinguish*	a) spengo, spegni, spegne, spegniamo, spegnete, spengono; b) spensi; c) spegnerò; d) spegnerei; e) spento
spendere *spend; make use of*	a) spendo; b) spesi; c) spenderò; d) spenderei; e) speso
spingere *push*	a) spingo; b) spinsi; c) spingerò; d) spingerei; e) spinto
stare *stand, remain*	a) sto, stai, sta, stiamo, state, stanno; b) stetti; c) starò; d) starei; e) stato

stendere *stretch*	→tendere
stringere *press, tighten*	a) stringo; b) strinsi; c) stringerò; d) stringerei; e) stretto
struggere *melt; torment*	a) struggo; b) strussi; c) struggerò; d) struggerei; e) strutto
succedere *happen, succeed*	a) succedo; b) successi; c) succederò; d) succederei; e) successo
tacere *be silent*	a) taccio, taci, tace, tacciamo, tacete, tacciono; b) tacqui; c) tacerò; d) tacerei; e) taciuto
tendere *stretch*	a) tendo; b) tesi; c) tenderò; d) tenderei; e) teso
tenere *keep*	a) tengo, tieni, tiene, teniamo, tenete, tengono; b) tenni; c) terrò; d) terrei; e) tenuto
tingere *dye*	a) tingo; b) tinsi; c) tingerò; d) tingerei; e) tinto
togliere *take away*	→cogliere
torcere *wring*	a) torco; b) torsi; c) torcerò; d) torcerei; e) torto
tradurre *translate*	→condurre
trarre *draw, haul in*	a) traggo, trai, trae, traiamo, traete, traggono; b) trassi; c) trarrò; d) trarrei; e) tratto
uccidere *kill*	a) uccido; b) uccisi; c) ucciderò; d) ucciderei; e) ucciso
udire *hear, listen to*	a) odo, odi, ode, udiamo, udite, odono; b) udii; c) udirò; d) udirei; e) udito
uscire *go, come out*	a) esco, esci, esce, usciamo, uscite, escono; b) uscii; c) uscirò; d) uscirei; e) uscito
valere *be worth*	a) valgo, vali, vale, valiamo, valete, valgono; b) valsi; c) varrò; d) varrei; e) valuto (valso)
vedere *see*	a) vedo; b) vidi; c) vedrò; d) vedrei; e) visto
venire *come, arrive*	a) vengo, vieni, viene, veniamo, venite, vengono; b) venni; c) verrò; d) verrei; e) venuto
vincere *win, conquer*	a) vinco; b) vinsi; c) vincerò; d) vincerei; e) vinto
vivere *live*	a) vivo; b) vissi; c) vivrò; d) vivrei; e) vissuto (vivuto)
volere *want*	a) voglio, vuoi, vuole, vogliamo, volete, vogliono; b) volli (volsi); c) vorrò; d) vorrei; e) voluto (volsuto)
volgere *turn*	a) volgo; b) volsi; c) volgerò; d) volgerei; e) volto

Italian Abbreviations

ab.	*abitanti*	inhabitants, population
abb.	*abbonamento*	subscription
a.C.	*avanti Cristo*	B.C.
A.C.I.	*Automobile Club d'Italia*	Italian Automobile Association
A.D.	*anno Domini*	Anno Domini
A.G.I.P.	*Azienda Generale Italiana Petroli*	Italian National Oil Company
all.	*allegato*	enclosure, enclosed
A.N.A.S.	*Azienda Nazionale Autonoma della Strada*	National Road Board
A.N.S.A.	*Azienda Nazionale Stampa Associata*	Italian News Agency
Avv.	*Avvocato*	lawyer, solicitor, barrister
C.A.I.	*Club Alpino Italiano*	Italian Alpine Club
cat.	*categoria*	category
Cav.	*Cavaliere*	title of nobility corresponding to knight
C.C.I.	*Camera di Commercio Internazionale*	International Chamber of Commerce
cfr.	*confronta*	compare
C.I.T.	*Compagnia Italiana Turismo*	Italian Tourist Information Office
c.m.	*corrente mese*	instant, of this month
Com. in Prov.	*Comune in provincia di...*	township in the province of...
C.O.N.I.	*Comitato Olimpico Nazionale Italiano*	Italian Olympic Games Committee
C.P.	*casella postale*	post office box
C.so	*Corso*	main street
c.c.	*conto corrente*	current account
d.C.	*dopo Cristo*	A.D.
dott., dr.	*dottore*	doctor
dott.ssa	*dottoressa*	lady doctor
dozz.	*dozzina*	dozen
ecc.	*eccetera*	and so on
Ed.	*editore*	publisher
EE	*Escursionisti Esteri*	licence plate for foreigners temporarily living in Italy
Fed.	*federale*	federal
F.S.	*Ferrovie dello Stato*	Italian State Railways

I.C.E.	*Istituto Italiano per il Commercio Estero*	Italian Institute for Foreign Trade
I.V.A.	*Imposta sul Valore Aggiunto*	VAT, value added tax
L., Lit.	*Lira italiana*	lira
mod.	*modulo*	form
n/, ns.	*nostro*	our(s)
p.	*pagina*	page
P.T.	*Poste & Telecomunicazioni*	Post and Telecommunications
P.za	*piazza*	square
racc.	*raccomandata*	registered (letter)
R.A.I.	*Radio Audizioni Italiane*	Italian Broadcasting Corporation
Rep.	*Repubblica*	republic
Rev.	*Reverendo*	reverend
S.	*Santo*	saint
S.E.	*Sua Eccellenza*	His/Her Excellency
sec.	*secolo*	century
Sig.	*Signor*	Mr.
Sig.na	*Signorina*	Miss
Sig.a	*Signora*	Mrs.
S.p.A.	*Società per Azioni*	Ltd., Inc.
S.r.l.	*Società a responsabilità limitata*	limited liability company
S.S.	*Sua Santità*	His Holiness
T.C.I.	*Touring Club Italiano*	Italian Touring Club
U.E.	*Union europea*	European Union
v/, vs.	*vostro*	your(s)
V.le	*Viale*	boulevard, avenue
v.p.	*vedi pagina*	see page
v.r.	*vedi retro*	P.T.O., please turn over

Numerals

Cardinal numbers

0	zero
1	uno
2	due
3	tre
4	quattro
5	cinque
6	sei
7	sette
8	otto
9	nove
10	dieci
11	undici
12	dodici
13	tredici
14	quattordici
15	quindici
16	sedici
17	diciassette
18	diciotto
19	diciannove
20	venti
21	ventuno
22	ventidue
28	ventotto
30	trenta
31	trentuno
32	trentadue
40	quaranta
50	cinquanta
60	sessanta
70	settanta
80	ottanta
90	novanta
100	cento
101	centuno
230	duecentotrenta
1.000	mille
1.001	milleuno
2.000	duemila
1.000.000	un milione

Ordinal numbers

1°	primo
2°	secondo
3°	terzo
4°	quarto
5°	quinto
6°	sesto
7°	settimo
8°	ottavo
9°	nono
10°	decimo
11°	undicesimo
12°	dodicesimo
13°	tredicesimo
14°	quattordicesimo
15°	quindicesimo
16°	sedicesimo
17°	diciassettesimo
18°	diciottesimo
19°	diciannovesimo
20°	ventesimo
21°	ventunesimo
22°	ventiduesimo
23°	ventitreesimo
24°	ventiquattresimo
30°	trentesimo
31°	trentunesimo
32°	trentaduesimo
33°	trentatreesimo
40°	quarantesimo
50°	cinquantesimo
60°	sessantesimo
70°	settantesimo
80°	ottantesimo
90°	novantesimo
100°	centesimo
101°	centunesimo
102°	centoduesimo
230°	duecentotrentesimo
1.000°	millesimo
1.001°	milleunesimo

Time

In everyday conversation the 12-hour clock is generally used, but you will notice that the 24-hour system is employed elsewhere (e.g., 14.00 = 2 p.m.).

If you have to indicate that it is a.m. or p.m., add *del mattino, del pomeriggio* or *di sera*.

otto del mattino	8 a.m.
due del pomeriggio	2 p.m.
otto di sera	8 p.m.

Days of the Week

domenica	Sunday	*giovedì*	Thursday
lunedì	Monday	*venerdì*	Friday
martedì	Tuesday	*sabato*	Saturday
mercoledì	Wednesday		

Some Basic Phrases	Alcune espressioni utili
Please.	Per favore.
Thank you very much.	Mille grazie.
Don't mention it.	Prego.
Good morning.	Buongiorno *(di mattina)*.
Good afternoon.	Buongiorno *(di pomeriggio)*.
Good evening.	Buona sera.
Good night.	Buona notte.
Good-bye.	Arrivederci.
See you later.	A più tardi.
Where is/Where are…?	Dov'è/Dove sono…?
What do you call this?	Come si chiama questo?
What does that mean?	Cosa significa?
Do you speak English?	Parla inglese?
Do you speak German?	Parla tedesco?
Do you speak French?	Parla francese?
Do you speak Spanish?	Parla spagnolo?
Do you speak Italian?	Parla italiano?
Could you speak more slowly, please?	Può parlare più adagio, per piacere?
I don't understand.	Non capisco.
Can I have…?	Posso avere…?
Can you show me…?	Può indicarmi…?
Can you tell me…?	Può dirmi…?
Can you help me, please?	Può aiutarmi, per piacere?
I'd like…	Vorrei…
We'd like…	Vorremmo…
Please give me…	Per favore, mi dia…
Please bring me…	Per favore, mi porti…
I'm hungry.	Ho fame.
I'm thirsty.	Ho sete.
I'm lost.	Mi sono perso.
Hurry up!	Si affretti!
There is/There are…	C'è/Ci sono…
There isn't/There aren't…	Non c'è/Non ci sono…

Arrival

Your passport, please.

Have you anything to declare?

No, nothing at all.

Can you help me with my luggage, please?

Where's the bus to the centre of town, please?

This way, please.

Where can I get a taxi?

What's the fare to…?

Take me to this address, please.

I'm in a hurry.

L'arrivo

Il passaporto, per favore.

Ha qualcosa da dichiarare?

No, non ho nulla.

Può prendere le mie valige, per favore?

Dov'è l'autobus per il centro della città, per favore?

Da questa parte, per piacere.

Dove posso trovare un taxi?

Quanto costa la corsa per…?

Mi porti a questo indirizzo, per favore.

Ho fretta.

Hotel

My name is…

Have you a reservation?

I'd like a room with a bath.

What's the price per night?

May I see the room?

What's my room number, please?

There's no hot water.

May I see the manager, please?

Did anyone telephone me?

Is there any mail for me?

May I have my bill (check), please?

L'albergo

Mi chiamo…

Ha fatto la prenotazione?

Vorrei una camera con bagno.

Qual è il prezzo per una notte?

Posso vedere la camera?

Qual è il numero della mia camera?

Non c'è acqua calda.

Posso vedere il direttore, per piacere?

Mi ha telefonato qualcuno?

C'è posta per me?

Posso avere il conto, per favore?

Eating out

Do you have a fixed-price menu?

May I see the menu?

Al ristorante

Avete un menù a prezzo fisso?

Posso vedere il menù a scelta?

May we have an ashtray, please?	Possiamo avere un portacenere, per favore?
Where's the toilet, please?	Dove sono i gabinetti, per favore?
I'd like an hors d'œuvre (starter).	Vorrei degli antipasti.
Have you any soup?	Ha un brodo?
I'd like some fish.	Vorrei del pesce.
What kind of fish do you have?	Che pesce ha?
I'd like a steak.	Vorrei una bistecca.
What vegetables have you got?	Quali verdure ha?
Nothing more, thanks.	Nient'altro. Grazie.
What would you like to drink?	Cosa desidera bere?
I'll have a beer, please.	Mi dia una birra, per piacere.
I'd like a bottle of wine.	Vorrei una bottiglia di vino.
May I have the bill (check), please?	Posso avere il conto, per piacere?
Is service included?	È compreso il servizio?
Thank you, that was a very good meal.	Grazie. Abbiamo mangiato molto bene.

Travelling

In viaggio

Where's the railway station, please?	Dove si trova la stazione, per favore?
Where's the ticket office, please?	Dove si trova lo sportello dei biglietti, per favore?
I'd like a ticket to...	Vorrei un biglietto per...
First or second class?	Di prima o di seconda classe?
First class, please.	Di prima classe, per piacere.
Single or return (one way or roundtrip)?	Andata o andata e ritorno?
Do I have to change trains?	Devo cambiare treno?
What platform does the train for... leave from?	Da che binario parte il treno per...?
Where's the nearest underground (subway) station?	Dov'è la più vicina stazione della metropolitana?
Where's the bus station, please?	Dov'è la stazione degli autobus, per piacere?

When's the first bus to…?	Quando passa il primo autobus per…?
Please let me off at the next stop.	Mi faccia scendere alla prossima fermata, per piacere.

Relaxing

Gli svaghi

What's on at the cinema (movies)?	Cosa danno al cinema?
What time does the film begin?	A che ora incomincia il film?
Are there any tickets for tonight?	Ci sono ancora posti liberi per questa sera?
Where can we go dancing?	Dove possiamo andare a ballare?

Meeting people

Incontri

How do you do.	Buongiorno.
How are you?	Come sta?
Very well, thank you. And you?	Molto bene. Grazie. E lei?
May I introduce…?	Posso presentarle…?
My name is…	Mi chiamo…
I'm very pleased to meet you.	Sono molto lieto di fare la sua conoscenza.
How long have you been here?	Da quanto tempo è qui?
It was nice meeting you.	Sono lieto di aver fatto la sua conoscenza.
Do you mind if I smoke?	Le disturba se fumo?
Do you have a light, please?	Mi fa accendere, per piacere?
May I get you a drink?	Posso offrirle da bere?
May I invite you for dinner tonight?	Posso invitarla a cena questa sera?
Where shall we meet?	Dove possiamo incontrarci?

Shops, stores and services

Negozi, grandi magazzini e altro

Where's the nearest bank, please?	Dov'è la banca più vicina, per favore?
Where can I cash some travellers' cheques?	Dove posso incassare dei travellers' cheque?

Can you give me some small change, please?

Potrebbe darmi della moneta spicciola, per favore?

Where's the nearest chemist's (pharmacy)?

Dov'è la più vicina farmacia?

How do I get there?

Come ci si può arrivare?

Is it within walking distance?

Ci si può andare anche a piedi?

Can you help me, please?

Può aiutarmi, per piacere?

How much is this? And that?

Quanto costa questo? E quello?

It's not quite what I want.

Non è quello che volevo.

I like it.

Questo mi piace.

Can you recommend something for sunburn?

Può consigliarmi qualcosa per una scottatura di sole?

I'd like a haircut, please.

Vorrei farmi tagliare i capelli, per favore.

I'd like a manicure, please.

Vorrei una manicure, per favore.

Street directions

Can you show me on the map where I am?

Indicazioni stradali

Può indicarmi sulla cartina dove mi trovo?

You are on the wrong road.

È sulla strada sbagliata.

Go/Walk straight ahead.

Continui diritto.

It's on the left/on the right.

È a sinistra/a destra.

Emergencies

Call a doctor quickly.

Urgenze

Chiami subito un medico.

Call an ambulance.

Chiami un'ambulanza.

Please call the police.

Per piacere, chiami la polizia.

inglese-italiano

english-italian

Introduzione

Questo dizionario è stato compilato in modo da rispondere quanto meglio possibile a necessità di ordine pratico. Sono state volontariamente omesse informazioni linguistiche ritenute non indispensabili. Le voci sono collocate in ordine alfabetico, siano esse costituite da una parola sola, o da più parole separate o no tra loro da una lineetta. Come unica eccezione a questa regola, alcune espressioni idiomatiche sono state classificate come voci principali nella posizione alfabetica della parola più significativa nell'espressione stessa. Quando ad una voce susseguono accezioni varie come espressioni e locuzioni particolari, esse sono egualmente collocate in ordine alfabetico.

Ad ogni vocabolo fa seguito la trascrizione fonetica (vedasi la Guida di pronuncia) la quale a sua volta precede, salvo eccezioni, la definizione della categoria grammaticale del vocabolo (nome, verbo, aggettivo, ecc.). Quando un vocabolo rappresenta più di una categoria, le varie traduzioni sono raggruppate dopo le rispettive categorie.

Quando irregolare, la forma plurale di un nome è sempre indicata, com'è pure indicata nei casi in cui il lettore possa emettere un dubbio.

La tilde (~) è usata per rappresentare una voce ogni qualvolta essa si ripeta, in forme plurali irregolari o in accezioni varie.

Nei plurali irregolari dei nomi composti, è scritta per intero solo la parte che cambia, mentre quella che rimane immutata è rappresentata da una lineetta.

Un verbo irregolare è segnalato da un asterisco (*) posto dinnanzi. Per dettagli, ci si può riferire all'elenco dei verbi irregolari.

Il dizionario segue le norme dell'ortografia britannica. Ogni vocabolo o significato di esso che sia prevalentemente americano è stato contrassegnato come tale (vedasi l'elenco delle abbreviazioni usate nel testo).

Abbreviazioni

adj	aggettivo	*num*	numerale
adv	avverbio	*p*	passato
Am	Americano	*pl*	plurale
art	articolo	*plAm*	plurale (Americano)
conj	congiunzione	*pp*	participio passato
f	femminile	*pr*	presente
fpl	femminile plurale	*pref*	prefisso
m	maschile	*prep*	preposizione
mpl	maschile plurale	*pron*	pronome
n	nome	*v*	verbo
nAm	nome (Americano)	*vAm*	verbo (Americano)

Guida della pronuncia

Ogni lemma di questa parte del dizionario è accompagnato da una trascrizione fonetica che ne indica la pronuncia e che si deve leggere come l'italiano. Diamo spiegazioni (sotto) solo per le lettere e i simboli ambigui o particolarmente difficili da comprendere.

Le lineette indicano le divisioni fra le sillabe, che sono stampate in *corsivo* quando si devono pronunciare accentuate.

Certo, i suoni delle due lingue non coincidono mai perfettamente, ma seguendo alla lettera le nostre indicazioni, potrete pronunciare le parole straniere in modo da farvi comprendere. Per facilitarvi il compito, talvolta le nostre trascrizioni semplificano leggermente il sistema fonetico della lingua pur riflettendo le differenze di suono essenziali.

Consonanti

ð	una s blesa come in rosa; mettete la punta della lingua contro i denti incisivi centrali superiori e soffiate leggermente facendo vibrare le corde vocali come per pronunciare **d**
gh	come in **gh**iro
h	come **c** nella pronunzia toscana di casa (**h**asa); espirate udibilmente, come se aveste appena fatto una corsa
ng	come **ng** in lu**ng**o, ma senza pronunciare la g finale
r	mettete la lingua nella posizione come per pronunciare ʒ (vedi sotto), poi aprite leggermente la bocca e abbassate la lingua
s	sempre sonora, come in rosa, mai come in si
ʃ	come **sc** in **sc**i
θ	come ð, ma senza far vibrare le corde vocali
ʒ	il suono dolce della g toscana; come **g** in **g**iro, ma senza far sentire la **d** che compone all'inizio tale suono

Vocali e dittonghi

æ	fra **a** in c**a**so ed **e** in b**e**lla
ê	come **e** in b**e**lla (aperta)
o	come in p**o**rta (aperta)
ô	come **o** in s**o**le (chiusa)
ö	un suono neutro, come la vocale di f**uo**co nei dialetti settentrionali («**foe**ch»)

1) Le vocali lunghe sono stampate doppie.

2) Le lettere rialzate (es. **ᵘi, uᵟ**) si devono pronunciare rapidamente.

3) Alcune parole inglesi derivanti dal francese hanno vocali nasali, che abbiamo trascritto col simbolo della vocale più **ng** (es. **ang**). Questo **ng** *non* si deve pronunciare: serve unicamente a indicare il suono nasale della vocale da pronunciare simultaneamente attraverso la bocca e il naso.

Pronuncia americana

La nostra trascrizione fonetica segue le norme usuali della pronunzia britannica. Benchè vi siano numerose variazioni secondo le regioni, l'inglese parlato in America presenta un certo numero di differenze generali. Eccone alcune:

1) La **r**, sia essa posta dinnanzi a consonante o in fine di parola, si pronunzia sempre (contrariamente all'usanza britannica).

2) In numerose parole (quali ad es. *ask*, *castle*, *laugh*, ecc.) **aa** diventa **ææ**.

3) Il suono britannico **o** si pronuncia **a**, spesso anche **oo**.

4) In vocaboli come *duty*, *tune*, *new*, ecc., **ᶦuu** diventa sovente una sola **uu**.

5) Infine, talune parole sono accentuate diversamente.

A

a (ei,ö) *art* (an) un *art*

abbey (*æ*-bi) *n* badia *f*

abbreviation (ö-brii-vi-*ei*-∫ön) *n* abbreviazione *f*

aberration (æ-bö-*rei*-∫ön) *n* aberrazione *f*

ability (ö-*bi*-lö-ti) *n* abilità *f*

able (*ei*-böl) *adj* capace; abile; *be ~ to* *essere in grado di; *sapere, *potere

abnormal (æb-*noo*-möl) *adj* anormale

aboard (ö-*bood*) *adv* a bordo

abolish (ö-*bo*-li∫) *v* abolire

abortion (ö-*boo*-∫ön) *n* aborto *m*

about (ö-*baut*) *prep* su; circa; intorno a; *adv* press'a poco, circa; attorno

above (ö-*bav*) *prep* su; *adv* sopra

abroad (ö-*brood*) *adv* all'estero

abscess (*æb*-ssèss) *n* ascesso *m*

absence (*æb*-ssönss) *n* assenza *f*

absent (*æb*-ssönt) *adj* assente

absolutely (*æb*-ssö-luut-li) *adv* assolutamente

abstain from (öb-*sstein*) *astenersi da

abstract (*æb*-sstrækt) *adj* astratto

absurd (öb-*ssööd*) *adj* assurdo

abundance (ö-*ban*-dönss) *n* abbondanza *f*

abundant (ö-*ban*-dönt) *adj* abbondante

abuse (ö-*bⁱuuss*) *n* abuso *m*

abyss (ö-*biss*) *n* abisso *m*

academy (ö-*kæ*-dö-mi) *n* accademia *f*

accelerate (ök-*ssè*-lö-reit) *v* accelerare

accelerator (ök-*ssè*-lö-rei-tö) *n* acceleratore *m*

accent (*æk*-ssönt) *n* accento *m*

accept (ök-*ssèpt*) *v* accettare; *accogliere

access (*æk*-ssèss) *n* accesso *m*

accessary (ök-*ssè*-ssö-ri) *n* complice *m*

accessible (ök-*ssè*-ssö-böl) *adj* accessibile

accessories (ök-*ssè*-ssö-ris) *pl* accessori *mpl*

accident (*æk*-ssi-dönt) *n* incidente *m*

accidental (æk-ssi-*dèn*-töl) *adj* fortuito

accommodate (ö-*ko*-mö-deit) *v* alloggiare

accommodation (ö-ko-mö-*dei*-∫ön) *n* sistemazione *f*, alloggio *m*

accompany (ö-*kam*-pö-ni) *v* accompagnare

accomplish (ö-*kam*-pli∫) *v* compiere; adempiere

in accordance with (in ö-*koo*-dönss ⁱiδ) in conformità con

according to (ö-*koo*-ding tuu) secondo

account (ö-*kaunt*) *n* conto *m*; resoconto *m*; *~ for* *rendere conto di;

on ~ of a causa di
accountable (ö-*kaun*-tö-böl) *adj* spiegabile
accurate (*æ*-k^{i}u-röt) *adj* accurato
accuse (ö-k^{i}uus) *v* accusare
accused (ö-k^{i}uusd) *n* accusato *m*
accustom (ö-*ka*-sstöm) *v* abituare
ache (eik) *v* *dolere; *n* dolore *m*
achieve (ö-*tfiiv*) *v* *raggiungere; effettuare
achievement (ö-*tfiiv*-mönt) *n* adempimento *m*
acid (*æ*-ssid) *n* acido *m*
acknowledge (ök-*no*-lid$_3$) *v* *riconoscere; *ammettere; confermare
acne (*æk*-ni) *n* acne *f*
acorn (*ei*-koon) *n* ghianda *f*
acquaintance (ö-k^u*ein*-tönss) *n* conoscenza *f*
acquire (ö-k^u*ai*ö) *v* *ottenere
acquisition (*æ*-k^{u}i-si-fön) *n* acquisizione *f*
acquittal (ö-k^{u}i-töl) *n* assoluzione *f*
acre (*ei*-kö) *n* acro *m*
across (ö-*kross*) *prep* attraverso; dall'altra parte di; *adv* dall'altra parte
act (ækt) *n* atto *m*; numero *m*; *v* agire; comportarsi; recitare
action (*æk*-fön) *n* azione *f*
active (*æk*-tiv) *adj* attivo; vivace
activity (æk-*ti*-vö-ti) *n* attività *f*
actor (*æk*-tö) *n* attore *m*
actress (*æk*-triss) *n* attrice *f*
actual (*æk*-tfu-öl) *adj* reale
actually (*æk*-tfu-ö-li) *adv* in realtà
acute (ö-k^{i}uut) *adj* acuto
adapt (ö-*dæpt*) *v* adattare
adaptor (ö-*dæp*-tö) *n* adattatore *m*
add (æd) *v* addizionare; *aggiungere
addition (ö-*di*-fön) *n* addizione *f*; aggiunta *f*
additional (ö-*di*-fö-nöl) *adj* supplementare; accessorio
address (ö-*drêss*) *n* indirizzo *m*; *v* in-

dirizzare; *rivolgersi a
addressee (æ-drê-*ssii*) *n* destinatario *m*
adequate (*æ*-di-k^{u}öt) *adj* adeguato; idoneo
adjective (*æ*-d$_3$ik-tiv) *n* aggettivo *m*
adjourn (ö-*d$_3$öön*) *v* rinviare
adjust (ö-*d$_3$asst*) *v* regolare; adattare
administer (öd-*mi*-ni-sstö) *v* somministrare
administration (öd-mi-ni-*sstrei*-fön) *n* amministrazione *f*
administrative (öd-*mi*-ni-sströ-tiv) *adj* amministrativo; ~ **law** diritto amministrativo
admiral (*æd*-mö-röl) *n* ammiraglio *m*
admiration (æd-mö-*rei*-fön) *n* ammirazione *f*
admire (öd-*mai*ö) *v* ammirare
admission (öd-*mi*-fön) *n* ingresso *m*; ammissione *f*
admit (öd-*mit*) *v* *ammettere; *riconoscere
admittance (öd-*mi*-tönss) *n* ammissione *f*; **no** ~ vietato l'ingresso
adopt (ö-*dopt*) *v* adottare
adorable (ö-*doo*-rö-böl) *adj* adorabile
adult (*æ*-dalt) *n* adulto *m*; *adj* adulto
advance (öd-*vaanss*) *n* avanzamento *m*; anticipo *m*; *v* avanzare; **in** ~ anticipatamente, in anticipo
advanced (öd-*vaansst*) *adj* avanzato
advantage (öd-*vaan*-tid$_3$) *n* vantaggio *m*
advantageous (æd-vön-*tei*-d$_3$öss) *adj* vantaggioso
adventure (öd-*vên*-tfö) *n* avventura *f*
adverb (*æd*-vööb) *n* avverbio *m*
advertisement (öd-*vöö*-tiss-mönt) *n* avviso *m*
advertising (*æd*-vö-tai-sing) *n* pubblicità *f*
advice (öd-*vaiss*) *n* consiglio *m*
advise (öd-*vais*) *v* consigliare

advocate (æd-võ-köt) *n* patrocinatore *m*

aerial (ê⁰-ri-öl) *n* antenna *f*

aeroplane (ê⁰-rö-plein) *n* aeroplano *m*

affair (ö-fê⁰) *n* affare *m* ; rapporto *m*, amoretto *m*

affect (ö-fêkt) *v* influenzare; riguardare

affected (ö-fêk-tid) *adj* affettato

affection (ö-fêk-ʃön) *n* affezione *f* ; affetto *m*

affectionate (ö-fêk-ʃö-nit) *adj* affettuoso

affiliated (ö-fi-li-ei-tid) *adj* associato

affirmative (ö-föö-mö-tiv) *adj* affermativo

affliction (ö-flik-ʃön) *n* afflizione *f*

afford (ö-food) *v* *permettersi

afraid (ö-freid) *adj* impaurito; *be ~ *aver paura

Africa (æ-fri-kö) Africa *f*

African (æ-fri-kön) *adj* africano

after (aaf-tö) *prep* dopo; *conj* dopo che

afternoon (aaf-tö-nuun) *n* pomeriggio *m* ; **this ~** oggi nel pomeriggio

afterwards (aaf-tö-ᵘöds) *adv* poi; in seguito

again (ö-ghên) *adv* ancora; di nuovo; **~ and again** ripetutamente

against (ö-ghênsst) *prep* contro

age (eidʒ) *n* età *f* ; vecchiaia *f* ; **of ~** maggiorenne; **under ~** minorenne

aged (ei-dʒid) *adj* attempato; anziano

agency (ei-dʒön-ssi) *n* agenzia *f* ; divisione *f*

agenda (ö-dʒên-dö) *n* agenda *f*

agent (ei-dʒönt) *n* agente *m*, rappresentante *m*

aggressive (ö-ghrê-ssiv) *adj* aggressivo

ago (ö-ghou) *adv* fa

agrarian (ö-ghrê⁰-ri-ön) *adj* agricolo

agree (ö-ghrii) *v* accordarsi; consentire; *corrispondere

agreeable (ö-ghrii-ö-böl) *adj* gradevole

agreement (ö-ghrii-mönt) *n* contratto *m* ; accordo *m* ; concordanza *f*

agriculture (æ-ghri-kal-tʃö) *n* agricoltura *f*

ahead (ö-hêd) *adv* avanti; **~ of** in testa a; *go ~ continuare; **straight ~** sempre diritto

aid (eid) *n* soccorso *m* ; *v* *assistere, aiutare

ailment (eil-mönt) *n* affezione *f* ; malattia *f*

aim (eim) *n* intento *m* ; **~ at** puntare su, mirare a; aspirare a

air (ê⁰) *n* aria *f* ; *v* arieggiare

air-conditioning (ê⁰-kön-di-ʃö-ning) *n* condizionamento dell'aria; **air-conditioned** *adj* ad aria condizionata

aircraft (ê⁰-kraaft) *n* (pl ~) velivolo *m* ; aereo *m*

airfield (ê⁰-fiild) *n* aerodromo *m*

air-filter (ê⁰-fil-tö) *n* filtro dell'aria

airline (ê⁰-lain) *n* linea aerea

airmail (ê⁰-meil) *n* posta aerea

airplane (ê⁰-plein) *nAm* aeroplano *m*

airport (ê⁰-poot) *n* aeroporto *m*

air-sickness (ê⁰-ssik-nöss) *n* mal d'aria

airtight (ê⁰-tait) *adj* a tenuta d'aria

airy (ê⁰-ri) *adj* arioso

aisle (ail) *n* navata laterale; passaggio *m*

alarm (ö-laam) *n* allarme *m* ; *v* allarmare

alarm-clock (ö-laam-klok) *n* sveglia *f*

album (æl-böm) *n* album *m*

alcohol (æl-kö-hol) *n* alcool *m*

alcoholic (æl-kö-ho-lik) *adj* alcoolico

ale (eil) *n* birra *f*

algebra (æl-dʒi-brö) *n* algebra *f*

Algeria (æl-dʒi⁰-ri-ö) Algeria *f*

Algerian (æl-*dȝi*ŏ-ri-ön) *adj* algerino

alien (*ei*-li-ön) *n* straniero *m*; *adj* straniero

alike (ö-*laik*) *adj* uguale, simile; *adv* ugualmente

alimony (*æ*-li-mö-ni) *n* alimenti

alive (ö-*laiv*) *adj* vivo, vivente

all (ool) *adj* tutto; ~ **in** tutto compreso; ~ **right!** va bene!; **at** ~ affatto

allergy (*æ*-lö-dȝi) *n* allergia *f*

alley (*æ*-li) *n* vicolo *m*

alliance (ö-*lai*-önss) *n* alleanza *f*

allot (ö-*lot*) *v* assegnare

allow (ö-*lau*) *v* *permettere; ~ **to** lasciare; *be allowed *essere permesso; *be allowed to *avere il permesso di

allowance (ö-*lau*-önss) *n* assegno *m*

all-round (ool-*raund*) *adj* universale

ally (*æ*-lai) *n* alleato *m*

almanac (*ool*-mö-næk) *n* almanacco *m*

almond (*aa*-mönd) *n* mandorla *f*

almost (*ool*-mousst) *adv* quasi

alone (ö-*loun*) *adv* solo

along (ö-*long*) *prep* lungo

aloud (ö-*laud*) *adv* ad alta voce

alphabet (*æl*-fö-bêt) *n* alfabeto *m*

already (ool-*rê*-di) *adv* già

also (*ool*-ssou) *adv* anche; pure

altar (*ool*-tö) *n* altare *m*

alter (*ool*-tö) *v* cambiare, modificare

alteration (ool-tö-*rei*-fön) *n* cambiamento *m*, modifica *f*

alternate (ool-*töö*-nöt) *adj* alternato

alternative (ool-*töö*-nö-tiv) *n* alternativa *f*

although (ool-*ðou*) *conj* benché, sebbene

altitude (*æl*-ti-tⁱuud) *n* altitudine *f*

alto (*æl*-tou) *n* (pl ~s) contralto *m*

altogether (ool-tö-*ghê*-ðö) *adv* interamente; in tutto

always (*ool*-ᵘeis) *adv* sempre

am (æm) *v* (pr be)

amaze (ö-*meis*) *v* stupire, *stupefare

amazement (ö-*meis*-mönt) *n* stupore *m*

ambassador (æm-*bæ*-ssö-dö) *n* ambasciatore *m*

amber (*æm*-bö) *n* ambra *f*

ambiguous (æm-*bi*-ghⁱu-öss) *adj* ambiguo; equivoco

ambitious (æm-*bi*-föss) *adj* ambizioso

ambulance (*æm*-bⁱu-lönss) *n* ambulanza *f*

ambush (*æm*-buf) *n* imboscata *f*

America (ö-*mê*-ri-kö) America *f*

American (ö-*mê*-ri-kön) *adj* americano

amethyst (*æ*-mi-θisst) *n* ametista *f*

amid (ö-*mid*) *prep* fra; tra, in mezzo a

ammonia (ö-*mou*-ni-ö) *n* ammoniaca *f*

amnesty (*æm*-ni-ssti) *n* amnistia *f*

among (ö-*mang*) *prep* tra; fra, in mezzo a; ~ **other things** tra l'altro

amount (ö-*maunt*) *n* quantità *f*; ammontare *m*, somma *f*; ~ **to** ammontare a

amuse (ö-*mⁱuus*) *v* divertire

amusement (ö-*mⁱuus*-mönt) *n* passatempo *m*, divertimento *m*

amusing (ö-*mⁱuu*-sing) *adj* divertente

anaemia (ö-*nii*-mi-ö) *n* anemia *f*

anaesthesia (æ-niss-*θii*-si-ö) *n* anestesia *f*

anaesthetic (æ-niss-*θê*-tik) *n* anestetico *m*

analyse (*æ*-nö-lais) *v* analizzare

analysis (ö-*næ*-lö-ssiss) *n* (pl -ses) analisi *f*

analyst (*æ*-nö-lisst) *n* analista *m*; psicoanalista *m*

anarchy (*æ*-nö-ki) *n* anarchia *f*

anatomy (ö-*næ*-tö-mi) *n* anatomia *f*

ancestor (*æn*-ssê-sstö) *n* antenato *m*

anchor (*æng*-kö) *n* ancora *f*

anchovy (æn-tʃö-vi) *n* acciuga *f*

ancient (*ein*-fönt) *adj* vecchio, antico; antiquato

and (ænd, önd) *conj* e

angel (*ein*-dʒöl) *n* angelo *m*

anger (æng-ghö) *n* collera *f*, rabbia *f*; ira *f*

angle (æng-ghöl) *v* pescare con l'amo; *n* angolo *m*

angry (æng-ghri) *adj* irato, arrabbiato

animal (æ-ni-möl) *n* animale *m*

ankle (æng-köl) *n* caviglia *f*

annex[1] (æ-nêkss) *n* dipendenza *f*; allegato *m*

annex[2] (ö-nêkss) *v* *annettere

anniversary (æ-ni-*vöö*-ssö-ri) *n* anniversario *m*

announce (ö-*naunss*) *v* annunziare

announcement (ö-*naunss*-mönt) *n* annunzio *m*, avviso *m*

annoy (ö-*noi*) *v* infastidire, annoiare

annoyance (ö-*noi*-önss) *n* noia *f*

annoying (ö-*noi*-ing) *adj* noioso

annual (æ-n¹u-öl) *adj* annuale; *n* annuario *m*

per annum (pör æ-nöm) all'anno

anonymous (ö-*no*-ni-möss) *adj* anonimo

another (ö-*na*-ðö) *adj* un altro

answer (*aan*-ssö) *v* *rispondere a; *n* risposta *f*

ant (ænt) *n* formica *f*

anthology (æn-*θo*-lö-dʒi) *n* antologia *f*

antibiotic (æn-ti-bai-*o*-tik) *n* antibiotico *m*

anticipate (æn-*ti*-ssi-peit) *v* *prevedere, anticipare; *prevenire

antifreeze (æn-ti-friis) *n* anticongelante *m*

antipathy (æn-*ti*-pö-θi) *n* antipatia *f*

antique (æn-*tiik*) *adj* antico; *n* anticaglia *f*; ~ **dealer** antiquario *m*

antiquity (æn-*ti*-k¹ö-ti) *n* Antichità *f*;

antiquities *pl* antichità *fpl*

antiseptic (æn-ti-*ssép*-tik) *n* antisettico *m*

antlers (ænt-lös) *pl* palco *m*

anxiety (æng-*sai*-ö-ti) *n* ansietà *f*

anxious (ængk-föss) *adj* ansioso; preoccupato

any (ê-ni) *adj* alcuno

anybody (ê-ni-bo-di) *pron* chiunque

anyhow (ê-ni-hau) *adv* in ogni modo

anyone (ê-ni-ᵘan) *pron* chiunque

anything (ê-ni-θing) *pron* qualunque cosa

anyway (ê-ni-ᵘei) *adv* in ogni caso

anywhere (ê-ni-ᵘêᵒ) *adv* dovunque; ovunque

apart (ö-*paat*) *adv* a parte, separatamente; ~ **from** a prescindere da

apartment (ö-*paat*-mönt) *nAm* appartamento *m*, alloggio *m*; ~ **house** *Am* blocco di appartamenti

aperitif (ö-*pê*-rö-tiv) *n* aperitivo *m*

apologize (ö-*po*-lö-dʒais) *v* scusarsi

apology (ö-*po*-lö-dʒi) *n* scusa *f*

apparatus (æ-pö-*rei*-töss) *n* dispositivo *m*, apparecchio *m*

apparent (ö-*pæ*-rönt) *adj* apparente; ovvio

apparently (ö-*pæ*-rönt-li) *adv* apparentemente; evidentemente

apparition (æ-pö-*ri*-fön) *n* apparizione *f*

appeal (ö-*piil*) *n* appello *m*

appear (ö-*piᵒ*) *v* sembrare; risultare; *apparire; presentarsi

appearance (ö-*piᵒ*-rönss) *n* apparenza *f*; aspetto *m*; ingresso *m*

appendicitis (ö-pên-di-*ssai*-tiss) *n* appendicite *f*

appendix (ö-*pên*-dikss) *n* (pl -dices, -dixes) appendice *f*

appetite (æ-pö-tait) *n* appetito *m*

appetizer (æ-pö-tai-sö) *n* stuzzichino *m*

appetizing (æ-pö-tai-sing) *adj* appetitoso

applause (ö-*ploos*) *n* applauso *m*

apple (æ-pöl) *n* mela *f*

appliance (ö-*plai*-önss) *n* apparecchio *m*

application (æ-pli-*kei*-fön) *n* applicazione *f*; richiesta *f*; domanda d'impiego

apply (ö-*plai*) *v* applicare; inoltrare una domanda d'impiego; applicarsi

appoint (ö-*point*) *v* designare, nominare

appointment (ö-*point*-mönt) *n* appuntamento *m*; nomina *f*

appreciate (ö-*prii*-fi-eit) *v* valutare; apprezzare

appreciation (ö-prii-fi-*ei*-fön) *n* apprezzamento *m*

approach (ö-*prouf*) *v* avvicinare; *n* impostazione *f*; accesso *m*

appropriate (ö-*prou*-pri-öt) *adj* adatto, appropriato

approval (ö-*pruu*-völ) *n* approvazione *f*; accordo *m*; **on ~** in prova

approve (ö-*pruuv*) *v* approvare

approximate (ö-*prok*-ssi-möt) *adj* approssimativo

approximately (ö-*prok*-ssi-möt-li) *adv* circa, approssimativamente

apricot (*ei*-pri-kot) *n* albicocca *f*

April (*ei*-pröl) aprile

apron (*ei*-prön) *n* grembiule *m*

Arab (æ-röb) *adj* arabo

arbitrary (*aa*-bi-trö-ri) *adj* arbitrario

arcade (aa-*keid*) *n* portico *m*, arcata *f*

arch (aatf) *n* arco *m*; arcata *f*

archaeologist (aa-ki-*o*-lö-dʒisst) *n* archeologo *m*

archaeology (aa-ki-*o*-lö-dʒi) *n* archeologia *f*

archbishop (aatf-*bi*-föp) *n* arcivescovo *m*

arched (aatft) *adj* arcato

architect (*aa*-ki-tĕkt) *n* architetto *m*

architecture (*aa*-ki-tĕk-tfö) *n* architettura *f*

archives (*aa*-kaivs) *pl* archivio *m*

are (aa) *v* (pr be)

area (*êô*-ri-ö) *n* area *f*; zona *f*; **~ code** prefisso *m*

Argentina (aa-dʒön-*tii*-nö) Argentina *f*

Argentinian (aa-dʒön-*ti*-ni-ön) *adj* argentino

argue (*aa*-ghⁱuu) *v* argomentare, *discutere; disputare

argument (*aa*-ghⁱu-mönt) *n* argomento *m*; discussione *f*; disputa *f*

arid (æ-rid) *adj* arido

***arise** (ö-*rais*) *v* *sorgere

arithmetic (ö-*riθ*-mö-tik) *n* aritmetica *f*

arm (aam) *n* braccio *m*; arma *f*; *v* armare

armchair (*aam*-tfêô) *n* poltrona *f*

armed (aamd) *adj* armato; **~ forces** forze armate

armour (*aa*-mö) *n* corazza *f*

army (*aa*-mi) *n* esercito *m*

aroma (ö-*rou*-mö) *n* aroma *m*

around (ö-*raund*) *prep* intorno a; *adv* intorno

arrange (ö-*reindʒ*) *v* ordinare, *mettere in ordine; organizzare

arrangement (ö-*reindʒ*-mönt) *n* accomodamento *m*

arrest (ö-*rêsst*) *v* arrestare; *n* arresto *m*

arrival (ö-*rai*-völ) *n* arrivo *m*

arrive (ö-*raiv*) *v* arrivare

arrow (æ-rou) *n* freccia *f*

art (aat) *n* arte *f*; abilità *f*; **~ collection** collezione d'arte; **~ exhibition** mostra d'arte; **~ gallery** galleria d'arte; **~ history** storia dell'arte; **arts and crafts** arti e mestieri; **~ school** accademia di belle arti

artery (*aa*-tö-ri) *n* arteria *f*

artichoke (aa-ti-tʃouk) n carciofo m

article (aa-ti-köl) n articolo m

artifice (aa-ti-fiss) n artificio m

artificial (aa-ti-fi-ſöl) adj artificiale

artist (aa-tisst) n artista m

artistic (aa-ti-sstik) adj artistico

as (æs) conj come; così; che; poiché; siccome; ~ from a partire da; da; ~ if come se

asbestos (æs-bê-sstoss) n amianto m

ascend (ö-ssénd) v *salire; *ascendere

ascent (ö-ssént) n ascensione f; ascesa f

ascertain (æ-ssö-tein) v constatare; accertarsi di, accertare

ash (æʃ) n cenere f

ashamed (ö-ſeimd) adj vergognoso; *be ~ *aver vergogna

ashore (ö-ſoo) adv a terra

ashtray (æſ-trei) n portacenere m

Asia (ei-ſö) Asia f

Asian (ei-ſön) adj asiatico

aside (ö-ssaid) adv da parte

ask (aassk) v domandare; pregare, *chiedere; invitare

asleep (ö-ssliip) adj addormentato

asparagus (ö-sspæ-rö-ghöss) n asparago m

aspect (æ-sspêkt) n aspetto m

asphalt (æss-fælt) n asfalto m

aspire (ö-sspaiᵒ) v aspirare

aspirin (æ-sspö-rin) n aspirina f

ass (æss) n asino m

assassination (ö-ssæ-ssi-nei-ſön) n assassinio m

assault (ö-ssoolt) v attaccare; aggredire

assemble (ö-ssêm-böl) v riunire; montare

assembly (ö-ssêm-bli) n riunione f, assemblea f

assignment (ö-ssain-mönt) n incarico m

assign to (ö-ssain) assegnare a; attribuire a

assist (ö-ssisst) v *assistere

assistance (ö-ssi-sstönss) n aiuto m; soccorso m, assistenza f

assistant (ö-ssi-sstönt) n assistente m

associate (ö-ssou-ſi-öt) n socio m; alleato m; v associare; ~ with frequentare

association (ö-ssou-ssi-ei-ſön) n associazione f

assort (ö-ssoot) v assortire

assortment (ö-ssoot-mönt) n assortimento m

assume (ö-ssiʲuum) v *assumere, *presumere

assure (ö-ſuᵒ) v assicurare

asthma (æss-mö) n asma f

astonish (ö-ssto-niʃ) v sbalordire

astonishing (ö-ssto-ni-ſing) adj sorprendente

astonishment (ö-ssto-niſ-mönt) n sorpresa f

astronomy (ö-sstro-nö-mi) n astronomia f

asylum (ö-ssai-löm) n asilo m; ospizio m

at (æt) prep in, da, a; verso

ate (êt) v (p eat)

atheist (ei-θi-isst) n ateo m

athlete (æθ-liit) n atleta m

athletics (æθ-lê-tikss) pl atletica f

Atlantic (öt-læn-tik) Atlantico m

atmosphere (æt-möss-fiᵒ) n atmosfera f

atom (æ-töm) n atomo m

atomic (ö-to-mik) adj atomico

atomizer (æ-tö-mai-sö) n atomizzatore m; spruzzatore m, vaporizzatore m

attach (ö-tætʃ) v attaccare; *annettere; attached to affezionato a

attack (ö-tæk) v *assalire; n attacco m

attain (ö-*tein*) *v* *raggiungere

attainable (ö-*tei*-nö-böl) *adj* raggiungibile; conseguibile

attempt (ö-*têmpt*) *v* tentare; provare; *n* tentativo *m*

attend (ö-*tênd*) *v* *assistere a; ~ **on** servire; ~ **to** accudire a, occuparsi di; prestare attenzione a

attendance (ö-*tên*-dönss) *n* frequenza *f*

attendant (ö-*tên*-dönt) *n* guardia *f*

attention (ö-*tên*-ſön) *n* attenzione *f*; ***pay** ~ *fare attenzione

attentive (ö-*tên*-tiv) *adj* attento

attic (*æ*-tik) *n* soffitta *f*

attitude (*æ*-ti-t'uud) *n* attitudine *f*

attorney (ö-*töö*-ni) *n* avvocato *m*

attract (ö-*trækt*) *v* *attrarre

attraction (ö-*træk*-ſön) *n* attrattiva *f*; attrazione *f*

attractive (ö-*træk*-tiv) *adj* attraente

auburn (*oo*-bön) *adj* castano

auction (*ook*-ſön) *n* asta *f*

audible (*oo*-di-böl) *adj* udibile

audience (*oo*-di-önss) *n* udienza *f*

auditor (*too*-di-tö) *n* uditore *m*

auditorium (oo-di-*too*-ri-öm) *n* auditorio *m*

August (*oo*-ghösst) agosto

aunt (aant) *n* zia *f*

Australia (o-*sstrei*-li-ö) Australia *f*

Australian (o-*sstrei*-li-ön) *adj* australiano

Austria (*o*-sstri-ö) Austria *f*

Austrian (*o*-sstri-ön) *adj* austriaco

authentic (oo-*θên*-tik) *adj* autentico

author (*oo*-θö) *n* autore *m*

authoritarian (oo-θo-ri-*tê*ᵒ-ri-ön) *adj* autoritario

authority (oo-*θo*-rö-ti) *n* autorità *f*; potere *m*

authorization (oo-θö-rai-*sei*-ſön) *n* autorizzazione *f*; permesso *m*

automatic (oo-tö-*mæ*-tik) *adj* automatico; ~ **teller** *Am* sportello automatica *f*

automation (oo-tö-*mei*-ſön) *n* automazione *f*

automobile (*oo*-tö-mö-biil) *n* automobile *f*; ~ **club** automobile club

autonomous (oo-*to*-nö-möss) *adj* autonomo

autopsy (*oo*-to-pssi) *n* necroscopia *f*

autumn (*oo*-töm) *n* autunno *m*

available (ö-*vei*-lö-böl) *adj* ottenibile, disponibile

avalanche (*æ*-vö-laanſ) *n* valanga *f*

avaricious (*æ*-vö-*ri*-ſöss) *adj* avaro

avenue (*æ*-vö-n'uu) *n* viale *m*

average (*æ*-vö-ridʒ) *adj* medio; *n* media *f*; **on the** ~ in media

aversion (ö-*vöö*-ſön) *n* avversione *f*

avert (ö-*vööt*) *v* *distogliere

avoid (ö-*void*) *v* evitare

await (ö-*ᵘeit*) *v* aspettare

awake (ö-*ᵘeik*) *adj* sveglio

***awake** (ö-*ᵘeik*) *v* svegliare

award (ö-*ᵘood*) *n* premio *m*; *v* aggiudicare

aware (ö-*ᵘê*ᵒ) *adj* consapevole

away (ö-*ᵘei*) *adv* via; ***go** ~ *andarsene

awful (*oo*-föl) *adj* terribile

awkward (*oo*-kᵘöd) *adj* imbarazzante; goffo

awning (*oo*-ning) *n* tenda di riparo

axe (*æ*kss) *n* ascia *f*

axle (*æ*k-ssöl) *n* asse *m*

B

baby (*bei*-bi) *n* piccino *m*; ~ **carriage** *Am* carrozzina *f*

babysitter (*bei*-bi-ssi-tö) *n* bambinaia *f*

bachelor (*bæ*-tſö-lö) *n* celibe *m*

back (bæk) *n* dorso *m*; *adv* indietro;
°go ~ tornare

backache (*bæ*-keik) *n* mal di schiena

backbone (*bæk*-boun) *n* spina dorsale

background (*bæk*-ghraund) *n* sfondo
m; istruzione *f*

backwards (*bæk*-^uöds) *adv* all'indietro

bacon (*bei*-kön) *n* lardo *m*

bacterium (bæk-*tii*-ri-öm) *n* (pl -ria)
batterio *m*

bad (bæd) *adj* cattivo; brutto

bag (bægh) *n* sacco *m*; borsetta *f*,
borsa *f*; valigia *f*

baggage (*bæ*-ghid3) *n* bagaglio *m*; ~
deposit office *Am* deposito bagagli; **hand ~** *Am* bagaglio a mano

bail (beil) *n* cauzione *f*

bailiff (*bei*-lif) *n* usciere *m*

bait (beit) *n* esca *f*

bake (beik) *v* infornare

baker (*bei*-kö) *n* panettiere *m*

bakery (*bei*-kö-ri) *n* panetteria *f*

balance (*bæ*-lönss) *n* equilibrio *m*;
bilancio *m*; saldo *m*

balcony (*bæl*-kö-ni) *n* balcone *m*

bald (boold) *adj* calvo

ball (bool) *n* palla *f*; ballo *m*

ballet (*bæ*-lei) *n* balletto *m*

balloon (bö-*luun*) *n* palloncino *m*

ballpoint-pen (*bool*-point-pên) *n* penna a sfera

ballroom (*bool*-ruum) *n* sala da ballo

bamboo (bæm-*buu*) *n* (pl ~s) bambù
m

banana (bö-*naa*-nö) *n* banana *f*

band (bænd) *n* banda *f*; benda *f*

bandage (*bæn*-did3) *n* fasciatura *f*

bandit (*bæn*-dit) *n* bandito *m*

bangle (*bæng*-ghöl) *n* braccialetto *m*

banisters (*bæ*-ni-stös) *pl* ringhiera *f*

bank (bængk) *n* riva *f*; banca *f*; *v* depositare; ~ **account** conto bancario

banknote (*bængk*-nout) *n* banconota
f

bank-rate (*bængk*-reit) *n* tasso di
sconto

bankrupt (*bængk*-rapt) *adj* fallito

banner (*bæ*-nö) *n* stendardo *m*

banquet (*bæng*-k^uit) *n* banchetto *m*

banqueting-hall (*bæng*-k^ui-ting-hool)
n sala da banchetto

baptism (*bæp*-ti-söm) *n* battesimo *m*

baptize (bæp-*tais*) *v* battezzare

bar (baa) *n* bar *m*; sbarra *f*

barber (*baa*-bö) *n* barbiere *m*

bare (bê^ö) *adj* nudo; spoglio

barely (*bê^ö*-li) *adv* appena

bargain (*baa*-ghin) *n* affare *m*; *v* mercanteggiare

baritone (*bæ*-ri-toun) *n* baritono *m*

bark (baak) *n* corteccia *f*; *v* abbaiare

barley (*baa*-li) *n* orzo *m*

barmaid (*baa*-meid) *n* barista *f*

barman (*baa*-mön) *n* (pl -men) barista
m

barn (baan) *n* granaio *m*

barometer (bö-*ro*-mi-tö) *n* barometro
m

baroque (bö-*rok*) *adj* barocco

barracks (*bæ*-rökss) *pl* caserma *f*

barrel (*bæ*-röl) *n* botte *f*, barile *m*

barrier (*bæ*-ri-ö) *n* barriera *f*

barrister (*bæ*-ri-sstö) *n* avvocato *m*

bartender (*baa*-tên-dö) *n* barista *m*

base (beiss) *n* base *f*; fondamento *m*;
v basare

baseball (*beiss*-bool) *n* baseball *m*

basement (*beiss*-mönt) *n* seminterrato
m

basic (*bei*-ssik) *adj* fondamentale

basilica (bö-*si*-li-kö) *n* basilica *f*

basin (*bei*-ssön) *n* bacino *m*, catino *m*

basis (*bei*-ssiss) *n* (pl bases) fondamento *m*, base *f*

basket (*baa*-sskit) *n* paniere *m*

bass¹ (beiss) *n* basso *m*

bass² (bæss) *n* (pl ~) branzino *m*

bastard (baa-sstöd) n bastardo m; mascalzone m

batch (bætʃ) n partita f

bath (baaθ) n bagno m; ~ **salts** sali da bagno; ~ **towel** asciugamano m

bathe (beið) v bagnarsi, *fare il bagno

bathing-cap (bei-ðing-kæp) n cuffia da bagno

bathing-suit (bei-ðing-ssuut) n costume da bagno

bathing-trunks (bei-ðing-trangkss) n mutandine da bagno

bathrobe (baaθ-roub) n accappatoio m

bathroom (baaθ-ruum) n stanza da bagno; gabinetto m

batter (bæ-tö) n impasto m

battery (bæ-tö-ri) n batteria f; accumulatore m

battle (bæ-töl) n battaglia f; lotta f, combattimento m; v combattere

bay (bei) n baia f; v latrare

*be (bii) v *essere

beach (biitʃ) n spiaggia f; **nudist** ~ spiaggia per nudisti

bead (biid) n perlina f; **beads** pl collana f; rosario m

beak (biik) n becco m

beam (biim) n raggio m; trave f

bean (biin) n fagiolo m

bear (bêö) n orso m

*bear (bêö) v portare; tollerare; sopportare

beard (biöd) n barba f

bearer (bêö-rö) n portatore m

beast (biisst) n animale m; ~ **of prey** animale da preda

*beat (biit) v picchiare; battere

beautiful (biuu-ti-föl) adj bello

beauty (biuu-ti) n bellezza f; ~ **parlour** salone di bellezza; ~ **salon** salone di bellezza; ~ **treatment** cura di bellezza

beaver (bii-vö) n castoro m

because (bi-kos) conj perché; poiché; ~ **of** in conseguenza di, a causa di

*become (bi-kam) v *divenire; *addirsi

bed (bêd) n letto m; ~ **and board** vitto e alloggio, pensione completa; ~ **and breakfast** alloggio e colazione

bedding (bê-ding) n biancheria da letto

bedroom (bêd-ruum) n camera da letto

bee (bii) n ape f

beech (biitʃ) n faggio m

beef (biif) n manzo m

beehive (bii-haiv) n alveare m

been (biin) v (pp be)

beer (biö) n birra f

beet (biit) n barbabietola f

beetle (bii-töl) n scarabeo m

beetroot (biit-ruut) n barbabietola f

before (bi-foo) prep prima di; davanti; conj prima che; adv prima; precedentemente

beg (bêgh) v mendicare; supplicare; *chiedere

beggar (bê-ghö) n mendicante m

*begin (bi-ghin) v cominciare; iniziare

beginner (bi-ghi-nö) n principiante m

beginning (bi-ghi-ning) n inizio m; principio m

on behalf of (on bi-haaf ov) a nome di, per conto di; a favore di

behave (bi-heiv) v comportarsi

behaviour (bi-hei-vïö) n comportamento m

behind (bi-haind) prep dietro; adv indietro

beige (beiʒ) adj beige

being (bii-ing) n essere m

Belgian (bêl-dʒön) adj belga

Belgium (bêl-dʒöm) Belgio m

belief (bi-*liif*) *n* fede *f*

believe (bi-*liiv*) *v* credere

bell (bêl) *n* campana *f*; campanello *m*

bellboy (*bêl*-boi) *n* fattorino d'albergo

belly (*bê*-li) *n* pancia *f*

belong (bi-*long*) *v* *appartenere

belongings (bi-*long*-ings) *pl* effetti personali

beloved (bi-*lavd*) *adj* amato

below (bi-*lou*) *prep* sotto; *adv* giù

belt (bêlt) *n* cinghia *f*; **garter ~** *Am* reggicalze *m*

bench (bêntʃ) *n* banco *m*

bend (bênd) *n* curva *f*; curvatura *f*

*****bend** (bênd) *v* curvare; **~ down** chinarsi

beneath (bi-*niiθ*) *prep* sotto; *adv* giù

benefit (*bê*-ni-fit) *n* profitto *m*, beneficio *m*; vantaggio *m*; *v* approfittare

bent (bênt) *adj* (pp bend) curvato

beret (*bê*-rei) *n* berretto *m*

berry (*bê*-ri) *n* bacca *f*

berth (bööθ) *n* cuccetta *f*

beside (bi-*ssaid*) *prep* vicino a

besides (bi-*ssaids*) *adv* inoltre; d'altronde; *prep* oltre a

best (bêsst) *adj* ottimo

bet (bêt) *n* scommessa *f*; posta *f*

*****bet** (bêt) *v* *scommettere

betray (bi-*trei*) *v* tradire

better (*bê*-tö) *adj* migliore

between (bi-*tᵁiin*) *prep* tra

beverage (*bê*-vö-ridʒ) *n* bevanda *f*

beware (bi-*ᵁêᵒ*) *v* guardarsi, *fare attenzione

bewitch (bi-*ᵁitʃ*) *v* stregare, incantare

beyond (bi-*ᶦond*) *prep* più in là di; oltre; in aggiunta a; *adv* al di là

bible (bai-böl) *n* bibbia *f*

bicycle (*bai*-ssi-köl) *n* bicicletta *f*; ciclo *m*

big (bigh) *adj* grande; voluminoso; grosso; importante

bile (bail) *n* bile *f*

bilingual (bai-*ling*-ghᵁöl) *adj* bilingue

bill (bil) *n* fattura *f*; conto *m*; *v* fatturare

billiards (*bil*-ᶦöds) *pl* biliardo *m*

*****bind** (baind) *v* legare

binding (*bain*-ding) *n* legatura *f*

binoculars (bi-*no*-kᶦö-lös) *pl* binocolo *m*

biology (bai-*o*-lö-dʒi) *n* biologia *f*

birch (böötʃ) *n* betulla *f*

bird (bööd) *n* uccello *m*

Biro (*bai*-rou) *n* penna a sfera

birth (bööθ) *n* nascita *f*

birthday (*bööθ*-dei) *n* compleanno *m*

biscuit (*biss*-kit) *n* biscottino *m*

bishop (*bi*-ʃöp) *n* vescovo *m*

bit (bit) *n* pezzetto *m*; poco *m*

bitch (bitʃ) *n* cagna *f*

bite (bait) *n* boccone *m*; morso *m*; puntura *f*

*****bite** (bait) *v* *mordere

bitter (*bi*-tö) *adj* amaro

black (blæk) *adj* nero; **~ market** mercato nero

blackberry (*blæk*-bö-ri) *n* mora *f*

blackbird (*blæk*-bööd) *n* merlo *m*

blackboard (*blæk*-bood) *n* lavagna *f*

black-currant (blæk-*ka*-rönt) *n* ribes nero

blackmail (*blæk*-meil) *n* ricatto *m*; *v* ricattare

blacksmith (*blæk*-ssmiθ) *n* fabbro *m*

bladder (*blæ*-dö) *n* vescica *f*

blade (bleid) *n* lama *f*; **~ of grass** filo d'erba

blame (bleim) *n* colpa *f*; biasimo *m*; *v* biasimare, rimproverare

blank (blængk) *adj* in bianco

blanket (*blæng*-kit) *n* coperta *f*

blast (blaasst) *n* esplosione *f*

blazer (*blei*-sö) *n* giacca sportiva

bleach (bliitʃ) *v* imbiancare

bleak (bliik) *adj* rigido

*bleed (bliid) *v* sanguinare; salassare

bless (blêss) *v* *benedire

blessing (blê-ssing) *n* benedizione *f*

blind (blaind) *n* avvolgibile *m*, persiana *f*; *adj* cieco; *v* abbagliare

blister (bli-stö) *n* bolla *f*

blizzard (bli-söd) *n* tormenta *f*

block (blok) *v* ostruire, bloccare; *n* ceppo *m*; ~ **of flats** caseggiato *m*

blonde (blond) *n* bionda *f*

blood (blad) *n* sangue *m*; ~ **pressure** pressione sanguigna

blood-poisoning (blad-poi-sö-ning) *n* setticemia *f*

blood-vessel (blad-vê-ssöl) *n* vaso sanguigno

blot (blot) *n* macchia *f*; **blotting paper** carta assorbente

blouse (blaus) *n* blusa *f*

blow (blou) *n* colpo *m*; raffica *f*

*blow (blou) *v* soffiare; tirare

blow-out (blou-aut) *n* foratura *f*

blue (bluu) *adj* blu; depresso

blunt (blant) *adj* ottuso; spuntato

blush (blaʃ) *v* arrossire

board (bood) *n* asse *f*; tavoletta *f*; pensione *f*; consiglio *m*; ~ **and lodging** pensione completa, vitto e alloggio

boarder (boo-dö) *n* pensionante *m*

boarding-house (boo-ding-hauss) *n* pensione *f*

boarding-school (boo-ding-sskuul) *n* convitto *m*

boast (bousst) *v* vantarsi

boat (bout) *n* battello *m*, barca *f*

body (bo-di) *n* corpo *m*

bodyguard (bo-di-ghaad) *n* guardia del corpo

bog (bogh) *n* palude *f*

boil (boil) *v* bollire; *n* foruncolo *m*

bold (bould) *adj* coraggioso; sfrontato, sfacciato

Bolivia (bö-li-vi-ö) Bolivia *f*

Bolivian (bö-li-vi-ön) *adj* boliviano

bolt (boult) *n* chiavistello *m*; bullone *m*

bomb (bom) *n* bomba *f*; *v* bombardare

bond (bond) *n* obbligazione *f*

bone (boun) *n* osso *m*; lisca *f*; *v* dissossare

bonnet (bo-nit) *n* cofano *m*

book (buk) *n* libro *m*; *v* prenotare; registrare, allibrare

booking (bu-king) *n* prenotazione *f*

bookmaker (buk-mei-kö) *n* allibratore *m*

bookseller (buk-ssê-lö) *n* libraio *m*

bookstand (buk-sstænd) *n* edicola *f*

bookstore (buk-sstoo) *n* libreria *f*

boot (buut) *n* stivale *m*; bagagliaio *m*

booth (buuð) *n* baracca *f*; cabina *f*

border (boo-dö) *n* confine *m*; bordo *m*

bore[1] (boo) *v* annoiare; trapanare; *n* seccatore *m*

bore[2] (boo) *v* (p bear)

boring (boo-ring) *adj* noioso

born (boon) *adj* nato

borrow (bo-rou) *v* *prendere in prestito; adottare

bosom (bu-söm) *n* petto *m*; seno *m*

boss (boss) *n* capo *m*, padrone *m*

botany (bo-tö-ni) *n* botanica *f*

both (bouθ) *adj* entrambi; **both ... and** sia ... sia

bother (bo-ðö) *v* infastidire, importunare; disturbarsi; *n* noia *f*

bottle (bo-töl) *n* bottiglia *f*; ~ **opener** apribottiglie *m*; **hot-water** ~ borsa dell'acqua calda

bottleneck (bo-töl-nêk) *n* ingorgo *m*

bottom (bo-töm) *n* fondo *m*; didietro *m*, sedere *m*; *adj* inferiore

bough (bau) *n* ramo *m*

bought (boot) *v* (p, pp buy)

boulder (*boul*-dö) *n* masso *m*

bound (baund) *n* limite *m*; *be ~ to *dovere; ~ **for** diretto a

boundary (*baun*-dö-ri) *n* limite *m*; frontiera *f*

bouquet (bu-*kei*) *n* mazzo *m*

bourgeois (*buô*-ʒ*u*aa) *adj* borghese

boutique (bu-*tiik*) *n* boutique *m*

bow[1] (bau) *v* inchinare

bow[2] (bou) *n* arco *m*; ~ **tie** cravattino *m*, cravatta a farfalla

bowels (bau*u*ls) *pl* intestino *m*, budella *fpl*

bowl (boul) *n* vaso *m*

bowling (*bou*-ling) *n* bowling *m*, gioco delle bocce; ~ **alley** pista di bocce

box[1] (bokss) *v* *fare del pugilato; **boxing match** partita di pugilato

box[2] (bokss) *n* scatola *f*

box-office (*bokss*-o-fiss) *n* botteghino *m*, biglietteria *f*

boy (boi) *n* ragazzo *m*; ragazzino *m*, fanciullo *m*; servo *m*; ~ **scout** giovane esploratore

bra (braa) *n* reggipetto *m*, reggiseno *m*

bracelet (*breiss*-lit) *n* braccialetto *m*

braces (*brei*-ssis) *pl* bretelle *fpl*

brain (brein) *n* cervello *m*; intelligenza *f*

brain-wave (*brein*-*u*eiv) *n* idea luminosa

brake (breik) *n* freno *m*; ~ **drum** tamburo del freno; ~ **lights** luci di arresto

branch (braantʃ) *n* ramo *m*; succursale *f*

brand (brænd) *n* marca *f*; marchio *m*

brand-new (brænd-*n*iuu) *adj* nuovo fiammante

brass (braass) *n* ottone *m*; ~ **band** *n* fanfara *f*

brassiere (*bræ*-siô) *n* reggipetto *m*, reggiseno *m*

brassware (*braass*-*u*êô) *n* ottoname *m*

brave (breiv) *adj* audace, coraggioso

Brazil (brö-*sil*) Brasile *m*

Brazilian (brö-*sil*-*i*ön) *adj* brasiliano

breach (briitʃ) *n* breccia *f*

bread (brêd) *n* pane *m*; **wholemeal** ~ pane integrale

breadth (brêdθ) *n* larghezza *f*

break (breik) *n* frattura *f*; intervallo *m*

*break (breik) *v* *rompere; ~ **down** guastarsi; analizzare

breakdown (*breik*-daun) *n* guasto *m*, avaria *f*

breakfast (*brêk*-fösst) *n* prima colazione

bream (briim) *n* (pl ~) abramide *m*

breast (brêsst) *n* seno *m*

breaststroke (*brêsst*-sstrouk) *n* nuoto a rana

breath (brêθ) *n* respiro *m*; fiato *m*

breathe (briið) *v* respirare

breathing (*brii*-ðing) *n* respirazione *f*

breed (briid) *n* razza *f*; specie *f*

*breed (briid) *v* allevare

breeze (briis) *n* brezza *f*

brew (bruu) *v* *fare la birra

brewery (*bruu*-ö-ri) *n* birreria *f*

bribe (braib) *v* *corrompere

bribery (*brai*-bö-ri) *n* corruzione *f*

brick (brik) *n* laterizio *m*, mattone *m*

bricklayer (*brik*-leiô) *n* muratore *m*

bride (braid) *n* sposa *f*

bridegroom (*braid*-ghruum) *n* sposo *m*

bridge (bridʒ) *n* ponte *m*; bridge *m*

brief (briif) *adj* breve

briefcase (*briif*-keiss) *n* cartella *f*

briefs (briifss) *pl* slip *mpl*, mutandine *fpl*

bright (brait) *adj* brillante; lucido; sveglio, intelligente

brill (bril) *n* rombo *m*

brilliant (*bril*-*i*önt) *adj* brillante

brim (brim) *n* orlo *m*
***bring** (bring) *v* portare; ~ **back** riportare; ~ **up** educare; sollevare
brisk (brissk) *adj* vivace
Britain (*bri*-tön) Gran Bretagna
British (*bri*-tiʃ) *adj* britannico; inglese
Briton (*bri*-tön) *n* britanno *m*; inglese *m*
broad (brood) *adj* largo; ampio, esteso; generale
broadcast (*brood*-kaasst) *n* emissione *f*
***broadcast** (*brood*-kaasst) *v* *trasmettere
brochure (brou-ʃuᵒ) *n* opuscolo *m*
broke[1] (brouk) *v* (p break)
broke[2] (brouk) *adj* squattrinato
broken (*brou*-kön) *adj* (pp break) guasto, rotto
broker (*brou*-kö) *n* mediatore *m*
bronchitis (brong-*kai*-tiss) *n* bronchite *f*
bronze (brons) *n* bronzo *m*; *adj* bronzeo
brooch (broutʃ) *n* spilla *f*
brook (bruk) *n* ruscello *m*
broom (bruum) *n* scopa *f*
brothel (*bro*-θöl) *n* bordello *m*
brother (*bra*-ðö) *n* fratello *m*
brother-in-law (*bra*-ðö-rin-loo) *n* (pl brothers-) cognato *m*
brought (broot) *v* (p, pp bring)
brown (braun) *adj* bruno
bruise (bruus) *n* livido *m*, contusione *f*; *v* ammaccare
brunette (bruu-*nêt*) *n* bruna *f*
brush (braʃ) *n* spazzola *f*; pennello *m*; *v* spazzolare
brutal (*bruu*-töl) *adj* brutale
bubble (*ba*-böl) *n* bolla *f*
bucket (*ba*-kit) *n* secchio *m*
buckle (*ba*-köl) *n* fibbia *f*
bud (bad) *n* bocciolo *m*
budget (*ba*-dʒit) *n* preventivo *m*, bilancio *m*

buffet (*bu*-fei) *n* buffé *m*
bug (bagh) *n* cimice *f*; *nAm* insetto *m*
***build** (bild) *v* costruire
building (*bil*-ding) *n* edificio *m*
bulb (balb) *n* bulbo *m*; **light** ~ lampadina *f*
Bulgaria (bal-*ghêᵒ*-ri-ö) Bulgaria *f*
Bulgarian (bal-*ghêᵒ*-ri-ön) *adj* bulgaro
bulk (balk) *n* massa *f*; maggior parte
bulky (*bal*-ki) *adj* voluminoso
bull (bul) *n* toro *m*
bullet (*bu*-lit) *n* pallottola *f*
bullfight (*bul*-fait) *n* corrida *f*
bullring (*bul*-ring) *n* arena *f*
bump (bamp) *v* urtare; cozzare; *n* urto *m*
bumper (*bam*-pö) *n* paraurti *m*
bumpy (*bam*-pi) *adj* accidentato
bun (ban) *n* panino *m*
bunch (bantʃ) *n* mazzo *m*; gruppo *m*
bundle (*ban*-döl) *n* fagotto *m*; *v* legare insieme, affastellare
bunk (bangk) *n* cuccetta *f*
buoy (boi) *n* boa *f*
burden (*böö*-dön) *n* peso *m*
bureau (*b'uᵒ*-rou) *n* (pl ~x, ~s) scrittoio *m*; *nAm* comò *m*
bureaucracy (b'uᵒ-*ro*-krö-ssi) *n* burocrazia *f*
burglar (*böö*-ghlö) *n* scassinatore *m*
burgle (*böö*-ghöl) *v* scassinare
burial (*bê*-ri-öl) *n* seppellimento *m*, sepoltura *f*
burn (böön) *n* bruciatura *f*
***burn** (böön) *v* *ardere; bruciare
***burst** (böösst) *v* scoppiare; spaccarsi
bury (*bê*-ri) *v* seppellire
bus (bass) *n* autobus *m*
bush (buʃ) *n* cespuglio *m*
business (*bis*-nöss) *n* affari, commercio *m*; azienda *f*, ditta *f*; mestiere *m*; affare *m*; ~ **hours** orario di

apertura, ore d'ufficio; ~ **trip** viaggio d'affari; **on** ~ per affari

businessman (*bis*-nöss-mön) *n* (pl -men) uomo d'affari

bust (basst) *n* busto *m*

bustle (*ba*-ssöl) *n* andirivieni *m*

busy (*bi*-si) *adj* occupato; animato, indaffarato

but (bat) *conj* ma; però; *prep* tranne

butcher (*bu*-tʃö) *n* macellaio *m*

butter (*ba*-tö) *n* burro *m*

butterfly (*ba*-tö-flai) *n* farfalla *f*; ~ **stroke** nuoto a farfalla

buttock (*ba*-tök) *n* natica *f*

button (*ba*-tön) *n* bottone *m*; *v* abbottonare

buttonhole (*ba*-tön-houl) *n* asola *f*

***buy** (bai) *v* comprare; acquistare

buyer (*bai*-ö) *n* compratore *m*

by (bai) *prep* da; con; vicino a

by-pass (*bai*-paass) *n* circonvallazione *f*; *v* girare intorno a

C

cab (kæb) *n* tassì *m*

cabaret (*kæ*-bö-rei) *n* cabaret *m*

cabbage (*kæ*-bidʒ) *n* cavolo *m*

cab-driver (*kæb*-drai-vö) *n* tassista *m*

cabin (*kæ*-bin) *n* cabina *f*; capanna *f*

cabinet (*kæ*-bi-nöt) *n* gabinetto *m*

cable (*kei*-böl) *n* cavo *m*; telegramma *m*; *v* telegrafare

cadre (*kaa*-dö) *n* quadro *m*

café (*kæ*-fei) *n* bar *m*

cafeteria (kæ-fö-*ti*ᵒ-ri-ö) *n* tavola calda

caffeine (*kæ*-fiin) *n* caffeina *f*

cage (keidʒ) *n* gabbia *f*

cake (keik) *n* dolce *m*; pasticceria *f*, torta *f*

calamity (kö-*læ*-mö-ti) *n* calamità *f*,

disastro *m*

calcium (*kæl*-ssi-öm) *n* calcio *m*

calculate (*kæl*-kⁱu-leit) *v* computare, calcolare

calculation (kæl-kⁱu-*lei*-ʃön) *n* calcolo *m*

calculator (kæl-kⁱu-*lei*-tö) *n* calcolatrice *f*

calendar (*kæ*-lön-dö) *n* calendario *m*

calf (kaaf) *n* (pl calves) vitello *m*; polpaccio *m*; ~ **skin** pelle di vitello

call (kool) *v* chiamare; telefonare; *n* appello *m*; visita *f*; telefonata *f*; *be called** chiamarsi; ~ **names** ingiuriare; ~ **on** visitare; ~ **up** *Am* telefonare

callus (*kæ*-löss) *n* callo *m*

calm (kaam) *adj* tranquillo, calmo; ~ **down** calmare

calorie (*kæ*-lö-ri) *n* caloria *f*

Calvinism (*kæl*-vi-ni-söm) *n* calvinismo *m*

came (keim) *v* (p come)

camel (*kæ*-möl) *n* cammello *m*

camera (*kæ*-mö-rö) *n* macchina fotografica; cinepresa *f*; ~ **shop** negozio di articoli fotografici

camp (kæmp) *n* campo *m*; *v* accamparsi

campaign (kæm-*pein*) *n* campagna *f*

camp-bed (kæmp-*bêd*) *n* lettino da campeggio, branda *f*

camper (*kæm*-pö) *n* campeggiatore *m*

camping (*kæm*-ping) *n* campeggio *m*; ~ **site** campeggio *m*

camshaft (*kæm*-ʃaaft) *n* albero a camme

can (kæn) *n* latta *f*; ~ **opener** apriscatole *m*

***can** (kæn) *v* *potere

Canada (*kæ*-nö-dö) *n* Canadà *m*

Canadian (kö-*nei*-di-ön) *adj* canadese

canal (kö-*næl*) *n* canale *m*

canary (kö-*nê*ᵒ-ri) *n* canarino *m*

cancel (*kæn*-ssöl) v annullare; *disdire

cancellation (kæn-ssö-*lei*-ʃön) n annullamento m

cancer (*kæn*-ssö) n cancro m

candelabrum (kæn-dö-*laa*-bröm) n (pl -bra) candelabro m

candidate (*kæn*-di-döt) n candidato m

candle (*kæn*-döl) n candela f

candy (*kæn*-di) nAm caramella f; dolciumi mpl; ~ store Am pasticceria f

cane (kein) n canna f; bastone m

canister (*kæ*-ni-sstö) n barattolo m

canoe (kö-*nuu*) n canoa f

canteen (kæn-*tiin*) n mensa f

canvas (*kæn*-völss) n tela di canapa

cap (kæp) n berretto m

capable (*kei*-pö-böl) adj capace

capacity (kö-*pæ*-ssö-ti) n capacità f; potenza f; abilità f

cape (keip) n mantella f; capo m

capital (*kæ*-pi-töl) n capitale f; capitale m; adj importante, capitale; ~ letter maiuscola f

capitalism (*kæ*-pi-tö-li-söm) n capitalismo m

capitulation (kö-pi-tⁱu-*lei*-ʃön) n capitolazione f

capsule (*kæp*-ssⁱuul) n capsula f

captain (*kæp*-tin) n capitano m; comandante m

capture (*kæp*-tʃö) v *far prigioniero, catturare; *prendere; n cattura f; presa f

car (kaa) n macchina f; ~ hire autonoleggio m; ~ park parcheggio m; ~ rental Am autonoleggio m

carafe (kö-*ræf*) n caraffa f

caramel (*kæ*-rö-möl) n caramella di zucchero

carat (*kæ*-röt) n carato m

caravan (*kæ*-rö-væn) n carovana f; carrozzone m

carburettor (kaa-bⁱu-*rê*-tö) n carburatore m

card (kaad) n cartoncino m; cartolina f

cardboard (*kaad*-bood) n cartone m; adj di cartone

cardigan (*kaa*-di-ghön) n giaccone m

cardinal (*kaa*-di-nöl) n cardinale m; adj cardinale, principale

care (kêᵒ) n cura f; preoccupazione f; ~ about preoccuparsi di; ~ for *voler bene; *take ~ of *aver cura di, occuparsi di

career (kö-*riᵒ*) n carriera f

carefree (*kêᵒ*-frii) adj spensierato

careful (*kêᵒ*-föl) adj attento; scrupoloso, accurato

careless (*kêᵒ*-löss) adj noncurante, trascurato

caretaker (*kêᵒ*-tei-kö) n custode m

cargo (*kaa*-ghou) n (pl ~es) carico m

carnival (*kaa*-ni-völ) n carnevale m

carp (kaap) n (pl ~) carpa f

carpenter (*kaa*-pin-tö) n falegname m

carpet (*kaa*-pit) n tappeto m

carriage (*kæ*-ridʒ) n vagone m; carrozza f

carriageway (*kæ*-ridʒ-ᵘei) n rotabile f

carrot (*kæ*-röt) n carota f

carry (*kæ*-ri) v portare; *condurre; ~ on continuare; proseguire; ~ out eseguire

carry-cot (*kæ*-ri-kot) n baby-pullman m

cart (kaat) n carro m

cartilage (*kaa*-ti-lidʒ) n cartilagine f

carton (*kaa*-tön) n scatolone m; stecca f

cartoon (kaa-*tuun*) n cartone animato

cartridge (*kaa*-tridʒ) n cartuccia f

carve (kaav) v tagliare; intagliare

carving (*kaa*-ving) n scultura in legno

case (keiss) n caso m; causa f; valigia *f*; astuccio *m*; **attaché** ~ porta-carte *m*; **in** ~ qualora; **in** ~ **of** in caso di

cash (kæʃ) *n* contanti *mpl*; *v* convertire, *riscuotere, incassare; ~ **dispenser** sportello automatica *f*

cashier (kæ-ʃiᵒ) *n* cassiere *m*; cassiera *f*

cashmere (kæʃ-miᵒ) *n* cachemire *m*

casino (kö-ssii-nou) *n* (pl ~s) casinò *m*

cask (kaassk) *n* barile *m*, botte *f*

cast (kaasst) *n* lancio *m*

*cast** (kaasst) *v* lanciare, gettare; **cast iron** ghisa *f*

castle (kaa-ssöl) *n* castello *m*

casual (kæ-ʒu-öl) *adj* informale; incidentale, fortuito

casualty (kæ-ʒu-öl-ti) *n* vittima *f*

cat (kæt) *n* gatto *m*

catacomb (kæ-tö-koum) *n* catacomba *f*

catalogue (kæ-tö-logh) *n* catalogo *m*

catarrh (kö-taa) *n* catarro *m*

catastrophe (kö-tæ-sströ-fi) *n* catastrofe *f*

*catch** (kætʃ) *v* acchiappare; afferrare; *cogliere

category (kæ-ti-ghö-ri) *n* categoria *f*

cathedral (kö-θii-dröl) *n* duomo *m*, cattedrale *f*

catholic (kæ-θö-lik) *adj* cattolico

cattle (kæ-töl) *pl* bestiame *m*

caught (koot) *v* (p, pp catch)

cauliflower (ko-li-flauᵒ) *n* cavolfiore *m*

cause (koos) *v* causare; provocare; *n* causa *f*; ragione *f*, motivo *m*; ~ **to** *indurre a

causeway (koos-ᵘei) *n* via selciata *f*

caution (koo-ʃön) *n* cautela *f*; *v* ammonire

cautious (koo-ʃöss) *adj* cauto

cave (keiv) *n* caverna *f*; spelonca *f*

cavern (kæ-vön) *n* caverna *f*

caviar (kæ-vi-aa) *n* caviale *m*

cavity (kæ-vö-ti) *n* cavità *f*

cease (ssiiss) *v* *smettere

ceiling (ssii-ling) *n* soffitto *m*

celebrate (ssé-li-breit) *v* celebrare

celebration (ssé-li-brei-ʃön) *n* celebrazione *f*

celebrity (ssi-lê-brö-ti) *n* celebrità *f*

celery (ssé-lö-ri) *n* sedano *m*

celibacy (ssé-li-bö-ssi) *n* celibato *m*

cell (ssêl) *n* cella *f*

cellar (ssé-lö) *n* cantina *f*

cellophane (ssé-lö-fein) *n* cellofan *m*

cement (ssi-mênt) *n* cemento *m*

cemetery (ssé-mi-tri) *n* cimitero *m*

censorship (ssên-ssö-ʃip) *n* censura *f*

centigrade (ssên-ti-ghreid) *adj* centigrado

centimetre (ssên-ti-mii-tö) *n* centimetro *m*

central (ssên-tröl) *adj* centrale; ~ **heating** riscaldamento centrale; ~ **station** stazione centrale

centralize (ssên-trö-lais) *v* centralizzare

centre (ssên-tö) *n* centro *m*

century (ssên-tʃö-ri) *n* secolo *m*

ceramics (ssi-ræ-mikss) *pl* terraglie *fpl*, ceramica *f*

ceremony (ssé-rö-mö-ni) *n* cerimonia *f*

certain (ssöö-tön) *adj* certo

certificate (ssö-ti-fi-köt) *n* attestato *m*; certificato *m*, atto *m*, diploma *m*

chain (tʃein) *n* catena *f*

chair (tʃêᵒ) *n* sedia *f*; seggio *m*

chairman (tʃêᵒ-mön) *n* (pl -men) presidente *m*

chalet (ʃæ-lei) *n* chalet *m*

chalk (tʃook) *n* creta *f*

challenge (tʃæ-löndʒ) *v* sfidare; *n* sfida *f*

chamber (tʃeim-bö) *n* camera *f*

chambermaid (*tʃeim*-bö-meid) *n* cameriera *f*

champagne (ʃæm-*pein*) *n* champagne *m*

champion (*tʃæm*-pˈön) *n* campione *m*; difensore *m*

chance (tʃaanss) *n* caso *m*; opportunità *f*, occasione *f*; rischio *m*; azzardo *m*; **by** ~ per caso

change (tʃeindʒ) *v* modificare, cambiare; cambiarsi; *n* cambiamento *m*, cambio *m*; spiccioli *mpl*

channel (*tʃæ*-nöl) *n* canale *m*; **English Channel** La Manica

chaos (*kei*-oss) *n* caos *m*

chaotic (kei-*o*-tik) *adj* caotico

chap (tʃæp) *n* tizio *m*

chapel (*tʃæ*-pöl) *n* chiesa *f*, cappella *f*

chaplain (*tʃæ*-plin) *n* cappellano *m*

character (*kæ*-rök-tö) *n* carattere *m*

characteristic (kæ-rök-tö-*ri*-sstik) *adj* tipico, caratteristico; *n* caratteristica *f*; tratto del carattere

characterize (*kæ*-rök-tö-rais) *v* caratterizzare

charcoal (*tʃaa*-koul) *n* carbone di legno

charge (tʃaadʒ) *v* *far pagare; incaricare; accusare; caricare; *n* costo *m*; carico *m*; accusa *f*; ~ **plate** *Am* carta di credito; **free of** ~ gratuito; **in** ~ **of** incaricato di; *take ~ of* incaricarsi di

charity (*tʃæ*-rö-ti) *n* carità *f*

charm (tʃaam) *n* incanto *m*, fascino *m*; amuleto *m*

charming (*tʃaa*-ming) *adj* affascinante

chart (tʃaat) *n* tabella *f*; diagramma *m*; carta nautica; **conversion** ~ tabella di conversione

chase (tʃeiss) *v* inseguire; scacciare, cacciare; *n* caccia *f*

chasm (*kæ*-söm) *n* baratro *m*

chassis (*ʃæ*-ssi) *n* (pl ~) telaio *m*

chaste (tʃeisst) *adj* casto

chat (tʃæt) *v* chiacchierare, ciarlare; *n* ciancia *f*, ciarlata *f*, chiacchierata *f*

chatterbox (*tʃæ*-tö-bokss) *n* chiacchierone *m*

chauffeur (*fou*-fö) *n* autista *m*

cheap (tʃiip) *adj* a buon mercato; economico

cheat (tʃiit) *v* ingannare; imbrogliare

check (tʃêk) *v* verificare, *rivedere; *n* quadretto *m*; *nAm* conto *m*; assegno *m*; **check!** scacco!; ~ **in** registrarsi; ~ **out** *disdire

check-book (*tʃêk*-buk) *nAm* libretto di assegni

checkerboard (*tʃê*-kö-bood) *nAm* scacchiera *f*

checkers (*tʃê*-kös) *plAm* gioco della dama

checkroom (*tʃêk*-ruum) *nAm* guardaroba *m*

check-up (*tʃê*-kap) *n* visita medica

cheek (tʃiik) *n* guancia *f*

cheek-bone (*tʃiik*-boun) *n* zigomo *m*

cheer (tʃiô) *v* acclamare; ~ **up** rallegrare

cheerful (*tʃiô*-föl) *adj* gaio, allegro

cheese (tʃiis) *n* formaggio *m*

chef (ʃêf) *n* capocuoco *m*

chemical (*kê*-mi-köl) *adj* chimico

chemist (*kê*-misst) *n* farmacista *m*; **chemist's** farmacia *f*

chemistry (*kê*-mi-sstri) *n* chimica *f*

cheque (tʃêk) *n* assegno *m*

cheque-book (*tʃêk*-buk) *n* libretto di assegni

chequered (*tʃê*-köd) *adj* quadrettato, scaccato

cherry (*tʃê*-ri) *n* ciliegia *f*

chess (tʃêss) *n* scacchi *mpl*

chest (tʃêsst) *n* petto *m*; torace *m*; baule *m*; ~ **of drawers** cassettone *m*

chestnut (*tʃéss*-nat) n castagna f

chew (tʃuu) v masticare

chewing-gum (*tʃuu*-ing-gham) n gomma da masticare

chicken (*tʃi*-kin) n pollo m; pulcino m

chickenpox (*tʃi*-kin-pokss) n varicella f

chief (tʃiif) n capo m; adj primo, principale

chieftain (*tʃiif*-tön) n capo m

chilblain (*tʃil*-blein) n gelone m

child (tʃaild) n (pl children) bambino m

childbirth (*tʃaild*-böö θ) n parto m

childhood (*tʃaild*-hud) n infanzia f

Chile (*tʃi*-li) Cile m

Chilean (*tʃi*-li-ön) adj cileno

chill (tʃil) n brivido m

chilly (*tʃi*-li) adj freddino

chimes (tʃaims) pl carillon m

chimney (*tʃim*-ni) n camino m

chin (tʃin) n mento m

China (*tʃai*-nö) Cina f

china (*tʃai*-nö) n porcellana f

Chinese (tʃai-*niis*) adj cinese

chink (tʃingk) n fessura f

chip (tʃip) n scheggia f; gettone m; v tagliare, scheggiare; **chips** patatine fritte

chiropodist (ki-*ro*-pö-disst) n callista m

chisel (*tʃi*-söl) n scalpello m

chives (tʃaivs) pl cipollina f

chlorine (*kloo*-riin) n cloro m

chock-full (tʃok-*ful*) adj gremito, pieno zeppo

chocolate (*tʃo*-klöt) n cioccolata f; cioccolatino m

choice (tʃoiss) n scelta f; selezione f

choir (kᵘaiᵒ) n coro m

choke (tʃouk) v soffocare; strozzare; n valvola dell'aria

*choose (tʃuus) v *scegliere

chop (tʃop) n cotoletta f, braciola f; v spaccare

Christ (kraisst) Cristo m

christen (*kri*-ssön) v battezzare

christening (*kri*-ssö-ning) n battesimo m

Christian (*kriss*-tʃön) adj cristiano; ~ **name** nome di battesimo

Christmas (*kriss*-möss) Natale m

chromium (*krou*-mi-öm) n cromo m

chronic (*kro*-nik) adj cronico

chronological (kro-nö-*lo*-dʒi-köl) adj cronologico

chuckle (*tʃa*-köl) v ridacchiare

chunk (tʃangk) n grosso pezzo

church (tʃöötʃ) n chiesa f

churchyard (*tʃöötʃ*-ˈaad) n camposanto m

cigar (ssi-*ghaa*) n sigaro m; ~ **shop** tabaccheria f

cigarette (ssi-ghö-*rêt*) n sigaretta f; ~ **tobacco** trinciato m

cigarette-case (ssi-ghö-*rêt*-keiss) n portasigarette m

cigarette-holder (ssi-ghö-*rêt*-houl-dö) n bocchino m

cigarette-lighter (ssi-ghö-*rêt*-lai-tö) n accendino m

cinema (*ssi*-nö-mö) n cinematografo m

cinnamon (*ssi*-nö-mön) n cannella f

circle (*ssöö*-köl) n cerchio m; circolo m; balconata f; v accerchiare, circondare

circulation (ssöö-kᵘu-*lei*-ʃön) n circolazione f; circolazione del sangue

circumstance (*ssöö*-köm-sstænss) n circostanza f

circus (*ssöö*-köss) n circo m

citizen (*ssi*-ti-sön) n cittadino m

citizenship (*ssi*-ti-sön-ʃip) n cittadinanza f

city (*ssi*-ti) n città f

civic (*ssi*-vik) adj civico

civil (*ssi*-völ) *adj* civile; cortese; ~ **law** diritto civile; ~ **servant** funzionario *m*

civilian (ssi-*vil*-¹ön) *adj* civile; *n* borghese *m*

civilization (ssi-vö-lai-*sei*-ʃön) *n* civiltà *f*

civilized (*ssi*-vö-laisd) *adj* civilizzato

claim (kleim) *v* rivendicare, reclamare; asserire; *n* rivendicazione *f*, pretesa *f*

clamp (klæmp) *n* morsa *f*; morsetto *m*

clap (klæp) *v* battere le mani, applaudire

clarify (*klæ*-ri-fai) *v* chiarire, chiarificare

class (klaass) *n* classe *f*

classical (*klæ*-ssi-köl) *adj* classico

classify (*klæ*-ssi-fai) *v* classificare

class-mate (*klaass*-meit) *n* compagno di classe

classroom (*klaass*-ruum) *n* aula *f*

clause (kloos) *n* clausola *f*

claw (kloo) *n* artiglio *m*

clay (klei) *n* argilla *f*

clean (kliin) *adj* puro, pulito; *v* nettare, pulire

cleaning (*klii*-ning) *n* pulizia *f*, pulitura *f*; ~ **fluid** smacchiatore *m*

clear (kliö) *adj* chiaro; *v* sgombrare

clearing (*kliö*-ring) *n* radura *f*

cleft (klêft) *n* crepa *f*

clergyman (*klöö*-dʒi-mön) *n* (pl -men) pastore *m*; chierico *m*

clerk (klaak) *n* commesso d'ufficio, impiegato *m*; scrivano *m*; segretario *m*

clever (*klê*-vö) *adj* intelligente; perspicace, sveglio

client (*klai*-önt) *n* cliente *m*

cliff (klif) *n* scoglio *m*, scogliera *f*

climate (*klai*-mit) *n* clima *m*

climb (klaim) *v* arrampicarsi; arrampicare

clinic (*kli*-nik) *n* clinica *f*

cloak (klouk) *n* mantello *m*

cloakroom (*klouk*-ruum) *n* spogliatoio *m*

clock (klok) *n* orologio *m*; **at ... o'-clock** alle ...

cloister (*kloi*-sstö) *n* monastero *m*

close¹ (klous) *v* *chiudere

close² (klouss) *adj* vicino

closet (*klo*-sit) *n* credenza *f*

cloth (kloθ) *n* stoffa *f*; panno *m*

clothes (klouðs) *pl* abiti, vestiti *mpl*

clothes-brush (*klouðs*-braʃ) *n* spazzola per vestiti

clothing (*klou*-ðing) *n* vestiti *mpl*

cloud (klaud) *n* nuvola *f*

cloud-burst (*klaud*-böösst) *n* nubifragio *m*

cloudy (*klau*-di) *adj* nuvoloso

clover (*klou*-vö) *n* trifoglio *m*

clown (klaun) *n* pagliaccio *m*

club (klab) *n* circolo *m*; associazione *f*; clava *f*, mazza *f*

clumsy (*klam*-si) *adj* goffo

clutch (klatʃ) *n* frizione *f*; stretta *f*

coach (koutʃ) *n* autobus *m*; vagone *m*; carrozza *f*; allenatore *m*

coachwork (*koutʃ*-ᵘöök) *n* carrozzeria *f*

coagulate (kou-æ-ghi¹u-leit) *v* coagulare

coal (koul) *n* carbone *m*

coarse (kooss) *adj* grossolano; volgare

coast (kousst) *n* costa *f*

coat (kout) *n* cappotto *m*, soprabito *m*

coat-hanger (*kout*-hæng-ö) *n* attaccapanni *m*

cobweb (*kob*-ᵘêb) *n* ragnatela *f*

cocaine (kou-*kein*) *n* cocaina *f*

cock (kok) *n* gallo *m*

cocktail (*kok*-teil) *n* cocktail *m*

coconut (*kou*-kö-nat) *n* noce di cocco

cod (kod) *n* (pl ~) merluzzo *m*

code (koud) *n* codice *m*

coffee (*ko*-fi) *n* caffè *m*

cognac (*ko*-n'æk) *n* cognac *m*

coherence (kou-*hi*ᵒ-rönss) *n* coerenza *f*

coin (koin) *n* moneta *f*

coincide (kou-in-*ssaid*) *v* *coincidere

cold (kould) *adj* freddo; *n* freddo *m*; raffreddore *m*; **catch a ~** *prendere un raffreddore

collapse (kö-*læpss*) *v* crollare

collar (*ko*-lö) *n* collare *m*; colletto *m*; **~ stud** bottoncino per colletto

collarbone (*ko*-lö-boun) *n* clavicola *f*

colleague (*ko*-liigh) *n* collega *m*

collect (kö-*lêkt*) *v* *raccogliere; rilevare, *andare a prendere; *fare una colletta

collection (kö-*lêk*-fön) *n* collezione *f*; levata *f*

collective (kö-*lêk*-tiv) *adj* collettivo

collector (kö-*lêk*-tö) *n* collezionista *m*; collettore *m*

college (*ko*-lidʒ) *n* collegio *m*

collide (kö-*laid*) *v* cozzare

collision (kö-*li*-ʒön) *n* scontro *m*, collisione *f*

Colombia (kö-*lom*-bi-ö) Colombia *f*

Colombian (kö-*lom*-bi-ön) *adj* colombiano

colonel (*köö*-nöl) *n* colonnello *m*

colony (*ko*-lö-ni) *n* colonia *f*

colour (*ka*-lö) *n* colore *m*; *v* colorare; **~ film** pellicola a colori

colourant (*ka*-lö-rönt) *n* tintura *f*

colour-blind (*ka*-lö-blaind) *adj* daltonico

coloured (*ka*-löd) *adj* di colore

colourful (*ka*-lö-föl) *adj* pieno di colore, colorito

column (*ko*-löm) *n* pilastro *m*, colonna *f*; rubrica *f*

coma (*kou*-mö) *n* coma *m*

comb (koum) *v* pettinare; *n* pettine *m*

combat (*kom*-bæt) *n* lotta *f*, combattimento *m*; *v* combattere

combination (kom-bi-*nei*-fön) *n* combinazione *f*

combine (köm-*bain*) *v* combinare; unire

*come (kam) *v* *venire; **~ across** incontrare; trovare

comedian (kö-*mii*-di-ön) *n* commediante *m*; comico *m*

comedy (*ko*-mö-di) *n* commedia *f*; **musical ~** commedia musicale

comfort (*kam*-föt) *n* agio *m*, comodità *f*, conforto *m*; consolazione *f*; *v* consolare

comfortable (*kam*-fö-tö-böl) *adj* confortevole, comodo

comic (*ko*-mik) *adj* comico

comics (*ko*-mikss) *pl* racconto a fumetti

coming (*ka*-ming) *n* venuta *f*

comma (*ko*-mö) *n* virgola *f*

command (kö-*maand*) *v* comandare; *n* ordine *m*

commander (kö-*maan*-dö) *n* comandante *m*

commemoration (kö-mê-mö-*rei*-fön) *n* commemorazione *f*

commence (kö-*mênss*) *v* iniziare

comment (*ko*-mênt) *n* commento *m*; *v* commentare

commerce (*ko*-mööss) *n* commercio *m*

commercial (kö-*möö*-föl) *adj* commerciale; *n* annunzio pubblicitario; **~ law** diritto commerciale

commission (kö-*mi*-fön) *n* comitato *m*

commit (kö-*mit*) *v* affidare, consegnare; *commettere, compiere

committee (kö-*mi*-ti) *n* commissione

f, comitato *m*

common (*ko*-mön) *adj* comune; abituale; ordinario

commune (*ko*-mⁱuun) *n* comune *f*

communicate (kö-*mⁱuu*-ni-keit) *v* comunicare

communication (kö-mⁱuu-ni-*kei*-ʃön) *n* comunicazione *f*

communism (*ko*-mⁱu-ni-söm) *n* comunismo *m*

communist (*ko*-mⁱu-nisst) *n* comunista *m*

community (kö-*mⁱuu*-nö-ti) *n* società *f*, comunità *f*

commuter (kö-*mⁱuu*-tö) *n* pendolare *m*

compact (*kom*-pækt) *adj* compatto

compact disc (*kom*-pækt dissk) *n* compact disc *m*; ~ **player** compact disc *m*

companion (köm-*pæ*-nⁱön) *n* compagno *m*

company (*kam*-pö-ni) *n* compagnia *f*; ditta *f*, società *f*

comparative (köm-*pæ*-rö-tiv) *adj* relativo

compare (köm-*pê^ö*) *v* paragonare

comparison (köm-*pæ*-ri-ssön) *n* paragone *m*

compartment (köm-*paat*-mönt) *n* scompartimento *m*

compass (*kam*-pöss) *n* bussola *f*

compel (köm-*pêl*) *v* *costringere

compensate (*kom*-pön-sseit) *v* compensare

compensation (kom-pön-*ssei*-ʃön) *n* compensazione *f*; indennità *f*

compete (köm-*piit*) *v* competere

competition (kom-pö-*ti*-ʃön) *n* gara *f*; concorrenza *f*

competitor (köm-*pê*-ti-tör) *n* concorrente *m*

compile (köm-*pail*) *v* compilare

complain (köm-*plein*) *v* lagnarsi

complaint (köm-*pleint*) *n* lagnanza *f*;

complaints book libro dei reclami

complete (köm-*pliit*) *adj* completo; *v* completare

completely (köm-*pliit*-li) *adv* interamente, totalmente, completamente

complex (*kom*-plêkss) *n* complesso *m*; *adj* intricato, complesso

complexion (köm-*plêk*-ʃön) *n* carnagione *f*

complicated (*kom*-pli-kei-tid) *adj* complicato

compliment (*kom*-pli-mönt) *n* complimento *m*; *v* complimentare, felicitarsi con

compose (köm-*pous*) *v* *comporre

composer (köm-*pou*-sö) *n* compositore *m*

composition (kom-pö-*si*-ʃön) *n* composizione *f*

comprehensive (kom-pri-*hên*-ssiv) *adj* comprensivo

comprise (köm-*prais*) *v* *comprendere, *contenere

compromise (*kom*-prö-mais) *n* compromesso *m*

compulsory (köm-*pal*-ssö-ri) *adj* obbligatorio

computer (köm-*pⁱuu*-tö) *n* computer *m*

conceal (kön-*ssiil*) *v* *nascondere

conceited (kön-*ssii*-tid) *adj* presuntuoso

conceive (kön-*ssiiv*) *v* concepire, *comprendere

concentrate (*kon*-ssön-treit) *v* concentrare

concentration (kon-ssön-*trei*-ʃön) *n* concentrazione *f*

conception (kön-*ssêp*-ʃön) *n* concezione *f*; concepimento *m*

concern (kön-*ssöön*) *v* riguardare, concernere; *n* ansietà *f*; faccenda *f*; azienda *f*, impresa *f*

concerned (kön-*ssöönd*) *adj* preoccupato; interessato

concerning (kön-*ssöö*-ning) *prep* riguardo a, riguardante

concert (*kon*-ssöt) *n* concerto *m*; ~ **hall** sala da concerti

concession (kön-*ssê*-[ön) *n* concessione *f*

concierge (kong-ssi-*ê^ö*₃) *n* portinaio *m*

concise (kön-*ssaiss*) *adj* conciso, breve

conclusion (köng-*kluu*-ʒön) *n* conclusione *f*

concrete (*kong*-kriit) *adj* concreto; *n* calcestruzzo *m*

concussion (köng-*ka*-[ön) *n* commozione cerebrale

condition (kön-*di*-[ön) *n* condizione *f*; stato *m*, forma *f*; circostanza *f*

conditional (kön-*di*-[ö-nöl) *adj* condizionale

conditioner (kön-*di*-[ö-nö) *n* balsamo *m*

condom (*kön*-döm) *n* condom *m*, preservativo *m*

conduct[1] (*kon*-dakt) *n* condotta *f*

conduct[2] (kön-*dakt*) *v* *condurre; guidare; *dirigere

conductor (kön-*dak*-tö) *n* conduttore *m*; direttore d'orchestra

confectioner (kön-*fêk*-[ö-nö) *n* pasticciere *m*

conference (*kon*-fö-rönss) *n* conferenza *f*

confess (kön-*fêss*) *v* *riconoscere; confessare; professare

confession (kön-*fê*-[ön) *n* confessione *f*

confidence (*kon*-fi-dönss) *n* fiducia *f*

confident (*kon*-fi-dönt) *adj* confidente

confidential (kon-fi-*dên*-[öl) *adj* confidenziale

confirm (kön-*fööm*) *v* confermare

confirmation (kon-fö-*mei*-[ön) *n* conferma *f*

confiscate (*kon*-fi-sskeit) *v* sequestrare, confiscare

conflict (*kon*-flikt) *n* conflitto *m*

confuse (kön-*f'uus*) *v* *confondere; **confused** *adj* confuso

confusion (kön-*f'uu*-ʒön) *n* confusione *f*

congratulate (köng-*ghræ*-t[u-leit) *v* congratularsi, felicitarsi con

congratulation (köng-ghræ-t[u-*lei*-[ön) *n* congratulazione *f*, felicitazione *f*

congregation (kong-ghri-*ghei*-[ön) *n* comunione *f*, congregazione *f*

congress (*kong*-ghrêss) *n* congresso *m*

connect (kö-*nêkt*) *v* *connettere; collegare

connection (kö-*nêk*-[ön) *n* relazione *f*; connessione *f*; coincidenza *f*

connoisseur (ko-nö-*ssöö*) *n* intenditore *m*

connotation (ko-nö-*tei*-[ön) *n* significato secondario

conquer (*kong*-kö) *v* conquistare; *vincere

conqueror (*kong*-kö-rö) *n* conquistatore *m*

conquest (*kong*-k^uêsst) *n* conquista *f*

conscience (*kon*-[önss) *n* coscienza *f*

conscious (*kon*-[öss) *adj* conscio

consciousness (*kon*-[öss-nöss) *n* coscienza *f*

conscript (*kon*-sskript) *n* coscritto *m*

consent (kön-*ssênt*) *v* consentire; acconsentire; *n* consenso *m*

consequence (*kon*-ssi-k^uönss) *n* conseguenza *f*

consequently (*kon*-ssi-k^uönt-li) *adv* conseguentemente

conservative (kön-*ssöö*-vö-tiv) *adj* conservatore

consider (kön-*ssi*-dö) *v* considerare; reputare, *ritenere

considerable (kön-*ssi*-dö-rö-böl) *adj* considerevole; notevole

considerate (kön-*ssi*-dö-röt) *adj* riguardoso

consideration (kön-ssi-dö-*rei*-[ön) *n*

considerazione *f*; riguardo *m*, attenzione *f*

considering (kön-*ssi*-dö-ring) *prep* considerato

consignment (kön-*ssain*-mönt) *n* spedizione *f*

consist of (kön-*ssisst*) consistere in

conspire (kön-*sspaiᵒ*) *v* cospirare

constant (*kon*-sstönt) *adj* constante

constipated (*kon*-ssti-pei-tid) *adj* stitico

constipation (kon-ssti-*pei*-ʃön) *n* stitichezza *f*

constituency (kön-*ssti*-tʃu-ön-ssi) *n* circoscrizione elettorale

constitution (kon-ssti-*tʹuu*-ʃön) *n* costituzione *f*

construct (kön-*sstrakt*) *v* costruire; edificare, fabbricare

construction (kön-*sstrak*-ʃön) *n* costruzione *f*; fabbricazione *f*; edificio *m*

consul (*kon*-ssöl) *n* console *m*

consulate (*kon*-ssʹu-löt) *n* consolato *m*

consult (kön-*ssalt*) *v* consultare

consultation (kon-ssöl-*tei*-ʃön) *n* consultazione *f*; consulta *f*; ~ **hours** *n* orario di ricevimento

consumer (kön-*ssʹuu*-mö) *n* consumatore *m*

contact (*kon*-tækt) *n* contatto *m*; accensione *f*; *v* contattare; ~ **lenses** lenti a contatto

contagious (kön-*tei*-dʒöss) *adj* contagioso

contain (kön-*tein*) *v* *contenere; *comprendere

container (kön-*tei*-nö) *n* recipiente *m*; cassa mobile

contemporary (kön-*têm*-pö-rö-ri) *adj* contemporaneo; di allora; *n* contemporaneo *m*

contempt (kön-*têmpt*) *n* disprezzo *m*,

disdegno *m*

content (kön-*tênt*) *adj* contento

contents (*kon*-têntss) *pl* contenuto *m*

contest (*kon*-têsst) *n* lotta *f*; competizione *f*

continent (*kon*-ti-nönt) *n* continente *m*

continental (kon-ti-*nên*-töl) *adj* continentale

continual (kön-*ti*-nʹu-öl) *adj* continuo

continue (kön-*ti*-nʹuu) *v* continuare; proseguire

continuous (kön-*ti*-nʹu-öss) *adj* continuo, ininterrotto

contour (*kon*-tuᵒ) *n* contorno *m*

contraceptive (kon-trö-*ssêp*-tiv) *n* anticoncezionale *m*

contract[1] (*kon*-trækt) *n* contratto *m*

contract[2] (kön-*trækt*) *v* *contrarre

contractor (kön-*træk*-tö) *n* imprenditore *m*

contradict (kon-trö-*dikt*) *v* *contraddire

contradictory (kon-trö-*dik*-tö-ri) *adj* contraddittorio

contrary (*kon*-trö-ri) *n* contrario *m*; *adj* contrario; **on the ~** al contrario

contrast (*kon*-traasst) *n* contrasto *m*; differenza *f*

contribution (kon-tri-*bʹuu*-ʃön) *n* contribuzione *f*

control (kön-*troul*) *n* controllo *m*; *v* controllare

controversial (kon-trö-*vöö*-ʃöl) *adj* controverso

convenience (kön-*vii*-nʹönss) *n* comodità *f*

convenient (kön-*vii*-nʹönt) *adj* comodo; conveniente

convent (*kon*-vönt) *n* convento *m*

conversation (kon-vö-*ssei*-ʃön) *n* discorso *m*, conversazione *f*

convert (kön-*vööt*) *v* convertire

convict[1] (kön-*vikt*) *v* dichiarare colpevole

convict[2] (*kon*-vikt) *n* condannato *m*

conviction (kön-*vik*-ſön) *n* convinzione *f*; condanna *f*

convince (kön-*vinss*) *v* *convincere

convulsion (kön-*val*-ſön) *n* convulsione *f*

cook (kuk) *n* cuoco *m*; *v* cucinare; preparare

cookbook (*kuk*-buk) *nAm* libro di cucina

cooker (*ku*-kö) *n* fornello *m*; **gas ~** cucina a gas

cookery-book (*ku*-kö-ri-buk) *n* libro di cucina

cookie (*ku*-ki) *nAm* biscotto *m*

cool (kuul) *adj* fresco; **cooling system** sistema di raffreddamento

co-operation (kou-o-pö-*rei*-ſön) *n* cooperazione *f*

co-operative (ko-*o*-pö-rö-tiv) *adj* cooperativo; cooperante, cooperatore; *n* cooperativa *f*

co-ordinate (kou-*on*-di-neit) *v* coordinare

co-ordination (kou-oo-di-*nei*-ſön) *n* coordinazione *f*

copper (*ko*-pö) *n* rame *m*

copy (*ko*-pi) *n* copia *f*; *v* copiare; imitare; **carbon ~** copia *f*

coral (*ko*-röl) *n* corallo *m*

cord (kood) *n* corda *f*; spago *m*

cordial (*koo*-di-öl) *adj* cordiale

corduroy (*koo*-dö-roi) *n* velluto a coste

core (koo) *n* nucleo *m*; torsolo *m*

cork (kook) *n* sughero *m*; tappo *m*

corkscrew (*kook*-sskruu) *n* cavatappi *m*

corn (koon) *n* granello *m*; frumento *m*, grano *m*; occhio di pernice, callo *m*; **~ on the cob** pannocchia di granturco

corner (*koo*-nö) *n* angolo *m*

cornfield (*koon*-fiild) *n* campo di grano

corpse (koopss) *n* cadavere *m*

corpulent (*koo*-p'u-lönt) *adj* corpulento; grasso, obeso

correct (kö-*rêkt*) *adj* esatto, corretto; *v* *correggere

correction (kö-*rêk*-ſön) *n* correzione *f*; rettifica *f*

correctness (kö-*rêkt*-nöss) *n* correttezza *f*

correspond (ko-ri-*sspond*) *v* *corrispondere

correspondence (ko-ri-*sspon*-dönss) *n* corrispondenza *f*

correspondent (ko-ri-*sspon*-dönt) *n* corrispondente *m*

corridor (*ko*-ri-doo) *n* corridoio *m*

corrupt (kö-*rapt*) *adj* corrotto; *v* *corrompere

corruption (kö-*rap*-ſön) *n* corruzione *f*

corset (*koo*-ssit) *n* busto *m*

cosmetics (kos-*mê*-tikss) *pl* cosmetici *mpl*

cost (kosst) *n* costo *m*; prezzo *m*

***cost** (kosst) *v* costare

cosy (*kou*-si) *adj* intimo, confortevole

cot (kot) *nAm* lettino da campeggio

cottage (*ko*-tidʒ) *n* villino *m*

cotton (*ko*-tön) *n* cotone *m*; di cotone

cotton-wool (*ko*-tön-ᵘul) *n* ovatta *f*

couch (kautʃ) *n* divano *m*

cough (kof) *n* tosse *f*; *v* tossire

could (kud) *v* (p can)

council (*kaun*-ssöl) *n* consiglio *m*

councillor (*kaun*-ssö-lö) *n* consigliere *m*

counsel (*kaun*-ssöl) *n* consiglio *m*

counsellor (*kaun*-ssö-lö) *n* consigliere *m*

count (kaunt) *v* contare; addizionare; *includere; considerare; *n* conte *m*

counter (*kaun*-tö) *n* banco *m*

counterfeit (*kaun*-tö-fiit) *v* falsificare

counterfoil (*kaun*-tö-foil) *n* talloncino *m*

counterpane (*kaun*-tö-pein) *n* copriletto *m*

countess (*kaun*-tiss) *n* contessa *f*

country (*kan*-tri) *n* paese *m*; campagna *f*; regione *f*; ~ **house** casa di campagna

countryman (*kan*-tri-mön) *n* (pl -men) compatriota *m*

countryside (*kan*-tri-ssaid) *n* campagna *f*

county (*kaun*-ti) *n* contea *f*

couple (*ka*-pöl) *n* coppia *f*

coupon (*kuu*-pon) *n* cedola *f*, tagliando *m*

courage (*ka*-ridʒ) *n* audacia *f*, coraggio *m*

courageous (kö-*rei*-dʒöss) *adj* valoroso, coraggioso

course (kooss) *n* rotta *f*; portata *f*; corso *m*; **intensive** ~ corso accelerato; **of** ~ naturalmente

court (koot) *n* tribunale *m*; corte *f*

courteous (*köö*-ti-öss) *adj* cortese

cousin (*ka*-sön) *n* cugina *f*, cugino *m*

cover (*ka*-vö) *v* *coprire; *n* rifugio *m*; coperchio *m*; copertina *f*; ~ **charge** prezzo del coperto

cow (kau) *n* vacca *f*

coward (*kau*-öd) *n* codardo *m*

cowardly (*kau*-öd-li) *adj* vile

cow-hide (*kau*-haid) *n* pelle di vacca

crab (kræb) *n* granchio *m*

crack (kræk) *n* schiocco *m*; fessura *f*; *v* schioccare; spaccare, incrinarsi

cracker (*kræ*-kö) *nAm* biscottino *m*

cradle (*krei*-döl) *n* culla *f*

cramp (kræmp) *n* crampo *m*

crane (krein) *n* gru *f*

crankcase (*krængk*-keiss) *n* basamento *m*

crankshaft (*krængk*-ʃaaft) *n* albero a gomiti

crash (kræʃ) *n* scontro *m*; *v* scontrarsi; precipitare; ~ **barrier** barriera di sicurezza

crate (kreit) *n* gabbia da imballaggio

crater (*krei*-tö) *n* cratere *m*

crawl (krool) *v* *andare carponi; *n* crawl *m*

craze (kreis) *n* mania *f*

crazy (*krei*-si) *adj* pazzo; sciocco, folle

creak (kriik) *v* cigolare

cream (kriim) *n* crema *f*; panna *f*; *adj* color crema

creamy (*krii*-mi) *adj* cremoso

crease (kriiss) *v* increspare; *n* piega *f*; grinza *f*

create (kri-*eit*) *v* creare

creature (*krii*-tʃö) *n* creatura *f*; essere *m*

credible (*krê*-di-böl) *adj* credibile

credit (*krê*-dit) *n* credito *m*; *v* accreditare; ~ **card** carta di credito

creditor (*krê*-di-tö) *n* creditore *m*

credulous (*krê*-dʰu-löss) *adj* credulo

creek (kriik) *n* insenatura *f*

*creep (kriip) *v* strisciare

creepy (*krii*-pi) *adj* ributtante, raccapricciante

cremate (kri-*meit*) *v* cremare

cremation (kri-*mei*-ʃön) *n* cremazione *f*

crew (kruu) *n* equipaggio *m*

cricket (*kri*-kit) *n* cricket *m*; grillo *m*

crime (kraim) *n* crimine *m*

criminal (*kri*-mi-nöl) *n* delinquente *m*, criminale *m*; *adj* criminale; ~ **law** diritto penale

criminality (kri-mi-*næ*-lö-ti) *n* criminalità *f*

crimson (*krim*-sön) *adj* cremisino

crippled (*kri*-pöld) *adj* zoppo

crisis (*krai*-ssiss) *n* (pl crises) crisi *f*

crisp (krissp) *adj* croccante

critic (*kri*-tik) *n* critico *m*

critical (*kri*-ti-köl) *adj* critico; precario

criticism (*kri*-ti-ssi-söm) n critica f

criticize (*kri*-ti-ssais) v criticare

crochet (*krou*-ʃei) v lavorare all'uncinetto

crockery (*kro*-kö-ri) n terraglie fpl, vasellame m

crocodile (*kro*-kö-dail) n coccodrillo m

crook (kruk) n raccolta f

crooked (*kru*-kid) adj tortuoso, storto; disonesto

crop (krop) n raccolta f

cross (kross) v attraversare; adj arrabbiato, imbronciato; n croce f

cross-eyed (*kross*-aid) adj strabico

crossing (*kro*-ssing) n traversata f; crocevia m; passaggio pedonale; passaggio a livello

crossroads (*kross*-rouds) n crocicchio m

crosswalk (*kross*-ᵘook) nAm passaggio pedonale

crow (krou) n cornacchia f

crowbar (*krou*-baa) n piede di porco

crowd (kraud) n massa f, folla f

crowded (*krau*-did) adj affollato

crown (kraun) n corona f; v incoronare; coronare

crucifix (*kruu*-ssi-fikss) n crocifisso m

crucifixion (kruu-ssi-*fik*-ʃön) n crocifissione f

crucify (*kruu*-ssi-fai) v *crocifiggere

cruel (*kru*ⁿl) adj crudele

cruise (kruus) n crociera f

crumb (kram) n briciola f

crusade (kruu-*sseid*) n crociata f

crust (krasst) n crosta f

crutch (kratʃ) n stampella f

cry (krai) v *piangere; gridare; n urlo m, grido m

crystal (*kri*-sstöl) n cristallo m; adj cristallino

Cuba (*kⁱuu*-bö) Cuba f

Cuban (*kⁱuu*-bön) adj cubano

cube (kⁱuub) n cubo m

cuckoo (*ku*-kuu) n cuculo m

cucumber (*kⁱuu*-köm-bö) n cetriolo m

cuddle (*ka*-döl) v vezzeggiare

cudgel (*ka*-dʒöl) n randello m

cuff (kaf) n polsino m

cuff-links (*kaf*-lingkss) pl gemelli mpl

cul-de-sac (*kal*-dö-ssæk) n vicolo cieco

cultivate (*kal*-ti-veit) v coltivare

culture (*kal*-tʃö) n cultura f; coltura f

cultured (*kal*-tʃöd) adj colto

cunning (*ka*-ning) adj furbo

cup (kap) n tazza f; coppa f

cupboard (*ka*-böd) n armadio m

curb (kööb) n orlo del marciapiede; v frenare

cure (kⁱuᵒ) v curare; n cura f; guarigione f

curio (*kⁱuᵒ*-ri-ou) n (pl ~s) curiosità f

curiosity (kⁱuᵒ-ri-*o*-ssö-ti) n curiosità f

curious (*kⁱuᵒ*-ri-öss) adj curioso; strano

curl (kööl) v ondulare; arricciare; n ricciolo m

curler (*köö*-lö) n bigodino m

curling-tongs (*köö*-ling-tongs) pl arricciacapelli m

curly (*köö*-li) adj ricciuto

currant (*ka*-rönt) n uva di Corinto; ribes m

currency (*ka*-rön-ssi) n valuta f; **foreign** ~ divisa estera

current (*ka*-rönt) n corrente f; adj corrente; **alternating** ~ corrente alternata; **direct** ~ corrente continua

curry (*ka*-ri) n curry m

curse (kööss) v bestemmiare; *maledire; n bestemmia f

curtain (*köö*-tön) n tenda f; sipario m

curve (kööv) n curva f; svolta f

curved (köövd) adj curvo

cushion (*ku*-ʃön) n cuscino m

custodian (ka-*sstou*-di-ön) n custode m

custody (*ka*-sstö-di) *n* detenzione *f*; custodia *f*; tutela *f*

custom (*ka*-sstöm) *n* costume *m*; abitudine *f*

customary (*ka*-sstö-mö-ri) *adj* usuale, solito, abituale

customer (*ka*-sstö-mö) *n* cliente *m*; avventore *m*

Customs (*ka*-sstöms) *pl* dogana *f*; ~ **duty** dazio *m*; ~ **officer** doganiere *m*

cut (kat) *n* incisione *f*; taglio *m*

***cut** (kat) *v* tagliare; *ridurre; ~ **off** tagliare; troncare

cutlery (*kat*-lö-ri) *n* posate *fpl*

cutlet (*kat*-löt) *n* costoletta *f*

cycle (*ssai*-köl) *n* ciclo *m*; bicicletta *f*

cyclist (*ssai*-klisst) *n* ciclista *m*

cylinder (*ssi*-lin-dö) *n* cilindro *m*; ~ **head** testa cilindro

cystitis (ssi-*sstai*-tiss) *n* cistite *f*

Czech (tʃêk) *adj* ceco

Czech Republic (tʃêk ri-*pa*-blik) Repubblica Ceca *f*

D

dad (dæd) *n* padre *m*

daddy (*dæ*-di) *n* papà *m*

daffodil (*dæ*-fö-dil) *n* narciso *m*

daily (*dei*-li) *adj* giornaliero, quotidiano; *n* quotidiano *m*

dairy (*dêô*-ri) *n* latteria *f*

dam (dæm) *n* argine *m*; diga *f*

damage (*dæ*-midʒ) *n* danno *m*; *v* danneggiare

damp (dæmp) *adj* umido; bagnato; *n* umidità *f*; *v* inumidire

dance (daanss) *v* ballare; *n* ballo *m*

dandelion (*dæn*-di-lai-ön) *n* soffione *m*

dandruff (*dæn*-dröf) *n* forfora *f*

Dane (dein) *n* danese *m*

danger (*dein*-dʒö) *n* pericolo *m*

dangerous (*dein*-dʒö-röss) *adj* pericoloso

Danish (*dei*-niʃ) *adj* danese

dare (dêô) *v* osare; sfidare

daring (*dêô*-ring) *adj* temerario

dark (daak) *adj* buio, oscuro; *n* oscurità *f*, buio *m*

darling (*daa*-ling) *n* amore *m*, caro *m*

darn (daan) *v* rammendare

dash (dæʃ) *v* precipitarsi; *n* lineetta *f*

dashboard (*dæf*-bood) *n* cruscotto *m*

data (*dei*-tö) *pl* dato *m*

date[1] (deit) *n* data *f*; appuntamento *m*; *v* datare; **out of** ~ fuori moda

date[2] (deit) *n* dattero *m*

daughter (*doo*-tö) *n* figlia *f*

dawn (doon) *n* alba *f*; aurora *f*

day (dei) *n* giorno *m*; **by** ~ di giorno; ~ **trip** giro *m*; **per** ~ al giorno; **the** ~ **before yesterday** avant'ieri

daybreak (*dei*-breik) *n* aurora *f*

daylight (*dei*-lait) *n* luce del giorno

dead (dêd) *adj* morto; deceduto

deaf (dêf) *adj* sordo

deal (diil) *n* accordo *m*, affare *m*

***deal** (diil) *v* distribuire; ~ **with** *v* trattare con; *fare affari con

dealer (*dii*-lö) *n* negoziante *m*, commerciante *m*

dear (diô) *adj* caro; diletto

death (dêθ) *n* morte *f*; ~ **penalty** pena di morte

debate (di-*beit*) *n* dibattito *m*

debit (*dê*-bit) *n* debito *m*

debt (dêt) *n* debito *m*

decaffeinated (dii-*kæ*-fi-nei-tid) *adj* decaffeinizzato

deceit (di-*ssiit*) *n* inganno *m*

deceive (di-*ssiiv*) *v* ingannare

December (di-*ssêm*-bö) *n* dicembre

decency (*dii*-ssön-ssi) *n* decenza *f*

decent (*dii*-ssönt) *adj* decente

decide (di-ssaid) v *decidere
decision (di-ssi-3ön) n decisione f
deck (dêk) n coperta f; ~ cabin cabina di coperta; ~ chair sedia a sdraio
declaration (dê-klö-rei-fön) n dichiarazione f
declare (di-klêö) v dichiarare; indicare
decoration (dê-kö-rei-fön) n ornamento m
decrease (dii-kriiss) v diminuire; *decrescere; n diminuzione f
dedicate (dê-di-keit) v dedicare
deduce (di-dʲuuss) v *dedurre
deduct (di-dakt) v *sottrarre
deed (diid) n azione f, atto m
deep (diip) adj profondo
deep-freeze (diip-friis) n congelatore m
deer (diö) n (pl ~) cervo m
defeat (di-fiit) v *sconfiggere; n sconfitta f
defective (di-fêk-tiv) adj difettoso
defence (di-fênss) n difesa f
defend (di-fênd) v *difendere
deficiency (di-fi-fön-ssi) n deficienza f
deficit (dê-fi-ssit) n deficit m
define (di-fain) v definire, determinare
definite (dê-fi-nit) adj determinato; esplicito
definition (dê-fi-ni-fön) n definizione f
deformed (di-foomd) adj deformato, deforme
degree (di-ghrii) n grado m; titolo m
delay (di-lei) v ritardare; differire; n indugio m, ritardo m; rinvio m
delegate (dê-li-ghöt) n delegato m
delegation (dê-li-ghei-fön) n delegazione f
deliberate¹ (di-li-bö-reit) v deliberare, ponderare

deliberate² (di-li-bö-röt) adj premeditato
deliberation (di-li-bö-rei-fön) n riflessione f, deliberazione f
delicacy (dê-li-kö-ssi) n ghiottoneria f
delicate (dê-li-köt) adj delicato
delicatessen (dê-li-kö-tê-ssön) n leccornia f; negozio di specialità gastronomiche
delicious (di-li-föss) adj squisito, delizioso
delight (di-lait) n diletto m, delizia f; v deliziare; delighted felicissimo
delightful (di-lait-föl) adj dilettevole, piacevolissimo
deliver (di-li-vö) v recapitare, consegnare; liberare
delivery (di-li-vö-ri) n consegna f; parto m; liberazione f; ~ van furgone m
demand (di-maand) v *richiedere, *esigere; n esigenza f; domanda f
democracy (di-mo-krö-ssi) n democrazia f
democratic (dê-mö-kræ-tik) adj democratico
demolish (di-mo-lif) v demolire
demolition (dê-mö-li-fön) n demolizione f
demonstrate (dê-mön-sstreit) v dimostrare; *fare una dimostrazione
demonstration (dê-mön-sstrei-fön) n dimostrazione f
den (dên) n tana f
Denmark (dên-maak) Danimarca f
denomination (di-no-mi-nei-fön) n denominazione f
dense (dênss) adj denso
dent (dênt) n ammaccatura f
dentist (dên-tisst) n dentista m
denture (dên-tfö) n dentiera f
deny (di-nai) v negare; rifiutare, ricusare
deodorant (dii-ou-dö-rönt) n deodo-

rante *m*

depart (di-*paat*) *v* *andarsene, partire; trapassare

department (di-*paat*-mönt) *n* sezione *f*, riparto *m*; ~ **store** grande magazzino

departure (di-*paa*-tſö) *n* partenza *f*

dependant (di-*pên*-dönt) *adj* dipendente

depend on (di-*pênd*) *dipendere da

deposit (di-*po*-sit) *n* versamento *m*; deposito *m*; sedimento *m*, giacimento *m*; *v* depositare

depository (di-*po*-si-tö-ri) *n* magazzino *m*

depot (*dê*-pou) *n* deposito *m*; *nAm* stazione *f*

depress (di-*prêss*) *v* *deprimere

depression (di-*prê*-ſön) *n* depressione *f*

deprive of (di-*praiv*) privare di

depth (dêpθ) *n* profondità *f*

deputy (*dê*-p¹u-ti) *n* deputato *m*; sostituto *m*

descend (di-*ssênd*) *v* *scendere

descendant (di-*ssên*-dönt) *n* discendente *m*

descent (di-*ssênt*) *n* discesa *f*

describe (di-*sskraib*) *v* *descrivere

description (di-*sskrip*-ſön) *n* descrizione *f*; connotati *mpl*

desert[1] (*dê*-söt) *n* deserto *m*; *adj* incolto, deserto

desert[2] (di-*sööt*) *v* disertare; lasciare

deserve (di-*sööv*) *v* meritare

design (di-*sain*) *v* progettare; *n* disegno *m*; scopo *m*

designate (*dê*-sigh-neit) *v* designare

desirable (di-*sai*°-rö-böl) *adj* desiderabile

desire (di-*sai*°) *n* desiderio *m*; *v* desiderare

desk (dêssk) *n* scrivania *f*; leggio *m*; banco di scuola

despair (di-*sspê*°) *n* disperazione *f*; *v* disperare

despatch (di-*sspætſ*) *v* spedire

desperate (*dê*-sspö-röt) *adj* disperato

despise (di-*sspais*) *v* disprezzare

despite (di-*sspait*) *prep* malgrado

dessert (di-*sööt*) *n* dolce *m*

destination (dê-ssti-*nei*-ſön) *n* destinazione *f*

destine (*dê*-sstin) *v* destinare

destiny (*dê*-ssti-ni) *n* destino *m*, sorte *f*

destroy (di-*sstroi*) *v* *distruggere

destruction (di-*sstrak*-ſön) *n* distruzione *f*; rovina *f*

detach (di-*tætſ*) *v* staccare

detail (*dii*-teil) *n* particolare *m*, dettaglio *m*

detailed (*dii*-teild) *adj* particolareggiato, dettagliato

detect (di-*têkt*) *v* *scoprire

detective (di-*têk*-tiv) *n* investigatore *m*; ~ **story** romanzo poliziesco

detergent (di-*töö*-dʒönt) *n* detergente *m*

determine (di-*töö*-min) *v* stabilire, determinare

determined (di-*töö*-mind) *adj* risoluto

detour (*dii*-tu°) *n* giro *m*; deviazione *f*

devaluation (dii-væl-¹u-*ei*-ſön) *n* svalutazione *f*

devalue (dii-*væl*-¹uu) *v* svalutare

develop (di-*vê*-löp) *v* sviluppare

development (di-*vê*-löp-mönt) *n* sviluppo *m*

deviate (*dii*-vi-eit) *v* deviare

devil (*dê*-völ) *n* diavolo *m*

devise (di-*vais*) *v* escogitare

devote (di-*vout*) *v* dedicare

dew (d¹uu) *n* rugiada *f*

diabetes (dai-ö-*bii*-tiis) *n* diabete *m*

diabetic (dai-ö-*bê*-tik) *n* diabetico *m*

diagnose (dai-ögh-*nous*) *v* diagnosticare; costatare

diagnosis (dai-ögh-*nou*-ssiss) *n* (pl -ses) diagnosi *f*

diagonal (dai-æ-ghö-nöl) *n* diagonale *f*; *adj* diagonale

diagram (*dai*-ö-ghræm) *n* diagramma *m*; schema *m*, grafico *m*

dialect (*dai*-ö-lêkt) *n* dialetto *m*

diamond (*dai*-ö-mönd) *n* diamante *m*

diaper (*dai*-ö-pö) *nAm* pannolino *m*

diaphragm (*dai*-ö-fræm) *n* membrana *f*

diarrhoea (dai-ö-*ri*-ö) *n* diarrea *f*

diary (*dai*-ö-ri) *n* agenda *f*; diario *m*

dictaphone (*dik*-tö-foun) *n* dittafono *m*

dictate (dik-*teit*) *v* dettare

dictation (dik-*tei*-jön) *n* dettato *m*

dictator (dik-*tei*-tö) *n* dittatore *m*

dictionary (*dik*-Jö-nö-ri) *n* dizionario *m*

did (did) *v* (p do)

die (dai) *v* *morire

diesel (*dii*-söl) *n* diesel *m*

diet (*dai*-öt) *n* dieta *f*

differ (*di*-fö) *v* differire

difference (*di*-fö-rönss) *n* differenza *f*; distinzione *f*

different (*di*-fö-rönt) *adj* differente; altro

difficult (*di*-fi-költ) *adj* difficile; fastidioso

difficulty (*di*-fi-köl-ti) *n* difficoltà *f*; pena *f*

***dig** (digh) *v* scavare

digest (di-*dʒêsst*) *v* digerire

digestible (di-*dʒê*-sstö-böl) *adj* digeribile

digestion (di-*dʒêss*-tjön) *n* digestione *f*

digit (*di*-dʒit) *n* numero *m*

digital (*di*-dʒi-töl) *adj* digitale

dike (daik) *n* diga *f*; argine *m*

dilapidated (di-*læ*-pi-dei-tid) *adj* de-

crepito

diligence (*di*-li-dʒönss) *n* zelo *m*, diligenza *f*

diligent (*di*-li-dʒönt) *adj* zelante, diligente

dilute (dai-*l'uut*) *v* allungare, diluire

dim (dim) *adj* pallido, opaco; oscuro, debole, offuscato

dine (dain) *v* pranzare

dinghy (*ding*-ghi) *n* barchetta *f*

dining-car (*dai*-ning-kaa) *n* vagone ristorante

dining-room (*dai*-ning-ruum) *n* sala da pranzo

dinner (*di*-nö) *n* pranzo *m*; cena *f*

dinner-jacket (*di*-nö-dʒæ-kit) *n* smoking *m*

dinner-service (*di*-nö-ssöö-viss) *n* servizio da tavola

diphtheria (dif-$\theta i^ö$-ri-ö) *n* difterite *f*

diploma (di-*plou*-mö) *n* diploma *m*

diplomat (*di*-plö-mæt) *n* diplomatico *m*

direct (di-*rêkt*) *adj* diretto; *v* *dirigere; amministrare

direction (di-*rêk*-jön) *n* direzione *f*; indicazione *f*; regia *f*; amministrazione *f*; **directional signal** *Am* indicatore di direzione; **directions for use** istruzioni per l'uso

directive (di-*rêk*-tiv) *n* direttiva *f*

director (di-*rêk*-tö) *n* direttore *m*; regista *m*

dirt (dööt) *n* sudiciume *m*

dirty (*döö*-ti) *adj* sozzo, sudicio, sporco

disabled (di-*ssei*-böld) *adj* inabilitato, invalido

disadvantage (dis-ssöd-*vaan*-tidʒ) *n* svantaggio *m*

disagree (dis-ssö-*ghrii*) *v* non *essere d'accordo, dissentire

disagreeable (dis-ssö-*ghrii*-ö-böl) *adj* sgradevole

disappear (di-ssö-*piᵒ*) v sparire

disappoint (di-ssö-*point*) v *deludere

disappointment (di-ssö-*point*-mönt) n delusione f

disapprove (di-ssö-*pruuv*) v disapprovare

disaster (di-saa-sstö) n disastro m; catastrofe f, sciagura f

disastrous (di-saa-sströss) adj disastroso

disc (dissk) n disco m; **slipped ~** ernia f

discard (di-sskaad) v scartare

discharge (diss-*tʃaadʒ*) v scaricare; **~ of** esonerare da

discipline (*di*-ssi-plin) n disciplina f

discolour (di-*sska*-lö) v scolorirsi

disconnect (di-sskö-*nêkt*) v *disgiungere; disinserire

discontented (di-sskön-*tên*-tid) adj scontento

discontinue (di-sskön-*ti*-nⁱuu) v *sospendere, cessare

discount (*di*-sskaunt) n sconto m, riduzione f

discover (di-*sska*-vö) v *scoprire

discovery (di-*sska*-vö-ri) n scoperta f

discuss (di-*sskass*) v *discutere; dibattere

discussion (di-*sska*-ʃön) n discussione f; conversazione f, dibattito m

disease (di-*siis*) n malattia f

disembark (di-ssim-*baak*) v sbarcare

disgrace (diss-*ghreiss*) n disonore m

disguise (diss-*ghais*) v travestirsi; travestimento m

disgusting (diss-*gha*-ssting) adj nauseante, disgustoso

dish (diʃ) n piatto m; pietanza f

dishonest (di-*sso*-nisst) adj disonesto

disinfect (di-ssin-*fêkt*) v disinfettare

disinfectant (di-ssin-*fêk*-tönt) n disinfettante m

dislike (di-*sslaik*) v detestare, non amare; n ripugnanza f, avversione f, antipatia f

dislocated (*di*-sslö-kei-tid) adj slogato

dismiss (diss-*miss*) v congedare

disorder (di-*ssoo*-dö) n disordine m; confusione f

dispatch (di-*sspætʃ*) v inviare, spedire

display (di-*ssplei*) v *mettere in mostra, *esporre; mostrare; n esposizione f, mostra f

displease (di-*sspliis*) v scontentare, *dispiacere

disposable (di-*sspou*-sö-böl) adj da buttare

disposal (di-*sspou*-söl) n disposizione f

dispose of (di-*sspous*) *disporre di

dispute (di-*sspⁱuut*) n disputa f; lite f, controversia f; v *discutere, disputare

dissatisfied (di-*ssæ*-tiss-faid) adj scontento

dissolve (di-*solv*) v *sciogliere

dissuade from (di-*ssᵘeid*) *dissuadere

distance (*di*-sstönss) n distanza f; **~ in kilometres** chilometraggio m

distant (*di*-sstönt) adj lontano

distinct (di-*sstingkt*) adj chiaro; distinto

distinction (di-*sstingk*-ʃön) n distinzione f, differenza f

distinguish (di-*ssting*-ghᵘiʃ) v *distinguere

distinguished (di-*ssting*-ghᵘiʃt) adj distinto

distress (di-*sstrêss*) n pericolo m; **~ signal** segnale di soccorso

distribute (di-*sstri*-bⁱuut) v distribuire

distributor (di-*sstri*-bⁱu-tö) n distributore m

district (*di*-sstrikt) n distretto m; regione f; quartiere m

disturb (di-*sstööb*) v importunare, disturbare

disturbance (di-*sstöö*-bönss) *n* disturbo *m*; tumulto *m*

ditch (ditʃ) *n* fosso *m*, fossato *m*

dive (daiv) *v* tuffare

diversion (dai-*vöö*-ʃön) *n* deviazione *f*; diversione *f*

divide (di-*vaid*) *v* *dividere; ripartire; separare

divine (di-*vain*) *adj* divino

division (di-*vi*-ʒön) *n* divisione *f*; reparto *m*

divorce (di-*vooss*) *n* divorzio *m*; *v* divorziare

dizziness (*di*-si-nöss) *n* capogiro *m*

dizzy (*di*-si) *adj* stordito

*do** (duu) *v* *fare; bastare

dock (dok) *n* bacino *m*; scalo *m*; *v* attraccare

docker (*do*-kö) *n* portuale *m*

doctor (*dok*-tö) *n* medico *m*, dottore *m*

document (*do*-kʲu-mönt) *n* documento *m*

dog (dogh) *n* cane *m*

dogged (*do*-ghid) *adj* ostinato

doll (dol) *n* bambola *f*

dome (doum) *n* cupola *f*

domestic (dö-*mê*-sstik) *adj* domestico; interno; *n* domestico *m*

domicile (*do*-mi-ssail) *n* domicilio *m*

domination (do-mi-*nei*-ʃön) *n* dominazione *f*

dominion (dö-*mi*-nʲön) *n* dominio *m*

donate (dou-*neit*) *v* donare

donation (dou-*nei*-ʃön) *n* donazione *f*

done (dan) *v* (pp do)

donkey (*dong*-ki) *n* asino *m*

donor (*dou*-nö) *n* donatore *m*

door (doo) *n* porta *f*; **revolving ~** porta girevole; **sliding ~** porta scorrevole

doorbell (*doo*-bêl) *n* campanello *m*

door-keeper (*doo*-kii-pö) *n* portinaio *m*

doorman (*doo*-mön) *n* (pl -men) portinaio *m*

dormitory (*doo*-mi-tri) *n* dormitorio *m*

dose (douss) *n* dose *f*

dot (dot) *n* punto *m*

double (*da*-böl) *adj* doppio

doubt (daut) *v* dubitare di, dubitare; *n* dubbio *m*; **without ~** senza dubbio

doubtful (*daut*-föl) *adj* dubbioso; incerto

dough (dou) *n* pasta *f*

down[1] (daun) *adv* giù; in giù, dabbasso, a terra; *adj* abbattuto; *prep* lungo, giù da; **~ payment** acconto *m*

down[2] (daun) *n* lanugine *f*

downpour (*daun*-poo) *n* acquazzone *m*

downstairs (daun-*sstêᵒs*) *adv* dabbasso

downstream (daun-*sstriim*) *adv* con la corrente

down-to-earth (daun-tu-*ööθ*) *adj* sensato

downwards (*daun*-ᵘöds) *adv* in giù, in discesa

dozen (*da*-sön) *n* (pl ~, ~s) dozzina *f*

draft (draaft) *n* tratta *f*

drag (drægh) *v* trascinare

dragon (*dræ*-ghön) *n* drago *m*

drain (drein) *v* prosciugare; drenare; *n* scolo *m*

drama (*draa*-mö) *n* dramma *m*; tragedia *f*; teatro *m*

dramatic (drö-*mæ*-tik) *adj* drammatico

dramatist (*dræ*-mö-tisst) *n* drammaturgo *m*

drank (drængk) *v* (p drink)

draper (*drei*-pö) *n* negoziante di stoffe

drapery (*drei*-pö-ri) *n* drapperia *f*

draught (draaft) *n* corrente d'aria;

draughts gioco della dama

draught-board (*draaft*-bood) *n* scacchiera *f*

draw (droo) *n* sorteggio *m*

***draw** (droo) *v* disegnare; tirare; ritirare; ~ **up** *redigere

drawbridge (*droo*-bridʒ) *n* ponte levatoio

drawer (*droo*-ö) *n* cassetto *m*; **drawers** mutande *fpl*

drawing (*droo*-ing) *n* disegno *m*

drawing-pin (*droo*-ing-pin) *n* puntina da disegno

drawing-room (*droo*-ing-ruum) *n* salotto *m*

dread (drêd) *v* temere; *n* timore *m*

dreadful (*drêd*-föl) *adj* terribile, spaventoso

dream (driim) *n* sogno *m*

***dream** (driim) *v* sognare

dress (drèss) *v* vestire; abbigliarsi, vestirsi, abbigliare; bendare; *n* abito femminile, vestito da donna

dressing-gown (*drê*-ssing-ghaun) *n* vestaglia *f*

dressing-room (*drê*-ssing-ruum) *n* camerino *m*

dressing-table (*drê*-ssing-tei-böl) *n* toletta *f*

dressmaker (*drèss*-mei-kö) *n* sarta *f*

drill (dril) *v* trapanare; addestrare; *n* trapano *m*

drink (dringk) *n* aperitivo *m*, bibita *f*

***drink** (dringk) *v* *bere

drinking-water (*dring*-king-ᵘoo-tö) *n* acqua potabile

drip-dry (drip-*drai*) *adj* non si stira, senza stiratura

drive (draiv) *n* strada *f*; scarrozzata *f*

***drive** (draiv) *v* guidare; *condurre

driver (*drai*-vö) *n* autista *m*

drizzle (*dri*-söl) *n* pioggerella *f*

drop (drop) *v* *far cadere; *n* goccia *f*

drought (draut) *n* siccità *f*

drowns (draun) *v* affogare; *be **drowned** affogarsi

drug (dragh) *n* narcotico *m*; farmaco *m*

drugstore (*dragh*-sstoo) *nAm* bar-emporio *m*, farmacia *f*; emporio *m*

drum (dram) *n* tamburo *m*

drunk (drangk) *adj* (pp drink) ubriaco

dry (drai) *adj* asciutto; *v* asciugare

dry-clean (drai-*kliin*) *v* pulire a secco

dry-cleaner's (drai-*klii*-nös) *n* tintoria *f*

dryer (*drai*-ö) *n* essiccatoio *m*

duchess (da-tʃiss) *n* duchessa *f*

duck (dak) *n* anitra *f*

due (dⁱuu) *adj* in arrivo; dovuto

dues (dⁱuus) *pl* diritti *mpl*

dug (dagh) *v* (p, pp dig)

duke (dⁱuuk) *n* duca *m*

dull (dal) *adj* monotono, noioso; smorto, pallido; smussato

dumb (dam) *adj* muto; ottuso, stupido

dune (dⁱuun) *n* duna *f*

dung (dang) *n* letame *m*

dunghill (*dang*-hil) *n* letamaio *m*

duration (dⁱu-*rei*-ʃön) *n* durata *f*

during (*dᵘuᵒ*-ring) *prep* durante

dusk (dassk) *n* crepuscolo *m*

dust (dasst) *n* polvere *f*

dustbin (*dasst*-bin) *n* pattumiera *f*

dusty (da-ssti) *adj* polveroso

Dutch (datʃ) *adj* olandese

Dutchman (*datʃ*-mön) *n* (pl -men) olandese *m*

dutiable (*dⁱuu*-ti-ö-böl) *adj* tassabile

duty (*dⁱuu*-ti) *n* dovere *m*; compito *m*; dazio *m*; **Customs** ~ tariffa doganale

duty-free (dⁱuu-ti-*frii*) *adj* franco di dazio

dwarf (dᵘoof) *n* nano *m*

dye (dai) *v* *tingere; *n* tintura *f*

dynamo (*dai*-nö-mou) *n* (pl ~s) dinamo f

dysentery (*di*-ssön-tri) *n* dissenteria *f*

E

each (iitf) *adj* ogni, ciascuno; ~ **other** l'un l'altro

eager (*ii*-ghö) *adj* desideroso, ansioso, impaziente

eagle (*ii*-ghöl) *n* aquila *f*

ear (iö) *n* orecchio *f*

earache (*iö*-reik) *n* mal d'orecchi

ear-drum (*iö*-dram) *n* timpano *m*

earl (ööl) *n* conte *m*

early (*öö*-li) *adj* mattutino

earn (öön) *v* guadagnare

earnest (*öö*-nisst) *n* serietà *f*

earnings (*öö*-nings) *pl* redditi, guadagni *mpl*

earring (*iö*-ring) *n* orecchino *m*

earth (ööθ) *n* terra *f*; suolo *m*

earthenware (*öö*-θön-uêⁿ) *n* terraglie *fpl*

earthquake (*ööθ*-kᵘeik) *n* terremoto *m*

ease (iis) *n* disinvoltura *f*, facilità *f*; agio *m*

east (iisst) *n* oriente *m*, est *m*

Easter (*ii*-sstö) Pasqua *f*

easterly (*ii*-sstö-li) *adj* orientale

eastern (*ii*-sstön) *adj* orientale

easy (*ii*-si) *adj* facile; comodo; ~ **chair** poltrona *f*

easy-going (*ii*-si-ghou-ing) *adj* facilone

*eat (iit) *v* mangiare; pranzare

eavesdrop (*iivs*-drop) *v* origliare

ebony (*ê*-bö-ni) *n* ebano *m*

eccentric (ik-*ssên*-trik) *adj* eccentrico

echo (*ê*-kou) *n* (pl ~es) eco *m/f*

eclipse (i-*klipss*) *n* eclissi *f*

economic (ii-kö-*no*-mik) *adj* economi-

co

economical (ii-kö-*no*-mi-köl) *adj* parsimonioso, economico

economist (i-*ko*-nö-misst) *n* economista *m*

economize (i-*ko*-nö-mais) *v* economizzare

economy (i-*ko*-nö-mi) *n* economia *f*

ecstasy (*êk*-sstö-si) *n* estasi *f*

Ecuador (*ê*-kᵘö-doo) Ecuador *m*

Ecuadorian (ê-kᵘö-*doo*-ri-ön) *n* ecuadoriano *m*

eczema (*êk*-ssi-mö) *n* eczema *m*

edge (êdʒ) *n* bordo *m*, margine *m*

edible (*ê*-di-böl) *adj* commestibile

edition (i-*di*-fön) *n* edizione *f*; **morning** ~ edizione del mattino

editor (*ê*-di-tö) *n* redattore *m*

educate (*ê*-dʒu-keit) *v* istruire, educare

education (ê-dʒu-*kei*-fön) *n* educazione *f*

eel (iil) *n* anguilla *f*

effect (i-*fêkt*) *n* risultato *m*, effetto *m*; *v* effettuare; **in** ~ in realtà

effective (i-*fêk*-tiv) *adj* efficace

efficient (i-*fi*-fönt) *adj* efficiente

effort (*ê*-föt) *n* sforzo *m*; tentativo *m*

egg (êgh) *n* uovo *m*

egg-cup (*êgh*-kap) *n* portauovo *m*

eggplant (*êgh*-plaant) *n* melanzana *f*

egg-yolk (*êgh*-ⁱouk) *n* tuorlo *m*

egoistic (ê-ghou-*i*-sstik) *adj* egoistico

Egypt (*ii*-dʒipt) Egitto *m*

Egyptian (i-*dʒip*-fön) *adj* egiziano

eiderdown (*ai*-dö-daun) *n* trapunta di piume *m*

eight (eit) *num* otto

eighteen (ei-*tiin*) *num* diciotto

eighteenth (ei-*tiin*θ) *num* diciottesimo

eighth (eitθ) *num* ottavo

eighty (*ei*-ti) *num* ottanta

either (*ai*-ðö) *pron* l'uno o l'altro;

either ... or o... o

elaborate (i-*læ*-bö-reit) v elaborare

elastic (i-*læ*-sstik) adj elastico; flessibile; elastico m

elasticity (ê-læ-*ssti*-ssö-ti) n elasticità f

elbow (*êl*-bou) n gomito m

elder (*êl*-dö) adj maggiore

elderly (*êl*-dö-li) adj anziano

eldest (*êl*-disst) adj maggiore

elect (i-*lêkt*) v *scegliere, *eleggere

election (i-*lêk*-fön) n elezione f

electric (i-*lêk*-trik) adj elettrico; ~ **razor** rasoio elettrico; ~ **cord** cordone elettrico

electrician (i-lêk-*tri*-fön) n elettricista m

electricity (i-lêk-*tri*-ssö-ti) n elettricità f

electronic (i-lêk-*tro*-nik) adj elettronico

elegance (*ê*-li-ghönss) n eleganza f

elegant (*ê*-li-ghönt) adj elegante

element (*ê*-li-mönt) n elemento m

elephant (*ê*-li-fönt) n elefante m

elevator (*ê*-li-vei-tö) nAm ascensore m

eleven (i-*lê*-vön) num undici

eleventh (i-*lê*-vönθ) num undicesimo

elf (êlf) n (pl elves) folletto m

eliminate (i-*li*-mi-neit) v eliminare

elm (êlm) n olmo m

else (êlss) adv altrimenti

elsewhere (êl-ss*ê*ö) adv altrove

elucidate (i-*luu*-ssi-deit) v delucidare

emancipation (i-mæn-ssi-*pei*-fön) n emancipazione f

embankment (im-*bæng*-mönt) n argine m

embargo (êm-*baa*-ghou) n (pl ~es) embargo m

embark (im-*baak*) v imbarcarsi; imbarcare

embarkation (êm-baa-*kei*-fön) n imbarco m

embarrass (im-*bæ*-röss) v imbarazzare; *mettere in imbarazzo; ostacolare

embassy (*êm*-bö-ssi) n ambasciata f

emblem (*êm*-blöm) n emblema m

embrace (im-*breiss*) v abbracciare; n abbraccio m

embroider (im-*broi*-dö) v ricamare

embroidery (im-*broi*-dö-ri) n ricamo m

emerald (*ê*-mö-röld) n smeraldo m

emergency (i-*möö*-dʒön-ssi) n caso di emergenza, emergenza f; stato di emergenza; ~ **exit** uscita di sicurezza

emigrant (*ê*-mi-ghrönt) n emigrante m

emigrate (*ê*-mi-ghreit) v emigrare

emigration (ê-mi-*ghrei*-fön) n emigrazione f

emotion (i-*mou*-fön) n commozione f, emozione f

emperor (*êm*-pö-rö) n imperatore m

emphasize (*êm*-fö-ssais) v sottolineare

empire (*êm*-pai⁶) n impero m

employ (im-*ploi*) v impiegare; utilizzare

employee (êm-ploi-*ii*) n salariato m, impiegato m

employer (im-*ploi*-ö) n datore di lavoro

employment (im-*ploi*-mönt) n impiego m, occupazione f; ~ **exchange** ufficio di collocamento

empress (*êm*-priss) n imperatrice f

empty (*êm*p-ti) adj vuoto; v vuotare

enable (i-*nei*-böl) v abilitare

enamel (i-*næ*-möl) n smalto m

enamelled (i-*næ*-möld) adj smaltato

enchanting (in-*tʃaan*-ting) adj affascinante, incantevole

encircle (in-*ssöö*-köl) v *cingere, circondare; accerchiare

enclose (ing-*klous*) *v* *accludere, allegare

enclosure (ing-*klou*-ʒö) *n* allegato *m*

encounter (ing-*kaun*-tö) *v* incontrare; *n* incontro *m*

encourage (ing-*ka*-ridʒ) *v* incoraggiare

encyclopaedia (ên-ssai-klö-*pii*-di-ö) *n* enciclopedia *f*

end (ênd) *n* fine *f*, estremità *f*; termine *m*; *v* finire; cessare

ending (*ên*-ding) *n* fine *f*

endless (*ênd*-löss) *adj* infinito

endorse (in-*dooss*) *v* vistare, girare

endure (in-*d*ⁱ*u*^ö) *v* sopportare

enemy (*ê*-nö-mi) *n* nemico *m*

energetic (ê-nö-*dʒê*-tik) *adj* energico

energy (*ê*-nö-dʒi) *n* energia *f*; forza *f*

engage (ing-*gheidʒ*) *v* *assumere; riservare; impegnarsi; **engaged** fidanzato; occupato

engagement (ing-*gheidʒ*-mönt) *n* fidanzamento *m*; impegno *m*; ~ **ring** anello di fidanzamento

engine (*ên*-dʒin) *n* macchina *f*, motore *m*; locomotrice *f*

engineer (ên-dʒi-*ni*^ö) *n* ingegnere *m*

England (*ing*-ghlönd) Inghilterra *f*

English (*ing*-ghliʃ) *adj* inglese

Englishman (*ing*-ghliʃ-mön) *n* (pl -men) inglese *m*

engrave (ing-*ghreiv*) *v* *incidere

engraver (ing-*ghrei*-vö) *n* incisore *m*

engraving (ing-*ghrei*-ving) *n* stampa *f*; incisione *f*

enigma (i-*nigh*-mö) *n* enigma *m*

enjoy (in-*dʒoi*) *v* godere, gustare

enjoyable (in-*dʒoi*-ö-böl) *adj* piacevole, gradevole, divertente; gustoso

enjoyment (in-*dʒoi*-mönt) *n* godimento *m*

enlarge (in-*laadʒ*) *v* ingrandire; ampliare

enlargement (in-*laadʒ*-mönt) *n* ingrandimento *m*

enormous (i-*noo*-möss) *adj* ingente, enorme

enough (i-*naf*) *adv* abbastanza; *adj* sufficiente

enquire (ing-*k*^u*ai*^ö) *v* informarsi; indagare

enquiry (ing-*k*^u*ai*^ö-ri) *n* informazione *f*; investigazione *f*; inchiesta *f*

enter (*ên*-tö) *v* entrare; *iscrivere

enterprise (*ên*-tö-prais) *n* impresa *f*

entertain (ên-tö-*tein*) *v* divertire, *intrattenere; ospitare

entertainer (ên-tö-*tei*-nö) *n* comico *m*

entertaining (ên-tö-*tei*-ning) *adj* divertente

entertainment (ên-tö-*tein*-mönt) *n* divertimento *m*, passatempo *m*

enthusiasm (in-*θ*ⁱ*uu*-si-æ-söm) *n* entusiasmo *m*

enthusiastic (in-θⁱuu-si-æ-*sstik*) *adj* entusiastico

entire (in-*tai*^ö) *adj* tutto, intero

entirely (in-*tai*^ö-li) *adv* interamente

entrance (*ên*-trönss) *n* entrata *f*; accesso *m*; ingresso *m*

entrance-fee (*ên*-trönss-fii) *n* ingresso *m*

entry (*ên*-tri) *n* entrata *f*; ingresso *m*; registrazione *f*; **no** ~ proibito passare

envelope (*ên*-vö-loup) *n* busta *f*

envious (*ên*-vi-öss) *adj* invidioso, geloso

environment (in-*vai*^ö-rön-mönt) *n* ambiente *m*; dintorni *mpl*

envoy (*ên*-voi) *n* inviato *m*

envy (*ên*-vi) *n* invidia *f*; *v* invidiare

epic (*ê*-pik) *n* poema epico; *adj* epico

epidemic (ê-pi-*dê*-mik) *n* epidemia *f*

epilepsy (*ê*-pi-lêp-ssi) *n* epilessia *f*

epilogue (*ê*-pi-logh) *n* epilogo *m*

episode (*ê*-pi-ssoud) *n* episodio *m*

equal (*ii*-k^uöl) *adj* uguale; *v* uguagliare

equality (i-kᵘo-lö-ti) n uguaglianza f
equalize (ii-kᵘö-lais) v pareggiare
equally (ii-kᵘö-li) adv ugualmente
equator (i-kᵘei-tö) n equatore m
equip (i-kᵘip) v equipaggiare
equipment (i-kᵘip-mönt) n equipaggiamento m
equivalent (i-kᵘi-vö-lönt) adj equivalente
eraser (i-rei-sö) n gomma per cancellare
erect (i-rêkt) v innalzare, *erigere; adj ritto, diritto
err (öö) v errare
errand (ê-rönd) n commissione f
error (ê-rö) n sbaglio m, errore m
escalator (ê-sskö-lei-tö) n scala mobile
escape (i-sskeip) v scappare; fuggire, sfuggire; n evasione f
escort¹ (ê-sskoot) n scorta f
escort² (i-sskoot) v scortare
especially (i-sspê-fö-li) adv soprattutto, specialmente
esplanade (ê-ssplö-neid) n spianata f
essay (ê-ssei) n saggio m; trattato m, componimento m
essence (ê-ssönss) n essenza f; nocciolo m, anima f
essential (i-ssên-föl) adj indispensabile; fondamentale, essenziale
essentially (i-ssên-fö-li) adv essenzialmente
establish (i-sstæ-bliʃ) v stabilire
estate (i-ssteit) n proprietà f
esteem (i-sstiim) n rispetto m, stima f; v stimare
estimate¹ (ê-ssti-meit) v *fare la stima, valutare
estimate² (ê-ssti-möt) n valutazione f
estuary (êss-tʃu-ö-ri) n estuario m
etcetera (êt-ssê-tö-rö) eccetera
etching (ê-tʃing) n acquaforte f
eternal (i-töö-nöl) adj eterno

eternity (i-töö-nö-ti) n eternità f
ether (ii-θö) n etere m
Ethiopia (i-θi-ou-pi-ö) Etiopia f
Ethiopian (i-θi-ou-pi-ön) adj etiopico
Europe (ᶦuö-röp) Europa f
European (ᶦuö-rö-pii-ön) adj europeo
evacuate (i-væ-kᶦu-eit) v evacuare
evaluate (i-væl-ᶦu-eit) v valutare
evaporate (i-væ-pö-reit) v evaporare
even (ii-vön) adj piano, piatto, uguale; costante; pari; adv anche
evening (iiv-ning) n sera f; ~ **dress** abito da sera
event (i-vênt) n evento m; caso m
eventual (i-vên-tʃu-öl) adj eventuale; finale
ever (ê-vö) adv mai; sempre
every (êv-ri) adj ciascuno, ogni
everybody (êv-ri-bo-di) pron ognuno
everyday (êv-ri-dei) adj quotidiano
everyone (êv-ri-ᶸan) pron ognuno
everything (êv-ri-θing) pron tutto
everywhere (êv-ri-ᶸêö) adv ovunque
evidence (ê-vi-dönss) n prova f
evident (ê-vi-dönt) adj evidente
evil (ii-völ) n male m; adj cattivo, malvagio
evolution (ii-vö-luu-ʃön) n evoluzione f
exact (igh-sækt) adj esatto
exactly (igh-sækt-li) adv precisamente
exaggerate (igh-sæ-dʒö-reit) v esagerare
examination (igh-sæ-mi-nei-ʃön) n esame m; indagine f; interrogazione f
examine (igh-sæ-min) v esaminare
example (igh-saam-pöl) n esempio m; **for** ~ per esempio
excavation (êkss-kö-vei-ʃön) n scavo m
exceed (ik-ssiid) v eccedere; superare
excel (ik-ssêl) v *eccellere
excellent (êk-ssö-lönt) adj ottimo, ec-

cellente

except (ik-*ssêpt*) *prep* eccetto, salvo

exception (ik-*ssêp*-ʃön) *n* eccezione *f*

exceptional (ik-*ssêp*-ʃö-nöl) *adj* straordinario, eccezionale

excerpt (*êk*-ssööpt) *n* brano *m*

excess (ik-*ssêss*) *n* eccesso *m*

excessive (ik-*ssê*-ssiv) *adj* eccessivo

exchange (ikss-*tʃeindʒ*) *v* scambiare, cambiare; *n* cambio *m*; borsa *f*; ~ **office** ufficio cambio; ~ **rate** corso del cambio

excite (ik-*ssait*) *v* eccitare

excitement (ik-*ssait*-mönt) *n* agitazione *f*, eccitazione *f*

exciting (ik-*ssai*-ting) *adj* eccitante

exclaim (ik-*sskleim*) *v* esclamare

exclamation (êk-ssklö-*mei*-ʃön) *n* esclamazione *f*

exclude (ik-*sskluud*) *v* *escludere

exclusive (ik-*sskluu*-ssiv) *adj* esclusivo

exclusively (ik-*sskluu*-ssiv-li) *adv* esclusivamente, unicamente

excursion (ik-*ssköö*-ʃön) *n* gita *f*, escursione *f*

excuse[1] (ik-*sskⁱuuss*) *n* scusa *f*

excuse[2] (ik-*sskⁱuuss*) *v* scusare

execute (*êk*-ssi-kⁱuut) *v* eseguire

execution (êk-ssi-*kⁱuu*-ʃön) *n* esecuzione *f*

executioner (êk-ssi-*kⁱuu*-ʃö-nö) *n* boia *m*

executive (igh-*sê*-kⁱu-tiv) *adj* esecutivo; *n* potere esecutivo; direttore *m*

exempt (igh-*ʒêmpt*) *v* dispensare, esentare; *adj* esente

exemption (igh-*sêmp*-ʃön) *n* esenzione *f*

exercise (*êk*-ssö-ssais) *n* esercizio *m*; *v* esercitare

exhale (êkss-*heil*) *v* esalare

exhaust (igh-*soosst*) *n* scappamento *m*; *v* esaurire; ~ **gases** gas di scarico

exhibit (igh-*si*-bit) *v* *esporre; esibire

exhibition (êk-ssi-*bi*-ʃön) *n* mostra *f*, esposizione *f*

exile (*êk*-ssail) *n* esilio *m*; esule *m*

exist (igh-*sisst*) *v* *esistere

existence (igh-*si*-sstönss) *n* esistenza *f*

exit (*êk*-ssit) *n* uscita *f*

exotic (igh-*so*-tik) *adj* esotico

expand (ik-*sspænd*) *v* *espandere; *estendere; allargare

expect (ik-*sspêkt*) *v* aspettare

expectation (êk-sspêk-*tei*-ʃön) *n* aspettativa *f*

expedition (êk- sspö-*di*-ʃön) *n* invio *m*; spedizione *f*

expel (ik-*sspêl*) *v* *espellere

expenditure (ik-*sspên*-di-tʃö) *n* spesa *f*

expense (ik-*sspênss*) *n* spesa *f*

expensive (ik-*sspên*-ssiv) *adj* caro; costoso

experience (ik-*sspⁱö*-ri-önss) *n* esperienza *f*; *v* provare, sperimentare; **experienced** esperto

experiment (ik-*sspê*-ri-mönt) *n* prova *f*, esperimento *m*; *v* sperimentare

expert (*êk*-sspööt) *n* perito *m*, esperto *m*; *adj* competente

expire (ik-*sspaiⁱö*) *v* spirare, finire, *scadere; espirare; **expired** scaduto

expiry (ik-*sspaiⁱö*-ri) *n* scadenza *f*

explain (ik-*ssplein*) *v* chiarire, spiegare

explanation (êk-ssplö-*nei*-ʃön) *n* schiarimento *m*, esplicazione *f*, spiegazione *f*

explicit (ik-*sspli*-ssit) *adj* categorico, esplicito

explode (ik-*ssploud*) *v* *esplodere

exploit (ik-*ssploit*) *v* sfruttare, utilizzare

explore (ik-*ssploo*) *v* esplorare

explosion (ik-*ssplou*-ʒön) *n* esplosione *f*

explosive (ik-*ssplou*-ssiv) *adj* esplosivo; *n* esplosivo *m*

export[1] (ik-*sspoot*) v esportare

export[2] (*êk*-sspoot) n esportazione f

exportation (êk-sspoo-*tei*-ʃön) n esportazione f

exports (*êk*-sspootss) pl esportazione f

exposition (êk-sspö-*si*-ʃön) n esposizione f

exposure (ik-*sspou*-ʒö) n privazioni fpl; esposizione f; ~ **meter** esposimetro m

express (ik-*ssprêss*) v *esprimere; manifestare; adj espresso; esplicito; ~ **train** treno direttissimo

expression (ik-*ssprê*-ʃön) n espressione f; manifestazione f

exquisite (ik-*ssku*ⁱ-sit) adj squisito

extend (ik-*sstênd*) v *estendere; allargare; accordare

extension (ik-*sstên*-ʃön) n prolungamento m; ampliamento m; telefono interno; ~ **cord** prolunga f

extensive (ik-*sstên*-ssiv) adj ampio; vasto

extent (ik-*sstênt*) n dimensione f

exterior (êk-*ssti*ⁱ-ri-ö) adj esterno; n esterno m

external (êk-*sstöö*-nöl) adj esteriore

extinguish (ik-*ssting*-ghuⁱʃ) v *spegnere, *estinguere

extort (ik-*sstoot*) v *estorcere

extortion (ik-*sstoo*-ʃön) n estorsione f

extra (*êk*-sströ) adj supplementare

extract[1] (ik-*sstrækt*) v *estrarre

extract[2] (*êk*-sstrækt) n passo m

extradite (*êk*-sströ-dait) v estradare

extraordinary (ik-*sstroo*-dön-ri) adj straordinario

extravagant (ik-*sstræ*-vö-ghönt) adj esagerato, stravagante

extreme (ik-*sstriim*) adj estremo; n estremo m

exuberant (igh-s*i*uu-bö-rönt) adj esuberante

eye (ai) n occhio m

eyebrow (*ai*-brau) n sopracciglio m

eyelash (*ai*-læʃ) n ciglio m

eyelid (*ai*-lid) n palpebra f

eye-pencil (*ai*-pên-ssöl) n matita per gli occhi

eye-shadow (*ai*-ʃæ-dou) n ombretto m

eye-witness (*ai*-ⁿit-nöss) n testimone oculare

F

fable (*fei*-böl) n favola f

fabric (*fæ*-brik) n stoffa f; struttura f

façade (fö-*ssaad*) n facciata f

face (feiss) n faccia f; v *far fronte a; ~ **massage** massaggio facciale; **facing** in faccia a

face-cream (*feiss*-kriim) n crema di bellezza

face-pack (*feiss*-pæk) n maschera di bellezza

face-powder (*feiss*-pau-dö) n cipria f

facility (fö-*ssi*-lö-ti) n agevolazione f

fact (fækt) n fatto m; **in** ~ infatti

factor (*fæk*-tö) n fattore m

factory (*fæk*-tö-ri) n fabbrica f

factual (*fæk*-tʃu-öl) adj reale

faculty (*fæ*-köl-ti) n potere m; capacità f, attitudine f, facoltà f

fad (fæd) n capriccio m

fade (feid) v scolorirsi, sbiadire

faience (fai-*aŋss*) n ceramica f, terracotta f

fail (feil) v fallire; mancare; tralasciare; bocciare; **without** ~ senz'altro

failure (*feil*-iö) n insuccesso m; fallimento m

faint (feint) v *svenire; adj fiacco, vago, debole

fair (fêⁱ) n fiera f; adj giusto, onesto;

biondo; bello

fairly (*fêᵒ*-li) *adv* alquanto, piuttosto, abbastanza

fairy (*fêᵒ*-ri) *n* fata *f*

fairytale (*fêᵒ*-ri-teil) *n* fiaba *f*

faith (feiθ) *n* fede *f*; fiducia *f*

faithful (*feiθ*-ful) *adj* fedele

fake (feik) *n* falsificazione *f*

fall (fool) *n* caduta *f*; *nAm* autunno *m*

***fall** (fool) *v* *cadere

false (foolss) *adj* falso; sbagliato, fallace, contraffatto; ~ **teeth** dentiera *f*

falter (*fool*-tö) *v* vacillare; balbettare

fame (feim) *n* rinomanza *f*, fama *f*; reputazione *f*

familiar (fö-*mil*-iö) *adj* familiare; confidenziale

family (*fæ*-mö-li) *n* famiglia *f*; ~ **name** cognome *m*

famous (*fei*-möss) *adj* famoso

fan (fæn) *n* ventilatore *m*; ventaglio *m*; tifoso *m*; ~ **belt** cinghia del ventilatore

fanatical (fö-*næ*-ti-köl) *adj* fanatico

fancy (*fæn*-ssi) *v* gradire, *aver voglia di; figurarsi, immaginare; *n* capriccio *m*; immaginazione *f*

fantastic (fæn-*tæ*-sstik) *adj* fantastico

fantasy (*fæn*-tö-si) *n* fantasia *f*

far (faa) *adj* lontano; *adv* molto; **by ~ di gran lunga; so ~** finora

far-away (*faa*-rö-ᵁei) *adj* distante

farce (faass) *n* farsa *f*, buffonata *f*

fare (fêᵒ) *n* spese di viaggio, prezzo del biglietto; vitto *m*, cibo *m*

farm (faam) *n* fattoria *f*

farmer (*faa*-mö) *n* fattore *m*; **farmer's wife** fattoressa *f*

farmhouse (*faam*-hauss) *n* cascina *f*

far-off (*faa*-rof) *adj* lontano

fascinate (*fæ*-ssi-neit) *v* affascinare

fascism (*fæ*-ʃi-söm) *n* fascismo *m*

fascist (*fæ*-ʃisst) *adj* fascistico; *n* fascista *m*

fashion (*fæ*-ʃön) *n* moda *f*; modo *m*

fashionable (*fæ*-ʃö-nö-böl) *adj* alla moda

fast (faasst) *adj* rapido, veloce; fisso

fast-dyed (faasst-*daid*) *adj* inalterabile al lavaggio, a tinta solida

fasten (*faa*-ssön) *v* allacciare; *chiudere

fastener (*faa*-ssö-nö) *n* fermaglio *m*

fat (fæt) *adj* grasso; *n* grasso *m*

fatal (*fei*-töl) *adj* fatale, mortale

fate (feit) *n* fato *m*, destino *m*

father (*faa*-ðö) *n* padre *m*

father-in-law (*faa*-ðö-rin-loo) *n* (pl fathers-) suocero *m*

fatherland (*faa*-ðö-lönd) *n* patria *f*

fatness (*fæt*-nöss) *n* pinguedine *f*

fatty (*fæ*-ti) *adj* untuoso

faucet (*foo*-ssit) *nAm* rubinetto *m*

fault (foolt) *n* colpa *f*; imperfezione *f*, difetto *m*, mancanza *f*

faultless (*foolt*-löss) *adj* impeccabile; perfetto

faulty (*fool*-ti) *adj* difettoso

favour (*fei*-vö) *n* favore *m*; *v* privilegiare, favorire

favourite (*fei*-vö-rit) *n* favorito *m*; *adj* preferito

fawn (foon) *adj* fulvo; *n* cerbiatto *m*

fax (fækss) *n* fax *m*; *v* mandare un fax

fear (fiᵒ) *n* timore *m*, paura *f*; *v* temere

feasible (*fii*-sö-böl) *adj* realizzabile

feast (fiisst) *n* festa *f*

feat (fiit) *n* prestazione *f*

feather (*fê*-ðö) *n* penna *f*

feature (*fii*-tʃö) *n* caratteristica *f*; tratto *m*

February (*fê*-bru-ö-ri) febbraio

federal (*fê*-dö-röl) *adj* federale

federation (fê-dö-*rei*-ʃön) *n* federazione f; confederazione f

fee (fii) n onorario m

feeble (fii-böl) adj fiacco

***feed** (fiid) v nutrire; **fed up with** stufo di

***feel** (fiil) v sentire; palpare; ~ **like** *aver voglia di

feeling (fii-ling) n sensazione f

fell (fêl) v (p fall)

fellow (fê-lou) n tipo m

felt[1] (fêlt) n feltro m

felt[2] (fêlt) v (p, pp feel)

female (fii-meil) adj femminile

feminine (fê-mi-nin) adj femminile

fence (fênss) n recinto m; steccato m; v tirare di scherma

fender (fên-dö) n paraurti m

ferment (föö-mênt) v fermentare

ferry-boat (fê-ri-bout) n traghetto m

fertile (föö-tail) adj fertile

festival (fê-ssti-völ) n festival m

festive (fê-sstiv) adj festivo

fetch (fêtʃ) v portare; *andare a prendere

feudal (fʲuu-döl) adj feudale

fever (fii-vö) n febbre f

feverish (fii-vö-riʃ) adj febbricitante

few (fʲuu) adj pochi

fiancé (fi-ang-ssei) n fidanzato m

fiancée (fi-ang-ssei) n fidanzata f

fibre (fai-bö) n fibra f

fiction (fik-ʃön) n finzione f

field (fiild) n campo m; settore m; ~ **glasses** binocolo m

fierce (fiöss) adj feroce; selvaggio, veemente

fifteen (fif-tiin) num quindici

fifteenth (fif-tiinθ) num quindicesimo

fifth (fifθ) num quinto

fifty (fif-ti) num cinquanta

fig (figh) n fico m

fight (fait) n combattimento m, lotta f

***fight** (fait) v combattere, lottare

figure (fi-ghö) n forma f, figura f; cifra f

file (fail) n lima f; raccolta di documenti; fila f

Filipino (fi-li-pii-nou) n filippino m

fill (fil) v riempire; ~ **in** completare; **filling station** distributore di benzina; ~ **out** Am completare, compilare; ~ **up** *fare il pieno

filling (fi-ling) n otturazione f; ripieno m

film (film) n film m; pellicola f; v filmare

filter (fil-tö) n filtro m

filthy (fil-θi) adj sordido, sudicio

final (fai-nöl) adj finale

finance (fai-nænss) v finanziare

finances (fai-næn-ssis) pl finanze fpl

financial (fai-næn-ʃöl) adj finanziario

finch (fintʃ) n fringuello m

***find** (faind) v trovare

fine (fain) n multa f; adj fino; bello; ottimo, meraviglioso; ~ **arts** belle arti

finger (fing-ghö) n dito m; **little** ~ mignolo m

fingerprint (fing-ghö-print) n impronta digitale

finish (fi-niʃ) v completare, finire; terminare; n termine m; traguardo m

Finland (fin-lönd) Finlandia f

Finn (fin) n finlandese m

Finnish (fi-niʃ) adj finlandese

fire (faiö) n fuoco m; incendio m; v sparare; licenziare

fire-alarm (faiö-rö-laam) n allarme d'incendio

fire-brigade (faiö-bri-gheid) n pompieri mpl

fire-escape (faiö-ri-sskeip) n scala di sicurezza

fire-extinguisher (faiö-rik-ssting-ghʷi-jö) n estintore m

fireplace (faiö-pleiss) n focolare m

fireproof (*faiᵒ*-pruuf) *adj* incombustibile

firm (fööm) *adj* saldo; solido; *n* ditta *f*

first (föösst) *num* primo; **at ~** prima; **al principio**; **~ name** nome *m*

first-aid (föösst-*eid*) *n* pronto soccorso; **~ kit** equipaggiamento di pronto soccorso; **~ post** posto di pronto soccorso

first-class (föösst-*klaass*) *adj* di prima qualità

first-rate (föösst-*reit*) *adj* ottimo, di prima qualità

fir-tree (*föö*-trii) *n* abete *m*

fish¹ (fiʃ) *n* (pl ~, ~es) pesce *m*; **~ shop** pescheria *f*

fish² (fiʃ) *v* pescare; pescare con l'amo; **fishing gear** attrezzi da pesca; **fishing hook** amo *m*; **fishing industry** pesca *f*; **fishing licence** permesso di pesca; **fishing line** lenza *f*; **fishing net** rete da pesca; **fishing rod** canna da pesca; **fishing tackle** attrezzi da pesca

fishbone (*fiʃ*-boun) *n* lisca *f*, spina di pesce

fisherman (*fi*-ʃö-mön) *n* (pl -men) pescatore *m*

fist (fisst) *n* pugno *m*

fit (fit) *adj* adatto; *n* attacco *m*; *v* *convenire; **fitting room** salottino di prova

five (faiv) *num* cinque

fix (fikss) *v* riparare

fixed (fiksst) *adj* fisso

fizz (fis) *n* effervescenza *f*

fjord (fⁱood) *n* fiordo *m*

flag (flægh) *n* bandiera *f*

flame (fleim) *n* fiamma *f*

flamingo (flö-*ming*-ghou) *n* (pl ~s, ~es) fenicottero *m*

flannel (*flæ*-nöl) *n* flanella *f*

flash (flæʃ) *n* baleno *m*

flash-bulb (*flæʃ*-balb) *n* lampada flash

flash-light (*flæʃ*-lait) *n* lampada portatile

flask (flaassk) *n* flacone *m*; **thermos ~** termos *m*

flat (flæt) *adj* piano, piatto; *n* appartamento *m*; **~ tyre** bucatura *f*

flavour (flei-vö) *n* gusto *m*; *v* condire

fleet (fliit) *n* flotta *f*

flesh (flêʃ) *n* carne *f*

flew (fluu) *v* (p fly)

flex (flêkss) *n* cordone elettrico

flexible (*flêk*-ssi-böl) *adj* flessibile; pieghevole

flight (flait) *n* volo *m*; **charter ~** volo charter

flint (flint) *n* pietrina *f*

float (flout) *v* galleggiare; *n* galleggiante *m*

flock (flok) *n* gregge *m*

flood (flad) *n* inondazione *f*; flusso *m*

floor (floo) *n* pavimento *m*; piano *m*; **~ show** spettacollo di varietà

florist (*flo*-risst) *n* fioraio *m*

flour (flauᵒ) *n* farina *f*

flow (flou) *v* *scorrere

flower (flauᵒ) *n* fiore *m*

flowerbed (*flauᵒ*-bêd) *n* aiola *f*

flower-shop (*flauᵒ*-ʃop) *n* negozio di fiori

flown (floun) *v* (pp fly)

flu (fluu) *n* influenza *f*

fluent (*fluu*-önt) *adj* fluente

fluid (*fluu*-id) *adj* fluido; *n* fluido *m*

flute (fluut) *n* flauto *m*

fly (flai) *n* mosca *f*; brachetta *f*

*fly (flai) *v* volare

foam (foum) *n* schiuma *f*; *v* spumare

foam-rubber (*foum*-ra-bö) *n* gommapiuma *f*

focus (*fou*-köss) *n* fuoco *m*

fog (fogh) *n* nebbia *f*

foggy (*fo*-ghi) *adj* nebbioso

foglamp (*fogh*-læmp) *n* fanale antinebbia

fold (fould) v piegare; n piega f

folk (fouk) n popolo m; ~ **song** canzone popolare

folk-dance (fouk-daanss) n danza popolare

folklore (fouk-loo) n folklore m

follow (fo-lou) v seguire; **following** adj successivo, seguente

*be fond of (bii fond ov) amare

food (fuud) n cibo m; mangiare m, vitto m; ~ **poisoning** intossicazione alimentare

foodstuffs (fuud-sstafss) pl alimentari mpl

fool (fuul) n idiota m, sciocco m; v beffare

foolish (fuu-liʃ) adj stolto, stupido; sciocco

foot (fut) n (pl feet) piede m; ~ **powder** talco per piedi; **on** ~ a piedi

football (fut-bool) n pallone m; ~ **match** partita di calcio

foot-brake (fut-breik) n freno a pedale

footpath (fut-paaθ) n sentiero m

footwear (fut-uêᵒ) n calzatura f

for (foo, fö) prep per; durante; a causa di, in conseguenza di; conj poiché

*forbid (fö-bid) v proibire

force (fooss) v *costringere, forzare; n forza f; **by** ~ per forza; **driving** ~ forza motrice

ford (food) n guado m

forecast (foo-kaasst) n previsione f; v *prevedere

foreground (foo-ghraund) n primo piano

forehead (fo-rêd) n fronte f

foreign (fo-rin) adj straniero; estraneo

foreigner (fo-ri-nö) n straniero m; forestiero m

foreman (foo-mön) n (pl -men) capo-

mastro m

foremost (foo-mousst) adj primo

foresail (foo-sseil) n vela di trinchetto

forest (fo-risst) n foresta f

forester (fo-ri-sstö) n guardia forestale

forge (foodʒ) v falsificare

*forget (fö-ghêt) v dimenticare

forgetful (fö-ghêt-föl) adj smemorato

*forgive (fö-ghiv) v perdonare

fork (fook) n forchetta f; bivio m; v biforcarsi

form (foom) n forma f; formulario m; classe f; v formare

formal (foo-möl) adj formale

formality (foo-mæ-lö-ti) n formalità f

former (foo-mö) adj antico; precedente; **formerly** anteriormente, già

formula (foo-miᵘ-lö) n (pl ~e, ~s) formula f

fort (foot) n forte m

fortnight (foot-nait) n quindicina di giorni

fortress (foo-triss) n fortezza f

fortunate (foo-tʃö-nöt) adj fortunato

fortune (foo-tʃuun) n ricchezza f; destino m, fortuna f

forty (foo-ti) num quaranta

forward (foo-uöd) adv in avanti, avanti; v inoltrare

fought (foot) v (p, pp fight)

foul (faul) adj sporco; perfido

found¹ (faund) v (p, pp find)

found² (faund) v fondare, istituire

foundation (faun-dei-ʃön) n fondazione f; ~ **cream** fondo tinta

fountain (faun-tin) n fontana f; sorgente f

fountain-pen (faun-tin-pên) n penna stilografica

four (foo) num quattro

fourteen (foo-tiin) num quattordici

fourteenth (foo-tiinθ) num quattordicesimo

fourth (fooθ) num quarto

fowl (faul) *n* (pl ~s, ~) pollame *m*

fox (fokss) *n* volpe *f*

foyer (*foi-ei*) *n* ridotto *m*

fraction (*fræk-*∫ön) *n* frazione *f*

fracture (*fræk-*t∫ö) *v* fratturare; *n* frattura *f*

fragile (*fræ-*dʒail) *adj* fragile

fragment (*frægh-*mönt) *n* frammento *m*; pezzo *m*

frame (freim) *n* cornice *f*; montatura *f*

France (fraanss) Francia *f*

franchise (*fræn-*t∫ais) *n* diritto elettorale

fraternity (frö-*töö-*nö-ti) *n* fraternità *f*

fraud (frood) *n* frode *f*

fray (frei) *v* sfilacciarsi

free (frii) *adj* libero; gratuito; ~ **of charge** gratuito; ~ **ticket** biglietto gratuito

freedom (*frii-*döm) *n* libertà *f*

*****freeze** (friis) *v* gelare; congelarsi

freezing (*frii-*sing) *adj* glaciale

freezing-point (*frii-*sing-point) *n* punto di congelamento

freight (freit) *n* carico *m*

freight-train (*freit-*trein) *nAm* treno merci

French (frênt∫) *adj* francese

Frenchman (*frênt∫-*mön) *n* (pl -men) francese *m*

frequency (*frii-*k*u*ön-ssi) *n* frequenza *f*

frequent (*frii-*k*u*önt) *adj* frequente

fresh (frê∫) *adj* fresco; ~ **water** acqua dolce

friction (*frik-*∫ön) *n* attrito *m*

Friday (*frai-*di) *n* venerdì *m*

fridge (fridʒ) *n* frigorifero *m*

friend (frênd) *n* amico *m*; amica *f*

friendly (*frênd-*li) *adj* affabile; amichevole

friendship (*frênd-*∫ip) *n* amicizia *f*

fright (frait) *n* paura *f*, spavento *m*

frighten (*frai-*tön) *v* spaventare

frightened (*frai-*tönd) *adj* spaventato; *****be ~** spaventarsi

frightful (*frait-*föl) *adj* terribile

fringe (frindʒ) *n* frangia *f*

frock (frok) *n* veste *f*

frog (frogh) *n* rana *f*

from (from) *prep* da

front (frant) *n* facciata *f*; **in ~ of** di fronte a

frontier (fran-tiö) *n* frontiera *f*

frost (frosst) *n* gelo *m*

froth (froθ) *n* schiuma *f*

frozen (*frou-*sön) *adj* congelato; ~ **food** cibo surgelato

fruit (fruut) *n* frutta *f*; frutto *m*

fry (frai) *v* *****friggere

frying-pan (*frai-*ing-pæn) *n* padella *f*

fuel (*f*uu-öl) *n* combustibile *m*; benzina *f*; ~ **pump** *Am* pompa di alimentazione

full (ful) *adj* pieno; ~ **board** pensione completa; ~ **stop** punto *m*; ~ **up** colmo

fun (fan) *n* divertimento *m*; scherzo *m*

function (*fangk-*∫ön) *n* funzione *f*

fund (fand) *n* fondi *m*

fundamental (fan-dö-*mên-*töl) *adj* fondamentale

funeral (*f*uu-nö-röl) *n* funerale *m*

funnel (*fa-*nöl) *n* imbuto *m*

funny (*fa-*ni) *adj* buffo, divertente; strano

fur (föö) *n* pelliccia *f*; ~ **coat** cappotto di pelliccia; **furs** pelliccia *f*

furious (*f*u*ö*-ri-öss) *adj* furibondo, furioso

furnace (*föö-*niss) *n* fornace *f*

furnish (*föö-*ni∫) *v* fornire, procurare; arredare, ammobiliare; ~ **with** *****provedere di

furniture (*föö-*ni-t∫ö) *n* mobilia *f*

furrier (*fa-*ri-ö) *n* pellicciaio *m*

further (*föö-*öö) *adj* più lontano; ulteriore

furthermore (*föö-ðö-moo*) *adv* inoltre

furthest (*föö-ðisst*) *adj* il più lontano

fuse (fᶦuus) *n* fusibile *m* ; miccia *f*

fuss (fass) *n* trambusto *m* ; scalpore *m*

future (fᶦuu-tʃö) *n* futuro *m* ; *adj* futuro

G

gable (*ghei-*böl) *n* frontone *m*

gadget (*ghæ-*dʒit) *n* aggeggio *m*

gaiety (*ghei-*ö-ti) *n* gaiezza *f*, allegria *f*

gain (ghein) *v* guadagnare ; *n* profitto *m*

gait (gheit) *n* andatura *f*, passo *m*

gale (gheil) *n* burrasca *f*

gall (ghool) *n* bile *f* ; ~ **bladder** cistifellea *f*

gallery (*ghæ-*lö-ɹi) *n* loggione *m* ; galleria *f*

gallop (*ghæ-*löp) *n* galoppo *m*

gallows (*ghæ-*lous) *pl* forca *f*

gallstone (*ghool-*sstoun) *n* calcolo biliare

game (gheim) *n* giuoco *m* ; selvaggina *f* ; ~ **reserve** riserva di selvaggina

gang (ghæng) *n* banda *f* ; squadra *f*

gangway (*ghæng-*ᵁei) *n* passarella *f*

gaol (dʒeil) *n* carcere *m*

gap (ghæp) *n* breccia *f*

garage (*ghæ-*raaʒ) *n* rimessa *f* ; *v* *mettere in rimessa

garbage (*ghaa-*bidʒ) *n* spazzatura *f*, immondizia *f*

garden (*ghaa-*dön) *n* giardino *m* ; **public** ~ giardino pubblico ; **zoological gardens** giardino zoologico

gardener (*ghaa-*dö-nö) *n* giardiniere *m*

gargle (*ghaa-*ghöl) *v* gargarizzare

garlic (*ghaa-*lik) *n* aglio *m*

gas (ghæss) *n* gas *m* ; *nAm* benzina *f* ; ~ **cooker** fornello a gas ; ~ **pump** *Am* pompa di benzina ; ~ **station** *Am* stazione di servizio ; ~ **stove** stufa a gas

gasoline (*ghæ-*ssö-liin) *nAm* benzina *f*

gastric (*ghæ-*sstrik) *adj* gastrico ; ~ **ulcer** ulcera gastrica

gasworks (*ghæss-*ᵁöökss) *n* officina del gas

gate (gheit) *n* cancello *m*

gather (*ghæ-*ðö) *v* *raccogliere ; *raccogliersi

gauge (gheidʒ) *n* misuratore *m*

gauze (ghoos) *n* garza *f*

gave (gheiv) *v* (p give)

gay (ghei) *adj* allegro ; vivace

gaze (gheis) *v* fissare

gazetteer (ghæ-sö-*tiᵒ*) *n* dizionario geografico

gear (ghiᵒ) *n* velocità *f* ; attrezzatura *f* ; **change** ~ cambiare marcia ; ~ **lever** leva del cambio

gear-box (*ghiᵒ-*bokss) *n* cambio di velocità

gem (dʒêm) *n* gioiello *m*, gemma *f*

gender (*dʒên-*dö) *n* genere *m*

general (*dʒê-*nö-röl) *adj* generale ; *n* generale *m* ; ~ **practitioner** medico generico ; **in** ~ in generale

generate (*dʒê-*nö-reit) *v* generare

generation (dʒê-nö-*rei-*jön) *n* generazione *f*

generator (*dʒê-*nö-rei-tör) *n* generatore *m*

generosity (dʒê-nö-*ro-*ssö-ti) *n* generosità *f*

generous (*dʒê-*nö-röss) *adj* munifico, generoso

genital (*dʒê-*ni-töl) *adj* genitale

genius (*dʒii-*ni-öss) *n* genio *m*

gentle (*dʒên*-töl) *adj* amabile; dolce, leggero; delicato

gentleman (*dʒên*-töl-mön) *n* (pl -men) signore *m*

genuine (*dʒê*-nⁱu-in) *adj* genuino

geography (dʒi-*o*-ghrö-fi) *n* geografia *f*

geology (dʒi-*o*-lö-dʒi) *n* geologia *f*

geometry (dʒi-*o*-mö-tri) *n* geometria *f*

germ (dʒöm) *n* germe *m*

German (*dʒöö*-mön) *adj* tedesco

Germany (*dʒöö*-mö-ni) Germania *f*

gesticulate (dʒi-*ssti*-kⁱu-leit) *v* gesticolare

*get (ghêt) *v* *ottenere; *andare a prendere; diventare; ~ **back** tornare; ~ **off** *scendere; ~ **on** montare; avanzare, progredire; ~ **up** alzarsi

ghost (ghousst) *n* spettro *m*; spirito *m*

giant (*dʒai*-önt) *n* gigante *m*

giddiness (*ghi*-di-nöss) *n* vertigine *f*

giddy (*ghi*-di) *adj* stordito

gift (ghift) *n* regalo *m*, dono *m*; talento *m*

gifted (*ghif*-tid) *adj* di talento

gigantic (dʒai-*ghæn*-tik) *adj* gigantesco

giggle (*ghi*-ghöl) *v* ridacchiare

gill (ghil) *n* branchia *f*

gilt (ghilt) *adj* dorato

ginger (*dʒin*-dʒö) *n* zenzero *m*

gipsy (*dʒip*-ssi) *n* zingaro *m*

girdle (*ghöö*-döl) *n* busto *m*

girl (ghööl) *n* ragazza *f*; ~ **guide** giovane esploratrice

*give (ghiv) *v* *dare; *porgere; ~ **away** tradire; ~ **in** cedere; ~ **up** desistere

glacier (*ghlæ*-ssi-ö) *n* ghiacciaio *m*

glad (ghlæd) *adj* lieto, contento; **gladly** con piacere, volentieri

gladness (*ghlæd*-nöss) *n* gioia *f*

glamorous (*ghlæ*-mö-röss) *adj* affascinante

glamour (*ghlæ*-mö) *n* fascino *m*

glance (ghlaanss) *n* occhiata *f*; *v* *dare un'occhiata

gland (ghlænd) *n* ghiandola *f*

glare (ghlêᵒ) *n* bagliore *m*; splendore *m*

glaring (*ghlêᵒ*-ring) *adj* abbagliante

glass (ghlaass) *n* bicchiere *m*; vetro *m*; di vetro; **glasses** occhiali *mpl*; **magnifying** ~ lente d'ingrandimento

glaze (ghleis) *v* smaltare

glen (ghlên) *n* gola *f*

glide (ghlaid) *v* scivolare

glider (*ghlai*-dö) *n* aliante *m*

glimpse (ghlimpss) *n* occhiata *f*; visione fugace; *v* *intravvedere

global (*ghlou*-böl) *adj* universale

globe (ghloub) *n* globo *m*

gloom (ghluum) *n* oscurità *f*

gloomy (*ghluu*-mi) *adj* cupo

glorious (*ghloo*-ri-öss) *adj* splendido

glory (*ghloo*-ri) *n* gloria *f*; onore *m*, lode *f*

gloss (ghloss) *n* lucentezza *f*

glossy (*ghlo*-ssi) *adj* lucido

glove (ghlav) *n* guanto *m*

glow (ghlou) *v* *ardere; *n* ardore *m*

glue (ghluu) *n* colla *f*

*go (ghou) *v* *andare; camminare; diventare; ~ **ahead** continuare; ~ **away** *andarsene; ~ **back** tornare; ~ **home** rincasare; ~ **in** entrare; ~ **on** continuare; ~ **out** *uscire; ~ **through** sopportare

goal (ghoul) *n* traguardo *m*, rete *f*

goalkeeper (*ghoul*-kii-pö) *n* portiere *m*

goat (ghout) *n* becco *m*, capra *f*

god (ghod) *n* dio *m*

goddess (*gho*-diss) *n* dea *f*

godfather (*ghod*-faa-öö) *n* padrino *m*

goggles (*gho*-ghöls) *pl* occhiali di protezione

gold (ghould) *n* oro *m*; ~ **leaf** oro laminato

golden (*ghoul*-dön) *adj* aureo

goldmine (*ghould*-main) *n* miniera d'oro

goldsmith (*ghould*-ssmiθ) *n* orefice *m*

golf (gholf) *n* golf *m*

golf-club (*gholf*-klab) *n* mazza da golf

golf-course (*gholf*-kooss) *n* campo di golf

golf-links (*gholf*-lingkss) *n* campo di golf

gondola (*ghon*-dö-lö) *n* gondola *f*

gone (ghon) *adv* (pp go) via

good (ghud) *adj* buono; virtuoso

good-bye! (ghud-*bai*) arrivederci!

good-humoured (ghud-*h'uu*-möd) *adj* di buon umore

good-looking (ghud-*lu*-king) *adj* di bell'aspetto

good-natured (ghud-*nei*-tſöd) *adj* gentile

goods (ghuds) *pl* merci; ~ **train** treno merci

good-tempered (ghud-*têm*-pöd) *adj* di buon umore

goodwill (ghud-ᵁil) *n* benevolenza *f*

goose (ghuuss) *n* (pl geese) oca *f*

gooseberry (*ghus*-bö-ri) *n* uva spina

goose-flesh (*ghuuss*-flêſ) *n* pelle d'oca

gorge (ghoodʒ) *n* gola *f*

gorgeous (*ghoo*-dʒöss) *adj* magnifico

gospel (*gho*-sspöl) *n* vangelo *m*

gossip (*gho*-ssip) *n* pettegolezzo *m*; *v* pettegolare

got (ghot) *v* (p, pp get)

gourmet (*ghuᵒ*-mei) *n* buongustaio *m*

gout (ghaut) *n* gotta *f*

govern (*gha*-vön) *v* governare

governess (*gha*-vö-niss) *n* governante *f*

government (*gha*-vön-mönt) *n* governo *m*

governor (*gha*-vö-nö) *n* governatore *m*

gown (ghaun) *n* vestito da donna

grace (ghreiss) *n* grazia *f*; perdono *m*

graceful (*ghreiss*-föl) *adj* grazioso

grade (ghreid) *n* classe *f*; *v* classificare

gradient (*ghrei*-di-önt) *n* inclinazione *f*

gradual (*ghræ*-dʒu-öl) *adj* graduale

graduate (*ghræ*-dʒu-eit) *v* diplomarsi

grain (ghrein) *n* granello *m*, frumento *m*, grano *m*

gram (ghræm) *n* grammo *m*

grammar (*ghræ*-mö) *n* grammatica *f*

grammatical (ghrö-*mæ*-ti-köl) *adj* grammaticale

gramophone (*ghræ*-mö-foun) *n* grammofono *m*

grand (ghrænd) *adj* imponente

granddad (*ghræn*-dæd) *n* nonno *m*

granddaughter (*ghræn*-doo-tö) *n* nipotina *f*, nipote *f*

grandfather (*ghræn*-faa-ðö) *n* nonno *m*

grandmother (*ghræn*-ma-ðö) *n* nonna *f*

grandparents (*ghræn*-pêᵒ-röntss) *pl* nonni

grandson (*ghræn*-ssan) *n* nipotino *m*, nipote *m*

granite (*ghræ*-nit) *n* granito *m*

grant (ghraant) *v* accordare; *concedere; *n* sussidio *m*, borsa *f*

grapefruit (*ghreip*-fruut) *n* pompelmo *m*

grapes (ghreipss) *pl* uva *f*

graph (ghræf) *n* grafico *m*

graphic (*ghræ*-fik) *adj* grafico

grasp (ghraassp) *v* afferrare; *n* stretta *f*

grass (ghraass) *n* erba *f*

grasshopper (*ghraass*-ho-pö) *n* cavalletta *f*

grate (ghreit) *n* grata *f*; *v* raspare

grateful (*ghreit*-föl) *adj* grato, riconoscente

grater (*ghrei*-tö) *n* grattugia *f*

gratis (*ghræ*-tiss) *adj* gratis

gratitude (*ghræ*-ti-t'uud) *n* gratitudine *f*

gratuity (ghrö-t'uu-ö-ti) *n* mancia *f*

grave (ghreiv) *n* tomba *f*; *adj* grave

gravel (*ghræ*-völ) *n* ghiaia *f*

gravestone (*ghreiv*-sstoun) *n* lapide *f*

graveyard (*ghreiv*-¹aad) *n* cimitero *m*

gravity (*ghræ*-vö-ti) *n* gravità *f*; serietà *f*

gravy (*ghrei*-vi) *n* sugo *m*

graze (ghreis) *v* pascolare; *n* escoriazione *f*

grease (ghriiss) *n* grasso *m*; *v* lubrificare

greasy (*ghrii*-ssi) *adj* grasso, unto

great (ghreit) *adj* grande; **Great Britain** Gran Bretagna

Greece (ghriiss) Grecia *f*

greed (ghriid) *n* cupidigia *f*

greedy (*ghrii*-di) *adj* avido; goloso

Greek (ghriik) *adj* greco

green (ghriin) *adj* verde; ~ **card** carta verde

greengrocer (*ghriin*-ghrou-ssö) *n* fruttivendolo *m*

greenhouse (*ghriin*-hauss) *n* serra *f*

greens (ghriins) *pl* verdura *f*

greet (ghriit) *v* salutare

greeting (*ghrii*-ting) *n* saluto *m*

grey (ghrei) *adj* grigio

greyhound (*ghrei*-haund) *n* levriere *m*

grief (ghriif) *n* cordoglio *m*; afflizione *f*, dolore *m*

grieve (ghriiv) *v* *affliggersi

grill (ghril) *n* griglia *f*; *v* cucinare alla griglia

grill-room (*ghril*-ruum) *n* rosticceria *f*

grin (ghrin) *v* ghignare; *n* smorfia *f*

*grind (ghraind) *v* macinare; tritare

grip (ghrip) *v* impugnare; *n* presa *f*, stretta *f*; *nAm* valigetta a mano *f*

grit (ghrit) *n* graniglia *f*

groan (ghroun) *v* gemere

grocer (*ghrou*-ssö) *n* droghiere *m*; **grocer's** drogheria *f*

groceries (*ghrou*-ssö-ris) *pl* alimentari *mpl*

groin (ghroin) *n* inguine *m*

groove (ghruuv) *n* solco *m*

gross¹ (ghrouss) *n* (pl ~) grossa *f*

gross² (ghrouss) *adj* rozzo; lordo

grotto (*ghro*-tou) *n* (pl ~es, ~s) grotta *f*

ground¹ (ghraund) *n* fondo *m*, terra *f*; ~ **floor** pianterreno *m*; **grounds** terreno *m*

ground² (ghraund) *v* (p, pp grind)

group (ghruup) *n* gruppo *m*

grove (ghrouv) *n* boschetto *m*

*grow (ghrou) *v* *crescere; coltivare; diventare

growl (ghraul) *v* brontolare

grown-up (*ghroun*-ap) *adj* adulto; *n* adulto *m*

growth (ghrouθ) *n* crescita *f*; escrescenza *f*

grudge (ghradʒ) *v* invidiare

grumble (*ghram*-böl) *v* brontolare

guarantee (ghæ-rön-*tii*) *n* garanzia *f*; cauzione *f*; *v* garantire

guarantor (ghæ-rön-*too*) *n* garante *m*

guard (ghaad) *n* guardiano *m*; *v* custodire

guardian (ghaa-di-ön) *n* tutore *m*

guess (ghêss) *v* indovinare; credere, congetturare; *n* congettura *f*

guest (ghêsst) *n* ospite *m*

guest-house (*ghêsst*-hauss) *n* pensione *f*

guest-room (*ghêsst*-ruum) *n* camera degli ospiti

guide (ghaid) *n* guida *f*; *v* guidare

guidebook (*ghaid*-buk) *n* guida *f*

guide-dog (*ghaid*-dogh) *n* cane guida

guilt (ghilt) *n* colpa *f*

guilty (*ghil*-ti) *adj* colpevole

guinea-pig (*ghi*-ni-pigh) *n* porcellino d'India

guitar (ghi-*taa*) *n* chitarra *f*

gulf (ghalf) *n* golfo *m*

gull (ghal) *n* gabbiano *m*

gum (gham) *n* gengiva *f*; gomma *f*; colla *f*

gun (ghan) *n* fucile *m*, rivoltella *f*; cannone *m*

gunpowder (*ghan*-pau-dö) *n* polvere da sparo

gust (ghasst) *n* raffica *f*

gusty (*gha*-ssti) *adj* ventoso

gut (ghat) *n* intestino *m*; **guts** coraggio *m*

gutter (*gha*-tö) *n* cunetta *f*

guy (ghai) *n* tipo *m*

gymnasium (dʒim-*nei*-si-öm) *n* (pl ~s, -sia) palestra *f*

gymnast (*dʒim*-næsst) *n* ginnasta *m*

gymnastics (dʒim-*næ*-sstikss) *pl* ginnastica *f*

gynaecologist (ghai-nö-*ko*-lö-dʒisst) *n* ginecologo *m*

H

haberdashery (*hæ*-bö-dæ-ʃö-ri) *n* merceria *f*

habit (*hæ*-bit) *n* abitudine *f*

habitable (*hæ*-bi-tö-böl) *adj* abitabile

habitual (hö-*bi*-tʃu-öl) *adj* consueto

had (hæd) *v* (p, pp have)

haddock (*hæ*-dök) *n* (pl ~) merluzzo *m*

haemorrhage (*hê*-mö-ridʒ) *n* emorragia *f*

haemorrhoids (*hê*-mö-roids) *pl* emorroidi *fpl*

hail (heil) *n* grandine *f*

hair (hêᵒ) *n* capello *m*; ~ **cream** brillantina *f*; ~ **gel** brillantina *f*; ~ **piece** toupet *m*; ~ **rollers** bigodini *mpl*

hairbrush (*hêᵒ*-braʃ) *n* spazzola per capelli

haircut (*hêᵒ*-kat) *n* taglio di capelli

hair-do (*hêᵒ*-duu) *n* capigliatura *f*, acconciatura *f*

hairdresser (*hêᵒ*-drê-ssö) *n* parrucchiere *m*

hair-dryer (*hêᵒ*-drai-ö) *n* asciugacapelli *m*

hair-grip (*hêᵒ*-ghrip) *n* forcina *f*

hair-net (*hêᵒ*-nêt) *n* reticella *f*

hair-oil (*hêᵒ*-roil) *n* olio per capelli

hairpin (*hêᵒ*-pin) *n* forcina *f*

hair-spray (*hêᵒ*-ssprei) *n* lacca per capelli

hairy (*hêᵒ*-ri) *adj* peloso

half¹ (haaf) *adj* mezzo; *adv* a metà

half² (haaf) *n* (pl halves) metà *f*

half-time (haaf-*taim*) *n* intervallo *m*

halfway (haaf-*ᵘei*) *adv* a mezza strada

halibut (*hæ*-li-böt) *n* (pl ~) ippoglosso *m*

hall (hool) *n* vestibolo *m*; sala *f*

halt (hoolt) *v* fermarsi

halve (haav) *v* dimezzare

ham (hæm) *n* prosciutto *m*

hamlet (*hæm*-löt) *n* frazione *f*

hammer (*hæ*-mö) *n* martello *m*

hammock (*hæ*-mök) *n* amaca *f*

hamper (*hæm*-pö) *n* paniere *m*

hand (hænd) *n* mano *f*; *v* *porgere; ~ **cream** crema per le mani

handbag (*hænd*-bægh) *n* borsetta *f*

handbook (*hænd*-buk) *n* manuale *m*

hand-brake (*hænd*-breik) *n* freno a mano

handcuffs (*hænd*-kafss) *pl* manette *fpl*

handful (*hænd*-ful) *n* manciata *f*

handicraft (*hæn*-di-kraaft) *n* lavoro manuale; artigianato *m*

handkerchief (*hæng*-kö-tʃif) *n* fazzoletto *m*

handle (*hæn*-döl) *n* manico *m*, impugnatura *f*; *v* maneggiare; trattare

hand-made (hænd-*meid*) *adj* fatto a mano

handshake (*hænd*-ʃeik) *n* stretta di mano

handsome (*hæn*-ssöm) *adj* avvenente

handwork (*hænd*-ᵘöök) *n* lavoro fatto a mano

handwriting (*hænd*-rai-ting) *n* scrittura *f*

handy (*hæn*-di) *adj* maneggevole

*hang (hæng) *v* *appendere; pendere

hanger (*hæng*-ö) *n* attaccapanni *m*

hangover (*hæng*-ou-vö) *n* malessere *m*

happen (*hæ*-pön) *v* *accadere, *succedere

happening (*hæ*-pö-ning) *n* evento *m*

happiness (*hæ*-pö-nöss) *n* felicità *f*

happy (*hæ*-pi) *adj* contento, felice

harbour (*haa*-bö) *n* porto *m*

hard (haad) *adj* duro; difficile; **hardly** appena

hardware (*haad*-ᵘêᵒ) *n* ferramenta *fpl*; ~ **store** negozio di ferramenta

hare (hêᵒ) *n* lepre *f*

harm (haam) *n* danno *m*; male *m*; *v* *nuocere

harmful (*haam*-föl) *adj* dannoso, nocivo

harmless (*haam*-löss) *adj* innocuo

harmony (*haa*-mö-ni) *n* armonia *f*

harp (haap) *n* arpa *f*

harpsichord (*haap*-ssi-kood) *n* clavicembalo *m*

harsh (haaʃ) *adj* aspro; severo; crudele

harvest (*haa*-visst) *n* raccolto *m*

has (hæss) *v* (pr have)

haste (heisst) *n* premura *f*, fretta *f*

hasten (*hei*-ssön) *v* affrettarsi

hasty (*hei*-ssti) *adj* frettoloso

hat (hæt) *n* cappello *m*; ~ **rack** attaccapanni *m*

hatch (hætʃ) *n* botola *f*

hate (heit) *v* detestare; odiare; *n* odio *m*

hatred (*hei*-trid) *n* odio *m*

haughty (*hoo*-ti) *adj* altezzoso

haul (hool) *v* trainare

*have (hæv) *v* *avere; *fare; ~ **to** *dovere

haversack (*hæ*-vö-ssæk) *n* bisaccia *f*

hawk (hook) *n* astore *m*; falcone *m*

hay (hei) *n* fieno *m*; ~ **fever** febbre del fieno

hazard (*hæ*-söd) *n* rischio *m*

haze (heis) *n* foschia *f*

hazelnut (*hei*-söl-nat) *n* nocciola *f*

hazy (*hei*-si) *adj* fosco; nebbioso

he (hii) *pron* egli

head (hêd) *n* testa *f*; capo *m*; *v* *dirigere; ~ **of state** capo di stato; ~ **teacher** direttore di scuola, preside *m*

headache (*hê*-deik) *n* mal di testa

heading (*hê*-ding) *n* titolo *m*

headlamp (*hêd*-læmp) *n* fanale *m*

headland (*hêd*-lönd) *n* promontorio *m*

headlight (*hêd*-lait) *n* faro *m*

headline (*hêd*-lain) *n* titolo *m*

headmaster (hêd-*maa*-sstö) *n* direttore di scuola; preside *m*

headquarters (hêd-*kᵘoo*-tös) *pl* quartiere generale

head-strong (*hêd*-sstrong) *adj* testardo

head-waiter (hêd-ᵘ*ei*-tö) *n* capocameriere *m*

heal (hiil) *v* guarire

health (hêlθ) *n* salute *f*; ~ **centre** centro sanitario; ~ **certificate** certificato di sanità

healthy (*hêl*-θi) *adj* sano

heap (hiip) *n* cumulo *m*, mucchio *m*

*hear (hiö) *v* *udire

hearing (*hiö*-ring) *n* udito *m*

heart (haat) *n* cuore *m*; nocciolo *m*; **by ~** a memoria; **~ attack** attacco cardiaco

heartburn (*haat*-böön) *n* bruciore di stomaco

hearth (haaθ) *n* focolare *m*

heartless (*haat*-löss) *adj* spietato

hearty (*haa*-ti) *adj* cordiale

heat (hiit) *n* calore *m*, caldo *m*; *v* scaldare; **heating pad** cuscino elettrico

heater (*hii*-tö) *n* riscaldatore *m*; **immersion ~** scaldacqua ad immersione

heath (hiiθ) *n* landa *f*

heathen (*hii*-öön) *n* pagano *m*

heather (*hê*-ðö) *n* erica *f*

heating (*hii*-ting) *n* riscaldamento *m*

heaven (*hê*-vön) *n* cielo *m*

heavy (*hê*-vi) *adj* pesante

Hebrew (*hii*-bruu) *n* ebraico *m*

hedge (hêdʒ) *n* siepe *f*

hedgehog (*hêdʒ*-hogh) *n* riccio *m*

heel (hiil) *n* tallone *m*; tacco *m*

height (hait) *n* altezza *f*; colmo *m*, culmine *m*

hell (hêl) *n* inferno *m*

hello! (hê-*lou*) ciao!

helm (hêlm) *n* timone *m*

helmet (*hêl*-mit) *n* casco *m*

helmsman (*hêlms*-mön) *n* timoniere *m*

help (hêlp) *v* aiutare; *n* aiuto *m*

helper (*hêl*-pö) *n* aiutante *m*

helpful (*hêlp*-föl) *adj* servizievole

helping (*hêl*-ping) *n* porzione *f*

hem (hêm) *n* orlo *m*

hemp (hêmp) *n* canapa *f*

hen (hên) *n* gallina *f*

henceforth (hênss-*fooθ*) *adv* d'ora innanzi

her (höö) *pron* la, le; *adj* suo

herb (hööb) *n* erba *f*

herd (hööd) *n* gregge *m*

here (hiö) *adv* qui; **~ you are** ecco

hereditary (hi-*rê*-di-tö-ri) *adj* ereditario

hernia (*höö*-ni-ö) *n* ernia *f*

hero (*hiö*-rou) *n* (pl ~es) eroe *m*

heron (*hê*-rön) *n* airone *m*

herring (*hê*-ring) *n* (pl ~, ~s) aringa *f*

herself (höö-*ssêlf*) *pron* si; essa stessa

hesitate (*hê*-si-teit) *v* esitare

heterosexual (hê-tö-rö-*ssêk*-ʃu-öl) *adj* eterosessuale

hiccup (*hi*-kap) *n* singhiozzo *m*

hide (haid) *n* pelle *f*

*hide (haid) *v* *nascondere; celare

hideous (*hi*-di-öss) *adj* orrendo

hierarchy (*haiö*-raa-ki) *n* gerarchia *f*

high (hai) *adj* alto

highway (*hai*-ᵘei) *n* via maestra; *nAm* autostrada *f*

hijack (*hai*-dʒæk) *v* dirottare

hijacker (*hai*-dʒæ-kö) *n* dirottatore *m*

hike (haik) *v* camminare

hill (hil) *n* collina *f*

hillside (*hil*-ssaid) *n* pendio *m*

hilltop (*hil*-top) *n* vetta *f*

hilly (*hi*-li) *adj* collinoso

him (him) *pron* lo, gli

himself (him-*ssêlf*) *pron* si; egli stesso

hinder (*hin*-dö) *v* ostacolare

hinge (hindʒ) *n* cardine *m*

hip (hip) *n* fianco *m*

hire (haiö) *v* noleggiare; **for ~** a nolo

hire-purchase (haiö-*pöö*-tʃöss) *n* vendita a rate

his (his) *adj* suo

historian (hi-*sstoo*-ri-ön) *n* storico *m*

historic (hi-*ssto*-rik) *adj* storico

historical (hi-*ssto*-ri-köl) *adj* storico

history (*hi*-sstö-ri) *n* storia *f*

hit (hit) *n* successo *m*

*****hit** (hit) *v* colpire; toccare

hitchhike (hitʃ-haik) *v* *fare l'autostop

hitchhiker (hitʃ-hai-kö) *n* autostoppista *m*

hoarse (hooss) *adj* roco, rauco

hobby (ho-bi) *n* passatempo *m*, hobby *m*

hobby-horse (ho-bi-hooss) *n* pallino *m*

hockey (ho-ki) *n* hockey *m*

hoist (hoisst) *v* issare

hold (hould) *n* stiva *f*

*****hold** (hould) *v* *tenere; conservare; ~ **on** *reggersi; ~ **up** *sostenere

hold-up (houl-dap) *n* rapina *f*

hole (houl) *n* buca *f*, buco *m*

holiday (ho-lö-di) *n* ferie *fpl*; festa *f*; ~ **camp** colonia di vacanze; ~ **resort** luogo di villeggiatura; **on** ~ **in** ferie

Holland (ho-lönd) Olanda *f*

hollow (ho-lou) *adj* vuoto

holy (hou-li) *adj* santo

homage (ho-midȝ) *n* omaggio *m*

home (houm) *n* casa *f*; ospizio *m*, abitazione *f*; *adv* a casa; **at** ~ **in** casa

home-made (houm-*meid*) *adj* casalingo

homesickness (houm-ssik-nöss) *n* nostalgia *f*

homosexual (hou-mö-*ssêk*-ʃu-öl) *adj* omosessuale

honest (o-nisst) *adj* onesto; sincero

honesty (o-ni-ssti) *n* onestà *f*

honey (ha-ni) *n* miele *m*

honeymoon (ha-ni-muun) *n* luna di miele

honk (hangk) *vAm* suonare il clacson

honour (o-nö) *n* onore *m*; *v* onorare, *rendere omaggio

honourable (o-nö-rö-böl) *adj* onorevole; onesto

hood (hud) *n* cappuccio *m*; *nAm* cofano *m*

hoof (huuf) *n* zoccolo *m*

hook (huk) *n* uncino *m*

hoot (huut) *v* suonare il clacson

hooter (huu-tö) *n* clacson *m*

hoover (huu-vö) *v* pulire con l'aspirapolvere

hop[1] (hop) *v* saltellare; *n* saltello *m*

hop[2] (hop) *n* luppolo *m*

hope (houp) *n* speranza *f*; *v* sperare

hopeful (houp-föl) *adj* speranzoso

hopeless (houp-löss) *adj* disperato

horizon (hö-*rai*-sön) *n* orizzonte *m*

horizontal (ho-ri-*son*-töl) *adj* orizzontale

horn (hoon) *n* corno *m*; clacson *m*

horrible (ho-ri-böl) *adj* orribile; spaventevole, atroce

horror (ho-rö) *n* raccapriccio *m*, orrore *m*

hors-d'œuvre (oo-*döövr*) *n* antipasto *m*

horse (hooss) *n* cavallo *m*

horseman (hooss-mön) *n* (pl -men) cavallerizzo *m*

horsepower (hooss-pauº) *n* cavallo vapore

horserace (hooss-reiss) *n* corsa di cavalli

horseradish (hooss-ræ-diʃ) *n* rafano *m*

horseshoe (hooss-ʃuu) *n* ferro di cavallo

horticulture (hoo-ti-kal-tʃö) *n* orticoltura *f*

hosiery (hou-ȝö-ri) *n* maglieria *f*

hospitable (ho-sspi-tö-böl) *adj* ospitale

hospital (ho-sspi-töl) *n* ospedale *m*

hospitality (ho-sspi-*tæ*-lö-ti) *n* ospitalità *f*

host (housst) *n* ospite *m*

hostage (ho-sstidȝ) *n* ostaggio *m*

hostel (*ho*-sstöl) *n* ostello *m*

hostess (*hou*-sstiss) *n* ospite *f*

hostile (*ho*-sstail) *adj* ostile

hot (hott) *adj* caldo

hotel (hou-*têl*) *n* albergo *m*

hot-tempered (hot-*têm*-pöd) *adj* irascibile

hour (au⁰) *n* ora *f*

hourly (*au⁰*-li) *adj* ogni ora

house (hauss) *n* casa *f*; abitazione *f*; immobile *m*; ~ **agent** agente immobiliare; ~ **block** *Am* isolato *m*; **public** ~ caffè *m*

houseboat (*hauss*-bout) *n* casa galleggiante

household (*hauss*-hould) *n* ménage *m*

housekeeper (*hauss*-kii-pö) *n* governante *f*

housekeeping (*hauss*-kii-ping) *n* faccende domestiche, faccende di casa

housemaid (*hauss*-meid) *n* domestica *f*

housewife (*hauss*-ᵘaif) *n* casalinga *f*

housework (*hauss*-ᵘöök) *n* lavori domestici

how (hau) *adv* come; che; ~ **many** quanto; ~ **much** quanto

however (hau-ê-vö) *conj* tuttavia, eppure

hug (hagh) *v* abbracciare; *n* abbraccio *m*

huge (hʲuudʒ) *adj* immenso, enorme

hum (ham) *v* canticchiare

human (*hʲuu*-mön) *adj* umano; ~ **being** essere umano

humanity (hʲu-*mæ*-nö-ti) *n* umanità *f*

humble (*ham*-böl) *adj* umile

humid (*hʲuu*-mid) *adj* umido

humidity (hʲu-*mi*-dö-ti) *n* umidità *f*

humorous (*hʲuu*-mö-röss) *adj* comico, spiritoso

humour (*hʲuu*-mö) *n* spirito *m*

hundred (*han*-dröd) *n* cento

Hungarian (hang-*ghêᵒ*-ri-ön) *adj* ungherese

Hungary (*hang*-ghö-ri) Ungheria *f*

hunger (*hang*-ghö) *n* fame *f*

hungry (*hang*-ghri) *adj* affamato

hunt (hant) *v* cacciare; *n* caccia *f*; ~ **for** cercare

hunter (*han*-tö) *n* cacciatore *m*

hurricane (*ha*-ri-kön) *n* uragano *m*; ~ **lamp** lanterna vento

hurry (*ha*-ri) *v* spicciarsi, affrettarsi; *n* fretta *f*; **in a** ~ in fretta

* **hurt** (hööt) *v* *dolere, ferire; *offendere

hurtful (*hööt*-föl) *adj* nocivo

husband (*has*-bönd) *n* marito *m*

hut (hat) *n* capanna *f*

hydrogen (*hai*-drö-dʒön) *n* idrogeno *m*

hygiene (*hai*-dʒiin) *n* igiene *f*

hygienic (hai-*dʒii*-nik) *adj* igienico

hymn (him) *n* inno *m*

hyphen (*hai*-fön) *n* lineetta *f*

hypocrisy (hi-*po*-krö-ssi) *n* ipocrisia *f*

hypocrite (*hi*-pö-krit) *n* ipocrita *m*

hypocritical (hi-pö-*kri*-ti-köl) *adj* ipocrita

hysterical (hi-*sstê*-ri-köl) *adj* isterico

I

I (ai) *pron* io

ice (aiss) *n* ghiaccio *m*

ice-bag (*aiss*-bægh) *n* borsa da ghiaccio

ice-cream (*aiss*-kriim) *n* gelato *m*

Iceland (*aiss*-lönd) Islanda *f*

Icelander (*aiss*-lön-dö) *n* islandese *m*

Icelandic (aiss-*læn*-dik) *adj* islandese

icon (*ai*-kon) *n* icona *f*

idea (ai-*diᵒ*) *n* idea *f*; trovata *f*, pensiero *m*; nozione *f*, concetto *m*

ideal (ai-*diᵒl*) *adj* ideale; *n* ideale *m*

identical (ai-*dên*-ti-köl) *adj* identico
identification (ai-dên-ti-fi-*kei*-ʃön) *n* identificazione *f*
identify (ai-*dên*-ti-fai) *v* identificare
identity (ai-*dên*-tö-ti) *n* identità *f*; ~ **card** carta d'identità
idiom (*i*-di-öm) *n* idioma *m*
idiomatic (i-di-ö-*mæ*-tik) *adj* idiomatico
idiot (*i*-di-öt) *n* idiota *m*
idiotic (i-di-*o*-tik) *adj* idiota
idle (*ai*-döl) *adj* ozioso; pigro; vano
idol (*ai*-döl) *n* idolo *m*
if (if) *conj* se
ignition (igh-*ni*-ʃön) *n* accensione *f*; ~ **coil** bobina di accensione
ignorant (*igh*-nö-rönt) *adj* ignorante
ignore (igh-*noo*) *v* ignorare
ill (il) *adj* ammalato; cattivo; malvagio
illegal (i-*lii*-ghöl) *adj* illegale
illegible (i-*lê*-dʒö-böl) *adj* illeggibile
illiterate (i-*li*-tö-röt) *n* analfabeta *m*
illness (*il*-nöss) *n* malattia *f*
illuminate (i-*luu*-mi-neit) *v* illuminare
illumination (i-luu-mi-*nei*-ʃön) *n* illuminazione *f*
illusion (i-*luu*-ʒön) *n* illusione *f*; inganno *m*
illustrate (*i*-lö-sstreit) *v* illustrare
illustration (i-lö-*sstrei*-ʃön) *n* illustrazione *f*
image (*i*-midʒ) *n* immagine *f*
imaginary (i-*mæ*-dʒi-nö-ri) *adj* immaginario
imagination (i-mæ-dʒi-*nei*-ʃön) *n* immaginazione *f*
imagine (i-*mæ*-dʒin) *v* immaginare; figurarsi
imitate (*i*-mi-teit) *v* imitare
imitation (i-mi-*tei*-ʃön) *n* imitazione *f*
immediate (i-*mii*-d'öt) *adj* immediato
immediately (i-*mii*-d'öt-li) *adv* subito, immediatamente

immense (i-*mênss*) *adj* smisurato, enorme, immenso
immigrant (*i*-mi-ghrönt) *n* immigrante *m*
immigrate (*i*-mi-ghreit) *v* immigrare
immigration (i-mi-*ghrei*-ʃön) *n* immigrazione *f*
immodest (i-*mo*-disst) *adj* immodesto
immunity (i-*m'uu*-nö-ti) *n* immunità *f*
immunize (*i*-m'u-nais) *v* immunizzare
impartial (im-*paa*-ʃöl) *adj* imparziale
impassable (im-*paa*-ssö-böl) *adj* impraticabile
impatient (im-*pei*-ʃönt) *adj* impaziente
impede (im-*piid*) *v* impedire
impediment (im-*pê*-di-mönt) *n* impedimento *m*
imperfect (im-*pöö*-fikt) *adj* imperfetto
imperial (im-*pi*ö-ri-öl) *adj* imperiale
impersonal (im-*pöö*-ssö-nöl) *adj* impersonale
impertinence (im-*pöö*-ti-nönss) *n* impertinenza *f*
impertinent (im-*pöö*-ti-nönt) *adj* impertinente, insolente
implement[1] (*im*-pli-mönt) *n* utensile *m*, strumento *m*
implement[2] (*im*-pli-mênt) *v* effettuare
imply (im-*plai*) *v* implicare; comportare
impolite (im-pö-*lait*) *adj* scortese
import[1] (im-*poot*) *v* importare
import[2] (*im*-poot) *n* importazione *f*; ~ **duty** dazio *m*
importance (im-*poo*-tönss) *n* rilievo *m*, importanza *f*
important (im-*poo*-tönt) *adj* rilevante, importante
importer (im-*poo*-tö) *n* importatore *m*
imposing (im-*pou*-sing) *adj* imponente
impossible (im-*po*-ssö-böl) *adj* impossibile
impotence (*im*-pö-tönss) *n* impotenza *f*

impotent (*im*-pö-tönt) *adj* impotente

impound (im-*paund*) *v* sequestrare

impress (im-*prêss*) *v* impressionare

impression (im-*prê*-ʃön) *n* impressione *f*

impressive (im-*prê*-ssiv) *adj* impressionante

imprison (im-*pri*-sön) *v* imprigionare

imprisonment (im-*pri*-sön-mönt) *n* imprigionamento *m*

improbable (im-*pro*-bö-böl) *adj* improbabile

improper (im-*pro*-pö) *adj* improprio

improve (im-*pruuv*) *v* migliorare

improvement (im-*pruuv*-mönt) *n* miglioramento *m*

improvise (*im*-prö-vais) *v* improvvisare

impudent (*im*-pⁱu-dönt) *adj* impudente

impulse (*im*-palss) *n* impulso *m*; stimolo *m*

impulsive (im-*pal*-ssiv) *adj* impulsivo

in (in) *prep* in; entro, su; *adv* dentro

inaccessible (i-næk-*ssê*-ssö-böl) *adj* inaccessibile

inaccurate (i-*næ*-kⁱu-röt) *adj* inesatto

inadequate (i-*næ*-di-kᵘöt) *adj* inadeguato

incapable (ing-*kei*-pö-böl) *adj* incapace

incense (*in*-ssênss) *n* incenso *m*

incident (*in*-ssi-dönt) *n* incidente *m*

incidental (in-ssi-*dên*-töl) *adj* incidentale

incite (in-*ssait*) *v* incitare

inclination (ing-kli-*nei*-ʃön) *n* inclinazione *f*

incline (ing-*klain*) *n* pendio *m*

inclined (ing-*klaind*) *adj* propenso, tendente; *be ~ to *v* *tendere

include (ing-*kluud*) *v* *comprendere, *includere

inclusive (ing-*kluu*-ssiv) *adj* compreso

income (*ing*-köm) *n* reddito *m*

income-tax (*ing*-köm-tækss) *n* imposta sul reddito

incompetent (ing-*kom*-pö-tönt) *adj* incompetente

incomplete (in-köm-*pliit*) *adj* incompleto

inconceivable (ing-kön-*ssii*-vö-böl) *adj* inconcepibile

inconspicuous (ing-kön-*sspi*-kⁱu-öss) *adj* insignificante

inconvenience (ing-kön-*vii*-nⁱönss) *n* scomodità *f*, inconveniente *m*

inconvenient (ing-kön-*vii*-nⁱönt) *adj* inconveniente; fastidioso

incorrect (ing-kö-*rêkt*) *adj* inesatto, scorretto

increase[1] (ing-*kriiss*) *v* aumentare; *salire, *accrescersi

increase[2] (*ing*-kriiss) *n* aumento *m*; incremento *m*

incredible (ing-*krê*-dö-böl) *adj* incredibile

incurable (ing-kⁱuᵒ-rö-böl) *adj* incurabile

indecent (in-*dii*-ssönt) *adj* indecente

indeed (in-*diid*) *adv* effettivamente

indefinite (in-*dê*-fi-nit) *adj* indefinito

indemnity (in-*dêm*-nö-ti) *n* risarcimento *m*, indennità *f*

independence (in-di-*pên*-dönss) *n* indipendenza *f*

independent (in-di-*pên*-dönt) *adj* indipendente; autonomo

index (*in*-dêkss) *n* indice *m*; *~ finger* indice *m*

India (*in*-di-ö) India *f*

Indian (*in*-di-ön) *adj* indiano; *n* indiano *m*

indicate (*in*-di-keit) *v* segnalare, indicare

indication (in-di-*kei*-ʃön) *n* indizio *m*, indicazione *f*

indicator (*in*-di-kei-tö) *n* freccia *f*

indifferent (in-*di*-fö-rönt) *adj* indifferente

indigestion (in-di-*dʒêss*-tʃön) *n* indigestione *f*

indignation (in-digh-*nei*-ʃön) *n* indignazione *f*

indirect (in-di-*rêkt*) *adj* indiretto

individual (in-di-*vi*-dʒu-öl) *adj* singolo, individuale; *n* singolo *m*, individuo *m*

Indonesia (in-dö-*nii*-si-ö) Indonesia *f*

Indonesian (in-dö-*nii*-si-ön) *adj* indonesiano

indoor (*in*-doo) *adj* in casa

indoors (in-*doos*) *adv* in casa

indulge (in-*daldʒ*) *v* cedere

industrial (in-*da*-sstri-öl) *adj* industriale; ~ **area** zona industriale

industrious (in-*da*-sstri-öss) *adj* laborioso

industry (*in*-dö-sstri) *n* industria *f*

inedible (i-*nê*-di-böl) *adj* immangiabile

inefficient (i-ni-*fi*-ʃönt) *adj* inefficace

inevitable (i-*nê*-vi-tö-böl) *adj* inevitabile

inexpensive (i-nik-*sspên*-ssiv) *adj* economico

inexperienced (i-nik-*sspiᵒ*-ri-önsst) *adj* inesperto

infant (*in*-fönt) *n* neonato *m*

infantry (*in*-fön-tri) *n* fanteria *f*

infect (in-*fêkt*) *v* infettare

infection (in-*fêk*-ʃön) *n* infezione *f*

infectious (in-*fêk*-ʃöss) *adj* contagioso

infer (in-*föö*) *v* *dedurre

inferior (in-*fiᵒ*-ri-ö) *adj* inferiore

infinite (*in*-fi-nöt) *adj* infinito

infinitive (in-*fi*-ni-tiv) *n* infinito *m*

infirmary (in-*föö*-mö-ri) *n* infermeria *f*

inflammable (in-*flæ*-mö-böl) *adj* infiammabile

inflammation (in-flö-*mei*-ʃön) *n* infiammazione *f*

inflatable (in-*flei*-tö-böl) *adj* gonfiabile

inflate (in-*fleit*) *v* gonfiare

inflation (in-*flei*-ʃön) *n* inflazione *f*

influence (*in*-flu-önss) *n* influenza *f*; *v* influire

influential (in-flu-*ên*-ʃöl) *adj* influente

influenza (in-flu-*ên*-sö) *n* influenza *f*

inform (in-*foom*) *v* informare; *mettere al corrente, comunicare

informal (in-*foo*-möl) *adj* informale

information (in-fö-*mei*-ʃön) *n* informazione *f*; ragguaglio *m*, comunicazione *f*; ~ **bureau** ufficio informazioni

infra-red (in-frö-*rêd*) *adj* infrarosso

infrequent (in-*frii*-kᵘönt) *adj* infrequente

ingredient (ing-*ghrii*-di-önt) *n* ingrediente *m*

inhabit (in-*hæ*-bit) *v* abitare

inhabitable (in-*hæ*-bi-tö-böl) *adj* abitabile

inhabitant (in-*hæ*-bi-tönt) *n* abitante *m*

inhale (in-*heil*) *v* aspirare

inherit (in-*hê*-rit) *v* ereditare

inheritance (in-*hê*-ri-tönss) *n* eredità *f*

initial (i-*ni*-ʃöl) *adj* iniziale; *n* iniziale *f*; *v* *apporre le iniziali

initiative (i-*ni*-ʃö-tiv) *n* iniziativa *f*

inject (in-*dʒêkt*) *v* iniettare

injection (in-*dʒêk*-ʃön) *n* iniezione *f*

injure (*in*-dʒö) *v* ferire; *offendere

injury (*in*-dʒö-ri) *n* ferita *f*; lesione *f*

injustice (in-*dʒa*-sstiss) *n* ingiustizia *f*

ink (ingk) *n* inchiostro *m*

inlet (*in*-lêt) *n* insenatura *f*

inn (in) *n* locanda *f*

inner (*i*-nö) *adj* interno; ~ **tube** camera d'aria

inn-keeper (*in*-kii-pö) *n* albergatore *m*

innocence (*i*-nö-ssönss) *n* innocenza *f*

innocent (*i*-nö-ssönt) *adj* innocente

inoculate (i-*no*-k'u-leit) *v* inoculare

inoculation (i-no-k'u-*lei*-∫ön) *n* inoculazione *f*

inquire (ing-k*u*ai*ö*) *v* informarsi, indagare

inquiry (ing-k*u*ai*ö*-ri) *n* domanda *f*, indagine *f*; inchiesta *f*; ~ **office** ufficio informazioni

inquisitive (ing-k*u*i-sö-tiv) *adj* inquisitivo

insane (in-*sein*) *adj* insano

inscription (in-*sskrip*-∫ön) *n* iscrizione *f*

insect (*in*-ssêkt) *n* insetto *m*; ~ **repellent** insettifugo *m*

insecticide (in-*ssêk*-ti-ssaid) *n* insetticida *m*

insensitive (in-*ssên*-ssö-tiv) *adj* insensibile

insert (in-*ssööt*) *v* inserire

inside (in-*ssaid*) *n* interno *m*; *adj* interno; *adv* dentro; *prep* dentro, dentro a; ~ **out** alla rovescia; **insides** interiora *fpl*

insight (*in*-ssait) *n* penetrazione *f*

insignificant (in-ssigh-*ni*-fi-könt) *adj* insignificante; irrilevante; futile

insist (in-*ssisst*) *v* insistere; persistere

insolence (*in*-ssö-lönss) *n* insolenza *f*

insolent (*in*-ssö-lönt) *adj* impertinente, insolente

insomnia (in-*ssom*-ni-ö) *n* insonnia *f*

inspect (in-*sspêkt*) *v* ispezionare

inspection (in-*sspêk*-∫ön) *n* ispezione *f*; controllo *m*

inspector (in-*sspêk*-tö) *n* ispettore *m*

inspire (in-*sspêkt*) *v* ispirare

install (in-*sstool*) *v* installare

installation (in-sstö-*lei*-∫ön) *n* installazione *f*

instalment (in-*sstool*-mönt) *n* rata *f*

instance (*in*-sstönss) *n* esempio *m*; caso *m*; **for** ~ per esempio

instant (*in*-sstönt) *n* istante *m*

instantly (*in*-sstönt-li) *adv* all'istante, subito, immediatamente

instead of (in-*sstêd* ov) invece di

instinct (*in*-sstingkt) *n* istinto *m*

institute (*in*-ssti-t'uut) *n* istituto *m*; istituzione *f*; *v* istituire

institution (in-ssti-*t'uu*-∫ön) *n* istituto *m*, istituzione *f*

instruct (in-*sstrakt*) *v* istruire

instruction (in-*sstrak*-∫ön) *n* istruzione *f*

instructive (in-*sstrak*-tiv) *adj* istruttivo

instructor (in-*sstrak*-tö) *n* istruttore *m*

instrument (*in*-sstru-mönt) *n* strumento *m*; **musical** ~ strumento musicale

insufficient (in-ssö-*fi*-∫önt) *adj* insufficiente

insulate (*in*-ss'u-leit) *v* isolare

insulation (in-ss'u-*lei*-∫ön) *n* isolamento *m*

insulator (in-ss'u-lei-tö) *n* isolatore *m*

insult[1] (in-*ssalt*) *v* insultare

insult[2] (*in*-ssalt) *n* insulto *m*

insurance (in-*∫u*ö-rönss) *n* assicurazione *f*; ~ **policy** polizza di assicurazione

insure (in-*∫u*ö) *v* assicurare

intact (in-*tækt*) *adj* intatto

intellect (*in*-tö-lêkt) *n* intelletto *m*

intellectual (in-tö-*lêk*-t∫u-öl) *adj* intellettuale

intelligence (in-*tê*-li-dʒönss) *n* intelligenza *f*

intelligent (in-*tê*-li-dʒönt) *adj* intelligente

intend (in-*tênd*) *v* *intendere

intense (in-*tênss*) *adj* intenso; veemente

intention (in-*tên*-∫ön) *n* intenzione *f*

intentional (in-*tên*-∫ö-nöl) *adj* intenzionale

intercourse (*in*-tö-kooss) *n* rapporto *m*

interest (*in*-trösst) *n* interesse *m*, interessamento *m*; *v* interessare

interesting (*in*-trö-ssting) *adj* interessante

interfere (in-tö-*fiö*) *v* interferire; ~ **with** intromettersi in

interference (in-tö-*fiö*-rönss) *n* interferenza *f*

interim (*in*-tö-rim) *n* interim *m*

interior (in-*tiö*-ri-ö) *n* interiore *m*

interlude (*in*-tö-luud) *n* intermezzo *m*

intermediary (in-tö-*mii*-d'ö-ri) *n* intermediario *m*

intermission (in-tö-*mi*-]ön) *n* intervallo *m*

internal (in-*töö*-nöl) *adj* interno

international (in-tö-*næ*-]ö-nöl) *adj* internazionale

interpret (in-*töö*-prit) *v* *fare da interprete; interpretare

interpreter (in-*töö*-pri-tö) *n* interprete *m*

interrogate (in-*tê*-rö-gheit) *v* interrogare

interrogation (in-tê-rö-*ghei*-]ön) *n* interrogatorio *m*

interrogative (in-tö-*ro*-ghö-tiv) *adj* interrogativo

interrupt (in-tö-*rapt*) *v* *interrompere

interruption (in-tö-*rap*-]ön) *n* interruzione *f*

intersection (in-tö-*ssêk*-]ön) *n* intersezione *f*

interval (*in*-tö-völ) *n* intervallo *m*

intervene (in-tö-*viin*) *v* *intervenire

interview (*in*-tö-v'uu) *n* intervista *f*

intestine (in-*tê*-sstin) *n* intestino *m*

intimate (*in*-ti-möt) *adj* intimo

into (*in*-tu) *prep* in

intolerable (in-*to*-lö-rö-böl) *adj* intollerabile

intoxicated (in-*tok*-ssi-kei-tid) *adj* ubriaco

intrigue (in-*triigh*) *n* intrigo *m*

introduce (in-trö-*d'uuss*) *v* presentare; *introdurre

introduction (in-trö-*dak*-]ön) *n* presentazione *f*; introduzione *f*

invade (in-*veid*) *v* *invadere

invalid[1] (*in*-vö-liid) *n* invalido *m*; *adj* invalido

invalid[2] (in-*væ*-lid) *adj* nullo

invasion (in-*vei*-3ön) *n* irruzione *f*, invasione *f*

invent (in-*vênt*) *v* inventare

invention (in-*vên*-]ön) *n* invenzione *f*

inventive (in-*vên*-tiv) *adj* inventivo

inventor (in-*vên*-tö) *n* inventore *m*

inventory (*in*-vön-tri) *n* inventario *m*

invert (in-*vööt*) *v* invertire

invest (in-*vêsst*) *v* investire

investigate (in-*vê*-ssti-gheit) *v* investigare

investigation (in-vê-ssti-*ghei*-]ön) *n* investigazione *f*

investment (in-*vêsst*-mönt) *n* investimento *m*

investor (in-*vê*-sstö) *n* finanziatore *m*

invisible (in-*vi*-sö-böl) *adj* invisibile

invitation (in-vi-*tei*-]ön) *n* invito *m*

invite (in-*vait*) *v* invitare

invoice (*in*-voiss) *n* fattura *f*

involve (in-*volv*) *v* *coinvolgere

inwards (*in*-ᵘöds) *adv* verso l'interno

iodine (*ai*-ö-diin) *n* iodio *m*

Iran (i-*raan*) Iran *m*

Iranian (i-*rei*-ni-ön) *adj* iraniano

Iraq (i-*raak*) Iraq *m*

Iraqi (i-*raa*-ki) *adj* iracheno

irascible (i-*ræ*-ssi-böl) *adj* irascibile

Ireland (*aiö*-lönd) Irlanda *f*

Irish (*aiö*-ri]) *adj* irlandese

Irishman (*aiö*-ri]-mön) *n* (pl -men) irlandese *m*

iron (*ai*-ön) *n* ferro *m*; ferro da stiro; di ferro; *v* stirare

ironical (ai-*ro*-ni-köl) *adj* ironico

ironworks (*ai*-ön-ᵘöökss) *n* ferriera *f*

irony (*ai⁰*-rö-ni) *n* ironia *f*

irregular (i-*rê*-gh'u-lö) *adj* irregolare

irreparable (i-*rê*-pö-rö-böl) *adj* irreparabile

irrevocable (i-*rê*-vö-kö-böl) *adj* irrevocabile

irritable (*i*-ri-tö-böl) *adj* irritabile

irritate (*i*-ri-teit) *v* irritare

is (is) *v* (pr be)

island (*ai*-lönd) *n* isola *f*

isolate (*ai*-ssö-leit) *v* isolare

isolation (ai-ssö-*lei*-[ö]n) *n* isolamento *m*

Israel (*is*-reil) Israele *m*

Israeli (is-*rei*-li) *adj* israeliano

issue (*i*-[fuu) *v* distribuire; *n* emissione *f*, tiratura *f*, edizione *f*; questione *f*, punto *m*; consequenza *f*, risultato *m*, conclusione *f*, esito *m*; uscita *f*

isthmus (*iss*-möss) *n* istmo *m*

Italian (i-*tæl*-'ön) *adj* italiano

italics (i-*tæ*-likss) *pl* caratteri corsivi

Italy (*i*-tö-li) Italia *f*

itch (it[) *n* prurito *m*; *v* prudere

item (*ai*-töm) *n* articolo *m*; punto *m*

itinerant (ai-*ti*-nö-rönt) *adj* ambulante

itinerary (ai-*ti*-nö-rö-ri) *n* itinerario *m*

ivory (*ai*-vö-ri) *n* avorio *m*

ivy (*ai*-vi) *n* edera *f*

J

jack (dʒæk) *n* cricco *m*

jacket (*dʒæ*-kit) *n* giacchetta *f*, giacca *f*; copertina *f*

jade (dʒeid) *n* giada *f*

jail (dʒeil) *n* prigione *f*

jailer (*dʒei*-lö) *n* carceriere *m*

jam (dʒæm) *n* marmellata *f*; ingorgo *m*

janitor (*dʒæ*-ni-tö) *n* portinaio *m*

January (*dʒæ*-n'u-ö-ri) gennaio

Japan (dʒö-*pæn*) Giappone *m*

Japanese (dʒæ-pö-*niis*) *adj* giapponese

jar (dʒaa) *n* giara *f*

jaundice (*dʒoon*-diss) *n* itterizia *f*

jaw (dʒoo) *n* mascella *f*

jealous (*dʒê*-löss) *adj* geloso

jealousy (*dʒê*-lö-ssi) *n* gelosia *f*

jeans (dʒiins) *pl* jeans *mpl*

jelly (*dʒê*-li) *n* gelatina *f*

jelly-fish (*dʒê*-li-fi[) *n* medusa *f*

jersey (*dʒöö*-si) *n* jersey *m*; maglione *m*

jet (dʒêt) *n* getto *m*; aviogetto *m*

jetty (*dʒê*-ti) *n* molo *m*

Jew (dʒuu) *n* ebreo *m*

jewel (*dʒuu*-öl) *n* gioiello *m*

jeweller (*dʒuu*-ö-lö) *n* gioielliere *m*

jewellery (*dʒuu*-öl-ri) *n* gioie; gioielli

Jewish (*dʒuu*-i[) *adj* ebraico

job (dʒob) *n* lavoro *m*; impiego *m*

jockey (*dʒo*-ki) *n* fantino *m*

join (dʒoin) *v* unire; unirsi a, associarsi; riunire

joint (dʒoint) *n* articolazione *f*; saldatura *f*; *adj* unito, congiunto

jointly (*dʒoint*-li) *adv* insieme

joke (dʒouk) *n* scherzo *m*

jolly (*dʒo*-li) *adj* allegro

Jordan (*dʒoo*-dön) Giordania *f*

Jordanian (dʒoo-*dei*-ni-ön) *adj* giordano

journal (*dʒöö*-nöl) *n* giornale *m*

journalism (*dʒöö*-nö-li-söm) *n* giornalismo *m*

journalist (*dʒöö*-nö-lisst) *n* giornalista *m*

journey (*dʒöö*-ni) *n* viaggio *m*

joy (dʒoi) *n* delizia *f*, gioia *f*

joyful (*dʒoi*-föl) *adj* allegro, gioioso

jubilee (*dʒuu*-bi-lii) *n* anniversario *m*

judge (dʒadʒ) *n* giudice *m*; *v* giudicare

judgment (*dʒadʒ*-mönt) *n* giudizio *m*

jug (dʒagh) *n* brocca *f*

juggler (*dʒa*-glö) *n* giocoliere *m*, giocoliera *f*

juice (dʒuuss) *n* succo *m*

juicy (*dʒuu*-ssi) *adj* succoso

July (dʒu-*lai*) luglio

jump (dʒamp) *v* saltare; *n* salto *m*

jumper (*dʒam*-pö) *n* golf *m*

junction (*dʒangk*-jön) *n* incrocio *m*; crocevia *m*

June (dʒuun) giugno

jungle (*dʒang*-ghöl) *n* giungla *f*

junior (*dʒuu*-n'ö) *adj* minore

junk (dʒangk) *n* spazzatura *f*

jury (*dʒuᵒ*-ri) *n* giuria *f*

just (dʒasst) *adj* giusto; esatto; *adv* appena; esattamente

justice (*dʒa*-sstiss) *n* giustizia *f*

justify (*dʒa*-ssti-fai) *v* giustificare

juvenile (*dʒuu*-vö-nail) *adj* giovanile

K

kangaroo (kæng-ghö-*ruu*) *n* canguro *m*

keel (kiil) *n* chiglia *f*

keen (kiin) *adj* appassionato; aguzzo

***keep** (kiip) *v* *tenere; *mantenere; continuare; ~ **away from** *tenersi lontano da; ~ **off** lasciar *stare; ~ **on** continuare; ~ **quiet** *tacere; ~ **up** perseverare; ~ **up with** *stare al passo con

keg (kêgh) *n* bariletto *m*

kennel (*kê*-nöl) *n* canile *m*

Kenya (*kê*-n'ö) Kenia *m*

kerosene (*kê*-rö-ssiin) *n* petrolio *m*

ketchup (*kê*-tʃap) *n* ketchup *m*

kettle (*kê*-töl) *n* bollitore *m*

key (kii) *n* chiave *f*

keyhole (*kii*-houl) *n* buco della serra-tura

khaki (*kaa*-ki) *n* kaki *m*

kick (kik) *v* tirare calci, *prendere a calci; *n* calcio *m*, pedata *f*

kick-off (ki-*kof*) *n* calcio d'inizio

kid (kid) *n* bambino *m*; capretto *m*; *v* stuzzicare

kidney (*kid*-ni) *n* rene *m*

kill (kil) *v* ammazzare, *uccidere

kilogram (*ki*-lö-ghræm) *n* chilo *m*

kilometre (*ki*-lö-mii-tö) *n* chilometro *m*

kind (kaind) *adj* gentile, benevolo; buono; *n* genere *m*

kindergarten (*kin*-dö-ghaa-tön) *n* giardino d'infanzia, asilo infantile

king (king) *n* re *m*

kingdom (*king*-döm) *n* regno *m*

kiosk (*kii*-ossk) *n* chiosco *m*

kiss (kiss) *n* bacio *m*; *v* baciare

kit (kit) *n* corredo *m*

kitchen (*ki*-tʃin) *n* cucina *f*; ~ **garden** orto *m*

kleenex (*klii*-nêkss) *n* fazzoletto di carta

knapsack (*næp*-ssæk) *n* zaino *m*

knave (neiv) *n* fante *m*

knee (nii) *n* ginocchio *m*

kneecap (*nii*-kæp) *n* rotula *f*

***kneel** (niil) *v* inginocchiarsi

knew (n'uu) *v* (p know)

knickers (*ni*-kös) *pl* mutandine *fpl*

knife (naif) *n* (pl knives) coltello *m*

knight (nait) *n* cavaliere *m*

***knit** (nit) *v* lavorare a maglia

knob (nob) *n* manopola *f*

knock (nok) *v* bussare; *n* colpo *m*; ~ **against** urtare contro; ~ **down** atterrare

knot (not) *n* nodo *m*; *v* annodare

***know** (nou) *v* *sapere, *conoscere

knowledge (*no*-lidʒ) *n* conoscenza *f*

knuckle (*na*-köl) *n* nocca *f*

L

label (*lei*-böl) *n* etichetta *f*; *v* etichettare

laboratory (lö-*bo*-rö-tö-ri) *n* laboratorio *m*

labour (*lei*-bö) *n* lavoro *m*; doglie *fpl*; *v* lavorare sodo, faticare; **labor permit** *Am* permesso di lavoro

labourer (*lei*-bö-rö) *n* operaio *m*

labour-saving (*lei*-bö-ssei-ving) *adj* che risparmia lavoro

labyrinth (*læ*-bö-rinθ) *n* labirinto *m*

lace (leiss) *n* merletto *m*; laccio *m*

lack (læk) *n* mancanza *f*; *v* mancare

lacquer (*læ*-kö) *n* lacca *f*

lad (læd) *n* giovane *m*, ragazzo *m*

ladder (*læ*-dö) *n* scala *f*

lady (*lei*-di) *n* signora *f*; **ladies' room** gabinetto per signore

lagoon (lö-*ghuun*) *n* laguna *f*

lake (leik) *n* lago *m*

lamb (læm) *n* agnello *m*

lame (leim) *adj* paralitico, zoppicante, zoppo

lamentable (*læ*-mön-tö-böl) *adj* lamentevole

lamp (læmp) *n* lampada *f*

lamp-post (*læmp*-pousst) *n* lampione *m*

lampshade (*læmp*-[eid) *n* paralume *m*

land (lænd) *n* paese *m*, terra *f*; *v* atterrare; sbarcare

landlady (*lænd*-lei-di) *n* affittacamere *f*

landlord (*lænd*-lood) *n* padrone di casa, proprietario *m*; affittacamere *m*

landmark (*lænd*-maak) *n* punto di riferimento; pietra miliare

landscape (*lænd*-sskeip) *n* paesaggio *m*

lane (lein) *n* vicolo *m*, sentiero *m*; corsia *f*

language (*læng*-gh^uidჳ) *n* lingua *f*; ~ **laboratory** laboratorio linguistico

lantern (*læn*-tön) *n* lanterna *f*

lapel (lö-*pêl*) *n* risvolta *f*

larder (*laa*-dö) *n* dispensa *f*

large (laadჳ) *adj* grande; spazioso

lark (laak) *n* allodola *f*

laryngitis (læ-rin-*dჳai*-tiss) *n* laringite *f*

last (laasst) *adj* ultimo; scorso; *v* durare; **at** ~ finalmente

lasting (*laa*-ssting) *adj* duraturo, durevole

latchkey (*lætʃ*-kii) *n* chiave di casa

late (leit) *adj* tardivo; in ritardo

lately (*leit*-li) *adv* ultimamente, recentemente

lather (*laa*-ðö) *n* schiuma *f*

Latin America (*læ*-tin ö-*mê*-ri-kö) America Latina

Latin-American (læ-tin-ö-*mê*-ri-kön) *adj* latino americano

latitude (*læ*-ti-tⁱuud) *n* latitudine *f*

laugh (laaf) *v* *ridere; *n* riso *m*

laughter (*laaf*-tö) *n* risata *f*

launch (loontʃ) *v* lanciare; *n* motonave *f*

launching (*loon*-tʃing) *n* varo *m*

launderette (loon-dö-*rêt*) *n* lavanderia automatica

laundry (*loon*-dri) *n* lavanderia *f*; bucato *m*

lavatory (*læ*-vö-tö-ri) *n* gabinetto *m*

lavish (*læ*-viʃ) *adj* prodigo

law (loo) *n* legge *f*; ~ **court** tribunale *m*

lawful (*loo*-föl) *adj* legale

lawn (loon) *n* prato *m*

lawsuit (*loo*-ssuut) *n* processo *m*, causa *f*

lawyer (*loo*-ⁱö) *n* avvocato *m*; giurista *m*

laxative (*læk*-ssö-tiv) *n* lassativo *m*

*lay (lei) v collocare, *mettere, posare; ~ **bricks** murare

layer (lei⁰) n strato m

layman (lei-mön) n profano m

lazy (lei-si) adj pigro

lead¹ (liid) n vantaggio m; guida f; guinzaglio m

lead² (lêd) n piombo m

*lead (liid) v *dirigere

leader (lii-dö) n leader m, dirigente m

leadership (lii-dö-ſip) n comando m

leading (lii-ding) adj dominante, principale

leaf (liif) n (pl leaves) foglia f

league (liigh) n lega f

leak (liik) n sgocciolamento m

leaky (lii-ki) adj perdente

lean (liin) adj magro

*lean (liin) v appoggiarsi

leap (liip) n salto m

*leap (liip) v balzare

leap-year (liip-¹jö⁰) n anno bisestile

*learn (löön) v imparare

learner (löö-nö) n principiante m

lease (liiss) n contratto di affitto; locazione f; v *dare in locazione, *dare in affitto; *prendere in affitto

leash (liiʃ) n guinzaglio m

least (liisst) adj minimo; **at** ~ almeno

leather (lê-ðö) n pelle f; di pelle

leave (liiv) n congedo m

*leave (liiv) v partire, lasciare; ~ **out** *omettere

Lebanese (lê-bö-niis) adj libanese

Lebanon (lê-bö-nön) Libano m

lecture (lêk-tʃö) n lezione f, conferenza f

left¹ (lêft) adj sinistro

left² (lêft) v (p, pp leave)

left-hand (lêft-hænd) adj sinistro, a sinistra

left-handed (lêft-hæn-did) adj mancino

leg (lêgh) n piede m, gamba f

legacy (lê-ghö-ssi) n legato m

legal (lii-ghöl) adj legittimo, legale; giuridico

legalization (lii-ghö-lai-sei-ſön) n legalizzazione f

legation (li-ghei-ſön) n legazione f

legible (lê-dʒi-böl) adj leggibile

legitimate (li-dʒi-ti-möt) adj legittimo

leisure (lê-ʒö) n comodo m

lemon (lê-mön) n limone m

lemonade (lê-mö-neid) n limonata f

*lend (lênd) v prestare

length (lêngθ) n lunghezza f

lengthen (lêng-θön) v allungare

lengthways (lêngθ-ᵘeis) adv per il lungo

lens (lêns) n lente f; **telephoto** ~ teleobbiettivo m; **zoom** ~ zoom m

leprosy (lê-prö-ssi) n lebbra f

less (lêss) adv meno

lessen (lê-ssön) v diminuire

lesson (lê-ssön) n lezione f

*let (lêt) v lasciare; affittare; ~ **down** *deludere

letter (lê-tö) n lettera f; ~ **of credit** lettera di credito; ~ **of recommendation** lettera di raccomandazione

letter-box (lê-tö-bokss) n cassetta postale

lettuce (lê-tiss) n lattuga f

level (lê-völ) adj piano; piatto, spianato; n livello m; livella f; v pareggiare, livellare; ~ **crossing** passaggio a livello

lever (lii-vö) n leva f

Levis (lii-vais) pl jeans mpl

liability (lai-ö-bi-lö-ti) n responsabilità f

liable (lai-ö-böl) adj responsabile; ~ **to** soggetto a

liberal (li-bö-röl) adj liberale; generoso, prodigo

liberation (li-bö-rei-ſön) n liberazione f

Liberia (lai-*bi⁰*-ri-ö) Liberia *f*
Liberian (lai-*bi⁰*-ri-ön) *adj* liberiano
liberty (*li*-bö-ti) *n* libertà *f*
library (*lai*-brö-ri) *n* biblioteca *f*
licence (*lai*-ssönss) *n* licenza *f*;
  driving ~ patente di guida; **~ number** *Am* numero di targa; **~ plate**
  Am targa automobilistica
license (*lai*-ssönss) *v* autorizzare
lick (lik) *v* leccare
lid (lid) *n* coperchio *m*
lie (lai) *v* mentire; *n* menzogna *f*
***lie** (lai) *v* *star disteso; **~ down**
  sdraiarsi
life (laif) *n* (pl lives) vita *f*; **~ insurance** assicurazione sulla vita
lifebelt (*laif*-bêlt) *n* cintura di salvataggio
lifetime (*laif*-taim) *n* vita *f*
lift (lift) *v* alzare, sollevare; *n* ascensore *m*
light (lait) *n* luce *f*; *adj* leggero; chiaro; **~ bulb** bulbo *m*
***light** (lait) *v* *accendere
lighter (*lai*-tö) *n* accendino *m*
lighthouse (*lait*-hauss) *n* faro *m*
lighting (*lai*-ting) *n* illuminazione *f*
lightning (*lait*-ning) *n* lampo *m*
like (laik) *v* *voler bene; gradire; *adj*
  simile; *conj* come
likely (*lai*-kli) *adj* probabile
like-minded (laik-*main*-did) *adj* unanime
likewise (*laik*-ᵁais) *adv* nello stesso
  modo, inoltre
lily (*li*-li) *n* giglio *m*
limb (lim) *n* membro *m*
lime (laim) *n* calce *f*; tiglio *m*; cedro
  m
limetree (*laim*-trii) *n* tiglio *m*
limit (*li*-mit) *n* limite *m*; *v* limitare
limp (limp) *v* zoppicare; *adj* floscio
line (lain) *n* riga *f*; tratto *m*; cordicella *f*; linea *f*; fila *f*; **stand in ~** *Am*

***fare la coda
linen (*li*-nin) *n* lino *m*; biancheria *f*
liner (*lai*-nö) *n* nave di linea
lingerie (*long*-3ö-rii) *n* biancheria *f*
lining (*lai*-ning) *n* fodera *f*
link (lingk) *v* collegare; *n* legame *m*;
  maglia *f*
lion (*lai*-ön) *n* leone *m*
lip (lip) *n* labbro *m*
lipsalve (*lip*-ssaav) *n* pomata per le
  labbra
lipstick (*lip*-sstik) *n* rossetto *m*
liqueur (li-*k'u⁰*) *n* liquore *m*
liquid (*li*-kᵁid) *adj* liquido; *n* liquido
  m
liquor (*li*-kö) *n* bevande alcooliche
liquorice (*li*-kö-riss) *n* liquirizia *f*
list (lisst) *n* elenco *m*; *v* elencare
listen (*li*-ssön) *v* sentire, ascoltare
listener (*liss*-nö) *n* ascoltatore *m*
literary (*li*-trö-ri) *adj* letterario
literature (*li*-trö-tfö) *n* letteratura *f*
litre (*lii*-tö) *n* litro *m*
litter (*li*-tö) *n* rifiuti; figliata *f*
little (*li*-töl) *adj* piccolo; poco
live¹ (liv) *v* *vivere; abitare
live² (laiv) *adj* vivo
livelihood (*laiv*-li-hud) *n* sussistenza *f*
lively (*laiv*-li) *adj* vivace
liver (*li*-vö) *n* fegato *m*
living-room (*li*-ving-ruum) *n* soggiorno
  m, salotto *m*
load (loud) *n* carico *m*; peso *m*; *v* caricare
loaf (louf) *n* (pl loaves) pagnotta *f*
loan (loun) *n* prestito *m*
lobby (*lo*-bi) *n* atrio *m*; ridotto *m*
lobster (*lob*-sstö) *n* aragosta *f*
local (*lou*-köl) *adj* locale; **~ call** chiamata locale; **~ train** treno locale
locality (lou-*kæ*-lö-ti) *n* località *f*
locate (lou-*keit*) *v* localizzare
location (lou-*kei*-fön) *n* posizione *f*
lock (lok) *v* *chiudere a chiave; *n* ser-

ratura *f*; chiusa *f*; ~ **up** *chiudere a chiave

locomotive (lou-kö-*mou*-tiv) *n* locomotiva *f*

lodge (lodʒ) *v* alloggiare; *n* padiglione da caccia

lodger (*lo*-dʒö) *n* inquilino *m*

lodgings (*lo*-dʒings) *pl* alloggio *m*

log (logh) *n* ceppo *m*

logic (*lo*-dʒik) *n* logica *f*

logical (*lo*-dʒi-köl) *adj* logico

lonely (*loun*-li) *adj* solitario

long (long) *adj* lungo; ~ **for** bramare; **no longer** non... più

longing (*long*-ing) *n* bramosia *f*

longitude (*lon*-dʒi-t¹uud) *n* longitudine *f*

look (luk) *v* guardare; sembrare, *aver l'aria; *n* occhiata *f*, sguardo *m*; aspetto *m*; ~ **after** occuparsi di, badare a; ~ **at** guardare; ~ **for** cercare; ~ **out** *stare attento, *fare attenzione; ~ **up** cercare

looking-glass (*lu*-king-ghlaass) *n* specchio *m*

loop (luup) *n* nodo scorsoio

loose (luuss) *adj* slegato

loosen (*luu*-ssön) *v* slegare

lord (lood) *n* lord *m*

lorry (*lo*-ri) *n* autocarro *m*

*lose** (luus) *v* *perdere, smarrire

loss (loss) *n* perdita *f*

lost (losst) *adj* smarrito; ~ **and found** oggetti smarriti; ~ **property office** ufficio oggetti smarriti

lot (lot) *n* fortuna *f*, sorte *f*; massa *f*, quantità *f*

lotion (*lou*-ʃön) *n* lozione *f*; **after-shave** ~ lozione dopo barba

lottery (*lo*-tö-ri) *n* lotteria *f*

loud (laud) *adj* forte, alto

loud-speaker (laud-*sspii*-kö) *n* altoparlante *m*

lounge (laundʒ) *n* salone *m*

louse (lauss) *n* (pl lice) pidocchio *m*

love (lav) *v* amare; *n* amore *m*; **in** ~ innamorato

lovely (*lav*-li) *adj* delizioso, splendido, bello

lover (*la*-vö) *n* amante *m*

love-story (*lav*-sstoo-ri) *n* storia d'amore

low (lou) *adj* basso; abbattuto; ~ **tide** bassa marea

lower (*lou*-ö) *v* abbassare; ribassare; calare; *adj* inferiore

lowlands (*lou*-lönds) *pl* bassopiano *m*

loyal (*loi*-öl) *adj* leale

lubricate (*luu*-bri-keit) *v* lubrificare

lubrication (luu-bri-*kei*-ʃön) *n* lubrificazione *f*; ~ **oil** lubrificante *m*; ~ **system** sistema lubrificante

luck (lak) *n* successo *m*, fortuna *f*; caso *m*; **bad** ~ sfortuna *f*

lucky (*la*-ki) *adj* fortunato; ~ **charm** portafortuna *m*

ludicrous (*luu*-di-kröss) *adj* irrisorio, ridicolo

luggage (*la*-ghidʒ) *n* bagaglio *m*; **hand** ~ bagaglio a mano; **left** ~ **office** deposito bagagli; ~ **rack** portabagagli *m*; ~ **van** bagagliaio *m*

lukewarm (*luuk*-ᵘoom) *adj* tiepido

lumbago (lam-*bei*-ghou) *n* lombaggine *f*

luminous (*luu*-mi-nöss) *adj* luminoso

lump (lamp) *n* nodo *m*, grumo *m*, pezzo *m*; protuberanza *f*; ~ **of sugar** zolletta di zucchero; ~ **sum** somma globale

lumpy (*lam*-pi) *adj* grumoso

lunacy (*luu*-nö-ssi) *n* pazzia *f*

lunatic (*luu*-nö-tik) *adj* pazzo; *n* pazzo *m*

lunch (lantʃ) *n* pranzo *m*, seconda colazione, colazione *f*

luncheon (*lan*-tʃön) *n* colazione *f*

lung (lang) *n* polmone *m*

lust (lasst) *n* concupiscenza *f*

luxurious (lagh-ʒuᵒ-ri-öss) *adj* lussuoso

luxury (*lak*-ʃö-ri) *n* lusso *m*

M

machine (mö-*ʃiin*) *n* apparecchio *m*, macchina *f*

machinery (mö-*ʃii*-nö-ri) *n* macchinario *m*; meccanismo *m*

mackerel (*mæ*-kröl) *n* (pl ~) sgombro *m*

mackintosh (*mæ*-kin-toʃ) *n* impermeabile *m*

mad (mæd) *adj* matto, pazzo, folle; rabbioso

madam (*mæ*-döm) *n* signora *f*

madness (*mæd*-nöss) *n* pazzia *f*

magazine (mæ-ghö-*siin*) *n* rivista *f*

magic (*mæ*-dʒik) *n* magia *f*; *adj* magico

magician (mö-*dʒi*-ʃön) *n* prestigiatore *m*

magistrate (*mæ*-dʒi-sstreit) *n* magistrato *m*

magnetic (mægh-*nê*-tik) *adj* magnetico

magneto (mægh-*nii*-tou) *n* (pl ~s) magnete *m*

magnificent (mægh-*ni*-fi-ssönt) *adj* magnifico; grandioso, splendido

magpie (*mægh*-pai) *n* gazza *f*

maid (meid) *n* cameriera *f*

maiden name (*mei*-dön neim) cognome da nubile

mail (meil) *n* posta *f*; *v* impostare; ~ **order** *Am* vaglia postale

mailbox (*meil*-bokss) *nAm* cassetta postale

main (mein) *adj* principale; maggiore; ~ **deck** ponte di coperta; ~ **line** linea principale; ~ **road** strada principale; ~ **street** via principale

mainland (*mein*-lönd) *n* terraferma *f*

mainly (*mein*-li) *adv* principalmente

mains (meins) *pl* linea elettrica principale

maintain (mein-*tein*) *v* *mantenere

maintenance (*mein*-tö-nönss) *n* manutenzione *f*

maize (meis) *n* granturco *m*

major (*mei*-dʒö) *adj* grande; maggiore; *n* maggiore *m*

majority (mö-*dʒo*-rö-ti) *n* maggioranza *f*

***make** (meik) *v* *fare; guadagnare; *riuscire; ~ **do with** arrangiarsi con; ~ **good** compensare; ~ **up** compilare

make-up (*mei*-kap) *n* trucco *m*

malaria (mö-*lêᵒ*-ri-ö) *n* malaria *f*

Malay (mö-*lei*) *n* malese *m*

Malaysia (mö-*lei*-si-ö) Malesia *f*

Malaysian (mö-*lei*-si-ön) *adj* malese

male (meil) *adj* maschio

malicious (mö-*li*-ʃöss) *adj* malevolo

malignant (mö-*ligh*-nönt) *adj* maligno

mallet (*mæ*-lit) *n* maglio *m*

malnutrition (mæl-n¹u-*tri*-ʃön) *n* denutrizione *f*

mammal (*mæ*-möl) *n* mammifero *m*

mammoth (*mæ*-möθ) *n* mammut *m*

man (mæn) *n* (pl men) uomo *m*; **men's room** gabinetto per signori

manage (*mæ*-nidʒ) *v* *dirigere; *riuscire

manageable (*mæ*-ni-dʒö-böl) *adj* maneggiabile

management (*mæ*-nidʒ-mönt) *n* direzione *f*; gestione *f*

manager (*mæ*-ni-dʒö) *n* capo *m*, direttore *m*

mandarin (*mæn*-dö-rin) *n* mandarino *m*

mandate (*mæn*-deit) *n* mandato *m*

manger (*mein*-dʒö) *n* mangiatoia *f*

manicure (*mæ*-ni-kʲuᵒ) *n* manicure *f*; *v* curare le unghie

mankind (*mæn*-*kaind*) *n* umanità *f*

mannequin (*mæ*-nö-kin) *n* indossatrice *f*

manner (*mæ*-nö) *n* modo *m*, maniera *f*; **manners** *pl* maniere

man-of-war (*mæ*-növ-ᵘ*oo*) *n* nave da guerra

manor-house (*mæ*-nö-hauss) *n* casa padronale

mansion (*mæn*-ʃön) *n* palazzo *m*

manual (*mæ*-nʲu-öl) *adj* manuale

manufacture (*mæ*-nʲu-*fæk*-tʃö) *v* confezionare, fabbricare

manufacturer (*mæ*-nʲu-*fæk*-tʃö-rö) *n* fabbricante *m*

manure (mö-*nʲu*ᵒ) *n* concime *m*

manuscript (*mæ*-nʲu-sskript) *n* manoscritto *m*

many (*mê*-ni) *adj* molti

map (mæp) *n* carta *f*; mappa *f*; pianta *f*

maple (*mei*-pöl) *n* acero *m*

marble (*maa*-böl) *n* marmo *m*; pallina *f*

March (maatʃ) *n* marzo

march (maatʃ) *v* marciare; *n* marcia *f*

mare (mê*ᵒ*) *n* cavalla *f*

margarine (maa-dʒö-*riin*) *n* margarina *f*

margin (*maa*-dʒin) *n* margine *m*

maritime (*mæ*-ri-taim) *adj* marittimo

mark (maak) *v* marcare; segnare; caratterizzare; *n* segno *m*; voto *m*; bersaglio *m*

market (*maa*-kit) *n* mercato *m*

market-place (*maa*-kit-pleiss) *n* piazza del mercato

marmalade (*maa*-mö-leid) *n* marmellata *f*

marriage (*mæ*-ridʒ) *n* matrimonio *m*

marrow (*mæ*-rou) *n* midollo *m*

marry (*mæ*-ri) *v* sposare; **married couple** coniugi *mpl*

marsh (maaʃ) *n* palude *f*

marshy (*maa*-ʃi) *adj* paludoso

martyr (*maa*-tö) *n* martire *m*

marvel (*maa*-völ) *n* meraviglia *f*; *v* meravigliarsi

marvellous (*maa*-vö-löss) *adj* meraviglioso

mascara (*mæ*-sskaa-rö) *n* mascara *m*

masculine (*mæ*-sskʲu-lin) *adj* maschile

mash (mæʃ) *v* schiacciare

mask (maassk) *n* maschera *f*

Mass (mæss) *n* messa *f*

mass (mæss) *n* massa *f*; ~ **production** produzione in serie

massage (*mæ*-ssaaʒ) *n* massaggio *m*; *v* massaggiare

masseur (*mæ*-ssöö) *n* massaggiatore *m*

massive (*mæ*-ssiv) *adj* massiccio

mast (maasst) *n* albero *m*

master (*maa*-sstö) *n* maestro *m*; padrone *m*; professore *m*, insegnante *m*; *v* dominare

masterpiece (*maa*-sstö-piiss) *n* capolavoro *m*

mat (mæt) *n* stuoia *f*; *adj* pallido, opaco

match (mætʃ) *n* fiammifero *m*; partita *f*; *v* intonarsi con

match-box (*mætʃ*-bokss) *n* scatola di fiammiferi

material (mö-*tiᵒ*-ri-öl) *n* materiale *m*; stoffa *f*; *adj* materiale

mathematical (*mæ*-θö-*mæ*-ti-köl) *adj* matematico

mathematics (*mæ*-θö-*mæ*-tikss) *n* matematica *f*

matrimonial (*mæ*-tri-*mou*-ni-öl) *adj* matrimoniale

matrimony (*mæ*-tri-mö-ni) *n* matrimonio *m*

matter (*mæ*-tö) *n* materia *f*; affare

m, questione *f*, faccenda *f*; *v* *avere importanza; **as a ~ of fact** effettivamente, infatti

matter-of-fact (mæ-tö-röv-*fækt*) *adj* prosaico

mattress (*mæ*-tröss) *n* materasso *m*

mature (mö-t'u°) *adj* maturo

maturity (mö-t'u°-rö-ti) *n* maturità *f*

mausoleum (moo-ssö-*lii*-öm) *n* mausoleo *m*

mauve (mouv) *adj* lilla

May (mei) maggio

*may (mei) *v* *potere

maybe (*mei*-bii) *adv* forse

mayor (mê°) *n* sindaco *m*

maze (meis) *n* labirinto *m*

me (mii) *pron* mi; me

meadow (*mê*-dou) *n* prato *m*

meal (miil) *n* pasto *m*

mean (miin) *adj* meschino; *n* media *f*

*mean (miin) *v* significare; *voler dire; *intendere

meaning (*mii*-ning) *n* significato *m*

meaningless (*mii*-ning-löss) *adj* insensato

means (miins) *n* mezzo *m*; **by no ~** in nessun modo

in the meantime (in ðö *miin*-taim) intanto, nel frattempo

meanwhile (*miin*-ᵁail) *adv* frattanto

measles (*mii*-söls) *n* morbillo *m*

measure (*mê*-ʒö) *v* misurare; *n* misura *f*

meat (miit) *n* carne *f*

mechanic (mi-*kæ*-nik) *n* meccanico *m*

mechanical (mi-*kæ*-ni-köl) *adj* meccanico

mechanism (*mê*-kö-ni-söm) *n* meccanismo *m*

medal (*mê*-döl) *n* medaglia *f*

mediaeval (mê-di-*ii*-völ) *adj* medievale

mediate (*mii*-di-eit) *v* *fare da intermediario

mediator (*mii*-di-ei-tö) *n* mediatore *m*

medical (*mê*-di-köl) *adj* medico

medicine (*méd*-ssin) *n* medicamento *m*; medicina *f*

meditate (*mê*-di-teit) *v* meditare

Mediterranean (mê-di-tö-*rei*-ni-ön) Mediterraneo *m*

medium (*mii*-di-öm) *adj* mediocre, medio

*meet (miit) *v* incontrare

meeting (*mii*-ting) *n* assemblea *f*, riunione *f*; incontro *m*

meeting-place (*mii*-ting-pleiss) *n* luogo di riunione

melancholy (*mê*-löng-kö-li) *n* malinconia *f*

mellow (*mê*-lou) *adj* polposo

melodrama (*mê*-lö-draa-mö) *n* melodramma *m*

melody (*mê*-lö-di) *n* melodia *f*

melon (*mê*-lön) *n* melone *m*

melt (mêlt) *v* *fondere

member (*mêm*-bö) *n* membro *m*; **Member of Parliament** deputato *m*

membership (*mêm*-bö-ʃip) *n* qualità di membro

memo (*mê*-mou) *n* (pl ~s) nota *f*

memorable (*mê*-mö-rö-böl) *adj* memorabile

memorial (mö-*moo*-ri-öl) *n* monumento commemorativo

memorize (*mê*-mö-rais) *v* imparare a memoria

memory (*mê*-mö-ri) *n* memoria *f*; ricordo *m*

mend (mênd) *v* rammendare, riparare

menstruation (mên-sstru-*ei*-ʃön) *n* mestruazione *f*

mental (*mên*-töl) *adj* mentale

mention (*mên*-ʃön) *v* nominare, menzionare; *n* citazione *f*, menzione *f*

menu (*mê*-nⁱuu) *n* carta *f*, menu *m*

merchandise (*möö*-tʃön-dais) *n* merce *f*, mercanzia *f*

merchant (*möö*-tʃönt) *n* commerciante *m*, mercante *m*

mercury (*möö*-k'u-ri) *n* mercurio *m*

mercy (*möö*-ssi) *n* misericordia *f*, clemenza *f*

mere (miᵒ) *adj* mero

merely (*miᵒ*-li) *adv* soltanto

merger (*möö*-dʒö) *n* fusione *f*

merit (*mê*-rit) *v* meritare; *n* merito *m*

mermaid (*möö*-meid) *n* sirena *f*

merry (*mê*-ri) *adj* allegro

merry-go-round (*mê*-ri-ghou-raund) *n* giostra *f*

mesh (mêʃ) *n* maglia *f*

mess (mêss) *n* disordine *m*; ~ **up** pasticciare

message (*mê*-ssidʒ) *n* commissione *f*, messaggio *m*

messenger (*mê*-ssin-dʒö) *n* messaggero *m*

metal (*mê*-töl) *n* metallo *m*; metallico

meter (*mii*-tö) *n* metro *m*

method (*mê*-θöd) *n* metodo *m*; ordine *m*

methodical (mö-*θo*-di-köl) *adj* metodico

methylated spirits (*mê*-θö-lei-tid sspiritss) alcool metilico

metre (*mii*-tö) *n* metro *m*

metric (*mê*-trik) *adj* metrico

Mexican (*mêk*-ssi-kön) *adj* messicano

Mexico (*mêk*-ssi-kou) Messico *m*

mezzanine (*mê*-sö-niin) *n* mezzanino *m*

microphone (*mai*-krö-foun) *n* microfono *m*

microwave oven (*mai*-krö-ᵘeiv a-vön) *n* forno a microonde *m*

midday (*mid*-dei) *n* mezzogiorno *m*

middle (*mi*-döl) *n* mezzo *m*; *adj* mezzo; **Middle Ages** medioevo *m*; ~ **class** ceto medio; **middle-class** *adj* borghese

midnight (*mid*-nait) *n* mezzanotte *f*

midst (midsst) *n* mezzo *m*

midsummer (*mid*-ssa-mö) *n* piena estate

midwife (*mid*-ᵘaif) *n* (pl -wives) levatrice *f*

might (mait) *n* potenza *f*

***might** (mait) *v* *potere

mighty (*mai*-ti) *adj* poderoso

migraine (*mi*-ghrein) *n* emicrania *f*

mild (maild) *adj* mite

mildew (*mil*-d'u) *n* muffa *f*

mile (mail) *n* miglio *m*

mileage (*mai*-lidʒ) *n* distanza in miglia

milepost (*mail*-pousst) *n* cartello indicatore

milestone (*mail*-sstoun) *n* pietra miliare

milieu (mii-l'öö) *n* ambiente *m*

military (*mi*-li-tö-ri) *adj* militare; ~ **force** forze militari

milk (milk) *n* latte *m*

milkman (*milk*-mön) *n* (pl -men) lattaio *m*

milk-shake (*milk*-ʃeik) *n* frappé *m*

milky (*mil*-ki) *adj* latteo

mill (mil) *n* macinino *m*; fabbrica *f*

miller (*mi*-lö) *n* mugnaio *m*

milliner (*mi*-li-nö) *n* modista *f*

million (*mil*-iön) *n* milione *m*

millionaire (mil-iö-nêᵒ) *n* milionario *m*

mince (minss) *v* tritare

mind (maind) *n* mente *f*; *v* *fare obiezione a; badare a, *fare attenzione

mine (main) *n* miniera *f*

miner (*mai*-nö) *n* minatore *m*

mineral (*mi*-nö-röl) *n* minerale *m*; ~ **water** acqua minerale

miniature (*min*-iö-tʃö) *n* miniatura *f*

minimum (*mi*-ni-möm) *n* minimo *m*

mining (*mai*-ning) *n* industria mineraria

minister (*mi*-ni-sstö) *n* ministro *m*;

pastore *m*; **Prime Minister** primo ministro

ministry (*mi*-ni-sstri) *n* ministero *m*

mink (mingk) *n* visone *m*

minor (*mai*-nö) *adj* piccolo, esiguo, minore; subordinato; *n* minorenne *m*

minority (mai-*no*-rö-ti) *n* minoranza *f*

mint (mint) *n* menta *f*

minus (*mai*-nöss) *prep* meno

minute[1] (*mi*-nit) *n* minuto *m*; **minutes** verbale *m*

minute[2] (mai-n'uut) *adj* minuto

miracle (*mi*-rö-köl) *n* miracolo *m*

miraculous (mi-*ræ*-k'u-löss) *adj* miracoloso

mirror (*mi*-rö) *n* specchio *m*

misbehave (miss-bi-*heiv*) *v* comportarsi male

miscarriage (miss-*kæ*-ridʒ) *n* aborto *m*

miscellaneous (mi-ssö-*lei*-ni-öss) *adj* misto

mischief (*miss*-tʃif) *n* birichinata *f*; male *m*, danno *m*, malizia *f*

mischievous (*miss*-tʃi-vöss) *adj* malizioso

miserable (*mi*-sö-rö-böl) *adj* misero, miserabile

misery (*mi*-sö-ri) *n* miseria *f*; bisogno *m*

misfortune (miss-*foo*-tʃên) *n* sfortuna *f*, avversità *f*

*mislay (miss-*lei*) *v* smarrire

misplaced (miss-*pleisst*) *adj* inopportuno; sbagliato

mispronounce (miss-prö-*naunss*) *v* pronunciar male

miss[1] (miss) *signorina f*

miss[2] (miss) *v* *rimpiangere

missing (*mi*-ssing) *adj* mancante; **~ person** persona scomparsa

mist (misst) *n* foschia *f*, nebbia *f*

mistake (mi-*ssteik*) *n* fallo *m*, sbaglio *m*, errore *m*

*mistake (mi-*ssteik*) *v* *confondere

mistaken (mi-*sstei*-kön) *adj* erroneo; **be ~** sbagliarsi

mister (*mi*-sstö) *n* signore *m*

mistress (*mi*-sströss) *n* signora *f*; padrona *f*; amante *f*

mistrust (miss-*trasst*) *v* diffidare di

misty (*mi*-ssti) *adj* nebbioso

*misunderstand (mi-ssan-dö-*sstænd*) *v* *fraintendere

misunderstanding (mi-ssan-dö-*sstæn*-ding) *n* malinteso *m*

misuse (miss-'*uuss*) *n* abuso *m*

mittens (*mi*-töns) *pl* muffole *fpl*

mix (mikss) *v* mescolare; **~ with** frequentare

mixed (miksst) *adj* misto

mixer (*mik*-ssö) *n* frullatore *m*

mixture (*mikss*-tʃö) *n* miscuglio *m*

moan (moun) *v* gemere

moat (mout) *n* fossato *m*

mobile (*mou*-bail) *adj* mobile

mock (mok) *v* canzonare

mockery (*mo*-kö-ri) *n* derisione *f*

model (*mo*-döl) *n* modello *m*; indossatrice *f*; *v* modellare, plasmare

moderate (*mo*-dö-röt) *adj* moderato; mediocre

modern (*mo*-dön) *adj* moderno

modest (*mo*-disst) *adj* riservato, modesto

modesty (*mo*-di-ssti) *n* modestia *f*

modify (*mo*-di-fai) *v* modificare

mohair (*mou*-hê[6]) *n* angora *f*

moist (moisst) *adj* bagnato, umido

moisten (*moi*-ssön) *v* inumidire

moisture (*moiss*-tʃö) *n* umidità *f*; **moisturizing cream** crema idratante

molar (*mou*-lö) *n* molare *m*

moment (*mou*-mönt) *n* attimo *m*, momento *m*

momentary (*mou*-mön-tö-ri) *adj* momentaneo

monarch (*mo*-nök·) *n* monarca *m*

monarchy (*mo*-nö-ki) *n* monarchia *f*

monastery (*mo*-nö-sstri) *n* monastero *m*

Monday (*man*-di) lunedì *m*

monetary (*ma*-ni-tö-ri) *adj* monetario; ~ **unit** unità monetaria

money (*ma*-ni) *n* denaro *m*; ~ **exchange** ufficio cambio; ~ **order** vaglia *m*

monk (mangk) *n* monaco *m*

monkey (*mang*-ki) *n* scimmia *f*

monologue (*mo*-no-logh) *n* monologo *m*

monopoly (mö-*no*-pö-li) *n* monopolio *m*

monotonous (mö-*no*-tö-nöss) *adj* monotono

month (manθ) *n* mese *m*

monthly (*man*θ-li) *adj* mensile; ~ **magazine** rivista mensile

monument (*mo*-n¹u-mönt) *n* monumento *m*

mood (muud) *n* umore *m*

moon (muun) *n* luna *f*

moonlight (*muun*-lait) *n* chiaro di luna

moor (mu°) *n* brughiera *f*, landa *f*

moose (muuss) *n* (pl ~, ~s) alce *m*

moped (*mou*-pêd) *n* micromotore *m*

moral (*mo*-röl) *n* morale *f*; *adj* morale; **morals** costumi *mpl*

morality (mö-*ræ*-lö-ti) *n* moralità *f*

more (moo) *adj* più; **once** ~ ancora una volta

moreover (moo-*rou*-vö) *adv* inoltre

morning (*moo*-ning) *n* mattino *m*, mattina *f*; ~ **paper** giornale del mattino; **this** ~ stamani

Moroccan (mö-*ro*-kön) *adj* marocchino

Morocco (mö-*ro*-kou) Marocco *m*

morphia (*moo*-fi-ö) *n* morfina *f*

morphine (*moo*-fiin) *n* morfina *f*

morsel (*moo*-ssöl) *n* pezzetto *m*

mortal (*moo*-töl) *adj* letale, mortale

mortgage (*moo*-ghidʒ) *n* ipoteca *f*

mosaic (mö-*sei*-ik) *n* mosaico *m*

mosque (mossk) *n* moschea *f*

mosquito (mö-*sskii*-tou) *n* (pl ~es) zanzara *f*

mosquito-net (mö-*sskii*-tou-nêt) *n* zanzariera *f*

moss (moss) *n* muschio *m*

most (mousst) *adj* il più; **at** ~ al massimo, tutt'al più; ~ **of all** soprattutto

mostly (*mousst*-li) *adv* per lo più

motel (mou-*têl*) *n* autostello *m*

moth (moθ) *n* tarma *f*

mother (*ma*-ðö) *n* madre *f*; ~ **tongue** lingua materna

mother-in-law (*ma*-ðö-rin-loo) *n* (pl mothers-) suocera *f*

mother-of-pearl (ma-ðö-röv-*pööl*) *n* madreperla *f*

motion (*mou*-ʃön) *n* moto *m*; mozione *f*

motive (*mou*-tiv) *n* movente *m*

motor (*mou*-tö) *n* motore *m*; *v* viaggiare in automobile; ~ **body** *Am* carrozzeria *f*; **starter** ~ avviatore *m*

motorbike (*mou*-tö-baik) *nAm* motorino *m*

motor-boat (*mou*-tö-bout) *n* motoscafo *m*

motor-car (*mou*-tö-kaa) *n* automobile *f*

motor-cycle (*mou*-tö-ssai-köl) *n* motocicletta *f*

motoring (*mou*-tö-ring) *n* automobilismo *m*

motorist (*mou*-tö-risst) *n* automobilista *m*

motorway (*mou*-tö-ᵘei) *n* autostrada *f*

motto (*mo*-tou) *n* (pl ~es, ~s) motto

m

mouldy (*moul*-di) *adj* ammuffito

mound (maund) *n* elevazione *f*

mount (maunt) *v* montare; *n* monte *m*

mountain (*maun*-tin) *n* montagna *f*; ~ **pass** passo *m*; ~ **range** catena di montagne

mountaineering (maun-ti-*niᵃ*-ring) *n* alpinismo *m*

mountainous (*maun*-ti-nöss) *adj* montagnoso

mourning (*moo*-ning) *n* lutto *m*

mouse (mauss) *n* (pl mice) topo *m*

moustache (mö-*sstaaʃ*) *n* baffi *mpl*

mouth (mauθ) *n* bocca *f*; fauci *fpl*; foce *f*

mouthwash (*mauθ*-ᵘoʃ) *n* acqua dentifricia

movable (*muu*-vö-böl) *adj* mobile

move (muuv) *v* *muovere; spostare; traslocare; *commuovere; *n* mossa *f*; trasloco *m*

movement (*muuv*-mönt) *n* movimento *m*

movie (*muu*-vi) *n* film *m*; **movies** *Am* cinema *m*; ~ **theater** *Am* cinema *m*

much (matʃ) *adj* molto; **as** ~ altrettanto; tanto

muck (mak) *n* melma *f*

mud (mad) *n* fango *m*

muddle (*ma*-döl) *n* imbroglio *m*, pasticcio *m*; *v* impasticciare

muddy (*ma*-di) *adj* fangoso

mud-guard (*mad*-ghaad) *n* parafango *m*

muffler (*maf*-lö) *nAm* silenziatore *m*

mug (magh) *n* boccale *m*, tazza *f*

mulberry (*mal*-bö-ri) *n* mora *f*

mule (m'uul) *n* mulo *m*

mullet (*ma*-lit) *n* triglia *f*

multiplication (mal-ti-pli-*kei*-ʃön) *n* moltiplicazione *f*

multiply (*mal*-ti-plai) *v* moltiplicare

mumps (mampss) *n* orecchioni *mpl*

municipal (m'uu-*ni*-ssi-pöl) *adj* municipale

municipality (m'uu-ni-ssi-*pæ*-lö-ti) *n* municipalità *f*

murder (*möö*-dö) *n* assassinio *m*; *v* assassinare

murderer (*möö*-dö-rö) *n* assassino *m*

muscle (*ma*-ssöl) *n* muscolo *m*

muscular (*ma*-sskᶦu-lö) *adj* muscoloso

museum (m'uu-*sii*-öm) *n* museo *m*

mushroom (*maʃ*-ruum) *n* fungo mangereccio; fungo *m*

music (*mᶦuu*-sik) *n* musica *f*; ~ **academy** conservatorio *m*

musical (*mᶦuu*-si-köl) *adj* musicale; commedia musicale

music-hall (*mᶦuu*-sik-hool) *n* teatro di varietà

musician (m'uu-*si*-ʃön) *n* musicista *m*

muslin (*mas*-lin) *n* mussolina *f*

mussel (*ma*-ssöl) *n* cozza *f*

*must (masst) *v* *dovere

mustard (*ma*-sstöd) *n* senape *f*

mute (m'uut) *adj* muto

mutiny (*mᶦuu*-ti-ni) *n* ammutinamento *m*

mutton (*ma*-tön) *n* montone *m*

mutual (*mᶦuu*-tʃu-öl) *adj* mutuo, reciproco

my (mai) *adj* mio

myself (mai-*ssêlf*) *pron* mi; io stesso

mysterious (mi-*ssti*º-ri-öss) *adj* misterioso

mystery (*mi*-sstö-ri) *n* enigma *m*, mistero *m*

myth (miθ) *n* mito *m*

N

nail (neil) *n* unghia *f*; chiodo *m*

nailbrush (*neil*-braʃ) *n* spazzolino per le unghie

nail-file (*neil*-fail) *n* limetta per le unghie

nail-polish (*neil*-po-liʃ) *n* smalto per unghie

nail-scissors (*neil*-ssi-sös) *pl* forbicine per le unghie

naïve (naa-*iiv*) *adj* ingenuo

naked (*nei*-kid) *adj* nudo; spoglio

name (neim) *n* nome *m*; *v* nominare; **in the ~ of** a nome di

namely (*neim*-li) *adv* cioè

nap (næp) *n* pisolino *m*

napkin (*næp*-kin) *n* tovagliolo *m*

nappy (*næ*-pi) *n* pannolino *m*

narcosis (naa-*kou*-ssiss) *n* (pl -ses) narcosi *f*

narcotic (naa-*ko*-tik) *n* narcotico *m*

narrow (*næ*-rou) *adj* angusto, stretto

narrow-minded (*næ*-rou-*main*-did) *adj* meschino

nasty (*naa*-ssti) *adj* antipatico, sgradevole

nation (*nei*-ʃön) *n* nazione *f*; popolo *m*

national (*næ*-ʃö-nöl) *adj* nazionale; statale; **~ anthem** inno nazionale; **~ dress** costume nazionale; **~ park** parco nazionale

nationality (næ-ʃö-*næ*-lö-ti) *n* nazionalità *f*

nationalize (*næ*-ʃö-nö-lais) *v* nazionalizzare

native (*nei*-tiv) *n* indigeno *m*; *adj* nativo; **~ country** patria *f*, paese natio; **~ language** lingua materna

natural (*næ*-tʃö-röl) *adj* naturale; innato

naturally (*næ*-tʃö-rö-li) *adv* naturalmente

nature (*nei*-tʃö) *n* natura *f*; indole *f*

naughty (*noo*-ti) *adj* cattivo

nausea (*noo*-ssi-ö) *n* nausea *f*

naval (*nei*-völ) *adj* navale

navel (*nei*-völ) *n* ombelico *m*

navigable (*næ*-vi-ghö-böl) *adj* navigabile

navigate (*næ*-vi-gheit) *v* navigare; governare

navigation (næ-vi-*ghei*-ʃön) *n* navigazione *f*

navy (*nei*-vi) *n* marina *f*

near (niö) *prep* vicino a; *adj* vicino

nearby (*niö*-bai) *adj* vicino

nearly (*niö*-li) *adv* quasi

neat (niit) *adj* lindo, curato; puro

necessary (*nê*-ssö-ssö-ri) *adj* necessario

necessity (nö-*ssê*-ssö-ti) *n* necessità *f*

neck (nêk) *n* collo *m*; **nape of the ~** nuca *f*

necklace (*nêk*-löss) *n* collana *f*

necktie (*nêk*-tai) *n* cravatta *f*

need (niid) *v* *occorrere, *aver bisogno di, bisognare; *n* bisogno *m*, necessità *f*; **~ to** *dovere

needle (*nii*-döl) *n* ago *m*

negative (*nê*-ghö-tiv) *adj* negativo; *n* negativa *f*

neglect (ni-*ghlêkt*) *v* trascurare; *n* negligenza *f*

neglectful (ni-*ghlêkt*-föl) *adj* negligente

negligee (*nê*-ghli-ʒei) *n* vestaglia *f*

negotiate (ni-*ghou*-ʃi-eit) *v* negoziare

negotiation (ni-ghou-ʃi-*ei*-ʃön) *n* trattativa *f*

Negro (*nii*-ghrou) *n* (pl ~es) negro *m*

neighbour (*nei*-bö) *n* vicino *m*

neighbourhood (*nei*-bö-hud) *n* vicinato *m*

neighbouring (*nei*-bö-ring) *adj* contiguo, adiacente

neither (*nai*-ðö) *pron* né l'uno né l'altro; **neither ... nor** né ... né

neon (*nii*-on) *n* neon *m*

nephew (*nê*-f'uu) *n* nipote *m*

nerve (nööv) *n* nervo *m*; audacia *f*

nervous (*nöö*-vöss) *adj* nervoso

nest (nêsst) *n* nido *m*

net (nêt) *n* rete *f*; *adj* netto

the Netherlands (*nê*-ðö-lönds) Paesi Bassi

network (*nêt*-ᵁöök) *n* rete *f*

neuralgia (n'u⁶-*rӕl*-dӡö) *n* nevralgia *f*

neurosis (n'u⁶-*rou*-ssiss) *n* nevrosi *f*

neuter (*n'uu*-tö) *adj* neutro

neutral (*n'uu*-tröl) *adj* neutrale

never (*nê*-vö) *adv* non... mai

nevertheless (nê-vö-ðö-*lêss*) *adv* tuttavia

new (n'uu) *adj* nuovo; **New Year** anno nuovo

news (n'uus) *n* notiziario *m*, novità *f*; notizie

newsagent (*n'uu*-sei-dӡönt) *n* giornalaio *m*

newspaper (*n'uus*-pei-pö) *n* giornale *m*

newsreel (*n'uus*-riil) *n* cinegiornale *m*

newsstand (*n'uus*-sstӕnd) *n* edicola *f*

New Zealand (n'uu *sii*-lönd) Nuova Zelanda

next (nêksst) *adj* prossimo; ~ **to** vicino a

next-door (nêksst-*doo*) *adv* accanto

nice (naiss) *adj* carino, bellino, piacevole; buono; simpatico

nickel (*ni*-köl) *n* nichelio *m*

nickname (*nik*-neim) *n* nomignolo *m*

nicotine (*ni*-kö-tiin) *n* nicotina *f*

niece (niiss) *n* nipote *f*

Nigeria (nai-*dӡi⁶*-ri-ö) Nigeria *f*

Nigerian (nai-*dӡi⁶*-ri-ön) *adj* nigeriano

night (nait) *n* notte *f*; sera *f*; **by ~** di notte; ~ **flight** volo notturno; ~

rate tariffa notturna; ~ **train** treno notturno

nightclub (*nait*-klab) *n* locale notturno

night-cream (*nait*-kriim) *n* crema per la notte

nightdress (*nait*-drêss) *n* camicia da notte

nightingale (*nai*-ting-gheil) *n* usignolo *m*

nightly (*nait*-li) *adj* notturno

nil (nil) *n* niente

nine (nain) *num* nove

nineteen (nain-*tiin*) *num* diciannove

nineteenth (nain-*tiin*θ) *num* diciannovesimo

ninety (*nain*-ti) *num* novanta

ninth (nainθ) *num* nono

nitrogen (*nai*-trö-dӡön) *n* azoto *m*

no (nou) no; *adj* nessuno; ~ **one** nessuno

nobility (nou-*bi*-lö-ti) *n* nobiltà *f*

noble (*nou*-böl) *adj* nobile

nobody (*nou*-bo-di) *pron* nessuno

nod (nod) *n* cenno con la testa; *v* annuire

noise (nois) *n* rumore *m*; baccano *m*, chiasso *m*

noisy (*noi*-si) *adj* rumoroso; sonoro

nominal (*no*-mi-nöl) *adj* nominale

nominate (*no*-mi-neit) *v* nominare

nomination (no-mi-*nei*-ӡön) *n* nomina *f*

none (nan) *pron* nessuno

nonsense (*non*-ssönss) *n* sciocchezza *f*

noon (nuun) *n* mezzogiorno *m*

normal (*noo*-möl) *adj* normale

north (nooθ) *n* nord *m*; settentrione *m*; *adj* settentrionale; **North Pole** polo Nord

north-east (nooθ-*iisst*) *n* nord-est *m*

northerly (*noo*-ðö-li) *adj* settentrionale

northern (*noo-*ðön) *adj* nordico

north-west (*nooθ-*ᵘésst) *n* nord-ovest *m*

Norway (*noo-*ᵘei) Norvegia *f*

Norwegian (*noo-*ᵘii-dʒön) *adj* norvegese

nose (nous) *n* naso *m*

nosebleed (*nous-*bliid) *n* rinorragia *f*

nostril (*no-*sstril) *n* narice *f*

not (not) *adv* non

notary (*nou-*tö-ri) *n* notaio *m*

note (nout) *n* appunto *m*, biglietto *m*; commento *m*; tono *m*; *v* annotare; osservare, notare

notebook (*nout-*buk) *n* taccuino *m*

noted (*nou-*tid) *adj* illustre

notepaper (*nout-*pei-pö) *n* carta da lettere

nothing (*na-*θing) *n* nulla *m*, niente

notice (*nou-*tiss) *v* rilevare, *accorgersi di, notare; *vedere; *n* avviso *m*, notizia *f*; attenzione *f*

noticeable (*nou-*ti-ssö-böl) *adj* percettibile; notevole

notify (*nou-*ti-fai) *v* notificare; avvisare

notion (*nou-*ʃön) *n* nozione *f*

notorious (nou-*too-*ri-öss) *adj* famigerato

nougat (*nuu-*ghaa) *n* torrone *m*

nought (noot) *n* zero *m*

noun (naun) *n* nome *m*

nourishing (*na-*ri-ʃing) *adj* nutriente

novel (*no-*völ) *n* romanzo *m*

novelist (*no-*vö-lisst) *n* romanziere *m*

November (nou-*vêm-*bö) novembre

now (nau) *adv* ora; adesso; ~ **and then** di tanto in tanto

nowadays (*nau-*ö-deis) *adv* oggigiorno

nowhere (*nou-*ᵘêᵒ) *adv* in nessun luogo

nozzle (*no-*söl) *n* becco *m*

nuance (nⁱuu-*angss*) *n* sfumatura *f*

nuclear (nⁱuu-kli-ö) *adj* nucleare; ~ **energy** energia nucleare

nucleus (nⁱuu-kli-öss) *n* nucleo *m*

nude (nⁱuud) *adj* nudo; *n* nudo *m*

nuisance (nⁱuu-ssönss) *n* seccatura *f*

numb (nam) *adj* intorpidito; intirizzito

number (*nam-*bö) *n* numero *m*; cifra *f*; quantità *f*

numeral (nⁱuu-mö-röl) *n* numerale *m*

numerous (nⁱuu-mö-röss) *adj* numeroso

nun (nan) *n* monaca *f*

nunnery (*na-*nö-ri) *n* convento *m*

nurse (nööss) *n* infermiera *f*; bambinaia *f*; *v* curare; allattare

nursery (*nöö-*ssö-ri) *n* camera dei bambini; nido *m*; vivaio *m*

nut (nat) *n* noce *f*; dado *m*

nutcrackers (*nat-*kræ-kös) *pl* schiaccianoci *m*

nutmeg (*nat-*mêgh) *n* noce moscata

nutritious (nⁱuu-*tri-*ʃöss) *adj* nutriente

nutshell (*nat-*ʃêl) *n* guscio di noce

nylon (*nai-*lon) *n* nailon *m*

O

oak (ouk) *n* quercia *f*

oar (oo) *n* remo *m*

oasis (ou-*ei-*ssiss) *n* (pl oases) oasi *f*

oath (ouθ) *n* giuramento *m*

oats (outss) *pl* avena *f*

obedience (ö-*bii-*di-önss) *n* ubbidienza *f*

obedient (ö-*bii-*di-önt) *adj* ubbidiente

obey (ö-*bei*) *v* ubbidire

object¹ (*ob-*dʒikt) *n* oggetto *m*; obiettivo *m*

object² (öb-*dʒêkt*) *v* obiettare; ~ **to** *opporsi a

objection (öb-*dʒêk-*ʃön) *n* obiezione *f*

objective (öb-*dʒêk*-tiv) *adj* oggettivo; *n* obiettivo *m*

obligatory (ö-*bli*-ghö-tö-ri) *adj* obbligatorio

oblige (ö-*blaidʒ*) *v* obbligare; ***be obliged to** *essere obbligato a; *dovere

obliging (ö-*blai*-dʒing) *adj* servizievole

oblong (*ob*-long) *adj* oblungo; *n* rettangolo *m*

obscene (öb-*ssiin*) *adj* osceno

obscure (öb-*ssk'u⁰*) *adj* scuro, oscuro, buio

observation (ob-sö-*vei*-fön) *n* osservazione *f*

observatory (öb-*söö*-vö-tri) *n* osservatorio *m*

observe (öb-*sööv*) *v* osservare

obsession (öb-*ssê*-fön) *n* ossessione *f*

obstacle (*ob*-sstö-köl) *n* ostacolo *m*

obstinate (*ob*-ssti-nöt) *adj* ostinato; caparbio

obtain (öb-*tein*) *v* conseguire, *ottenere

obtainable (öb-*tei*-nö-böl) *adj* ottenibile

obvious (*ob*-vi-öss) *adj* ovvio

occasion (ö-*kei*-ʒön) *n* occasione *f*; motivo *m*

occasionally (ö-*kei*-ʒö-nö-li) *adv* ogni tanto, occasionalmente

occupant (*o*-k'u-pönt) *n* occupante *m*

occupation (o-k'u-*pei*-fön) *n* occupazione *f*

occupy (*o*-k'u-pai) *v* occupare

occur (ö-*köö*) *v* *succedere, capitare, *accadere

occurrence (ö-*ka*-rönss) *n* evento *m*

ocean (*ou*-fön) *n* oceano *m*

October (ok-*tou*-bö) ottobre

octopus (*ok*-tö-pöss) *n* polipo *m*

oculist (*o*-k'u-lisst) *n* oculista *m*

odd (od) *adj* bizzarro, strano; dispari

odour (*ou*-dö) *n* odore *m*

of (ov, öv) *prep* di

off (of) *adv* via; *prep* giù da

offence (ö-*fênss*) *n* reato *m*; offesa *f*, scandalo *m*

offend (ö-*fênd*) *v* *offendere; trasgredire

offensive (ö-*fên*-ssiv) *adj* offensivo; insultante; *n* offensiva *f*

offer (*o*-fö) *v* *offrire; presentare; *n* offerta *f*

office (*o*-fiss) *n* ufficio *m*; funzione *f*; ~ **hours** ore d'ufficio

officer (*o*-fi-ssö) *n* ufficiale *m*

official (ö-*fi*-föl) *adj* ufficiale

off-licence (*of*-lai-ssönss) *n* spaccio di liquori

often (*o*-fön) *adv* spesso

oil (oil) *n* olio *m*; petrolio *m*; **fuel** ~ nafta *f*; ~ **filter** filtro dell'olio; ~ **pressure** pressione dell'olio

oil-painting (oil-*pein*-ting) *n* pittura ad olio

oil-refinery (*oil*-ri-fai-nö-ri) *n* raffineria di petrolio

oil-well (*oil*-uêl) *n* pozzo di petrolio

oily (*oi*-li) *adj* oleoso

ointment (*oint*-mönt) *n* unguento *m*

okay! (ou-*kei*) d'accordo!

old (ould) *adj* vecchio; ~ **age** vecchiaia *f*

old-fashioned (ould-*fæ*-fönd) *adj* antiquato

olive (*o*-liv) *n* oliva *f*; ~ **oil** olio d'oliva

omelette (*om*-löt) *n* frittata *f*

ominous (*o*-mi-nöss) *adj* sinistro

omit (ö-*mit*) *v* *omettere

omnipotent (om-*ni*-pö-tönt) *adj* onnipotente

on (on) *prep* su; a

once (uanss) *adv* una volta; **at** ~ **subito**; ~ **more** ancora una volta

oncoming (*on*-ka-ming) *adj* imminente

one (ᵁan) *num* uno; *pron* uno

oneself (ᵁan-*ssélf*) *pron* sé stesso

onion (a-n'ön) *n* cipolla *f*

only (oun-li) *adj* solo; *adv* solo, soltanto, solamente; *conj* però

onwards (on-ᵁöds) *adv* avanti

onyx (o-nikss) *n* onice *f*

opal (ou-pöl) *n* opale *m*

open (ou-pön) *v* *aprire; *adj* aperto; franco

opening (ou-pö-ning) *n* apertura *f*

opera (o-pö-rö) *n* opera *f*; ~ house teatro dell'opera

operate (o-pö-reit) *v* agire, funzionare; operare

operation (o-pö-*rei*-fön) *n* funzionamento *m*; operazione *f*

operator (o-pö-rei-tö) *n* centralinista *f*

operetta (o-pö-*rê*-tö) *n* operetta *f*

opinion (ö-*pi*-n'ön) *n* parere *m*, opinione *f*

opponent (ö-*pou*-nönt) *n* avversario *m*

opportunity (o-pö-*t'uu*-nö-ti) *n* opportunità *f*, occasione *f*

oppose (ö-*pous*) *v* *opporsi

opposite (o-pö-sit) *prep* di fronte a; *adj* contrario, opposto

opposition (o-pö-*si*-fön) *n* opposizione *f*

oppress (ö-*prêss*) *v* *opprimere

optician (op-*ti*-fön) *n* ottico *m*

optimism (*op*-ti-mi-söm) *n* ottimismo *m*

optimist (*op*-ti-misst) *n* ottimista *m*

optimistic (op-ti-*mi*-sstik) *adj* ottimistico

optional (*op*-fö-nöl) *adj* facoltativo

or (oo) *conj* o

oral (oo-röl) *adj* orale

orange (o-rind3) *n* arancia *f*; *adj* arancione

orchard (oo-tföd) *n* frutteto *m*

orchestra (oo-ki-sströ) *n* orchestra *f*;

~ seat *Am* poltrona d'orchestra

order (oo-dö) *v* comandare; ordinare; *n* ordine *m*; comando *m*; ordinazione *f*; in ~ in ordine; in ~ to allo scopo di; made to ~ fatto su misura; out of ~ fuori uso; postal ~ vaglia postale

order-form (oo-dö-foom) *n* modulo di ordinazione

ordinary (oo-dön-ri) *adj* solito, ordinario

ore (oo) *n* minerale *m*

organ (oo-ghön) *n* organo *m*

organic (oo-*ghæ*-nik) *adj* organico

organization (oo-ghö-nai-*sei*-fön) *n* organizzazione *f*

organize (oo-ghö-nais) *v* organizzare

Orient (oo-ri-önt) *n* oriente *m*

oriental (oo-ri-*ên*-töl) *adj* orientale

orientate (oo-ri-ön-teit) *v* orientarsi

origin (o-ri-d3in) *n* origine *f*; discendenza *f*, provenienza *f*

original (ö-*ri*-d3i-nöl) *adj* autentico, originale

originally (ö-*ri*-d3i-nö-li) *adv* originariamente

orlon (oo-lon) *n* orlon *m*

ornament (oo-nö-mönt) *n* ornamento *m*

ornamental (oo-nö-*mên*-töl) *adj* ornamentale

orphan (oo-fön) *n* orfano *m*

orthodox (oo-θö-dokss) *adj* ortodosso

ostrich (o-sstritf) *n* struzzo *m*

other (a-ðö) *adj* altro

otherwise (a-ðö-ᵁais) *conj* altrimenti; *adv* altrimenti

*ought to (oot) *dovere

our (auᵒ) *adj* nostro

ourselves (auᵒ-*ssêlvs*) *pron* ci; noi stessi

out (aut) *adv* fuori; ~ of fuori di, da

outbreak (aut-breik) *n* scoppio *m*

outcome (aut-kam) *n* risultato *m*

*outdo (aut-*duu*) v superare

outdoors (aut-*doos*) adv all'aperto

outer (*au*-tö) adj esterno

outfit (*aut*-fit) n equipaggiamento m

outline (*aut*-lain) n contorno m; v abbozzare

outlook (*aut*-luk) n prospettiva f; punto di vista

output (*aut*-put) n produzione f

outrage (*aut*-reidȝ) n oltraggio m

outside (aut-*ssaid*) adv fuori; prep fuori di; n esteriore m, esterno m

outsize (*aut*-ssais) n taglia fuori misura

outskirts (*aut*-ssköötss) pl sobborgo m

outstanding (aut-*sstæn*-ding) adj eminente

outward (*aut*-ᵘöd) adj esterno

outwards (*aut*-ᵘöds) adv al di fuori

oval (*ou*-völ) adj ovale

oven (*a*-vön) n forno m

over (*ou*-vö) prep sopra; oltre; adv al di sopra; giù; adj finito; ~ **there** laggiù

overall (*ou*-vö-rool) adj globale

overalls (*ou*-vö-rools) pl tuta f

overcast (*ou*-vö-kaasst) adj coperto

overcoat (*ou*-vö-kout) n soprabito m

*overcome (ou-vö-*kam*) v *vincere

overdue (ou-vö-*d'uu*) adj in ritardo; arretrato

overgrown (ou-vö-*ghroun*) adj coperto di fogliame

overhaul (ou-vö-*hool*) v revisionare

overhead (ou-vö-*hêd*) adv in su

overlook (ou-vö-*luk*) v trascurare

overnight (ou-vö-*nait*) adv di notte

overseas (ou-vö-*ssiis*) adj oltremarino

oversight (*ou*-vö-ssait) n svista f

*oversleep (ou-vö-*ssliip*) v dormire troppo

overstrung (ou-vö-*sstrang*) adj esausto

*overtake (ou-vö-*teik*) v oltrepassare;

no overtaking divieto di sorpasso

over-tired (ou-vö-*tai*ᵒd) adj esausto

overture (*ou*-vö-tʃö) n ouverture f

overweight (*ou*-vö-ᵘeit) n soprappeso m

overwhelm (ou-vö-ᵘ*êlm*) v *sopraffare, schiacciare

overwork (ou-vö-ᵘ*öök*) v lavorare troppo

owe (ou) v *dovere; **owing to** a motivo di, a causa di

owl (aul) n gufo m

own (oun) v *possedere; adj proprio

owner (*ou*-nö) n proprietario m

ox (okss) n (pl oxen) bue m

oxygen (*ok*-ssi-dȝön) n ossigeno m

oyster (*oi*-sstö) n ostrica f

P

pace (peiss) n andatura f; passo m; velocità f

Pacific Ocean (pö-*ssi*-fik *ou*-ʃön) Oceano Pacifico

pacifism (*pæ*-ssi-fi-söm) n pacifismo m

pacifist (*pæ*-ssi-fisst) n pacifista m

pack (pæk) v imballare; ~ **up** imballare

package (*pæ*-kidȝ) n pacco m

packet (*pæ*-kit) n pacchetto m

packing (*pæ*-king) n imballaggio m

pad (pæd) n cuscinetto m; blocco per appunti

paddle (*pæ*-döl) n remo m

padlock (*pæd*-lok) n lucchetto m

pagan (*pei*-ghön) adj pagano; n pagano m

page (peidȝ) n pagina f

page-boy (*peidȝ*-boi) n paggio m

pail (peil) n secchio m

pain (pein) n dolore m; **pains** pena f

painful (*pein*-fŏl) *adj* penoso
painless (*pein*-lŏss) *adj* indolore
paint (peint) *n* colore *m*; *v* pitturare; verniciare
paint-box (*peint*-bokss) *n* scatola di colori
paint-brush (*peint*-braʃ) *n* pennello *m*
painter (*pein*-tö) *n* pittore *m*
painting (*pein*-ting) *n* pittura *f*
pair (pêᵒ) *n* paio *m*
Pakistan (paa-ki-*sstaan*) Pakistan *m*
Pakistani (paa-ki-*sstaa*-ni) *adj* pachistano
palace (*pæ*-löss) *n* palazzo *m*
pale (peil) *adj* pallido; chiaro
palm (paam) *n* palma *f*
palpable (*pæl*-pö-böl) *adj* palpabile
palpitation (pæl-pi-*tei*-ʃön) *n* palpitazione *f*
pan (pæn) *n* tegame *m*
pane (pein) *n* vetro *m*
panel (*pæ*-nöl) *n* pannello *m*
panelling (*pæ*-nö-ling) *n* rivestimento a pannelli
panic (*pæ*-nik) *n* panico *m*
pant (pænt) *v* ansimare
panties (*pæn*-tis) *pl* mutandine *fpl*, mutande *fpl*
pants (pæntss) *pl* mutande *fpl*; *plAm* calzoni *mpl*
pant-suit (*pænt*-ssuut) *n* giacca e calzoni
panty-hose (*pæn*-ti-hous) *n* calzamaglia *f*
paper (*pei*-pö) *n* carta *f*; giornale *m*; di carta; **carbon** ~ carta carbone; ~ **bag** sacchetto *m*; ~ **napkin** tovagliolo di carta; **typing** ~ carta da macchina; **wrapping** ~ carta da imballaggio
paperback (*pei*-pö-bæk) *n* libro in brossura
paper-knife (*pei*-pö-naif) *n* tagliacarte *m*

parade (pö-*reid*) *n* parata *f*
paraffin (*pæ*-rö-fin) *n* petrolio *m*
paragraph (*pæ*-rö-ghraaf) *n* capoverso *m*, paragrafo *m*
parakeet (*pæ*-rö-kiit) *n* parrocchetto *m*
paralise (*pæ*-rö-lais) *v* paralizzare
parallel (*pæ*-rö-lêl) *adj* parallelo; *n* parallela *f*
parcel (*paa*-ssöl) *n* pacco *m*, pacchetto *m*
pardon (*paa*-dön) *n* perdono *m*; grazia *f*
parents (*pêᵒ*-röntss) *pl* genitori *mpl*
parents-in-law (*pêᵒ*-röntss-in-loo) *pl* suoceri
parish (*pæ*-riʃ) *n* parrocchia *f*
park (paak) *n* parco *m*; *v* posteggiare
parking (*paa*-king) *n* parcheggio *m*; **no** ~ divieto di sosta; ~ **fee** tariffa del parcheggio; ~ **light** luce di posizione; ~ **lot** *Am* parcheggio *m*; ~ **meter** parchimetro *m*; ~ **zone** zona di parcheggio
parliament (*paa*-lö-mönt) *n* parlamento *m*
parliamentary (paa-lö-*mên*-tö-ri) *adj* parlamentare
parrot (*pæ*-röt) *n* pappagallo *m*
parsley (*paa*-ssli) *n* prezzemolo *m*
parson (*paa*-ssön) *n* pastore *m*
parsonage (*paa*-ssö-nidʒ) *n* presbiterio *m*
part (paat) *n* parte *f*; pezzo *m*; *v* separare; **spare** ~ pezzo di ricambio
partial (*paa*-ʃöl) *adj* parziale
participant (paa-*ti*-ssi-pönt) *n* partecipante *m*
participate (paa-*ti*-ssi-peit) *v* partecipare
particular (pö-*ti*-kʲu-lö) *adj* speciale, particolare; esigente; **in** ~ in particolare
parting (*paa*-ting) *n* addio *m*; scrimi-

natura f

partition (paa-*ti*-ʃön) n divisorio m

partly (*paat*-li) adv in parte

partner (*paat*-nö) n compagno m; socio m

partridge (*paa*-tridʒ) n pernice f

party (*paa*-ti) n partito m; festa f; gruppo m

pass (paass) v *trascorrere, passare, sorpassare; vAm oltrepassare; **no passing** Am divieto di sorpasso; ~ **by** passare accanto; ~ **through** attraversare

passage (*pæ*-ssidʒ) n passaggio m; traversata f; brano m

passenger (*pæ*-ssön-dʒö) n passeggero m; ~ **car** Am vagone m; ~ **train** treno passeggeri

passer-by (paa-ssö-*bai*) n passante m

passion (*pæ*-ʃön) n passione f; collera f

passionate (*pæ*-ʃö-nöt) adj appassionato

passive (*pæ*-ssiv) adj passivo

passport (*paass*-poot) n passaporto m; ~ **control** controllo passaporti; ~ **photograph** foto per passaporto

password (*paass*-ᵁööd) n parola d'ordine

past (paasst) n passato m; adj scorso, passato; prep lungo, al di là di

paste (peisst) n pasta f; v incollare

pastry (*pei*-sstri) n pasticceria f; ~ **shop** pasticceria f

pasture (*paass*-tʃö) n pascolo m

patch (pætʃ) v rappezzare

patent (*pei*-tönt) n brevetto m

path (paaθ) n sentiero m

patience (*pei*-ʃönss) n pazienza f

patient (*pei*-ʃönt) adj paziente; n paziente m

patriot (*pei*-tri-öt) n patriota m

patrol (pö-*troul*) n pattuglia f; v pattugliare; sorvegliare

pattern (*pæ*-tön) n disegno m

pause (poos) n pausa f; v *interrompersi

pave (peiv) v lastricare, pavimentare

pavement (*peiv*-mönt) n marciapiede m; pavimento m

pavilion (pö-*vil*-ᶦön) n padiglione m

paw (poo) n zampa f

pawn (poon) v impegnare; n pedina f

pawnbroker (*poon*-brou-kö) n prestatore su pegno

pay (pei) n salario m, paga f

***pay** (pei) v pagare; *rendere; ~ **attention to** *stare attento a; **paying** rimunerativo; ~ **off** saldare; ~ **on account** pagare a rate

pay-desk (*pei*-dèssk) n cassa f

payee (pei-*ii*) n beneficiario m

payment (*pei*-mönt) n pagamento m

pea (pii) n pisello m

peace (piiss) n pace f

peaceful (*piiss*-föl) adj pacifico

peach (piitʃ) n pesca f

peacock (*pii*-kok) n pavone m

peak (piik) n vetta f; cima f; ~ **hour** ora di punta; ~ **season** alta stagione

peanut (*pii*-nat) n arachide f

pear (pêᵒ) n pera f

pearl (pööl) n perla f

peasant (*pê*-sönt) n contadino m

pebble (*pê*-böl) n ciottolo m

peculiar (pi-*kᶦuul*-ᶦö) adj strano; speciale, particolare

peculiarity (pi-kᶦuu-li-æ-rö-ti) n singolarità f

pedal (*pê*-döl) n pedale m

pedestrian (pi-*dê*-sstri-ön) n pedone m; **no pedestrians** vietato ai pedoni; ~ **crossing** passaggio pedonale

pedicure (*pê*-di-kᶦuᵒ) n pedicure m

peel (piil) v sbucciare; n buccia f

peep (piip) v spiare

peg (pêgh) n gancio m

pelican (*pê*-li-kön) *n* pellicano *m*

pelvis (*pêl*-viss) *n* bacino *m*

pen (pèn) *n* penna *f*

penalty (*pê*-nöl-ti) *n* penalità *f*; pena *f*; ~ **kick** calcio di rigore

pencil (*pên*-ssöl) *n* matita *f*

pencil-sharpener (*pên*-ssöl-ʃaap-nö) *n* temperamatite *m*

pendant (*pên*-dönt) *n* pendente *m*

penetrate (*pê*-ni-treit) *v* penetrare

penguin (*pêng*-ghᵘin) *n* pinguino *m*

penicillin (pê-ni-*ssi*-lin) *n* penicillina *f*

peninsula (pö-*nin*-ssᵘu-lö) *n* penisola *f*

penknife (*pên*-naif) *n* (pl -knives) temperino *m*

pension¹ (*pang*-ssi-ong) *n* pensione *f*

pension² (*pên*-ʃön) *n* pensione *f*

people (*pii*-pöl) *pl* gente *f*; *n* popolo *m*

pepper (*pê*-pö) *n* pepe *m*

peppermint (*pê*-pö-mint) *n* menta peperina

perceive (pö-*ssiiv*) *v* percepire

percent (pö-*ssênt*) *n* percento *m*

percentage (pö-*ssên*-tidʒ) *n* percentuale *f*

perceptible (pö-*ssêp*-ti-böl) *adj* percettibile

perception (pö-*ssêp*-ʃön) *n* percezione *f*

perch (pöötʃ) (pl ~) pesce persico

percolator (*pöö*-kö-lei-tö) *n* filtro *m*

perfect (*pöö*-fikt) *adj* perfetto

perfection (pö-*fêk*-ʃön) *n* perfezione *f*

perform (pö-*foom*) *v* compiere, eseguire

performance (pö-*foo*-mönss) *n* rappresentazione *f*

perfume (*pöö*-fⁱuum) *n* profumo *m*

perhaps (pö-*hæpss*) *adv* forse

peril (*pê*-ril) *n* pericolo *m*

perilous (*pê*-ri-löss) *adj* pericoloso

period (*piᵒ*-ri-öd) *n* epoca *f*, periodo *m*; punto *m*

periodical (piᵒ-ri-*o*-di-köl) *n* periodico *m*; *adj* periodico

perish (*pê*-riʃ) *v* perire

perishable (*pê*-ri-ʃö-böl) *adj* deperibile

perjury (*pöö*-dʒö-ri) *n* spergiuro *m*

permanent (*pöö*-mö-nönt) *adj* duraturo, permanente; stabile, fisso; ~ **press** stiratura permanente; ~ **wave** permanente *f*

permission (pö-*mi*-ʃön) *n* permesso *m*, autorizzazione *f*; licenza *f*

permit¹ (pö-*mit*) *v* *permettere

permit² (*pöö*-mit) *n* permesso *m*

peroxide (pö-*rok*-ssaid) *n* acqua ossigenata *m*

perpendicular (pöö-pön-*di*-kⁱu-lö) *adj* perpendicolare

Persia (*pöö*-ʃö) Persia *f*

Persian (*pöö*-ʃön) *adj* persiano

person (*pöö*-ssön) *n* persona *f*; **per ~** per persona

personal (*pöö*-ssö-nöl) *adj* personale

personality (pöö-ssö-*næ*-lö-ti) *n* personalità *f*

personnel (pöö-ssö-*nêl*) *n* personale *m*

perspective (pö-*sspêk*-tiv) *n* prospettiva *f*

perspiration (pöö-sspö-*rei*-ʃön) *n* traspirazione *f*, sudore *m*

perspire (pö-*sspaiᵒ*) *v* traspirare, sudare

persuade (pö-ss*ᵘeid*) *v* *persuadere; *convincere

persuasion (pö-ss*ᵘei*-ʒön) *n* convinzione *f*

pessimism (*pê*-ssi-mi-söm) *n* pessimismo *m*

pessimist (*pê*-ssi-misst) *n* pessimista *m*

pessimistic (pê-ssi-*mi*-sstik) *adj* pessimistico

pet (pêt) *n* animale domestico; cocco

m; favorito

petal (*pé*-töl) *n* petalo *m*

petition (pi-*ti*-jön) *n* petizione *f*

petrol (*pê*-tröl) *n* benzina *f*; ~ **pump** pompa di benzina; ~ **station** distributore di benzina; ~ **tank** serbatoio di benzina

petroleum (pi-*trou*-li-öm) *n* petrolio *m*

petty (*pê*-ti) *adj* piccolo, futile, insignificante; ~ **cash** moneta spicciola

pewit (*pii*-ᵘit) *n* pavoncella *f*

pewter (*pⁱuu*-tö) *n* peltro *m*

phantom (*fæn*-töm) *n* fantasma *m*

pharmacology (faa-mö-*ko*-lö-dʒi) *n* farmacologia *f*

pharmacy (*faa*-mö-ssi) *n* farmacia *f*

phase (feis) *n* fase *f*

pheasant (*fê*-sönt) *n* fagiano *m*

Philippine (*fi*-li-ipain) *adj* filippino

Philippines (*fi*-li-piins) *pl* Isole Filippine

philosopher (fi-*lo*-ssö-fö) *n* filosofo *m*

philosophy (fi-*lo*-ssö-fi) *n* filosofia *f*

phone (foun) *n* telefono *m*; *v* telefonare

phonetic (fö-*nê*-tik) *adj* fonetico

photo (*fou*-tou) *n* (pl ~s) foto *f*

photocopy (*fou*-tö-ko-pi) *n* fotocopia *f*; *v* fotocopiare

photograph (*fou*-tö-ghraaf) *n* fotografia *f*; *v* fotografare

photographer (fö-*to*-ghrö-fö) *n* fotografo *m*

photography (fö-*to*-ghrö-fi) *n* fotografia *f*

phrase (freis) *n* frase *f*

phrase-book (*freis*-buk) *n* manuale di conversazione

physical (*fi*-si-köl) *adj* fisico

physician (fi-*si*-jön) *n* medico *m*

physicist (*fi*-si-ssisst) *n* fisico *m*

physics (*fi*-sikss) *n* fisica *f*

physiology (fi-si-*o*-lö-dʒi) *n* fisiologia *f*

pianist (*pii*-ö-nisst) *n* pianista *m*

piano (pi-*æ*-nou) *n* pianoforte *m*; **grand** ~ pianoforte a coda

pick (pik) *v* *cogliere; *scegliere; *n* scelta *f*; ~ **up** *raccogliere; rilevare; **pick-up van** camionetta *f*

pick-axe (*pi*-kækss) *n* piccone *m*

pickles (*pi*-köls) *pl* sottaceti *mpl*

picnic (*pik*-nik) *n* picnic *m*; *v* *fare un picnic

picture (*pik*-tjö) *n* pittura *f*; illustrazione *f*, stampa *f*; figura *f*, quadro *m*; ~ **postcard** cartolina illustrata; **pictures** cinema *m*

picturesque (pik-tjö-*rêssk*) *adj* pittoresco

piece (piiss) *n* pezzo *m*

pier (piᵒ) *n* molo *m*

pierce (piᵒss) *v* perforare

pig (pigh) *n* maiale *m*; porco *m*

pigeon (*pi*-dʒön) *n* piccione *m*

pig-headed (pigh-*hê*-did) *adj* testardo

piglet (*pigh*-löt) *n* porcellino *m*

pigskin (*pigh*-sskin) *n* pelle di cinghiale

pike (paik) (pl ~) luccio *m*

pile (pail) *n* mucchio *m*; *v* ammucchiare; **piles** *pl* emorroidi *fpl*

pilgrim (*pil*-ghrim) *n* pellegrino *m*

pilgrimage (*pil*-ghri-midʒ) *n* pellegrinaggio *m*

pill (pil) *n* pillola *f*

pillar (*pi*-lö) *n* pilastro *m*, colonna *f*

pillar-box (*pi*-lö-bokss) *n* buca delle lettere

pillow (*pi*-lou) *n* guanciale *m*

pillow-case (*pi*-lou-keiss) *n* federa *f*

pilot (*pai*-löt) *n* pilota *m*

pimple (*pim*-pöl) *n* pustoletta *f*

pin (pin) *n* spillo *m*; *v* appuntare; **bobby** ~ *Am* fermaglio per capelli

pincers (*pin*-ssös) *pl* tenaglie *fpl*

pinch (pintʃ) *v* pizzicare

pineapple (*pai*-næ-pöl) *n* ananas *m*

ping-pong (*ping*-pong) *n* tennis da tavolo

pink (pingk) *adj* rosa

pioneer (pai-ö-*ni*ŏ) *n* pioniere *m*

pious (*pai*-öss) *adj* pio

pip (pip) *n* seme *m*

pipe (paip) *n* pipa *f*; tubatura *f*; ~ **cleaner** curapipe *m*; ~ **tobacco** tabacco da pipa

pirate (*pai*ŏ-rŏt) *n* pirata *m*

pistol (*pi*-sstöl) *n* pistola *f*

piston (*pi*-sstön) *n* stantuffo *m*; ~ **ring** anello per stantuffo

piston-rod (*pi*-sstön-rod) *n* asta dello stantuffo

pit (pit) *n* buca *f*; miniera *f*

pitcher (*pi*-tʃö) *n* brocca *f*

pity (*pi*-ti) *n* pietà *f*; *v* provare compassione per, compatire; **what a pity!** peccato!

placard (*plæ*-kaad) *n* affisso *m*

place (pleiss) *n* posto *m*; *v* posare, *porre; ~ **of birth** luogo di nascita; *take ~ *aver luogo

plague (pleigh) *n* flagello *m*

plaice (pleiss) (pl ~) passera di mare

plain (plein) *adj* chiaro; ordinario, semplice; *n* pianura *f*

plan (plæn) *n* progetto *m*; pianta *f*; *v* progettare

plane (plein) *adj* piano; *n* aereo *m*; ~ **crash** incidente aereo

planet (*plæ*-nit) *n* pianeta *m*

planetarium (plæ-ni-*tê*ŏ-ri-öm) *n* planetario *m*

plank (plængk) *n* asse *f*

plant (plaant) *n* pianta *f*; impianto *m*; *v* piantare

plantation (plæn-*tei*-ʃön) *n* piantagione *f*

plaster (*plaa*-sstŏ) *n* stucco *m*, gesso *m*; cerotto *m*

plastic (*plæ*-sstik) *adj* plastico; *n* plastica *f*

plate (pleit) *n* piatto *m*; lamiera *f*

plateau (*plæ*-tou) *n* (pl ~x, ~s) altopiano *m*

platform (*plæt*-foom) *n* banchina *f*

platinum (*plæ*-ti-nöm) *n* platino *m*

play (plei) *v* giocare; sonare; *n* gioco *m*; rappresentazione teatrale; **one-act** ~ commedia in un atto; ~ **truant** marinare la scuola

player (pleiŏ) *n* giocatore *m*

playground (*plei*-ghraund) *n* cortile di ricreazione

playing-card (*plei*-ing-kaad) *n* carta da gioco

playwright (*plei*-rait) *n* drammaturgo *m*

plea (plii) *n* difesa *f*

plead (pliid) *v* perorare

pleasant (*plê*-sönt) *adj* gradevole, simpatico, piacevole

please (pliis) per favore; *v* *piacere; **pleased** lieto; **pleasing** gradevole

pleasure (*plê*-ȝö) *n* diletto *m*, divertimento *m*, piacere *m*

plentiful (*plên*-ti-föl) *adj* abbondante

plenty (*plên*-ti) *n* abbondanza *f*

pliers (plaiŏs) *pl* pinze *fpl*

plimsolls (*plim*-ssöls) *pl* scarpe da ginnastica

plot (plot) *n* congiura *f*, complotto *m*; trama *f*; appezzamento *m*

plough (plau) *n* aratro *m*; *v* arare

plucky (*pla*-ki) *adj* coraggioso

plug (plagh) *n* spina *f*; ~ **in** *connettere

plum (plam) *n* susina *f*

plumber (*pla*-mö) *n* idraulico *m*

plump (plamp) *adj* grassottello

plural (*plu*ŏ-röl) *n* plurale *m*

plus (plass) *prep* più

pneumatic (nⁱuu-*mæ*-tik) *adj* pneumatico

pneumonia (nⁱuu-*mou*-ni-ö) *n* polmonite *f*

poach (poutʃ) v cacciare di frodo

pocket (po-kit) n tasca f

pocket-book (po-kit-buk) n portafoglio m

pocket-comb (po-kit-koum) n pettine tascabile

pocket-knife (po-kit-naif) n (pl -knives) temperino m

pocket-watch (po-kit-ᵘotʃ) n orologio da tasca

poem (pou-im) n poema m

poet (pou-it) n poeta m

poetry (pou-i-tri) n poesia f

point (point) n punto m; punta f; v additare; ~ **of view** punto di vista; ~ **out** indicare

pointed (poin-tid) adj appuntato

poison (poi-sön) n veleno m; v avvelenare

poisonous (poi-sö-nöss) adj velenoso

Poland (pou-lönd) Polonia f

Pole (poul) n polacco m

pole (poul) n palo m

police (pö-liiss) pl polizia f

policeman (pö-liiss-mön) n (pl -men) agente m, poliziotto m

police-station (pö-liiss-sstei-ʃön) n posto di polizia

policy (po-li-ssi) n politica f; polizza f

polio (pou-li-ou) n polio f, poliomielite f

Polish (pou-liʃ) adj polacco

polish (po-liʃ) v lucidare

polite (pö-lait) adj cortese

political (pö-li-ti-köl) adj politico

politician (po-li-ti-ʃön) n uomo politico

politics (po-li-tikss) n politica f

pollution (pö-luu-ʃön) n contaminazione f, inquinamento m

pond (pond) n stagno m

pony (pou-ni) n cavallino m

poor (puö) adj povero; misero; scadente

pope (poup) n Papa m

poplin (po-plin) n popelina f

pop music (pop mᶦuu-sik) musica pop

poppy (po-pi) n rosolaccio m; papavero m

popular (po-pᶦu-lö) adj popolare

population (po-pᶦu-lei-ʃön) n popolazione f

populous (po-pᶦu-löss) adj popoloso

porcelain (poo-ssö-lin) n porcellana f

porcupine (poo-kᶦu-pain) n porcospino m

pork (pook) n carne di maiale

port (poot) n porto m; babordo m

portable (poo-tö-böl) adj portatile

porter (poo-tö) n facchino m; portiere m

porthole (poot-houl) n boccaporto m

portion (poo-ʃön) n porzione f

portrait (poo-trit) n ritratto m

Portugal (poo-tᶦu-ghöl) Portogallo m

Portuguese (poo-tᶦu-ghiis) adj portoghese

position (pö-si-ʃön) n posizione f; situazione f; atteggiamento m

positive (po-sö-tiv) adj positivo; n positiva f

possess (pö-sêss) v *possedere; **possessed** adj indemoniato

possession (pö-sê-ʃön) n possesso m; **possessions** possedimenti mpl

possibility (po-ssö-bi-lö-ti) n possibilità f

possible (po-ssö-böl) adj possibile; eventuale

post (pousst) n palo m; impiego m; posta f; v impostare; **post-office** ufficio postale

postage (pou-sstidʒ) n affrancatura f; ~ **paid** franco di porto; ~ **stamp** francobollo m

postcard (pousst-kaad) n cartolina f; cartolina illustrata

poster (pou-sstö) n cartellone m,

poster *m*

poste restante (pousst rê-*sstangt*) fermo posta

postman (*pousst*-mön) *n* (pl -men) postino *m*

post-paid (pousst-*peid*) *adj* porto franco

postpone (pö-*sspoun*) *v* rimandare

pot (pot) *n* pentola *f*

potato (pö-*tei*-tou) *n* (pl ~es) patata *f*

pottery (*po*-tö-ri) *n* ceramica *f*; stoviglie *fpl*

pouch (pautʃ) *n* sacchetto *m*

poulterer (*poul*-tö-rö) *n* pollivendolo *m*

poultry (*poul*-tri) *n* pollame *m*

pound (paund) *n* libbra *f*

pour (poo) *v* versare

poverty (*po*-vö-ti) *n* povertà *f*

powder (*pau*-dö) *n* polvere *f*; ~ **compact** portacipria *m*; **talc** ~ talco *m*

powder-puff (*pau*-dö-paf) *n* piumino da cipria

powder-room (*pau*-dö-ruum) *n* gabinetto per signore

power (pauº) *n* potenza *f*, energia *f*; potere *m*

powerful (*pauº*-föl) *adj* potente, poderoso; forte

powerless (*pauº*-löss) *adj* impotente

power-station (*pauº*-sstei-ʃön) *n* centrale elettrica

practical (*præk*-ti-köl) *adj* pratico

practically (*præk*-ti-kli) *adv* praticamente

practice (*præk*-tiss) *n* pratica *f*

practise (*præk*-tiss) *v* praticare; esercitarsi

praise (preis) *v* lodare; *n* elogio *m*

pram (præm) *n* carrozzina *f*

prawn (proon) *n* gambero *m*, aragostina *f*

pray (prei) *v* pregare

prayer (prêº) *n* preghiera *f*

preach (priitʃ) *v* predicare

precarious (pri-*kêº*-ri-öss) *adj* precario

precaution (pri-*koo*-ʃön) *n* precauzione *f*

precede (pri-*ssiid*) *v* precedere

preceding (pri-*ssii*-ding) *adj* precedente

precious (*prê*-ʃöss) *adj* prezioso

precipice (*prê*-ssi-piss) *n* precipizio *m*

precipitation (pri-ssi-pi-*tei*-ʃön) *n* precipitazione *f*

precise (pri-*ssaiss*) *adj* preciso, esatto; meticoloso

predecessor (*prii*-di-sse-ssö) *n* predecessore *m*

predict (pri-*dikt*) *v* *predire

prefer (pri-*föö*) *v* preferire

preferable (*prê*-fö-rö-böl) *adj* preferibile

preference (*prê*-fö-rönss) *n* preferenza *f*

prefix (*prii*-fikss) *n* prefisso *m*

pregnant (*prêgh*-nönt) *adj* incinta

prejudice (*prê*-dʒö-diss) *n* pregiudizio *m*

preliminary (pri-*li*-mi-nö-ri) *adj* preliminare

premature (*prê*-mö-tʃuº) *adj* prematuro

premier (*prêm*-iº) *n* primo ministro

premises (*prê*-mi-ssiss) *pl* stabile *m*

premium (*prii*-mi-öm) *n* premio *m*

prepaid (prii-*peid*) *adj* pagato in anticipo

preparation (prê-pö-*rei*-ʃön) *n* preparazione *f*

prepare (pri-*pêº*) *v* preparare

preposition (prê-pö-*si*-ʃön) *n* preposizione *f*

prescribe (pri-*sskraib*) *v* *prescrivere

prescription (pri-*sskrip*-ʃön) *n* ricetta *f*

presence (*prê*-sönss) *n* presenza *f*

present¹ (*prê*-sönt) *n* regalo *m*, dono

_m_; presente _m_; _adj_ attuale; presente

present² (pri-_sênt_) _v_ presentare

presently (_prê_-sönt-li) _adv_ a momenti, subito

preservation (prê-sö-_vei_-ſön) _n_ preservazione _f_

preserve (pri-_sööv_) _v_ conservare; *mettere in conserva

president (_prê_-si-dönt) _n_ presidente _m_

press (prêss) _n_ stampa _f_; _v_ schiacciare, premere; stirare; ~ **conference** conferenza stampa

pressing (_prê_-ssing) _adj_ pressante, urgente

pressure (_prê_-ſö) _n_ pressione _f_; tensione _f_; **atmospheric** ~ pressione atmosferica

pressure-cooker (_prê_-ſö-ku-kö) _n_ pentola a pressione

prestige (prê-_sstiiʒ_) _n_ prestigio _m_

presumable (pri-_s^iuu_-mö-böl) _adj_ presumibile

presumptuous (pri-_samp_-ſöss) _adj_ presuntuoso

pretence (pri-_tênss_) _n_ pretesa _f_

pretend (pri-_ténd_) _v_ *fingere, *pretendere

pretext (_prii_-têksst) _n_ pretesto _m_

pretty (_pri_-ti) _adj_ bello, carino; _adv_ alquanto, piuttosto, abbastanza

prevent (pri-_vênt_) _v_ impedire; *prevenire

preventive (pri-_vên_-tiv) _adj_ preventivo

previous (_prii_-vi-öss) _adj_ precedente, anteriore, previo

pre-war (prii-_ᵘoo_) _adj_ d'anteguerra

price (praiss) _v_ prezzare; ~ **list** listino prezzi

priceless (_praiss_-löss) _adj_ inestimabile

price-list (_praiss_-lisst) _n_ prezzo _m_

prick (prik) _v_ *pungere

pride (praid) _n_ fierezza _f_

priest (priisst) _n_ prete _m_

primary (_prai_-mö-ri) _adj_ primario; primo, principale; elementare

prince (prinss) _n_ principe _m_

princess (prin-_ssêss_) _n_ principessa _f_

principal (_prin_-ssö-pöl) _adj_ principale; _n_ preside _m_, direttore _m_

principle (_prin_-ssö-pöl) _n_ principio _m_

print (print) _v_ stampare; _n_ positiva _f_; stampa _f_; **printed matter** stampe

prior (prai⁰) _adj_ anteriore

priority (prai-_o_-rö-ti) _n_ precedenza _f_, priorità _f_

prison (_pri_-sön) _n_ prigione _f_

prisoner (_pri_-sö-nö) _n_ detenuto _m_, prigioniero _m_; ~ **of war** prigioniero di guerra

privacy (_prai_-vö-ssi) _n_ intimità _f_

private (_prai_-vit) _adj_ privato; personale

privilege (_pri_-vi-lidʒ) _n_ privilegio _m_

prize (prais) _n_ premio _m_; ricompensa _f_

probable (_pro_-bö-böl) _adj_ probabile

probably (_pro_-bö-bli) _adv_ probabilmente

problem (_pro_-blöm) _n_ problema _m_

procedure (prö-_ssii_-dʒö) _n_ procedimento _m_

proceed (prö-_ssiid_) _v_ procedere

process (_prou_-ssêss) _n_ procedimento _m_, processo _m_

procession (prö-_ssê_-ſön) _n_ processione _f_, corteo _m_

proclaim (prö-_kleim_) _v_ proclamare

produce¹ (prö-_d^uuss_) _v_ *produrre

produce² (_prod_-^uuss) _n_ prodotto _m_

producer (prö-_d^uu_-ssö) _n_ produttore _m_

product (_pro_-dakt) _n_ prodotto _m_

production (prö-_dak_-ſön) _n_ produzione _f_

profession (prö-_fê_-ſön) _n_ professione _f_

professional (prö-_fê_-ſö-nöl) _adj_ professionale

professor (prö-*fé*-ssö) n professore m

profit (*pro*-fit) n profitto m, guadagno m; vantaggio m; v approfittare

profitable (*pro*-fi-tö-böl) adj fruttuoso

profound (prö-*faund*) adj profondo

programme (*prou*-ghræm) n programma m

progress[1] (*prou*-ghréss) n progresso m

progress[2] (prö-*ghréss*) v progredire

progressive (prö-*ghré*-ssiv) adj progressista; progressivo

prohibit (prö-*hi*-bit) v proibire

prohibition (prou-i-*bi*-Jön) n divieto m

prohibitive (prö-*hi*-bi-tiv) adj proibitivo

project (*pro*-dʒèkt) n piano m, progetto m

promenade (pro-mö-*naad*) n corso m

promise (*pro*-miss) n promessa f; v *promettere

promote (prö-*mout*) v *promuovere

promotion (prö-*mou*-Jön) n promozione f

prompt (prompt) adj sollecito, pronto

pronoun (*prou*-naun) n pronome m

pronounce (prö-*naunss*) v pronunciare

pronunciation (prö-nan-ssi-*ei*-Jön) n pronuncia f

proof (pruuf) n prova f

propaganda (pro-pö-*ghæn*-dö) n propaganda f

propel (prö-*pêl*) v propulsare

propeller (prö-*pê*-lö) n elica f

proper (*pro*-pö) adj giusto; decente, conveniente, adatto, appropriato

property (*pro*-pö-ti) n proprietà f

prophet (*pro*-fit) n profeta m

proportion (prö-*poo*-Jön) n proporzione f

proportional (prö-*poo*-Jö-nöl) adj proporzionale

proposal (prö-*pou*-söl) n proposta f

propose (prö-*pous*) v *proporre

proposition (pro-pö-*si*-Jön) n proposta f

proprietor (prö-*prai*-ö-tö) n proprietario m

prospect (*pro*-sspèkt) n prospettiva f

prospectus (prö-*sspêk*-töss) n prospetto m

prosperity (pro-*sspê*-rö-ti) n prosperità f

prosperous (*pro*-sspö-röss) adj fiorente

prostitute (*pro*-ssti-t'uut) n prostituta f

protect (prö-*têkt*) v *proteggere

protection (prö-*têk*-Jön) n protezione f

protein (*prou*-tiin) n proteina f

protest[1] (*prou*-tèsst) n protesta f

protest[2] (prö-*têsst*) v protestare

Protestant (*pro*-ti-sstönt) adj protestante

proud (praud) adj fiero; orgoglioso

prove (pruuv) v dimostrare, provare; mostrarsi

proverb (*pro*-vööb) n proverbio m

provide (prö-*vaid*) v fornire, *provvedere; **provided that** purché

province (*pro*-vinss) n provincia f

provincial (prö-*vin*-Jöl) adj provinciale

provisional (prö-*vi*-ʒö-nöl) adj provvisorio

provisions (prö-*vi*-ʒöns) pl provvisioni fpl

prune (pruun) n prugna secca

psychiatrist (ssai-*kai*-ö-trisst) n psichiatra m

psychic (*ssai*-kik) adj psichico

psychoanalyst (ssai-kou-*æ*-nö-lisst) n psicoanalista m

psychological (ssai-ko-*lo*-dʒi-köl) adj psicologico

psychologist (ssai-*ko*-lö-dʒisst) n psi-

cologo m
psychology (ssai-*ko*-lö-dʒi) *n* psicologia *f*
pub (pab) *n* taverna *f*; bar *m*
public (*pa*-blik) *adj* pubblico; generale; *n* pubblico *m*; ~ **garden** giardino pubblico; ~ **house** taverna *f*
publication (pa-bli-*kei*-fön) *n* pubblicazione *f*
publicity (pa-*bli*-ssö-ti) *n* pubblicità *f*
publish (*pa*-bliʃ) *v* pubblicare
publisher (*pa*-bli-ʃö) *n* editore *m*
puddle (*pa*-döl) *n* pozzanghera *f*
pull (pul) *v* tirare; ~ **out** partire; ~ **up** fermarsi
pulley (*pu*-li) *n* (pl ~s) carrucola *f*
Pullman (*pul*-mön) *n* vettura pullman
pullover (*pu*-lou-vö) *n* maglione *m*
pulpit (*pul*-pit) *n* cattedra *f*, pulpito *m*
pulse (palss) *n* polso *m*
pump (pamp) *n* pompa *f*; *v* pompare
punch (pantʃ) *v* sferrare pugni; *n* pugno *m*
punctual (*pangk*-tʃu-öl) *adj* puntuale
puncture (*pangk*-tʃö) *n* foratura *f*, bucatura *f*
punctured (*pangk*-tʃöd) *adj* bucato
punish (*pa*-niʃ) *v* punire
punishment (*pa*-niʃ-mönt) *n* punizione *f*
pupil (*p'uu*-pöl) *n* scolaro *m*
puppet-show (*pa*-pit-ʃou) *n* rappresentazione di marionette
purchase (*pöö*-tʃöss) *v* comprare; *n* compera *f*, acquisto *m*; ~ **price** prezzo d'acquisto; ~ **tax** tassa di scambio
purchaser (*pöö*-tʃö-ssö) *n* compratore *m*
pure (p'u⁰) *adj* casto, puro
purple (*pöö*-pöl) *adj* porporino
purpose (*pöö*-pöss) *n* proposito *m*, fine *m*, intenzione *f*; **on** ~ apposta

purse (pööss) *n* borsellino *m*
pursue (pö-*ss'uu*) *v* perseguire
pus (pass) *n* pus *m*
push (puʃ) *n* urto *m*, spinta *f*; *v* *spingere; *farsi largo
push-button (*puʃ*-ba-tön) *n* pulsante *m*
* **put** (put) *v* collocare, posare, *mettere; *porre; ~ **away** *mettere a posto; ~ **off** rinviare; ~ **on** indossare; ~ **out** *spegnere
puzzle (*pa*-söl) *n* rompicapo *m*; enigma *m*; *v* imbarazzare; **jigsaw** ~ puzzle
puzzling (*pas*-ling) *adj* imbarazzante
pyjamas (pö-*dʒaa*-mös) *pl* pigiama *m*

Q

quack (k⁰æk) *n* medicone *m*, ciarlatano *m*
quail (k⁰eil) *n* (pl ~, ~s) quaglia *f*
quaint (k⁰eint) *adj* bizzarro; antiquato
qualification (k⁰o-li-fi-*kei*-fön) *n* qualifica *f*; riserva *f*, restrizione *f*
qualified (*k⁰o*-li-faid) *adj* qualificato; competente
qualify (*k⁰o*-li-fai) *v* *addirsi
quality (*k⁰o*-lö-ti) *n* qualità *f*; caratteristica *f*
quantity (*k⁰on*-tö-ti) *n* quantità *f*; numero *m*
quarantine (*k⁰o*-rön-tiin) *n* quarantena *f*
quarrel (*k⁰o*-röl) *v* litigare; *n* litigio *m*, lite *f*
quarry (*k⁰o*-ri) *n* cava *f*
quarter (*k⁰oo*-tö) *n* quarto *m*; trimestre *m*; quartiere *m*; ~ **of an hour** quarto d'ora
quarterly (*k⁰oo*-tö-li) *adj* trimestrale

quay (kii) *n* molo *m*

queen (kᵘiin) *n* regina *f*

queer (kᵘiⁿ) *adj* singolare, strano; bizzarro

query (kᵘjⁿ-ri) *n* domanda *f*; *v* domandare; *mettere in dubbio

question (kᵘêss-tʃön) *n* questione *f*; problema *m*; *v* interrogare; *mettere in dubbio; ~ **mark** punto interrogativo

queue (kⁱuu) *n* coda *f*; *v* *fare la coda

quick (kᵘik) *adj* svelto

quick-tempered (kᵘik-têm-pöd) *adj* irascibile

quiet (kᵘai-öt) *adj* quieto, calmo, tranquillo; *n* quiete *f*, tranquillità *f*

quilt (kᵘilt) *n* coperta *f*

quinine (kᵘi-niin) *n* chinino *m*

quit (kᵘit) *v* cessare, *smettere

quite (kᵘait) *adv* interamente, completamente; alquanto, abbastanza, piuttosto; assai, molto

quiz (kᵘis) *n* (pl ~zes) quiz *m*

quota (kᵘou-tö) *n* quota *f*

quotation (kᵘou-tei-ʃön) *n* citazione *f*; ~ **marks** virgolette *fpl*

quote (kᵘout) *v* citare

R

rabbit (ræ-bit) *n* coniglio *m*

rabies (rei-bis) *n* rabbia *f*

race (reiss) *n* gara *f*, corsa *f*; razza *f*

race-course (reiss-kooss) *n* pista da corsa, ippodromo *m*

race-horse (reiss-hooss) *n* cavallo da corsa

race-track (reiss-træk) *n* pista da corsa

racial (rei-ʃöl) *adj* razziale

racket (ræ-kit) *n* chiasso *m*

racquet (ræ-kit) *n* racchetta *f*

radiator (rei-di-ei-tö) *n* radiatore *m*

radical (ræ-di-köl) *adj* radicale

radio (rei-di-ou) *n* radio *f*

radish (ræ-diʃ) *n* ravanello *m*

radius (rei-di-öss) *n* (pl radii) raggio *m*

raft (raaft) *n* zattera *f*

rag (rægh) *n* straccio *m*

rage (reidʒ) *n* furore *m*, rabbia *f*; *v* infierire

raid (reid) *n* irruzione *f*

rail (reil) *n* ringhiera *f*, sbarra *f*

railing (rei-ling) *n* inferriata *f*

railroad (reil-roud) *nAm* strada ferrata, ferrovia *f*

railway (reil-ᵘei) *n* ferrovia *f*

rain (rein) *n* pioggia *f*; *v* *piovere

rainbow (rein-bou) *n* arcobaleno *m*

raincoat (rein-kout) *n* impermeabile *m*

rainproof (rein-pruuf) *adj* impermeabile

rainy (rei-ni) *adj* piovoso

raise (reis) *v* sollevare; aumentare; allevare, coltivare; *riscuotere; *nAm* aumento *m*

raisin (rei-sön) *n* uvetta *f*

rake (reik) *n* rastrello *m*

rally (ræ-li) *n* raduno *m*

ramp (ræmp) *n* rampa *f*

ramshackle (ræm-[æ-köl) *adj* sgangerato

rancid (ræn-ssid) *adj* rancido

rang (ræng) *v* (p ring)

range (reindʒ) *n* portata *f*

range-finder (reindʒ-fain-dö) *n* telemetro *m*

rank (rængk) *n* ceto *m*; fila *f*

ransom (ræn-ssöm) *n* riscatto *m*

rape (reip) *v* violentare

rapid (ræ-pid) *adj* veloce, rapido

rapids (ræ-pids) *pl* rapida *f*

rare (rêⁿ) *adj* raro

rarely (*rê^ö*-li) *adv* raramente

rascal (*raa*-ssköl) *n* birbante *m*, monello *m*

rash (ræʃ) *n* esantema *m*, eruzione *f*; *adj* avventato, sconsiderato

raspberry (*raas*-bö-ri) *n* lampone *m*

rat (ræt) *n* ratto *m*

rate (reit) *n* prezzo *m*, tariffa *f*; velocità *f*; **at any ~** ad ogni modo, comunque; **~ of exchange** corso del cambio

rather (*raa*-ðö) *adv* abbastanza, alquanto; piuttosto

ration (*ræ*-ʃön) *n* razione *f*

rattan (ræ-*tæn*) *n* malacca *f*

raven (*rei*-vön) *n* corvo *m*

raw (roo) *adj* crudo; **~ material** materia prima

ray (rei) *n* raggio *m*

rayon (*rei*-on) *n* raion *m*

razor (*rei*-sö) *n* rasoio *m*

razor-blade (*rei*-sö-bleid) *n* lama di rasoio

reach (riitʃ) *v* *raggiungere; *n* portata *f*

reaction (ri-*æk*-ʃön) *n* reazione *f*

***read** (riid) *v* *leggere

reading (*rii*-ding) *n* lettura *f*

reading-lamp (*rii*-ding-læmp) *n* lampada da tavolo

reading-room (*rii*-ding-ruum) *n* sala di lettura

ready (*rê*-di) *adj* pronto

ready-made (*rê*-di-*meid*) *adj* confezionato

real (ri^öl) *adj* reale

reality (ri-æ-lö-ti) *n* realtà *f*

realizable (*ri^ö*-lai-sö-böl) *adj* realizzabile

realize (*ri^ö*-lais) *v* realizzare; attuare

really (*ri^ö*-li) *adv* davvero, veramente; in realtà

rear (ri^ö) *n* parte posteriore; *v* allevare

rear-light (ri^ö-*lait*) *n* fanalino posteriore

reason (*rii*-sön) *n* causa *f*, ragione *f*; senso *m*; *v* ragionare

reasonable (*rii*-sö-nö-böl) *adj* ragionevole

reassure (rii-ö-*ʃu^ö*) *v* tranquillizzare

rebate (*rii*-beit) *n* riduzione *f*, sconto *m*

rebellion (ri-*bêl*-¹ön) *n* rivolta *f*, ribellione *f*

recall (ri-*kool*) *v* ricordarsi; richiamare; revocare

receipt (ri-*ssiit*) *n* ricevuta *f*; ricevimento *m*

receive (ri-*ssiiv*) *v* ricevere

receiver (ri-*ssii*-vö) *n* ricevitore *m*

recent (*rii*-ssönt) *adj* recente

recently (*rii*-ssönt-li) *adv* di recente, recentemente

reception (ri-*ssêp*-ʃön) *n* ricevimento *m*; accoglienza *f*; **~ office** ufficio ricevimento

receptionist (ri-*ssêp*-ʃö-nisst) *n* capo ufficio ricevimento

recession (ri-*ssê*-ʃön) *n* recessione *f*

recipe (*rê*-ssi-pi) *n* ricetta *f*

recital (ri-*ssai*-töl) *n* recital *m*

reckon (*rê*-kön) *v* *fare i calcoli; considerare; credere

recognition (rê-kögh-*ni*-ʃön) *n* riconoscimento *m*

recognize (*rê*-kögh-nais) *v* *riconoscere

recollect (rê-kö-*lêkt*) *v* ricordarsi

recommence (rii-kö-*mênss*) *v* ricominciare

recommend (rê-kö-*mênd*) *v* raccomandare; consigliare

recommendation (rê-kö-mên-*dei*-ʃön) *n* raccomandazione *f*

reconciliation (rê-kön-ssi-li-*ei*-ʃön) *n* riconciliazione *f*

record[1] (*rê*-kood) *n* disco *m*; primato

m; registrazione *f*; **long-playing ~** microsolco *m*

record[2] (ri-*kood*) *v* registrare

recorder (ri-*koo*-dö) *n* magnetofono *m*

recording (ri-*koo*-ding) *n* registrazione *f*

record-player (*rê*-kood-plei⁶) *n* giradischi *m*

recover (ri-*ka*-vö) *v* ricuperare; guarire

recovery (ri-*ka*-vö-ri) *n* guarigione *f*

recreation (rê-kri-*ei*-fön) *n* ricreazione *f*, svago *m*; **~ centre** centro di ricreazione; **~ ground** campo di gioco

recruit (ri-*kruut*) *n* recluta *f*

rectangle (*rêk*-tæng-ghöl) *n* rettangolo *m*

rectangular (rêk-*tæng*-ghi'u-lö) *adj* rettangolare

rector (*rêk*-tö) *n* pastore *m*

rectory (*rêk*-tö-ri) *n* presbiterio *m*

rectum (*rêk*-töm) *n* retto *m*

recycle (ri-*ssai*-köl) *v* riciclare

red (rêd) *adj* rosso

reduce (ri-*d'uuss*) *v* *ridurre, diminuire

reduction (ri-*dak*-fön) *n* ribasso *m*, riduzione *f*

redundant (ri-*dan*-dönt) *adj* ridondante

reed (riid) *n* giunco *m*

reef (riif) *n* banco *m*

reference (*rêf*-rönss) *n* referenza *f*, riferimento *m*; relazione *f*; **with ~ to** riguardo a

refer to (ri-*föö*) rimandare a

refill (*rii*-fil) *n* ricambio *m*

refinery (ri-*fai*-nö-ri) *n* raffineria *f*

reflect (ri-*flêkt*) *v* *riflettere

reflection (ri-*flêk*-fön) *n* riflesso *m*; immagine riflessa

reflector (ri-*flêk*-tö) *n* riflettore *m*

reformation (rê-fö-*mei*-fön) *n* riforma *f*

refresh (ri-*frêf*) *v* rinfrescare

refreshment (ri-*frêf*-mönt) *n* rinfresco *m*

refrigerator (ri-*fri*-dʒö-rei-tö) *n* frigorifero *m*

refund[1] (ri-*fand*) *v* rimborsare

refund[2] (*rii*-fand) *n* rimborso *m*

refusal (ri-*f'uu*-söl) *n* rifiuto *m*

refuse[1] (ri-*f'uus*) *v* rifiutare

refuse[2] (*rê*-f'uuss) *n* immondizia *f*

regard (ri-*ghaad*) *v* considerare; osservare; *n* riguardo *m*; **as regards** per quanto riguarda

regarding (ri-*ghaa*-ding) *prep* riguardo a; in relazione a

regatta (ri-*ghæ*-tö) *n* regata *f*

régime (rei-*ʒiim*) *n* regime *m*

region (*rii*-dʒön) *n* regione *f*

regional (*rii*-dʒö-nöl) *adj* regionale

register (*rê*-dʒi-sstö) *v* registrarsi; raccomandare; **registered letter** raccomandata *f*

registration (rê-dʒi-*sstrei*-fön) *n* registrazione *f*; **~ form** foglio di registrazione; **~ number** numero di targa; **~ plate** targa automobilistica

regret (ri-*ghrêt*) *v* *rimpiangere; *n* rimpianto *m*

regular (*rê*-ghi'u-lö) *adj* regolato, regolare; normale

regulate (*rê*-ghi'u-leit) *v* regolare

regulation (rê-ghi'u-*lei*-fön) *n* regolamento *m*; regolamentazione *f*

rehabilitation (rii-hö-bi-li-*tei*-fön) *n* rieducazione *f*

rehearsal (ri-*höö*-ssöl) *n* prova *f*

rehearse (ri-*hööss*) *v* *fare le prove

reign (rein) *n* regno *m*; *v* regnare

reimburse (rii-im-*bööss*) *v* *rendere, rimborsare

reindeer (*rein*-di⁶) *n* (pl ~) renna *f*

reject (ri-*dʒêkt*) *v* rifiutare, *respingere; rigettare

relate (ri-*leit*) v raccontare

related (ri-*lei*-tid) adj congiunto

relation (ri-*lei*-fön) n relazione f, attinenza f; parente m

relative (*rê*-lö-tiv) n parente m; adj relativo

relax (ri-*lækss*) v rilassarsi

relaxation (ri-læk-*ssei*-fön) n rilassamento m

reliable (ri-*lai*-ö-böl) adj fidato

relic (*rê*-lik) n reliquia f

relief (ri-*liif*) n sollievo m; aiuto m; rilievo m

relieve (ri-*liiv*) v mitigare; *dare il cambio

religion (ri-*li*-dʒön) n religione f

religious (ri-*li*-dʒöss) adj religioso

rely on (ri-*lai*) contare su

remain (ri-*mein*) v *rimanere; restare

remainder (ri-*mein*-dö) n avanzo m, resto m, residuo m

remaining (ri-*mei*-ning) adj rimanente

remark (ri-*maak*) n osservazione f; v osservare

remarkable (ri-*maa*-kö-böl) adj notevole

remedy (*rê*-mö-di) n rimedio m

remember (ri-*mêm*-bö) v ricordarsi

remembrance (ri-*mêm*-brönss) n ricordo m

remind (ri-*maind*) v *far ricordare

remit (ri-*mit*) v *rimettere

remittance (ri-*mi*-tönss) n rimessa f

remnant (*rêm*-nönt) n resto m, rimanenza f, residuo m

remote (ri-*mout*) adj distante, remoto

removal (ri-*muu*-völ) n spostamento m

remove (ri-*muuv*) v spostare

remunerate (ri-*m¹uu*-nö-reit) v rimunerare

remuneration (ri-*m¹uu*-nö-*rei*-fön) n rimunerazione f

renew (ri-*n¹uu*) v rinnovare

rent (rênt) v affittare; n affitto m

repair (ri-*pêᵒ*) v riparare; n restauro m

reparation (rê-pö-*rei*-fön) n riparazione f

*repay (ri-*pei*) v rimborsare

repayment (ri-*pei*-mönt) n rimborso m

repeat (ri-*piit*) v ripetere

repellent (ri-*pê*-lönt) adj ripugnante, repellente

repentance (ri-*pên*-tönss) n pentimento m

repertory (*rê*-pö-tö-ri) n repertorio m

repetition (rê-pö-*ti*-fön) n ripetizione f

replace (ri-*pleiss*) v sostituire

reply (ri-*plai*) v *rispondere; n risposta f; in ~ in risposta

report (ri-*poot*) v riferire; presentarsi; n relazione f, rapporto m

reporter (ri-*poo*-tö) n corrispondente m

represent (rê-pri-*sênt*) v rappresentare; raffigurare

representation (rê-pri-sên-*tei*-fön) n rappresentanza f

representative (rê-pri-*sên*-tö-tiv) adj rappresentativo

reprimand (*rê*-pri-maand) v rimproverare

reproach (ri-*prout*f) n rimprovero m; v rimproverare

reproduce (rii-prö-*d¹uuss*) v *riprodurre

reproduction (rii-prö-*dak*-fön) n riproduzione f

reptile (*rêp*-tail) n rettile m

republic (ri-*pa*-blik) n repubblica f

republican (ri-*pa*-bli-kön) adj repubblicano

repulsive (ri-*pal*-ssiv) adj ributtante

reputation (rê-p¹u-*tei*-fön) n reputazione f; fama f

request (ri-k^{u}êsst) n richiesta f; domanda f; v *richiedere

require (ri-k^{u}ai^ö) v *esigere

requirement (ri-k^{u}ai^ö-mönt) n esigenza f

requisite (rê-k^{u}i-sit) adj richiesto

rescue (ré-ssk'uu) v salvare; n salvataggio m

research (ri-ssööt∫) n ricerca f

resemblance (ri-sêm-blönss) n somiglianza f

resemble (ri-sêm-böl) v assomigliare a

resent (ri-sênt) v risentirsi per

reservation (rê-sö-vei-∫ön) n prenotazione f

reserve (ri-sööv) v riservare; prenotare; n riserva f

reserved (ri-söövd) adj riservato

reservoir (rê-sö-v^{u}aa) n serbatoio m

reside (ri-said) v abitare

residence (rê-si-dönss) n residenza f; ~ **permit** permesso di soggiorno

resident (rê-si-dönt) n residente m; adj residente; interno

resign (ri-sain) v *dimettersi

resignation (rê-sigh-nei-∫ön) n dimissioni fpl

resin (rê-sin) n resina f

resist (ri-sisst) v resistere

resistance (ri-si-sstönss) n resistenza f

resolute (rê-sö-luut) adj risoluto, deciso

respect (ri-sspêkt) n rispetto m; stima f, deferenza f; v rispettare

respectable (ri-sspêk-tö-böl) adj rispettabile

respectful (ri-sspêk-föl) adj rispettoso

respective (ri-sspêk-tiv) adj rispettivo

respiration (rê-sspö-rei-∫ön) n respirazione f

respite (rê-sspait) n dilazione f

responsibility (ri-sspon-ssö-bi-lö-ti) n responsabilità f

responsible (ri-sspon-ssö-böl) adj responsabile

rest (rêsst) n riposo m; resto m; v riposarsi

restaurant (rê-sstö-rong) n ristorante m

restful (rêsst-föl) adj riposante

rest-home (rêsst-houm) n casa di riposo

restless (rêsst-löss) adj inquieto; irrequieto

restrain (ri-sstrein) v *contenere, *trattenere

restriction (ri-sstrik-∫ön) n restrizione f

result (ri-salt) n risultato m; conseguenza f; esito m; v risultare

resume (ri-s'uum) v *riprendere

résumé (rê-s'u-mei) n riassunto m

retail (rii-teil) v vendere al minuto; ~ **trade** commercio al minuto, vendita al minuto

retailer (rii-tei-lö) n dettagliante m; rivenditore m

retina (rê-ti-nö) n retina f

retired (ri-tai^{ö}d) adj pensionato

return (ri-töön) v ritornare; n ritorno m; ~ **flight** volo di ritorno; ~ **journey** viaggio di ritorno

reunite (rii-'uu-nait) v riunire

reveal (ri-viil) v svelare, rivelare

revelation (rê-vö-lei-∫ön) n rivelazione f

revenge (ri-vênd3) n vendetta f

revenue (rê-vö-n'uu) n entrate, reddito m

reverse (ri-vööss) n contrario m; rovescio m; marcia indietro; rivolgimento m; adj inverso; v *far marcia indietro

review (ri-v'uu) n recensione f; rivista f

revise (ri-vais) v revisionare

revision (ri-vi-3ön) n revisione f

revival (ri-*vai*-völ) *n* ripristino *m*

revolt (ri-*voult*) *v* rivoltarsi; *n* ribellione *f*, rivolta *f*

revolting (ri-*voul*-ting) *adj* stomachevole, rivoltante, disgustoso

revolution (rê-vö-*luu*-ʃön) *n* rivoluzione *f*

revolutionary (rê-vö-*luu*-ʃö-nö-ri) *adj* rivoluzionario

revolver (ri-*vol*-vö) *n* rivoltella *f*

revue (ri-*v*ʲuu) *n* rivista *f*

reward (ri-*ᵘood*) *n* ricompensa *f*; *v* ricompensare

rheumatism (*ruu*-mö-ti-söm) *n* reumatismo *m*

rhinoceros (rai-*no*-ssö-röss) *n* (pl ~, ~es) rinoceronte *m*

rhubarb (*ruu*-baab) *n* rabarbaro *m*

rhyme (raim) *n* rima *f*

rhythm (*ri*-ðöm) *n* ritmo *m*

rib (rib) *n* costola *f*

ribbon (*ri*-bön) *n* nastro *m*

rice (raiss) *n* riso *m*

rich (ritʃ) *adj* ricco

riches (*ri*-tʃis) *pl* ricchezza *f*

riddle (*ri*-döl) *n* indovinello *m*

ride (raid) *n* corsa *f*

*****ride** (raid) *v* *andare in macchina; cavalcare

rider (*rai*-dö) *n* cavallerizzo *m*

ridge (ridʒ) *n* cresta *f*

ridicule (*ri*-di-kʲuul) *v* ridicolizzare

ridiculous (ri-*di*-kʲu-löss) *adj* ridicolo

riding (*rai*-ding) *n* equitazione *f*

riding-school (*rai*-ding-sskuul) *n* scuola di equitazione

rifle (*rai*-föl) *v* fucile *m*

right (rait) *n* diritto *m*; *adj* corretto, giusto; retto; destro; equo; **all right!** va bene!; *** be ~ ***avere ragione; ~ **of way** precedenza *f*

righteous (*rai*-tʃöss) *adj* giusto

right-hand (*rait*-hænd) *adj* destro

rightly (*rait*-li) *adv* giustamente

rim (rim) *n* cerchione *m*; orlo *m*

ring (ring) *n* anello *m*; cerchio *m*; pista *f*

*****ring** (ring) *v* suonare; ~ **up** telefonare

rinse (rinss) *v* sciacquare; *n* sciacquata *f*

riot (*rai*-öt) *n* sommossa *f*

rip (rip) *v* strappare

ripe (raip) *adj* maturo

rise (rais) *n* aumento *m*; altura *f*; rialzo *m*; ascesa *f*

*** rise** (rais) *v* alzarsi; *sorgere; *salire

rising (*rai*-sing) *n* insurrezione *f*

risk (rissk) *n* rischio *m*; pericolo *m*; *v* rischiare

risky (*ri*-sski) *adj* rischioso

rival (*rai*-völ) *n* rivale *m*; concorrente *m*; *v* rivaleggiare

rivalry (*rai*-völ-ri) *n* rivalità *f*; concorrenza *f*

river (*ri*-vö) *n* fiume *m*; ~ **bank** argine *m*

riverside (*ri*-vö-ssaid) *n* lungofiume *m*

roach (routʃ) *n* (pl ~) lasca *f*

road (roud) *n* strada *f*; ~ **fork** *n* bivio *m*; ~ **map** carta stradale; ~ **system** rete stradale; ~ **up** strada in riparazione

roadhouse (*roud*-hauss) *n* locanda *f*

roadside (*roud*-ssaid) *n* margine della strada; ~ **restaurant** locanda *f*

roadway (*roud*-ᵘei) *nAm* rotabile *f*

roam (roum) *v* vagabondare

roar (roo) *v* mugghiare, ruggire; *n* ruggito *m*, rombo *m*

roast (rousst) *v* *cuocere arrosto, arrostire

rob (rob) *v* rubare

robber (*ro*-bö) *n* ladro *m*

robbery (*ro*-bö-ri) *n* rapina *f*, furto *m*

robe (roub) *n* abito femminile; veste *f*

robin (*ro*-bin) *n* pettirosso *m*

robust (rou-*basst*) *adj* robusto

rock (rok) *n* roccia *f*; *v* dondolare

rocket (*ro*-kit) *n* razzo *m*

rocky (*ro*-ki) *adj* roccioso

rod (rod) *n* barra *f*, stecca *f*

roe (rou) *n* uova di pesce

roll (roul) *v* rotolare; *n* rotolo *m*; panino *m*

roller-skating (*rou*-lö-sskei-ting) *n* pattinaggio a rotelle

Roman Catholic (*rou*-mön kæ-θö-lik) cattolico

romance (rö-*mænss*) *n* idillio *m*

romantic (rö-*mæn*-tik) *adj* romantico

roof (ruuf) *n* tetto *m*; **thatched** ~ tetto di paglia

room (ruum) *n* camera *f*, stanza *f*; spazio *m*, vano *m*; ~ **and board** vitto e alloggio; ~ **service** servizio in camera; ~ **temperature** temperatura ambientale

roomy (*ruu*-mi) *adj* spazioso

root (ruut) *n* radice *f*

rope (roup) *n* corda *f*

rosary (*rou*-sö-ri) *n* rosario *m*

rose (rous) *n* rosa *f*; *adj* rosa

rotten (*ro*-tön) *adj* marcio

rouge (ruuʒ) *n* rossetto *m*

rough (raf) *adj* malagevole

roulette (ruu-*lét*) *n* roulette *f*

round (raund) *adj* rotondo; *prep* attorno a, intorno a; *n* ripresa *f*; ~ **trip** *Am* andata e ritorno

roundabout (*raun*-dö-baut) *n* rotonda *f*

rounded (*raun*-did) *adj* arrotondato

route (ruut) *n* rotta *f*

routine (ruu-*tiin*) *n* abitudine *f*

row[1] (rou) *n* fila *f*; *v* remare

row[2] (rau) *n* lite *f*

rowdy (*rau*-di) *adj* turbolento

rowing-boat (*rou*-ing-bout) *n* barca a remi

royal (*roi*-öl) *adj* reale

rub (rab) *v* strofinare

rubber (*ra*-bö) *n* caucciù *m*; gomma per cancellare; ~ **band** elastico *m*

rubbish (*ra*-biʃ) *n* immondizia *f*; sciocchezza *f*, stupidaggini *fpl*; **talk** ~ *dire stupidaggini

rubbish-bin (*ra*-biʃ-bin) *n* pattumiera *f*

ruby (*ruu*-bi) *n* rubino *m*

rucksack (*rak*-ssæk) *n* zaino *m*

rudder (*ra*-dö) *n* timone *m*

rude (ruud) *adj* grossolano

rug (ragh) *n* tappeto *m*

ruin (*ruu*-in) *v* rovinare; *n* rovina *f*

ruination (ruu-i-*nei*-ʃön) *n* rovina *f*

rule (ruul) *n* regola *f*; regime *m*, governo *m*, dominio *m*; *v* dominare, governare; **as a** ~ generalmente, di norma

ruler (*ruu*-lö) *n* monarca *m*, sovrano *m*; riga *f*

Rumania (ruu-*mei*-ni-ö) Romania *f*

Rumanian (ruu-*mei*-ni-ön) *adj* romeno

rumour (*ruu*-mö) *n* diceria *f*

***run** (ran) *v* *correre; ~ **into** incontrare

runaway (*ra*-nö-ᵘei) *n* fuggitivo *m*

rung (ran) *V* (pp ring)

runway (*ran*-ᵘei) *n* pista di decollo

rural (*ruᵒ*-röl) *adj* rurale

ruse (ruus) *n* astuzia *f*

rush (raʃ) *v* affrettarsi; *n* giunco *m*

rush-hour (*raʃ*-auᵒ) *n* ora di punta

Russia (*ra*-ʃö) Russia *f*

Russian (*ra*-ʃön) *adj* russo

rust (rasst) *n* ruggine *f*

rustic (*ra*-sstik) *adj* rustico

rusty (*ra*-ssti) *adj* arrugginito

S

saccharin (*ssæ*-kö-rin) *n* saccarina *f*

sack (ssæk) *n* sacco *m*

sacred (*ssei*-krid) *adj* sacro

sacrifice (*ssæ*-kri-faiss) *n* sacrificio *m*; *v* sacrificare

sacrilege (*ssæ*-kri-lidʒ) *n* sacrilegio *m*

sad (ssæd) *adj* triste; mesto, afflitto, malinconico

saddle (*ssæ*-döl) *n* sella *f*

sadness (*ssæd*-nöss) *n* tristezza *f*

safe (sseif) *adj* sicuro; *n* cassaforte *f*

safety (*sseif*-ti) *n* sicurezza *f*

safety-belt (*sseif*-ti-bēlt) *n* cintura di sicurezza

safety-pin (*sseif*-ti-pin) *n* spillo di sicurezza

safety-razor (*sseif*-ti-rei-sö) *n* rasoio *m*

sail (sseil) *v* navigare; *n* vela *f*

sailing-boat (*ssei*-ling-bout) *n* barca a vela

sailor (*ssei*-lö) *n* marinaio *m*

saint (sseint) *n* santo *m*

salad (*ssæ*-löd) *n* insalata *f*

salad-oil (*ssæ*-löd-oil) *n* olio da tavola

salary (*ssæ*-lö-ri) *n* stipendio *m*, salario *m*

sale (sseil) *n* vendita *f*; **clearance ~** svendita *f*; **for ~** in vendita; **sales** saldi; **sales tax** tassa di scambio

saleable (*ssei*-lö-böl) *adj* vendibile

salesgirl (*sseils*-ghööl) *n* commessa *f*

salesman (*sseils*-mön) *n* (pl -men) commesso *m*

salmon (*ssæ*-mön) *n* (pl ~) salmone *m*

salon (*ssæ*-long) *n* salone *m*

saloon (ssö-*luun*) *n* bar *m*

salt (ssoolt) *n* sale *m*

salt-cellar (*ssoolt*-ssê-lö) *n* saliera *f*

salty (*ssool*-ti) *adj* salato

salute (ssö-*luut*) *v* salutare

salve (ssaav) *n* unguento *m*

same (sseim) *adj* stesso

sample (*ssaam*-pöl) *n* campione *m*

sanatorium (ssæ-nö-*too*-ri-öm) *n* (pl ~s, -ria) sanatorio *m*

sand (ssænd) *n* sabbia *f*

sandal (*ssæn*-döl) *n* sandalo *m*

sandpaper (*ssænd*-pei-pö) *n* carta vetrata

sandwich (*ssæn*-ᵘidʒ) *n* tramezzino *m*

sandy (*ssæn*-di) *adj* sabbioso

sanitary (*ssæ*-ni-tö-ri) *adj* sanitario; **~ towel** pannolino igienico

sapphire (*ssæ*-faiö) *n* zaffiro *m*

sardine (ssaa-*diin*) *n* sardina *f*

satchel (*ssæ*-tʃöl) *n* cartella *f*

satellite (*ssæ*-tö-lait) *n* satellite *m*

satin (*ssæ*-tin) *n* raso *m*

satisfaction (ssæ-tiss-*fæk*-ʃön) *n* appagamento *m*, soddisfazione *f*

satisfy (*ssæ*-tiss-fai) *v* *soddisfare; **satisfied** accontentato, soddisfatto

Saturday (*ssæ*-tö-di) sabato *m*

sauce (ssooss) *n* salsa *f*

saucepan (*ssooss*-pön) *n* casseruola *f*

saucer (*ssoo*-ssö) *n* piattino *m*

Saudi Arabia (ssau-di-ö-*rei*-bi-ö) Arabia Saudita

Saudi Arabian (ssau-di-ö-*rei*-bi-ön) *adj* saudita

sauna (*ssoo*-nö) *n* sauna *f*

sausage (*sso*-ssidʒ) *n* salsiccia *f*

savage (*ssæ*-vidʒ) *adj* selvaggio

save (sseiv) *v* salvare; risparmiare

savings (*ssei*-vings) *pl* risparmi *mpl*; **~ bank** cassa di risparmio

saviour (*ssei*-v'ö) *n* salvatore *m*

savoury (*ssei*-vö-ri) *adj* saporito; piccante

saw¹ (ssoo) *v* (p see)

saw² (ssoo) *n* sega *f*

sawdust (*ssoo*-dasst) *n* segatura *f*

saw-mill (*ssoo*-mil) *n* segheria *f*

*say (ssei) *v* *dire

scaffolding (*sskæ*-föl-ding) *n* impalcatura *f*

scale (sskeil) *n* scala *f*; scala musicale; squama *f*; **scales** *pl* bilancia *f* scandal (*sskæn*-döl) n scandalo m

Scandinavia (sskæn-di-*nei*-vi-ö) Scandinavia f

Scandinavian (sskæn-di-*nei*-vi-ön) adj scandinavo

scapegoat (*sskeip*-ghout) n capro espiatorio

scar (sskaa) n cicatrice f

scarce (sskê°ss) adj scarso

scarcely (*sskê°*-ssli) adv scarsamente

scarcity (sskê°-ssö-ti) n penuria f

scare (sskê°) v spaventare; n spavento m

scarf (sskaaf) n (pl ~s, scarves) sciarpa f, scialle m

scarlet (*sskaa*-löt) adj scarlatto

scary (sskê°-ri) adj allarmante

scatter (*sskæ*-tö) v sparpagliare

scene (ssiin) n scena f

scenery (*ssii*-nö-ri) n paesaggio m

scenic (*ssii*-nik) adj pittoresco

scent (ssênt) n profumo m

schedule (/é-d¹uul) n orario m

scheme (sskiim) n schema m; progetto m

scholar (*ssko*-lö) n erudito m; allievo m

scholarship (ssko-lö-ſip) n borsa di studio

school (sskuul) n scuola f

schoolboy (*sskuul*-boi) n scolaro m

schoolgirl (*sskuul*-ghööl) n scolara f

schoolmaster (*sskuul*-maa-sstö) n insegnante m, maestro m

schoolteacher (*sskuul*-tii-tſö) n insegnante m

science (*ssai*-önss) n scienza f

scientific (ssai-ön-*ti*-fik) adj scientifico

scientist (*ssai*-ön-tisst) n scienziato m

scissors (*ssi*-sös) pl forbici fpl

scold (sskould) v riprovare; inveire

scooter (*sskuu*-tö) n scooter m; monopattino m

score (sskoo) n punteggio m; v marcare

scorn (sskoon) n scherno m, disprezzo m; v disprezzare

Scot (sskot) n scozzese m

Scotch (sskotſ) adj scozzese; scotch tape nastro gommato

Scotland (*sskot*-lönd) Scozia f

Scottish (*ssko*-tiſ) adj scozzese

scout (sskaut) n boy-scout m

scrap (sskræp) n pezzetto m

scrap-book (*sskræp*-buk) n album per ritagli

scrape (sskreip) v raschiare

scrap-iron (*sskræ*-pai°n) n rottame di ferro

scratch (sskrætſ) v scalfire, graffiare; n scalfittura f, graffio m

scream (sskriim) v urlare, strillare; n strillo m, grido m

screen (sskriin) n riparo m; video m, schermo m

screw (sskruu) n vite f; v avvitare

screw-driver (*sskruu*-drai-vö) n cacciavite m

scrub (sskrab) v strofinare; n cespuglio m

sculptor (*sskalp*-tö) n scultore m

sculpture (*sskalp*-tſö) n scultura f

sea (ssii) n mare m

sea-bird (*ssii*-bööd) n uccello marino

sea-coast (*ssii*-kousst) n litorale m

seagull (*ssii*-ghal) n gabbiano m

seal (ssiil) n sigillo m; foca f

seam (ssiim) n cucitura f

seaman (*ssii*-mön) n (pl -men) marinaio m

seamless (*ssiim*-löss) adj senza cucitura

seaport (*ssii*-poot) n porto di mare

search (ssöötſ) v cercare; perquisire, perlustrare; n ricerca f

searchlight (*ssöötſ*-lait) n riflettore m

seascape (*ssii*-sskeip) n marina f

sea-shell (*ssii*-ſêl) n conchiglia f

seashore (ssii-ʃoo) n riva del mare

seasick (ssii-ssik) adj sofferente di mal di mare

seasickness (ssii-ssik-nöss) n mal di mare

seaside (ssii-ssaid) n riva del mare; ~ **resort** stazione balneare

season (ssii-sön) n stagione f; **high** ~ alta stagione; **low** ~ bassa stagione; **off** ~ fuori stagione

season-ticket (ssii-sön-ti-kit) n abbonamento m

seat (ssiit) n sedia f; posto m; sede f

seat-belt (ssiit-bêlt) n cintura di sicurezza

sea-urchin (ssii-öö-tʃin) n riccio di mare

sea-water (ssii-ᵘoo-tö) n acqua di mare

second (ssê-könd) num secondo; n secondo m; istante m

secondary (ssê-kön-dö-ri) adj secondario; ~ **school** scuola media

second-hand (ssê-könd-hænd) adj d'occasione

secret (ssii-kröt) n segreto m; adj segreto

secretary (ssê-krö-tri) n segretaria f; segretario m

section (ssêk-ʃön) n sezione f; scomparto m, reparto m

secure (ssi-kʲuᵒ) adj sicuro; v assicurarsi

security (ssi-kʲuᵒ-rö-ti) n sicurezza f; cauzione f

sedate (ssi-deit) adj composto

sedative (ssê-dö-tiv) n sedativo m

seduce (ssi-dʲuuss) v *sedurre

*** see** (ssii) v *vedere; capire, *rendersi conto; ~ **to** occuparsi di

seed (ssiid) n semenza f

*** seek** (ssiik) v cercare

seem (ssiim) v sembrare, *parere

seen (ssiin) v (pp see)

seesaw (ssii-ssoo) n altalena f

seize (ssiis) v afferrare

seldom (ssêl-döm) adv raramente

select (ssi-lêkt) v selezionare, *scegliere; adj selezionato, scelto

selection (ssi-lêk-ʃön) n scelta f, selezione f

self-centred (ssêlf-ssên-töd) adj egocentrico

self-employed (ssêl-fim-ploid) adj indipendente

self-evident (ssêl-fê-vi-dönt) adj lampante

self-government (ssêlf-gha-vö-mönt) n autogoverno m

selfish (ssêl-fiʃ) adj egoista

selfishness (ssêl-fiʃ-nöss) n egoismo m

self-service (ssêlf-ssöö-viss) n self-service m

*** sell** (ssêl) v vendere

semblance (ssêm-blönss) n apparenza f

semi- (ssê-mi) semi-

semicircle (ssê-mi-ssöö-köl) n semicerchio m

semi-colon (ssê-mi-kou-lön) n punto e virgola

senate (ssê-nöt) n senato m

senator (ssê-nö-tö) n senatore m

*** send** (ssênd) v mandare, spedire; ~ **back** rinviare, rispedire; ~ **for** *far venire; ~ **off** spedire

senile (ssii-nail) adj senile

sensation (ssên-ssei-ʃön) n sensazione f

sensational (ssên-ssei-ʃö-nöl) adj sensazionale

sense (ssênss) n senso m; discernimento m, ragione f; significato m; v percepire; ~ **of honour** sentimento dell'onore

senseless (ssênss-löss) adj insensato

sensible (ssên-ssö-böl) adj ragionevole

sensitive (*ssên*-ssi-tiv) *adj* sensibile

sentence (*ssên*-tönss) *n* frase *f*; sentenza *f*; *v* condannare

sentimental (ssên-ti-*mên*-töl) *adj* sentimentale

separate[1] (*ssê*-pö-reit) *v* separare

separate[2] (*ssê*-pö-röt) *adj* distinto, separato

separately (*ssê*-pö-röt-li) *adv* a parte

September (ssêp-*têm*-bö) settembre

septic (*ssêp*-tik) *adj* settico; *****become ~ infiammarsi

sequel (*ssii*-kʉöl) *n* continuazione *f*

sequence (*ssii*-kʉönss) *n* successione *f*; serie *f*

serene (ssö-*riin*) *adj* calmo; sereno

serial (*ssiö*-ri-öl) *n* romanzo a puntate

series (*ssiö*-riis) *n* (pl ~) serie *f*

serious (*ssiö*-ri-öss) *adj* serio

seriousness (*ssiö*-ri-öss-nöss) *n* serietà *f*

sermon (*ssöö*-mön) *n* sermone *m*

serum (*ssiö*-röm) *n* siero *m*

servant (*ssöö*-vönt) *n* servitore *m*

serve (ssööv) *v* servire

service (*ssöö*-viss) *n* servizio *m*; ~ **charge** servizio *m*; ~ **station** distributore di benzina

serviette (ssöö-vi-*êt*) *n* tovagliolo *m*

session (*ssê*-ʃön) *n* sessione *f*

set (ssêt) *n* assieme *m*, gruppo *m*

*****set** (ssêt) *v* *****mettere; ~ **menu** pranzo a prezzo fisso; ~ **out** partire

setting (*ssê*-ting) *n* scenario *m*; ~ **lotion** fissatore per capelli

settle (*ssê*-töl) *v* sistemare, fissare; ~ **down** sistemarsi

settlement (*ssê*-töl-mönt) *n* accomodamento *m*, aggiustamento *m*, accordo *m*

seven (*ssê*-vön) *num* sette

seventeen (ssê-vön-*tiin*) *num* diciassette

seventeenth (ssê-vön-*tiinθ*) *num* diciassettesimo

seventh (*ssê*-vönθ) *num* settimo

seventy (*ssê*-vön-ti) *num* settanta

several (*ssê*-vö-röl) *adj* diversi, parecchi

severe (ssi-*viö*) *adj* violento, rigoroso, severo

sew (ssou) *v* cucire; ~ **up** suturare

sewer (*ssuu*-ö) *n* fogna *f*

sewing-machine (*ssou*-ing-mö-ʃiin) *n* macchina da cucire

sex (ssêkss) *n* sesso *m*

sexton (*ssêk*-sstön) *n* sagrestano *m*

sexual (*ssêk*-ʃu-öl) *adj* sessuale

sexuality (ssêk-ʃu-æ-lö-ti) *n* sessualità *f*

shade (ʃeid) *n* ombra *f*; tinta *f*

shadow (*ʃæ*-dou) *n* ombra *f*

shady (*ʃei*-di) *adj* ombreggiato

*****shake** (ʃeik) *v* agitare

shaky (*ʃei*-ki) *adj* vacillante

*****shall** (ʃæl) *v* *****dovere

shallow (*ʃæ*-lou) *adj* poco profondo

shame (ʃeim) *n* vergogna *f*; disonore *m*; **shame!** vergogna!

shampoo (ʃæm-*puu*) *n* shampoo *m*

shamrock (*ʃæm*-rok) *n* trifoglio *m*

shape (ʃeip) *n* forma *f*; *v* formare

share (ʃêö) *v* *****condividere; *n* parte *f*; azione *f*

shark (ʃaak) *n* pescecane *m*

sharp (ʃaap) *adj* affilato

sharpen (*ʃaa*-pön) *v* affilare

shave (ʃeiv) *v* *****radere

shaver (*ʃei*-vö) *n* rasoio elettrico

shaving-brush (*ʃei*-ving-braʃ) *n* pennello da barba

shaving-cream (*ʃei*-ving-kriim) *n* crema da barba

shaving-soap (*ʃei*-ving-ssoup) *n* sapone da barba

shawl (ʃool) *n* scialle *m*

she (ʃii) *pron* essa

shed (ʃēd) n baracca f

*shed (ʃēd) v versare; *diffondere

sheep (ʃiip) n (pl ~) pecora f

sheer (ʃiᵒ) adj assoluto, puro; fino, trasparente, sottile

sheet (ʃiit) n lenzuolo m; foglio m; lamina f

shelf (ʃēlf) n (pl shelves) scaffale m

shell (ʃēl) n conchiglia f; guscio m

shellfish (ʃēl-fiʃ) n crostaceo m

shelter (ʃēl-tö) n riparo m, rifugio m; v riparare

shepherd (ʃê-pöd) n pastore m

shift (ʃift) n squadra f

*shine (ʃain) v brillare; scintillare, risplendere

ship (ʃip) n nave f; v spedire; shipping line linea di navigazione

shipowner (ʃi-pou-nö) n armatore m

shipyard (ʃip-¹aad) n cantiere navale

shirt (ʃööt) n camicia f

shiver (ʃi-vö) v tremare, rabbrividire; n brivido m

shivery (ʃi-vö-ri) adj infreddolito

shock (ʃok) n scossa f; v *scuotere; ~ absorber ammortizzatore m

shocking (ʃo-king) adj urtante

shoe (ʃuu) n scarpa f; gym shoes scarpe da ginnastica; ~ polish lucido per scarpe

shoe-lace (ʃuu-leiss) n stringa per scarpe

shoemaker (ʃuu-mei-kö) n calzolaio m

shoe-shop (ʃuu-ʃop) n calzoleria f

shook (ʃuk) v (p shake)

*shoot (ʃuut) v sparare

shop (ʃop) n negozio m; v *fare la spesa; ~ assistant commesso m; shopping bag borsa per la spesa; shopping centre centro commerciale

shopkeeper (ʃop-kii-pö) n negoziante m

shop-window (ʃop-ᵘin-dou) n vetrina f

shore (ʃoo) n riva f, sponda f

short (ʃoot) adj corto; basso; ~ circuit corto circuito

shortage (ʃoo-tidʒ) n carenza f, mancanza f

shortcoming (ʃoot-ka-ming) n deficienza f

shorten (ʃoo-tön) v raccorciare

shorthand (ʃoot-hænd) n stenografia f

shortly (ʃoot-li) adv presto, tra breve, prossimamente

shorts (ʃootss) pl calzoncini mpl; plAm mutande fpl

short-sighted (ʃoot-ssai-tid) adj miope

shot (ʃot) n sparo m; iniezione f; sequenza f

*should (ʃud) v *dovere

shoulder (ʃoul-dö) n spalla f

shout (ʃaut) v urlare, gridare; n grido m

shovel (ʃa-völ) n pala f

show (ʃou) n rappresentazione f, spettacolo m; esposizione f

*show (ʃou) v mostrare; *far vedere, esibire; dimostrare

show-case (ʃou-keiss) n bacheca f

shower (ʃauᵒ) n doccia f; acquazzone m, precipitazione f

showroom (ʃou-ruum) n sala di esposizione

shriek (ʃriik) v strillare; n strillo m

shrimp (ʃrimp) n gamberetto m

shrine (ʃrain) n santuario m

*shrink (ʃringk) v *restringersi

shrinkproof (ʃringk-pruuf) adj irrestringibile

shrub (ʃrab) n arbusto m

shudder (ʃa-dö) n brivido m

shuffle (ʃa-föl) v mescolare

*shut (ʃat) v *chiudere; ~ in *rinchiudere

shutter (ʃa-tö) n imposta f, persiana f

shy (ʃai) *adj* schivo, timido

shyness (ʃai-nöss) *n* timidezza *f*

Siam (ssai-*æm*) Siam *m*

Siamese (ssai-ö-*miis*) *adj* siamese

sick (ssik) *adj* ammalato; nauseato

sickness (ssik-nöss) *n* male *m*; nausea *f*

side (ssaid) *n* lato *m*; parte *f*; **one-sided** *adj* unilaterale

sideburns (ssaid-bööns) *pl* basette *fpl*

sidelight (ssaid-lait) *n* luce laterale

side-street (ssaid-sstriit) *n* traversa *f*

sidewalk (ssaid-ᵘook) *nAm* marciapiede *m*

sideways (ssaid-ᵘeis) *adv* lateralmente

siege (ssiidʒ) *n* assedio *m*

sieve (ssiv) *n* setaccio *m*; *v* setacciare

sift (ssift) *v* vagliare

sight (ssait) *n* vista *f*; veduta *f*, spettacolo *m*; curiosità *f*

sign (ssain) *n* segno *m*; gesto *m*, cenno *m*; *v* *sottoscrivere, firmare

signal (ssigh-nöl) *n* segnale *m*; segno *m*; *v* segnalare

signature (ssigh-nö-tʃö) *n* firma *f*

significant (ssigh-*ni*-fi-könt) *adj* significativo

signpost (ssain-pousst) *n* cartello indicatore

silence (ssai-lönss) *n* silenzio *m*; *v* *far tacere

silencer (ssai-lön-ssö) *n* silenziatore *m*

silent (ssai-lönt) *adj* silenzioso; *be ~ *tacere

silk (ssilk) *n* seta *f*

silken (ssil-kön) *adj* di seta

silly (ssi-li) *adj* grullo, sciocco

silver (ssil-vö) *n* argento *m*; d'argento

silversmith (ssil-vö-ssmiθ) *n* argentiere *m*

silverware (ssil-vö-ᵘê̂ᵒ) *n* argenteria *f*

similar (ssi-mi-lö) *adj* analogo, simile

similarity (ssi-mi-*læ*-rö-ti) *n* rassomiglianza *f*

simple (ssim-pöl) *adj* ingenuo, semplice; ordinario

simply (ssim-pli) *adv* semplicemente

simulate (ssi-mᶦu-leit) *v* simulare

simultaneous (ssi-möl-*tei*-ni-öss) *adj* simultaneo

sin (ssin) *n* peccato *m*

since (ssinss) *prep* da; *adv* da allora; *conj* dacché; poiché

sincere (ssin-*ssiᵒ*) *adj* sincero

sinew (ssi-nᶦuu) *n* tendine *m*

***sing** (ssing) *v* cantare

singer (ssing-ö) *n* cantante *m*

single (ssing-ghöl) *adj* singolo; celibe

singular (ssing-ghᶦu-lö) *n* singolare *m*; *adj* strano

sinister (ssi-ni-sstö) *adj* sinistro

sink (ssingk) *n* lavello *m*

***sink** (ssingk) *v* affondare

sip (ssip) *n* sorsetto *m*

siphon (ssai-fön) *n* sifone *m*

sir (ssöö) *n* signore *m*

siren (ssaiᵒ-rön) *n* sirena *f*

sister (ssi-sstö) *n* sorella *f*

sister-in-law (ssi-sstö-rin-loo) *n* (pl sisters-) cognata *f*

***sit** (ssit) *v* *sedere; ~ **down** *sedersi

site (ssait) *n* sito *m*; posizione *f*

sitting-room (ssi-ting-ruum) *n* soggiorno *m*

situated (ssi-tʃu-ei-tid) *adj* situato

situation (ssi-tʃu-*ei*-ʃön) *n* situazione *f*; ubicazione *f*

six (ssikss) *num* sei

sixteen (ssikss-*tiin*) *num* sedici

sixteenth (ssikss-*tiin*θ) *num* sedicesimo

sixth (ssikssθ) *num* sesto

sixty (ssikss-ti) *num* sessanta

size (ssais) *n* grandezza *f*, misura *f*; dimensione *f*; formato *m*

skate (sskeit) *v* pattinare; *n* pattino *m*

skating (*sskei*-ting) *n* pattinaggio *m*

skating-rink (*sskei*-ting-ringk) *n* pista di pattinaggio

skeleton (*sské*-li-tön) *n* scheletro *m*

sketch (sskêtʃ) *n* disegno *m*, schizzo *m*; *v* disegnare, abbozzare

sketch-book (*sskêtʃ*-buk) *n* album da disegno

ski¹ (sskii) *v* sciare

ski² (sskii) *n* (pl ~, ~s) sci *m*; ~ **boots** scarponi da sci; ~ **pants** calzoni da sci; ~ **poles** *Am* bastoni da sci; ~ **sticks** bastoni da sci

skid (sskid) *v* scivolare

skier (*sskii*-ö) *n* sciatore *m*

skiing (*sskii*-ing) *n* sci *m*

ski-jump (*sskii*-dʒamp) *n* salto con gli sci

skilful (*sskil*-föl) *adj* esperto, destro, abile

ski-lift (*sskii*-lift) *n* teleferica per sciatori

skill (sskil) *n* abilità *f*

skilled (sskild) *adj* abile; esperto

skin (sskin) *n* pelle *f*; buccia *f*; ~ **cream** crema per la pelle

skip (sskip) *v* saltellare; *omettere

skirt (sskööt) *n* gonna *f*

skull (sskal) *n* cranio *m*

sky (sskai) *n* cielo *m*; aria *f*

skyscraper (*sskai*-sskrei-pö) *n* grattacielo *m*

slack (sslæk) *adj* lento

slacks (sslækss) *pl* calzoni *mpl*

slam (sslæm) *v* sbattere

slander (*sslaan*-dö) *n* calunnia *f*

slant (sslaant) *v* inclinare

slanting (*sslaan*-ting) *adj* obliquo, pendente, inclinato

slap (sslæp) *v* schiaffeggiare; *n* schiaffo *m*

slate (ssleit) *n* ardesia *f*

slave (ssleiv) *n* schiavo *m*

sledge (sslêdʒ) *n* slitta *f*

sleep (ssliip) *n* sonno *m*

* **sleep** (ssliip) *v* dormire

sleeping-bag (*sslii*-ping-bægh) *n* sacco a pelo

sleeping-car (*sslii*-ping-kaa) *n* vagone letto

sleeping-pill (*sslii*-ping-pil) *n* sonnifero *m*

sleepless (*ssliip*-löss) *adj* insonne

sleepy (*sslii*-pi) *adj* assonnato

sleeve (ssliiv) *n* manica *f*; busta *f*

sleigh (sslei) *n* slitta *f*

slender (*sslên*-dö) *adj* snello

slice (sslaiss) *n* fetta *f*

slide (sslaid) *n* scivolata *f*; scivolo *m*; diapositiva *f*

* **slide** (sslaid) *v* slittare

slight (sslait) *adj* leggero; scarso

slim (sslim) *adj* snello; *v* dimagrire

slip (sslip) *v* scivolare; scappare; *n* svista *f*; sottoveste *f*

slipper (*ssli*-pö) *n* ciabatta *f*, pantofola *f*

slippery (*ssli*-pö-ri) *adj* viscido, sdrucciolevole

slogan (*sslou*-ghön) *n* motto *m*, slogan *m*

slope (ssloup) *n* pendio *m*; *v* pendere

sloping (*sslou*-ping) *adj* inclinato

sloppy (*sslo*-pi) *adj* disordinato

slot (sslot) *n* fessura *f*

slot-machine (*sslot*-mö-ʃiin) *n* distributore automatico

slovenly (*ssla*-vön-li) *adj* sciatto

slow (sslou) *adj* ottuso, lento; ~ **down** rallentare

sluice (ssluuss) *n* chiusa *f*

slum (sslam) *n* quartiere povero

slump (sslamp) *n* calo di prezzo

slush (sslaʃ) *n* neve fangosa

sly (sslai) *adj* astuto

smack (ssmæk) *v* picchiare; *n* ceffone *m*

small (ssmool) *adj* piccolo; scarso

smallpox (*ssmool*-pokss) *n* vaiolo *m*

smart (ssmaat) *adj* elegante; sveglio, intelligente

smell (ssmêl) *n* odore *m*

*****smell** (ssmêl) *v* odorare; puzzare

smelly (*ssmê*-li) *adj* puzzolente

smile (ssmail) *v* *sorridere; *n* sorriso *m*

smith (ssmiθ) *n* fabbro *m*

smoke (ssmouk) *v* fumare; *n* fumo *m*; **no smoking** vietato fumare

smoker (*ssmou*-kö) *n* fumatore *m*; scompartimento per fumatori

smoking-compartment (*ssmou*-king-köm-paat-mönt) *n* compartimento per fumatori

smoking-room (*ssmou*-king-ruum) *n* sala per fumatori

smooth (ssmuuð) *adj* levigato, piano, liscio; morbido

smuggle (*ssma*-ghöl) *v* contrabbandare

snack (ssnæk) *n* spuntino *m*

snack-bar (*ssnæk*-baa) *n* tavola calda

snail (ssneil) *n* lumaca *f*

snake (ssneik) *n* serpente *m*

snapshot (*ssnæp*-ʃot) *n* istantanea *f*

sneakers (*ssnii*-kös) *plAm* scarpe da ginnastica

sneeze (ssniis) *v* starnutire

sniper (*ssnai*-pö) *n* franco tiratore

snooty (*ssnuu*-ti) *adj* arrogante

snore (ssnoo) *v* russare

snorkel (*ssnoo*-köl) *n* respiratore *m*

snout (ssnaut) *n* muso *m*

snow (ssnou) *n* neve *f*; *v* nevicare

snowstorm (*ssnou*-sstoom) *n* tormenta *f*

snowy (*ssnou*-i) *adj* nevoso

so (ssou) *conj* dunque; *adv* così; talmente; and ~ **on** e così via; ~ **far** finora; ~ **that** così che, affinché

soak (ssouk) *v* ammollare, inzuppare

soap (ssoup) *n* sapone *m*; ~ **powder** sapone in polvere

sober (*ssou*-bö) *adj* sobrio; assennato

so-called (ssou-*koold*) *adj* cosiddetto

soccer (*sso*-kö) *n* calcio *m*; ~ **team** squadra *f*

social (*ssou*-ʃöl) *adj* sociale

socialism (*ssou*-ʃö-li-söm) *n* socialismo *m*

socialist (*ssou*-ʃö-lisst) *adj* socialista; *n* socialista *m*

society (ssö-*ssai*-ö-ti) *n* società *f*; associazione *f*; compagnia *f*

sock (ssok) *n* calza *f*

socket (*sso*-kit) *n* portalampada *m*

soda-water (*ssou*-dö-ᵘoo-tö) *n* acqua di seltz

sofa (*ssou*-fö) *n* sofà *m*

soft (ssoft) *adj* morbido; ~ **drink** bibita analcoolica

soften (*sso*-fön) *v* ammorbidire

soil (ssoil) *n* suolo *m*; terreno *m*, terra *f*

soiled (ssoild) *adj* sudicio

sold (ssould) *v* (p, pp sell); ~ **out** esaurito

solder (*ssol*-dö) *v* saldare

soldering-iron (*ssol*-dö-ring-aiⁿn) *n* saldatore *m*

soldier (*ssoul*-dʒö) *n* militare *m*, soldato *m*

sole[1] (ssoul) *adj* unico

sole[2] (ssoul) *n* suola *f*; sogliola *f*

solely (*ssoul*-li) *adv* esclusivamente

solemn (*sso*-löm) *adj* solenne

solicitor (ssö-*li*-ssi-tö) *n* procuratore legale, avvocato *m*

solid (*sso*-lid) *adj* robusto, solido; massiccio; *n* solido *m*

soluble (*sso*-lᵘu-böl) *adj* solubile

solution (ssö-*luu*-ʃön) *n* soluzione *f*

solve (ssolv) *v* *risolvere

sombre (*ssom*-bö) *adj* tetro

some (ssam) *adj* alcuni, qualche; *pron* alcuni, taluni; una parte; ~

day un giorno o l'altro; ~ **more** ancora; ~ **time** un giorno

somebody (*ssam*-bŏ-di) *pron* qualcuno

somehow (*ssam*-hau) *adv* in un modo o nell'altro

someone (*ssam*-ᵘan) *pron* qualcuno

something (*ssam*-θing) *pron* qualcosa

sometimes (*ssam*-taims) *adv* qualche volta

somewhat (*ssam*-ᵘot) *adv* alquanto

somewhere (*ssam*-ᵘê̂ᵒ) *adv* in qualche posto

son (ssan) *n* figlio *m*

song (ssong) *n* canzone *f*

son-in-law (*ssa*-nin-loo) *n* (pl sons-) genero *m*

soon (ssuun) *adv* presto, tra poco; **as** ~ **as** non appena

sooner (*ssuu*-nö) *adv* piuttosto

sore (ssoo) *adj* indolenzito; *n* piaga *f*; ulcera *f*; ~ **throat** mal di gola

sorrow (*sso*-rou) *n* tristezza *f*, dolore *m*, dispiacere *m*

sorry (*sso*-ri) *adj* spiacente; **sorry!** scusa!, scusate!, scusi!

sort (ssoot) *v* classificare, assortire; *n* genere *m*, specie *f*; **all sorts of** ogni sorta di

soul (ssoul) *n* anima *f*; spirito *m*

sound (ssaund) *n* suono *m*; *v* suonare; *adj* solido

soundproof (*ssaund*-pruuf) *adj* insonorizzato

soup (ssuup) *n* minestra *f*

soup-plate (*ssuup*-pleit) *n* scodella *f*

soup-spoon (*ssuup*-sspuun) *n* cucchiaio da minestra

sour (ssauᵒ) *adj* agro

source (ssooss) *n* sorgente *f*

south (ssauθ) *n* sud *m*; **South Pole** polo Sud

South Africa (ssauθ æ-fri-kö) Africa del Sud

south-east (ssauθ-*iisst*) *n* sud-est *m*

southerly (*ssa*-ðö-li) *adj* meridionale

southern (*ssa*-ðön) *adj* meridionale

south-west (ssauθ-ᵘêsst) *n* sud-ovest *m*

souvenir (*ssuu*-vö-niᵒ) *n* ricordo *m*

sovereign (*ssov*-rin) *n* sovrano *m*

*sow (ssou) *v* seminare

spa (sspaa) *n* stazione termale

space (sspeiss) *n* spazio *m*; distanza *f*; *v* spaziare

spacious (*sspei*-föss) *adj* spazioso

spade (sspeid) *n* zappa *f*, vanga *f*

Spain (sspein) Spagna *f*

Spaniard (*sspæ*-niᵒd) *n* spagnolo *m*

Spanish (*sspæ*-nif) *adj* spagnolo

spanking (*sspæng*-king) *n* sculacciata *f*

spanner (*sspæ*-nö) *n* chiave fissa

spare (sspêᵒ) *adj* di riserva, disponibile; *v* *fare a meno di; ~ **part** pezzo di ricambio; ~ **room** camera degli ospiti; ~ **time** tempo libero; ~ **tyre** pneumatico di ricambio; ~ **wheel** ruota di ricambio

spark (sspaak) *n* scintilla *f*

sparking-plug (*sspaa*-king-plagh) *n* candela d'accensione

sparkling (*sspaa*-kling) *adj* scintillante; spumante

sparrow (*sspæ*-rou) *n* passero *m*

spasm (*sspæ*-söm) *n* spasmo *m*

*speak (sspiik) *v* parlare

speaker (*sspii*-kö) *n* parlatore *m*; altoparlante *m*

spear (sspiᵒ) *n* lancia *f*

special (*sspê*-föl) *adj* particolare, speciale; ~ **delivery** per espresso

specialist (*sspê*-fö-lisst) *n* specialista *m*

speciality (sspê-fi-æ-lö-ti) *n* specialità *f*

specialize (*sspê*-fö-lais) *v* specializzarsi

specially (*sspê-ʃö-li*) *adv* particolarmente

species (*sspii-ʃiis*) *n* (pl ~) specie *f*

specific (*sspö-ssi-fik*) *adj* specifico

specimen (*sspê-ssi-mön*) *n* esemplare *m*

speck (*sspêk*) *n* macchiolina *f*

spectacle (*sspêk-tö-köl*) *n* spettacolo *m*; **spectacles** occhiali *mpl*

spectator (*sspêk-tei-tö*) *n* spettatore *m*

speculate (*sspê-k¹u-leit*) *v* speculare

speech (*sspiit*) *n* parola *f*; discorso *m*; linguaggio *m*

speechless (*sspiit-löss*) *adj* muto

speed (*sspiid*) *n* velocità *f*; rapidità *f*, fretta *f*; **cruising** ~ velocità di crociera; ~ **limit** limite di velocità; ~ **up** *v* accelerare

*****speed** (*sspiid*) *v* *correre; *correre troppo

speeding (*sspii-ding*) *n* eccesso di velocità

speedometer (*sspii-do-mi-tö*) *n* tachimetro *m*

spell (*sspêl*) *n* incanto *m*

*****spell** (*sspêl*) *v* compitare

spelling (*sspê-ling*) *n* ortografia *f*

*****spend** (*sspênd*) *v* *spendere; impiegare

sphere (*ssfiô*) *n* sfera *f*

spiced (*sspaisst*) *adj* condito

spicy (*sspai-ssi*) *adj* piccante

spider (*sspai-dö*) *n* ragno *m*; **spider's web** ragnatela *f*

*****spill** (*sspil*) *v* *spandere

*****spin** (*sspin*) *v* filare; *far girare

spinach (*sspi-nidʒ*) *n* spinaci *mpl*

spine (*sspain*) *n* spina dorsale

spinster (*sspin-sstö*) *n* zitella *f*

spire (*sspaiô*) *n* guglia *f*

spirit (*sspi-rit*) *n* spirito *m*; fantasma *m*; umore *m*; **spirits** bevande alcooliche; morale *m*; ~ **stove** fornello a spirito

spiritual (*sspi-ri-tʃu-öl*) *adj* spirituale

spit (*sspit*) *n* sputo *m*, saliva *f*; spiedo *m*

*****spit** (*sspit*) *v* sputare

in spite of (in sspait ov) nonostante, malgrado

spiteful (*sspait-föl*) *adj* malevolo

splash (*ssplæʃ*) *v* schizzare

splendid (*ssplên-did*) *adj* magnifico, splendido

splendour (*ssplên-dö*) *n* splendore *m*

splint (*ssplint*) *n* stecca *f*

splinter (*ssplin-tö*) *n* scheggia *f*

*****split** (*ssplit*) *v* *fendere

*****spoil** (*sspoil*) *v* guastare; viziare

spoke¹ (*sspouk*) *v* (p speak)

spoke² (*sspouk*) *n* raggio *m*

sponge (*sspandʒ*) *n* spugna *f*

spook (*sspuuk*) *n* spettro *m*

spool (*sspuul*) *n* rocchetto *m*

spoon (*sspuun*) *n* cucchiaio *m*

spoonful (*sspuun-ful*) *n* cucchiaiata *f*

sport (*sspoot*) *n* sport *m*

sports-car (*sspootss-kaa*) *n* macchina sportiva

sports-jacket (*sspootss-dʒæ-kit*) *n* giacchetta sportiva

sportsman (*sspootss-mön*) *n* (pl -men) sportivo *m*

sportswear (*sspootss-ᵘêᵒ*) *n* abbigliamento sportivo

spot (*sspot*) *n* chiazza *f*, macchia *f*; località *f*, luogo *m*

spotless (*sspot-löss*) *adj* immacolato

spotlight (*sspot-lait*) *n* proiettore *m*

spotted (*sspo-tid*) *adj* chiazzato

spout (*sspaut*) *n* getto *m*

sprain (*ssprein*) *v* *storcere; *n* distorsione *f*

*****spread** (*ssprêd*) *v* *stendere

spring (*sspring*) *n* primavera *f*; molla *f*; sorgente *f*

springtime (*sspring-taim*) *n* primavera

f

sprouts (ssprautss) *pl* cavolini *mpl*

spy (sspai) *n* spia *f*

squadron (ssk⁼o-drön) *n* squadriglia *f*

square (ssk⁼êô) *adj* quadrato; *n* quadrato *m*; piazza *f*

squash (ssk⁼oʃ) *n* succo di frutta

squirrel (ssk⁼i-röl) *n* scoiattolo *m*

squirt (ssk⁼ööt) *n* zampillo *m*

stable (sstei-böl) *adj* stabile; *n* stalla *f*

stack (sstæk) *n* pila *f*

stadium (sstei-di-öm) *n* stadio *m*

staff (sstaaf) *n* personale *m*

stage (ssteidȝ) *n* scena *f*; stadio *m*, fase *f*; tappa *f*

stain (sstein) *v* macchiare; *n* macchia *f*; **stained glass** vetro colorato; ~ **remover** smacchiatore *m*

stainless (sstein-löss) *adj* immacolato; ~ **steel** acciaio inossidabile

staircase (sstêô-keiss) *n* scala *f*

stairs (sstêôs) *pl* scala *f*

stale (ssteil) *adj* raffermo

stall (sstool) *n* bancarella *f*; poltrona d'orchestra

stamina (sstæ-mi-nö) *n* vigore *m*

stamp (sstæmp) *n* francobollo *m*; timbro *m*; *v* affrancare; pestare; ~ **machine** distributore automatico di francobolli

stand (sstænd) *n* banco *m*; tribuna *f*

***stand** (sstænd) *v* *stare in piedi

standard (sstæn-död) *n* norma *f*; normale; ~ **of living** livello di vita

stanza (sstæn-sö) *n* strofa *f*

staple (sstei-pöl) *n* graffetta *f*

star (sstaa) *n* stella *f*

starboard (sstaa-böd) *n* tribordo *m*

starch (sstaatʃ) *n* amido *m*; *v* inamidare

stare (sstêô) *v* fissare

starling (sstaa-ling) *n* stornello *m*

start (sstaat) *v* cominciare; *n* inizio *m*; **starter motor** avviatore *m*

starting-point (sstaa-ting-point) *n* punto di partenza

state (ssteit) *n* stato *m*; *v* affermare **the States** Stati Uniti

statement (ssteit-mönt) *n* dichiarazione *f*

statesman (ssteitss-mön) *n* (pl -men) uomo di stato

station (sstei-ʃön) *n* stazione *f*; posto *m*

stationary (sstei-ʃö-nö-ri) *adj* stazionario

stationer's (sstei-ʃö-nös) *n* cartoleria *f*

stationery (sstei-ʃö-nö-ri) *n* cartoleria *f*

station-master (sstei-ʃön-maa-sstô) *n* capostazione *m*

statistics (sstö-ti-sstikss) *pl* statistica *f*

statue (sstæ-tʃuu) *n* statua *f*

stay (sstei) *v* *rimanere, *stare; soggiornare, *trattenersi; *n* soggiorno *m*

steadfast (sstêd-faast) *adj* fermo

steady (sstê-di) *adj* stabile

steak (ssteik) *n* bistecca *f*

***steal** (sstiil) *v* rubare

steam (sstiim) *n* vapore *m*

steamer (sstii-mö) *n* piroscafo *m*

steel (sstiil) *n* acciaio *m*

steep (sstiip) *adj* ripido

steeple (sstii-pöl) *n* campanile *m*

steering-column (ssti⁰-ring-ko-löm) *n* piantone di guida

steering-wheel (ssti⁰-ring-⁼iil) *n* volante *m*

steersman (ssti⁰s-mön) *n* (pl -men) timoniere *m*

stem (sstêm) *n* gambo *m*

stenographer (sstê-no-ghrò-fö) *n* stenografo *m*

step (sstêp) *n* passo *m*; scalino *m*; *v* camminare

stepchild (sstêp-tʃaild) *n* (pl -children) figliastro *m*

stepfather (sstêp-faa-ðö) n patrigno m

stepmother (sstêp-ma-ðö) n matrigna f

stereo (sstê-ri-ou) n sistema stereofonico m; riproduzione stereofonica f

sterile (sstê-rail) adj sterile

sterilize (sstê-ri-lais) v sterilizzare

steward (sstⁱuu-öd) n steward m

stewardess (sstⁱuu-ö-dêss) n hostess f

stick (sstik) n bastone m

*** stick** (sstik) v appiccicare, incollare

sticky (ssti-ki) adj appiccicaticcio

stiff (sstif) adj rigido

still (sstil) adv ancora; comunque; adj tranquillo

stillness (sstil-nöss) n quiete f

stimulant (ssti-mⁱu-lönt) n stimolante m

stimulate (ssti-mⁱu-leit) v stimolare

sting (ssting) n puntura f

*** sting** (ssting) v *pungere

stingy (sstin-dʒi) adj taccagno

*** stink** (sstink) v puzzare

stipulate (ssti-pⁱu-leit) v stipulare

stir (sstöö) v *muovere; mescolare

stirrup (ssti-röp) n staffa f

stitch (sstitʃ) n punto m, fitta f

stock (sstok) n scorta f; v *tenere in magazzino; ~ **exchange** borsa valori, borsa f; ~ **market** borsa f; **stocks and shares** titoli

stocking (ssto-king) n calza f

stole[1] (sstoul) v (p steal)

stole[2] (sstoul) n stola f

stomach (ssta-mök) n stomaco m

stomach-ache (ssta-mö-keik) n mal di pancia, mal di stomaco

stone (sstoun) n sasso m, pietra f; pietra preziosa; nocciolo m; di pietra; **pumice** ~ pietra pomice

stood (sstud) v (p, pp stand)

stop (sstop) v *smettere; terminare, cessare; n fermata f; **stop!** alt!

stopper (ssto-pö) n tappo m

storage (sstoo-ridʒ) n magazzinaggio m

store (sstoo) n riserva f; bottega f; v immagazzinare

store-house (sstoo-hauss) n magazzino m

storey (sstoo-ri) n piano m

stork (sstook) n cicogna f

storm (sstoom) n tempesta f

stormy (sstoo-mi) adj tempestoso

story (sstoo-ri) n racconto m

stout (sstaut) adj grosso, obeso, corpulento

stove (sstouv) n stufa f; cucina f

straight (sstreit) adj dritto; onesto; adv dritto; ~ **ahead** sempre diritto; ~ **away** direttamente, subito; ~ **on** avanti dritto

strain (sstrein) n fatica f; sforzo m; v forzare; filtrare

strainer (sstrei-nö) n colapasta m

strange (sstreindʒ) adj strano; bizzarro

stranger (sstrein-dʒö) n straniero m; estraneo m

strangle (sstræng-ghöl) v strangolare

strap (sstræp) n cinghia f

straw (sstroo) n paglia f

strawberry (sstroo-bö-ri) n fragola f

stream (sstriim) n ruscello m; corrente f; v *scorrere

street (sstriit) n strada f

streetcar (sstriit-kaa) nAm tram m

street-organ (sstrii-too-ghön) n organetto di Barberia

strength (sstrêngθ) n resistenza f, forza f

stress (sstrêss) n tensione f; accento m; v sottolineare

stretch (sstrêtʃ) v *tendere; n segmento m

strict (sstrikt) adj severo; rigido

strife (sstraif) n lotta f

strike (*sstraik*) *n* sciopero *m*

*strike (*sstraik*) *v* picchiare; colpire; scioperare; ammainare

striking (*sstrai*-king) *adj* impressionante, notevole, vistoso

string (*sstring*) *n* spago *m*; corda *f*

strip (*sstrip*) *n* striscia *f*

stripe (*sstraip*) *n* stria *f*

striped (*sstraipt*) *adj* striato

stroke (*sstrouk*) *n* colpo *m*

stroll (*sstroul*) *v* passeggiare; *n* passeggiata *f*

strong (*sstrong*) *adj* forte; robusto

stronghold (*sstrong*-hould) *n* roccaforte *f*

structure (*sstrak*-tʃö) *n* struttura *f*

struggle (*sstra*-ghöl) *n* combattimento *m*, lotta *f*; *v* lottare

stub (*sstab*) *n* matrice *f*

stubborn (*sst*-bön) *adj* cocciuto

student (*ssti̍uu*-dönt) *n* studente *m*; studentessa *f*

study (*ssta*-di) *v* studiare; *n* studio *m*

stuff (*sstaf*) *n* sostanza *f*; roba *f*

stuffed (*sstaft*) *adj* ripieno

stuffing (*ssta*-fing) *n* ripieno *m*

stuffy (*ssta*-fi) *adj* stantio

stumble (*sstam*-böl) *v* inciampare

stung (*sstang*) *v* (p, pp sting)

stupid (*ssti̍uu*-pid) *adj* stupido

style (*sstail*) *n* stile *m*

subject¹ (*ssab*-dʒikt) *n* soggetto *m*; suddito *m*; ~ **to** soggetto a

subject² (ssöb-*dʒêkt*) *v* *sottomettere

submit (ssöb-*mit*) *v* *sottomettersi

subordinate (ssö-*boo*-di-nöt) *adj* subalterno; secondario

subscriber (ssöb-*sskrai*-bö) *n* abbonato *m*

subscription (ssöb-*sskrip*-ʃön) *n* abbonamento *m*

subsequent (*ssab*-ssi-kᵘönt) *adj* successivo

subsidy (*ssab*-ssi-di) *n* sovvenzione *f*

substance (*ssab*-sstönss) *n* sostanza *f*

substantial (ssöb-*sstæn*-ʃöl) *adj* materiale; reale; sostanziale

substitute (*ssab*-ssti-ti̍uut) *v* sostituire; *n* sostituto *m*

subtitle (*ssab*-tai-töl) *n* sottotitolo *m*

subtle (*ssa*-töl) *adj* sottile

subtract (ssöb-*trækt*) *v* *sottrarre

suburb (*ssa*-bööb) *n* sobborgo *m*

suburban (ssö-*böö*-bön) *adj* suburbano

subway (*ssab*-ᵁei) *nAm* metropolitana *f*

succeed (ssök-*ssiid*) *v* *riuscire; *succedere

success (ssök-*ssêss*) *n* successo *m*

successful (ssök-*ssêss*-föl) *adj* riuscito

succumb (ssö-*kam*) *v* soccombere

such (ssatʃ) *adj* simile, tale; *adv* così; ~ **as** come

suck (ssak) *v* succhiare

sudden (*ssa*-dön) *adj* improvviso

suddenly (*ssa*-dön-li) *adv* improvvisamente

suede (ssᵘeid) *n* pelle scamosciata

suffer (*ssa*-fö) *v* *soffrire; subire

suffering (*ssa*-fö-ring) *n* sofferenza *f*

suffice (ssö-*faiss*) *v* bastare

sufficient (ssö-*fi*-fönt) *adj* bastante, sufficiente

suffrage (*ssa*-fridʒ) *n* suffragio *m*

sugar (*ʃu*-ghö) *n* zucchero *m*

suggest (ssö-*dʒêsst*) *v* suggerire

suggestion (ssö-*dʒêss*-tʃön) *n* suggerimento *m*

suicide (*ssuu*-i-ssaid) *n* suicidio *m*

suit (ssuut) *v* *convenire; adattare; *addirsi; *n* vestito da uomo *m*

suitable (*ssuu*-tö-böl) *adj* adeguato, adatto

suitcase (*ssuut*-keiss) *n* valigia *f*

suite (ssᵘiit) *n* appartamento *m*

sum (ssam) *n* somma *f*

summary (*ssa*-mö-ri) *n* sommario *m*,

sunto *m*

summer (*ssa*-mö) *n* estate *f*; ~ **time** orario estivo

summit (*ssa*-mit) *n* vetta *f*

summons (*ssa*-möns) *n* (pl ~es) citazione *f*

sun (ssan) *n* sole *m*

sunbathe (*ssan*-beið) *v* *fare il bagno di sole

sunburn (*ssan*-böön) *n* abbronzatura *f*

Sunday (*ssan*-di) domenica *f*

sun-glasses (*ssan*-ghlaa-ssis) *pl* occhiali da sole

sunlight (*ssan*-lait) *n* luce del sole

sunny (*ssa*-ni) *adj* soleggiato

sunrise (*ssan*-rais) *n* aurora *f*

sunset (*ssan*-ssêt) *n* tramonto *m*

sunshade (*ssan*-ſeid) *n* ombrellino *m*

sunshine (*ssan*-ſain) *n* luce del sole

sunstroke (*ssan*-sstrouk) *n* colpo di sole

suntan oil (*ssan*-tæn-oil) olio abbronzante

superb (ssu-*pööb*) *adj* grandioso, superbo

superficial (ssuu-pö-*fi*-ſöl) *adj* superficiale

superfluous (ssu-*pöö*-flu-öss) *adj* superfluo

superior (ssu-*pi*ᵒ-ri-ö) *adj* migliore, maggiore, superiore

superlative (ssu-*pöö*-lö-tiv) *adj* superlativo; *n* superlativo *m*

supermarket (*ssuu*-pö-maa-kit) *n* supermercato *m*

superstition (ssuu-pö-*ssti*-ſön) *n* superstizione *f*

supervise (*ssuu*-pö-vais) *v* *soprintendere

supervision (ssuu-pö-*vi*-ʒön) *n* soprintendenza *f*, sorveglianza *f*

supervisor (*ssuu*-pö-vai-sö) *n* ispettore *m*

supper (*ssa*-pö) *n* cena *f*

supple (*ssa*-pöl) *adj* pieghevole, flessibile, agile

supplement (*ssa*-pli-mönt) *n* supplemento *m*

supply (ssö-*plai*) *n* rifornimento *m*, fornitura *f*; provvista *f*; offerta *f*; *v* fornire

support (ssö-*poot*) *v* appoggiare, *sostenere; *n* sostegno *m*; ~ **hose** calze elastiche

supporter (ssö-*poo*-tö) *n* tifoso *m*

suppose (ssö-*pous*) *v* *supporre; **supposing that** supposto che

suppository (ssö-*po*-si-tö-ri) *n* supposta *f*

suppress (ssö-*prêss*) *v* *reprimere

surcharge (*ssöö*-tſaadʒ) *n* supplemento *m*

sure (ſuᵒ) *adj* sicuro

surely (*ſuᵒ*-li) *adv* certamente

surface (*ssöö*-fiss) *n* superficie *f*

surf-board (*ssööf*-bood) *n* acquaplano *m*

surgeon (*ssöö*-dʒön) *n* chirurgo *m*; **veterinary** ~ veterinario *m*

surgery (*ssöö*-dʒö-ri) *n* operazione *f*; consultorio *m*

surname (*ssöö*-neim) *n* cognome *m*

surplus (*ssöö*-plöss) *n* eccedenza *f*

surprise (ssö-*prais*) *n* sorpresa *f*; meraviglia *f*; *v* *sorprendere; stupire

surrender (ssö-*rên*-dö) *v* *arrendersi; *n* resa *f*

surround (ssö-*raund*) *v* circondare

surrounding (ssö-*raun*-ding) *adj* circostante

surroundings (ssö-*raun*-dings) *pl* dintorni *mpl*

survey (*ssöö*-vei) *n* rassegna *f*

survival (ssö-*vai*-völ) *n* sopravvivenza *f*

survive (ssö-*vaiv*) *v* *sopravvivere

suspect¹ (ssö-*sspêkt*) *v* sospettare;

*supporre

suspect² (ssa-sspèkt) *n* indiziato *m*

suspend (ssö-sspènd) *v* *sospendere

suspenders (ssö-sspên-dös) *plAm* bretelle *fpl*; **suspender belt** reggicalze *m*

suspension (ssö-sspên-[ö]n) *n* molleggio *m*, sospensione *f*; ~ **bridge** ponte sospeso

suspicion (ssö-sspi-[ö]n) *n* sospetto *m*

suspicious (ssö-sspi-[ö]ss) *adj* sospetto; sospettoso

sustain (ssö-sstein) *v* sopportare

Swahili (ssü ö-hii-li) *n* swahili *m*

swallow (ssü o-lou) *v* ingoiare, inghiottire; *n* rondine *f*

swam (ssü æm) *v* (p swim)

swamp (ssü omp) *n* palude *f*

swan (ssü on) *n* cigno *m*

swap (ssü op) *v* barattare

***swear** (ssü ê ô) *v* giurare; bestemmiare

sweat (ssü êt) *n* sudore *m*; *v* sudare

sweater (ssü ê-tö) *n* maglione *m*

Swede (ssü iid) *n* svedese *m*

Sweden (ssü ii-dön) Svezia *f*

Swedish (ssü ii-di[ʃ]) *adj* svedese

***sweep** (ssü iip) *v* scopare

sweet (ssü iit) *adj* dolce; *n* caramella *f*; dolce *m*; **sweets** dolciumi *mpl*

sweeten (ssü ii-tön) *v* zuccherare

sweetheart (ssü iit-haat) *n* amore *m*

sweetshop (ssü iit-[ʃ]op) *n* pasticceria *f*

swell (ssü êl) *adj* magnifico

***swell** (ssü êl) *v* gonfiare

swelling (ssü ê-ling) *n* gonfiore *m*

swift (ssü ift) *adj* rapido

***swim** (ssü im) *v* nuotare

swimmer (ssü i-mö) *n* nuotatore *m*

swimming (ssü i-ming) *n* nuoto *m*; ~ **pool** piscina *f*

swimming-trunks (ssü i-ming-trangkss) *n* mutandine da bagno

swim-suit (ssü im-ssuut) *n* costume da bagno

swindle (ssü in-döl) *v* truffare; *n* truffa *f*

swindler (ssü in-dlö) *n* truffatore *m*

swing (ssü ing) *n* altalena *f*

***swing** (ssü ing) *v* dondolare

Swiss (ssü iss) *adj* svizzero

switch (ssü it[ʃ]) *n* interruttore *m*; *v* cambiare; ~ **off** *spegnere; ~ **on** *accendere

switchboard (ssü it[ʃ]-bood) *n* quadro di distribuzione

Switzerland (ssü it-ssö-lönd) Svizzera *f*

sword (ssood) *n* spada *f*

swum (ssü am) *v* (pp swim)

syllable (ssi-lö-böl) *n* sillaba *f*

symbol (ssim-böl) *n* simbolo *m*

sympathetic (ssim-pö-θê-tik) *adj* cordiale, comprensivo

sympathy (ssim-pö-θi) *n* simpatia *f*; compassione *f*

symphony (ssim-fö-ni) *n* sinfonia *f*

symptom (ssim-töm) *n* sintomo *m*

synagogue (ssi-nö-ghogh) *n* sinagoga *f*

synonym (ssi-nö-nim) *n* sinonimo *m*

synthetic (ssin-θê-tik) *adj* sintetico

syphon (ssai-fön) *n* sifone *m*

Syria (ssi-ri-ö) Siria *f*

Syrian (ssi-ri-ön) *adj* siriano

syringe (ssi-rind3) *n* siringa *f*

syrup (ssi-röp) *n* sciroppo *m*

system (ssi-sstöm) *n* sistema *m*; **decimal** ~ sistema decimale

systematic (ssi-sstö-mæ-tik) *adj* sistematico

T

table (*tei*-böl) *n* tavola *f*; tabella *f*; ~ **of contents** indice *m*; ~ **tennis** ping-pong *m*

table-cloth (*tei*-böl-kloθ) *n* tovaglia *f*

tablespoon (*tei*-böl-sspuun) *n* cucchiaio *m*

tablet (*tæ*-blit) *n* pasticca *f*

taboo (tö-*buu*) *n* tabù *m*

tactics (*tæk*-tikss) *pl* tattica *f*

tag (tægh) *n* etichetta *f*

tail (teil) *n* coda *f*

tail-light (*teil*-lait) *n* luce posteriore

tailor (*tei*-lö) *n* sarto *m*

tailor-made (*tei*-lö-meid) *adj* fatto su misura

***take** (teik) *v* *prendere; accompagnare; capire; afferrare; ~ away portar via; *togliere, levare; ~ off decollare; ~ out *togliere; ~ over rilevare; ~ place *aver luogo; ~ up occupare

take-off (*tei*-kof) *n* decollo *m*

tale (teil) *n* storia *f*, racconto *m*

talent (*tæ*-lönt) *n* attitudine *f*, talento *m*

talented (*tæ*-lön-tid) *adj* dotato

talk (took) *v* parlare; *n* conversazione *f*

talkative (*too*-kö-tiv) *adj* loquace

tall (tool) *adj* alto; lungo

tame (teim) *adj* mansueto, addomesticato; *v* addomesticare

tampon (*tæm*-pön) *n* tampone *m*

tangerine (tæn-dȝö-*riin*) *n* mandarino *m*

tangible (*tæn*-dȝi-böl) *adj* tangibile

tank (tængk) *n* serbatoio *m*

tanker (*tæng*-kö) *n* petroliera *f*

tanned (tænd) *adj* abbronzato

tap (tæp) *n* rubinetto *m*; colpetto *m*; *v* bussare

tape (teip) *n* nastro *m*; **adhesive ~** nastro adesivo; cerotto *m*

tape-measure (*teip*-mê-ȝö) *n* centimetro *m*, metro a nastro

tape-recorder (*teip*-ri-koo-dö) *n* magnetofono *m*

tapestry (*tæ*-pi-sstri) *n* arazzo *m*, tappezzeria *f*

tar (taa) *n* catrame *m*

target (*taa*-ghit) *n* bersaglio *m*

tariff (*tæ*-rif) *n* tariffa *f*

tarpaulin (taa-*poo*-lin) *n* tela cerata

task (taassk) *n* compito *m*

taste (teisst) *n* gusto *m*; *v* *sapere; assaggiare

tasteless (*teisst*-löss) *adj* insipido

tasty (*tei*-ssti) *adj* gustoso, saporito

taught (toot) *v* (p, pp teach)

tavern (*tæ*-vön) *n* taverna *f*

tax (tækss) *n* tassa *f*; *v* tassare

taxation (tæk-*ssei*-fön) *n* imposta *f*

tax-free (*tækss*-frii) *adj* esente da tassa

taxi (*tæk*-ssi) *n* tassì *m*; ~ **rank** posteggio di autopubbliche; ~ **stand** *Am* posteggio di autopubbliche

taxi-driver (*tæk*-ssi-drai-vö) *n* tassista *m*

taxi-meter (*tæk*-ssi-mii-tö) *n* tassametro *m*

tea (tii) *n* tè *m*; merenda *f*

***teach** (tiitf) *v* insegnare

teacher (*tii*-tfö) *n* docente *m*, insegnante *m*; professoressa *f*; maestro *m*

teachings (*tii*-tfings) *pl* insegnamento *m*

tea-cloth (*tii*-kloθ) *n* canovaccio per stoviglie

teacup (*tii*-kap) *n* tazzina da tè

team (tiim) *n* squadra *f*

teapot (*tii*-pot) *n* teiera *f*

tear[1] (tiö) *n* lacrima *f*

tear[2] (têö) *n* strappo *m*; *tear *v* strappare

tear-jerker (*tiö*-dȝöö-kö) *n* sdolcinatura *f*

tease (tiis) *v* stuzzicare

tea-set (*tii*-ssét) *n* servizio da tè

tea-shop (*tii*-fop) *n* sala da tè

teaspoon (*tii*-sspuun) *n* cucchiaino *m*

teaspoonful (*tii*-sspuun-ful) *n* cucchiaino *m*

technical (*têk*-ni-köl) *adj* tecnico

technician (têk-*ni*-∫ön) *n* tecnico *m*

technique (têk-*niik*) *n* tecnica *f*

technology (têk-*no*-lö-dʒi) *n* tecnologia *f*

teenager (*tii*-nei-dʒö) *n* adolescente *m*

teetotaller (tii-*tou*-tö-lö) *n* astemio *m*

telegram (*tê*-li-ghræm) *n* telegramma *m*

telegraph (*tê*-li-ghraaf) *v* telegrafare

telephone (*tê*-li-foun) *n* telefono *m*; ~ **book** *Am* elenco telefonico; ~ **booth** cabina telefonica; ~ **call** chiamata *f*; ~ **directory** elenco telefonico; ~ **exchange** centralino *m*; ~ **operator** telefonista *f*

telephonist (ti-*lê*-fö-nisst) *n* telefonista *f*

television (tê-li-vi-ʒön) *n* televisione *f*; ~ **set** televisore *m*; **cable** ~ TV cavo *f*; **satellite** ~ TV satellite *m*

telex (*tê*-lêkss) *n* telex *m*

*****tell** (têl) *v* *dire; raccontare

temper (*têm*-pö) *n* stizza *f*

temperature (*têm*-prö-tʃö) *n* temperatura *f*

tempest (*têm*-pisst) *n* tempesta *f*

temple (*têm*-pöl) *n* tempio *m*; tempia *f*

temporary (*têm*-pö-rö-ri) *adj* provvisorio, temporaneo

tempt (têmpt) *v* tentare

temptation (têmp-*tei*-∫ön) *n* tentazione *f*

ten (tên) *num* dieci

tenant (*tê*-nönt) *n* inquilino *m*

tend (tênd) *v* *tendere a; badare a; ~ **to** *tendere a

tendency (*tên*-dön-ssi) *n* inclinazione *f*, tendenza *f*

tender (*tên*-dö) *adj* delicato, dolce; tenero

tendon (*tên*-dön) *n* tendine *m*

tennis (*tê*-niss) *n* tennis *m*; ~ **shoes** scarpe da tennis

tennis-court (*tê*-niss-koot) *n* campo di tennis

tense (tênss) *adj* teso

tension (*tên*-∫ön) *n* tensione *f*

tent (tênt) *n* tenda *f*

tenth (tênθ) *num* decimo

tepid (*tê*-pid) *adj* tiepido

term (tööm) *n* termine *m*; periodo *m*; condizione *f*

terminal (*töö*-mi-nöl) *n* termine *m*

terrace (*tê*-röss) *n* terrazza *f*

terrain (tê-*rein*) *n* terreno *m*

terrible (*tê*-ri-böl) *adj* tremendo, spaventoso, terribile

terrific (tö-*ri*-fik) *adj* formidabile

terrify (*tê*-ri-fai) *v* sgomentare; **terrifying** spaventevole

territory (*tê*-ri-tö-ri) *n* territorio *m*

terror (*tê*-rö) *n* terrore *m*

terrorism (*tê*-rö-ri-söm) *n* terrorismo *m*

terrorist (*tê*-rö-risst) *n* terrorista *m*

terylene (*tê*-rö-liin) *n* terital *m*

test (têsst) *n* prova *f*, esame *m*; *v* provare, saggiare

testify (*tê*-ssti-fai) *v* testimoniare

text (têksst) *n* testo *m*

textbook (*têkss*-buk) *n* manuale *m*

textile (*têkss*-sstail) *n* tessuto *m*

texture (*têkss*-tʃö) *n* struttura *f*

Thai (tai) *adj* tailandese

Thailand (*tai*-lænd) Tailandia *f*

than (ðæn) *conj* che

thank (θæŋk) *v* ringraziare; ~ **you** grazie

thankful (*θæŋk*-föl) *adj* riconoscente

that (ðæt) *adj* quello; *pron* quello; che; *conj* che

thaw (θoo) *v* disgelarsi; *n* disgelo *m*

the (ðö,ði) *art* il *art*; **the ... the** più ... più

theatre ($\theta i^ö$-tö) *n* teatro *m*

theft (θéft) *n* furto *m*

their ($\delta \hat{e}^ö$) *adj* loro

them (δêm) *pron* li; loro

theme (θiim) *n* tema *m*, argomento *m*

themselves (δöm-*ssêlvs*) *pron* si; essi stessi

then (δên) *adv* allora; in seguito, poi; dunque

theology (θi-*o*-lö-d$\check{3}$i) *n* teologia *f*

theoretical ($\theta i^ö$-*rê*-ti-köl) *adj* teorico

theory ($\theta i^ö$-ri) *n* teoria *f*

therapy ($\theta \hat{e}$-rö-pi) *n* terapia *f*

there ($\delta \hat{e}^ö$) *adv* là; di là

therefore ($\delta \hat{e}^ö$-foo) *conj* quindi

thermometer (θö-*mo*-mi-tö) *n* termometro *m*

thermostat ($\theta öö$-mö-sstæt) *n* termostato *m*

these (δiis) *adj* questi

thesis (θii-ssiss) *n* (pl theses) tesi *f*

they (δei) *pron* essi

thick (θik) *adj* spesso; denso

thicken (θi-kön) *v* ispessire

thickness (θik-nöss) *n* spessore *m*

thief (θiif) *n* (pl thieves) ladro *m*

thigh (θai) *n* coscia *f*

thimble (θim-böl) *n* ditale *m*

thin (θin) *adj* sottile; magro

thing (θing) *n* cosa *f*

*think (θingk) *v* pensare; *riflettere; ~ **of** pensare a; ricordare; ~ **over** ripensare

thinker (θing-kö) *n* pensatore *m*

third (θööd) *num* terzo

thirst (θöösst) *n* sete *f*

thirsty (θöö-ssti) *adj* assetato

thirteen (θöö-*tiin*) *num* tredici

thirteenth (θöö-*tiinθ*) *num* tredicesimo

thirtieth ($\theta öö$-ti-öθ) *num* trentesimo

thirty ($\theta öö$-ti) *num* trenta

this (δiss) *adj* questo; *pron* questo

thistle (θi-ssöl) *n* cardo *m*

thorn (θoon) *n* spina *f*

thorough (θa-rö) *adj* minuzioso, accurato

thoroughbred (θa-rö-brêd) *adj* purosangue

thoroughfare (θa-rö-fê^ö) *n* strada maestra, arteria *f*

those (δous) *adj* quei; *pron* quelli

though (δou) *conj* sebbene, quantunque, benché; *adv* comunque

thought¹ (θoot) *v* (p, pp think)

thought² (θoot) *n* pensiero *m*

thoughtful (θoot-föl) *adj* pensieroso; premuroso

thousand (θau-sönd) *num* mille

thread (θrêd) *n* filo *m*; refe *m*; *v* infilare

threadbare (θrêd-bê^ö) *adj* liso

threat (θrêt) *n* minaccia *f*

threaten (θrê-tön) *v* minacciare; **threatening** minaccioso

three (θrii) *num* tre

three-quarter (θrii-*k^{u}oo*-tö) *adj* tre quarti

threshold (θrê-$\int$ould) *n* soglia *f*

threw (θruu) *v* (p throw)

thrifty (θrif-ti) *adj* parsimonioso

throat (θrout) *n* gola *f*; collo *m*

throne (θroun) *n* trono *m*

through (θruu) *prep* attraverso

throughout (θruu-*aut*) *adv* dappertutto

throw (θrou) *n* tiro *m*

*throw (θrou) *v* lanciare, gettare, buttare

thrush (θra$\int$) *n* tordo *m*

thumb (θam) *n* pollice *m*

thumbtack (θam-tæk) *nAm* puntina da disegno

thump (θamp) *v* *percuotere

thunder (θan-dö) *n* tuono *m*; *v* tuonare

thunderstorm (θan-dö-sstoom) *n* temporale *m*

thundery (*θan*-dö-ri) *adj* temporalesco

Thursday (*θöös*-di) giovedì *m*

thus (ðass) *adv* così

thyme (taim) *n* timo *m*

tick (tik) *n* segno *m*;

ticket (*ti*-kit) *n* biglietto *m*; contravvenzione *f*; ~ **collector** controllore *m*; ~ **machine** biglietteria automatica

tickle (*ti*-köl) *v* solleticare

tide (taid) *n* marea *f*; **high** ~ alta marea; **low** ~ bassa marea

tidings (*tai*-dings) *pl* notizie

tidy (*tai*-di) *adj* ordinato; ~ **up** riordinare

tie (tai) *v* annodare, legare; *n* cravatta *f*

tiger (*tai*-ghö) *n* tigre *f*

tight (tait) *adj* stretto; attillato; *adv* strettamente

tighten (*tai*-tön) *v* serrare; *stringere; *restringersi

tights (taitss) *pl* calzamaglia *f*

tile (tail) *n* mattonella *f*; tegola *f*

till (til) *prep* fino a; *conj* finché non, finché

timber (*tim*-bö) *n* legname *m*

time (taim) *n* tempo *m*; volta *f*; **all the** ~ continuamente; **in** ~ in tempo; ~ **of arrival** ora di arrivo; ~ **of departure** ora di partenza

time-saving (*taim*-ssei-ving) *adj* che fa risparmiare tempo

timetable (*taim*-tei-böl) *n* orario *m*

timid (*ti*-mid) *adj* timido

timidity (ti-*mi*-dö-ti) *n* timidezza *f*

tin (tin) *n* stagno *m*; barattolo *m*, latta *f*; **tinned food** conserve *fpl*

tinfoil (*tin*-foil) *n* stagnola *f*

tin-opener (*ti*-nou-pö-nö) *n* apriscatole *m*

tiny (*tai*-ni) *adj* minuscolo

tip (tip) *n* punta *f*; mancia *f*

tire[1] (tai*ö*) *n* pneumatico *m*

tire[2] (tai*ö*) *v* stancare

tired (tai*ö*d) *adj* affaticato, stanco; ~ **of** stufo di

tiring (*tai*ö-ring) *adj* faticoso

tissue (*ti*-ʃuu) *n* tessuto *m*; fazzoletto di carta

title (*tai*-töl) *n* titolo *m*

to (tuu) *prep* fino a; a, per, da, verso; allo scopo di

toad (toud) *n* rospo *m*

toadstool (*toud*-sstuul) *n* fungo *m*

toast (tousst) *n* crostino *m*; brindisi *m*

tobacco (tö-*bæ*-kou) *n* (pl ~s) tabacco *m*; ~ **pouch** astuccio per tabacco

tobacconist (tö-*bæ*-kö-nisst) *n* tabaccaio *m*; **tobacconist's** tabaccheria *f*

today (tö-*dei*) *adv* oggi

toddler (*tod*-lö) *n* bimbo *m*

toe (tou) *n* dito del piede

toffee (*to*-fi) *n* caramella *f*

together (tö-*ghê*-ðö) *adv* insieme

toilet (*toi*-löt) *n* gabinetto *m*; ~ **case** astuccio di toeletta

toilet-paper (*toi*-löt-pei-pö) *n* carta igienica

toiletry (*toi*-lö-tri) *n* articoli da toeletta

token (*tou*-kön) *n* segno *m*; prova *f*; gettone *m*

told (tould) *v* (p, pp tell)

tolerable (*to*-lö-rö-böl) *adj* tollerabile

toll (toul) *n* pedaggio *m*

tomato (tö-*maa*-tou) *n* (pl ~es) pomodoro *m*

tomb (tuum) *n* tomba *f*

tombstone (*tuum*-sstoun) *n* pietra sepolcrale

tomorrow (tö-*mo*-rou) *adv* domani

ton (tan) *n* tonnellata *f*

tone (toun) *n* tono *m*; timbro *m*

tongs (tongs) *pl* pinze *fpl*

tongue (tang) *n* lingua *f*

tonic (*to*-nik) *n* tonico *m*

tonight (tö-*nait*) *adv* stanotte, stasera

tonsilitis (ton-ssö-*lai*-tiss) *n* tonsillite *f*

tonsils (*ton*-ssöls) *pl* tonsille *fpl*

too (tuu) *adv* troppo; anche

took (tuk) *v* (p take)

tool (tuul) *n* attrezzo *m*, arnese *m*; ~ **kit** cassetta degli arnesi

toot (tuut) *vAm* suonare il clacson

tooth (tuuθ) *n* (pl teeth) dente *m*

toothache (*tuu*-θeik) *n* mal di denti

toothbrush (*tuuθ*-braʃ) *n* spazzolino da denti

toothpaste (*tuuθ*-peisst) *n* dentifricio *m*

toothpick (*tuuθ*-pik) *n* stuzzicadenti *m*

toothpowder (*tuuθ*-pau-dö) *n* polvere dentifricia

top (top) *n* cima *f*; parte superiore; coperchio *m*; sommo; **on ~ of** in cima a; ~ **side** lato superiore

topcoat (*top*-kout) *n* soprabito *m*

topic (*to*-pik) *n* soggetto *m*

topical (*to*-pi-köl) *adj* attuale

torch (tootʃ) *n* torcia *f*; lampadina tascabile

torment¹ (too-*mênt*) *v* tormentare

torment² (*too*-mênt) *n* tormento *m*

torture (*too*-tʃö) *n* tortura *f*; *v* torturare

toss (toss) *v* gettare

tot (tot) *n* bimbetto *m*

total (*tou*-töl) *adj* totale; completo, assoluto; *n* totale *m*

totalitarian (tou-tæ-li-*têᵃ*-ri-ön) *adj* totalitario

totalizator (*tou*-tö-lai-sei-tö) *n* totalizzatore *m*

touch (tatʃ) *v* toccare; colpire; *n* contatto *m*, tocco *m*; tatto *m*

touching (*ta*-tʃing) *adj* commovente

tough (taf) *adj* duro

tour (tuᵒ) *n* gita turistica

tourism (*tuᵒ*-ri-söm) *n* turismo *m*

tourist (*tuᵒ*-risst) *n* turista *m*; ~ **class** classe turistica; ~ **office** ufficio turistico

tournament (*tuᵒ*-nö-mönt) *n* torneo *m*

tow (tou) *v* trainare

towards (tö-ᵘoods) *prep* verso

towel (tauᵒl) *n* asciugamano *m*

towelling (*tauᵒ*-ling) *n* spugna *f*

tower (tauᵒ) *n* torre *f*

town (taun) *n* città *f*; ~ **centre** centro della città; ~ **hall** municipio *m*

townspeople (*tauns*-pii-pöl) *pl* cittadinanza *f*

toxic (*tok*-ssik) *adj* tossico

toy (toi) *n* giocattolo *m*

toyshop (*toi*-ʃop) *n* negozio di giocattoli

trace (treiss) *n* traccia *f*; *v* rintracciare

track (træk) *n* binario *m*; pista *f*

tractor (*træk*-tö) *n* trattore *m*

trade (treid) *n* commercio *m*; mestiere *m*; *v* commerciare

trademark (*treid*-maak) *n* marchio di fabbrica

trader (*trei*-dö) *n* mercante *m*

tradesman (*treids*-mön) *n* (pl -men) commerciante *m*

trade-union (treid-ᶦ*uu*-nᶦön) *n* sindacato *m*

tradition (trö-*di*-ʃön) *n* tradizione *f*

traditional (trö-*di*-ʃö-nöl) *adj* tradizionale

traffic (*træ*-fik) *n* traffico *m*; ~ **jam** ingorgo *m*; ~ **light** semaforo *m*

trafficator (*træ*-fi-kei-tö) *n* indicatore di direzione

tragedy (*træ*-dʒö-di) *n* tragedia *f*

tragic (*træ*-dʒik) *adj* tragico

trail (treil) *n* traccia *f*, sentiero *m*

trailer (*trei*-lö) *n* rimorchio *m*; *nAm* roulotte *f*

train (trein) *n* treno *m*; *v* ammaestrare, addestrare; **stopping ~** accelerato *m*; **through ~** treno diretto

training (*trei*-ning) *n* addestramento *m*

trait (treit) *n* tratto *m*

traitor (*trei*-tö) *n* traditore *m*

tram (træm) *n* tram *m*

tramp (træmp) *n* vagabondo *m*, barbone *m*; *v* vagabondare

tranquil (*træng*-k^{u}il) *adj* tranquillo

tranquillizer (*træng*-k^{u}i-lai-sö) *n* tranquillante *m*

transaction (træn-*sæk*-ʃön) *n* transazione *f*

transatlantic (træn-söt-*læn*-tik) *adj* transatlantico

transfer (trænss-*föö*) *v* trasferire

transform (trænss-*foom*) *v* trasformare

transformer (trænss-*foo*-mö) *n* trasformatore *m*

transition (træn-*ssi*-ʃön) *n* transizione *f*

translate (trænss-*leit*) *v* *tradurre

translation (trænss-*lei*-ʃön) *n* traduzione *f*

translator (trænss-*lei*-tö) *n* traduttore *m*

transmission (træns-*mi*-ʃön) *n* trasmissione *f*

transmit (træns-*mit*) *v* *trasmettere

transmitter (træns-*mi*-tö) *n* trasmettitore *m*

transparent (træn-*sspê*ᵒ-rönt) *adj* trasparente

transport[1] (*træn*-sspoot) *n* trasporto *m*

transport[2] (træn-*sspoot*) *v* trasportare

transportation (træn-sspoo-*tei*-ʃön) *n* trasporto *m*

trap (træp) *n* trappola *f*

trash (træʃ) *n* robaccia *f*; **~ can** *Am* pattumiera *f*

travel (*træ*-völ) *v* viaggiare; **~ agency** agenzia viaggi; **~ agent** agente di viaggio; **~ insurance** assicurazione viaggi; **travelling expenses** spese di viaggio

traveller (*træ*-vö-lö) *n* viaggiatore *m*; **traveller's cheque** assegno turistico

tray (trei) *n* vassoio *m*

treason (*trii*-sön) *n* tradimento *m*

treasure (*trê*-zö) *n* tesoro *m*

treasurer (*trê*-zö-rö) *n* tesoriere *m*

treasury (*trê*-zö-ri) *n* Tesoro *m*

treat (triit) *v* trattare

treatment (*triit*-mönt) *n* trattamento *m*

treaty (*trii*-ti) *n* trattato *m*

tree (trii) *n* albero *m*

tremble (*trêm*-böl) *v* tremare; vibrare

tremendous (tri-*mên*-döss) *adj* enorme

trespass (*trêss*-pöss) *v* trasgredire

trespasser (*trêss*-pö-ssö) *n* trasgressore *m*

trial (traiᵒl) *n* processo *m*; prova *f*

triangle (*trai*-æng-ghöl) *n* triangolo *m*

triangular (trai-*æng*-gh^{i}u-lö) *adj* triangolare

tribe (traib) *n* tribù *f*

tributary (*tri*-b^{i}u-tö-ri) *n* braccio *m*

tribute (*tri*-b^{i}uut) *n* omaggio *m*

trick (trik) *n* tiro *m*; trucco *m*

trigger (*tri*-ghö) *n* grilletto *m*

trim (trim) *v* raccorciare

trip (trip) *n* gita *f*, viaggio *m*

triumph (*trai*-ömf) *n* trionfo *m*; *v* trionfare

triumphant (trai-*am*-fönt) *adj* trionfante

trolley-bus (*tro*-li-bass) *n* filobus *m*

troops (truupss) *pl* truppe *fpl*

tropical (*tro*-pi-köl) *adj* tropicale

tropics (*tro*-pikss) *pl* tropici *mpl*

trouble (*tra*-böl) *n* preoccupazione *f*, pena *f*, guaio *m*; *v* disturbare

troublesome (*tra*-böl-ssöm) *adj* molesto

trousers (*trau*-sös) *pl* pantaloni *mpl*

trout (traut) *n* (pl ~) trota *f*

truck (trak) *nAm* autocarro *m*

true (truu) *adj* vero; reale, autentico; leale, fedele

trumpet (*tram*-pit) *n* tromba *f*

trunk (trangk) *n* baule *m*; tronco *m*; *nAm* bagagliaio *m*; **trunks** *pl* calzoncini *mpl*

trunk-call (*trangk*-kool) *n* interurbana *f*

trust (trasst) *v* fidarsi; *n* fiducia *f*

trustworthy (*trasst*-ᵁöö-ði) *adj* fidato

truth (truuθ) *n* verità *f*

truthful (*truuθ*-föl) *adj* veritiero

try (trai) *v* tentare; sforzarsi; *n* tentativo *m*; ~ **on** provare

tube (t¹uub) *n* tubo *m*; tubetto *m*

tuberculosis (t¹uu-böö-k¹u-*lou*-ssiss) *n* tubercolosi *f*

Tuesday (*t¹uus*-di) martedì *m*

tug (tagh) *v* rimorchiare; *n* rimorchiatore *m*; strattone *m*

tuition (t¹uu-*i*-∫ön) *n* insegnamento *m*

tulip (*t¹uu*-lip) *n* tulipano *m*

tumbler (*tam*-blö) *n* bicchiere *m*

tumour (*t¹uu*-mö) *n* tumore *m*

tuna (*t¹uu*-nö) *n* (pl ~, ~s) tonno *m*

tune (t¹uun) *n* aria *f*, melodia *f*; ~ **in** sintonizzare

tuneful (*t¹uun*-föl) *adj* melodioso

tunic (*t¹uu*-nik) *n* tunica *f*

Tunisia (t¹uu-*ni*-si-ö) Tunisia *f*

Tunisian (t¹uu-*ni*-si-ön) *adj* tunisino

tunnel (*ta*-nöl) *n* galleria *f*

turbine (*töö*-bain) *n* turbina *f*

turbojet (töö-bou-*dʒ*êt) *n* aereo a reazione

Turk (töök) *n* turco *m*

Turkey (*töö*-ki) Turchia *f*

turkey (*töö*-ki) *n* tacchino *m*

Turkish (*töö*-ki∫) *adj* turco; ~ **bath** bagno turco

turn (töön) *v* voltare; *volgere, girare; *n* cambiamento *m*, giro *m*; tornante *m*; turno *m*; ~ **back** ritornare; ~ **down** *respingere; ~ **into** trasformarsi in; ~ **off** *chiudere; ~ **on** *accendere; *aprire; ~ **over** *capovolgere; ~ **round** voltare; rigirarsi

turning (*töö*-ning) *n* svolta *f*

turning-point (*töö*-ning-point) *n* punto decisivo

turnover (*töö*-nou-vö) *n* giro d'affari; ~ **tax** tassa sugli affari

turnpike (*töön*-paik) *nAm* strada a pedaggio

turpentine (*töö*-pön-tain) *n* trementina *f*

turtle (*töö*-töl) *n* tartaruga *f*

tutor (*t¹uu*-tö) *n* precettore *m*; tutore *m*

tuxedo (tak-*ssii*-dou) *nAm* (pl ~s, ~es) smoking *m*

tweed (t¹iid) *n* tweed *m*

tweezers (t¹ii-sös) *pl* pinzette *fpl*

twelfth (t¹êlfθ) *num* dodicesimo

twelve (t¹êlv) *num* dodici

twentieth (*t¹ên*-ti-öθ) *num* ventesimo

twenty (*t¹ên*-ti) *num* venti

twice (t¹aiss) *adv* due volte

twig (t¹igh) *n* ramoscello *m*

twilight (*t¹ai*-lait) *n* crepuscolo *m*

twine (t¹ain) *n* spago *m*

twins (t¹ins) *pl* gemelli *mpl*; **twin beds** letti gemelli

twist (t¹isst) *v* *torcere; *n* torsione *f*

two (tuu) *num* due

two-piece (tuu-*piiss*) *adj* in due pezzi

type (taip) *v* dattilografare; *n* tipo *m*

typewriter (*taip*-rai-tö) *n* macchina da scrivere

typewritten (*taip*-ri-tön) dattiloscritto

typhoid (*tai*-foid) *n* tifoidea *f*

typical (*ti*-pi-köl) *adj* caratteristico, tipico

typist (*tai*-pisst) *n* dattilografa *f*

tyrant (*taiÒ*-rönt) *n* tiranno *m*

tyre (taiÒ) *n* copertone *m*; ~ **pressure** pressione gomme

U

ugly (*a*-ghli) *adj* brutto

ulcer (*al*-ssö) *n* ulcera *f*

ultimate (*al*-ti-möt) *adj* ultimo

ultraviolet (al-trö-*vaiÒ*-löt) *adj* ultravioletto

umbrella (am-*brê*-lö) *n* ombrello *m*

umpire (*am*-paiÒ) *n* arbitro *m*

unable (a-*nei*-böl) *adj* incapace

unacceptable (a-nök-*ssêp*-tö-böl) *adj* inaccettabile

unaccountable (a-nö-*kaun*-tö-böl) *adj* inesplicabile

unaccustomed (a-nö-*ka*-sstömd) *adj* non abituato

unanimous (ᴵuu-*næ*-ni-möss) *adj* unanime

unanswered (a-*naan*-ssöd) *adj* senza risposta

unauthorized (a-*noo*-θö-raisd) *adj* illecito

unavoidable (a-nö-*voi*-dö-böl) *adj* inevitabile

unaware (a-nö-ᵘ*êÒ*) *adj* incosciente

unbearable (an-*bêÒ*-rö-böl) *adj* insopportabile

unbreakable (an-*brei*-kö-böl) *adj* infrangibile

unbroken (an-*brou*-kön) *adj* intatto

unbutton (an-*ba*-tön) *v* sbottonare

uncertain (an-*ssöö*-tön) *adj* incerto

uncle (*ang*-köl) *n* zio *m*

unclean (an-*kliin*) *adj* sudicio

uncomfortable (an-*kam*-fö-tö-böl) *adj* scomodo

uncommon (an-*ko*-mön) *adj* insolito, raro

unconditional (an-kön-*di*-[ö-nöl) *adj* incondizionato

unconscious (an-*kon*-[öss) *adj* inconscio

uncork (an-*kook*) *v* stappare

uncover (an-*ka*-vö) *v* *scoprire

uncultivated (an-*kal*-ti-vei-tid) *adj* incolto

under (*an*-dö) *prep* sotto

underestimate (an-dö-*rê*-ssti-meit) *v* sottovalutare

underground (*an*-dö-ghraund) *adj* sotterraneo; *n* metropolitana *f*

underline (an-dö-*lain*) *v* sottolineare

underneath (an-dö-*niiθ*) *adv* sotto

underpants (*an*-dö-pæntss) *plAm* mutandine *fpl*

undershirt (*an*-dö-[ööt) *n* maglietta *f*

undersigned (*an*-dö-ssaind) *n* sottoscritto *m*

*understand (an-dö-*sstænd*) *v* *comprendere, capire

understanding (an-dö-*sstæn*-ding) *n* comprensione *f*

*undertake (an-dö-*teik*) *v* *intraprendere

undertaking (an-dö-*tei*-king) *n* impresa *f*

underwater (*an*-dö-ᵘoo-tö) *adj* subacqueo

underwear (*an*-dö-ᵘêÒ) *n* biancheria personale

undesirable (an-di-*saiÒ*-rö-böl) *adj* indesiderabile

*undo (an-*duu*) *v* *disfare

undoubtedly (an-*dau*-tid-li) *adv* indubbiamente

undress (an-*drêss*) *v* spogliarsi

undulating (*an*-dᴵu-lei-ting) *adj* ondulato

unearned (a-*nöönd*) *adj* non meritato

uneasy (a-*nii*-si) *adj* inquieto

uneducated (a-*nê*-dʲu-kei-tid) *adj* incolto

unemployed (a-nim-*ploid*) *adj* disoccupato

unemployment (a-nim-*ploi*-mönt) *n* disoccupazione *f*

unequal (a-*nii*-kᵘöl) *adj* ineguale

uneven (a-*nii*-vön) *adj* ineguale, ruvido; irregolare

unexpected (a-nik-*sspêk*-tid) *adj* inatteso, inaspettato

unfair (an-*fê*ᵃ) *adj* disonesto, ingiusto

unfaithful (an-*feiθ*-föl) *adj* infedele

unfamiliar (an-fö-*mil*-ʲö) *adj* sconosciuto

unfasten (an-*faa*-ssön) *v* slacciare

unfavourable (an-*fei*-vö-rö-böl) *adj* sfavorevole

unfit (an-*fit*) *adj* disadatto

unfold (an-*fould*) *v* spiegare

unfortunate (an-*foo*-tʃö-nöt) *adj* sfortunato

unfortunately (an-*foo*-tʃö-nöt-li) *adv* disgraziatamente, sfortunatamente

unfriendly (an-*frênd*-li) *adj* poco gentile

unfurnished (an-*föö*-niʃt) *adj* non ammobiliato

ungrateful (an-*ghreit*-föl) *adj* ingrato

unhappy (an-*hæ*-pi) *adj* infelice

unhealthy (an-*hêl*-θi) *adj* malsano

unhurt (an-*hööt*) *adj* incolume

uniform (*ʲuu*-ni-foom) *n* uniforme *f*; *adj* uniforme

unimportant (a-nim-*poo*-tönt) *adj* insignificante

uninhabitable (a-nin-*hæ*-bi-tö-böl) *adj* inabitabile

uninhabited (a-nin-*hæ*-bi-tid) *adj* disabitato

unintentional (a-nin-*tên*-ʃö-nöl) *adj* involontario

union (*ʲuu*-nʲön) *n* unione *f*; lega *f*, confederazione *f*

unique (*ʲuu*-*niik*) *adj* unico

unit (*ʲuu*-nit) *n* unità *f*

unite (*ʲuu*-*nait*) *v* unire

United States (ʲuu-*nai*-tid ssteitss) Stati Uniti

unity (*ʲuu*-nö-ti) *n* unità *f*

universal (*ʲuu*-ni-*vöö*-ssöl) *adj* generale, universale

universe (*ʲuu*-ni-vööss) *n* universo *m*

university (*ʲuu*-ni-*vöö*-ssö-ti) *n* università *f*

unjust (an-*dʒasst*) *adj* ingiusto

unkind (an-*kaind*) *adj* sgarbato, scortese

unknown (an-*noun*) *adj* ignoto

unlawful (an-*loo*-föl) *adj* illegale

unleaded (an-*lê*-did) *adj* senza piombo

unlearn (an-*löön*) *v* disimparare

unless (ön-*lêss*) *conj* a meno che

unlike (an-*laik*) *adj* dissimile

unlikely (an-*lai*-kli) *adj* improbabile

unlimited (an-*li*-mi-tid) *adj* sconfinato, illimitato

unload (an-*loud*) *v* scaricare

unlock (an-*lok*) *v* *aprire

unlucky (an-*la*-ki) *adj* sfortunato

unnecessary (an-*nê*-ssö-ssö-ri) *adj* superfluo

unoccupied (a-*no*-kʲu-paid) *adj* vacante

unofficial (a-nö-*fi*-föl) *adj* ufficioso

unpack (an-*pæk*) *v* *disfare

unpleasant (an-*plê*-sönt) *adj* increscioso, spiacevole; sgradevole

unpopular (an-*po*-pʲu-lö) *adj* impopolare

unprotected (an-prö-*têk*-tid) *adj* indifeso

unqualified (an-*kᵘo*-li-faid) *adj* incompetente

unreal (an-*ri*ᵃ*l*) *adj* irreale

unreasonable (an-*rii*-sö-nö-böl) *adj* irragionevole

unreliable (an-ri-*lai*-ö-böl) *adj* non fidato

unrest (an-*rêsst*) *n* agitazione *f*; inquietudine *f*

unsafe (an-*sseif*) *adj* malsicuro

unsatisfactory (an-ssæ-tiss-*fæk*-tö-ri) *adj* insoddisfacente

unscrew (an-*sskruu*) *v* svitare

unselfish (an-*ssêl*-fiʃ) *adj* disinteressato

unskilled (an-*sskild*) *adj* non qualificato

unsound (an-*ssaund*) *adj* malsano

unstable (an-*sstei*-böl) *adj* instabile

unsteady (an-*sstê*-di) *adj* barcollante, malfermo; vacillante

unsuccessful (an-ssök-*ssêss*-föl) *adj* infruttuoso

unsuitable (an-*ssuu*-tö-böl) *adj* inadatto

unsurpassed (an-ssö-*paasst*) *adj* insuperato

untidy (an-*tai*-di) *adj* disordinato

untie (an-*tai*) *v* slacciare

until (ön-*til*) *prep* fino a, finché

untrue (an-*truu*) *adj* falso

untrustworthy (an-*trasst*-ᵘöö-ði) *adj* malfido

unusual (an-*ˈuu*-ʒu-öl) *adj* inconsueto, insolito

unwell (an-ᵘêl) *adj* indisposto

unwilling (an-ᵘi-ling) *adj* restio

unwise (an-ᵘais) *adj* incauto

unwrap (an-*ræp*) *v* *disfare

up (ap) *adv* verso l'alto, in su, su

upholster (ap-*houl*-sstö) *v* tappezzare

upkeep (*ap*-kiip) *n* mantenimento *m*

uplands (*ap*-lönds) *pl* altopiano *m*

upon (ö-*pon*) *prep* su

upper (a-pö) *adj* superiore

upright (*ap*-rait) *adj* diritto; *adv* in piedi

upset (ap-*ssêt*) *v* turbare; *adj* coster-

nato

upside-down (ap-ssaid-*daun*) *adv* sottosopra

upstairs (ap-*sstêᵒs*) *adv* di sopra; su

upstream (ap-*sstriim*) *adv* contro corrente

upwards (*ap*-ᵘods) *adv* in su

urban (*öö*-bön) *adj* urbano

urge (ööds) *v* stimolare; *n* impulso *m*

urgency (*öö*-dʒön-ssi) *n* urgenza *f*

urgent (*öö*-dʒönt) *adj* urgente

urine (*ˈuᵒ*-rin) *n* urina *f*

Uruguay (*ˈuᵒ*-rö-ghᵘai) Uruguay *m*

Uruguayan (*ˈuᵒ*-rö-*ghᵘai*-ön) *adj* uruguaiano

us (ass) *pron* ci

usable (*ˈuu*-sö-böl) *adj* usabile

usage (*ˈuu*-sidʒ) *n* usanza *f*

use¹ (*ˈuus*) *v* usare; ***be used to** *essere abituato a; ~ **up** consumare

use² (*ˈuuss*) *n* uso *m*; utilità *f*; ***be of** ~ giovare

useful (*ˈuuss*-föl) *adj* utile

useless (*ˈuuss*-löss) *adj* inutile

user (*ˈuu*-sö) *n* utente *m*

usher (a-ʃö) *n* usciere *m*

usherette (a-ʃö-*rêt*) *n* maschera *f*

usual (*ˈuu*-ʒu-öl) *adj* solito

usually (*ˈuu*-ʒu-ö-li) *adv* abitualmente

utensil (*ˈuu*-*tên*-ssöl) *n* arnese *m*, utensile *m*

utility (*ˈuu*-*ti*-lö-ti) *n* utilità *f*

utilize (*ˈuu*-ti-lais) *v* utilizzare

utmost (*at*-mousst) *adj* estremo

utter (a-tö) *adj* completo, totale; *v* *emettere

V

vacancy (*vei*-kön-ssi) *n* posto libero

vacant (*vei*-könt) *adj* vacante

vacate (vö-*keit*) *v* sgombrare

vacation (vö-*kei*-ʃön) *n* vacanza *f*
vaccinate (*væk*-ssi-neit) *v* vaccinare
vaccination (væk-ssi-*nei*-ʃön) *n* vaccinazione *f*
vacuum (*væ*-k'u-öm) *n* vuoto *m*; *vAm* pulire con l'aspirapolvere; ~ **cleaner** aspirapolvere *m*; ~ **flask** termos *m*
vagrancy (*vei*-ghrön-ssi) *n* vagabondaggio *m*
vague (veigh) *adj* vago
vain (vein) *adj* vano; inutile; **in** ~ inutilmente, invano
valet (*væ*-lit) *n* cameriere *m*, valletto *m*
valid (*væ*-lid) *adj* valido
valley (*væ*-li) *n* valle *f*
valuable (*væ*-l'u-böl) *adj* prezioso; **valuables** *pl* valori
value (*væ*-l'uu) *n* valore *m*; *v* valutare
valve (vælv) *n* valvola *f*
van (væn) *n* furgone *m*
vanilla (vö-*ni*-lö) *n* vaniglia *f*
vanish (*væ*-niʃ) *v* sparire
vapour (*vei*-pö) *n* vapore *m*
variable (*vê*ᵒ-ri-ö-böl) *adj* variabile
variation (vêᵒ-ri-*ei*-ʃön) *n* variazione *f*; mutamento *m*
varied (*vê*ᵒ-rid) *adj* assortito
variety (vö-*rai*-ö-ti) *n* varietà *f*; ~ **show** spettacolo di varietà; ~ **theatre** teatro di varietà
various (*vê*ᵒ-ri-öss) *adj* vari, parecchi
varnish (*vaa*-niʃ) *n* lacca *f*, vernice *f*; *v* verniciare
vary (*vê*ᵒ-ri) *v* differire, variare; cambiare
vase (vaas) *n* vaso *m*
vaseline (*væ*-ssö-liin) *n* vasellina *f*
vast (vaasst) *adj* immenso, vasto
vault (voolt) *n* volta *f*; camera blindata
veal (viil) *n* vitello *m*

vegetable (*vê*-dʒö-tö-böl) *n* verdura *f*; ~ **merchant** fruttivendolo *m*
vegetarian (vê-dʒi-*tê*ᵒ-ri-ön) *n* vegetariano *m*
vegetation (vê-dʒi-*tei*-ʃön) *n* vegetazione *f*
vehicle (*vii*-ö-köl) *n* veicolo *m*
veil (veil) *n* velo *m*
vein (vein) *n* vena *f*; **varicose** ~ vena varicosa
velvet (*vêl*-vit) *n* velluto *m*
velveteen (vêl-vi-*tiin*) *n* velluto di cotone
venerable (*vê*-nö-rö-böl) *adj* venerabile
venereal disease (vi-*ni*ᵒ-ri-öl di-*siis*) malattia venerea
Venezuela (vê-ni-sᵘ*ei*-lö) Venezuela *m*
Venezuelan (vê-ni-sᵘ*ei*-lön) *adj* venezolano
ventilate (*vên*-ti-leit) *v* ventilare; aerare
ventilation (vên-ti-*lei*-ʃön) *n* ventilazione *f*; aerazione *f*
ventilator (*vên*-ti-lei-tö) *n* ventilatore *m*
venture (*vên*-tʃö) *v* arrischiare
veranda (vö-*ræn*-dö) *n* veranda *f*
verb (vööb) *n* verbo *m*
verbal (*vöö*-böl) *adj* verbale
verdict (*vöö*-dikt) *n* sentenza *f*, verdetto *m*
verge (vöödʒ) *n* bordo *m*
verify (*vê*-ri-fai) *v* verificare
verse (vööss) *n* verso *m*
version (*vöö*-ʃön) *n* versione *f*; traduzione *f*
versus (*vöö*-ssöss) *prep* contro
vertical (*vöö*-ti-köl) *adj* verticale
vertigo (*vöö*-ti-ghou) *n* vertigine *f*
very (*vê*-ri) *adv* assai, molto; *adj* vero, preciso; estremo
vessel (*vê*-ssöl) *n* nave *f*, vascello *m*; recipiente *m*

vest (vêsst) *n* maglia *f*; *nAm* panciotto *m*

veterinary surgeon (vê-tri-nö-ri ssöö-dʒön) veterinario *m*

via (vaiö) *prep* via

viaduct (vaiö-dakt) *n* viadotto *m*

vibrate (vai-breit) *v* vibrare

vibration (vai-brei-[ö]n) *n* vibrazione *f*

vicar (vi-kö) *n* vicario *m*

vicarage (vi-kö-ridʒ) *n* presbiterio *m*

vice-president (vaiss-prê-si-dönt) *n* vicepresidente *m*

vicinity (vi-ssi-nö-ti) *n* prossimità *f*, vicinanza *f*

victim (vik-tim) *n* vittima *f*

victory (vik-tö-ri) *n* vittoria *f*

videocassette (vi-di-ou-kö-sset) *n* videocassetta *f*; ~ **recorder** videoregistratore *m*

view (vˡuu) *n* vista *f*; parere *m*, opinione *f*; *v* guardare

view-finder (vˡuu-fain-dö) *n* mirino *m*

vigilant (vi-dʒi-lönt) *adj* vigilante

villa (vi-lö) *n* villa *f*

village (vi-lidʒ) *n* villaggio *m*

villain (vi-lön) *n* furfante *m*

vine (vain) *n* vite *f*

vinegar (vi-ni-ghö) *n* aceto *m*

vineyard (vin-ˡöd) *n* vigna *f*

vintage (vin-tidʒ) *n* vendemmia *f*

violation (vaiö-lei-[ö]n) *n* violazione *f*

violence (vaiö-lönss) *n* violenza *f*

violent (vaiö-lönt) *adj* violento; intenso, impetuoso

violet (vaiö-löt) *n* violetta *f*; *adj* violetto

violin (vaiö-lin) *n* violino *m*

virgin (vöö-dʒin) *n* vergine *f*

virtue (vöö-tʃuu) *n* virtù *f*

visa (vii-sö) *n* visto *m*

visibility (vi-sö-bi-lö-ti) *n* visibilità *f*

visible (vi-sö-böl) *adj* visibile

vision (vi-ʒön) *n* visione *f*

visit (vi-sit) *v* visitare; *n* visita *f*;

visiting hours ore di visita

visitor (vi-si-tö) *n* visitatore *m*

vital (vai-töl) *adj* vitale

vitamin (vi-tö-min) *n* vitamina *f*

vivid (vi-vid) *adj* vivido

vocabulary (vö-kæ-bˡu-lö-ri) *n* vocabolario *m*; glossario *m*

vocal (vou-köl) *adj* vocale

vocalist (vou-kö-lisst) *n* cantante *m*

voice (voiss) *n* voce *f*

void (void) *adj* nullo

volcano (vol-kei-nou) *n* (pl ~es, ~s) vulcano *m*

volt (voult) *n* volt *m*

voltage (voul-tidʒ) *n* voltaggio *m*

volume (vo-lˡum) *n* volume *m*

voluntary (vo-lön-tö-ri) *adj* volontario

volunteer (vo-lön-tiö) *n* volontario *m*

vomit (vo-mit) *v* rigettare, vomitare

vote (vout) *v* votare; *n* voto *m*; votazione *f*

voucher (vau-tʃö) *n* buono *m*, ricevuta *f*

vow (vau) *n* promessa *f*, giuramento *m*; *v* giurare

vowel (vauˡl) *n* vocale *f*

voyage (voi-idʒ) *n* viaggio *m*

vulgar (val-ghö) *adj* volgare; popolano, triviale

vulnerable (val-nö-rö-böl) *adj* vulnerabile

vulture (val-tʃö) *n* avvoltoio *m*

W

wade (ˡueid) *v* guadare

wafer (ˡuei-fö) *n* ostia *f*

waffle (ˡuo-föl) *n* cialda *f*

wages (ˡuei-dʒis) *pl* stipendio *m*

waggon (ˡuæ-ghön) *n* vagone *m*

waist (ˡueisst) *n* vita *f*

waistcoat (ˡueiss-kout) *n* panciotto *m*

wait (ᵘeit) v aspettare; ~ **on** servire

waiter (ᵘei-tö) n cameriere m

waiting (ᵘei-ting) n attesa f

waiting-list (ᵘei-ting-lisst) n lista di attesa

waiting-room (ᵘei-ting-ruum) n sala d'aspetto

waitress (ᵘei-triss) n cameriera f

***wake** (ᵘeik) v svegliare; ~ **up** destarsi, svegliarsi

walk (ᵘook) v camminare; passeggiare; n passeggiata f; andatura f; **walking** a piedi

walker (ᵘoo-kö) n camminatore m

walking-stick (ᵘoo-king-sstik) n bastone da passeggio

wall (ᵘool) n muro m; parete f

wallet (ᵘo-lit) n portafoglio m

wallpaper (ᵘool-pei-pö) n carta da parati

walnut (ᵘool-nat) n noce f

waltz (ᵘoolss) n valzer m

wander (ᵘon-dö) v errare, vagare

want (ᵘont) v *volere; desiderare; n bisogno m; scarsezza f, mancanza f

war (ᵘoo) n guerra f

warden (ᵘoo-dön) n custode m, guardiano m

wardrobe (ᵘoo-droub) n guardaroba m

warehouse (ᵘêᵒ-hauss) n magazzino m, deposito m

wares (ᵘêᵒs) pl merci

warm (ᵘoom) adj caldo; v scaldare

warmth (ᵘoomθ) n calore m

warn (ᵘoon) v avvisare

warning (ᵘoo-ning) n avvertimento m

wary (ᵘêᵒ-ri) adj prudente

was (ᵘos) v (p be)

wash (ᵘoʃ) v lavare; ~ **and wear** non si stira; ~ **up** lavare i piatti

washable (ᵘo-fö-böl) adj lavabile

wash-basin (ᵘoʃ-bei-ssön) n lavandino m

washing (ᵘo-ʃing) n lavaggio m; bucato m

washing-machine (ᵘo-ʃing-mö-ʃiin) n lavatrice f

washing-powder (ᵘo-ʃing-pau-dö) n detersivo m

washroom (ᵘoʃ-ruum) nAm toletta f

wash-stand (ᵘoʃ-sstænd) n lavandino m

wasp (ᵘossp) n vespa f

waste (ᵘeisst) v sprecare; n spreco m; adj incolto

wasteful (ᵘeisst-föl) adj spendereccio

wastepaper-basket (ᵘeisst-pei-pö-baasskit) n cestino m

watch (ᵘotʃ) v guardare, osservare; *tenere d'occhio; n orologio m; ~ **out** *stare in guardia

watch-maker (ᵘotf-mei-kö) n orologiaio m

watch-strap (ᵘotf-sstræp) n cinturino da orologio

water (ᵘoo-tö) n acqua f; **iced** ~ acqua ghiacciata; **running** ~ acqua corrente; ~ **pump** pompa ad acqua; ~ **ski** sci d'acqua

water-colour (ᵘoo-tö-ka-lö) n acquerello m

watercress (ᵘoo-tö-krêss) n crescione m

waterfall (ᵘoo-tö-fool) n cascata f

watermelon (ᵘoo-tö-mê-lön) n anguria f

waterproof (ᵘoo-tö-pruuf) adj impermeabile

water-softener (ᵘoo-tö-ssof-nö) n addolcitore m

waterway (ᵘoo-tö-ᵘei) n via d'acqua

watt (ᵘot) n watt m

wave (ᵘeiv) n ricciolo m, onda f; v sventolare

wave-length (ᵘeiv-lêngθ) n lunghezza d'onda

wavy (ᵘei-vi) adj ondulato

wax (ᵘækss) *n* cera *f*

waxworks (ᵘækss-ᵘöökss) *pl* museo delle cere

way (ᵘei) *n* maniera *f*, modo *m*; via *f*; lato *m*, direzione *f*; distanza *f*; **any ~** comunque; **by the ~** a proposito; **one-way traffic** senso unico; **out of the ~** remoto; **the other ~ round** alla rovescia; **~ back** ritorno *m*; **~ in** entrata *f*; **~ out** uscita *f*

wayside (ᵘei-ssaid) *n* margine della strada

we (ᵘii) *pron* noi

weak (ᵘiik) *adj* debole; diluito

weakness (ᵘiik-nöss) *n* debolezza *f*

wealth (ᵘêlθ) *n* ricchezza *f*

wealthy (ᵘêl-θi) *adj* ricco

weapon (ᵘê°-pön) *n* arma *f*

***wear** (ᵘê°) *v* indossare, vestire; **~ out** logorare

weary (ᵘi°-ri) *adj* affaticato, stanco

weather (ᵘê-ðö) *n* tempo *m*; **~ forecast** bollettino meteorologico

***weave** (ᵘiiv) *v* tessere

weaver (ᵘii-vö) *n* tessitore *m*

wedding (ᵘê-ding) *n* sposalizio *m*, matrimonio *m*

wedding-ring (ᵘê-ding-ring) *n* fede *f*

wedge (ᵘêdʒ) *n* cuneo *m*

Wednesday (ᵘêns-di) mercoledì *m*

weed (ᵘiid) *n* erbaccia *f*

week (ᵘiik) *n* settimana *f*

weekday (ᵘiik-dei) *n* giorno feriale

weekend (ᵘii-kênd) *n* fine-settimana

weekly (ᵘii-kli) *adj* settimanale

***weep** (ᵘiip) *v* *piangere

weigh (ᵘei) *v* pesare

weighing-machine (ᵘei-ing-mö-ʃiin) *n* bilancia *f*

weight (ᵘeit) *n* peso *m*

welcome (ᵘêl-köm) *adj* benvenuto; *n* accoglienza *f*; *v* *accogliere

weld (ᵘêld) *v* saldare

welfare (ᵘêl-fê°) *n* benessere *m*

well[1] (ᵘêl) *adv* bene; *adj* sano; **as ~ pure**, come pure; **as ~ as** come pure; **well!** ebbene!

well[2] (ᵘêl) *n* pozzo *m*

well-founded (ᵘêl-faun-did) *adj* fondato

well-known (ᵘêl-noun) *adj* noto

well-to-do (ᵘêl-tö-duu) *adj* agiato

went (ᵘênt) *v* (p go)

were (ᵘöö) *v* (p be)

west (ᵘêsst) *n* occidente *m*, ovest *m*

westerly (ᵘê-sstö-li) *adj* occidentale

western (ᵘê-sstön) *adj* occidentale

wet (ᵘêt) *adj* bagnato; umido

whale (ᵘeil) *n* balena *f*

wharf (ᵘoof) *n* (pl ~s, wharves) molo *m*

what (ᵘot) *pron* che cosa; quello che; **~ for** perché

whatever (ᵘo-tê-vö) *pron* qualsiasi

wheat (ᵘiit) *n* frumento *m*

wheel (ᵘiil) *n* ruota *f*

wheelbarrow (ᵘiil-bæ-rou) *n* carriola *f*

wheelchair (ᵘiil-tʃê°) *n* sedia a rotelle

when (ᵘên) *adv* quando; *conj* qualora, quando

whenever (ᵘê-nê-vö) *conj* ogniqualvolta

where (ᵘê°) *adv* dove; *conj* dove

wherever (ᵘê°-rê-vö) *conj* dovunque

whether (ᵘê-ðö) *conj* se; **whether ... or** se ... o

which (ᵘitʃ) *pron* quale; che

whichever (ᵘi-tʃê-vö) *adj* qualsiasi

while (ᵘail) *conj* mentre; *n* istante *m*

whilst (ᵘailsst) *conj* mentre

whim (ᵘim) *n* ghiribizzo *m*, capriccio *m*

whip (ᵘip) *n* frusta *f*; *v* sbattere

whiskers (ᵘi-sskös) *pl* basette *fpl*

whisper (ᵘi-sspö) *v* mormorare; *n* sussurro *m*

whistle (ᵘi-ssöl) v fischiare; n fischio m

white (ᵘait) adj bianco

whitebait (ᵘait-beit) n pesciolino m

whiting (ᵘai-ting) n (pl ~) merlano m

Whitsun (ᵘit-ssön) Pentecoste f

who (huu) pron chi; che

whoever (huu-ê-vö) pron chiunque

whole (houl) adj completo, intero; intatto; n totale m

wholesale (houl-sseil) n ingrosso m; ~ **dealer** grossista m

wholesome (houl-ssöm) adj salubre

wholly (houl-li) adv completamente

whom (huum) pron a chi

whore (hoo) n puttana f

whose (huus) pron il cui; di chi

why (ᵘai) adv perché

wicked (ᵘi-kid) adj scellerato

wide (ᵘaid) adj vasto, largo

widen (ᵘai-dön) v allargare

widow (ᵘi-dou) n vedova f

widower (ᵘi-dou-ö) n vedovo m

width (ᵘidθ) n larghezza f

wife (ᵘaif) n (pl wives) consorte f, moglie f

wig (ᵘigh) n parrucca f

wild (ᵘaild) adj selvatico; feroce

will (ᵘil) n volontà f; testamento m

***will** (ᵘil) v *volere

willing (ᵘi-ling) adj compiacente

willingly (ᵘi-ling-li) adv volentieri

will-power (ᵘil-pau⁶) n forza di volontà

***win** (ᵘin) v *vincere

wind (ᵘind) n vento m

***wind** (ᵘaind) v zigzagare; caricare, *avvolgere

winding (ᵘain-ding) adj serpeggiante

windmill (ᵘind-mil) n mulino a vento

window (ᵘin-dou) n finestra f

window-sill (ᵘin-dou-ssil) n davanzale m

windscreen (ᵘind-sskriin) n parabrezza m; ~ **wiper** tergicristallo m

windshield (ᵘind-ʃiild) nAm parabrezza m; ~ **wiper** Am tergicristallo m

windy (ᵘin-di) adj ventoso

wine (ᵘain) n vino m

wine-cellar (ᵘain-ssê-lö) n cantina f

wine-list (ᵘain-lisst) n lista dei vini

wine-merchant (ᵘain-möö-tʃönt) n mercante di vini

wine-waiter (ᵘain-ᵘei-tö) n cantiniere m

wing (ᵘing) n ala f

winkle (ᵘing-köl) n chiocciola di mare

winner (ᵘi-nö) n vincitore m

winning (ᵘi-ning) adj vincente; **winnings** pl vincita f

winter (ᵘin-tö) n inverno m; ~ **sports** sport invernali

wipe (ᵘaip) v strofinare, asciugare; spazzare

wire (ᵘai⁶) n filo m; filo di ferro

wireless (ᵘai⁶-löss) n radio f

wisdom (ᵘis-döm) n saggezza f

wise (ᵘais) adj saggio

wish (ᵘiʃ) v desiderare; n desiderio m

witch (ᵘitʃ) n strega f

with (ᵘið) prep con; presso; per

***withdraw** (ᵘið-droo) v ritirare

within (ᵘi-ðin) prep dentro; adv all'interno

without (ᵘi-ðaut) prep senza

witness (ᵘit-nöss) n testimone m

wits (ᵘitss) pl ragione f

witty (ᵘi-ti) adj spiritoso

wolf (ᵘulf) n (pl wolves) lupo m

woman (ᵘu-mön) n (pl women) donna f

womb (ᵘuum) n utero m

won (ᵘan) v (p, pp win)

wonder (ᵘan-dö) n miracolo m; stupore m; v *chiedersi

wonderful (ᵘan-dö-föl) adj stupendo, meraviglioso; delizioso

wood (ᵘud) n legno m; bosco m

wood-carving (ᵘud-kaa-ving) n scultura in legno

wooded (ᵘu-did) adj boscoso

wooden (ᵘu-dön) adj di legno; ~ **shoe** zoccolo m

woodland (ᵘud-lönd) n terreno boscoso

wool (ᵘul) n lana f; **darning** ~ lana da rammendo

woollen (ᵘu-lön) adj di lana

word (ᵘööd) n parola f

wore (ᵘoo) v (p wear)

work (ᵘöök) n lavoro m; attività f; v lavorare; funzionare; **working day** giorno lavorativo; ~ **of art** opera d'arte; ~ **permit** permesso di lavoro

worker (ᵘöö-kö) n lavoratore m

working (ᵘöö-king) n funzionamento m

workman (ᵘöök-mön) n (pl -men) operaio m

works (ᵘöökss) pl fabbrica f

workshop (ᵘöök-ʃop) n officina f

world (ᵘööld) n mondo m; ~ **war** guerra mondiale

world-famous (ᵘööld-fei-möss) adj di fama mondiale

world-wide (ᵘööld-ᵘaid) adj mondiale

worm (ᵘööm) n verme m

worn (ᵘoon) adj (pp wear) consumato

worn-out (ᵘoon-aut) adj usato

worried (ᵘa-rid) adj preoccupato

worry (ᵘa-ri) v preoccuparsi; n ansia f, preoccupazione f

worse (ᵘööss) adj peggiore; adv peggio

worship (ᵘöö-ʃip) v venerare; n culto m

worst (ᵘöösst) adj pessimo; adv peggio

worsted (ᵘu-sstid) n lana pettinata

worth (ᵘööθ) n valore m; *be ~ *valere; *be worth-while *valer la pena

worthless (ᵘööθ-löss) adj senza valore

worthy of (ᵘöö-ði öv) degno di

would (ᵘud) v (p will) *solere

wound¹ (ᵘuund) n ferita f; v *offendere, ferire

wound² (ᵘaund) v (p, pp wind)

wrap (ræp) v *avvolgere

wreck (rêk) n relitto m; v *distruggere

wrench (rêntʃ) n chiave f; storta f; v *storcere

wrinkle (ring-köl) n ruga f

wrist (risst) n polso m

wrist-watch (risst-ᵘotʃ) n orologio da polso

***write** (rait) v *scrivere; **in writing** per iscritto; ~ **down** annotare

writer (rai-tö) n scrittore m

writing-pad (rai-ting-pæd) n blocco per appunti, blocco di carta da lettere

writing-paper (rai-ting-pei-pö) n carta da lettere

written (ri-tön) adj (pp write) per iscritto

wrong (rong) adj erroneo, sbagliato; n torto m; v *fare un torto; *be ~ *avere torto

wrote (rout) v (p write)

X

Xmas (kriss-möss) Natale

X-ray (êkss-rei) n radiografia f; v radiografare

Y

yacht (¹ot) *n* panfilo *m*
yacht-club (¹*ot*-klab) *n* circolo nautico
yachting (¹*o*-ting) *n* sport velico
yard (¹aad) *n* cortile *m*
yarn (¹aan) *n* filo *m*
yawn (¹oon) *v* sbadigliare
year (¹¡ö) *n* anno *m*
yearly (¹¡ö-li) *adj* annuale
yeast (¹iisst) *n* lievito *m*
yell (¹èl) *v* strillare; *n* strillo *m*
yellow (¹*ê*-lou) *adj* giallo
yes (¹èss) sì
yesterday (¹*ê*-sstö-di) *adv* ieri
yet (¹èt) *adv* ancora; *conj* eppure, pe-
ò, ma
yield (¹iild) *v* *rendere; cedere
yoke (¹ouk) *n* giogo *m*
yolk (¹ouk) *n* tuorlo *m*
you (¹uu) *pron* tu; ti; Lei; Le; voi; vi
young (¹ang) *adj* giovane
your (¹oo) *adj* Suo; tuo; vostro, vostri

yourself (¹oo-*ssêlf*) *pron* ti; tu stesso;
Lei stesso
yourselves (¹oo-*ssêlvs*) *pron* vi; voi
stessi
youth (¹uuθ) *n* gioventù *f*; ~ hostel
ostello della gioventù

Z

zeal (siil) *n* zelo *m*
zealous (sê-löss) *adj* zelante
zebra (*sii*-brö) *n* zebra *f*
zenith (*sê*-niθ) *n* zenit *m*; apice *m*
zero (*si*ö-rou) *n* (pl ~s) zero *m*
zest (sêsst) *n* gusto *m*
zinc (singk) *n* zinco *m*
zip (sip) *n* chiusura lampo; ~ code
Am codice postale
zipper (*si*-pö) *n* chiusura lampo
zodiac (*sou*-di-æk) *n* zodiaco *m*
zone (soun) *n* zona *f*
zoo (suu) *n* (pl ~s) giardino zoologico
zoology (sou-*o*-lö-dʒi) *n* zoologia *f*

Lessico gastronomico

Cibi

à la carte secondo la lista delle vivande

almond mandorla

anchovy acciuga

angel food cake dolce a base di albumi

angels on horseback ostriche avvolte in fettine di pancetta, cotte alla griglia e servite su pane tostato

appetizer stuzzichino

apple mela

~ **charlotte** torta di mele coperta con fette di pane

~ **dumpling** mela ricoperta di pasta e cotta nel forno

~ **sauce** salsa di mele

apricot albicocca

Arbroath smoky eglefino affumicato

artichoke carciofo

asparagus asparago

~ **tip** punta d'asparago

aspic gelantina

assorted assortito

aubergine melanzana

bacon pancetta

~ **and eggs** uova con pancetta

bagel panino a forma di corona

baked al forno

~ **Alaska** omelette alla norvegese; dessert con gelato alla vaniglia e meringhe

~ **beans** fagioli bianchi con salsa di pomodoro

~ **potato** patate cotte al forno con la buccia

Bakewell tart crostata con mandorle e marmellata di lamponi

baloney varietà di mortadella

banana banana

~ **split** banana tagliata a metà e servita con gelato, noci, sciroppo o cioccolata

barbecue 1) carne di manzo tritata, servita in un panino con salsa di pomodoro piccante 2) pasto all'aperto a base di carne ai ferri fatta al momento

~ **sauce** salsa di pomodoro molto piccante

barbecued ai ferri

basil basilico

bass branzino

bean fagiolo

beef manzo

~ **olive** involtino di manzo

beefburger medaglione di carne di manzo ai ferri, servito in un panino

beet, beetroot barbabietola

bilberry mirtillo

bill conto

~ **of fare** menù, lista delle vivande

biscuit 1) biscotto, pasticcino (GB) 2) panino (US)

black pudding sanguinaccio

blackberry mora

blackcurrant ribes nero

bloater aringa salata e affumicata

blood sausage sanguinaccio

blueberry mirtillo

boiled bollito

Bologna (sausage) mortadella

bone osso

boned disossato

Boston baked beans piatto di fagioli bianchi, cotti con pancetta e zucchero grezzo

Boston cream pie torta a strati, ripiena di crema e con glassa al cioccolato

brains cervella

braised brasato

bramble pudding budino di more a cui possono essere aggiunte mele tagliate a pezzetti

braunschweiger specie di paté di fegato

bread pane

breaded impanato

breakfast prima colazione

bream pagello

breast petto

brisket punta di petto

broad bean grossa fava

broth brodo

brown Betty torta di mele con spezie, coperta di uno strato di pasta frolla

brunch pasto abbondante, preso in tarda mattinata, che riunisce la colazione e il pranzo

brussels sprout cavolino di Bruxelles

bubble and squeak frittelle di purea di patate e di cavolo, a volte con pezzetti di manzo

bun 1) panino al latte con frutta secca (GB) 2) varietà di panino (US)

butter burro

buttered imburrato

cabbage cavolo

Caesar salad insalata con crostini all'aroma d'aglio, acciughe e formaggio grattugiato

cake torta, dolce

cakes pasticcini, biscotti

calf vitello

Canadian bacon filetto di maiale affumicato, tagliato a fette sottili

canapé panino imbottito

cantaloupe melone

caper cappero

capercaillie, capercailzie gallo cedrone

caramel caramello

carp carpa

carrot carota

cashew noce di acagiù

casserole casseruola; stufato

catfish pesce gatto

catsup ketchup, salsa di pomodoro con aceto e spezie

cauliflower cavolfiore

celery sedano

cereal fiocchi di mais, avena o altri cereali, serviti con latte freddo e zucchero

 hot ∼ pappa di cereali calda

chateaubriand filetto di manzo di prima scelta cotto ai ferri

check il conto

Cheddar (cheese) formaggio di pasta dura, grasso e di gusto leggermente acido

cheese formaggio

 ∼ **board** piatto di formaggio

 ∼ **cake** dolce al formaggio doppia panna

cheeseburger amburghese con una fetta di formaggio fuso, servito in un panino

chef's salad insalata di prosciutto, pollo, uova sode, pomodoro, lattuga e formaggio

cherry ciliegia

chestnut castagna

chicken pollo

chicory 1) indivia (GB) 2) cicoria (US)

chili con carne piatto a base di manzo tritato, fagioli borlotti e pepe di Caienna

chili pepper pepe di Caienna

chips 1) patate fritte (GB) 2) patatine (US)

chitt(er)lings trippa di maiale

chive erba cipollina

chocolate cioccolato

~ **pudding** 1) budino al cioccolato (GB) 2) spuma al cioccolato (US)

choice scelta

chop cotoletta, braciola

~ **suey** piatto a base di carne o di pollo, verdure e riso

chopped sminuzzato, tritato

chowder zuppa densa di pesce, di frutti di mare o di carne

Christmas pudding budino a base di frutta candita, scorza di limone, cedro; a volte alla fiamma

cinnamon cannella

chutney salsa indiana molto piccante

clam vongola, tellina

club sandwich panino imbottito con pancetta, pollo, pomodoro, lattuga e maionese; a diversi strati

cobbler crostata di frutta, ricoperta di pasta frolla

cock-a-leekie soup minestra di pollo e di porri

coconut noce di cocco

cod merluzzo

Colchester oyster la più pregiata ostrica inglese

cold cuts/meat affettati

coleslaw insalata di cavolo

compote composta, conserva

condiment condimento

consommé brodo ristretto

cooked cotto

cookie biscotto

corn 1) grano (GB) 2) granturco (US)

~ **on the cob** pannocchia di granturco

cornflakes fiocchi di granturco

corned beef carne di manzo in scatola

cottage cheese formaggio bianco, fresco

cottage pie carne tritata ricoperta di cipolle e purea di patate, il tutto passato al forno

course portata

cover charge coperto

crab granchio

cranberry varietà di mirtillo

~ **sauce** marmellata di mirtilli rossi, servita con carne e selvaggina

crawfish, crayfish 1) gambero di fiume 2) aragosta (GB) 3) scampo (US)

cream 1) crema, panna 2) dessert 3) zuppa densa

~ **cheese** formaggio doppia panna

~ **puff** bignè

creamed potatoes patate tagliate a dadi, in besciamella

creole alla creola; piatto preparato con salsa di pomodoro molto ɹiccante, peperoni, cipolle e servito con riso

cress crescione

crisps patatine

croquette polpetta

crumpet panino leggero di forma rotonda, tostato e imburrato

cucumber cetriolo

Cumberland ham prosciutto inglese molto rinomato

Cumberland sauce gelatina di ribes, con vino, succo d'arancia e spezie

cupcake varietà di pasticcino

cured salato, affumicato, marinato (pesce o carne)

currant 1) uva sultanina 2) ribes

curried con curry

custard crema, sformato

cutlet cotoletta, scaloppina

dab genere di pesce, simile alla sogliola

Danish pastry pasticceria danese

date dattero

Derby cheese tipo di formaggio piccante

devilled alla diavola; condimento molto piccante

devil's food cake torta al cioccolato, molto sostanziosa

devils on horseback prugne secche cotte nel vino rosso e ripiene di mandorle e di acciughe, avvolte nella pancetta, passate alla griglia e servite su pane tostato

Devonshire cream crema cagliata

diced tagliato a dadi

diet food cibo dietetico

dill aneto

dinner cena

dish piatto

donut, doughnut frittella a forma di ciambella

double cream doppia panna,

panna intera

Dover sole sogliola di Dover, molto rinomata

dressing 1) condimento per insalata 2) ripieno per tacchino (US)

Dublin Bay prawn scampo

duck anitra

duckling anatroccolo

dumpling gnocchetto di pasta, bollito

Dutch apple pie torta di mele, ricoperta da un impasto di burro e zucchero grezzo

éclair pasticcino glassato ripieno di crema

eel anguilla

egg uovo

　boiled ∼ alla coque

　fried ∼ al tegame

　hard-boiled ∼ sodo

　poached ∼ in camicia

　scrambled ∼ strapazzato

　soft-boiled ∼ molle

eggplant melanzana

endive 1) cicoria, insalata riccia (GB) 2) indivia (US)

entrecôte costata

entrée 1) antipasto (GB) 2) piatto principale (US)

escalope scaloppina

fennel finocchio

fig fico

fillet filetto di carne o di pesce

finnan haddock eglefino affumicato

fish pesce

　∼ **and chips** pesce fritto con contorno di patatine fritte

　∼ **cake** polpette di pesce

flan crostata alla frutta

flapjack frittella dolce e spessa

flounder passerino

forcemeat ripieno, farcia

fowl pollame
frankfurter wurstel
French bean fagiolino verde
French bread sfilatino (pane)
French dressing 1) condimento per insalata a base di olio e aceto (GB) 2) condimento per insalata un po' denso, con ketchup (US)
french fries patatine fritte
French toast fette di pane imbevute di uova battute e fritte in padella, servite con marmellata o zucchero
fresh fresco
fricassée fricassea
fried fritto
fritter frittella
frogs' legs cosce di rana
frosting glassa
fruit frutto
fry frittura
galantine galantina
game cacciagione
gammon prosciutto affumicato
garfish aguglia di mare, luccio
garlic aglio
garnish contorno
gherkin cetriolino
giblets rigaglie
ginger zenzero
goose oca
   ~**berry** uva spina
grape uva
   ~**fruit** pompelmo
grated grattugiato
gravy sugo a base di carne
grayling temolo
green bean fagiolino verde
green pepper peperone verde
green salad insalata verde
greens verdura
grilled alla griglia, ai ferri
grilse salmone giovane

grouse starna
gumbo 1) legume di origine africana 2) piatto creolo a base di *okra* con pomodori e carne o pesce
haddock eglefino
haggis frattaglie di pecora (o di vitello) tagliate a pezzetti e mescolate con fiocchi d'avena
hake baccalà
half mezzo, metà
halibut passera, pianuzza
ham prosciutto
   ~ **and eggs** uova con prosciutto
hamburger polpetta di carne di manzo tritata e cipolla, servita in un panino
hare lepre
haricot bean fagiolo
hash carne tritata o sminuzzata; piatto di carne sminuzzata, con patate e verdure
hazelnut nocciola
heart cuore
herb erbe, odori
herring aringa
home-made fatto in casa
hominy grits specie di polenta
honey miele
   ~**dew melon** melone molto dolce dalla polpa verde-gialla
hors-d'œuvre antipasto
horse-radish rafano
hot 1) caldo 2) piccante
   ~ **cross bun** brioche a forma di croce, con uvetta e ricoperta di una glassa (per la Quaresima)
   ~ **dog** wurstel caldo in un panino
huckleberry mirtillo
hush puppy frittella di farina di mais e di cipolle
ice-cream gelato
iced glassato, gelato

icing glassa
Idaho baked potato qualità di patata specialmente adatta per essere cotta al forno
Irish stew stufato di montone con cipolle e patate
Italian dressing condimento per insalata a base di olio e aceto
jam marmellata
jellied in gelatina
Jell-O dolce di gelatina
jelly gelatina
Jerusalem artichoke topinambur
John Dory orata
jugged hare lepre in salmì
juice succo
juniper berry bacca di ginepro
junket latte cagliato zuccherato
kale cavolo ricciuto
kedgeree pesce sminuzzato, accompagnato da riso, uova e burro
kidney rognone
kipper aringa affumicata
lamb agnello
Lancashire hot pot stufato di cotolette e rognoni d'agnello, con patate e cipolle
larded lardellato
lean magro
leek porro
leg coscetto, coscia
lemon limone
  ~ **sole** sogliola
lentil lenticchia
lettuce lattuga, lattuga cappuccina
lima bean specie di grossa fava
lime limoncino verde
liver fegato
loaf pagnotta
lobster astice
loin lombata
Long Island duck anitra di Long Island, molto rinomata

low-calorie povero in calorie
lox salmone affumicato
lunch pranzo
macaroon amaretto
macaroni maccheroni
mackerel sgombro
maize granturco, mais
mandarin mandarino
maple syrup sciroppo d'acero
marinade salsa di aceto e spezie
marinated marinato
marjoram maggiorana
marmalade marmellata d'arance
marrow midollo
  ~ **bone** osso con midollo
marshmallow caramella gelatinosa e gommosa
marzipan pasta di mandorle
mashed potatoes purea di patate
mayonnaise maionese
meal pasto
meat carne
  ~ **ball** polpetta di carne
  ~ **loaf** polpettone cotto al forno e servito a fette
  ~ **pâté** pasticcio di carne
medium (done) cotto a puntino
melon melone
melted fuso
Melton Mowbray pie pasticcio a base di carne
meringue meringa
milk latte
mince trito
  ~ **pie** dolce ripieno di frutta
minced tritato
  ~ **meat** carne tritata
mint menta
minute steak bistecca cotta velocemente a fuoco vivo da ambo le parti
mixed misto
  ~ **grill** spiedini con salsicce, fegatini, rognoni, cotolette e pan-

cetta, passati alla griglia

molasses melassa

morel spugnolo (fungo)

mousse 1) dolce o dessert a base di panna o albumi battuti 2) spuma leggera di carne o di pesce

mulberry mora

mullet triglia, muggine

mulligatawny soup minestra di pollo, molto piccante, di origine indiana

mushroom fungo

muskmelon varietà di melone

mussel mitilo, cozza

mustard mostarda, senape

mutton montone

noodle taglierini

nut noce

oatmeal (porridge) pappa d'avena

oil olio

okra baccelli di *gumbo* utilizzati per rendere dense zuppe, minestre e stufati

olive oliva

omelet frittata

onion cipolla

orange arancia

ox tongue lingua di bue

oxtail coda di bue

oyster ostrica

pancake frittella

paprika paprica

Parmesan (cheese) parmigiano

parsley prezzemolo

parsnip pastinaca

partridge pernice

pastry pasta, pasticcino

pasty polpetta, pasticcio

pea pisello

peach pesca

peanut arachide

  ~ **butter** burro di arachidi

pear pera

pearl barley orzo perlato

pepper pepe

  ~ **mint** menta piperita

perch pesce persico

persimmon kaki

pheasant fagiano

pickerel piccolo luccio

pickle 1) sottaceto 2) negli US si riferisce solo al cetriolino

pickled sott'aceto

pie pasticcio o torta, spesso ricoperta da uno strato di pasta, ripiena di carne, verdura, frutta o crema alla vaniglia

pig maiale

pigeon piccione

pike luccio

pineapple ananas

plaice passerino, pianuzza

plain liscio, al naturale

plate piatto

plum susina, prugna

  ~ **pudding** budino a base di frutta candita, scorza di limone, cedro; a volte alla fiamma

poached in camicia, affogato

popover piccolo dolce di pasta farcito alla frutta

pork maiale

porridge pappa di fiocchi d'avena o preparata con farina di altri cereali

porterhouse steak equivalente di bistecca alla fiorentina

pot roast arrosto brasato

potato patata

  ~ **chips** 1) patatine fritte (GB) 2) patatine (US)

  ~ **in its jacket** patata cotta con la buccia

potted shrimps gamberetti serviti in piccoli stampi con burro fuso aromatizzato

poultry pollame

prawn gambero

prune prugna secca
ptarmigan pernice delle nevi
pudding budino, sformato
pumpernickel pane di segale integrale
pumpkin zucca
quail quaglia
quince mela cotogna
rabbit coniglio
radish ravanello
rainbow trout trota fario
raisin uva passa
rare poco cotto, al sangue
raspberry lampone
raw crudo
red mullet triglia
red (sweet) pepper peperone rosso
redcurrant ribes rosso
relish condimento a base di verdura sott'aceto sminuzzata
rhubarb rabarbaro
rib (of beef) costola di manzo
rib-eye-steak grossa bistecca
rice riso
rissole polpetta di carne o di pesce avvolta in pasta frolla
river trout trota di torrente
roast(ed) arrosto
Rock Cornish hen galletto specialmente adatto per essere preparato arrosto
roe uova di pesce
roll panino
rollmop herring filetto di aringa, arrotolato attorno a un cetriolo, marinato nel vino bianco
round steak girello di manzo
Rubens sandwich carne tritata su toast, con crauti, emmental, condimento per insalata; servita calda
rump steak bistecca di girello
rusk pane biscottato
rye bread pane di segale

saddle la parte del dorso di un animale macellato
saffron zafferano
sage salvia
salad insalata
  ~ bar vasta scelta di insalate
  ~ cream condimento per insalata a base di panna, leggermente dolce
  ~ dressing condimento per insalata
salami salame
salmon salmone
  ~ trout trota salmonata
salt sale
salted salato
sardine sardina
sauce salsa, sugo
sauerkraut crauti
sausage salsiccia
sauté(ed) rosolato, fritto in padella
scallop 1) conchiglia S. Giacomo 2) scaloppina di vitello
scone focaccia di pasta leggera a base di farina d'avena o d'orzo
Scotch broth brodo di manzo o di agnello con verdure sminuzzate
Scotch woodcock crostino coperto di uova strapazzate e acciughe
sea bass spigola
sea kale cavolo di mare
seafood frutti di mare, pesce
(in) season (di) stagione
seasoning condimento
service servizio
  ~ charge prezzo del servizio
  ~ (not) included servizio (non) compreso
set menu menù a prezzo fisso
shad alosa, salacca (genere di sardina)
shallot scalogno
shellfish crostaceo
sherbet sorbetto

shoulder spalla
shredded wheat fiocchi d'avena serviti a colazione
shrimp gamberetto
silverside (of beef) controgirello
sirloin steak bistecca di lombo di manzo
skewer spiedino
slice fetta
sliced a fette
sloppy Joe carne di manzo tritata con salsa di pomodoro piccante, servita in un panino
smelt eperlano
smoked affumicato
snack spuntino
sole sogliola
soup minestra, zuppa
sour agro, acido
soused herring aringa marinata in aceto e spezie
spare rib costola di maiale o manzo
spice spezia
spinach spinacio
spiny lobster aragosta
(on a) spit (allo) spiedo
sponge cake pan di Spagna
sprat spratto (piccola aringa)
squash zucca
starter antipasto
steak and kidney pie stufato di manzo e rognoni, coperto di pasta
steamed cotto a vapore
stew stufato, in umido
Stilton (cheese) uno dei più rinomati formaggi inglesi a venatura blu
strawberry fragola
string bean fagiolino
stuffed ripieno, farcito
stuffing ripieno, farcia
suck(l)ing pig maialino da latte

sugar zucchero
sugarless senza zucchero
sundae varietà di cassata con noci, crema e talora sciroppo
supper cena
swede specie di rapa
sweet dolce, torta
 ~ **corn** granturco bianco
 ~ **potato** patata dolce
sweetbread animella
Swiss cheese emmental
Swiss roll brioche alla crema o marmellata
Swiss steak fetta di manzo brasata con legumi e spezie
T-bone steak bistecca di manzo formata dal filetto e dal controfiletto separati da un'osso a forma di T
table d'hôte menù a prezzo fisso
tangerine specie di mandarino
tarragon dragoncello, estragone
tart torta di frutta
tenderloin filetto di carne
Thousand Island dressing condimento per insalata a base di maionese, peperoni, olive e uova sode
thyme timo
toad-in-the-hole carne di manzo o salsiccia avvolta in pasta e cotta al forno
toasted tostato
 ~ **cheese** crostino spalmato di formaggio fuso
tomato pomodoro
tongue lingua
tournedos medaglione di filetto
treacle melassa
trifle genere di zuppa inglese; charlotte allo sherry o al brandy con mandorle, marmellata e panna montata
tripe trippa

trout trota
truffle tartufo
tuna, tunny tonno
turbot rombo
turkey tacchino
turnip rapa
turnover calzone ripieno
turtle tartaruga
underdone poco cotto, al sangue
vanilla vaniglia
veal vitello
  ~ **bird** involtino di vitello
  ~ **escalope** scaloppina di vitello
vegetable verdura
  ~ **marrow** zucchino
venison cacciagione, capriolo
vichyssoise zuppa fredda a base di panna, patate e porri
vinegar aceto
Virginia baked ham prosciutto americano, steccato con chiodi di garofano, cotto al forno e decorato con fette di ananas, ciliege e glassato con lo sciroppo di questi frutti
vol-au-vent pasticcino di pasta sfoglia ripieno di carne o altro

intingolo
wafer cialda
waffle sorta di cialda calda
walnut noce
water ice sorbetto
watercress crescione
watermelon cocomero, anguria
well-done ben cotto
Welsh rabbit/rarebit formaggio fuso su un toast
whelk buccina (mollusco)
whipped cream panna montata
whitebait bianchetti
Wiener schnitzel scaloppina impanata
wine list lista dei vini
woodcock beccaccia
Worcestershire sauce salsa piccante a base di aceto e soia
York ham uno dei più rinomati prosciutti inglesi, servito a fette sottili
Yorkshire pudding sformato a base di farina, latte e uova cotto con sugo di manzo; si mangia col rosbif
zwieback fettine di pane biscottato

Bevande

ale birra scura, leggermente dolce, fermentata ad alta temperatura
  bitter ~ scura, amara e forte
  brown ~ scura in bottiglia, leggermente dolce
  light ~ chiara in bottiglia
  mild ~ scura alla spina, dal gusto spiccato
  pale ~ chiara in bottiglia
applejack acquavite di mele
Athol Brose bevanda scozzese composta da whisky, mele e talora fiocchi di avena
Bacardi cocktail cocktail al rum e

al gin, con sciroppo di melagrana e succo di limone verde

barley water bibita rinfrescante a base di orzo e aromatizzata con limone

barley wine birra scura a forte gradazione alcoolica

beer birra

  bottled ~ in bottiglia

  draft, draught ~ alla spina

black velvet champagne con *stout* (servito spesso con le ostriche)

bloody Mary vodka con succo di pomodoro e spezie

bourbon whisky americano, distillato soprattutto dal granturco

brandy 1) appellazione generica dell'acquavite distillata dall'uva o da altra frutta 2) cognac

  ~ **Alexander** acquavite, crema di cacao e panna

British wines vini fatti con uva (o succo d'uva) importata in Gran Bretagna

cherry brandy liquore di ciliege

chocolate latte al cacao

cider sidro

  ~ **cup** miscuglio di sidro, spezie, zucchero e ghiaccio

claret vino rosso di Bordeaux

cobbler *long drink* ghiacciato, a base di frutta, al quale si aggiunge vino o altra bevanda alcoolica

coffee caffè

  ~ **with cream** con panna

  black ~ nero

  caffeine-free ~ decaffeinato

  white ~ con latte

cordial cordiale

cream panna

cup bevanda rinfrescante composta da vino molto freddo, seltz, liquore, e guarnita con una fetta

di limone, di arancia o di cetriolo

daiquiri bevanda composta da rum, succo di limone verde e di ananasso

double doppia quantità

Drambuie liquore fatto da whisky e miele

dry martini 1) vermuth secco (GB) 2) cocktail al gin con un po' di vermuth secco (US)

egg-nog bevanda preparata con rum e altro liquore forte, tuorli battuti e zucchero

gin and it gin e vermut italiano

gin-fizz bevanda composta da gin, zucchero, succo di limone e soda

ginger ale bevanda non alcoolica allo zenzero

ginger beer bevanda leggermente alcoolica a base di zenzero e zucchero

grasshopper bevanda composta da crema di menta, crema di cacao e panna

Guinness (stout) birra molto scura e dal gusto dolciastro, ad alta gradazione di malto e luppolo

half pint misura di capacità: circa 0,3 litri

highball whisky o altri superalcoolici con acqua gasata o con *ginger ale*

iced ghiacciato

Irish coffee caffè con zucchero, un po' di whisky irlandese e ricoperto di panna montata

Irish Mist liquore irlandese a base di whisky e miele

Irish whiskey whisky irlandese, più secco dello *scotch*, fatto non solo da orzo ma anche da segale, avena e grano

juice succo

lager birra chiara e leggera, servita molto fredda

lemon squash succo di limone

lemonade limonata

lime juice succo di limoncini verdi

liqueur liquore

liquor bevanda molto alcoolica

long drink bevanda alcoolica allungata con acqua o acqua tonica e ghiaccio

madeira madera

Manhattan bevanda a base di whisky americano, vermut secco e angostura

milk latte

~ **shake** frappè

mineral water acqua minerale

mulled wine vin brûlé; vino caldo con spezie

neat liscio

old-fashioned bevanda a base di whisky, zucchero, angostura e ciliege al maraschino

on the rocks con cubetti di ghiaccio

Ovaltine Ovomaltina

Pimm's cup(s) bevanda alcoolica con aggiunta di succo di frutta e talvolta seltz

~ **No. 1** a base di gin

~ **No. 2** a base di whisky

~ **No. 3** a base di rum

~ **No. 4** a base di acquavite

pink champagne champagne rosé

pink lady cocktail composto da albumi, calvados, succo di limone, succo di melagrana e gin

pint misura di capacità: circa 0,6 litri

port (wine) porto

porter birra scura e amara

quart misura di capacità: 1,14 litri

(US 0,95 litri)

root beer bevanda gasata e analcoolica dolce, ricavata da erbe e radici varie

rye (whiskey) whisky di segale, più forte e più aspro del *bourbon*

scotch (whisky) miscuglio di whisky di grano e d'orzo

screwdriver vodka e succo d'arancia

shandy *bitter ale* con l'aggiunta di limonata o di *ginger beer*

sherry xeres

short drink bevanda alcoolica liscia

shot piccola dose di whisky o di altro liquore

sloe gin-fizz liquore di prugnola con soda e succo di limone

soda water acqua gasata, seltz

soft drink bevanda analcoolica

spirits bevande molto alcooliche

stinger cognac e crema di menta

stout birra scura, aromatizzata fortemente con il luppolo

straight liscio

tea tè

toddy grog, ponce

Tom Collins bevanda a base di gin, succo di limone, acqua di seltz e zucchero

tonic (water) acqua brillante, acqua tonica

water acqua

whisky sour bevanda a base di whisky, succo di limone, zucchero e soda

wine vino

dry ~ secco

red ~ rosso

rosé ~ rosato, rosatello

sparkling ~ spumante

sweet ~ dolce

white ~ bianco

Mini-grammatica

L'articolo

L'articolo determinativo (il, lo, la, i, gli, le) ha una sola forma: *the.*

the room, the rooms	la camera, le camere

L'articolo indeterminativo (un, una, uno) ha due forme: *a,* che si usa davanti a consonante, *an,* che si usa davanti a vocale e *h* muta.

a coat	un cappotto
an umbrella	un ombrello
an hour	un'ora

Some (del, dello, della, dei, degli, delle) indica una quantità o un numero indefiniti.

I'd like some water, please.	Vorrei dell'acqua, per favore.
Please bring me some biscuits.	Per favore, portami dei biscotti.

Any si usa nelle frasi negative e nelle interrogative.

There isn't any soap.	Non c'è del sapone.
Do you have any stamps?	Avete dei francobolli?
Is there any message for me?	C'è un messaggio per me?

Il sostantivo

Il plurale della maggior parte dei sostantivi si forma aggiungendo *-(e)s* alla forma del singolare.

cup — cups (tazza — tazze)	**dress — dresses** (abito — abiti)

Nota: se un sostantivo termina con *-y* preceduta da una consonante, la desinenza del plurale sarà *-ies*, se la *-y* è preceduta da una vocale, il sostantivo segue la regola generale.

lady — ladies (signora — signore)	**key — keys** (chiave — chiavi)

Alcuni plurali irregolari:

man — men (uomo/uomini)	**foot — feet** (piede/-i)
woman — women (donna/-e)	**tooth — teeth** (dente/-i)
child — children (bambino/-il)	**mouse — mice** (topo/-i)

Il complemento del nome (genitivo)

1. Il possessore è una persona: se il sostantivo non termina in *-s,* si aggiunge *'s.*

the boy's room	la camera del ragazzo
the children's clothes	gli abiti dei bambini

Se il sostantivo termina in *s,* si aggiunge l'apostrofo (').

the boys' room	la camera dei ragazzi

2. Il possessore non è una persona: si usa la preposizione *of:*

the key of the door	la chiave della porta

L'aggettivo

Gli aggettivi di solito precedono il sostantivo.

a large brown suitcase   una grande valigia marrone

Vi sono due modi per formare il comparativo e il superlativo degli aggettivi:

1. Gli aggettivi di una sillaba e molti aggettivi di due sillabe aggiungono *-(e)r* ed *-(e)st*.

small (piccolo) — **smaller** — **smallest**
pretty (carino) — **prettier** — **prettiest***

2. Gli aggettivi di tre o più sillabe e alcuni aggettivi di due sillabe (in particolare quelli che terminano in *-ful* e *-less*) formano il comparativo e il superlativo con *more* e *most*.

expensive (caro) — **more expensive** — **most expensive**
careful (attento) — **more careful** — **most careful**

Alcune forme irregolari:

good (buono)	better	best
bad (cattivo)	worse	worst
little (poco)	less	least
much/many (molto)	more	most

L'avverbio

Numerosi avverbi si formano aggiungendo *-ly* all'aggettivo.

quick — **quickly**   veloce — velocemente
slow — **slowly**   lento — lentamente

Il pronome

	Soggetto	Complemento (dir./indir.)	Possessivo 1	2
Singolare				
1ª persona	I	me	my	mine
2ª persona	you	you	your	yours
3ª persona (m.)	he	him	his	his
(f.)	she	her	her	hers
(n.)	it	it	its	—
Plurale				
1ª persona	we	us	our	ours
2ª persona	you	you	your	yours
3ª persona	they	them	their	theirs

Nota: in inglese non c'è distinzione come in italiano fra il «tu» e il «Lei». Si usa una sola forma: *you.*

---

*La *y* diventa *i* quando è preceduta da una consonante.

Il pronome personale complemento si usa anche dopo le preposizioni.

| **Give it to me.** | Dammelo. |
| **He came with us.** | È venuto con noi. |

La forma 1 del possessivo corrisponde a «mio», «tuo», ecc., la forma 2 a «il mio», «il tuo», ecc.

| **Where's my key?** | Dov'è la mia chiave? |
| **That's not mine.** | Non è la mia. |

L'aggettivo dimostrativo

This (questo; plurale *these*) si riferisce a una cosa vicina nello spazio o nel tempo. *That* (quello; plurale *those*) si riferisce a una cosa più lontana.

| **Is this seat taken?** | È occupato questo posto? |

Verbi ausiliari

a) **to be** (essere)

	Forma contratta	Negativo — forme contratte		
I am	I'm		I'm not	o
you are	you're	you're not		you aren't
he is	he's	he's not		he isn't
she is	she's	she's not		she isn't
it is	it's	it's not		it isn't
we are	we're	we're not		we aren't
you are	you're	you're not		you aren't
they are	they're	they're not		they aren't

Interrogativo: **Am I? Are you? Is he?** ecc.

Nota: nella lingua corrente si usano quasi sempre le forme contratte.

Le forme «c'è» e «ci sono» si traducono: **there is** (**there's**) e **there are**.

b) **to have** (avere)

	Contrazione		Contrazione
I have	I've	we have	we've
you have	you've	you have	you've
he/she/it has	he's/she's/it's	they have	they've

| Negazione: | **I have not (I haven't)** |
| Interrogazione: | **Have you? — Has he?** |

c) **to do** (fare)

	Negativo contratto		Negativo contratto
I do	I don't	we do	we don't
you do	you don't	you do	you don't
he/she/it does	he/she/it doesn't	they do	they don't

Interrogazione: **Do you? Does he/she/it?**

Altri verbi

L'infinito si usa per tutte le persone del tempo presente; si aggiunge solo *-(e)s* alla terza persona singolare.

	to love (amare)	to come (venire)	to go (andare)
I	love	come	go
you	love	come	go
he/she/it	loves	comes	goes
we	love	come	go
you	love	come	go
they	love	come	go

La negazione si forma per mezzo dell'ausiliare *do/does* + *not* + verbo all'infinito.

We do not (don't) like this hotel.	Non ci piace questo albergo.
She does not (doesn't) smoke.	Ella non fuma.

L'interrogazione si forma con l'ausiliare *do* + soggetto + infinito.

Do you like it?	Ti piace?
Does he live here?	Egli vive qui?

Presente continuo

Si forma con il verbo *to be* (essere) + il participio presente del verbo coniugato. Il participio presente si forma aggiungendo *-ing* all'infinito (eliminando la *-e* finale quando c'è). Il presente continuo si impiega solo con certi verbi, in quanto indica un'azione o uno stato che sta avvenendo nel momento in cui si parla.

What are you doing?	Cosa stai facendo?
I'm writing a letter.	Sto scrivendo una lettera.

Imperativo

L'imperativo (singolare e plurale) ha la stessa forma dell'infinito (senza *to*). La negazione si forma con *don't*.

Please bring me some water.	Per favore, portami dell'acqua.
Don't be late.	Non essere in ritardo.

Verbi irregolari inglesi

Vi elenchiamo qui di seguito i verbi irregolari inglesi. I verbi composti o quelli con prefisso si coniugano come i verbi semplici, es. *mistake* e *overdrive* si coniugano come *take* e *drive*.

Infinito	Passato remoto	Participio passato	
arise	arose	arisen	*alzare*
awake	awoke	awoken	*svegliare*
be	was	been	*essere*
bear	bore	borne	*portare*
beat	beat	beaten	*battere*
become	became	become	*diventare*
begin	began	begun	*cominciare*
bend	bent	bent	*curvare*
bet	bet	bet	*scommettere*
bid	bade/bid	bidden/bid	*comandare*
bind	bound	bound	*legare*
bite	bit	bitten	*mordere*
bleed	bled	bled	*sanguinare*
blow	blew	blown	*soffiare*
break	broke	broken	*rompere*
breed	bred	bred	*allevare*
bring	brought	brought	*portare*
build	built	built	*costruire*
burn	burnt/burned	burnt/burned	*bruciare*
burst	burst	burst	*scoppiare*
buy	bought	bought	*comprare*
can*	could	—	*potere*
cast	cast	cast	*gettare*
catch	caught	caught	*afferrare*
choose	chose	chosen	*scegliere*
cling	clung	clung	*aderire*
clothe	clothed/clad	clothed/clad	*vestire*
come	came	come	*venire*
cost	cost	cost	*costare*
creep	crept	crept	*strisciare*
cut	cut	cut	*tagliare*
deal	dealt	dealt	*trattare*
dig	dug	dug	*scavare*
do (he does)	did	done	*fare*
draw	drew	drawn	*tirare*
dream	dreamt/dreamed	dreamt/dreamed	*sognare*
drink	drank	drunk	*bere*
drive	drove	driven	*guidare*
dwell	dwelt	dwelt	*abitare*
eat	ate	eaten	*mangiare*
fall	fell	fallen	*cadere*

* indicativo presente

feed	fed	fed	*nutrire*
feel	felt	felt	*sentire*
fight	fought	fought	*combattere*
find	found	found	*trovare*
flee	fled	fled	*fuggire*
fling	flung	flung	*gettare*
fly	flew	flown	*volare'*
forsake	forsook	forsaken	*abbandonare*
freeze	froze	frozen	*gelare*
get	got	got	*ottenere*
give	gave	given	*dare*
go	went	gone	*andare*
grind	ground	ground	*macinare*
grow	grew	grown	*crescere*
hang	hung	hung	*appendere*
have	had	had	*avere*
hear	heard	heard	*udire*
hew	hewed	hewed/hewn	*spaccare*
hide	hid	hidden	*nascondere*
hit	hit	hit	*colpire*
hold	held	held	*tenere*
hurt	hurt	hurt	*dolere*
keep	kept	kept	*tenere*
kneel	knelt	knelt	*inginocchiarsi*
knit	knitted/knit	knitted/knit	*congiungere*
know	knew	known	*conoscere*
lay	laid	laid	*posare*
lead	led	led	*dirigere*
lean	leant/leaned	leant/leaned	*inclinare*
leap	leapt/leaped	leapt/leaped	*balzare*
learn	learnt/learned	learnt/learned	*imparare*
leave	left	left	*lasciare*
lend	lent	lent	*prestare*
let	let	let	*permettere*
lie	lay	lain	*giacere*
light	lit/lighted	lit/lighted	*accendere*
lose	lost	lost	*perdere*
make	made	made	*fare*
may*	might	—	*potere*
mean	meant	meant	*significare*
meet	met	met	*incontrare*
mow	mowed	mowed/mown	*falciare*
must*	—	—	*dovere*
ought (to)*	—	—	*dovere*
pay	paid	paid	*pagare*
put	put	put	*mettere*
read	read	read	*leggere*
rid	rid	rid	*sbarazzare*
ride	rode	ridden	*cavalcare*

* indicativo presente

ring	rang	rung	*suonare*
rise	rose	risen	*sorgere*
run	ran	run	*correre*
saw	sawed	sawn	*segare*
say	said	said	*dire*
see	saw	seen	*vedere*
seek	sought	sought	*cercare*
sell	sold	sold	*vendere*
send	sent	sent	*mandare*
set	set	set	*mettere*
sew	sewed	sewed/sewn	*cucire*
shake	shook	shaken	*scuotere*
shall*	should	—	*dovere*
shed	shed	shed	*spandere*
shine	shone	shone	*splendere*
shoot	shot	shot	*sparare*
show	showed	shown	*mostrare*
shrink	shrank	shrunk	*restringere*
shut	shut	shut	*chiudere*
sing	sang	sung	*cantare*
sink	sank	sunk	*affondare*
sit	sat	sat	*sedere*
sleep	slept	slept	*dormire*
slide	slid	slid	*scivolare*
sling	slung	slung	*scagliare*
slink	slunk	slunk	*sgattaiolare*
slit	slit	slit	*fendere*
smell	smelled/smelt	smelled/smelt	*fiutare*
sow	sowed	sown/sowed	*seminare*
speak	spoke	spoken	*parlare*
speed	sped/speeded	sped/speeded	*affrettarsi*
spell	spelt/spelled	spelt/spelled	*compitare*
spend	spent	spent	*spendere*
spill	spilt/spilled	spilt/spilled	*versare*
spin	spun	spun	*(far) girare*
spit	spat	spat	*sputare*
split	split	split	*spaccare*
spoil	spoilt/spoiled	spoilt/spoiled	*viziare*
spread	spread	spread	*spargere*
spring	sprang	sprung	*scattare*
stand	stood	stood	*stare in piedi*
steal	stole	stolen	*rubare*
stick	stuck	stuck	*ficcare*
sting	stung	stung	*pungere*
stink	stank/stunk	stunk	*puzzare*
strew	strewed	strewed/strewn	*spargere*
stride	strode	stridden	*camminare a grandi passi*
strike	struck	struck/stricken	*percuotere*

---

* indicativo presente

string	strung	strung	*legare*
strive	strove	striven	*sforzarsi*
swear	swore	sworn	*giurare*
sweep	swept	swept	*scopare*
swell	swelled	swollen	*gonfiare*
swim	swam	swum	*nuotare*
swing	swung	swung	*dondolare*
take	took	taken	*prendere*
teach	taught	taught	*insegnare*
tear	tore	torn	*stracciare*
tell	told	told	*dire*
think	thought	thought	*pensare*
throw	threw	thrown	*gettare*
thrust	thrust	thrust	*spingere*
tread	trod	trodden	*calpestare*
wake	woke/waked	woken/waked	*svegliare*
wear	wore	worn	*indossare*
weave	wove	woven	*tessere*
weep	wept	wept	*piangere*
will*	would	—	*volere*
win	won	won	*vincere*
wind	wound	wound	*avvolgere*
wring	wrung	wrung	*torcere*
write	wrote	written	*scrivere*

---

* indicativo presente

Abbreviazioni inglesi

AA	*Automobile Association*	Automobile Club Britannico
AAA	*American Automobile Association*	Automobile Club Americano
ABC	*American Broadcasting Company*	società privata radio-televisiva americana
A.D.	*anno Domini*	A.D.
Am.	*America; American*	America; americano
a.m.	*ante meridiem (before noon)*	di mattina (00.00–12.00)
Amtrak	*American railroad corporation*	società di ferrovie americana
AT & T	*American Telephone and Telegraph Company*	società americana dei telefoni e telegrafi
Ave.	*avenue*	viale
BBC	*British Broadcasting Corporation*	Radio-Televisione Britannica
B.C.	*before Christ*	a.C.
bldg.	*building*	edificio
Blvd.	*boulevard*	viale
B.R.	*British Rail*	ferrovie britanniche
Brit.	*Britain; British*	Gran Bretagna; britannico
Bros.	*brothers*	fratelli
¢	*cent*	1/100 di dollaro
Can.	*Canada; Canadian*	Canada; canadese
CBS	*Columbia Broadcasting System*	società privata radio-televisiva americana
CID	*Criminal Investigation Department*	polizia giudiziaria britannica
CNR	*Canadian National Railway*	ferrovie nazionali canadesi
c/o	*(in) care of*	presso (negli indirizzi)
Co.	*company*	compagnia
Corp.	*corporation*	tipo di società
CPR	*Canadian Pacific Railways*	società di ferrovie canadesi
D.C.	*District of Columbia*	Distretto Federale della Columbia (Washington, D.C.)
DDS	*Doctor of Dental Science*	dentista
dept.	*department*	reparto, sezione
e.g.	*for instance*	per esempio
Eng.	*England; English*	Inghilterra; inglese
EU	*European Union*	Unione europea

excl.	*excluding; exclusive*	esclusivo, non compreso
ft.	*foot/feet*	piede/piedi
GB	*Great Britain*	Gran Bretagna
H.E.	*His/Her Excellency; His Eminence*	Sua Eccellenza; Sua Eminenza
H.H.	*His Holiness*	Sua Santità
H.M.	*His/Her Majesty*	Sua Maestà
H.M.S.	*Her Majesty's ship*	nave della marina reale inglese
hp	*horsepower*	cavallo (vapore)
Hwy	*highway*	strada a grande scorrimento
i.e.	*that is to say*	cioè
in.	*inch*	pollice (2,54 cm)
Inc.	*incorporated*	tipo di società anonima americana
incl.	*including, inclusive*	inclusivo, compreso
£	*pound sterling*	lira sterlina
L.A.	*Los Angeles*	Los Angeles
Ltd.	*limited*	società anonima
M.D.	*Doctor of Medicine*	Dottore in Medicina
M.P.	*Member of Parliament*	deputato
mph	*miles per hour*	miglia all'ora
Mr.	*Mister*	Signor
Mrs.	*Missis*	Signora
Ms.	*Missis/Miss*	Signora/Signorina
nat.	*national*	nazionale
NBC	*National Broadcasting Company*	società privata radio-televisiva americana
No.	*number*	numero
N.Y.C.	*New York City*	città di New York
O.B.E.	*Officer (of the Order) of the British Empire*	Ufficiale (dell'Ordine) dell'Impero Britannico
p.	*page; penny/pence*	pagina; 1/100 di lira sterlina
p.a.	*per annum*	per anno
Ph.D.	*Doctor of Philosophy*	Dottore in Filosofia
PLC	*public limited company*	Società per azioni
p.m.	*post meridiem (after noon)*	del pomeriggio o della sera (12.00–24.00)
PO	*Post Office*	ufficio postale
POO	*post office order*	mandato postale
pop.	*population*	abitanti
P.T.O.	*please turn over*	vedi retro
RAC	*Royal Automobile Club*	Real Automobile Club Inglese

RCMP	*Royal Canadian Mounted Police*	polizia reale canadese a cavallo
Rd.	*road*	strada
ref.	*reference*	riferimento
Rev.	*reverend*	reverendo della chiesa anglicana
RFD	*rural free delivery*	distribuzione della posta in campagna
RR	*railroad*	ferrovia
RSVP	*please reply*	si prega rispondere
$	*dollar*	dollaro
Soc.	*society*	società
St.	*saint ; street*	santo ; strada
STD	*Subscriber Trunk Dialling*	telefono automatico
UN	*United Nations*	N.U., Nazioni Unite
UPS	*United Parcel Service*	servizio spedizione pacchi americano
US	*United States*	Stati Uniti
USS	*United States Ship*	nave della marina americana
VAT	*value added tax*	I.V.A.
VIP	*very important person*	V.I.P., persona molto importante
Xmas	*Christmas*	Natale
yd.	*yard*	iarda (91,44 cm)
YMCA	*Young Men's Christian Association*	A.C.D.G.
YWCA	*Young Women's Christian Association*	U.C.D.G.
ZIP	*ZIP code*	codice di avviamento postale

Numeri

Numeri cardinali		Numeri ordinali	
0	zero	1st	first
1	one	2nd	second
2	two	3rd	third
3	three	4th	fourth
4	four	5th	fifth
5	five	6th	sixth
6	six	7th	seventh
7	seven	8th	eighth
8	eight	9th	ninth
9	nine	10th	tenth
10	ten	11th	eleventh
11	eleven	12th	twelfth
12	twelve	13th	thirteenth
13	thirteen	14th	fourteenth
14	fourteen	15th	fifteenth
15	fifteen	16th	sixteenth
16	sixteen	17th	seventeenth
17	seventeen	18th	eighteenth
18	eighteen	19th	nineteenth
19	nineteen	20th	twentieth
20	twenty	21st	twenty-first
21	twenty-one	22nd	twenty-second
22	twenty-two	23rd	twenty-third
23	twenty-three	24th	twenty-fourth
24	twenty-four	25th	twenty-fifth
25	twenty-five	26th	twenty-sixth
30	thirty	27th	twenty-seventh
40	forty	28th	twenty-eighth
50	fifty	29th	twenty-ninth
60	sixty	30th	thirtieth
70	seventy	40th	fortieth
80	eighty	50th	fiftieth
90	ninety	60th	sixtieth
100	a/one hundred	70th	seventieth
230	two hundred and thirty	80th	eightieth
		90th	ninetieth
1,000	a/one thousand	100th	hundredth
10,000	ten thousand	230th	two hundred and thirtieth
100,000	a/one hundred thousand		
1,000,000	a/one million	1,000th	thousandth

L'ora

I Britannici e gli Americani usano il sistema di dodici ore. L'espressione *a.m. (ante meridiem)* indica le ore che precedono mezzogiorno e *p.m. (post meridiem)* quelle fino a mezzanotte. Tuttavia in Inghilterra gli orari sono di più in più indicati alla maniera continentale.

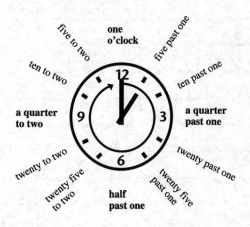

I'll come at seven a.m.	Verrò alle 7 (del mattino).
I'll come at two p.m.	Verrò alle 2 (del pomeriggio).
I'll come at eight p.m.	Verrò alle 8 (di sera).

I giorni della settimana

Sunday	domenica	*Thursday*	giovedì
Monday	lunedì	*Friday*	venerdì
Tuesday	martedì	*Saturday*	sabato
Wednesday	mercoledì		

Notes

Appunti

Appunti

Appunti

Conversion tables/
Tavole di trasformazione

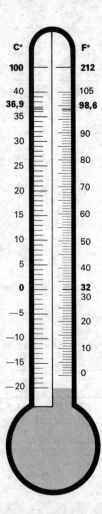

Metres and feet
The figure in the middle stands for both metres and feet, e.g. 1 metre = 3.281 ft. and 1 foot = 0.30 m.

Metri e piedi
I numeri al centro del seguente specchietto valgono sia per i metri sia per i piedi. Es.: 1 metro = 3,281 piedi e 1 piede = 0,30 m.

Metres/Metri		Feet/Piedi
0.30	**1**	3.281
0.61	**2**	6.563
0.91	**3**	9.843
1.22	**4**	13.124
1.52	**5**	16.403
1.83	**6**	19.686
2.13	**7**	22.967
2.44	**8**	26.248
2.74	**9**	29.529
3.05	**10**	32.810
3.66	**12**	39.372
4.27	**14**	45.934
6.10	**20**	65.620
7.62	**25**	82.023
15.24	**50**	164.046
22.86	**75**	246.069
30.48	**100**	328.092

Temperature
To convert Centigrade to Fahrenheit, multiply by 1.8 and add 32.
To convert Fahrenheit to Centigrade, subtract 32 from Fahrenheit and divide by 1.8.

Temperatura
Per trasformare i gradi centigradi in Fahrenheit moltiplicare i centigradi per 1,8 e aggiungere 32.
Per convertire i Fahrenheit in centigradi sottrarre 32 dai Fahrenheit e dividere per 1,8.